Church Missionary Society

The Church Missionary Intelligencer

1860

Church Missionary Society

The Church Missionary Intelligencer
1860

ISBN/EAN: 9783337369675

Printed in Europe, USA, Canada, Australia, Japan

Cover: Foto ©Lupo / pixelio.de

More available books at **www.hansebooks.com**

THE CHURCH MISSIONARY INTELLIGENCER,

A MONTHLY JOURNAL

OF

MISSIONARY INFORMATION.

VOL. XI.

"BEHOLD, I HAVE SET BEFORE THEE AN OPEN DOOR, AND NO MAN CAN SHUT IT."—*REVELATION* III. 8.

LONDON:
SEELEY, JACKSON, AND HALLIDAY, FLEET STREET,
AND G. SEELEY, HANOVER STREET, HANOVER SQUARE;
HATCHARD AND CO., PICCADILLY;
AND J. NISBET AND CO., BERNERS STREET.

1860.

W. M. WATTS, CROWN COURT, TEMPLE BAR.

CONTENTS.

Africa.

DISCOVERIES IN EAST AFRICA.

Explorations of the Rev. J. Rebmann in 1848—His discovery of the Snow Mountain, Kilimandjaro.	25
Dr. Krapf's visits to Ukambani—His discovery of Mount Kenia, and subsequent perils in the wilderness.	26
Difficulties of the routes to the interior now diminishing—Remarks on the Masai and Wakuafi.	27, 28
Usambara, and its facilities for exploration—Residence there of the Rev. J. Erhardt.	29
Early rumours, collected by the Missionaries, of a great lake in the interior—Consequent measures of the Geographical Society.	29, 30
Expedition of Captains Burton and Speke—Their progress westward from the Sea—Discovery of the Mountains of the Moon and Lake Tanganyika.	30, 31
The lake crossed to Kivira—Traffic for ivory—Journey to Uvira.	31—33
Unnatural effects of slavery—The East Africans as free labourers—Information gained respecting the great lake Nyanza—Departure of the caravan—Villages and scenery of the Uniamesi country.	34—36
Discovery of the Lake Nyanza—(the Niassa of the Missionaries), by Captain Speke, on the 3rd of August 1858—Probable extent of it and its river tributaries.	36, 37
Return of the expedition—Face of the country.	37, 38
Expeditions of the Egyptian Government to discover the source of the Nile—Journeys of Knoblecher, &c.	38
Phenomena of the Nile regions—Discrepancies in the scientific observations of travellers—the difficulty solved.	39, 40
Recent explorations of Petherick—Proceedings at the Geographical Society, January 8, 1859.	41
Testimony of Captain Speke to the labours of the Church Missionaries, and to their travels, as first advancing East-African discovery.	41, 42

LIVINGSTONE'S DISCOVERIES IN AFRICA.

Dr. Livingstone's departure from Kuruman in June 1849—Discovery of Lake Ngami.	42
Commencement of the long journey—Linyanti—Ascent of the rivers Leeambye and Leeba.	43, 44
Journey overland—The Balonda—Portuguese traders—Face of the country—The Quango valley.	44, 45
Arrival at the Atlantic—Return journey—Progress down the Barotse valley.	45, 46
Journey to the East Coast—Water route to the sea—Discovery of the Victoria Falls—The Falls described—Arrival at the mouth of the Zambesi.	46, 47
Plan for formation of Mission stations—Livingstone's recent discoveries of the River Shire and Lake Shirwa—Letter from him to the Church Missionary Society, inviting its co-operation.	47, 48

.*.* *Vide* also "Recent Intelligence."

CONTENTS.

Mediterranean.

"*" *Vide* "Recent Intelligence," and the article—"Missionary deductions from the Parables," under head "Miscellaneous."

India.

MISSIONARY ACTION IN THE PUNJAB.

	Page
Extracts from the Journal of the Rev. J. Leighton, Missionary at Umritsur, from December 31, 1858 to February 20, 1859	21—24

OUDE—ITS HISTORY.

Introduction—Physical features of Oude	49
Sketch of the history of Oude—Early connexions with England	49, 50
Profligacy of the native Court—Remonstrances of successive Governors-General	50
Cession of the Southern Doab to the East-India Company in 1801—Yearly subsidy paid to the Company—New Treaty	51
Oude from 1814 to 1822—Continued profligacy	51, 52
Nuseerood Deen and his wives—Interview between the King and Lord Combermere at Lucknow in 1827	52, 53
Barbaric magnificence of the Court—Suspicious death of the King	53
Moonna Jan elected King—British interference—Coronation of Mohammed Ali Shah	54
Accession of Wajid Alice Shah, the last King of Oude, in 1847—his character and habits	54, 55
Revenue System of the Country—Instances of judicial oppression and suffering under Dursun Sing and Rughbur Sing, official collectors of tribute	55, 56
History of Man Sing—his conduct during the Mutiny of 1857—opposite conduct of the Rajah of Bulrampore	57

OUDE AS IT WAS BEFORE THE ANNEXATION.

Lucknow as visited by Bishop Heber in 1824	73
Lucknow of our own times—The Residency and its prospect—The Imambara and Hall of Chandeliers—Reckless expenditure of the Kings	73—75
The Choke or main street of the old city—Lucknow a Sodom	75
Panorama seen from the roof of the Chutter Munzil	76
Extortions of the native rulers—Oppressions of the Talookdars and robber gangs of the country	77
Desolation of districts following misrule—Absence of wealthy men in the rural districts and consequent overpopulation and depravity of the capital	78, 79
Sufferings of the peasantry—Restoration by the British Government of the forfeited Estates to the Talookdars—Sunnud (Note)	79, 80
Female Infanticide in Oude—Scarcity of Marriageable Women—Customs at the murder of the babe	80—82
Continued apathy at the Court—Rise of the Jungle fastnesses	82
Question of the Annexation—Minute of Lord Dalhousie, &c.	83
Opposite opinion—Proposed new treaty with the East-India Company, and Proclamation	84
Interview of the British Resident with the Prime Minister of Oude, January 30, 1856	84, 85
Interview with the Queen-Mother, February 1st	85, 86
Interview with the King, February 4th	86—88
Royal Proclamation, and subsequent departure of the King to Calcutta to lay his case before the Governor-General	88

CONTENTS.

INDIA—WHAT IS TO BE OUR POLICY?

	Page
Two questions of primary importance—	
1. What is the extent of Christian liberty Government officials in India may practice?	58
Spirit of inquiry in the 24th Regiment of Punjabee Infantry—Action of officers, and prohibition of Government—Letter of Rev. R. Clark, Nov. 2, 1859	58, 59
2. Is the policy of Government Education in India to be changed?	60
Need of alteration, and permission for scholars to read the Bible	60
Native employés, and how they should be obtained—Remarks on Education debarred of a Christian tone	61, 62
Bible examinations at Benares, January 1857—Communications of H. C. Tucker, Esq.	62—64
Details of the examination, and results—Reflections	64, 65
Instances of success following an open Christian policy	66
Speech of Colonel Edwardes at Shrewsbury	66—70
How India must be elevated	70, 71

THE POPULATION OF EASTERN BENGAL.

Extracts from the Forty-sixth Report of the Calcutta Bible Society . 71, 72

GONDWANA AND ITS ABORIGINAL TRIBES.

Position of Gondwana in India—Its physical features, divisions of the country, and inhabitants . . . 145, 146

The Gonds—
The district they inhabit—Divisions of the people—The Bennia and the Malia Gonds . . . 146, 147
Dress, agriculture, &c.—Religious opinions—Legend of the creation—Tradition of the Fall of Man . . . 147, 148
Human sacrifices—Invocation of Tari Pennu—Government suppression of the rite . . . 148, 149
The Puttooa tribes—their pursuits . . . 149
The Mica Mines of Behar—Mode of opening a mine—Uses of the mica, &c. . 150, 151
Duty of Christians as regards these people . . . 151

The Hill Tribes of the Upper Godavery—
Paper by Colonel Cotton respecting the Koiys, and the facilities for Missionary action among them . . . 151—153
Missionary efforts at Nagpore, Jubbulpore, &c. . . . 153

Bhagulpore—
Description by Captain Sherwill—Situation, climate, soil, vegetation, &c. . 154, 155
Towns of the country—The Mundar Hill . . . 155
People of the Kurrukpore, Purbutpara, and other Pergunnahs . . . 156, 157

The Santhals—
Their features, food, dress, and religion—Prayers for preservation—Government . . . 157, 158
Sherwill's journey through the Raj Mahal hills—His notices of the people, their manners and customs; scenery of the country, vegetation, agriculture, geology, &c. . . . 158—162
Commencement of Missionary operations in 1850—The Santhal outbreak—Evidence of influence of Missions on the people . . . 162
Grants-in-aid allowed to Christian schools in 1854—Withdrawal of the grant in 1857—Remarks . . . 162, 163
Extracts from the journal of the Rev. T. E. Hallett, Missionary among the Santhals, Dec. 1859 . . . 163—168

CONTENTS.

THE REVIVAL IN NORTH TINNEVELLY.

	Page
Introduction—General features of Revivals	175, 176
Itinerating Mission of North Tinnevelly, its extent, &c.	176
The Revival—	
Letter of the Rev. W. T. Satthianadhen, March 27, 1860	177
Letter of the Rev. A. Dibb, May 15	177
The Work at Vageikulam—Letters of Rev. D. Fenn	178—182
Letter of the Rev. W. Gray, May 14	182—185
Additional later information—Letter of Rev. W. Gray, May 21—Extract from his Journal, May 18	185—188
Letter of Rev. W. T. Satthianadhen, May 25—Letter of Rev. W. Gray, June 1	188, 189
Differences between the present Revival and former ones	265
The movement among the Retty caste in 1841—Remarks of Rev. G. Pettitt	265
Recent testimonies from North Tinnevelly — Letter from Rev. A. Dibb, September 15	266
Letter from Rev. A. Valpy, September 7	266—269
Mission House at Surandei—"Agastya's Hill"—Traditions of Agastya	269

CUSTOMS OF THE HINDUS AND MUSSULMANS OF INDIA.

Opening remarks—Hindu ceremonies on the last day of the month	92, 93
Festivals of the Ehath, Ekadashee—Auspicious days	93, 94
The Beas Pooja—Anniversary of Krishna's birth	94, 95
The Goorea-teohar—The Raki-teohar, The Skunka-choth and the Tej	95, 96
Ceremonies of the Ununth and the Dussurah Leela—Tradition of Ramchund and Leta—Its theatrical representation yearly in Bengal	116—118
The Dewalee—The Sunka Nath and its origin—The Busunth, the Hoolee, &c.	118—120
Indian customs regarding Births	142
Marriages	142—144
Deaths	189—191
Belief as to the after state of the Soul	191
Hindu Beggars	192

*** *Vide* also "Recent Intelligence."

China.

ENGLISH POLICY ON THE COAST OF CHINA.

The new disturbances on the Chinese coast—Remarks	97, 98
Injustice of British action with the Chinese—The opium traffic	98
Voyages of the "Lord Amherst" and "Sylph" along the coast, in 1832, with opium	99
Diplomacy up to 1841—Cause of the war—Blockade of Canton and bombardments of Tinghae, &c.—Sufferings of the wounded, and self-slaughter of the Mantchus	99, 100
Close of the war—Stipulations as to the traffic—Treaty of 1843	100, 101
The question of opening the city of Canton to foreigners—Native unwillingness—Letters of Lord Palmerston disadvising the attempt to force entrance	101, 102
Interview between the Chinese Commissioner, Seu, and Governor Bonham	102, 103
Official correspondence of 1849—Apparent settlemnt of the question—Honours conferred on Seu by the Emperor	103, 104
Commemorative temple near Canton, with its inscriptions—Governor Yeh	105
Correspondence with Consul Bowring and the authorities in 1854, respecting the entrance into Canton	106, 107

CONTENTS.

	Page
Change of sentiment in the Home Ministry in 1854 respecting Canton—Further correspondence—Yeh's determination not to open the city	107—109
Seizure of the "Arrow" in October 1856—Immediate and violent action of the British—Yeh's remonstrances—Public notification	109—111
Convention at Bocca Tigris, April 1846—Remarks	121
Etiquette of Chinese Diplomacy connected with British—which should yield? Necessity for a just perception of our position with China	122, 123
Recapitulation of events to 1856—Seizure of the Dutch Folly—Yeh's yamun fired upon—His consequent proclamation offering a reward for each Englishman slain	124
Attempt at pacification—Yeh's reply—Offensive operations resumed—Notification of Mr. Consul Parkes	124, 125
Address from the whole of the inhabitants of Canton to the British authorities—Translation of the document	126
Deputation from the city—Surrender of Yeh demanded	127
Seizure of the Bogue and Shamun Forts—Further correspondence	127, 128
Destruction of the British Factories by the Chinese—Retirement of the Admiral	128
Question of Foreign Ambassadors at Pekin—Imperial reply to Lord Macartney in 1793—Remarks	128—130

THE TAI-PINGS.

Sketch of the insurgent rebellion in China since 1851	278
The skirmish with Lord Elgin in 1858—Reduction of cities	278, 279
Fall of Hang-chow and Soo-chow—Description of Soo-chow—Present ruinous and desolate state of these once flourishing towns	279, 280
Suicides at Shanghae—Characteristics of the Chinese mind	280, 281
Deputation of Missionaries to Hung-jin, the minister of the rebel king at Soo-chow—Remarks	281, 282
Intention of the insurgents to capture Shanghae—Proclamation and replies	282, 283
The Rev. J. S. Burdon's narrative of an interview with the Kan wang (Hung-jin),	233
The million New Testaments for China sent out by the people of England—Early history of the Kan wang	283, 284
Start from Shanghae—Kwun shan—I-ting—Arrival at Soo-chow	284, 285
Treatment at the gate—Admittance—Appearance of the city—Detention at the house of Lieu-ta-jin	285
Interview with the Kan wang—His appearance—Leading points of the conversation—Errors of the insurgents in doctrine and practice	286—288
Christian worship performed by the Kan wang—Departure	283

NINGPO—A GLANCE AT THE SOCIAL LIFE OF CHINA.

Ningpo, its situation and importance—Characteristics of the City within and without the walls	211, 212
The Temples of Ningpo—Milne's account of the Seu Tsoo and other Monasteries—A Mohammedan Mosque in China	213, 214
The domestic life of the Chinese—The suicidal mania—Infanticide—Parental murders	214, 215
Romish Missions in Ningpo and Shanghae—A question for the Protestant Church,	215, 216

*** *Vide* also the article, "Missionary deductions from the Parables," and "Recent Intelligence."

CONTENTS.

New Zealand.

NEW ZEALAND—THE EPISCOPATE, THE CHURCH MISSIONARY SOCIETY, AND THE NATIVE RACE.

	Page
Advantageous position of New Zealand—Points of identity between it and the British Isles	1
Fertility and natural features of the country—Paucity of the population	2
Can Britons and Maoris ever blend into one united people?	2, 3
Retrospect—Implanting of Christianity in New Zealand—Its success	3, 4
Arrival of the Bishop; his testimony to the success of the Church Missions	4
Colonization scheme in 1833; Remarks by the late D. Coates, Esq., and the Rev. J. Beecham—Formation of the New-Zealand Company	4, 5
Precipitate action of the Company—Treaty of Waitangi—Native Insurrection—Pacification	6, 7
Creation of the Episcopate—Remarks—Requisitions of the Bishop—Ecclesiastical relations of the Church Missionary Society	8, 9
Establishment of a lengthened Diaconate—Collegiate schemes—Extracts from letters of Missionaries	9, 10
Clouded aspect of the Mission—Conference of the Church Missionary Society with the Bishop and the Governor—Decision of the Committee—Minute of Sir G. Grey	11, 12
Assembly of the Synod at Wellington, March 1859—Unanimous Resolutions passed on the occasion	12, 13
The Native Race—their Christianity, capabilities for industry and for military tuition	14—16
Causes of decrease among the Maoris—Explanations	16, 17
Educational Missionary Institutions in New Zealand at Auckland, Otaki, &c.	17
Government of the Country—Privileges of the Natives—their neglect of them—Duties of their Teachers	18, 19
Extract from the Address of the Bishop of Waiapu to the Wellington Synod	20
Resolutions adopted by the Parent Committee as a Response to the Resolutions of the Synod	20, 21

CHRISTIANITY IN ITS INFLUENCE ON THE COLONIZATION OF NEW ZEALAND.

Colonization and native races—The Maori and the European	217, 218
Christianity in New Zealand preparing the way for the settler—Zeal of the early Missionaries	218, 219
Instances of the influence of Religion in New-Zealand History—The Treaty of Waitangi	220
Recognition of the Treaty by British Statesmen—Extracts of letters and speeches of Lord J. Russell, Sir Robert Peel, &c.	220—222
Native law as to tenure of Land—Tribes of the island and their subdivisions	222, 223
Attempts to wrest land from Natives by Europeans in 1840, and results—Subsequent proceedings	223, 224
Heke's insurrection—Rumours from England—Fresh outbreak—Panic at Auckland	224
Preservation of the Colony—Celebration of peace	225, 226
New Constitution—Right of the native to legislate in the Parliament, and its overrulement	226, 227
Governor Grey's return home—Early proceedings of the New-Zealand Parliament—The direction of native affairs vested solely in the Governor	227
The Governor's concessions to the House—Memorandum of the Secretary for Native Affairs, September, 20, 1858	228, 229
The Seal granted to New Zealand, its devices—Remarks	229

CONTENTS.

THE WAR IN NEW ZEALAND.

	Page
Meeting of tribes at Ngaruawahia—State of feeling in the Colony respecting the Governor's policy	229, 230
The King-Meeting in May—Description of the proceedings	230, 231
Events at Taranaki—Colonel Gold's attack—Repulse of the British	232
Mutual distrust between the races—Extract from a Memorandum of the Bishop of New Zealand, May 8, 1860	233, 234
Settlers' desire for native land—Meeting at Auckland—Despatch of an exploring party into the interior	234—236
Correspondence on the subject—Conclusions to by drawn from its tenor	235—237
Governor Browne to the Duke of Newcastle, September 20, 1859—Memorandum of the Assistant Native Secretary—Letter of Rev. R. Maunsell in the "New Zealander"	237—239
What is to be the issue of the war?—Despatch of Lord Carnarvon	239, 240
Closing remarks—the duty of Christians at home with regard to the present juncture	240

COLONIAL NEW ZEALAND.

	Page
Natural advantages of New Zealand—Harbours of the Northern Island	241
Gradual physical alterations of coast lines in the Provinces of Wellington, &c.—Mountains of the country	241, 242
Vegetation of New Zealand—its forest scenery and wooded elevations	242, 243
Water and water power—Cultivable nature and fecundity of the land—climate—fruits	244, 245
Extent of land acquired from the natives—Native depopulation of the Middle Island	246
Provinces of the Middle Island—The Nelson or Northern Province—its ports, rivers, and capabilities	246, 247
The Canterbury or Central Province—Settlements, &c.—Lyttelton—Christ Church—Population	247
Otago or Southern Province—Dunedin—Invercargill—Southern Island	248
Natural Ocean Docks of Otago—Extract from the Admiralty Blue Book—Population	248, 249
Colonial population of the Middle Island—Its general resources	249
Provinces of the Northern Island;—The Wellington Province—Population—Town of Wellington and outlying districts	249, 250
Province of New Plymouth—Population—Natural features—Mount Egmont—Taranaki	250, 251
Letter of Mr. Fox protesting against the Memorial in favour of the Governor's proceedings in respect to the native outbreak	251, 252
Province of Auckland—Population, &c.—Position and advantages of the capital	252, 253
The demand for land by the Auckland Colonists considered—Statement of the Superintendent, and reply to the Chief Commissioner—Remarks	253, 254
Speech of Mr. Forsaith, June 4, 1859—Remarks on Emigration—Supposititious reply of a Maori to an unreasonable emigrant	254, 255
Further investigation of the subject—Real cause of the restlessness at Auckland—Territorial Rights' Bill	255, 256
The Credit System at Auckland—Concluding Observations	256, 257

⁎ *Vide* also "Recent Intelligence."

CONTENTS.

North-West America.

RUPERT'S LAND—ITS PROSPECTS.

	Page
The Red-River Colony sixteen years ago—Gradual openings of intercourse with the United States and Canada	111, 112
The overland Canadian route by Dog Lake, Rainy Lake, and Lake of the Woods, to Red River	112
Importation of whisky to the colony—Extract from letter of Rev. W. W. Kirkby	113
Religious condition of St. Andrew's—Conservative power of true Christianity—Remarks by the Rev. A. Cowley	114, 115
Extract from the Journal of the Rev. J. Horden, of Moose—Missionary diffusiveness—Visit of the Bishop of Rupert's Land to English River	115, 116
Tour of the Earl of Southesk through the colony—Interesting discovery made by him	116
Progressiveness of Missionary Action—Extracts from the Journal of Rev. H. Budd	130, 131
Extracts from the Journal of the Rev. T. H. Fleming of a journey of 500 miles in snow-shoes	132, 133
Efforts of Rome in the extreme North—Extract from Archdeacon Hunter's Journal	133
Extracts from the Charge of the Bishop of Rupert's Land, delivered in January 1860	133—141

*** *Vide* also "Recent Intelligence."

Rome.

DISMISSAL OF MISSIONARIES TO THEIR SPHERES OF LABOUR.

Instructions of the Committee delivered March 12th, to the Rev. J. Bilderbeck, the Rev. J. C. Taylor, and the Rev. R. H. Weakley	89—92

VALEDICTION OF MISSIONARIES, AND INSTRUCTIONS ADDRESSED TO THEM.

Introductory Remarks	257
Instructions to Missionaries	258—264

CONTENTS.

Miscellaneous.

MISSIONARY DEDUCTIONS FROM THE PARABLES.

	Page
The string of parables in Matthew xiii., and their main subject	169
The Wheat and the Tares—The Field of the World—Remarks	169—171
The disturbances in Mount Lebanon—The locality described	171
The Druzes and the Maronites—Asaad-el-Shidiak, the Martyr—Tribe contentions, Labours of the American Missionaries—Formation of Churches at Beyrout and Hashbeyia—Hindrances	172
	172, 173
Insurrection of the Druzes—Fall of, and slaughter at Hashbeyia, Deir-el-Kamr, &c.—What is to be the issue?	173—175
The Chinese Question—Remarks on the British policy towards that nation	193, 194
Appeal of the Four Powers—Oliphant's account of the presentation at Soochow	194—196
Macartney's Embassy of 1793—The journey to Pekin—Performance of the "Kotow"—Journey towards Tartary—The great wall	196, 197
Arrival of Macartney at Zhehol—Office of the "Board of Rights"—Appearance of the Emperor—Presentation of the Gold Box	197, 198
Return to Pekin—The Emperor's answer—Departure of the Embassy	198, 199
Lord Amherst's Visit in 1816—Davis's Account of his reception	199, 200
Late efforts to obtain permission for a British Minister to reside at Pekin—Signing of the Treaty	201, 202
Letters of the Chinese Commissioners to Lord Elgin—Lord Elgin to Lord Malmesbury, November 5, 1858—Instructions to Mr. Bruce	202—204
Action of the Russian Government—Remarks—Memorandum of a conversation with a Chinese from Pekin	204, 205
The Action at the Peiho—Mr. Bruce to Lord Malmesbury, July 13, 1859—Chinese treatment of the American Minister	205—208
England's duty to China at this emergency, political and religious—Native Memorial to the Emperor on the subject of Christianity	208, 209
The 29th Article of the American Treaty—Proclamation against Romish Christianity in the Kiang-si province—Persecution of Native Converts	210, 211
The Seed, the word of God—God's revelation to man	270
The "Essays and Reviews from Oxford"—their direct object and tendency	270
The language of the "Essays" aggressive on the authority of revelation	271
Dr. William's Review—his summary mode of explaining away the miracles and prophecies of Scripture	272
The third "Essay"—its object—General remarks on the series	272—273
Various efforts to counteract the teaching of revelation—The true medium	273, 274
Weapons of attack against the truth—the Gospel its own defence	274, 275
Peculiar and valuable properties of the Seed	275, 276
Analogy between the natural and the spiritual Seed	276, 277

Illustrations.

(Engraved by Johnston.)

Pa in the Hutt District, New Zealand	1
Panoramic View of Lucknow	49
Burning the dead in North India	93
Western Gate, Pekin	97
Church, &c., of the Bishop of Rupert's Land, Red River	131
A Mica Mine in Behar	145
The Great Tank at Strivilliputthur, North Tinnevelly	175
The Great Wall of China	193
Stage erected at the Bay of Islands in 1849, to celebrate peace	217
A New Zealand forest	241
View from the Mission Bungalow, Surandei	265

CONTENTS.

Recent Intelligence.

Supplement to January Number—Extract from the "Bombay Guardian."
    Letter of Rev. W. A. Russell, Ningpo.
  February—Financial Affairs.
    Letter of Rev. J. Rebmann, Mombas.
    Christianity among the Natives of India.
    Sir C. Wood on the Madras Memorial.
    Festival of St. Francis Xavier at Goa.
    Departure and return home of Missionaries.
  March—Financial system of the Society.
    Letter of Rev. C. C. Mengé, Western India.
    Ordinations in Tinnevelly—Letter of Rev. P. S. Royston.
    Candidates for Ordination.
    Death of a Missionary.
  April—Success of Mr. Williams, Native Protestant Missionary in Turkey.
    Letter of Rev. J. Vaughan, Burdwan.
    Letter of Rev. A. Strawbridge, Umritsur.
    Letter of Rev. R. Clark, Peshawur.
    Letter of Rev. P. P. Schaffter, Tinnevelly.
    Dismissal, return home, death, and ordination of Missionaries.
  May—Prayer Meeting in January—Letters from Rupert's Land and China.
    Letter of Mr. Smith, Ishaga, Yoruba.
    Extract from the "Iwe Irohin."
    Letter of Rev. J. P. Mengé, Lucknow.
    Return home, departure, and ordination of Missionaries.
  June—Sixty-first Anniversary of the Society—Annual Sermon and Meetings, Movers and Seconders, Resolutions, Committee, Finances, and Conclusion of Report.
    Lord Stratford De Redcliffe and Lord Wodehouse on Protestantism in Turkey.
  July—Petition of the Society respecting Bible Schools in India.
    Letter of Rev. J. Vaughan, Burdwan.
    The Swinging Festival—Extract from "Allen's Indian Mail."
    Dismissal, departure, and return home of Missionaries.
  August—Presentation of the Petition of the Society respecting the Bible in Indian Schools.
    Finances of the Society.
    Destruction of the Missionary Premises at Magbeli, West Africa.
    Extract from the "Bombay Guardian."
  September—Minute of the Governor-General of India on the promulgation of Christianity by Military Officers.
    Candidates for ordination.
  October—Progress of Christianity among the Kols.
    Missionary Meeting at Victoria, Vancouver's Island.
    Notes on the Indians at ditto.
    Return home, departure, and ordination of Missionaries.
  November—Expected arrival of Prince Alfred at Sierra Leone.
    Religion of the Chinese Insurgents—Letter of a Missionary.
    The Taranaki outbreak, New Zealand—Letter of Rev. R. Burrows.
    Return home of a Missionary.
  December—Visit of Missionaries to the Kan wang.
    The Slave-trade.
    Dismissal, departure, and return home of Missionaries.

PA IN THE HUTT DISTRICT, NEW ZEALAND.

Church Missionary Intelligencer.

NEW ZEALAND—THE EPISCOPATE, THE CHURCH MISSIONARY SOCIETY, AND THE NATIVE RACE.

NEW ZEALAND has been designated the Britain of the South, and assuredly if the possible future of New Zealand might be concluded from her advantageous position and natural endowments, there would be no enthusiasm in affirming that she will yet prove to be the Great Britain of the southern hemisphere. The points of identity between these widely-separated island groups are interesting and remarkable. They each consist of two leading islands, with their satellites, of which, in the New-Zealand group, Stewart's island, about half the size of Perthshire, is the principal. The New-Zealand isles extend from north to south eight hundred miles; and if the two great islands of the British archipelago were placed to the north and south of each other, instead of to the east and west, their longitudinal extension would be about the same. New Zealand is more approximated to the equator than the isles of the United Kingdom; the most northern point of New Zealand, that which is nearest the equator, being in 34° 10′ south latitude, and that of the British isles reaching a little to the south of 50° north latitude. Yet are they both within the limits of the temperate zone, and fitted to be the homes of energetic races. The position of the United Kingdom is influential and commanding, as regards the coasts and kingdoms that border on the Great Atlantic with the gulfs and bays; nor is that of New Zealand less so as respects the Pacific and its shores and islands. "Close to the west she has the busy marts and markets of Australia. Close on the north, the thousand Polynesian islands, slumbering in their summer seas, and needing but the touch of magic steam to open new worlds to our commerce. She stands on the great Panama highway from Europe to the southern gold-fields. Within easy sail, on the one side, she reaches the Dutch and Spanish colonies, China, and our Indian possessions; on the other, California, Mexico, Chili, and Peru. She stands in the centre of the Austral Ocean, mid-way between ocean's greatest capes, Cape Horn and Good Hope; and so before the doors of Australia, that every wool and gold ship has to pass within sight of her southern shores." And as thus placed in a position of great importance, so she is gifted with an indented coast line of great extent, from whence commercial relations may radiate forth to the ends of the earth. In this respect the New-Zealand isles can compete favourably with our British home: "being more generally indented with estuaries and deep bays, they have a sea-board exceeding considerably that of the islands of Great Britain." The position of Auckland, the capital, is, in this respect, one of admirable selection. "About 150 miles from the north cape, the northern island of New Zealand is almost intersected by two large estuaries, which indent the coast so deeply on either side, that the waters are separated only by a narrow isthmus. On the eastern side is the estuary of the Manukau; on the other side, lying deep in the south-western extremity of the estuary of the Thames, and completely shut in by a group of small islands, is the land-locked harbour of the Waitemata." Studded with islands of various size and form, its outline broken by numerous deep bays and jutting headlands, it presents the appearance of an English lake, and "is seen to greatest advantage on one of those rare days when a perfect calm prevails, with a deep but soft blue sky, studded here and there with fields of snow-white silvery clouds, seen through a glistening atmosphere. Thus seen, under all the advantages of light, colouring, and repose, the harbour presents a scene of placid beauty, which it would tax the imagination to surpass."[*]

Nor is the interior less richly endowed. As to its surface character generally, it may be classified as a "wooded-highland country, with some half-dozen noble plains, and thousands of brook-watered villages, dells, and dales." The soil, though light, is often rich, "and the fertility of the earth, quadrupled by

---

[*] Swainson's "New Zealand and its Colonization," p. 216.

the genial climate, literally produces a wilderness of vegetation. Sea-spray crags, shore margins, plains, valleys, hill-sides, mountain-steeps, are alike clothed with perpetual verdure; and the expression 'smothered in vegetation,' is not a mere figure of speech when applied to New Zealand, but a term truly descriptive of the country."* "In those features which constitute the foundation of fine scenery, New Zealand is unsurpassed by any country in the world. She displays noble forests, snow-capped mountains, shooting up 10,000 feet from a sea of green, and wooded up to the line of snow, tracts of rolling champaign country, dells, valleys, rivers, and rivulets innumerable." Nor is this mere beauty. "New Zealand is a fertile cultivable country, where plough, and sickle, and mill would singularly enrich and brighten the landscape." Taranaki, under the shadow of the snow-peaked Mount Egmont, with its neatly-thatched cottages, farm buildings, and its abundant wool and farm produce; the grassy plains of Ahuriri and Wairarapa, clothed with rich pasturage for sheep; Nelson, with its settled climate and opening gold-fields; Canterbury, with its extensive grass plains and great agricultural capabilities; the well-watered and well-wooded Otago, with its superior advantages for pastoral pursuits, and its valuable harbours;—these are some of the more familiar points of the New Zealand of our day. Of the climate it may suffice to say, that it is "favourable alike to the preservation of robust health, and to the improvement of weak health;" a climate most congenial to all pastoral and agricultural pursuits; one in which every English domestic animal thrives and fattens; and one in which every English grain, grass, fruit, and flowers, attains full development and perfection. "But besides growing nearly all the fruits of Europe, the climate has been proved to have the singular power of maturing crops of both potatoes and Indian corn. In scarcely any other country are maize and potatoes found to flourish in the same climate, the growth of Indian corn being commonly confined to the country of the vine."

But what avail abundant resources, the fertile soil, and the numerous and capacious harbours, unless there be present the active and industrious population, turning to account the gifts of God's providence, making the solitude re-echo with the voice of man, and causing the earth and sea to yield forth their treasures? In this consists the great defect under which New Zealand labours—the paucity of its population. It is not land that is wanted, but people to possess it. The entire population of New Zealand at the present moment amounts to no more than 120,000 souls. Man, therefore, is the element of prosperity which is most needed, which is most scarce and most valuable, and all available means should be adopted to improve and strengthen the existing stock, if so be it may increase and multiply, and replenish the earth.

The 120,000 occupants of New Zealand consist of two distinct races—an aboriginal people, the Maories, and Europeans brought thither by emigration; the former exceeding the latter in the proportion of seven to five. Of the value of the European population, no man doubts. They are mainly our own countrymen, who have gone forth from our own shores; and if only they forget not the faith of their fathers, and be guided in their actions by the fear of God, and submission to his revealed will, we doubt not they will be blessed and prospered. That the settlers who have raised new homesteads on far New-Zealand's shore, and have taken root in that their adopted country, should desire an increase of their numbers by emigration, is most natural; nor can we be surprised when writers urge the importance of attracting population to an infant colony where there is "one human being to 1600 acres of fertile wilderness." But it is, we hesitate not to say, a great mistake so exclusively to regard this source of increase, as to ignore and set aside, as of no value, the aboriginal population.

But can these two races, so distinct in origin, and so removed from one another in their respective conditions of semi-barbarism and civilization, ever so blend as to become an united and happy people? Is amalgamation possible? Or, before such an issue can be reached, shall not the old catastrophe be acted over again, and the inferior race become extinguished in the presence of the superior one? This is the problem that, at the present moment, waits solution in New Zealand.

The question is asked, Is its possible that two distinct portions of the human race, in the opposite conditions of civilization and barbarism, can be brought into immediate contact without the destruction of the uncivilized race? We believe it to be possible, quite possible, if only Christianity in its purity and power be on the spot to counteract those antipathies which repel, and induce those sympathies which attract and invite. We are too

---

* Hursthouse, "New Zealand," vol. i. pp. 95, 96.

well aware of the blood-stained annals of colonization; but they have been so because Christianity has been either entirely absent from the scene, or present in name only, without the power. The European without Christianity has been alike dangerous to the native, whether as friend or foe. As a friend, he slew him by his vices; as a foe, he slew him by the sword. But where Christianity, in its purity and power, is on the spot to mediate, a different result may be expected, and the two streams, derived from sources so widely remote, may meet and blend under wholesome influences, so as to form one united and prosperous population. Instances are on record in which the European, covetous of the patrimony of some heathen tribe, has cast aside all restraints of religion and conscience, and pursued, at whatever cost, his grasping scheme, until the native race, crushed and enfeebled in the contest, has been left like the sick man, whose vital powers rapidly fail, and the moment of dissolution is momentarily expected. Yet even then, although apparently too late, its arrival deferred to the last moment, Christianity has come, and administered reviving cordials, and the sick man nigh unto death has been restored, and the old stock, re-invigorated, has thrown out fresh shoots, and, under a new condition, promises to be more fruitful and vigorous than it was before. So it has been with the remnants of the Apallachian tribes on the United-States frontier. Broken in repeated conflicts with the white man, they " have received teachers, and applied their efforts to master the problem of civilization. They have also admitted the axiom, that the Indian communities cannot exist, in prosperity, within the boundaries of the States. One tribe after another has consented to dispose of their lands and improvements, and, carrying along their teachers and the arts, have removed to the west of the Mississippi, and to the waters of the Missouri. A revival and very striking improvement of their condition has been the result, with all the industrial and temperate tribes. They have erected schools and academies with a part of their annuities; they raise large stocks of cattle and horses; they cultivate extensive fields of Indian corn and the cereal grains; they erect substantial dwelling-houses and farms; they build mills, and manufactories of articles of first necessity; they have, to a considerable extent, adopted the European costume and the English language. The principal tribes have organized systems of government, courts, and civil codes. The writings of their public men compare very well with those of politicians of the frontier States and Territories. Men of learning and piety conduct their system of education, and, in the most advanced tribes, no small per-centage of the population, as compared with European communities in that region, are shown to have adopted Christianity."*

Christianity in New Zealand was more advantageously circumstanced than in the conflicts between the colonists of America and the native races. It had there preceded formal colonization. It had laid hold on the mind of the native, and acquired influence over it, which it was enabled to use for good, to control his fiery passions, and guide him in comparative safety through the most critical period of his national existence. No one can duly reflect on what Christianity has effected in New Zealand, without feeling encouraged as to the future. Whatever new difficulties may arise, they cannot surely be greater than those which have been already overcome.

What was New Zealand when the first Missionaries went there? What a land of horrors! In reading the annals of its earlier history, one feels in the midst of fiends rather than of men. It is almost impossible to conceive that human beings could have so deteriorated, and become so shameless and so pitiless, so intensely bloodthirsty and indescribably revolting in their practices. We shrink from retracing the outlines of that earthly pandemonium, or lighting up again the lurid fires around which the cannibal held his horrid feast. No wonder they are but the remnant of a nation. When we remember that they went forward to their wars prompted by a double appetite—the lust for revenge and the lust for human flesh—the wonder is, not that so few survived, but that any survived at all. Twenty and seven years back, when Missionaries, amidst u ntold difficulties and dangers, were persevering in a work which many pronounced to be hopeless, the desolating traces of mutual slaughter were but too plainly discernible. Marks of former settlements might be seen, all swept as with the besom of destruction. No one can tell what the Missionaries had to endure in those dark times. Yet there they were, amidst all that was disheartening and repulsive, first the Church Missionary, and then the Wesleyan Missionary. They stood alone in this valley of death. There was no church in its integrity sent out in those days; no episcopate, founded at the expense of several thousand pounds, was thought necessary to initiate the

* " Schoolcraft."

work; the dogma had not yet been enunciated, that the preaching of the Gospel is unavailing, and carries with it no blessing, unless accredited by the presence of a bishop. Evangelists went forth, depending not on organization, but on the teaching and preaching of Jesus Christ, and Him crucified; and that simplicity of procedure God blessed. Before the bishop arrived, the steep wall-side had been climbed, the level summit reached, and Christianity, although made known only by simple presbyters, had attained acknowledged influence over the people. The subduing power of the cross had been felt, and many, whose names might well be Legion, might be seen sitting at the feet of Jesus, clothed, and in their right mind.

"On his first arrival in the country, fifteen years ago, the Bishop of New Zealand was struck with their orderly observance of religious ordinances. In February 1843, he wrote, 'I held my first confirmation, at which 325 natives were confirmed; and a more orderly, and, I hope, impressive ceremony, could not have been conducted in any church in England; the natives coming up in parties to the communion-table, and audibly repeating the answer, 'Ewakoatia ana e ahua' ('I do confess'). It was a most striking sight to see a church filled with native Christians, ready at my first invitation to obey the ordinances of their religion. On the following Sunday, 300 native communicants assembled at the Lord's table, though the rain was unceasing; and some of them came two days' journey for this purpose.' On another occasion 'a noble congregation, amounting to at least 1000, assembled amidst the ruins of the chapel (recently blown down). They came up in the most orderly way, in parties, headed by the native chiefs and teachers, and took their places on the ground with all the regularity of so many companies of soldiers. We were placed under an awning made of tents, but the congregation sat in the sun. The gathering of this body of people, their attentive manner, and the deep sonorous uniformity of their responses, was most striking.'"*

That was a wondrous change: the great mass of an independent and savage people moved to submit themselves to an influence which they had long despised, numbers of them honestly embracing Christianity, in a thorough change of heart and an earnest abandonment of their heathen practices. That marked and memorable result, under circumstances of peculiar difficulty, gave an impulse to the modern Missionary efforts of the church which continues to be felt to this very day. It encouraged the friends of Missions to expect results greater than we had yet ventured to hope for; and with New Zealand inscribed on their banners, Missionary agencies went forward to the conflict with a strong expectance, not merely of future, but of present success. In the achievements, then, of the past may we not often find encouragement as to the difficulties of the future?

But just as our affairs in New Zealand assumed this improved and encouraging aspect, a new difficulty arose: colonization commenced, and the tide of emigration set in strongly on the shores of New Zealand. Many of the most earnest friends of the Maori race dreaded such a movement, and earnestly deprecated it. We can scarcely wonder at this, when we remember the horrors which had too frequently attended that procedure. A Committee of the House of Commons on Aborigines had been appointed in the Session of 1833, and renewed in that of 1835. Men of experience and character bore their testimony to the calamitous results of European contact with native races, except through the medium of an active and restraining Christianity. On that occasion Mr. Dandeson Coates, the then Secretary of the Church Missionary Society, expressed himself forcibly on the subject of the colonization of New Zealand—

"Speaking with reference to New Zealand, I would suggest the importance of the firm establishment of British influence on the minds of the native chiefs. They are at present extremely well disposed towards England; they look to England, and regard this country as a point of reference, as a friendly power. They are disposed, therefore, to receive suggestions and recommendations; and in this way the British Government, without exceeding their appropriate limits, might, I apprehend, materially facilitate the social, moral, and religious improvement of the New-Zealanders, by its influence on the minds of the native chiefs. But in saying this, I wish to add most distinctly, a protest, if I might venture to employ such a term, against the colonization of New Zealand on the part of the Government; because, though I do not conceive colonization to be necessarily productive of destructive consequences, yet it has so generally led to that result, that there is nothing that I should deprecate more than the colonization of New Zealand by this country. And this the more especially, as, by the agency of Christian Missions—there being a Mission of the Wesleyan, as well as of

---

* "Swainson," pp. 31, 32.

the Church Missionary Society in operation there—a process is going on by which those general interpositions of the Government that I have referred to would secure, so far as any human means can secure, the moral, social, and religious improvement of the people, and preserve them entire as a distinct race."

Another gentleman, the Rev. J. Beecham, of the Wesleyan Missionary Society, pointed out, in his evidence, the special feature in the existing system of colonization, which he considered most productive of injury.

"When I read some of our Acts of Parliament which relate to the formation of our colonies, I find that the lands of certain countries are sold to the colonists, without any reference whatever to the aboriginal inhabitants: the very countries which, at the times when the Acts are passed, are occupied by various aboriginal tribes, are all disposed of as though they were waste and uninhabited regions. Now I must confess I have never yet been able to see the equity of such a proceeding. I have ever thought, and must still continue to think, unless eternal justice itself should change, that this is essentially and morally wrong; and that our colonization system is thus based upon a principle of unrighteousness. This I regard as the original cause of many of the evils of which we complain: a great proportion of the ill consequences resulting from intercourse between the colonists and the natives are to be traced to this very source. I do not see what else can follow than very disastrous results. The colonists and the natives are necessarily brought into painful collision at the very outset: the one seeks to obtain possession of the lands secured to them by Act of Parliament; the other to keep possession of those very lands which are theirs by a prior right; and what is the consequence? The whole history of colonization tells us. The natives have to retire, but they retire with irritated feelings, and in the spirit of revenge; and thus the foundation is laid, as the natural consequence of the wrong principle on which our colonization is based: the foundation, I say, is laid of a system of painful and angry intercourse between the colonists and the natives for years to come."

There were, however, in England, men of different opinions. They were resolved to colonize, and New Zealand, no longer now the New Zealand of the "Boyd" massacre, was selected as the most suitable and promising field. In 1837 an association was formed in London for this express purpose. The first efforts of its members was to induce the Government to erect the New-Zealand isles into a British colony. Disappointed, for a time, in this hope, they then resolved to send their agents to New Zealand, purchase land, and prepare the way for emigrants; "and, calculating on the success of their agent, they proceeded at once to offer, for sale by lottery, in England, the right of selection amongst the lands thus anticipated to be acquired by them..... And though officially warned that their proceedings would not be sanctioned by the Government, the New-Zealand Company found purchasers in England to the amount of more than 100,000*l.*"

Hitherto the policy of the Government had been to leave untouched the independence of New Zealand, and to confine its action to cultivating friendly relations with the chiefs, and exercising an influence over them for their good. But now they felt themselves necessitated to pursue other measures; and, to "protect the natives, to avert a war of races, and to rescue the emigrants themselves from the evils of a lawless state of society, it was now resolved to adopt the most effectual measures for establishing among them a settled form of civil government."

In order that such effectual protection might be rendered, it became necessary that the Queen should be acknowledged as the Sovereign of the country; and Captain Hobson was charged with the delicate duty of bringing these negotiations to a successful issue. The result was, the treaty of Waitangi, signed by a large portion of the chiefs, by which, on the express conditions that their territorial rights should be respected, they ceded the sovereignty of the islands to the Queen. In fulfilment of such stipulations, the English Government, instead of acting upon the unjust principle of appropriating at their convenience, and without due compensation, the lands of aboriginal tribes, proceeded to render a fair equivalent for such lands as it required; and, during the two and a-half years of Governor Hobson's administration "considerable tracts of land became, by purchase, the demesne lands of the Crown." "An experiment was about to be tried, deeply affecting the interests of humanity." A pledge had been "given by the ministers of the Crown that the natives of these islands should, if possible, be saved from that process of extermination, under which uncivilized tribes had hitherto disappeared, when brought into contact with civilization;" and the British Government was, for the first time in earnest, about to try the experiment, whether a fragment of the great human family, long sunk in heathen darkness, could be raised from its state of social degradation, and maintained and preserved as a civilized people."*

The precipitate action of the New-Zealand Company had, however, already laid the foundation of coming troubles. The Company's titles were defective. "When their purchasers proceeded to take actual possession of the land, natives from various parts of the country, who had not been parties to the sale, came forward to assert their rights, and, regarding the Company's settlers as unauthorized intruders, actually opposed their occupation of the land; while the colonists, ignorant of the native law of property, naturally viewed the claims put forward by the natives as but a pretext for acts of violence, and for making extortionate demands."

The British Government refused to be responsible for proceedings which it had never sanctioned, nay, which it had expressly disclaimed. We must refer such of our readers as desire a further insight into the proceedings of the New-Zealand Land Company to Mr. Swainson's recent work on New Zealand, where they will find facts stated of the most painful nature. The settlers were placed in a most unhappy position, consigned either to idleness and poverty, or to attempt to possess themselves of lands, their title to which was denied by the natives. At length the first collision ensued in July 1843, in the Wairau valley, about seventy miles from Nelson, in which "upwards of twenty Europeans, including nearly all the leading members of the Nelson settlement, were tomahawked or shot."

That collision aroused the slumbering distrust of the native chiefs and people. They feared that their lands would be wrested from them. On the part of the Bay-of-Islands' natives in particular, other causes of dissatisfaction existed. They found that, by the selection of Auckland as a capital, trade had decreased on their part of the coast, while the duties levied on imported goods increased the price of such articles as they needed. Unhappily, too, about this time the House of Commons had violated the stipulations of Waitangi, by a resolution "that measures already ripe for mischief, with an effect that may be readily imagined."

Heki, a chief of the Bay of Islands, who had been the first to sign the treaty, now raised the standard of independence. Kororarika was taken and sacked, the royal flag-staff was cut down, the military block-house was taken, the soldiers, seamen, and the whole population of the settlement, abandoned it, and, the places of worship being spared, the other buildings, with scarcely an exception, were sacked, plundered, and destroyed. Reinforcements of British troops arrived, and war ensued, but the Maories held their fortified pa, in spite of a spirited attack, and repulsed their assailants with heavy loss. The disaffection spread from north to south. The settlers were driven from the valley of the Hutt. In the town of Wellington the colonists were kept in arms for weeks together, keeping watch and ward, in daily expectation of attack; and it is hardly too much to affirm that Wellington owed its safety at that moment to a single individual, the Rev. Octavius Hadfield, Missionary of the Church Missionary Society at Otaki. "At Wanganui the out-settlers were driven in; houses, in the settlement itself, and within gunshot of a fortified military post, were plundered and destroyed, and the Queen's troops, during a period of several weeks, could only show themselves outside of their own stockade at the hazard of being shot."

It was a most critical moment. There was reason to apprehend that a large proportion of the Maori population throughout the island would rise in sympathy with Heki, on the north, and other chiefs in the south and west. Had they done so, what would have been the position of the settlers? The central area of the island, its mountain-fastnesses and strong positions, were occupied by the Maories, well supplied with fire-arms: there was not one of them who was not familiar with the use of a musket. Independent of any regular commissariat, they could "move rapidly from place to place, either across the country, or by paths where ordinary European troops would be unable to follow them, and,

them within easy reach of a superior native force." The Maories, had there been a national rising, such as Ireland has often witnessed, might have cut them off in detail, and, had they been the Maories of former days, they would have done so. But a new controlling power had been introduced amongst them. The light of Christian truth had penetrated many a dark heart, and given them new views of things. Its restraining influence was felt on their consciences. The New Testament was in circulation amongst them in their own tongue: they had taught themselves to read it, and numbers of them read it diligently. The Bishop and Missionaries were earnest and active. Influential meetings were held. It was shown them that their fears were groundless, and that there was no intention on the part of the British Government to set aside the treaty of Waitangi, and seize their lands. It pleased God to bless these efforts. Strong as was the sympathy with Heki, the exertions of the mediating parties—those whom the natives recognized as spiritual men, the teachers of the Gospel of peace, in whom they had confidence—were more powerful. The disaffected feelings of the moment evaporated in a few outbreaks in different parts of the island, which, left unsupported by the native masses, languished, and were, after a time, put out. The agitation gradually subsided, and the Maories settled down in contented submission to the British rule. That was an eventful crisis, one to be remembered, in which New Zealand was conserved from an overwhelming calamity by the action of the Gospel.

We would warn our readers against another version of these facts—that which describes the New-Zealand Company as the innocent and injured party, and throws the blame of the collision between the races on the Government and the Missionaries. We cannot accept that view. The facts of the case, when examined, entirely disprove it. We believe the Government to have been actuated by a real desire to act justly and impartially towards all parties; and we believe that the Missionaries may with truth be pronounced to be the benefactors of both races. We do not say there were no mistakes made. We cannot undertake to justify every step which every Missionary thought himself free to take. There were, no doubt, some things done which had far better been otherwise. But this we say, that but for the knowledge of Christian truth which the natives had received through the Missionaries of the two Societies in London, and the moral pressure which could thus be brought to bear upon them in the hour of danger, not all the military force which the authorities, at that remote point, could have collected from the mother-country and the adjoining colonies, would have sufficed to prevent scenes of bloodshed which would have laid waste the country, and put back for many a day the rising prosperity of New Zealand. As it was, the effect of these disturbances was highly prejudicial: emigration to New Zealand almost entirely ceased.

New Zealand now entered on a new phase of its history, and became exposed to new trials. In 1851 the Australian gold discoveries took place, and it seemed at first as if the influence of this event would be highly prejudicial to New Zealand. "The news which arrived by every mail of the prizes drawn by hundreds in the Australian gold-fields naturally excited the minds of the settlers in New Zealand, and rendered them impatient until they had tried their fortunes in the golden lottery; and for several months every vessel carried away numbers of the more adventurous and unsettled of the male population. As soon, however, as the first excitement had passed away, instead of fearing the effects of the recent gold discoveries, tho settlers perceived a rapidly-increasing market close at hand for all their surplus produce; and they were soon convinced that in New Zealand itself they had a certain means of transmuting the materials around them into gold, by supplying the market of the neighbouring colonies; and they have now, for several years been in the enjoyment of uninterrupted prosperity."*

In this industrial impulse the natives largely shared: gold, the proceeds of the sale of lands and grain produce, came largely into their hands, and native Christianity became exposed to a test severer than any which it had yet experienced. With the opportunity of acquiring wealth came the collateral opportunity of expending it on evil gratifications to which they had hitherto been strangers. The ungodly white men presented himself with his low vices; and grog-shops, opening in increasing numbers, tempted the natives to drunkenness and its attendant evils.

Let us consider in what state of preparedness this new trial found the native church. The Episcopate had now been nine years in the islands. No sooner had New Zealand been created into a colony than the ecclesiastical authorities in England decided on the establishment of an episcopal see at the seat of Government in that country. In that movement the Church Missionary Society heartily

---

* "Swainson," pp. 192, 193.

concurred. A great impression had been made upon the native mind, and that impression needed to be so deepened and strengthened, that it might prove to be, not a momentary glow of pleasing excitement, but such a real alteration in the native character as might be lasting and influential. It needed that the work should be followed up, and that promptly and energetically; that the Missionary agency should be made in all respects as effective as possible, and have afforded to it every facility of free action; and that amidst the increasing pressure of new inquirers, the European Missionaries should be supplemented, as quickly as was consistent with safe action, by a native pastorate, which might bring home the preaching of the Gospel to the little groups of New Zealanders, who now, encouraged by the prevalence of peace, were deserting the old pas, and dispersing themselves over the face of the country for purposes of cultivation. At such a crisis the advent of the Episcopate was most opportune. Hitherto, for the discharge of episcopal functions, the native church was entirely dependent on the occasional visit of the Bishop of Australia; but the transfer of the Episcopate to the spot gave to the native church, and the Missionaries who served it, an ecclesiastical basis of their own, to which they might recur as cases of necessity arose; and thus new vigour be infused into all departments of this work. Nine years was a considerable period in which much of these hopes might have been realized, and the ship rigged and in all respects fitted to meet the coming storm. We desire to touch as lightly as possible on this part of the subject. Of earnestness and conscientiousness of purpose we feel assured there was no lack in any quarter; the errors were those of the judgment. At the same time we should be untrue to ourselves, and untrue to our subject, did we not frankly express our conviction that, at the end of the nine years, the Mission had not derived from the Episcopate that increased measure of effectiveness which had been expected.

The Episcopate required the surrender of principles of action which the more mature experience of the Society had taught it to be essential to Missionary success. And yet the new principles on which the Episcopate had decided to act may easily be collected from published documents. The bishop, soon after his arrival in the island, issued a notice in these words — "Every clergyman, acting under a licence within the diocese, is required to be prepared to minister to the English settlers within his district, as well as to the native people, as occasion may require." A letter addressed to the Secretary of the Gospel-Propagation Society, dated November 2, 1852, expressed decision—"I require every town clergyman to learn the native language, and be ready to minister to the spiritual wants of the Aborigines; and I find it will be necessary also to establish the converse rule—that every Missionary to the natives shall also be ready to minister to the English settlers; for, in this country, English and natives will live side by side, unless some rupture, which God avert, should take place between the two races." Now it had long been an established principle of the Church Missionary Society, that its Missionaries, as a general rule, should abstain from ministering to their own countrymen. It was a decision formed on long experiences of the working of Missions in various fields of labour, which all combined to testify—that it is not possible to invest a Missionary with permanent relations to Europeans, except to the detriment of his proper work, the evangelization of the natives, and their establishment in a profession of Christianity.

Another point of discrepancy may be referred to. It will be found in the same letter from the Bishop to the Secretary of the Gospel-Propagation Society, dated Nov. 2, 1842—

"In carrying into effect the various plans which I have felt to be necessary for the establishment of a sound church system in this country, I have been continually reminded of the confidence reposed in me by the Committee, which has enabled me to act with decision in many cases where delay would seriously have injured the future prospects of the church. It is impossible to foresee what may be the peculiar position of this colony from year to year: even the course of population cannot be predicted: the relations with the native people involve a new element of uncertainty. If I had been fettered with strict rules, and obliged to refer every question to England; or if every clergyman were at liberty to communicate directly with the Society, instead of looking up to me as the *director of his duties*, and *the source of his emoluments*, I could never have met the changes which, even in one year, have completely altered many of the arrangements which I at first formed."

Now, that the Society should thus entirely abdicate its own functions by surrendering to other hands the direction of its own Missionaries, selected by itself, sent out and maintained by it in the islands, thus reducing itself to a mere instrument for the collection of the necessary funds, is incompatible with the principles laid down in the paper on the ecclesiastical relations of the Society, appended to the Thirty-ninth Report, in which it is provided that its Missionaries, when intra-diocesan, must be under the bishop's licence, and that by granting or withholding his licence, the Bishop has the power of expressing his approbation, or otherwise, of the location to which the Missionary is appointed; but which as expressly reserves to the Society, "the superintendence of Missionaries in their labours among the heathen," and more especially the two points of income and location, "the Society continuing to be the paymaster, and proposing removals and changes to the bishop." In his location the Missionary is under episcopal superintendence and jurisdiction, but the selection of the place of labour must rest primarily with the Society, although, in the decision which may be come to, the judgment and wishes of the bishop always receive due consideration.

Again, the attempt was made to establish in New Zealand a lengthened diaconate. Several of the Society's Missionaries were kept in deacons' orders for nearly ten or fourteen years, notwithstanding the entreaties and applications of the Committee; and these ministers, being at the time in charge of large districts, containing many hundred native communicants, there not unfrequently occurred an interval of twelve months before the sacrament of the Lord's supper could be administered by the visit of some distant Missionary in full orders, and many aged and infirm persons were wholly cut off from an ordinance which, by the native Christians of New Zealand, is greatly prized.

Nor were the Missionaries supplemented as they might have been by the effective action of a native pastorate. The Episcopate, immediately on its arrival, had taken into its own hands the preparation of candidates for the ministry, as well European as native. A college was established, through which every candidate for holy orders was required to pass; and a similar institution, which had been commenced by the Church Missionary Society, was consequently closed. But not until a period of eleven years from the introduction of the Episcopate had the first native been ordained. Eventually the Episcopal College proved a failure, and the preparation of candidates for the ministry reverted to the Church Missionaries. And thus it happened, that, at a time when the Mission stood in need of a complete organization, and full effectiveness of action, it was found in a crippled state, and ill fitted to cope with the emergencies of the moment. The Missionaries, in their reports, very frankly express the difficulties under which they laboured.

A European catechist, subsequently ordained, but whose ordination had been long delayed, and who, as a catechist, had to meet, in the best way he could, the requirements of a large district, complains—

"I am sorry to say the (Romish) priests have gained a considerable advantage here, from the weak state in which this district has always been left. No ordained minister having been placed here, our people always have been, and still are, put to great inconvenience for the administration of baptism and the Lord's supper, and are thus become a reproach to their Popish neighbours. They are consequently much discouraged; and, as I have before remarked, some of them have joined the Papists. I hear, indeed, that the Rev. Christopher Davies has been appointed to Wakatane by the Bishop; but, as he is only in deacons' orders, this will not facilitate the administration of the sacrament of the Lord's supper."*

A Missionary who had laboured effectively in the Mission from the year 1830, but who was not admitted into Priests' orders until 1852, remarks—

"What, then, remains, but to urge upon the consideration of that branch of the Christian church to which we belong, more comprehensive measures than have hitherto been adopted for evangelizing New Zealand? And, to be effective, these measures must include the organization of a system that shall gather into the bosom of the church—not negatively, but operatively—the thousands who, having received baptism in infancy, are growing up in ignorance and disregard of all that belongs to their baptismal vow. This must soon be done, or we shall have done nothing. Everywhere the first steps have been taken, firstfruits have been gathered in: but the harvest has not been secured, and the seed-corn for the coming season is left to mildew, if not to perish."†

Archdeacon W. Williams, now Bishop of Waiapu, refers to the same great defect at a later period (1854)—

"The natives of Turanga have been generally an industrious people, and the stimulus communicated to them by the large demand for wheat at Auckland, and the high prices given for it, have led them to cultivate more

* "Church Missionary Record," October, 1852, p. 234.
† Ibid., November 1853, p. 267.

extensively, and has thrown into their hands a large amount of property. Temporal prosperity has led to worldly-mindedness and all its attendant evils. An avaricious spirit has been engendered, and—grasping at more, like the dog and the shadow—they believed that by buying vessels for themselves, and taking their own grain to Auckland, they should realise a much greater gain. About twelve of these vessels, averaging between twenty and thirty tons, have been purchased by the natives between East Cape and Turanga; but nine have been wrecked, partly for want of skill, partly because there are no proper harbours to shelter them along the coast. But this is the least evil. Those natives who have thus been led to hold intercourse with the English towns have always been injured in their morality. They copy from our own countrymen an indifference to religion, and pick up all other vices which are so common in an English community. There is now, unhappily, a disposition to indulge in drinking, which is fostered by the English traders, who, notwithstanding the heavy penalties enforced by the law upon all persons who supply the natives with spirits, nevertheless distribute great quantities among them. Thus, after a lapse of fourteen years since the Gospel was brought to this part of the island, there is more apparent difficulty meeting us at every step than when we first came among them. When the Gospel message was new to the people, there was astonishing favour shown towards it: "they heard the word gladly." But by-and-bye many were offended, when they found that they were still subject to tribulation and affliction; and in the case of many, we have to mourn that, under the influence of the care of the world, and the deceitfulness of riches, the word is choked, and becometh unfruitful. Hence is seen the necessity of constant exertion, and of the faithful declaration of the Gospel. If in an English parish, much, under God, depends upon the labours of the clergyman, and, where he is remiss, the people fall back into a state of spiritual darkness, much more is care required where we have to encounter the influence of old superstitions and of new temptations. But what means have we for carrying out that which is required, where one Missionary has an extent of country to attend to which is fifty or sixty miles in length?"*

Another Missionary, in deacons' orders in a remote and extensive district, pointedly suggests the remedy—

"Some of our best and well-tried Christian teachers, of fifteen or twenty years' standing, should be ordained deacons while we have strength to pursue our work and overlook them. There should be one ordained native at Whangape immediately. We cannot personally attend to this district more than a very few times in a year; and a native teacher without a salary cannot be expected to attend to the duties required, for those duties would engross all his time. The Whangape district is a fine place to try a native deacon in the ministry. There are a few teachers at Herekino, five miles nearer our settlement; but as they do not attend our meetings but a few times, they are but weak, i. e. they do not visit about. It wants one invested with authority to preach, &c. Himeona is the teacher that I should recommend to be ordained, if he would consent, for I have not spoken yet to him on this subject, although I have made it known that I wish him to go to Whangape.

"The Lord's supper ought to be administered in all the suitable chapels in the district, and that every three months. Such is the nature of the times for worldly-mindedness, that our Christian natives are in the utmost danger of falling away unless we can often, both in the word and sacraments, set the Lord before them. New Zealand indeed, at this time, wants Bishops and Missionaries who will feel for the souls of the people, and not in any ways seek their own glory, but that of the great Shepherd who has laid down his life for the sheep. Neither bishops, priests, nor deacons, are ordained or consecrated to seek any thing else but the glory of Christ and the salvation of perishing souls; and what is our duty but to lead our people, the sheep of Christ's flock, into green or budding pastures? We, who are witnesses of the state of things, at least in the north of New Zealand, are fully aware that the present state is far from being a healthy one. We are altogether too weak or too short of hands, and a better state of things is needed; a brotherly and Missionary consultation should take place, and inquiry should be made whether a few of the best of the teachers could not or should not be ordained, &c. May God bless what I have suggested!"*

The Mission then, unhappily, had not been brought into full organization and effectiveness. It came to pass, therefore, that when the time of trial arrived, and, like children caught by glittering toys, the Maories were tempted to leave their first love, and be-

---

* "Church Missionary Record," Oct. 1853, p. 236.

* "Church Missionary Record," September 1855, p. 211.

come careless and worldly, it had not the vigour which was requisite to meet the emergencies of the moment, and native Christianity deteriorated. The crop, which in its first abundant spring had looked so promising, appeared, as it grew, disfigured with many evils, the product of a seed which the great enemy had sown. The vice of drunkenness, alike the evidence and melancholy consequence of religious declension, spread widely and rapidly, and the entire work assumed a sombre aspect. Multiplied testimonies might be adduced, but our space precludes enlargement on this point, and we must confine ourselves to such as have been already placed before our readers.

This was indeed a dark period in the history of the Mission. The hand of God's displeasure seemed to rest heavily on the native church. Sickness was abroad to an unprecedented extent. Whooping-cough, influenza, measles, wrought sad havoc amongst the native race, especially amongst the younger portion of them; and the fact, as stated by one of the Missionaries,* that, "in those residences where drunkenness and thefts were carried on, and where the greatest lukewarmness amongst the Christian party existed, the number of deaths" have been about seven to one of other places, is one of special emphasis as regards New Zealand, for it points to this as a settled axiom, that the preservation of the native race depends on the continued and efficacious action of Christianity on their hearts and lives; and that a declension amongst them, from whatever cause, of this conserving influence, must prove to be the death-warrant of the race.

It was at this crisis in the history of the Mission that the Bishop of New Zealand and the Governor, Sir George Grey, visited this country, and had an interview with the Committee of the Church Missionary Society. The Bishop, in his address on that occasion, expressed his conviction that the time had fully come for the Church Missionary Society to withdraw from New Zealand, and leave the future management of the native church in the hands of the ecclesiastical authorities; and in order to enable the Society to effect this with a due regard to the best interests of the natives, and with a full assurance to themselves that those interests would continue to be regarded with every solicitude, and carried forward on the Society's own principles, the Bishop set forward his plan of making a division of the diocese, and using his influence to obtain the appointment of three of the elder and most experienced Missionaries of the Society to the new sees, proposing, with the unhesitating spirit of personal self-sacrifice which has characterized all his proceedings, to divide with such of the associate bishops as were not otherwise sufficiently provided for, the annuity of 600*l*., which, since its formation, the New-Zealand Episcopate has received from the funds of the Church Missionary Society. That proposal was placed before the Committee, and became the subject of grave and prolonged deliberation. It was in no self-regarding spirit that its members addressed themselves to it but with a simple desire to ascertain what might be their duty before God. It led to a review of all the circumstances of the Mission, and the conclusion to which they came was, that they were not at liberty to retire from the Mission field of New Zealand, or abandon the measure of influence, which, as the result of long experience, of prolonged labours, and a costly expenditure, they had acquired amongst the native race; that their work was not complete, for as yet but one native had been admitted to holy orders, and the native church remained unprovided with a native pastorate. As to the appointment of new bishops, and the promotion of some of their own Missionaries to that office, the Committee was willing to concur, and that with a view to the more rapid development of the Mission.

Preparatory measures, moreover, it was ready to adopt; to diminish its annual grants, and to throw the native church more upon self-supporting efforts, so that when the mature moment did arrive, the Society might, without embarrassment, retire from a field once overrun with heathenism, but happily reclaimed and brought under Christian cultivation; but with reference to any immediate abandonment of its position, the Committee felt that the time was not come; and its feelings on this important question will be found expressed in two paragraphs from the Annual Report of 1855-56.

"The present is a great crisis in the New-Zealand Mission: the natives are in danger of losing their 'first love.' Some time back they were, as a people recently awakened from spiritual death, most anxious for instruction, and desirous of learning more and more of the Lord Jesus, that they might serve Him. Since then, riches have increased, and they are tempted to set their hearts upon them, to the neglect of the 'durable riches and righteousness' which Christ has to give. In some parts of the island, grog-shops which

---

* Rev. James Hamlin. Vide "Church Missionary Record," 1855, p. 241.

the white men have opened are much frequented. The New Zealander, who, as a heathen, was abstemious, is in danger, as a professing Christian, of becoming a drunkard.

"But the Committee do not despond. The Gospel is 'the power of God unto salvation to every one that believeth,' yesterday, to-day, and for ever. It brought the New Zealanders out of the pit of heathenism into the glorious liberty of the children of God; and it is as able to preserve them amidst the temptations of nominal Christianity or Romish apostasy. It is clear, however, that they still need the stay and support of their first spiritual guides, and that the Missionaries cannot be at present diminished in number. The Society, which has been honoured of God to bring a nation into the Christian church, must still stand by them in the critical hour of this struggle, that the truth of the Gospel may continue with them."

To this decision the Committee was strongly moved by the opinion of the Governor, Sir George Grey, which remains recorded in the following minute, corrected by himself—

"Sir George Grey stated that he had visited nearly every station of the Society, and could speak with confidence of the great and good work accomplished by it in New Zealand; that he believed that out of the native population, estimated by himself at nearly 100,000, there were not more than 1000 who did not make a profession of Christianity; that though he had heard doubts expressed about the Christian character of individuals, yet no one doubted the effect of Christianity upon the mass of the people, which had been evidenced in their social improvement, their friendly intercourse with Europeans, and their attendance upon divine worship; that there was in many places a readiness on the part of the natives to contribute one-tenth of the produce of their labour for the support of their Christian teachers, and to make liberal grants of land for the endowment of the schools; that some of the native teachers were, and many, by means of the schools, might be, qualified for acting as native pastors, if admitted to holy orders, and might be trusted, in such a position, to carry on the good work among their countrymen, and even to go out as native Missionaries to other islands of the Pacific; that the great want in the native church at present was a consolidation of the work, and its establishment upon a basis of self support; that it was impossible for a single bishop to accomplish such a work, from the extent and geographical isolation of the different parts of the diocese; that he understood it was the opinion of the bishop that there should be four bishoprics in the Northern Island, in which opinion he concurred; that the most suitable persons to be appointed to the new sees were those he understood to have been recommended by the bishop, namely, three of the elder Missionaries of the Society, who had commenced the work, and brought it to its present state; that the appointment of these gentlemen would, he believed, give satisfaction; that he believed nothing could induce the Missionaries to desert 'the natives; that they would rather give up their salaries, and throw themselves upon native resources; that they possessed the full confidence of the natives, and were thoroughly acquainted with their character: but that, if the Society were now wholly to withdraw from New Zealand, the work would, he believed, fall to pieces, and the Mission do an injury to Christianity; whereas, if the work should be consolidated and perfected, as he hoped, the conversion of New Zealand would become one of the most encouraging facts in the modern history of Christianity, and a pattern of the way in which it might be established in all other heathen countries."*

We dwell upon this topic, because "the Committee of the Church Missionary Society has been often censured for retaining the management of its Missions, instead of resigning them into the hands of the bishops. Even the warm friends of the Society have been sometimes disposed to blame the Committee for a too sensitive jealousy of ecclesiastical authority: they have thought that such authority, exercised on the spot, must be better able to direct and invigorate the Mission than a lay Committee sitting in London."

This question has now, we rejoice to say, reached a final decision.

"A Synod of the whole church was at length assembled in Wellington in March and April 1859, on which occasion Bishop Selwyn formally brought forward the question in his opening address to the Synod, stating his conviction that the time was come when 'it would be found impossible to carry on a double government for the Colonial and Missionary Church;' adding, 'It is now more than six years since a large public meeting at this place concurred unanimously in the following Resolution—

"'That this Meeting, gratefully acknowledging the vast benefits which, under Divine Providence, have been conferred upon the New-Zealand islands by the Church Mis-

---

* Church Missionary Society's Report, 1853-54, p. 153.

sionary Society, authorize Archdeacon Hadfield to communicate with the Society, in order to ascertain whether they would be willing to resign into the hands of the clergy and laity of the district of Wellington their present charge of the native settlements in that district, and upon what conditions they would assist in forming a fund for the permanent endowment of native parishes and schools.'

"'I would earnestly recommend to this Synod the adoption of a Resolution of a similar kind, including the whole field of the Society's Mission in New Zealand.'

"Instead of complying with this earnest recommendation of Bishop Selwyn, the Synod passed Resolutions without a division, in which they declared that '*there has never been a period when the native race more urgently required the undiminished efforts of the Church Missionary Society than at the present moment.*'

"The Resolutions of the Synod *in extenso* were the following—

"'1. This Synod wishes to avow its sense of the responsibility resting upon the church in these islands to extend, as far as in it lies, the knowledge of our blessed Lord and Saviour, and the enjoyment of his means of grace, to every creature within this ecclesiastical province, and to the heathen beyond.

"'2. This Synod desires to record its conviction that it is the duty of every member of the church to give, according as God hath prospered him, to the furtherance of these objects, and that it is the duty of every clergyman to bring these obligations periodically before his flock, with the view of stimulating their bounty.

"'3. This Synod commends to the several Diocesan Synods the early consideration of measures for securing a regular contribution from the congregations of their several dioceses, and for apportioning the same to the several objects—

"'(1) Missions to the settlers in thinly peopled districts.

"'(2) Missions to the natives within each diocese.

"'(3) The existing Missionary endeavours amongst the heathen of the Pacific Islands, which have hitherto been carried on by the Bishop of New Zealand.

"'(4) That with a view to the spiritual wants of the natives of New Zealand, the time has now arrived, in the opinion of this Synod, when the natives should themselves be stimulated to further efforts for the support of the church in New Zealand.

"'(5) That it is due to the Church Missionary Society to communicate to them the Resolutions which have been passed by the Synod with reference to measures for drawing out the contributions of this church in support of Home and Foreign Missions, and to accompany the communication with a grateful recognition of their labours for the evangelization of the aborigines of these islands; and with the expression of the opinion of this Synod, that since the colonization of New Zealand, there has never been a period when the native race more urgently required the undiminished efforts of the Church Missionary Society than at the present moment.'

"It will be seen that these Resolutions propose measures for drawing out local contributions on behalf of Missions in New Zealand, as well as elsewhere; but they couple with such local efforts, their desire to retain the agency of the Church Missionary Society. It must be observed, also, that the Society has of late years withdrawn all pecuniary support to the Mission, beyond the payment of the salaries of its European agents; and that it has also forewarned its friends in New Zealand that they cannot supply fresh agents, or continue those salaries, when the present Missionaries are removed. These points were explained to the Synod in a speech of Bishop Williams immediately before the Resolutions were passed. It may therefore be fairly presumed that the Synod desires the continuance of the general superintendence of the Mission by the Parent Committee in London, especially for the maintenance of those Missionary principles, on which, under God, the great success of the Mission has been accomplished.

"The Committee beg to draw the attention of the friends of the Society to this very gratifying testimony to the value of the Society's action in a Mission, even when, so far as the Europeans are concerned, the church is fully organized. The sentiment of Bishop Selwyn and his friends is repeated in many forms by the writers of a section of our church. The demand for Missionary bishops is avowedly grounded upon such opinions. And yet, in a Synod of five bishops, eight representative clergymen, and thirteen representative laymen, these sentiments are formally overruled; the transfer of the Mission to the bishops, clergy, and laity, is virtually deprecated; and the continued action of the Church Missionary Society is urgently invited."

We may well pause here to inquire what are the circumstances in the existing condition of New Zealand which decided so influential a Synod to give expression to a judgment of such solemnity, that, "since the colonization of New Zealand, there has never been a period when the native race more urgently required the undiminished efforts of the Church Missionary Society than at the present moment."

Severe as the test was to which native Christianity has been exposed, and that with so little to back it up, it has nevertheless survived, and is again enkindling. Such was the declension at one time, that some feared that it would die out with the first generation of converts, and never have sufficient vigour to obtain amongst their children. We thank God it has not been so. These are encouraging indications, enough to assure us that the blessing of the Lord will not be withheld from prayerful and earnest efforts put forth for the spiritual welfare of the Maori race. Archdeacon Henry Williams writes— "There has been a more general interest amongst the people in seeking for divine knowledge than has appeared for some years past. We hope a good work is going on." Another, the Rev. R Maunsell observes— "I trust there are signs of spiritual life among my people generally." Another, the Rev. S. M. Spencer — "It is to be hoped, from recent indications observable in various places, that the natives, as a people, will ere long settle into a more regular community than ever." Another, the Rev. T. S. Grace, at Taupo—"The year now closed has been marked by a steady progress rather than by any thing particularly striking. There has been an increased attention to spiritual things; attendance of the adult classes for scriptural instruction has greatly increased; candidates for baptism have become numerous; some of the native teachers have shown more diligence in their work; and a growing interest has been manifested in our industrial school."

But there is a feature in connexion with them which may well call forth our sympathy—the native race is decreasing. "In some few districts the population has increased within the last few years; in others, again, it has been nearly stationary; but more generally it has been decreasing, and there is no longer any doubt that the Maori race are fewer in number than they were twenty years ago. There is a sensible diminution also in the number of very aged venerable-looking men. In almost every part of the country the sexes are unequal, the males predominating. And the children are still comparatively few. The average number of children born is, indeed, in many cases, considerable; but they commonly die young. In some parts of the country the children are reported to be 'healthy and numerous;' but more commonly they are found to be 'decreasing and few.' Some years ago the influenza carried off a considerable number of the natives, of all ages; and more recently the measles proved still more destructive. Small-pox has not yet shown itself in the country, and great efforts have been made to prepare for it by a general vaccination of the people. In one respect their constitution appears to have improved; owing, probably, to the use of wheaten bread, and to a general improvement in their diet: they certainly appear less scrofulous than before."*

Perhaps in the estimation of some persons this may be deemed a matter of little moment. "They are decreasing," it will be said, " by a natural process, and perhaps, on the whole, it is better it should be so. They will pass away, and leave the land for the occupation of a superior race." The friends of Missions may be excused if they cannot take so apathetic a view of their decline. We have been with them from the moment of their birth into a Christian profession, and have watched over them amidst the perils and fluctuations of their childhood; and we should like to see them, for the honour of the Gospel, grow up into a Christian manhood, blessed in themselves, and a blessing to other races throughout the wide Pacific. These, however, may be thought to be parental sympathies, weak, although pardonable.

But are the Maories of no value as a national element? or, like the Australian blacks, are they a wilful and degraded remnant, impossible to civilize, and indisposed to receive instruction; mere denizens of the wilderness, frequenting the forest depths, shunning the white man, or, when brought into communication with him, susceptible only of the evils of his character, and reluctant to the imitation of what is good? Let us hear some recent and important testimony as to their industrial and productive capabilities.

"Owing to the ignorance which has generally prevailed in England of the value of their labour, and of the extent to which the native population are engaged in industrial pursuits, the importance of these islands as a dependency of the Crown is commonly estimated with reference only to the number of the English settlers, without taking into account their native inhabitants; who, instead of being occupied as formerly in a state of constant and destructive warfare, are now peaceable and industrious, and occupied in

---

* "Swainson," pp. 12, 13.

various departments of productive industry: acquiring property to a considerable amount, the owners of the greater portion of the soil, the principal producers of the wheat grown within the province, and large and increasing consumers of British manufactures.

"In seasons of harvest the English settlers are largely dependent upon the labour of the natives for mowing, hay-making, reaping, threshing, &c; and experience has proved them to be capable, not only of acquiring skill in various descriptions of handicraft work, but, under judicious superintendence, of steady application to laborious pursuits. During the disturbance in the south, native labour was chiefly made use of in the construction of the military roads; and about 300 natives were engaged upon the work. In the course of a year they earned upwards of 3020*l.*, and felled about twenty miles in length by 120 feet in width of dense forest; constructed seven miles of bridle-road, chiefly cut out of the side of steep hills and precipices, and helped to construct six miles of carriage-road; taking part in every operation, such as bridge-making, sloping, draining, metalling, &c.

"The amount of property now possessed by the New Zealanders is certainly remarkable. The Bay of Plenty and the Taupo and Rotorua districts have a native population estimated to amount to above 8000. In the year 1857 the natives of these districts alone had upwards of 3000 acres of land in wheat, 3000 acres in potatoes, nearly 2000 acres in maize, and upwards of 1000 acres planted with kumeras. They owned nearly 1000 horses, 200 head of cattle, and 5000 pigs, four water-mills, and ninety-six ploughs. They were also the owners of forty-three small coasting vessels, averaging nearly twenty tons each, and upwards of 900 canoes. In the course of the same year the natives of the east coast (a tract of country extending from the East Cape to Turanga, about fifty miles) supplied 46,000 bushels of wheat to the English traders, of the marketable value of 13,000*l.* From a distance of nearly a hundred miles the natives of the north supply the markets of Auckland with the produce of their industry; brought partly by land-carriage, partly by small coasting-craft, and partly by canoes. In the course of a single year, 1792 canoes entered the harbour of Auckland, bringing to market by this means alone 200 tons of potatoes, 1400 baskets of onions, 1700 baskets of maize, 1200 baskets of peaches, 1200 tons of firewood, 45 tons of fish, and 1300 pigs, besides flax, poultry, kauri gum, and vegetables."*

Is it not, then, worth while to put forth an energetic effort to maintain the race? or shall we leave them to their fate, and suffer the depopulating process to waste them away? And yet circumstances might arise of such a nature as to make the New Zealander of value, even in the eyes of those who have hitherto regarded him as no better than a worthless refuse, fit only to give place to the advancing footsteps of the white settler. Let it be remembered that their military capabilities are of a superior kind, and that when they have taken up arms against us, as has been the case, they have proved themselves to be no contemptible adversaries.

"They have long been well supplied with fire-arms. There is not a single man amongst them who is not familiar with the musket, and warfare has been the business of their lives. Instead of wearing a conspicuous dress, and standing to be shot at like a target, they frequently, when engaged in skirmishing, disencumber themselves of every stitch of clothing, well contented to have strapped about their persons a plentiful supply of dry ball-cartridges. Thus unencumbered, they dodge about from cover to cover, skilfully availing themselves of every tuft and inequality in the ground, and move away the moment they have delivered their fire. From lengthened experience they have become good tactitians; when opposed to us they can always choose their fighting ground, and invariably show great wisdom in the choice. The are independent of any regular commissariat, and can move rapidly from place to place, either across country, or by paths where ordinary European troops would be unable to follow them; and, when closely pressed, they have always a dense forest, or some inaccessible fastness to fall back upon. The idea was formerly entertained, that a single well-armed Englishman was sufficient to put to flight a horde of naked savages, but recent experience in New Zealand and at the Cape has done much to dispel this dangerous illusion; and it is now admitted that, on their own ground, the Maories, man for man, are fully a match even for disciplined English troops. In knowledge of the art of war, and in the planning of a regular campaign, they excel the North-American Indians, and for irregular bush-fighting they are better armed and equipped than the much-drilled, tight-laced, belted British soldier."*

Suppose, then, an European war should break out? Such an event, unhappily, is by no means improbable. Our own defensive preparations demonstrate sufficiently the national feeling on the subject, and the deep conviction that a crisis might supervene in

---

* "Swainson," pp. 63-66.

* "Swainson," pp. 152-154.

which every Briton, who could bear arms, would be summoned forth to defend our hearths and homes, is covering the face of the land with rifle corps. Suppose the heavens should become suddenly overcast, and Great Britain find herself in the presence of a formidable combination for her overthrow, isolated from all alliances, and thrown entirely on her own resources, and that amidst the strain and pressure of the conflict she was compelled, for the moment, to leave her colonies to defend themselves: if such a crisis should arrive, would the Maories be worthless, and of no value? The New-Zealand group occupies a commanding position. Invaders, possessed of that point, could easily coerce and overcome the gold colonies, and dominate over the South Pacific. Just at the moment when the English Government decided on the assumption of the sovereignty of those isles, another European nation had similarly decided, and had sent out an expedition for that purpose, which, had it not been anticipated by the English Mission, would have planted the standard of France on their shores. If considered valuable then, surely they are not less so now. An expedition might be fitted out by a hostile power, and, our fleets being evaded, an enemy's force be landed on the New-Zealand shore. Should such a crisis ever supervene, we hesitate not to say, that, with the Maories still numerous, physically strong, loyal, and well affected to the British rule, the colonists might set at defiance the most powerful efforts that could be put forth for the subjugation of those islands. The Englishman and the native, occupying in concert the rugged ascents from the coasts into the interior, would present so formidable a resistance as to render it impossible for an invading force to effect a passage, and would so harrass it, when encamped upon the shore, as to compel it to a quick retreat.

But to what may the decrease of the Maories be attributed? To their domestic habits, which are injurious to health, and sufficient to account for the prevalence of epidemics and the destruction of youthful life. "The great majority of the people are still living in a rude uncivilised state; their habitations are small, and, for want of chimneys and fire-places, their persons, their garments, and every thing belonging to them, become perfectly saturated with the pungent odour of wood smoke. Finger-forks are still in common use, and they are by no means extravagant in the use of soap."*

Another writer, with somewhat of graphic freedom, describes the domestic habits of the natives—

"A tribe generally lives together in little communities of from 50 to 200 individuals, in various villages (pas), scattered over their district. These villages, planted on some hill or precipice near the coast, or perched on some river's cliff, cover half an acre to two or three acres of ground. A common pa consists of two or three rows (two or three feet apart) of stout split paling, ten to twelve feet high, lashed with flax and creepers to posts and cross rails, entered by two or three narrow posterns, and divided by similar paling into numerous little labyrinth-like passages, courts, and squares.

"Here we find built the houses — little rush-and-pole verandah-huts, devoid of window, door, or chimney, and displaying the firebrands smoking on the floor. Here, too, are stacks of fuel, the warepuni, some chief's or rich man's better house, and perchance a bell-decked wooden chapel. Here, too, is the larder — bits of kumera and potatoes, maize and wheat, dried eels, roots and berries, stowed aloft on shelves or poles, away from rat and dog. Here, too, will congregate the hundred pests of the village—yelping curs and shrillest cocks, monstrous cats, fleas by bushels, a goat or two, pet calves and foals, intrusive pigs, the mocking tui, caged but clamorous, and the gloomy kaka, tied to his pole, and bewailing his fate in indignant screams, like Hiawatha's felon raven."*

In another place the same writer adds— "There are no people in the world whom a knowledge of common things would benefit more than the New Zealanders. The Maori will gorge on grease, oil, eels, and rancid fish, till he has induced or aggravated scrofula; and will hold night arguments in his foul warepuni, and then rush out and sit in the damp night blast to check perspiration and cool himself, till he has induced consumption."†

There are other causes of decrease which we cannot particularly specify, but which may also be found among their domestic habits. Suffice it to say, that they need to feel that girlhood marriages produce a sickly offspring, and that infants, in order that they may live, need to be well cared for. Maori mothers require to be taught how white mothers manage their children. The Maori men require to be taught that "the woman is the weaker vessel, and should only do indoor work; and that the sight of a girl staggering

---

* "Swainson," p. 27.

* Hursthouse, "Great Britain of the South," vol. i, pp. 170, 171.
† Ibid., pp. 184, 185.

along for a dozen miles under a sixty-pound potato-kit, would be disgusting even among the wretched blackfellows of Australia.

And how comes it that they are Christians, and yet so defective in their domestic habits? Because, first, impressions have not been sufficiently followed up, and Christian truth brought *home* to them in that clearness and power of application which would have enabled its influence to pervade, and correct, and improve all the details of domestic life. Because they have wanted amongst them living models; not merely European Christians, whose peculiar habits and mode of living they ascribe to their race, and consequently never intended for their imitation; but native Christians, so trained and educated as to be sufficiently in advance of them to lead them on, and yet not too much in advance of them, lest they be discouraged; men no longer content to live in a warepuni, to eat their meals *aus doits*, to accept as an article of diet putrid maize, and to abstain from the washing of their persons as a waste of time; men who should be able to show their countrymen that improved habits belong not to race, but to Christianity, and ought to have place in a Christian Maori as well as in a Christian Englishman. Had there been raised up a well-qualified native agency, pastors and catechists, this desideratum would have been supplied. This is a defect which must be remedied, and that as promptly as possible, if the decrease of the native race is to be arrested. Mr. Hursthouse, from whose work we have already quoted, recommends that intelligent settlers should be located in the different villages as "training exemplars." They must be natives and religious teachers, or they will have but few copyists.

Here, then, is a good work in which the Church Missionary Society has to render important help—the raising up promptly and effectively of a well-qualified agency, and to this work it has already with energy applied itself. The admirable institution of the Rev. R. Maunsell is labouring towards this pressing and important object. Archdeacon Kissling, near Auckland, has been selected by the bishop to train native theological students for ordination, and receive them for this purpose from the various Missionary districts. The Bishop of Waiapu, on his visit to this country in 1852-53, had especially committed to him, by the Committee, this important trust, and, in conjunction with his son, the Rev. L. Williams, who, having graduated at Oxford, was sent forth in 1854, with a special reference to this object, he has put forth measures of such a nature as to enable him to express his hope that, "If our present plans can be continued without interruption, there is every reason to believe that a better class of schoolmasters for the villages will be provided, as well as pastors, who may gradually fill up the vacancies which occur. Already many applications have been made for natives who have been some time in the school, to take charge of distant villages, for the people begin to appreciate their superiority over the old teachers. We see much reason to rejoice in our prospect. God has raised up assistance for us in quarters from which we did not expect it; and it is abundantly clear that his good hand is with us, and that his blessing will accompany our efforts."

At Otaki, Archdeacon Hadfield's station, in the diocese of Wellington, a similar effort has been commenced. A graduate of Cambridge, of high standing, who has devoted himself to the work of education in the higher branches, has been appointed to the charge of a new collegiate school. With these various institutions in active operation we trust that native candidates for ordination, of suitable qualifications, will rapidly increase; and when we remember that, as the Bishop of New Zealand stated in his opening address to the first general Synod, "The great object for which the Missionary diocese at Waiapu has been constituted is, to widen the basis of native ordination," we feel secure in the future close relations of the Episcopate and the Society; that there will be no more misapprehensions or unhappy discrepancies of judgment of such a nature as to impede necessary action; but that both will harmoniously co-operate for the consolidation of the native church, and the conservation of the native race; and that the serious defect under which that church has laboured, and to which the evils and discouragements of this Mission may be mainly traced—the want of a native pastorate—will soon and for ever be removed.

And there is another reason why we earnestly desire this more universal diffusion of regular Christian instruction and Christian ordinances throughout the land, and a closer application of the truth to the hearts and consciences of the natives, so as to move them to more decided self-improvement in their personal and domestic traits, namely, that on this depends the maintenance of peace between the races, and the continued prosperity of New Zealand. At present there is between them no amalgamation.

"For the purposes of trade the natives constantly, and in large numbers, frequent our English settlements, but the two races really live apart; and, with the exception of the Missionaries, and a few isolated settlers, few have sufficient knowledge of the language, superstitions, and social life of the native race, to be able to form a judgment of their real character. .... The Maori is impatient of injustice, yet amenable to reason, and possesses more common sense and judgment than the mass of a European community."*

And yet to these races *conjointly* Great Britain has confided the government of their common country. The new constitution given in 1853 recognises the political rights of the native as fully as those of the settler.

"The elective franchise, as prescribed by the constitution, is without distinction of race, and every man of the age of twenty-one, or upwards, who owns land to the value of 50*l.*, or who holds land on lease to the value of 10*l.* a year, or, being a householder, occupying a tenement in a town of the annual value of 10*l.*, or a tenement in the country of the annual value of 5*l.*, if duly registered, is not only qualified to vote at the election of a member of the House of Representatives and of the Provincial Council, and also of the superintendant of the province, but to be himself elected to the office of superintendant, or as a member of the Provincial or General Legislature, or both."

But the native race has not as yet accepted these responsibilities, nor has it in the slightest degree identified itself with the governing action of the country. "They take no part in the exercise of the elective franchise, nor exercise any influence on party combinations." There is not yet sufficient assimilation between the races. "By some friend of the race, a well-disposed native is occasionally invited to a meal at an English table; and he uniformly conducts himself with studied and scrupulous propriety; ... but, both by their language, and by their widely different modes of life, the two races are still entirely kept apart."

The result is, that the administration of political affairs rests entirely in the hands of on recognised rights; danger, lest the native become irritated, and fall back on the law of might. This danger became more apparent when the principle of ministerial responsibility was introduced, and the continuance in office of the advisers of the Crown was made to depend on their being able to command a majority of votes in the House of Assembly. It then became necessary to limit the application of this principle of government, so far as the natives were concerned, and to leave entirely in the hands of the Governor the direction of native affairs. The justice of such an arrangement is apparent.

"A ministry, chosen by and from the elected representatives of the Europeans, can have no claims to absolute authority over the Maori race; and, while the colonists claim for themselves self-government, representative institutions, and irresponsible ministry, they cannot in reason refuse to the native race that form of government which they prefer, viz. that the management of their affairs should be left, as heretofore, in the hands of the representative of the Crown. And the just and generous course would be to ascertain what amount of annual revenue is contributed by the native race; to pay into the general treasury that proportion of the income which is due to works and objects in which both races have a common interest; and to place the surplus at the disposal of the Governor for strictly native purposes: thus placing the native race in the position of a distant province, paying to the general Government a certain portion of the revenue, and retaining the remainder for its own local expenditure. Such were some of the reasons assigned for retaining still in the hands of Her Majesty's representative the immediate government of the native race."

"The natives of New Zealand ceded their independence, not to the English settlers, but confidingly to the justice and wisdom of the British Crown; and the British Government became morally responsible for their just and paternal government. They know little, and they care less, about a responsible ministry— here to-day and gone to-morrow; a ministry whom they hardly know by name, and for

This, however, is not the case. "Subject to a charge of 7000*l.* a year for native purposes, the revenues of the colony are at the disposal of a legislature in which the natives themselves are not immediately represented, and over which they have, practically, no control, while the Governor of the colony can carry on the management of native affairs on his own responsibility, and by means of officers appointed by himself, only so far as he may be supplied with funds by an annual vote of the Colonial Legislature."*

Evidently this is but a temporary arrangement, and cannot be of long duration. "It may be received as a law, as constant in its operation as the law of gravitation, that the powers of the Governor on native questions will constantly be liable to be limited and encroached upon by the popular representatives, and that if the Governor is to hold his own, there will be a constant state of antagonism between the representative of the Crown and the ministers of the people."†

When this safeguard is removed, what shall be the issue? That, under God, will depend on the condition of improvement which the native race shall have attained under the ameliorating influence of Christian instruction. The happiest results may be produced on both races by a number of well-educated Christian natives, brought forward into the responsible positions of Christian pastors. It would give their own race confidence, and convince the European that the Maories are improvable, and not lightly to be thrown away. The European Missionaries and native pastors would constitute a point of junction at which the two races would meet each other on terms of assimilation and equality, and from this the process of amalgamation would really commence. We feel persuaded, that not only the conservation of the native race, but the maintenance of peace between the European and Maori sections of the population, depends, under God, on a more energetic and rapid development of the resources of the native church than we have yet witnessed.

With such important interests at stake, and relations so intricate to be adjusted, no influence, from whatever quarter, which is of the right kind, and capable in a great or less degree of controlling men's minds for good, can possibly be spared, especially the influence of a body of men who have been deeply interested in and intimately conversant with the native race from the time when they were to a man heathen. The Episcopate has thought that, in order to the right management of ecclesiastical affairs, it is desirable that they should be left entirely in its own hands and under its own control; and that a body like the Church Missionary Society had better abdicate its functions, and withdraw from all interference with the progress of Christianity in New Zealand. But is this a well-founded persuasion? Are the decisions of the Episcopate always unerring? Have there been no mistakes, no errors in judgment? And although a check, a remonstrance, when authority is going forward too hastily in one direction, may be far from agreeable, is it not timely and most useful? Is there no advantage in the continued relationship to New Zealand of a body constituted like the Committee of the Church Missionary Society, far removed from those local prejudices and influences which so often bias the judgment of the most gifted men; a body whose decisions are not the product of a single mind, or of a mind whose advisers are always of a deferential character, but of a number of Christian men, who frankly speak their sentiments, take different views of the same subject, check and compare those views, correct by this reciprocal action what is erroneous in one another's judgment, and whose decisions at the last are almost always the expression of an unanimous opinion? We do not wonder that the Synod, in a deliberate and recorded Resolution, deprecated the withdrawal of the Society.

"It is generally found in other important undertakings, as well as in Missions, that those who superintend the work at a distance are in a position better fitted for the maintenance of the right principles of action than those who are involved in all the details of the work. A pressing practical difficulty will often suggest a compromise of principle, or at least obscure its importance and countervail its influence.

"In the great work of evangelizing the heathen, questions occur in the case of every tribe of the human race, identical in their nature, and capable of only one true solution, but so various in their aspect, and often so complicated, that the Missionary who has only dealt with them under one form may be easily perplexed and deceived, while a judgment formed upon a wider experience will at once supply the right answer. Among these questions, none are more liable to be misunderstood by the agents on the spot than those which relate to the proper treatment of the native race."

The truth of these remarks is strikingly confirmed by the Bishop of Waiapu in his address to the Synod—

---

* "Swainson" p. 375.   † Ibid., p. 378

"It has been proposed, that in the districts where the population consists of a mixture of the races, the clergyman who has charge of our own countrymen shall be also held responsible for the native race, but experience tells us in most cases the system will not work. A clergyman, whose special care is the white population, having withal a new language to learn, finds that the charge is difficult; and while the English settlers will have seven-eighths of his attention, the natives will scarcely receive the remaining portion. The only remedy for this state of things is to raise up a native pastorate, and I am thankful to be able to state, for the information of the Synod, that there is every prospect that this provision will be made. There is already the Rev. Rota Waitoa at the East Cape, who has now been several years a native clergyman, much respected by his countrymen, over whom he exercises a most beneficial influence. Then, again, there is the Rev. Riwai Te Ahu. He, too, is a most satisfactory instance to show how well the plan of a native pastorate is likely to succeed. There are many other natives also preparing for ordination at the central schools at Turanga, Auckland, and elsewhere. One great difficulty must be the means of support for a native ministry: but the subject of endowment has been already before the natives, and there are many who enter into it with spirit. Among the natives of East Cape many contributions have been brought together, and more than 100l. now forms the basis of a fund to which those members of our church who are able to do so will do well to add. I trust, therefore, it will be recognised as a duty resting upon the church in general to promote the establishment of a native pastorate, and that this subject will be recommended by the Synod to the consideration of the several Diocesan Synods."

Our readers will now be prepared to appreciate the Resolutions which were adopted by the Parent Committee as a response to the Resolutions of the Synod in New Zealand.

"Resolved, 1. That this Committee receive with great satisfaction the Resolutions passed April 4, 1859, in the Synod of Bishops, Clergy, and Laity, of the branch of the United Church of England and Ireland in New Zealand, especially that which states—

'That it is due to the Church Missionary Society to communicate to them the resolutions which have been passed by the Synod with reference to measures for drawing out the contributions of this church in support of home and foreign Missions, and to accompany the communication with a grateful recognition of their labours for the evangelization of the aborigines of these islands, and with the expression of the opinion of the Synod, that, since the colonization of New Zealand, there has never been a period when the native race more urgently required the undimished efforts of the Church Missionary Society than at the present moment.'

"2. That, as the Synod have accompanied their Resolution with measures for drawing out local support for Missions, and as this Committee have frequently explained, in printed documents, the necessity of gradually withdrawing its pecuniary grants from New Zealand, which the Bishop of Waiapu brought under the notice of the Synod, explaining the principle on which such withdrawal would be carried into effect,—this Committee accept the Resolution of the Synod as especially inviting the continuance of the Society's aid by counsel, sympathy, and prayer, in upholding the spiritual and Missionary principles which have ever characterized its proceedings: they regard the resolution as also inviting the Society to retain the direct control of its pecuniary grants, as long as they may be continued,—of the lands held by the Society in trust for the native church,—and of the educational establishments which may be supported by its endowments.

"3. That this Committee recognises many advantages which Missionaries and settlers, commingled in any land with aborignal races, may derive from a direct and intimate connexion with a central Missionary body in a long-established Christian church; such a central body being able to gather experience from many fields, and being familiar with questions which everywhere arise between different races, brought together to co-operate in the same work. More especially they recognise the benefits of such connexion when cemented by a common and supreme value for the truth of the Gospel of the grace of God, and for those Protestant and evangelical principles in which consist the strength and harmony of the United Church of England and Ireland.

"That this Committee, therefore, cordially respond to the appeal of the Synod, and trust, in reliance upon the grace of Christ, that they may do so without impairing the principles of independence and of self-support in the native church: more particularly, they are prepared to act throughout New Zealand upon the plan agreed upon with the Bishop of Wellington and Archdeacon Hadfield, in their late interview with the Committee, October 19th, 1858, namely, to keep up the efficiency of the Society's educational establishments for the preparation of native teachers, and to employ its European Missionaries, and a few native assistants, in working out the complete organization of native congregations and of native-Christian institutions.

"5. That, for the effectual carrying out of the purposes already described, the Parent Committee, on their part, invite the formation of local Church Missionary Committees, or Associations; the object of which Committees shall be to collect funds for Missionary purposes, and to hold direct communication with the Parent Committee on various matters connected with the native congregations, as well as on measures for bringing those, who are still 'without,' into the fold of Christ."

MISSIONARY ACTION IN THE PUNJAB.

The following notes refer to a preaching tour carried out by one of our Umritsur Missionaries, the Rev. James Leighton, in a circuit round about Umritsur, one of the most populous portions of the territory beyond the Sutlej. The census of January 1, 1855, brought out very remarkably the rapid and great alternations of sparseness and density of population, for which the Punjab districts are remarkable. Two districts may be observed in the same division, perhaps adjoining each other, yet exhibiting an extreme diversity in this respect: thus, in the Lahore division we have Sealkote, with a population per square mile of 479·37, and Googranwalla of 147·47. This arises from the varied surface of the Punjab, "the submontane portion only being fertile, and the remainder a wild tract, with exceptional strips of cultivation." Thus the Baree Doab, in which the capital cities, Lahore and Umritsur are situated, is fertile towards the north, but, towards the centre and south, elevated and covered with brushwood, the margin near the rivers only being fringed with cultivation. It is in remedial of this inequality of productive power, by affording the means of irrigation, that the Baree Doab canal is being constructed.

"*Dec.* 31, 1858—I left Umritsur this afternoon, about half-past four P.M, to reach my tent at Nangli, four miles distant, for the be present at a service which we proposed to hold under a tree at the entrance to the village.

"*Jan.* 2: *Lord's-day* — Before breakfast I found eight respectable men, with as many, apparently, of a poorer class, come to pay their respects. No Missionary having been in these villages before, I suppose they concluded me to be a Government officer. Their custom is to bring a rupee, which they put upon a cloth in their hands, as a token of respect and submission. This is touched by the person to whom it is offered, as a sign of acceptance, but not taken. These people could ill afford to lose so much. Paulus, the catechist, begun to talk with them, explaining the object of my visit, and introduced some of the chief facts of Christ's life, and the commandment of the Sabbath. I then read to them the parables of the prodigal son, the lost sheep, and the lost piece of money, with application, and promised to visit their villages in the course of the day.

"*Jan.* 17 — To Sangatpur, where, immediately upon our arrival, about twenty men came to converse. I seated them on two carpets for a quiet address. They asked what the custom of our country is in regard to marriage. After telling them the social view of the matter, I read and explained to them the duties of husbands and wives as contained in 1 Peter and the Epistle to the Ephesians; also the duties of servants and

light. He was present at the latter part of this meeting, and after the others had gone away, I asked him some questions, to ascertain whether he had read them. His answers evinced a very attentive reading ; *e.g.* as to what is necessary to any one wishing to enter the fold of Christ; the three kinds of sin; the lust of the flesh, the lust of the eye, and the pride of life. He mentioned of his own accord the substance of St. John v., Christ's healing the man at the pool of Bethesda. 'Oh that this soul might be given me in the day of Christ.

"*Jan.* 20 — To Ram Das, eight miles. The country is now very beautiful, and the road through the fields tolerable. It is the season when the wheat is about a foot high. Another plant, which overtops the wheat, and bears a yellow flower, is sown along with it. This is now in full beauty, and often, as far as the eye can reach, on all sides large fields of this wave in the breeze. They now pull up the yellow plant for food for the cattle, cutting it in pieces, and mixing it with chopped straw. This reminds us of two things in Scripture— the mingling of tares with the wheat and the command in Leviticus xix. 19, Deut. xxii. 9, 10, 'Thou shalt not sow thy field with mingled seed.'

"*Jan.* 22—After a short walk this morning, groups of twenty or twenty-five assembled near the tent to hear, at different intervals during the day. We are thus literally sequestrated from other pursuits, and constantly talking with others upon religious subjects. Altogether, the whole town is moved, of which we had proof in the evening. The smooth reception hitherto met with I felt to be too gentle for much real work to be going on, and was therefore not sorry to see more opposition in the evening. We chose a place near another gate, where very quickly we had as many hearers as we could have wished for, from this other side of the village. I was speaking from Isaiah liii., showing the prophecies of Christ's character and work, with their fulfilment, and had nearly done, when a pundit, respectably dressed, but quite excited and rude, attempted to stop us. I told him to say what he had to say, but this

take the people away. About two-thirds, however, remained, and we finished our subject, our hearers evidently better disposed towards us for the man's violence and insults.

"*Jan.* 23: *Lord's-day* — In the evening, once more preached at the place where we had been disturbed the day before. The interest was not diminished, and we had as large a number as before. I preached upon the Apostle Paul's success at Ephesus, and the burning of the sorcerers' books; after which Paulus spoke upon the comfort given to those who suffer for Christ's sake. (2 Cor. i.). In this town we had thus given three full days to regular preaching, besides constant assemblies round the tent-door, so that, as Paulus remarked, "the preaching was going on from morning to night." What was to be the result?

"*Jan.* 24—We left Ram Das for Narowal. The prospect of preaching in Narowal came before my mind with much solemnity, and a deep sense of my inability to set forth the Gospel message as I should wish. It is a small town, and important in its neighbourhood, the centre of one of the pergunnahs of the Umritsur district: the population about 6000 or 7000. It has a good many brick buildings: the chief bazaars and streets are clean and respectable, but the remainder narrow and undrained. Paulus' forefathers were Lambardars of the place, and he himself held a position of authority here under Runjeet Singh. He was present fighting in most of the battles between the English and the Sikhs ten years ago. He settled in Sealkote as shopkeeper, where he heard the Gospel from Mr. Fitzpatrick, and, shortly after, came to Umritsur seeking baptism. He is a man of somewhat different character from most native Christians, especially those who have been brought up as orphans with Missionaries. Unassuming and unobtrusive, with a firm grasp upon the essential truths and evidences of the Gospel, he has an independence of character and strength which enable him to stand alone, and an aggressive spirit of Missionary action, which he is able to support by a close acquaintance with the Koran, and some knowledge of the Hindu Shasters accompanies the Missionaries of Umritsur on their tours. Blessed be that grace which gave Umritsur so efficient a convert at the commencement of its Mission. He has now several friends whom he regards as inquirers, and for whom he never ceases to pray. Some of them are in other villages, which I hope to visit with him. My first object in coming here now is to preach in the town; a second object is to ascertain what openings there may be for a Christian vernacular school.

"After much prayer we went to the bazar to preach this morning. I could not induce the people to sit upon the carpet I spread for them, so some stood on the right, some on the left, some sat in the shop-stalls on the opposite side of the bazaar, and some on the tops of the houses, which were of one story. At the first address I explained to them the Scripture meaning of salvation, pointing out the means which God has ordained for it in his dear Son. There was no opposition.

"*Jan.* 27--29—Preaching in the city generally one part of the day, and the other visiting some neighbouring village. On the 28th I visited Jessore, four miles distant, which is an interesting village. About fifty hearers, to whom I spoke of the way in which we should approach God in prayer, from the parable of the Pharisee and the publican. The interest was remarkable, and encouraged me to visit the place again. The preaching in Narowal itself is attended as I never saw preaching attended before so continuously. We have preached generally twice, sometimes three times, and even four times, at the same places, and thus gone almost through the town; still the interest is not diminished.

"*Feb.* 3—To-day one of Paulus' inquiring friends has come from Zufferwal, sixteen miles. His mind is fully made up as to Christianity, and he will read with me to-night for further instruction. He is a man of humble spirit and respectable position in life.

"*Feb.* 4—Read last night and this morning with Jiwan, the new disciple, the 1st

proposed the ordeal of poison as a test of Christianity, offering to become a Christian in case it should not take effect. Jiwan's younger brother came forward to answer him, saying, first, that this could be no proof of a religion, since it was the nature of poison to kill; and secondly, that it was written, 'Thou shalt not tempt the Lord thy God.' It appears, that at the time of the mutiny he was known as a reader of the Scriptures, and the people began to abstain from associating with him, and wished to exclude him from their wells. Upon this the Tahseeldar asked him if he had not Christian books. At that time, he said, he had the three volumes of the Scriptures in Urdu, the Tariq-ul-Hayat, and several smaller tracts. The Tahseeldar told him if he would give up the books he would give him a certificate of orthodoxy, which would secure him access to the wells, and participation in the hukka (a great test of social intercourse). He said that he took the Tahseeldar three small tracts, and denied having more, as he was challenged with having; and, upon his return home, resolved to brave the danger if search should be made, and refuse to give them up. Since that time, he said, he had kept the Scriptures closely shut up in a box, and only read them when his shop was shut at night and he was alone. He appears now stronger in faith, and would, I have every reason to believe, gain much strength by his baptism. He kneels and prays with us as the other Christians do. By profession he is a doctor and attar, and has a shop for the sale of medicines, sherbet, &c., which supports his whole family, including mother, brother, wife, &c. A prominent part of instruction to him has been the tribulation everywhere spoken of in the Scriptures as the lot of those who would live godly in Christ Jesus; at the same time I have set before him the joy and peace which are in believing.

"*Feb.* 6—Yesterday Jiwan explained to me his views of baptism. He had, he said, to return to Zufferwal in consequence of the death of a relative, where he would talk with his brother about the step he proposed to take,

in instructing them, and enable them to witness a good confession before many witnesses!

"*Feb.* 7--9 — Preaching regularly in the bazaars, and instructing Paulus' sons. On Sunday evening a very violent storm of wind and rain, with thunder and lightning, flooded us, and on Monday we took refuge in the tahseel in the city, now empty. Here we are at least dry, though, as there are no windows, and only shutters, which admit drafts of air, we are not in other respects very comfortable. But this is what, as Missionaries we must make up our minds to.

"*Feb.* 10 — Went to Zufferwal, sixteen miles. Here Jiwan and his brother Haima live. We met them in the bazaar as we entered, and Jiwan came with us to get a place for the rawti (a small tent), and then went to get some dinner cooked for us. In the evening his brother also came, and the spirit and conversation of both showed at once that the work of grace had begun in their minds, and was forming them into the character of the true children of God. Our discourse was very sweet and pleasant of the things of God. The night was spent in reading the Scriptures, prayer, and exhorting one another. Both evinced an enlarged and accurate acquaintance with the Scripture, but especially the younger, about twenty years old. He is of an inquiring and thoughtful mind, very quiet in perceiving the bearing of any principle, and cautious in accepting what he has not thoroughly considered. I loved him very much. As there were others in the tent, I took him out alone and asked him whether he loved Christ. He replied with much fervour, "Sir, I do love Him: I spake the truth, I do love Him." He then mentioned one or two difficulties in his mind, arising from apparent discrepancies, or various readings in the Bible, which he was anxious to have removed. It was evident, I think, that Christ was beginning to be formed in him the hope of glory, and he had decided to make a public profession of faith in Christ.

I felt I could only commit them to that grace which had already enlightened their hearts, and pray that He who had been the Author would also be the Finisher of their faith.

"*Feb.* 13 — In the evening, after tea, we had evening prayers; present, Paulus, Jiwan, Haima, Jawahir Messeeb, a catechist of the Sealkote Mission, passing through, an inquirer going with him, and a relative of Paulus, called Ghulam Nabee. This latter had come to talk with Paulus, and being present when we begun our service, he was invited to stay. This he did, listening to the prayers and sermon very attentively. I explained and applied Coloss. iii.12,13, ' Put on, therefore, as the elect of God, holy and beloved, bowels of mercies, kindness, humbleness of mind, longsuffering, &c.,' which was part of the epistle for the day. It was the the first time four of our number had ever joined in worship. May they be preserved to join in that assembly above who worship God day and night without ceasing!

"*Feb.* 14 — To-day being fixed for our return, Jiwan and Haima were early with us to pay us a parting visit. I asked them again if they had decided upon their baptism, and they gave me the same promise as before. We then spoke of several parts of God's word, relating to their danger as living among strangers to God's covenant, the wiles of Satan, and the necessity of looking to Jesus as all in all. Then, reading Acts xx., we committed them to God and the word of his grace, which is able to build them up, and give them an inheritance among all them that are sanctified.

"*Feb.* 20 — Preached to the native Christians (Umritsur) from Ephesians iii. 1—6. In the evening, after service, Sadiq begged me to remember his anxiety for baptism, and as I felt it better not to delay, he was received into the church by the name of Sadiq Masiee, a truly humble convert, I believe, conscious of his sinful nature, and his need of Christ, and desirous of living to the Saviour's praise. He begged to be allowed to spend the night with me, to be quite alone, without any other conversation from the native Christians. His mind is extremely tender: he needs much care and tender watching. The Lord give him strength equal to his day! He continued his education in the Mission school, and privately with me, until it shall appear to what work it may please God to call him.

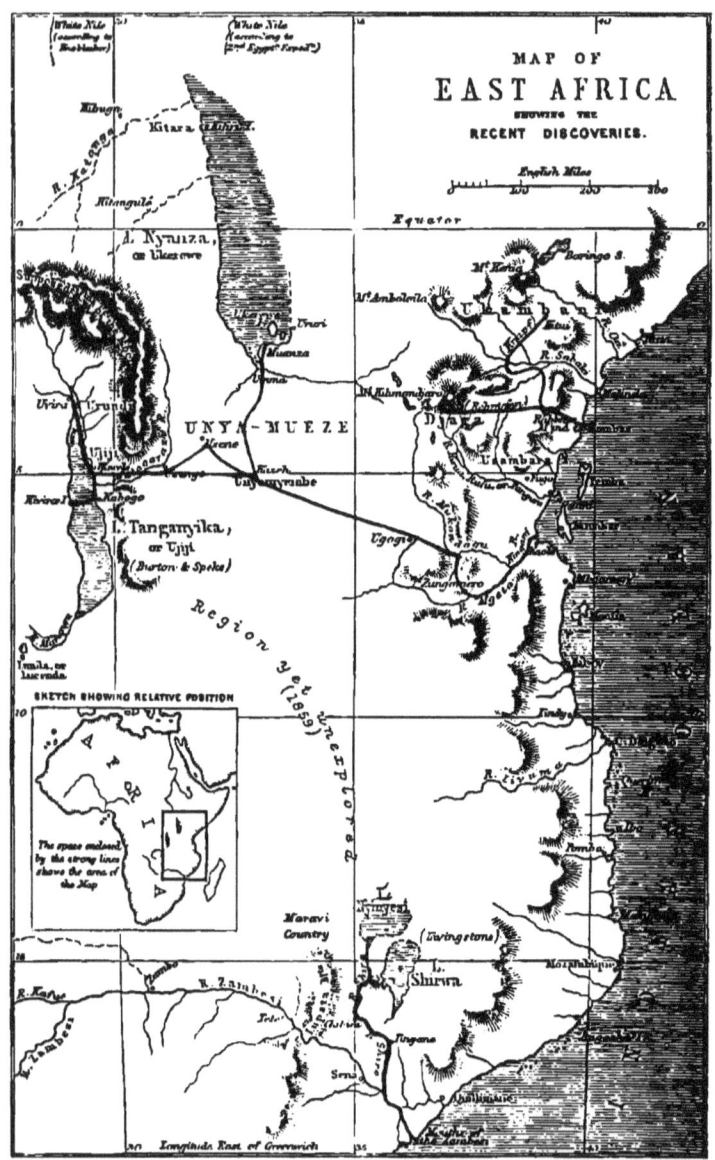

DISCOVERIES IN EAST AFRICA.*

In the early part of the year 1843, the Missionaries of the Church Missionary Society were expelled from Abyssinia, and some of them were transferred to the Western-India Mission. One from amongst the number, Dr. Krapf, was unwilling to leave East Africa. While residing in Shoa, his attention had been directed to the heathen Galla tribes who lie to the south of Abyssinia, and who form one of the most powerful and remarkable nations in Central Africa. He resolved on attempting to reach them from the coast, and selected, as his place of observation and temporary residence, Mombas, a small island at the mouth of the Tuaca river, and in about 4° south latitude. In June 1846 he was joined by the Rev. J. Rebmann, and a Mission station was immediately formed on the mainland amongst the Wanicas, a people with whom Dr. Krapf had been for some time previously on friendly intercourse, so as to acquire their good opinion. Finding themselves in a new region, the Missionaries felt anxious to learn something of the surrounding countries and their inhabitants, with a view to the extension of their labours, and exploratory tours were commenced. To these we shall briefly refer. One was undertaken to Jagga in April 1848. Seven days' journey in a westerly direction through the wilderness brought Mr. Rebmann to the Bura mountain, which consisted of several ranges stretching parallel to each other, from south to north, for about a three days' journey. Ascending the second range, he felt as if he was once more walking on the Jura mountains in the canton of Basle, so cool was the air, so beautiful the country. Five days subsequently (May 11th), the mountains of Jagga rose to view, and one amongst them, eminent above its fellows, crowned, as the monarch of the group, with a silver diadem of snow.

Of this mountain they had heard at Mombas. Strange stories were in circulation respecting it: that it was a silver mountain, but inaccessible, on account of evil spirits, by whom many persons attempting to ascend it had been killed. In November of the same year Mr. Rebmann again left Rabbai Mpia with the intention of penetrating to Kukuyi, a country north-west of Jagga. His previous visit to Jagga had been in the rainy season, and Kilimandjaro, as the mountain was called, obscured with clouds, was only occasionally visible. In November it was the middle of the dry season, and the route which he pursued conducted him within eighteen miles of the foot of Kilimandjaro. Under such favourable circumstances the great mountain was distinctly visible, even by moonlight, and the cold was as severe as in Europe during November. The country, which he traversed was intersected by valleys of from 1500 to 2000 feet deep, through which ran perennial streams, not less than twelve of them being crossed in one and a half-days' journey. It was while resident in the territory of Jagga that Mr. Rebmann first heard mention made of certain lakes in the interior—one called Rō, in or near the country Itandu, where the Kilimandjaro is still visible, and another on the north-west foot of that mountain. The country of Uniamesi, as lying more to the westward, and occupying a vast tract of Central Africa, was also referred to. It appeared, however, that the customary route to these central regions did not lie through Jagga.

Although not the usual road, still the hope was entertained, that through Jagga access might be found to Uniamesi, more especially as the king had promised an escort to protect our travellers from the wandering Masai and Wakuafi. In April 1849, Mr. Rebmann set out on his third journey to the Jagga districts. It was the rainy season: the rivers were swollen, and the route perilous and fatiguing. The ruler, instead of showing friendship, proved to be a heartless robber, and the Missionary, disappointed in his expectations, with much difficulty returned to the coast.

---

* The accompanying Map, carefully compiled from several sources, will be found to illustrate all the points discussed in this article. The routes of Krapf and Rebmann are indicated by a red line: those of Burton and Speke by a blue line nearly intersecting the Map. At the top of the Map will be found the White Nile, as laid down severally by Knoblecher and by Werne (of the second Egyptian Expedition), who each penetrated southward to about the same degree of latitude, but differ as to the meridian in which the river is to be placed. The still more recent traveller, Petherick, to whom also we allude, appears to have made his way to the Equator, passing somewhere between the routes of his predecessors, but his direction is not yet laid down precisely. We are indebted for the courtesy of the Royal Geographical Society for being able to present our readers with as yet unpublished discoveries in the regions of the River Shire and the Lake Shirwa from a sketch-map by Dr. Livingstone, whose route in that direction is indicated by a blue line near the bottom of the Map. This portion of the Map illustrates the other article in the present Number.

It now appeared desirable to visit Ukambani, an extensive country to the north-west of Mombas, and, in November 1849, Dr. Krapf set forth on this lengthened journey, accompanied by a small party of Wanika bearers. After passing through the wilderness, Mount Maunga was reached, from the summit of which an extensive prospect presented itself. Amongst other distinctive features, the snow-capped Kilimandjaro was seen towering over the high mountains of Bura and Ndara. Its dome-like head, glittering with transparent whiteness, was visible on several occasions, and did not fail to present itself to the attention of the Missionary at every spot which was somewhat elevated. While in Ukambani, Dr. Krapf heard of a great river, which one of his Wanika bearers had crossed on a journey from Jagga through the Wakuafi wilderness to Kikuyu. On that occasion he expressed his conviction that important discoveries remained to be made in these latitudes, and that future geographers would wonder at the simple manner in which the countries of Central Africa are connected. He adverted to the fact, that, as to their sources, the Nile, the Tchadda, the Congo, the Kilimani, all point towards the Equator, and the extensive territory of Uniamesi, which might be rendered, by interpretation, "Possession of the moon." In the great lake of Uniamesi, or at no great distance from it, they might be found to take their rise.

From Kivoi, the Wanika chief, whose guest he was, Dr. Krapf was informed of another snow-mountain in Kikuyu. This mountain, which the natives called Kenia, was said to be the living fountain of many rivers. Kivoi also made mention of a *bahari*, or sea, which he placed to the north of Kikuyu, according to the information received by him from the Wakamba hunters. This chief also referred to a fire mountain in the Wakuafi country, to the north-west of the Kenia mountain.

Doubts have been cast on the existence of snow-capped mountains in these equatorial regions. With respect to one of them, however, the Kilimandjaro, no room seems to be left for uncertainty. It has been seen by two Missionaries, and that repeatedly, and from different points of view. One of them, in his journeying, came sufficiently near its base, as not only to see it, but to feel the cold temperature; and if he approached no nearer than eighteen miles, it was simply because, beyond that point, through the superstitious fears of the people, the land was uninhabited.

Respecting the Kenia, we have not the same amount of testimony. Dr. Krapf describes it on his first visit to Ukambani. Kivoi conducted him to an elevated spot, about four miles distance from his hamlet, from whence "I enjoyed the great pleasure of distinctly seeing the Kenia. The sky being clear, I got a full sight of the snow-mountain, which I had been told by Kivoi is situated between Kikuyu and Uembu. It stretches from east to north-west by west. It appears to be like a gigantic wall, on whose summit I observed two immense towers or horns. These, which are at a short distance from each other, gave the mountain a grand and majestic appearance." On his second visit, however, the Kenia was not seen. On approaching the Dana river, Dr. Krapf says, "Before us lay the mountains of Mbé and Uembu eastward. In the west we saw the high Kikuyu mountains, whose termination and highest point is the Ndurkenia, which mountain I did not, however, see at present distinctly, for it was covered with clouds."

In June 1851, Dr. Krapf proceeded on a second visit to Ukambani, for the purpose of commencing a Mission among the Wakamba on the elevated plain of Yata. The sufferings and dangers of this attempt were extreme. On this passage through the wilderness the Missionary and his bearers were attacked by the Aendi, a predatory tribe of the lower country of the Bura. On arriving at Yata, the Wanika bearers whom he had engaged to build him a good cottage, refused to fulfil their agreement, and prepared to return home, after hastily constructing a miserable hut. Under these circumstances, Dr. Krapf found himself obliged to defer for a time the commencement of the Mission. Before, however, his return to Rabbai, with a view to more successful arrangements, he proposed to spend some time in exploring the country of Ukambani. An excursion to the river Dana, lying three days' journey north of Kitui, the hamlet of the chief Kivoi, was decided upon; this river, which falls into the sea under the name of the Osi, being reported to flow from the Kenia mountain. This expedition proved calamitous. The caravan was attacked by robbers, Kivoi slain, and his companions having fled in all directions, our Missionary found himself alone in a wild and unknown country. Devoured by thirst, he was constrained to seek the river, which he found to be, although in the dry season, 150 feet in width, and six or seven in depth. From thence, amidst excessive perils and privations, he made his way to the coast.

It had been a great object with our Missionaries to reach the central region of Uniamesi, and with this, amongst other objects, Mr. Rebmann had penetrated thrice to Jagga;

but beyond that point, as we have seen, no advance could be made, partly through the jealousy and avariciousness of the rulers, who wished to monopolize the white man, and appropriate to themselves all that might be gained from him; but also because of the wild Masai and Wakuafi tribes, whose predatory habits rendered travelling unsafe beyond the western frontier of Jagga. Disappointed in that direction, the Missionaries concluded that "Ukambani would be more likely to present a thoroughfare to Uniamesi, because the Wakamba themselves are great travellers;" and on Dr. Krapf's first visit to Ukambani, this idea seemed to be confirmed, the chief, Kivoi, having offered to convey him 300 miles beyond Ukambani to Kikuyu, Mbé, Uembu, and other countries. The results, however, of the second visit showed that he had promised more than he was able to accomplish, and that access to Uniamesi was as impracticable through Ukambani as through Jagga. The wild Masai and Wakuafi rove over the territory which extends between the Kenia and the Kilimandjaro, and have hitherto rendered that route so unsafe, that in carrying on their ivory traffic the Arabs of the coast prefer the circuitous route by Unyanyambe. Captain Speke, however, states that the difficulties of the route through Ukambani are diminishing.

"That commerce does make wonderful improvements on the barbarous habits of the Africans, can now be seen in the Masai country, and the countries extending north-westward from Mombas up through Kikuyu into the interior, where the process has been going on during the last few years. There even the roving wild pastorals, formerly untamable, are now gradually becoming reduced to subjection; and they no doubt will, ere long, have as strong a desire for cloths and other luxuries as any other civilized beings, from the natural desire to equal in comfort and dignity of appurtenances those whom they now must see constantly passing through their country. Caravans are penetrating farther, and going in greater numbers, every succeeding year, in those directions, and Arab merchants say that those countries are everywhere healthy. The best proof we have that the district is largely productive is the fact that the caravans and competition increase on those lines more and more every day."*

If this route permanently and safely open,

the facilities of access to the great Victoria Nyanza will be greatly increased, and happily the commercial advantages of intercourse with the interior are of sufficient promise to induce the Arab traders to brave the difficulties.

It may be suitable here to say something respecting these wild Masai and Wakuafi, who have hitherto been the scourge and terror of the more peaceable tribes of Eastern Africa.

"The Wakuafi and Masai," says Krapf, "who call themselves 'Orloikob, or 'Loikob,' 'loigob' (in the singular, 'Orloiksbani'), that is, possessors of the land, aborigines, primeval inhabitants—occupy a flat region in the interior of Eastern Africa. They extend from about two degrees north of the Equator to about four degrees south of it. The names 'Wakuafi' and 'Masai' are given them by the tribes of the coast. Their language diverges widely from the great South-African section (which I call the Orphno-Hamitic), and has, on the contrary, regarded lexicographically, some affinity with a very ancient Arabic language, termed by me the Cushite Arabic. Their way of life is nomadic. Where they find water and grass, there they encamp, often for months together. They live entirely on milk, butter, honey, and the flesh of cows, goats, and sheep, and of the game which they hunt down. They have a great distaste for agriculture, believing that the nourishment afforded by cereals enfeebles, and is only suited to the despised tribes of the mountains; while to feed on flesh and milk gives strength and courage. When cattle fail them, they make raids on the tribes which they know to be in possession of herds of beeves. They say that Engai (Heaven, God) gave them all that exists in the way of cattle, and that no other nation ought to possess any. Wherever there is a herd of cattle, thither the Wakuafi and Masai are commissioned to proceed and seize it. Agreeably with this fundamental faith, they undertake expeditions for hundreds of leagues to attain their object. They make forays into the territories of the Wakamba, the Galla, the Wadschagga, and even of the Wanika on the sea-coast. They are dreaded as warriors, laying all waste with fire and sword, so that the weaker tribes do not venture to resist them in the open field, but leave them in possession of their herds, and seek only to save themselves by the quickest possible flight.

"The arms of the Masai and Wakuafi consist of a spear, a large long shield, and a club, round and thick at the top, hurling

---

* Captain Speke's Discovery of the Victoria Nyanza, the supposed source of the Nile—"Blackwood's Magazine," Nov. 1859.

which, with the greatest precision, at a distance of from fifty to seventy paces, they can dash out the brains of the enemy. It is this weapon, above all, which strikes terror into the East Africans, the Suahelis with their muskets not excepted. The Wakuafi conceal themselves behind their long shields, until they come close enough to the enemy to make good use of their clubs. They conquer or die: death having no terrors for them."

Happily for the weaker African tribes, these two brother-tribes are possessed by a deadly hatred toward each other. If united, none of the East-African tribes, not even the Gallas, could withstand them.

"As regards the physical conformation of the Masai and Wakuafi," Dr. Krapf continues, "their forms are tall and slender, with handsome and rather light-complexioned features. Their greatest resemblance is to the Somali, who are considered Mohammedanized Gallas, and who, divided into many tribes, inhabit the eastern coast of Africa from the river Dschub northward to the Bay of Tadschurra. From their beauty of form, the Masai and Wakuafi slaves, especially the young females, are much sought after by the Arabs and Suahelis of the coast. They grow much attached to their Mohammedan masters, provided always that the latter do not require from them any labour (field-work, for instance) which is repugnant to their inclinations and habits.

"The Wakuafi and Masai consider themselves as pastoral tribes, the exclusive possessors of the plains and deserts, and the springs and rivers therein. But they do not attack the inhabitants of the mountains, so long as these confine themselves to the mountains, and refrain from descending into the level country to turn it to agricultural and pastoral account. It is said, however, that very recently they have resolved to take possession of the mountain Kadiaro, to facilitate their freebooting expeditions against the Galla, Wanika, and Suahelis, and to exclude these tribes of the coast from access to the interior. . . . .

"Like all East Africans, the Wakuafi and Masai are passionately fond of tobacco, but use it more to snuff than to smoke. They procure it principally from Kikuyu, Dschagga, and Usambara, countries with which they have some connexion. They also obtain it, as well as clothes, glass beads copper wire, &c., from the Suaheli traders, who, in caravans from 600 to 1000 men strong (most of them armed with muskets), venture into the countries of the Wakuafi and Masai to fetch ivory, but are often nearly all slain. . . . .

"As regards the religious conceptions of the Masai and Wakuafi, they appear, like other East Africans, to have a vague idea of a Supreme Being, whom they call Engai, which primarily denotes 'rain, the sky.' This highest of beings dwells on the White Mountain, whence comes the water or the rain, which is so indispensable to their meadows and herds. But according to the notion of the Wakuafi, between the Engai and themselves there is an intermediary being, the Neiterkob, who is, as it were, the mediator between God and man; and it is therefore to him that the Wakuafi first turn to gain a hearing from the Engai, when, as already mentioned, they pray for rain, health, victory, and cattle. What conceptions they entertain of evil spirits, and how far their souls are subjugated by a fear of these, I have not been able to learn. Probably they do not, in this respect, differ much from other Africans; for the dread of evil spirits is the invariable accompaniment of fallen man, so long as he does not learn to know and to experience in Christ Jesus a reconciled God and Father."

Disappointed in the hope of commencing Missionary operations in Jagga or Ukambani, the Missionaries looked toward the kingdom of Usambara, lying south-west from Mombas. In 1844, when visiting Zanzibar, the Pangani river, Tanga, Wasseen, and other places on the coast, Dr. Krapf had marked its lofty mountains, and wished, even then, to visit its king and people; and in the year 1848 he had succeeded in doing so. His interview with the king Kmeri was, on the whole, favourable, the sable ruler having granted him permission to come and teach his people.

After his return from his second journey to Ukambani, Dr. Krapf decided on again proceeding to Usambara, in the hope of obtaining from the king a renewal and confirmation of the favourable answer given by him in 1848, and the assignment of some specific locality where Missionary efforts might be at once commenced. Accordingly, in the early part of 1852, he again visited Kmeri at his capital, Fuga, and had allotted to him the maritime districts of Tengue, Pembina, and Pangani, as the first places to be occupied.

Usambara is a mountainous country, the ranges being very steep and eave-shaped, and their summits not admitting of many inhabitants or much cultivation, only villages, groves, and plaintain-plantations being found on the heights. Dr. Krapf suffered much from the continual windings, and the ascents or descents of the country. "Here we skirted a precipice, there we had only a shrub or some tufts of grass to lay hold upon is clambering up the precipitous path." On returning, a different road was selected: by keeping to the south and south-east our traveller succeeded in leaving behind the mountain region, and, descending into the valley of Kerenge, reached the mouth of the Panguni without difficulty.

Of the importance of Usambara as a central position, and affording a door of access to the interior, Dr. Krapf was led to form a favourable opinion. "My journey has shown that there is no country of East Africa better situated than Usambara, whence the Missionary has so much space for extending his operations. He may proceed to Pare, to Jagga, to Unguena, and Ngu, to the Masai and Wakuafi country, or to Uniamesi. There is a road to all these quarters."

In August 1853, the Rev. J. Erhardt proceeded to Fuga to present himself to Kmeri, as the Missionary that had been long promised to come and dwell amongst his people, and labour for their instruction and improvement. On the frontier he was soon surrounded by a strange mixture of races, anxious to see the Msungu— "the naked Mkamba, with his red-painted body; the proud Maegua, wrapped in his highly-coloured cloth; the tall, thin Mdigo, firmly grasping his bow and arrows; with a few skin-clad Wabondei."

In ascending Muango, the highest mountain-range of Bondei, he experienced the same difficulties as his predecessor—

"Muango is a very deceptive mountain: in looking up we always flattered ourselves that, after having cleared a certain promontory, we should have mounted the whole; but hill was towered upon hill, and mount upon mount, so that when the sun went down we had not seen the end of hills yet. The steep sides of the mountain are covered with gigantic grass, far more luxuriant than the plain. Trees of large dimensions and valuable wood are only now and then to be seen, underwood being very scarce. At some parts the wild grape has got the ascendancy over the grass, and produced very good-sized black grapes. On the higher parts of the mountain we met with very large isolated blocks of stone, lying and hanging about in every direction. At some places they are even piled up to considerable heights. It was curious to me to find that they were the very same kind of sandstone, some even with very similar holes, as those I had seen in the wilderness. .... The west side of this mountain is steeper and richer in water than the east. .... Towards the north I saw the horizon-bound wilderness, and towards the south a fine lake and the plain of the Rufa."

Finding a continued residence at Kmeri's court impracticable, Mr. Erhardt, in 1854, selected Tanga, on the coast, as his place of residence, applying himself to the study of the languages, and conversing with the men of various races by whom Tanga is frequented. There he found himself in that part of the coast from whence caravans start for the interior; and, in conversation with him, the ivory-traders spoke of the great lake of Uniamesi. Of this Dr. Krapf had heard when on his second visit to Ukambani. At Kivoi's house he became acquainted with a merchant from Uembu, a country lying, according to his informant, two days' distance across the Dana, in a northerly direction, the mountain Ndurkenia, or Kirenia, in the language of the Wakuafi and Uembu people, being five more days' distance from Uembu. From the Ndurkenia, or White Mountain, several rivers are described as having their course, the Dana, the Tumbiri, and the Nsaruddi; the two former having their course towards the Indian Ocean; the latter running down into a lake on the north-eastern side of the Kenia, from whence it flowed north-east into a much larger lake, called Baringa.

Again, in the beginning of 1850, when voyaging along the coast from Mombas to the southern extremity of the Imaum of Muscat's dominions, at a village called Mtotána, Dr. Krapf met with a considerable number of Waniamesi. They had spent three months in coming down to the coast with ivory and slaves. These men all made mention of a great lake, which they described as increasing and decreasing, or as being subject to periods of flood and contraction.

At Tanga, again, Mr. Erhardt heard native testimony on this point. Being one of the starting-points from the coast into the interior, he found himself there, as well as at Fuga, Kmeri's capital, brought into communication with caravan-leaders, Arabs, Suahelis, ivory-merchants, and slave-dealers, who visited him in his tent, and freely communicated to him what they knew of the interior; and it certainly did seem remarkable, "that persons journeying into the interior, all from very different starting-points, along a tract of coast extending some six degrees of latitude, should represent themselves, at very varying points of distance from the coast, as arriving at a bahari, or inland sea." Their statements also indicated, not two lakes, but one only, the lake Niassa being, according to their view, simply a prolongation of the lake of Uniamesi.

Mr. Rebmann, at Kisuludini, the Mission-station at Mombas, had obtained similar shreds of information from a man in his service, who had been a slave at Mombas, and who described his native country as lying two days' west from a lake, which, by the tribes who reside on its banks, is called Niansha, or Ninja. He had been used to go often to the lake, in search of a species of palm, of the leaves of which the natives made mats, bags, &c., as also to buy cotton, which is grown near the lake, and of which a coarse kind of cloth is prepared. The lake, from his description of it, and from more recent information, would appear to be the Niassa lake, yet he called it the Niansha. Thus names and descriptions were all confused. The two Missionaries resolved all the descrepancies and difficulties into one enormous inland sea, a map of which, as an approximation to the reality, appeared in our volume for 1856. This vast body of water was spread over an area extending from the equator to 13° south latitude, and from the 24° to the 35° of east longitude; the apex of the broad portion lying on the 27° east longitude, and the extremity of the tail-like projection to the south, touching the 35° east longitude, the shores being eastern and western shores, until, about the 8° and 10° of south latitude, they respectively curve to the east, and, having considerably approached each other and diminished the breadth of the water, they become north and south shores, until they approach the 36° of east longitude, when still nearing each other, they curve to north and south, and terminate in a tail-like prolongation. This enormous and strangely-shaped sea, in which, as we now perceive, not less, perhaps, than three distinct bodies of water were confused, received as many names as belonged to its supposed constituent members, being in one part the Ukerewe sea, then the Nianja, and also, by corruption, the Niassa, the whole being designated the Uniamesi sea.

Now, when we published Mr. Erhardt's map, which had previously appeared in the "Calwer-blatt," and also in a Number of the "Proceedings of the Royal Geographical Society of London," we presented it simply as a compilation from native sources, and as shadowing out the existence of phenomena in this portion of the African interior which would repay investigation. This was the object we had in view. We extract one paragraph from our Number for August 1856—"The statements of our Missionaries, and the objections urged against them, are before our readers. Without pledging ourselves to the accuracy of all their views, and making due allowance for the uncertainty connected with native reports, enough remains to arrest the attention of scientific men. Is it impossible to ascertain what is the fact? Have not geographical problems of much less interest and importance elicited repeated expeditions and persevering efforts at discovery?" The investigation which we thus pleaded for has been carried out, through the energy and perseverance of the Royal Geographical Society, and the results are before us in the deeply-interesting discoveries of Captains Burton and Speke.

"Many," writes Captain Speke, "may remember the excitement produced by an extraordinary map, and a more extraordinary lake figuring upon it, of a rather slug-like shape, which drew forth risible observations from all who entered the Royal Geographical Society's rooms in the year 1856. In order to ascertain the truthfulness of the said map, the Royal Geographical Society appointed Captain Burton to investigate this monster piece of water, represented as extending from the equator to 14° south latitude, as having a breadth of two to three hundred miles, and as lying at a distance of seven hundred miles inland west from Zanzibar.

"As Captain Burton and myself had been engaged on a former occasion exploring the Somali country in Eastern Africa together, he invited me to join him in these investigations."[*]

Kaolé, a village on the mainland, a little south of the Kingani river, was the coast starting-point of the expedition. The "caravan consisted of an Arab called Shayk Said, the Ras-cafila (head of the caravan), some porters of the Wanyamuézi tribe, and a host of donkeys for riding" and the transport of goods. Besides these, there were some negroes hired through the medium of an Hindi merchant, who carried muskets, and were in other ways useful. The lowland between the coast-range and the sea was first passed. It is described as diversified with flats and terraces, well-peopled and cultivated, and rich in forests and large tropical vegetation. At about one hundred miles distant from the seashore, the east coast range of mountains was reached, which extends from 9° north latitude down nearly to the Cape of Good Hope. These hills, nowhere exceeding 6000 feet in elevation, are in lines and masses, intersected by valleys, through which the rivers of the east coast find their way. Descending westward, our travellers reached an elevated plateau, chiefly wild forest, and with comparatively few inhabitants. It extends westward two hundred

---

[*] "Blackwood," September 1859.

and twenty miles, its average altitude being from 2500 to 4000 feet. Here were found the Wagogo and Wanyamuézi tribes, "who live in huts of a very civilized appearance, and far more comfortable than those possessed by any other interior clan." In the centre of the Wanyamuézi tribe lies Kazeh, an Arab dépôt, in south latitude 5° and east longitude 33°, "the immediate district of which is called Unyanyembo." From this point the caravans diverge to the different points, west, north, and south, where they are accustomed to meet and traffic with the tribes of the interior. There our travellers remained a month. Proceeding "westwards in the height of the monsoon, they passed through a country highly cultivated, producing rice, sugar-cane, and all Indian productions, the people weaving their cotton into loin cloths." One remarkable feature of this region was its gradual decline westwards, amounting to 1800 feet in one hundred and forty-five miles. After travelling along this decline about one hundred and fifty miles, our travellers ascended a mountain-spur, and, from the summit of the ridge, beheld the magnificent lake they were in search of. There it lay, overshadowed, as to its northern half, by a large crescent-shaped mass of mountains, which our travellers did not hesitate to recognise as the true Mountains of the Moon. Their disposition around the lake at once showed the appropriateness of the name, and the reason why they were so designated. At the north end of the lake the mountain mass is large and deep, but it throws out horns on either flank in a crescent shape, so as to stretch southward down the east and west side of the lake. The lake itself "lying between 3° and 8° south latitude, and 29° east longitude, has a length of three hundred miles, and is from thirty to forty broad in its centre, but tapers towards each end. The surface-level, as I ascertained by the temperature of boiling water, is only eighteen hundred feet, and it appears quite sunk into the lap of these mountains. It lies in a trough-like or synclinal depression, draining the waters of all the surrounding districts into its own bosom. Its waters are very sweet, and abound with delicious fish in great variety. Its shores are thickly inhabited by numerous tribes of the true Negro breed, amongst which the most conspicuous are the Wabembe cannibals, into whose territory no Arabs durst ever venture."*

Ujiji was the first place which they sought to reach, being the hamlet on the eastern shore which the Arabs chiefly frequent. It had been known to our Missionaries on the coast as the starting-point for row-boats, to cross the lake to the opposite shore, and our travellers found it to be the only district where canoes were obtainable. These were, however, nothing save little cockle-shell things, made out of the hollowed trunks of trees, liable to be driven ashore by a heavy gust, an event which might prove to be very serious, as the tribes around the coast were all in a state of hostility with each other. The native boatmen were therefore afraid to commit themselves to them, except for short distances and on a friendly beat. At length a boat was obtained at an exorbitant price—a long, "narrow canoe, hollowed out of the trunk of a single tree These vessels are mostly built from large timbers, growing in the district of Uguhba, on the western side of the lake. The savages fell them, lop off the branches and ends to the length required, and then, after covering the upper surface with wet mud, as the tree lies upon the ground, they set fire to and smoulder out its interior, until nothing but a case remains, which they finish up by paring out with roughly-constructed hatchets. The seats of these canoes are bars of wood tied transversely to the length."†

On examination, it was found to require considerable repairs before it could be considered seaworthy; and while these were going forward, Captain Speke occupied himself in recruiting his health, which, as well as Captain Burton's, had suffered severely since they had left the elevated plateau, and descended into the richly-productive regions which bordered the lake. He visited frequently the market at Ujiji. "The market is held between the hours of ten A.M. and four P.M. near the port, and consists of a few temporary huts, composed of grass and branches hastily tied together. Most of these are thrown up day by day. The commodities brought for sale are fish, flesh, tobacco, palm-oil, and spirits, different kinds of potatoes, artichokes, several sorts of beans, plantains, melons, cotton, sugar-cane, a variety of pulse and vegetables, and ivories, and sometimes slaves."‡

The party in the boat consisted of six of Captain Speke's people and twenty naked savage sailors. They pulled southward along the eastern shore, now along a low shelving beach, now hugging a bold bluff, the foreground being backed by small well-wooded hills, and densely wooded to the water's edge.

---

* "Blackwood," September 1859.
† "Blackwood," September 1859.
‡ Ibid.

"Could but a little civilized art, as whitewashed houses, well-trained gardens, and the like, vary these ever-green hills and trees, and diversify the unceasing monotony of hill and dale, and dale and hill—of green trees, green grass—green grass, green trees—so wearisome in their luxuriance, what a paradise of beauty would this place present! The deep blue waters of the lake in contrast with the vegetation and large brown rocks form everywhere an object of intense attraction; but the appetite soon wearies of such profusion, without the contrast of more sober tints, or the variety incidental to a populous and inhabited country. There are said to be some few scattered villages concealed in these dense jungles extending away in the background, but how the shores should be so desolate strikes one with much surprise. The naturally excessive growth of all vegetable life is sufficient proof of the soil's capabilities. Unless in former times this beautiful country has been harrassed by neighbouring tribes, and despoiled of its men and cattle to satisfy the spoilers and sell to distant markets, its present state appears quite incomprehensible. In hazarding this conjecture, it might be thought that I am taking an extreme view of the case; but when we see everywhere in Africa what one slave-hunt or cattle-lifting party can effect, it is not unreasonable to imagine that this was most probably the cause of such utter desolation here. These war-parties lay waste the tracts they visit for endless time. Indeed, until the effects of slavery and the so-called *free labour* are suppressed in Africa, we may expect to find such places in a similarly melancholy state."*

Animal life was most abundant. Crocodiles frequented the lake; hippopotami were also numerous. On the shores might be seen herds of wild buffaloes, horned like the Cape ones. The trail of elephants was also occasionally visible, and antelopes were sprung. At length they neared that part of the lake which, as being the narrowest, is selected as the crossing-place for canoes, the starting-points being Kabogo on the west shore, and Kasengé on the east. Kivira, an island near the western shore, with the Ugubha mountains in the background, was reached after fourteen hours occupied in crossing. From the summit of this island a good view of the lake was obtained.

"Kivira Island is a massive hill, about five miles long by two or three broad, and is irregularly shaped. In places there are high flats, formed in terraces, but generally the steeps are abrupt and thickly wooded. The mainland immediately west is a promontory, at the southern extremity of the Ugubha mountains, on the western coast of the Tanganyika; and the island is detached from it by so narrow a strip of water, that unless you obtained a profile view, it might easily be mistaken for a headland. The population is considerable, and they live in mushroom huts, situated on the high flats and easier slopes, where they cultivate the manioc, sweet potato, maize, millet, various kinds of pulse, and all the common vegetables in general use about the country. Poultry abounds in the villages. The dress of the people is simple, consisting of small black monkey-skins, cat-skins, and the furs of any vermin they can get. These are tucked under a waist-strap, and, according to the number they possess, go completely or only half-way round the body, the animals' heads hanging in front and the tails always depending gracefully below. These monkeys are easily captured when the maize is ripe, by a number of people stealthily staking small square nets in contiguous lines all round the fields which these animals may be occupied in robbing, and then with screams and yells, flinging sticks and stones, the hunters rush upon the affrighted thieves, till, in their hurry and confusion to escape, they become irretrievably entangled in the meshes."*

At Kasenge Captain Speke was the guest of an Arab, Shaykh Hamed biu Sulayyimi, by whom a tempting offer was made to him to prosecute his researches westward of the lake. The Shaykh was about to march in a few days about a hundred miles to the south-west, to a country called Urawa, a territory belonging to Sultan Keyombo. Uruwwa is about half-way across the continent, and thus the line of exploration from the east would be brought near to those which have been traced by Livingstone. The roads were described "as easy to travel over, for the track lay across an undulating country, intersected by many small insignificant streams, which only contribute to fertilize the land, and present no obstacles whatever. The line is cheap, and affords provisions in abundance."

The proceedings of this Shaykh may serve to show how research is going forward from the east coast, and the Arabs induced to penetrate further and further into the central area. "It may appear odd that men should go so far into the interior of Africa to procure ivory, when undoubtedly much is to be found at places not half so distant from Zanzibar; but the reason of it is simple. The nearer coun-

---

* "Blackwood," September 1859.

* "Blackwood," September 1859.

tries have become so overstocked with beads and cloth, that ivory there has risen to so great a price, it does not pay its transport Hence every succeeding year finds the Arabs penetrating farther inland."*

On Captain Speke's return to Ujiji, Kannina, the chief of that district, having some ivory business to transact with the Sultan of Uvira, a district on the northern and western shore of the lake, agreed to take the exploratory party thither in two canoes, and show them a large river, the Rusizi, which Shaykh Hamed had described as running out of the lake, but which Captain Speke felt assured must flow into it.

"I feel convinced that he was romancing when talking of the northern rivers' flow, not only because the northern end of the lake is encircled by high hills—the concave of the Mountains of the Moon—but because the lake's altitude is so much less than that of the adjacent plateaus. Indeed, the waters of the lake are so low as to convey the impression that the trough they lie in has been formed by volcanic agency."†

On arriving, however, at Uvira, Kannina could not be persuaded to go any further, although "the remaining distance to the river could have been accomplished in about six hours' paddling." But the Sultan's son, who visited them soon after their arrival, assured them that the river drained the high mountains to the north, and discharged its waters into the lake.

"I should not have been satisfied with this counter-statement alone (knowing, as everybody must who travels amongst unenlightened men, that they have a proverbial habit of describing a river's flow to be the opposite of what it is), had I not ascended some neighbouring heights, and observed the mountains increasing in size as they extended away to the northward, and effectually closing in this low lake, which is not quite half the altitude of the surface-level of the general interior plateau, and cannot, therefore, under any circumstances, have an overflow of water."‡

The districts around the lake appear to contain a considerable population, although diminished by slave-hunts, which depress the people, and discourage them from any effort to improve their condition.

"In consequence of these slave-hunts the country is kept in such a state of commotion that no one thinks it worth his while to make accumulations of property, and consequently the negroes now only live for the day, and keep no granaries, never thinking of exerting themselves to better their condition. Without doubt it is mainly owing to this unfortunate influence of slavery on African society that we have been kept so long ignorant of the vast resources of Eastern and Central Africa—a vast field, full of resources, which would be of so much value to Zanzibar and neighbouring India, were it only properly developed."*

Of the demoralizing influence of slave-trading transactions, and the fearful way in which they dry up natural affection, and harden each man's heart against his fellow, some painful evidences will be found in the following description of the people of Kasengé—

"The population is very considerable. They are extremely filthy in their habits, and are incessantly inquisitive, as far at least as gratifying their idle curiosity is concerned. From having no industrial occupations, they will stand for hours and hours together, watching any strange object, and are, in consequence, an infinite pest to any stranger coming near them. In appearance they are not much unlike the Kaffir, resembling that tribe both in size, height, and general bearing, having enlarged lips, flattish noses, and frizzly woolly hair. They are very easily amused, and generally wear smiling faces. The women are better dressed than the men, having a cloth round the body, fastened under the arms, and reaching below the knees, and generally beads, brass necklaces, or other ornaments, while the latter only wear a single goat-skin slung game-bag fashion over the shoulder, or, when they possess it, a short cloth tied kilt fashion round the waist. They lie about their huts like swine, with little more animation on a warm day than the pig has when basking in a summer's sun. The mothers of those savage people have infinitely less affection than many savage beasts of my acquaintance. I have seen a mother bear, galled by constant fire, obstinately meet her death, by repeatedly returning under a shower of bullets, endeavouring to rescue her young from the grasp of intruding men. But here, for a simple loin-cloth or two, human mothers eagerly exchanged their little offspring, delivering them into perpetual bondage to my Belooch soldiers."†

Capt. Speke disallows the possibility of natives of Africa being procurable as free labourers. The state of society is not such as to "induce the negroes to leave their easy homes and

---

* "Blackwood," September 1859.
† Ibid.   ‡ Ibid. Oct. 1859.

* "Blackwood," September 1859.
† Ibid.

seek for hard service abroad. Nothing is more foreign to their inclinations. Nor can men be found willing to exile themselves as free labourers in any part of these African regions. In the first place, the negro has as great an antipathy to work as a mad dog has to water: he will avoid it by every stratagem within his power."*

"When a market for free labourers is once opened—when the draining poultice is once applied to Africa's exterior—then the interior will assuredly be drained of all its working men, and become more a waste than ever. To supply the markets with those free cattle becomes so lucrative a means of gain, that merchants would stick at no expedient in endeavouring to secure them. The country, so full as we have seen it of all the useful necessaries of life, able to supply our markets and relieve our people by cheapening all commodities, would, if slavery were only permitted to increase, soon be devastated for the very minor consideration of improving a few small islands in the Indian Ocean. On the contrary, slavery has only to be suppressed entirely, and the country would soon yield one hundredfold more than ever it has done before. The merchants themselves are aware of this, for every Hindi on the coast with whom I ever spoke on the subject of slavery, seemed confident that the true prosperity of Africa would only commence with the cessation of slavery."†

Our travellers returned to Kazeh by the end of June, and there Capt. Speke occupied himself in preparations for a still more arduous undertaking. His Arab host at Kazeh, on his first arrival there, had told him of another great body of interior water, which he called the Ukerewe Sea, and had urged that he should journey there instead of to the smaller waters of Ujiji.

This man very distinctly described the particulars of his journey to Kibuga, supposed to be in 2° north latitude, and 31° east long., where he had remained with king Sunna for three years. "Starting from Unyanyembé, he approached the lake, and entered the Karagwah district, the only difficulty which he experienced on the march arising from the Wasoe tribe, who are situated at the beginning of the Karagwah district." This district, "a mountainous tract of land, containing several high spurs of hills, the eastern buttresses of those *Lunæ montes*, and washed on the flanks by the Ukerewe Sea, is bounded on the north by the Kitangura river, beyond which the Wanyoros territory, crescent shape, lies, with the horns directed eastward. Amidst them, situate in the concave or lake side, are the Wagandas," whose capital is Kibuga. The Kitangura river constitutes the northern boundary of the Karagwah district. It was described by the native informant as very "great, with much water flowing from Urundi, a district in the Mountains of the Moon, and pursuing a north-easterly course towards the lake. Besides lesser streams, one other large river was passed, the Katonga, like the rest coming from the west, and flowing towards the lake. It has a span of 2000 yards, and is very deep when full; but sinks and is very sluggish in the dry season." From a Hindu merchant called Musa, Captain Speke obtained still further information. He spoke of "a third large river to the northward of the line, lying north beyond Uganda: it is much larger than the Katonga, and is generally called the Usoga river, because it waters that district." "He produced a negro slave of the Wanyoro tribe who had been to Usoga, and had seen the river in question This man called the river Kivira, and described it as being much broader, deeper, and stronger in its current than either the Katonga or Kitangura river; that it came from the generally acknowledged direction of the lake, and that it intersected stony, hilly ground on its passage to the north-west. This river Kivira I now believe (although I must confess at first I did not) is the Nile itself; for on a subsequent occasion, when talking to a very respectable Suaheli merchant, by name Shaykh Abdullah bin Nasib, about the Nyanza, he corroborated the story about the mariners, who are said to keep logs and use sextants, and mentioned that he had heard of a tribe called Bari, living on the Kivira river. Now the Bari people mentioned by him are evidently those which have long since been known to us as a tribe living on the Nile in latitude 4° north, and longitude 32° east, and described by the different Egyptian expeditions sent up the Nile to discover its source. M. Ferdinand Werne (says Dr. Beke) has published an account of the second expedition's proceedings, in which he took part; and which, it appears, succeeded in getting further up the river than either of the others. 'The author states that, according to Lacono, king of Bari, the course of the river continues thence southwards a distance of thirty days' journey.' This, by Dr. Beke's computation, places the source of the Nile just where I have since discovered the Nyanza's southern extremity to be, in the second degree south longitude, lying in the Uniamesi country. Here we see how sin-

---

* "Blackwood," Sept. 1859. † Ibid.

gularly all the different informers' statements blend together, in substantiating my opinion that the Nyanza is the great reservoir or fountain-head of that mighty stream that floated father Moses on his first adventurous sail—the Nile. Even Ptolemy, we see, is right in stating that the Nile is fed by the waters coming from the Mountains of the Moon: and though he has not placed those mountains exactly where they should be on his map—from not understanding the true disposition of the various physical geographical features which occupy that part of Africa—still it is wonderfully near the truth for an hypothetical production."*

In following out the native accounts which Captain Speke collected, we have unavoidably anticipated much of the subsequent narrative. We cannot be surprised, if, with such information before him, he decided to undertake a second expedition in search of the great lake, which the Arabs declared to be "both broader and longer than the Tanganyika, and which they call Ukarewe, after the island where their caravans go for ivory." The details of this expedition, which are deeply interesting, will be found in Blackwood's Magazine for October and November of last year. To that publication we must refer our readers, as our digest of the various incidents must be very brief.

The caravan, which, from severe illness, Captain Burton was unable to accompany, left Kazeh on July 9th, 1858. They first passed through the cultivated plain of Unyanyembé, where the comfortable structure of the villages arrested attention. " As is the case in all central Uniamesi, they form a large hollow square, the walls of which are their huts, ranged on all sides of it in a sort of street, consisting of two walls, the breadth of an ordinary room, which is partitioned off to a convenient size by interior walls of the same earth-construction as the exterior ones, or as our Sepoys' lines are made in India. The roof is flat, and serves as a store-place for keeping sticks to burn, drying grain, pumpkins, mushrooms, or any vegetables they may have. Most of these compartments contain the families of the villagers, together with their poultry, brewing utensils, cooking apparatus, stores of grain, and any thing they possess. The remainder contain their flocks and herds, principally goats and cows, for sheep do not breed well in the country, and their flesh is not much approved of by the people. What few sheep there are appear to be an offshoot from the Persian stock. They have a very scraggy appearance, and show but the slightest signs of the fat-rumped proportions of their ancestors. The cows, unlike the noble Tanganyika ones, are small and short-horned, and are of a variety of colours. They carry a hump like the Brahminy bull, but give very little milk. In front of nearly every house you see large slabs of granite, the stones on which the jowari is ground by women, who, kneeling before them, rub the grain down to flour with a smaller stone, which they hold with both hands at once. Thus rubbing and grinding away, their bodies sway monotonously to and fro, while they cheer the time by singing and droning in cadence to the motion of their bodies." *

Beyond the limits of Uniamesi proper the dwellings of the population deteriorate. "They consist of a number of mushroom-shaped grass huts, surrounded by a tall slender palisading, and having streets or passages of the same wooden construction, some winding, some straight, and others crosswise, with outlets at certain distances leading into the different courts, each court usually containing five or six huts, partitioned off with poles as the streets are. These courts serve for dividing the different families, uncles and cousins occupying some, whilst slaves and their relatives live in others. Besides this, they have their cattle-yards. If the site of the village be on moist or soft ground, it is usual, in addition to the palisading, to have it further fortified by a maur or evergreen fence."†

As they advanced the scenery varied: sometimes there were extensively-cultivated plains, where flesh, milk, eggs, and every variety of vegetable abounded; at other times the country lay "in long waves, crested with cropping little hills, thickly clad with small trees and brushwood. In the hollows of these waves the cultivation is very abundant." The population was occasionally so dense as to astonish the coast people by whom Captain Speke was attended. In the Msalala district the road is described as tolerably thronged with them: they had heard that Msungu was passing by, and came, many of them, a long way to see him.

On his return journey the same fact is adverted to. "This country being full of sweet springs, accounts for the denseness of the population and numberless herds of cattle. To look upon its resources, one is struck with amazement at the waste of the world: if, instead of this district being in the hands of its present owners, it were ruled by a few scores of Eu-

---

* "Blackwood," October 1859.

* "Blackwood," October 1859.
† Ibid.

ropeans, what an entire revolution a few years would bring forth! An extensive market would be opened to the world, the present nakedness of the land would have a covering, and industry and commerce would clear the way for civilization and enlightenment. At present the natural inert laziness and ignorance of the people is their own and their country's bane. They are all totally unaware of the treasures at their feet. This dreadful sloth is in part engendered by the excessive bounty of the land in its natural state; by the little want of clothes or other luxuries, in consequence of the congenial temperature; and from the people having no higher object in view than the first-coming meal, and no other stimulus to exertion by example or any thing else."*

Captain Speke eulogizes the climate. On the 27th of July he says—

"To walk till breakfast, nine A.M., every morning, I find a luxury, and thence till noon I ride with pleasure; but the next three hours, though pleasant in a hut, are too warm to be agreeable under hard exertion. The evenings and the mornings, again, are particularly serene, and the night, after ten P.M., so cold as to render a blanket necessary. But then you must remember that all the country about these latitudes, on this meridian, 33° east, is at an altitude of 3500 to 4000 feet."†

Yet it must be remembered, that during the first eight months of their residence in East Africa our travellers suffered much from sickness. "The climate is a paradox quite beyond my solving, unless the numerous and severe maladies that we all suffered from, during the first eight months of our explorations, may be attributed to too much exposure; and even that does not solve the problem. To all appearance the whole of the country to the westward of the east-coast range is high, dry, and healthy. No unpleasant exhalations pollute the atmosphere; there are no extremes of temperature; the air is neither too hot nor too cold; and a little care in hutting, dressing, and diet, should obviate any evil effects of exposure. Springs of good water, and wholesome food, are everywhere obtainable. Flies and musquitos, the great Indian pests, are scarcely known, and the tsetse of the south nowhere exists."‡

On the 26th, after passing some village cultivations, they "entered a waterless wilderness of thorn and tree forest, with some long and broad plains of tall grass intersecting the line of march. These flats very much resemble some we crossed when travelling close to and parallel with the Malagarazi river; for by the cracked and flawy nature of the ground, now parched up by a constant drought, it shows that this part gets inundated in the wet season. Indeed, this peculiar grassy flat formation suggests the proximity of a river everywhere in Africa; and I felt sure, as afterwards proved true, that a river was not far from us. The existence of animal life is another warranty of water being near: elephants and buffaloes cannot live a day without it."*

On the 30th a sheet of water was discernible, which " proved to be a creek, the southern point of the Great Nyanza." Along this creek they advanced, the country having "a mixed and large population of smiths, agriculturists, and herdsmen, residing in the flats and depressions which lie between the scattered little hills. During the rainy season, when the lake swells, and the country becomes super-saturated, the inundations are so great that all travelling becomes suspended."†

The creek continued to increase in breadth as it extended northward, until it had attained very considerable dimensions, with "many little islands, well-wooded elevations, standing boldly out of its waters, which, together with the hill-dotted country around, afforded a most agreeable prospect." The route was sometimes "close by the creek, at other times winding between small hills, the valleys of which were thickly inhabited by both agricultural and pastoral people. Here some small perennial streams, exuding from springs by the base of these hills, meander through the valleys, and keep all vegetable life in a constant state of verdant freshness."‡

At length, on August 3d, from an elevated point, " the vast expanse of the pale-blue waters of the Nyanza" burst suddenly on the view. "It was early morning. The distant sea-line of the north horizon was defined in the calm atmosphere between the north and west points of the compass; but even this did not afford me any idea of the breadth of the lake, as an archipelago of islands, each consisting of a single hill, rising to a height of 200 or 300 feet above the water, intersected the line of vision to the left; while on the right the western horn of the Ukerewé Island cut off any further view of its distant waters to the eastward of north."

"This view was one which, even in a well-known and explored country, would have

---

* "Blackwood," November 1859.
† Ibid. Oct. 1859.   ‡ Ibid. Nov. 1859.

* "Blackwood," Oct. 1859.   † Ibid.   ‡ Ibid.

arrested the traveller by its peaceful beauty. The islands, each swelling in a gentle slope to a rounded summit, clothed with wood between the rugged angular closely-cropping rocks of granite, seemed mirrored in the calm surface of the lake; on which I here and there detected a small black speck, the tiny canoe of some Muanza fisherman. On the gently shelving plain below me, blue smoke curled above the trees, which here and there partially concealed villages and hamlets, their brown thatched roofs contrasting with the emerald green of the beautiful milk-bush, the coral branches of which cluster in such profusion round the cottages, and form alleys and hedgerows about the villages as ornamental as any garden shrub in England. But the pleasure of the mere view vanished in the presence of those more intense and exciting emotions which are called up by the consideration of the commercial and geographical importance of the prospect before me. I no longer felt any doubt that the lake at my feet gave birth to that interesting river, the source of which has been the subject of so many explorers."*

Captain Speke stayed his advance northward at a point 220 miles distant from Kazeh. There, from the summit of a small hill, which he called Observatory Hill, he was enabled to take compass-bearings of all the principal features of the lake.

"On facing to the W.N.W., I could only see a sea horizon; and, on inquiring how far back the land lay, was assured that, beyond the island of Ukerewé, there was an equal expanse of it east and west, and that it would be more than double the distance of the little hill before alluded to, or from eighty to one hundred miles in breadth. On my inquiring about the lake's length, the man faced to the north, and began nodding his head to it; at the same time he kept throwing forward his right hand, and, making repeated snaps of his fingers, endeavoured to indicate something immeasurable; and added, that nobody knew, but he thought it probably extended to the end of the world."†

Such, then, is the great inland sea of Equatorial Africa, so long bruited in native reports and Missionary journals, and now at length proved to be a reality.

"The Nyanza, as we now see, is a large expansive sheet of water, flush with the basial surface of the country, and lies between the Mountains of the Moon (on its western side), having, according to Dr. Krapf, snowy Kenia on its eastern flank. Dr. Krapf tells us of a large river flowing down from the western side of this snowy peak, and trending away to the north-west, in a direction, as will be seen by the map, leading right into my lake. Now, returning again to the western side, we find that the Nyanza is plentifully supplied by those streams coming from the *Lunæ Montes*, of which the Arabs, one and all, give such consistent and concise accounts; and the flowings of which, being north-easterly, must, in course of time and distance, commingle with those north-westerly off-flowings, before mentioned, of Mons Kenia. My impression is, after hearing everybody's story on the matter, that these streams enter at opposite sides of the lake, on the northern side of the Equator, and are consequently very considerable feeders to it."*

On the return journey the general features of the country were carefully observed. Its capabilities and resources are highly spoken of.

"The flats and hollows are well peopled, and cattle and cultivation are everywhere abundant. The stone, soil, and aspect of this tract is uniform throughout. The stone is chiefly granite, the rugged rocks of which lie like knobs of sugar over the surface of the little hills, intermingled with sandstone in a highly ferruginous state; whilst the soil is an accumulation of sand the same colour as the stone, a light brownish grey, and appears as if it were formed of disintegrated particles of the rocks worn off by time and weathering. Small trees and brushwood cover all the outcropping hills; and palms on the plains, though few and widely spread, prove that water is very near the surface. Springs, too, are numerous, and generally distributed. The mean level of the country between Unyanyembé and the lake is 3767 feet; that of the lake itself, 3750. The tribes, as a rule, are well disposed towards all strangers, and wish to extend their commerce. Their social state rather represents a conservative than a radical disposition; and their government is a sort of semi-patriarchal-feudal arrangement, and, like a band of robbers, all hold together from feeling the necessity of mutual support. Bordering the south of the lake, there are vast fields of iron; cotton is also abundant; and every tropical plant or tree could grow: those that do exist, even rice, vegetate in the utmost luxuriance. Cattle are very abundant, and hides fill every house. On the east of the lake ivory is said to be very abundant and cheap; and on the west we hear of many advantages which are especially worthy of

---

* "Blackwood", October 1859.
† Ibid.

* "Blackwood," October 1859.

our notice. The Karagwa hills overlooking the lake are high, cold, and healthy, and have enormous droves of cattle bearing horns of stupendous size; and ivory, fine timber, and all the necessaries of life, are to be found in great profusion there. Again, beyond the equator, of the kingdom of Uganda we hear from everybody a rapturous account. That country evidently swarms with people who cultivate coffee and all the common grains, and have large flocks and herds, even greater than what I have lately seen. Now if the Nyanza be really the Nile's fount, which I sincerely believe to be the case, what an advantage this will be to the English merchant on the Nile, and what a field is open to the world, if, as I hope will be the case, England does not neglect this discovery!"*

In the above paragraph, Captain Speke connects the discoveries which have been made from the south with those which have approached the Equator from the north. How near have the latter approximated, and what may be the amount of territory which intervenes between the recognised points of discovery?

There have been several expeditions sent forth by the Egyptian Government. The first originated with Mohammed Ali. When nearly eighty years of age, actuated by a desire to see the auriferous country of Fazokl, which, although insignificant in its yield, had been depicted as a new El Dorado, he had not hesitated to undertake a journey of 700 leagues. While resting awhile at Khartoum, his thoughts were carried towards the mysterious sources of the river, lying hid in the profound depths of the African continent. The Europeans by whom he was surrounded urged him to such an enterprise, and the exploration of the White River was resolved upon. But the first expedition was exclusively Egyptian, only one European, without assigned duties or authority, accompanying it. Destitute of every thing of a scientific character, no dependence could be placed on the observations which were made, and which were so incorrect, that Selim, the commandant, supposed he had reached 8½° latitude, N., when, in reality, he had not attained the sixth parallel.

This was followed by a second expedition, in which more attention was paid to scientific matters. Two French engineers in the Egyptian service, Messrs. D'Arnaud and Sabatier, were charged with the astronomical observations; another European was adjoined as naturalist; and a German physician was permitted to accompany the expedition as a passenger. To this person, Mr. Werne, we are indebted for the only detailed record of its proceedings. This expedition took place in 1840 and 1841; and scarcely had the vessels returned to Khartoum, in April 1841, when they set sail on a third expedition, of which M. D'Arnaud had again the scientific direction. This effort does not appear to have reached so far south as its predecessor.

Ever since 1848, when D'Arnaud's expedition returned to Cairo, the Egyptian Government has been intending a new effort in search of the sources of the White Nile, but although always contemplated, it has never been realized.

From other sources, however, new information has been obtained respecting the countries of the White River. Some has been furnished by Europeans, whom the gum and ivory traffic have brought, for fifteen years, to the uttermost limits of the discoveries made by the Egyptian expedition. M. Brun Rollet, a Sardinian subject of Savoyard origin, belongs to the first category. Without being a man of science, Mr. Brun Rollet was far from illiterate; the detached observations that have been received from him, and, finally, the volume which he has published on the higher region of the river, alike contain most interesting information. The greater part relates to the tribes with whom the traveller was brought into direct communication, or with whom he became acquainted through the report of natives. Information has also been acquired by the Romish Missionaries, who, with the usual activity of their system, have been pushed up the Nile. The Romish Mission to Central Africa was begun ten years ago by the Pontifical Government of Pius IX. An Austrian monk, the Rev. Ignatius Knoblecher, had the direction of it. He arrived at Balenia, the extreme point of the Egyptian discoveries, towards the middle of January 1850, and there he founded an establishment from whence Romish teaching was to radiate into the surrounding countries. A short notice of Mr. Knoblecher's journey has been printed from his letters, which contains remarks and statements as to the course of the river, and the population on its banks. The most considerable part, however, of the materials collected by him have not been published, and his astronomical observations have been withheld, which were the more necessary, as his notations are very different from those given by the Egyptian expedition of 1840. One of the priests of the Mission at Balenia, Angelo Vinco, has collected, during a residence of many years, much valuable

---

* "Blackwood," November 1859.

information on the countries and populations situated farther south, towards the Equator. Angelo, as well as Knoblecher, and M. Brun Rollet, have all, at short intervals, paid the fatal tribute from which so few Europeans escape in a tropical climate.

Let us now glance at some of the phenomena of these regions. When we take in, at one look, the Nile basin in its enormous extent, we see that the territory of this king of the African rivers divides itself into two large regions, perfectly distinct and separate, and of about equal lengths—southward from the Equator to the 17° N. latitude, the region of periodical rains; northwards, from the seventeenth parallel to the Mediterranean below the thirty-second, the region deprived of rain. This is a striking demarcation, because this great climatological division produced by the annual path of the sun from one tropic to the other, corresponds exactly with the physical division of the basin of the Nile. The zone of rains is also the region of the highest tributaries of the river; for in the rainless zone, during a course of more than 500 leagues, the Nile receives not a single river, not a single brook even. In the upper part of the basin, over an extent of from 400 to 500 miles, there spreads out, as an immense fan, the vast network of confluent rivers, some descending from unknown heights near the Equator, others rolling through deep cuttings of the Abyssinian plateau, all of them watering countries where animal and vegetable life are most abundant. In the lower half, on the contrary, the waters of the Nile, shut up into one solitary channel, flow on silently through the arid waters of Egypt and Nubia, where, within the narrow space just bordering on the river, there alone is fertility. The last confluent of the Upper Nile, the Atbara or Astabazza, joins itself to the river between the 17° and 18° N. latitude, at about the limit of the region of tropical rains. There the aridity of the sandy plains meets and mingles with the verdant vegetation of the first pasture lands. But if we ascend 2° or 3° farther south, to the plains where the white and blue rivers meet, the two great upper arms of the Nile, there the splendid vegetation of the tropics, at once displays itself.

M. Rüsseger, ascending from Khartoum to Elais, thus depicts the magnificent vigour of nature in this latitude—"The aspect that the river presents on approaching Elais is the very type of tropical beauty: an immense extent of water, all covered with islands thickly planted with trees, and wooded on both banks. You can see nothing but water and the sombre green of the forests of mimosas that the axe has never touched. Climbing plants, with brilliant flowers, meet and intertwine in such a way as to render the woods impenetrable: the trees, that stretch their branches far over the river, completely cover the shore. Crocodiles and hippopotami appear in great numbers."

It is much to be regretted that the extreme point of discoveries on the White River, among the Baris, is far from being satisfactorily determined, although at many different times astronomical observations have been made upon it. This is because these observations—a little in the latitude, and a great deal in the longitude—differ almost incredibly. This may be judged of by the following statements—

	N. Lat.	E. Long. from Paris.
The little island of Tshanker, the extreme boundary of the expedition of 1846, is, according to M. D'Arnaud	4 · 42	29 · 18
Or, according to a previous estimate by the same traveller	— · —	29 · 42
According to Selim Bimbachi, the Egyptian Commander of the same expedition (Worne, p. 311)	4 · 35	30 · 05
According to M. Werne's Map	4 · 04	30 · 05
But according to Rev. Mr. Knoblecher (Periodical of the Paris Geographical Society, 1852, p. 27) the same spot is fixed at	4 · 37	26 · 20

In the latitude assigned to the island the greatest differences amount to scarcely 40 minutes—two-thirds of a degree; but it is very different with regard to the longitude. Between the statement of M. D'Arnaud (whether it was formed from direct observation, or from an estimate, we know not) and the observation of Mr. Knoblecher, the difference is one of three degrees and more. This difference increases by 45 minutes, or three-fourths of a degree, if we compare them with M. Werne's chart, whose statement M. Kiepert, the learned geographer of Berlin, followed. It is clear that the actual state of practical astronomy does not admit of such anomalies. One of the two figures, at least, is stained by a grave error.

The difference of opinon is of so much the more importance, inasmuch as it completely changes the aspect and course of the White River. According to the calculations of M. D'Arnaud and Selim, the river, from the marshy lake of Bahr-el-Ghazal, pursues a course to the south-east, as far as the island of Tshanker. According to Knoblecher, the valley, notwithstanding slight variations, ascends direct south.

From the island of Tshanker, hills and ranges of hills appeared as a panorama dispersed about from east to west by north, with an elevation of from 600 to 3000 feet. The highest range, called Kugelu, appeared to the south-west, at a distance of about twenty hours, and beyond this Werne thought that other peaks were discernible. The Bari people all pointed south as the quarter from whence the Nile came, and as having its course amongst those granite ranges. "This," Captain Speke observes, is "equivalent to saying it comes from the Nyanza, as it lies exactly on the place thus specified." The conclusion, then, seems to be, that the Kivira is the Nile, which has its source in these interior waters. It may be observed that Dr. Krapf speaks of three rivers, which, according to native report, had their sources in the Kenia—the Dana, the Tumbiri, and Nsaradda, of which the two former were supposed to find their way to the Indian Ocean, and the latter to enter a large lake to the north-east. Now it is singular that at the isle of Tshanker the Nile is called the Tubirih, and we incline with Dr. Beke in thinking that in Dr. Krapf's account the Tumbiri and Nsaradda ought to have changed places.

On leaving the Uganda district, which is a high interior plateau, the Kivira is said to become rapid and boisterous, and such it appeared to be when emerging, at the island of Tshanker, from the rock and interrupted channel, through which, by rapids and cataracts, it had forced its way. "The river bed," says Werne, "beginning from hence, appears to be generally of a more rocky nature, for we perceive, even from the rocks on the island of Tshanker, breakers in the stream up the river;" and again, "the river here formerly broke violently through its projecting base, isolated Mount Lugi, which is like a half-demolished pyramid, and rushed down like a powerful waterfall." The sudden drop of the country to the northward from the lake region would at once account for this rush of water.

A difficulty has been suggested in assuming an identity between the Kivira, or river of Uganda, and Tubiri, or the river of the Bari, or, as it becomes in its further progress, the Bahr-el-Abiad, or White Nile; namely that the Nile in Lower Egypt begins to rise in June, and continues rising until September, and that this is irreconcileable with the monsoon in those lake regions of Central Africa, which are represented by Captains Burton and Speke " to have commenced in the autumn — a monsoon that could not produce a rise of the Nile in June."*

A reference to Captain Speke's journal as published in Blackwood's Magazine, at once removes this difficulty. On their return from the Tanganyika lake, they reached, early in June, the ferry on the river Malagazezi, the largest river on the eastern shore. "We found its appearance very different from what it was on our former visit, at the beginning of the monsoon. Then its waters were contained within its banks, of no considerable width; but now, although the rains had ceased here long ago, the river had not only overflowed its banks, but had submerged nearly all the valley in which it lies to the extent at least of a mile or more." A reference to the previous portion of the journal shows that the time of his first visit was on March 5th: that then was the beginning of the monsoon. Now it is remarkable that Werne, writing from the Bari country, says, under date of January 28th, "Rain begins here in two months' time."† As, therefore, Sir Roderick Murchison observed on the occasion of the meeting of June 13th, "the tropical rains cause these upland lakes and rivers to swell and burst their banks at a period which tallies very well with the rise of the Nile at Cairo."

In tracing the progress of discovery up the Nile, we have extracted largely from the "Bulletin de la Société de Geographie" for 1859, and we agree with the writer of that periodical in the conviction expressed by him, that in the region of the Upper Nile many researches as to detail, many verifications of statements and discoveries of importance, remain to be made; but that henceforth the field for investigation is clearly defined, and of limited extent. Captain Speke has reached nearly to the second parallel of south latitude, and the Egyptian discoveries to the 4½° north latitude. The native reports collected by Captain Speke shadow forth the physical features which will meet the eye of the first European explorer. A sailing boat, so constructed as to be capable of being taken to pieces, thus to be carried on asses to Unyanyembe, and thence to the southern shore of the Nyanza, and there put together, would with ease solve this interesting problem, and open to our view the mysteries of inner Africa. Compared with the explorations of Park, Denham, Clapperton, Barth, Krapf, and Livingstone, what remains to be

---

* "Proceedings of Royal Geographical Society." June 13th, 1859.

† Werne. Sources of Nile, Vol. II. p. 81.

done is of small extent; yet is it the keystone of the arch, and gives completion to all that has been already done.

The *resumé* of a paper read before a crowded meeting of the Royal Geographical Society on Monday January 8th of the present year, may here with propriety be added. It is entitled—"Journey up the White Nile to the Equator, and Travels in the interior of Africa, in the years 1857-58, by Mr. J. Petherick, Her Majesty's Consul at Khartoum." On the author's first expedition, in 1853, he reached the extreme limits of the Bahr el Ghazal, where he met opposition, which, on account of the cowardice of his men, he was unable to overcome; but in the next year he effected a landing, and, by establishing stations in that and the following year on his route, he believes that he actually penetrated as far as the Equator. Starting from Khartoum in December 1857, the author passed, on the 30th, Eleis, the last Egyptian settlement on the White Nile, leaving which they proceeded for two days through an uninhabited and unfertile country, when they reached, on the eastern bank, the Shillook, a fishing and commercial tribe; and on the western the Dinker, a nomadic tribe, its deadly enemy. The large island of Daenab was next passed, whence, proceeding through a level, well-wooded, and thickly-inhabited country, they arrived off the mouth of the Sobat, at its mouth about 100 yards wide, and which is supposed to have its source in the Galla and Berri countries. The Giraffe river, scarcely half the size of the Sobat, flowing from the S. E., was next passed: continuing to steer W. by a little N., they came to a large basin, into which the White Nile flows from the south. This lake is an accumulation of numberless rivulets and streams, overgrown with strong reeds, abounding in hippopotami in such profusion as to make a passage between them appear impossible. From here they continued their navigation to the Island of Kyt, whence they proceeded further into the interior by land, passing through the country of the Djour tribe. The natives hitherto met with are strictly pastoral, but they now entered a latitude where the tsetse fly abounds, and consequently cattle cannot exist: therefore the Djour tribe, as well as all the more southerly ones, are agricultural in their habits. Pursuing their journey amid numerous obstacles and perils, the author calculates that, having marched twenty-five days from the shore of the lake, in a direct line, the latitude of the Equator was reached. The general character of the country through which he passed is eminently fertile. In some places maize or millet, cotton of good staple, yarns, &c., are grown, and iron ore exists and is extensively worked by the Djour tribe.

"The President (Earl de Grey and Ripon), in proposing a vote of thanks to Mr. Petherick, stated that Her Majesty's Government had granted 2500*l.*, to be paid to the Society's bankers, and to be expended by the Council on behalf of the Eastern African Expedition, under the command of Captain Speke, and the President expressed a hope that these two explorers, one proceeding from the south and the other from the north, would, at some not far distant day, again meet, after having completed their respective undertakings, and satisfactorily traced the course of the Nile."

One extract more will conclude our *resumé* of these most interesting and important discoveries. It contains a special reference to the labours of our own Missionaries in East Africa, and indicates what may prove to be a suitable field for the prosecution of future efforts.

"I must now (after expressing a fervent hope that England especially, and the civilized world generally, will not neglect this land of promise) call attention to the marked fact, that the Church Missionaries, residing for many years at Zanzibar, are the prime and first promoters of this discovery. They have been, for years past, doing their utmost, with simple sincerity, to Christianize this negro land, and promote a civilized and happy state of existence for these benighted beings. During their sojourn among these blackamoors, they heard from Arabs and others of many of the facts I have now stated, but only in a confused way, such as might be expected in information derived from an uneducated people. Amongst the more important disclosures made by the Arabs was the constant reference to a large lake or inland sea, which their caravans were in the habit of visiting. It was a singular thing that, at whatever part of the coast the Missionaries arrived, on inquiring from the travelling merchants where they went to, they one and all started to an inland sea, the dimensions of which were such that nobody could give any estimate of its length or width. The directions they travelled in pointed north-west, west, and south-west, and their accounts seemed to indicate a single sheet of water extending from the Line down to 14° south latitude—a sea of about 840 miles in length, with an assumed breadth of two hundred to three hundred miles. In fact, from this great combination of testimony that water lay generally in a continuous line from the Equator up to 14° south latitude, and from not being able to gain information of there being any territorial separations to the said water, they very naturally, and, I may add, fortunately, created that monster slug of an inland sea which so much attracted the attention of the geographical world in 1855-56, and caused our being sent out to Africa. The good that may result from this little, yet happy incident, will, I trust, prove proportionately as large and fruitful as the produce from the symbolical grain of mustard-seed; and nobody knows or believes in this more fully than one of the chief promoters of this exciting investigation, Dr. Rebmann. From these late explorations, he feels convinced, as he has oftentimes told me, that the first step has been taken in the right direction for the development of the commercial resources of the country, the spread of civilization, and the extension of our geographical knowledge.

"As many churchmen, Missionaries and others, have begged me to publish what facilities are open to the better prosecution of their noble ends in this wild country, I would certainly direct their attention to the Karagwah district, in preference to any other. There they will find, I feel convinced, a fine healthy country; a choice of ground from the mountain-top to the level of the lake, capable of affording them every comfort of life which an isolated place can produce; and, being the most remote region from the coast, they would have less interference from the Mohammedan communities that reside by the sea . . . . . . As that country must be cold in consequence of its great altitude, the people would, much sooner than in the hotter and more enervating lowlands, learn any lessons of industry they might be taught."*

* "Blackwood," November 1859.

LIVINGSTONE'S DISCOVERIES IN AFRICA.

As our map embraces a portion of Livingstone's discoveries, we have thought that a digest of his extraordinary explorations might with advantage be appended to the previous article.

Dr. Livingstone's first Missionary station was at Kuruman, in the Bechuana country, about 700 miles from Cape Town, and there, and at two other stations—Chonuane and Kolobeng—he continued engaged in Missionary labours amongst the Bakwenis or Bechuanas, until the year 1849. Northward extended the vast flat called the Kalahari Desert, a region destitute of running water, although intersected by the beds of ancient rivers. Over these tracts roam prodigious herds of antelopes, in whose tracks follow the Bushmen, or Bakalahari, preying upon them as they move from place to place, and thus checking their inordinate increase. Lake Ngami had been heard of through native reports, and its exact position pointed out. In June 1849, Dr. Livingstone, accompanied by Messrs. Oswell and Murray, set out on an exploratory journey across the desert, striking, on the 4th of July, the Zouga, and reaching, on the 1st of August, the Lake Ngami. Its elevation was found to be not more than 2000 feet above sea-level, so that, in reaching it, the travellers had descended 2000 feet from Kolobeng. This shallow sheet of water spreads over an area of from seventy-five to one hundred geographical miles in circumference, and may be regarded as "the southern and lowest part of the great river system beyond, in which large tracts of country are inundated annually by tropical rains. A little of that water which, in the countries farther north, produces inundation, comes as far south as 20° 20′, the latitude of the upper end of the lake, and, instead of flooding the country, falls into the lake as into a reservoir."

Penetrating still further, Dr. Livingstone, in the year 1850, reached the Makololo country, and was kindly and hospitably received by their great chief, Sebituane. Into this district, and amongst these people, the slave-dealer had just entered, and Dr. Livingstone conceived the idea of arresting the spread of that deadly pestilence which has inflicted such evils on Africa, by introducing civilized commerce, and using, for this purpose, the waters of the great Zambesi, which this expedition had discovered to him. But the hope of using Kolobeng as a *point d'appui* was soon ended. In 1852 the Boers invaded the Bechuana country, ruining that Christian settlement, and breaking up the entire Missionary organization which had cost him years of labour.

The resolution to which Dr. Livingstone

came was prompt and decisive. Proceeding to Cape Town, he embarked his family in a homeward ship for England, and started on that long and arduous exploration, which occupied him from 1852 to 1856. After a journey of eleven months in the ponderous bullock-waggon of South Africa, he reached Linyanti, the capital of the Makololo, in May 1853, and was kindly received by Sekeletu, the son and successor of the deceased Sebituane. His great object was to induce the co-operation of this chief, and from his tribe to procure the volunteers and helps, without which further exploration was impossible. It is remarkable that Dr. Livingstone met in this region a party of Arabs from Zanzibar, a fact confirmatory of the statements made in our previous article, as to the great extent of country over which these men extend their journeys in prosecution of traffic, which never fails eventually to assume a slave-trading character. Dr. Livingstone had an interview with these men, who professed their dislike of the Portuguese, because they eat pigs, and of the English, because of their forcible interference with the slave-trade.

Dr. Livingstone now avowed his intention of endeavouring to reach Loanda, on the west coast, and a "picho," or assembly, was held, to determine the action of the Makololo. Some of the old divines croaked, and endeavoured to persuade their people from uniting in an expedition which they predicted would prove disastrous. "Where is he taking you to?" they exclaimed: "the white man is throwing you away: your garments already smell of blood." But the popular voice was in his favour, and a band of twenty-seven men were appointed to accompany him.

The party now prepared themselves for their start, and certainly never did a body of men voluntarily set forth on so serious an undertaking, with so spare an outfit: "a few biscuits, a few pounds of tea and sugar, and about twenty of coffee," constituted the provision stock. That of clothes was equally scanty, consisting of one small tin canister, about fifteen inches square, filled with spare shirting, trousers, and shoes, to be used when they reached civilized life, with some others in a bag, which were expected to wear out on the way. Three other boxes of the same size contained—one, some medicines; a second, some books; and the third, a magic lantern, which proved to be very useful. Three muskets for his people, a rifle and double-barrelled smooth bore for himself, were all the fire-arms which our traveller took with him, although on these and their ammunition depended, under God, the supplies of food. The money-chest, with its store, was 20 lbs. of beads, worth about forty shillings. "I had a secret conviction," observes Dr. Livingstone, "that if I did not succeed it would not be for lack of the 'nick-nacks' advertized as indispensable for travellers, but from want of 'pluck,' or because a large array of baggage excited the cupidity of the tribes through whose country we wished to pass."

Leaving Linyanti on November 11th, 1853, they embarked on the tortuous Chobe, and paddled along its windings until they reached its confluence with the Leeambye, when they commenced the ascent of the latter river. The generous order of Sekeletu secured for them kind treatment, and their progress was delayed by the supplies of food from the different villages. The banks of the river appeared to great advantage. Many trees were putting on their fresh green leaves, their lighter green contrasting beautifully with the motsouri or moyela, now covered with pink plums as large as cherries. New birds fluttered among the forest trees, and the musical notes of some of them sounded pleasantly beside the harsh voice of the little green, yellow-shouldered parrots of the country. Numbers of iguanos sat sunning themselves on overhanging branches; large alligators, with a heavy plunge, glided away as the canoes came suddenly round a bend of the stream; while in the deep reaches of the river were seen large herds of hippopotami. Thus they advanced along the Barotse valley, the people of every village treating them most liberally, and presenting oxen, butter, milk, and meal, more than could be stowed away in the canoes.

In speaking of the human inhabitants of these interesting regions, Dr. Livingstone observes—

"I shall not often advert to their depravity. My practice has always been to apply the remedy with all possible earnestness, but never allow my own mind to dwell on the dark shades of men's characters. I have never been able to draw pictures of guilt, as if that could awaken Christian sympathy. The evil is there. But all around in this fair creation are scenes of beauty, and to turn from these to ponder on deeds of sin, cannot promote a healthy state of the faculties. I attribute much of the bodily health I enjoy to following the plan adopted by most physicians, who, while engaged in active, laborious efforts to assist the needy, at the same time follow the delightful studies of some department of natural history. The human misery and sin we endeavour to alleviate and cure, may be likened to the sickness and impurity of some of the back slums of great cities. One contents himself by ministering to the sick, and trying to remove causes without remaining longer in the filth than is necessary for his work; another, equally anxious for the public good, stirs up every cesspool, that he may describe its reeking vapours, and, by long contact with impurities, becomes himself infected, sickens, and dies."[*]

On December 27th the party reached the confluence of the Leeba and Leeambye, latitude 14° 10' 52" S., longitude 23° 35' 40" E.

They now began to ascend in a N. W. direction the placid Leeba, winding its way slowly through the most charming meadows. The trees were covered with a profusion of the freshest foliage, and were planted in groups of such a pleasant, graceful culture, that nothing could be done to improve them. Trees in flower brought to remembrance the pleasant fragrance of hawthorn hedges, and the flowers, unlike the scentless or nauseously-smelling tribes of the south, emitted sweet odours.

"On January the 1st, 1854, when crossing the confluence of the Leeba and Makondo, one of my men picked up a bit of steel watch-chain of English manufacture, and we were informed that this was the spot where the Mambari cross in coming to Masiko. . . . .

"These Mambari are very enterprising merchants: when they mean to trade with a town, they deliberately begin the affair by building huts, as if they knew that little business could be transacted without a liberal allowance of time for palaver. They bring Manchester goods into the heart of Africa: these cotton prints look so wonderful that the Makololo could not believe them to be the work of mortal hands. On questioning the Mambari they were answered that English manufactures came out of the sea, and beads were gathered on its shore. To Africans our cotton-mills are fairy dreams. 'How can the irons spin, weave, and print so beautifully?' Our country is like what Taprobane was to our ancestors — a strange realm of light, whence came the diamond, muslin, and peacocks: an attempt at explanation of our manufactures usually elicits the expression, 'Truly, ye are gods!'"[†]

On January 10th, at the solicitation of the chiefs of the Balonda, they left their canoes, and prosecuted their route on foot.

As they advanced north, the forests became more dense, so that the sunlight was veiled by the deep gloom. Large climbing plants, like boa-constrictors, entwined themselves around the trunks and branches of gigantic trees. It was now the rainy season, and this sufficed to complete the marked contrast which existed between this region and the arid and treeless flats of the Kalahari desert.

In this Balonda territory, every village had its idols near it for protection, so that when they came to an idol in the woods, they knew themselves to be within a quarter of an hour of human habitations. "One very ugly idol we passed rested on a horizontal beam, placed on two upright posts. This beam was furnished with two loops of cord, as of a chain, to suspend offerings before it."

On January 16th they encountered two Portuguese traders, having with them a gang of young female slaves in chains. It was the first time the Makololo had seen slaves in chains. "They are not men," they exclaimed, "who treat their children so."

Such was the prevalence of rain and the cloudiness of the atmosphere, that Dr. Livingstone only obtained one observation during his journey through the Balonda territory, and that gave longitude 22° 57' east, and latitude 12° 6' 6" south. Again and again did he take out his instruments, and, when all was prepared, the stars became suddenly obscured. Heavy night and early morning rains kept pouring down, until his tent became so thin as to admit the rain in a thin mist.

They had now reached the water-shed which divides the southern and northern rivers, consisting, not of a mountain-range, but of vast plains, or table-land, covered with swamps, and shallow lakes, its height at the swampy Lake Dilolo, which lies on one part of the summit-level, being not more than 4000 feet.

Proceeding in a N. N. W. direction, they entered a district in which the rivers flowed northerly into the Kasai, or Loké, and descended into the first deep valley which they had seen since leaving Kolobeng. The country generally assumed this furrowed character, the slopes of the valleys being full of bogs or oozing fountains, which slowly discharged their moisture into the streams below. On the 27th of February they struck a part of the Kasai, "a beautiful river, and very much like the Clyde in Scotland," winding slowly amidst sylvan vegetation, or rich meadows, covered with tall grass. "The men pointed out its course, and said, 'Though you sail along it for months, you will turn without seeing an end of it.'"

The tribes which they met with after pass-

---

[*] " Livingstone's Travels," p. 259.
[†] " Ibid. p. 271.

ing the great water-shed were very different from their friends the Makololo, or the people of the Barotse valley. They were unfriendly and suspicious, each chief demanding payment for permission to pass through his country, and, rather than forego his claim, prepared to resort to acts of violence. Dr. Livingstone was suffering under an attack of fever of great severity. Yet at such time wise and intrepid action was most needful. The little party moved in a compact body, for defence, none being allowed to straggle, passing thus through miles of gloomy forest in gloomier silence. At length, on March 30th, they came to a sudden descent from the high valley-indented land over which they had been travelling.

"Before us lay the valley of the Quángo. If you sit on the spot where Mary Queen of Scots viewed the battle of Langside, and look down on the vale of Clyde, you may see, in miniature, the glorious sight which a much greater and richer valley presented to our view. It is about a hundred miles broad, clothed with dark forest, except where the light-green grass covers meadow-lands on the Quángo, which here and there glances out in the sun as it wends its way to the north. The opposite side of this great valley appears like a range of lofty mountains, and the descent into it about a mile, which, measured perpendicularly, may be from a thousand to twelve hundred feet. Emerging from the gloomy forests of Loanda, this magnificent prospect made us all feel as if a weight had been lifted off our eyelids. A cloud was passing across the middle of the valley, from which rolling thunder pealed, while above all was glorious sunlight; and when we went down to the part where we saw it passing, we found that a very heavy thunder-shower had fallen under the path of the cloud; and the bottom of the valley, which, from above, seemed quite smooth, we discovered to be intersected and furrowed by great numbers of deep-cut streams. Looking back from below, the descent appears as the edge of a table-land, with numerous indented dells and spurs jutting out all along, giving it a serrated appearance. Both the top and sides of the sierra are covered with trees, but large patches of the more perpendicular parts are bare, and exhibit the red soil, which is general over the region we have now entered."*

Entering the Portuguese territory, they pursued their way, until at length the boundless ocean lay before them. The Makololo were filled with awe as they beheld it. "We marched along with our father," they said, "believing that what the ancients had told us was true, that the world has no end; but all at once the world said to us, 'I am finished; there is no more of me.'"

After a rest of four months at Loanda, they started on September 20th, 1854, on their return journey. We shall not attempt to trace the intermediate marches, which at length brought them to the Leeba and its tributaries in the month of July. Their progress down the Barotse valley was quite an ovation. The women came forth to meet them, making their curious dancing gestures and loud lulliloos.

"Some carried a mat and stick, in imitation of a spear and shield. Others rushed forward and kissed the hands and cheeks of the different persons of their acquaintance among us, raising such a dust that it was quite a relief to get to the men assembled, and sitting, with proper African decorum, in the kotla. We were looked upon as men risen from the dead, for the most skilful of their diviners had pronounced us to have perished long ago. After many expressions of joy at meeting, I arose, and, thanking them, explained the causes of our long delay, but left the report to be made by their own countrymen. . . . The following day we observed as our thanksgiving to God for his goodness in bringing us all back in safety to our friends. My men decked themselves out in their best, and I found, that although their goods were finished, they had managed to save suits of European clothing, which, being white, with their red caps, gave them rather a dashing appearance. They tried to walk like the soldiers they had seen in Loanda, and called themselves my 'braves' (batlabani). During the service they all sat with their guns over their shoulders, and excited the unbounded admiration of the women and children. I addressed them all on the goodness of God in preserving us from all the dangers of strange tribes and disease. We had a similar service in the afternoon. The men gave us two fine oxen for slaughter, and the women supplied us abundantly with milk, meal, and butter. It was all quite gratuitous, and I felt ashamed that I could make no return. My men explained the total expenditure of our means, and the Libontese answered gracefully, 'It does not matter: you have opened a path for us, and we shall have sleep.' Strangers came flocking from a distance, and seldom empty-handed. Their presents I distributed amongst my men.

---

* "Livingstone's Travels," p. 360.

"Our progress down the Barotse valley was just like this. Every village gave us an ox, and sometimes two. The people were wonderfully kind. I felt, and still feel, most deeply grateful, and tried to benefit them in the only way I could, by imparting the knowledge of that Saviour who can comfort and supply them in the time of need, and my prayer is, that He may send his good Spirit to instruct them and lead them into his kingdom. Even now, I earnestly long to return, and make some recompense to them for their kindness. In passing them on our way to the north, their liberality might have been supposed to be influenced by the hope of repayment on our return, for the white man's land is imagined to be the source of every ornament they prize most. But though we set out from Loanda with a considerable quantity of goods, hoping both to pay our way through the stingy Chiboque, and to make presents to the kind Balonda, and still more generous Makololo, the many delays caused by sickness made us expend all my stock, and all the goods my men procured by their own labour at Loanda, and we returned to the Makololo as poor as when we set out. Yet no distrust was shown, and my poverty did not lessen my influence. They saw that I had been exerting myself for their benefit alone, and even my men remarked, 'Though we return as poor as we went, we have not gone in vain.' They began immediately to collect tusks of hippopotami and other ivory for a second journey."*

Thus safely brought back, after incredible hardships, Dr. Livingstone still felt that his undertaking was incomplete. He wished to open out the interior to salutary influences from the Christian world, and for this purpose it was necessary that he should prove its accessibility from the east coast, as well as demonstrate the probability of communicating with Loanda on the west. The great question was, to which part of the eastern coast should he direct his steps.

The Arabs from Zanzibar reported the character of the country over which they had travelled as consisting of swampy steppes. They spoke also of a shallow lake, called Tanganyénka, which required three days to pass it in canoes; and this was said to be connected with another further north, named Kalagwe (Karagwah), and which Dr. Livingstone supposed might be the Nyanja of the Maravi. They assured him also of the peaceable state of the country, and that the powerful chiefs to the N.E. of the Cazembe would not object to his passing through their country. They mentioned also that the path which they followed, at the end of ten days beyond Cazembe wound around the extremity of Lake Tanganyénka.

Livingstone's object, however, was a water route to the sea, and he resolved to move along the course of the Zambesi. Accordingly, on November the 3d, 1855, he bade adieu to Linyanti, accompanied by Sekeletu and about 200 followers. On their way the Victoria Falls were visited, a scene of overwhelming wonders. At a distance of five or six miles, columns of vapour appeared, rising high into the air, exactly as when tracts of grass are burned in Africa. In a light canoe Dr. Livingstone was paddled to an island in the midst of the river, and on the edge of the lip over which the water rolls. Looking from thence, the vast body of water seemed to lose itself in the earth, the opposite lip of the fissure, into which it disappeared, being only eighty feet distant. This fissure is a rent or crack made in the hard basaltic rock of the Zambesi, from the right to the left bank, and thence prolonged from the left bank, through thirty or forty miles of hill. A stream of a thousand yards broad, leaping down a hundred feet, becomes suddenly compressed into this rocky trench, and, indignant at the snare into which it has fallen, rushes, boiling and foaming, through the hills. "If one imagines the Thames filled with low tree-covered hills immediately beyond the tunnel, extending as far as Gravesend; the bed of black basaltic rock instead of London mud; and a fissure made therein from one end of the tunnel to the other, down through the keystones of the arch, and prolonged from the left end of the tunnel through thirty miles of hills; the pathway being 100 feet down from the bed of the river instead of what it is, with the lips of the fissure from 80 to 100 feet apart; then fancy the Thames leaping bodily into the gulf; and forced there to change its direction, and flow from the right to the left bank; and then rush boiling and roaring through the hills,—he may have some idea of what takes place at this, the most wonderful sight I had seen in Africa. In looking down into the fissure on the right of the island, one sees nothing but a dense white cloud, which, at the time we visited the spot, had two bright rainbows on it. (The sun was on the meridian, and the declination about equal to the latitude of the place.) From the cloud rushed up a great jet of vapour exactly like steam, and it mounted 200 or 300 feet high: there condensing, it changed its hue to that of dark smoke, and

---

* "Livingstone's Travels," p. 493.

came back in a constant shower, which soon wetted us to the skin. This shower falls chiefly on the opposite side of the fissure, and a few yards back from the lip there stands a straight hedge of evergreen trees, whose leaves are always wet. From their roots a number of little rills run back into the gulf; but as they flow down the steep wall there, the column of vapour, in its ascent, licks them up clean off the rock, and away they mount again. They are constantly running down, but never reach the bottom.

"On the left of the island we see the water at the bottom, a white, rolling mass, moving away to the prolongation of the fissure, which branches off near the left bank of the river. A piece of the rock has fallen off a spot on the left of the island, and juts out from the water below, and from it I judged the distance which the water falls to be about 100 feet. The walls of this gigantic crack are perpendicular, and composed of one homogeneous mass of rock. The edge of that side over which the water falls is worn off two or three feet, and pieces have fallen away, so as to give it somewhat of a serrated appearance. That over which the water does not fall is quite straight, except at the left corner, where a rent appears, and a piece seems inclined to fall off. Upon the whole, it is nearly in the state in which it was left at the period of its formation. The rock is dark brown in colour, except about ten feet from the bottom, which is discoloured by the annual rise of the water to that or a greater height. On the left side of the island we have a good view of the mass of water which causes one of the columns of vapour to ascend, as it leaps quite clear of the rock, and forms a thick unbroken fleece all the way to the bottom. Its whiteness gave the idea of snow, a sight I had not seen for many a day. As it broke into (if I may use the term) pieces of water, all rushing on in the same direction, each gave off several rays of foam, exactly as bits of steel, when burnt in oxygen gas, give off rays of sparks. The snow-white sheet seemed like myriads of small comets rushing on in one direction, each of which left behind its nucleus rays of foam. I never saw the appearance referred to noticed elsewhere. It seemed to be the effect of the mass of water leaping at once clear of the rock, and but slowly breaking up into spray."*

As they advanced eastward, they found themselves ascending. Dr. Livingstone, from this and other phenomena, concludes that the central area, from the Victoria Falls, westward as far as the ridge beyond Lebebe, and southwards as far as Lake Ngami and the Zouga, was one large fresh-water lake. "There is abundant evidence of the existence and extent of this vast lake on the longitude indicated, and stretching from 17' to 20' south latitude." "The whole of these lakes was let out by means of cracks or fissures made in the subtending sides by the upheaval of the country. The fissure made at Victoria Falls let out the water of this great valley, and left a patch in what was, probably, a deepish portion, and is now called Lake Ngami."

Leaving the Zambesi, Dr. Livingstone and his party struck northward into the hilly country of the Batoka. On Jan. 5th, 1856, their eyes were again gladdened by the sight of the waters of the Zambesi, presenting a breadth greater than above the falls. They journeyed along the left bank of the river; but now their experience became unhappily similar to that which they had met on the western side of the continent. As they approached the coast the natives, in consequence of hostilities between them and the Portuguese, became unfriendly, and distrust and danger supervened. About a mile from the confluence of the Loanga and the Zambesi, they crossed the river, expecting every instant to be attacked by the natives: but from this they were happily preserved; and although on more than one occasion danger was imminent, they were enabled to avoid any collision with the tribes, and reached Tete in safety, Dr. Livingstone embarking on board H.M. "Frolic" on July 12th, 1856.

As the practical results of these explorations, Dr. Livingstone contemplated the formation of stations on the Zambesi, beyond the Portuguese territory. The highlands on the borders of the central basin are comparatively healthy, and afford a favourable position on which a chain of Missionary stations might be so formed as to strengthen and sustain each other.

Since his return to the Zambesi, we have received from Dr. Livingstone the following letter, in which he refers to new discoveries, and invites the co-operation of the Church Missionary Society—

"*Senna, May* 15, 1859.

"We have just returned from the discovery of a magificent lake, called Shirwa, separated by a partition of only a few miles from Nyinyesi (Nyassa, Uniamesi, or Nyanja), and not more than thirty from one part of the navigable Shire; and one of the first thoughts that entered my mind after gazing on the broad blue waters, and admiring the lofty cloud-covered mountains that surround it, was,

---

* "Livingstone's Travels," pp. 520—522.

'Now this is what the Church Missionary Society has been thinking of for many years—a field in Eastern Africa for planting the Gospel beyond the unfriendly coast tribes. I shall write to Mr. Venn about it by the first opportunity.'

"Our first visit up the Shire created great alarm, for the people had never been visited by Portuguese, and a steamer was a more formidable sight to the Mang-anja than a comet would be to the hysteric among ourselves. We allowed that alarm to subside, and, on our second visit, found the people all so friendly, that we left the vessel with a chief, called Chibisa (16° 2' latitude S., and longitude 35° 2'). Dr. Kirk, and fifteen Makololo, proceeded with me on foot through a high mountainous region of the Shire. After a fortnight of very zigzag tramping, for we had to go from one little-great man's village to another, we at last got near to Zomba, or Dzomba, a mountain (inhabited) quite 6000 feet high, but not standing on the lake. On crossing its southern talus on the 14th of April, we got a distant view of Lake Shirwa eastwards, and, on the 18th, stood on its shores. A goodly sight it is, surrounded on all sides by lofty mountains, and is itself 2000 feet above the level of the sea. On looking away northwards from a point up a hill, we have 26° of watery horizon. There is a mountain island in it, and two points, like little islands, rise fifty or sixty miles away above the horizon there. To a person there, Zomba will appear in the lake. It is of a pear shape, some thirty miles broad, and has a prolongation south of our point of view (15° 23' S. latitude, 35° 25' E. longitude), which, by ascending a branch of the Shire, called Ruo, we can approach within thirty miles. It has no known outlet, and its waters are slightly bitter. There is a small partition between it and Nyinyesi, 'stars' (a prettier name than Nyanja, 'a river or great water' only, is it not?) of only five or six miles. We saw the waves dashing on the rocks on one part of the shore, exactly as on the sea-shore. It contains plenty of fish, alligators, hippopotami, and, as we found in wading into it, leeches.

"The people have no fire-arms, and pointed out a pass in the mountain range Milanje, eastward, through which a tribe with guns came to attack them. They were all friendly, except a party of Bajana, or Ajana, who are in the habit of taking slaves down to Quilimane. They thought us Portuguese, but changed their conduct instantly on learning that we were English. The others were alarmed, but we got abundance of provisions at a cheap rate. I have never seen so much land under cotton as here, and every one spins it; but we want the agents that Sierra Leone has supplied to Western Africa to guide the people to lawful commerce. The first time we came up the Shire we bought specimens of their cotton, and this time they brought it in bags; and, were there an agency, I have no doubt a trade, which would render the visits of Bajana slave-traders unfruitful, would spring up. We were accompanied by one of Chibisa's people as a guide, but he was useful only as making it known that we came from a man of influence. He is a sensible man, and would treat any white man well, and he has influence with all the people in the north, with whom his family is traditionally connected.

"We returned to the vessel after twenty-two days' march. Dr. Kirk and I slept on the ground: our beds were usually wet with the dew, and we were soaked in dew from the tall grass which overhangs the paths every morning; yet we returned in perfect health. The country being high, it is much colder than we found it in descending between 2000 and 3000 feet into the valley of the Shire. We have had several cases of fever, but none fatal. The severity of the disease is to us, who are well provided for, nothing compared with what I experienced before: the cases seemed more like common colds than fever at first: they have become more severe lately, during the unhealthy period of the year, but are quite amenable to proper treatment.

"DAVID LIVINGSTONE."

OUDE—ITS HISTORY.

On the re-establishment of British authority in Oude, and the suppression of the insurrection there, that province was entered by Christian Missionaries, and constitutes now a new and important field of our Society's operations: and assuredly, in no part of the wide-spread earth did there ever exist a more urgent need for the tranquillizing influences of the Gospel of peace.

It becomes our duty to introduce more especially to our readers this new scene of labour, where difficulties await us, and glorious victories remain to be achieved, and to commend it to their interest and prayers.

Oude is a strip of territory extending from the base of the sub-Himalaya, in a direction from north-west to south-east, until it reaches the Ganges. Its greatest length is about 270, and its breadth 160 miles. Its general character is that of a plain, marked by a slight declination as it extends from the mountain to the river. It is intersected by numerous streams, the direction of whose course coincides with the slope of the country, the principal of which, inclusive of the frontier stream of the Ganges, are the Surjoo, Gogra, Chowka, Goomtee, and Saee. These, with numerous lesser streams and tributaries, watering the country from the Himalayan chain and Tarae forest, and "flowing gently through the country towards the Ganges, without cutting very deeply into the soil, always keep the water near the surface, and available in all quarters, and in any quantity, for purposes of irrigation. Never was there a country more favoured by nature, or more susceptible of improvement under judicious management. There is hardly an acre of ground that is not capable of good culture." It is generally well timbered, studded with groves and fine solitary trees in great perfection. The bandha, or misletoe, upon the mhowa and mango trees, when in full blossom, adds much to their beauty. "The soil is good, and the surface everywhere capable of tillage, with little labour or outlay; for the jungle, where it prevails the most, is of grass and the small pulas trees, which may be easily uprooted. The whole surface of Oude is indeed like a gentleman's park of the most beautiful description, as far as the surface of the ground and the foliage, &c." The Hindu, in planting, uses a great variety of trees, and when, in consequence of limited space, a selection requires to be made, he chooses the most sacred, which are, at the same time, the most useful and ornamental. "Nothing can be more beautiful than one of those groves, surrounded by fields teeming with rich spring crops, and studded here and there with fine single banyan, peepul, tamarind, mhowa, and cotton trees, which, in such positions, attain their highest perfection, as if anxious to display their greatest beauties where they can be seen to the most advantage. Each tree has there free space for its roots, which have the advantage of water supplied to the fields around in irrigation, and a free current of air, whose moisture is condensed upon its leaves and stems by their cooler temperature, while its carbonic acid and ammonia are absorbed and appropriated to their exclusive use. Its branches, unincommoded by the proximity of other trees, spread out freely, and attain their utmost size and beauty."

Yet with all these natural advantages, never was there a country where anarchy and confusion so generally prevailed. An unusual blight seemed to rest upon it, and neither life nor property were secure. A glance at its history will explain the causes of this.

When, in 1720, the Emperor Mohammed Shah determined to free himself from the thraldom of the Syuds, he was powerfully aided by Saadut Khan. This man, originally a merchant of Khorassan, had risen to a military command, and, on the successful issue of the conspiracy against the Syuds, became a person of importance, and was appointed to be the Governor of Oude, a position which he retained until his death in 1739. He was the progenitor of the kings of Oude. He was succeeded by his nephew, Sufder Jung; and on his death, in 1754, Shuja-ood-Dowlah became Nawab-Vizier of Oude.

In 1763, the English having quarrelled with their own élève, Meer Cossim, Governor of Bengal, the Viceroy of Oude took the field in his favour. Defeated in successive battles at Patna, Buxar, and Calpy, he repaired to the English camp, and threw himself on the mercy of the conquerors. It had been intended to deprive him of his territories, but Clive, on a personal interview, reversed the decision, and reinstated him on the condition of his paying the expenses of the war, and restoring to the Mogul Emperor the districts of Allahabad and Corah, of which he had possessed himself. Five years subsequently, intelligence having reached the Government that the Nawab was preparing to repossess himself by force of the surrendered districts, he was compelled to sign a treaty which limited his army to 35,000 men,* the Company guaranteeing the defence of his territory against foreign invasion. Stipulations of this nature virtually rendered him a vassal of the East-India Company, as the paramount authority, and in this light the Sovereigns of Oude must be regarded; nor are the subsequent treaties entered into with them intelligible except on this basis. Subsequently to this treaty, the districts of Allahabad, with the consent of the English, were annexed to Oude, which was still further aggrandized by the addition of Rohilcund, the Rohilla forces having been defeated by British troops sent by Mr. Warren Hastings to the assistance of the Nawab-Vizier.†

Shuja-ood-Dowlah dying in 1775, was succeeded by his son, Asuf-ood-Dowlah, with whom fresh treaties were formed. A brigade of British troops, for defensive purposes, was to be at his disposal, in return for which he ceded to the East-India Company, Benares, Juanpore, and some contiguous districts, stipulating also a yearly payment of 312,000*l.* in maintenance of the auxiliary force. From this impost, in 1799, he prayed to be exonerated, on the plea of the failure of revenue. Lord Cornwallis, in his reply, declared, "that the disorder of his State, and the dissipation of his revenues, were the effect of his own conduct, which had failed, not so much from incapacity as from the detestable choice which he had made of the Ministers of his power and the participators of his confidence." The Governor-General availed himself of this opportunity to remind the Nawab that the treaties into which he had entered were of a nature to render him eventually, and necessarily, a vassal of the Company.

The following rebuke, addressed by Lord Cornwallis to this Viceroy in 1793, proves how grievously the province was suffering under his mal-administration.

"On my return from the war in the Dekhan, I had the mortification to find that, after a period of five years, the evils which prevailed at the beginning of that time had increased; that your finances had fallen into a worse state by an enormous accumulated debt; that the same oppressions continue to be exercised by rapacious and overgrown Amils towards the ryots; and that not only the subjects and merchants of your own dominions, but those residing under the Company's protection, suffered many exactions, contrary to the commercial treaty, from the custom-house officers, from Zemindars, Amils, and others.

"As in a state the evils that are practised by the lower classes of men are to be attributed to the example held out to them by their superiors, and to their connivance or their weak government; so am I obliged to represent, that all the oppressions and extortions caused by the Amils on the peasantry take their source in the connivance and irregularities of the administration of Lucknow."*

On the death of Asuf-ood-Dowlah, in 1797, a pretended son was raised to the musnud, whose brief term of power was ended by the accession of Saadut Ali, brother of the preceding Viceroy.

This Nawab, persisting in the same course of oppression and reckless expenditure, was urged by the Governor-General to retrenchment and reform. His reply was, the expression of a desire on his part to resign, a proposal to which the Marquis of Wellesley hastened to accede as an arrangement the most desirable for Oude and for the British Government. "The proposition of the Vizier is pregnant with such benefit, not only to the Company, but to the inhabitants of Oude, that his Lordship thinks it cannot be too much encouraged, and that there are no circumstances which should be allowed to impede the accomplishment of the grand object which leads to it. This object his Lordship considers to be the acquisition by the Company of the exclusive authority, civil and military, over the dominions of Oude."†

But the Nawab had no intention of abdicating; and the province continuing to suffer, the Governor-General again remonstrated in 1801.

"The causes of increasing defalcation of the revenue are manifest, and daily acquire new strength. Had the territories of Oude been subject to the frequent or occasional devastations of any enemy or by other calamities which impair the public prosperity, the rapid decline of the Vizier's revenue might be imputed to other causes than a defective administration; but no such calamitous visitations have afflicted the province of Oude; which, in consequence of the protection which it derives from the presence of the British forces, has been maintained, together with all the Company's possessions on this side of India, in the uninterrupted enjoyment of peace. . . . . While the territories of the Company have been advancing progressively, during the last ten years, in prosperity, population, and opulence, the dominions of the Vizier, although enjoying equal advan-

---

* Blue Book, p. 201.   † Ibid. p. 76.   * Blue Book, p. 78.   † Ibid. p. 79.

tages of tranquillity and security, have rapidly and progressively declined. None of the evils have been diminished under His Excellency's government: on the contrary, their daily increase and aggravation are notorious, and must be progressive, to the utter ruin of the resources of Oude, unless the vicious system of native administration be immediately abandoned. The Vizier must now be prepared for the active and decided interference of the British Government in the affairs of this country."*

In 1801 Saadut Ali, being unable to pay the augmented subsidy, and other sums chargeable to him on account of the defensive arrangements with the Company, the pecuniary subsidy was commuted for a territorial cession, and the Southern Doab, together with the districts of Allahabad, Azimgurh, Western Gorruckpore, &c., were ceded to the East-India Company. It is rather amusing to observe the gloss put upon this transaction in a paper published at Calcutta, and purporting to be a reply from the ex-king to various charges brought against the Oude administration.

Nawab Saadut Ali showed himself more favourably disposed to the British Government, inasmuch as he, at first, added to the sum of 56,77,668 rupees, which was the amount given to the British Government every year on account of the subsidiary force during his predecessor's reign, the sum of 19,22,362 rupees; and afterwards, for the greater satisfaction of the British Government, made over to the Hon. East-India Company certain districts of his dominions which yielded the sum of 135,23,474 rupees, in order that thereby the aforesaid expenses, as well as the wages of other people and collection expenses might be defrayed.

The true cause of this liberality, which was not required of him by former treaties, was merely this: in those times the East-India Company possessed but a few districts, and those yielding a very small revenue; besides, the southern and eastern districts of India were then under their native rulers: "hence the expenditure of the Company so exceeded their income, that the British Government always found it difficult to pay their forces."†

In the new treaty of 1801 there were clear and definite engagements entered into by the contracting parties. By the 6th article "the Nawab-Vizier engaged that he would establish in his reserved dominions such a system of administration, to be carried into effect by his own officers, as should be conducive to the prosperity of his subjects, and be calculated to secure the lives and prosperity of the inhabitants; and His Excellency," it was added, "will always advise and act in conformity to the counsel of the officers of the East-India Company.

"The British Government, upon its part, bound itself, by the 3d article of the treaty, to defend the territories which will remain to His Excellency the Vizier against all foreign and domestic enemies, provided always that it be in the power of the Company's Government to station the British troops in such part of His Excellency's dominions as shall appear to the said Government most expedient."*

Ghazee-ood-Deen succeeded his father in 1814, and, with the consent of the British Government, assumed the title of king. But the increase of dignity thus conferred upon him was more than counterbalanced by the degradation which he experienced at the hands of his chief wife, the Padshah Begum, an imperious and furious character, " whose frequent ebullitions often disfigured the king's robes and vests, and left even the hair of his head and chin unsafe." In these domestic broils the king's son, Nuseer-ood Deen Hyder, always took the part of his adopted mother, the Padshah Begum. " His natural mother had died soon after his birth ; and people suspected that the Padshah Begum had her put to death, that she might have no rival in his affections, and she had an entire ascendancy over him, acquired by every species of enervating indulgencies."

Under such rulers no administrative improvement could be expected. Such was the anarchy that prevailed in Oude] during the years1815—1822, " that the British troops were constantly employed against the refractory Zemindars, and, in the beginning of 1822, more than seventy of their forts were occupied and dismantled by the British troops. Nor were the unassisted means of the Oude Government able to suppress gangs of armed robbers, who haunted the jungles, and made frequent and desperate inroads into the British territory: their lurking-places were occasionally penetrated and their villages destroyed ; but the connivance of the Oude police, and the secret encouragement of the neighbouring Zemindars, sheltered them from any pursuit or punishment.

" Between 1815 and 1820 there had been forty gang robberies on the frontiers adjacent to Oude, in which forty persons were killed, and one hundred and seventy wounded, and

---

* Blue Book, p. 79.

property carried off to the amount of 1,14,000 rupees. In 1820, 400 of these marauders traversed the British territory for more than 300 miles from the Oude frontier, and, near Moughyr, plundered the boats of a merchant of Calcutta, carrying bullion to the extent of a lakh and a half of rupees."*

The British Government now found itself inconvenienced by engagements having reference to the employment of the subsidiary force. The Sovereign was exacting and unjust; and when his subjects, irritated by his arbitrary conduct, ventured on resistance, they were coerced by the strong arm of British power. A limitation as to the services on which the troops of the Company were to be employed becoming necessary, it was decided, in November 1824, "that our troops were to be actively and energetically employed in the Oude territory in cases of real commotion and disorder; but that when their aid was required by the King of Oude, the British Government was clearly entitled, as well as morally obliged, to satisfy itself, by whatever means it might deem necessary, that its assistance was about to be yielded in support of right and justice, and not to effectuate injustice and extortion."

In 1820 the Governor-General had an interview with the King of Oude, in the hope of inducing him to amend the administration of the country. In the October of the following year Ghazee-ood Deen died.

His son, Nuseer-ood Deen succeeded him. This prince, impaired in his constitution by drinking and other vicious indulgences, in which he had been encouraged in early life by the Padshah Begum, was incapable of taking any useful part in the management of public affairs.

He had for his consort a grand-daughter of the Emperor of Delhi, a very beautiful young woman of exemplary character; but other wives were soon associated with her, amongst others, Dojaree, a woman of low origin and disreputable antecedents. She was introduced into the palace as wet-nurse to the new-born prince Moonna Jan, whose mother's name was Afzul Mahal. The king elevated her to be his chief consort, under the title of Mulika Zamanee, Queen of the Age; and such was her influence over him, that she persuaded him to declare her son, Kywan Jan, who was three years old when she entered the palace, to be his eldest son and heir apparent to the throne. It was this youth who, in this assumed rank, was sent to meet Lord Combermere at Lucknow in 1827. A lively description of this scene, drawn up by a military officer in attendance on the Commander-in-Chief, may serve to lighten the prosaic character of this historical sketch.

"The two cavalcades approached, met and blended themselves in one; an impenetrable cloud of dust, the never-failing accompaniment of an Indian suwarree, hiding the rencontre of the British and Mussulman chiefs from the gaze of the spectators. The young prince having quitted his own howdah for that of the commander-in-chief, the whole procession rushed on together in one compact mass of about forty elephants. The two escorts led the way, followed by a pedestrian crowd of chobdars or mace-bearers, standards, heralds calling the high-sounding titles of the boy-prince, and led horses richly caparisoned. On front, flanks, and rear we were surrounded by a cloud of picturesque-looking cavaliers, who were constantly employed in displaying their horsemanship and dexterity in the use of the spear and sword, by curvetting and careering at each other in mimic jousts, with the most noble disregard of banks, ditches, and uneven ground.

"The whole scene was highly interesting and striking. The dark and close-serried column of elephants, caparisoned with flowing jhools and coloured cloth, and brocade deeply fringed; the splendid howdahs of the Mussulmans, many of them panelled with plates of silver and gilt; the complete contrast of the splendid shawls and ample-flowing drapery of the natives with the stiff, angular, scarlet coats of the English, as the wearers, riding side by side, conversed courteously from their lofty seats; add to this the wild, fierce, and disorderly array of the Lucknow cavalry, compared with the disciplined regularity of our own escort, the discordant clashing of the British and native bands of music, which seemed vying with each other for the mastery in sound, and the continual glitter of hundreds of banneroles of gold and silver tissues; and we were in possession of materials for amusement and interest, which were scarcely exhausted ere we arrived at camp."

A special day having been indicated by the soothsayers as auspicious for the purpose, the Commander-in-Chief made his *entrée* into Lucknow. "About two miles from the town we encountered His Majesty of Oude, accompanied by a numerous and splendid retinue. The king and the Commander-in-Chief, after a fraternal embrace, continued their march in the same howdah. Our cavalcade was most formidably augmented by this last reinforcement, and must have presented an imposing spectacle to the myriads of lookers-on as we entered the city. The king Nuseer-

---

* Blue Book, pp. 80, 81.

ood Deen Hyder, is a plain, vulgar-looking man, of about twenty-six years of age, his stature about five feet nine inches, and his complexion rather unusually dark. His Majesty's mental endowments, pursuits, and amusements are by no means of an elevated or dignified order, although his deficiencies are, in some measure, supplied by the abilities and shrewdness of his minister,* who is, however, an unexampled rogue, displaying it in his countenance with such perspicuity of development as would satisfy the most sceptical unbeliever in Lavater. He is detested by all ranks, with the exception of his royal master, who reposes the most perfect confidence in him.

"On arriving at the palace, we sat down to breakfast with the king and his courtiers. The king was splendidly attired in a tunic of green velvet, and girded with a costly shawl. He wore a diamond turban, and his person was profusely ornamented with necklaces, earrings, and armlets, of the most brilliant diamonds, emeralds, and pearls. After breakfast we adjourned to the state-chamber, an ill-proportioned, indifferent room. The throne is, however, beautifully decorated with embroidery in seed-pearl. Here his majesty presented the Commander-in-Chief with his portrait set in diamonds, and suspended to a string of pearls and emeralds."†

The barbaric magnificence of this monarch's court may be conceived on reading the following sketch of one of his wives, the Taj Mahal. "Her dress was of gold and scarlet brocade, and her hair was literally strewed with pearls, which hung down upon her neck in long single strings, terminating in large pearls, which mixed with and hung as low as her hair, which was curled on each side of her head in long ringlets, like Charles the Second's beauties. On her forehead she wore a small gold circlet, from which depended and hung, half-way down, large pearls interspersed with emeralds. Above this was a paradise-plume, from which strings of pearls were carried over the head. Her earrings were immense gold rings, with pearls and emeralds suspended stood behind her couch to arrange her head-dress, when, in moving, her pearls got entangled in the immense robe of scarlet and gold she had thrown around her."*

Such, then, was Nuseer-ood Deen Hyder, his character, court, and administration. He had become estranged from the imperious Padshah Begum, his adopted mother, and, to annoy her, had declared the young prince, Moonna Jan, to whom she was much attached, not to be his son. Banished from the palace, she and the boy had apartments assigned them in the Residency; and there she pursued the same course as with his father, developing to the utmost all the unhappy tendencies of his character.

Amidst the intrigues and selfish interests which kept the palace in continued agitation, the unhappy monarch felt his life to be insecure, and often declared that he should die of poison. "For some time before his death he had a small well in the palace, over which he kept his own lock and key; and he kept the same over the jar in which he drew the water from it for his own drinking. The keys were suspended by a gold chain around his neck." Vain precautions! The king was taken suddenly ill, and on hastening to the palace, the Resident found him lying dead upon his bed, but his body was still warm, and Dr. Stevenson opened a vein in one arm. Blood flowed freely from it, but no other sign of life could be discovered. His features were placid, and betrayed no sign of his having suffered any pain; and the servants in attendance declared that the only sign of suffering they had heard was a slight shriek to which the king gave utterance before he expired; that after that shriek he neither moved, spoke, nor showed any sign whatever of life. His majesty had been unwell for three weeks, but no one had any apprehension of danger from the symptoms. Two females, sisters of the king's prime-favourite Duljeet, from whose hands alone the king would receive any drink, are generally supposed to have poisoned him, at the instigation of the minister, Nuseer having called for some sherbet a short time before his death, which was given

nied by his eldest surviving son, Amjud Allee Shah, and his two grandsons, one of them, Wajid Allee Shah, the present ex-king.

But the Padshah Begum was on the alert. Knowing that Moonna Jan was the late king's son, and rightful heir to the throne, and ambitious of the power which her influence over him would enable her to wield, could his succession be secured, she resolved to strike boldly for the prize, and before the Resident could take decisive measures to arrest her advance, at the head of a large mass of armed followers, rushed towards the palace. In vain were the gates closed: a furious elephant, urged on by his driver, burst them in, and the courts and rooms of the palace were soon filled by her retainers. Moonna Jan was placed on the throne; the band struck up "God save the king," being answered from without by salvos of artillery, the crowd within and without shouting their congratulations at the top of their voices, and every man who had a sword, spear, musket, or matchlock, flourishing it in the air amidst a thousand torches. In vain the Resident remonstrated: he was dragged to the foot of the throne, and commanded, on pain of death, to offer his congratulations. It was with difficulty that some, fearful of the consequences if his life were lost amidst the tumult, extricated him from his dangerous position, and led him from without the palace.

At length British troops were moved up to the scene of action. Artillery was brought to bear upon the throne-room and the other halls of the bara-duree, and, after six or seven rounds of grape, the halls were stormed, the soldiers, on entering the throne-room, firing at their own figures, which they saw reflected in a large mirror behind the throne. Several of the insurgents were killed or wounded. Moonna Jan was found concealed in a small room under the throne, and the Begum in an adjoining apartment, and Nuseer-ood Dowlah, who, with his family, had been in extreme danger, was crowned so soon as the slain had been removed out of the throne-room.

But the crisis was not over. The old man was not popular. The ministry, aware of the peculations of which they had been guilty, were afraid of his business-habits, and their being compelled to disgorge their ill-gotten gain. Others disliked, some his prudence, some his parsimony: a sudden insurrection seemed not improbable; and the Resident, feeling the necessity of prompt action, at a moment's notice sent off the Begum and the young prince, under a strong escort, to the fort of Chunar.

On the subsiding of the agitation, and the

under the title of Mohammed Ali Shah, a new treaty was executed between him and the British Government, the seventh article of which provided, that if the king failed to rectify the disorders of his dominions, the British Government reserved to itself the "right of appointing its own officers to the management of whatever portions of the kingdom of Oude as were suffering from misrule, and for so long a period as it might deem necessary, the surplus receipts being paid into the king's treasury, and a faithful account of receipts and expenditure rendered to his majesty."* With this provision were coupled certain military regulations which the Home Government disallowed. Of this the Oude authorities were made aware. But they were left in ignorance of the fact that the entire treaty had been disannulled. Lord Dalhousie, in his despatch to Sir James Outram, January 23, 1856, admits that this very necessary communication "had been inadvertently neglected."†

In 1842 the old king died, and was succeeded by his son, Umjid Allee Shah. These reigns were as barren of remedial measures as their predecessors. In February 1847 Umjid Allee Shah died, and the last king of Oude, Wajid Allee Shah, was placed upon the throne. In October of the same year Lord Hardinge, in a personal interview with the king, solemnly assured him "that the British had, as a paramount power, a duty to perform towards the cultivators of the soil, and that unless the king adopted a proper arrangement in the revenue and judicial departments of his Government, so as to correct abuses now existing, it would be imperative on the British Government to carry out the orders of the Court of Directors." A period of two years was specified as affording sufficient opportunity for checking and eradicating the worst abuses. In a memorandum carefully drawn up and explained to the king, reference was made to the treaty of 1837, as confirming that of 1801, and not only giving the British Government the *right* to interfere, but declaring it to be the intention of the Government to interfere, if necessary, for the purpose of securing good government in Oude." The particular nature of the interference intended was also specified. It consisted "in placing the Oude territories under the direct management of officers of the British Government."‡ Lord Hardinge also stated his indisposedness to act immediately on the power vested in him, and expressed his earnest hope that the king would preclude the necessity of so ex-

---

* Blue Book, p. 81.   † Ibid. p. 248.
‡ Sleeman's "Journey through Oude," vol. ii.

treme a measure by the speedy correction of existing abuses.

His majesty's character and habits were not, however, such as to encourage the prospect of improvement. Nothing could be more low or dissolute. Singers and females provided for his amusement occupied all his time. These singers were all Domes, the lowest of the low-castes of India. These men, with the eunuchs, became the virtual sovereigns of the country, and on them the minister was entirely dependent. They meddled in all affairs, and influenced the king's decisions in every reference made to him. Colonel Sleeman, in a letter dated August 1853, reproaches the king with the misrule which prevailed—" Your minister has dismissed all the news-writers, who formerly were attached to Amils of districts to report their proceedings, on the ground that such officers are unnecessary in districts under the *amanee*, or trust-management system, so that you can never learn the sufferings of the people, much less afford redress. . . . . In regard to affairs in the city of Lucknow, your eunuchs, your fiddlers, your poets, and your majesty's creatures, plunder the people here, as much as your Amils plunder them in the distant districts."*

It may here be suitable to break off for a time from these historical dottings, to a consideration of the revenue system which prevailed under the kings of Oude, and the sufferings which, in consequence, were inflicted upon the people. This will throw open to us the whole interior of the country; and when we have made ourselves sufficiently acquainted with it, the annexation and its consequences will with propriety close the subject.

The territorial revenues of Oude were derived from four sources—the Khalsa, or crown estates; Huzoor Tehseel, wherein the landholders paid direct to Government; districts comprising the estates of Talookdars and Zemindars the revenues of which were held in *izarah*, or under contract; and districts, similarly composed, held under *amanee*, or trust-management.

Of these, the Khalsa estates, through mismanagement and misrule, became gradually lost without the intervention of local agents, and this mode of management was more successful and popular in Oude than any other. Abuses, however, crept into it. The Dewan and his subordinates were in the habit of increasing the rents, and if this was not acquiesced in, the Dewan threatened to make over the estate to the Chuckladars, and to subject its proprietor to all the miseries and extortions of the wretched farming system.

The third—the contract or farming system —was alike disadvantageous to the Government and injurious to the people. The object of the contractor was to extort as much as possible during the term of his contract.

A sketch of one family will suffice to show what an amount of oppression these contractors were capable of. Mungul, a Brahmin, residing with his father-in-law at Pullea, 112 miles north-west from Lucknow, had four sons. The eldest of them, Bukhtawar Sing, was a trooper in the Honourable Company's 8th Regiment of Light Cavalry. While home on furlough, being a young man and very handsome, he attracted the notice of Saadut Ali, king of Oude, and having saved his life on one occasion, he became one of his favourite orderlies, and rose to the command of a squadron. His three brothers, through his influence, were introduced into the Oude service; and one of them, Dursun Sing, obtained, in 1814, the command of a regiment. The estate of a court favourite, who had fallen into disgrace, was let, under contract, to Dursun Sing; and before six years had expired, by rack-renting, lending on mortgage, and other fraudulent and violent means, he succeeded in dispossessing most of the proprietors of their lands. He pursued the same course in other districts which came under him as contractor. He imposed upon the lands he coveted rates which he knew they could never pay; took all the property of the proprietors for rent, or for the wages of the mounted and foot soldiers whom he placed over them, or quartered upon their villages to enforce his demands; seized any neighbouring banker or capitalist whom he could lay hold of, and, by confinement and harsh treatment, made him stand security for the suffer-

Dursun Sing was the favourite agent of the Oude Government. When the court found the barons in any district refractory, they gave it in contract to him, and he, being strong in troops, plundered and kept down the great landholders, and protected the cultivators, and even the smaller landed proprietors, whose estates could be conveniently added to his own.

Amongst others thus aggressed upon was the young Rajah of Bulrampore. When a child, he had been obliged to fly into the British territories from the oppression of a previous collector; and now that he had reached manhood, he came under the iron rod of Dursun Sing. Taking advantage of the young Rajah's absence, Dursun attacked his castle, killing many of the people, and carrying away property to the amount of 200,000 rupees. The young Rajah fled into Nepaul, where he was pursued, and again attacked by the collector. Complaints from the court of Nepaul, for this infringement of territory, were addressed to the king of Oude and his ministers, and these being sustained by the British Resident, resulted in the banishment of Dursun. This took place in March 1844. In the following May he was recalled, and appointed Inspector-General of all the Oude dominions, with power to make a settlement of the land revenue at an increased rate, and generally to rectify the disorders which had so long prevailed. How he would have conducted himself in his new position may be judged of by his antecedents; but the judgments of God intervened, and death closed his history in August 1844.

His son, Rughbur Sing, succeeded to his government, of whom it might be said with truth, that, in the way of oppression and cruelty, his little finger was thicker than his father's loins. The atrocities perpetrated by this man are scarcely credible.

An old Rajpoot proprietor, Rajah Hurdut Sahae, venturing to resist him, was overwhelmed, his town of Bondee plundered, and 1000 captives, of all ages and sexes, were subjected to all manner of torture, until they paid the required ransom.

But this was only the prelude to worse atrocities. Overtures of reconciliation were made to the Rajah and his people, until all were thrown off their guard; when, at a given signal, bands of plunderers went forth. "All towns and villages on the estates were spoiled, and fifteen hundred men, and about five hundred women and children, were brought in prisoners, with no less than eighty thousand animals of all kinds. There were twenty-five thousand head of cattle; and horses, rest. All, with the men, women, and children, were driven off pell mell a distance of twenty miles, to Busuntpore, in the Hurhurpore district. . . . For three days heavy rain continued to fall. Pregnant women were beaten on by the troops with bludgeons and the butt-ends of muskets and matchlocks. Many of them gave premature birth to children, and died on the road, and many children were trodden to death by animals on the road, which was crowded for more than ten miles." At Busuntpore the force was divided into two parties, for the purpose or torturing the surviving prisoners, till they consented to sign bonds for the payment of such sums as might be demanded of them. Beharee Lal, Rughbur's principal agent, presided over the first party, in which they were tortured from daybreak until noon. They were tied up and flogged; had red-hot ramrods thrust into their flesh; their tongues were pulled out with hot pincers, and pierced through; and when all would not do, they were taken to the agent who presided over the other party, to be tortured again until evening. He sat with a savage delight to witness this brutal scene, and invent new kinds of torture. No less than seventy men, besides women and children, perished at Busuntpore from torture and starvation, "and their bodies were left to rot in the mud, as their friends were afraid to approach them."*

This is only one of numberless atrocities perpetrated under the contract system.

Remonstrances against the cruelty of this man continued to be urged by the Resident, until, at length, Rughbur Sing was banished, and retired into the British territories, to Zureedabad in the Juanpore district, where he had purchased property, and where he was residing in 1857.

Man Sing, his brother, then became the head of the family. His name figures in recent events. "In 1854 and 1855 serious disturbances broke out at Fyzabad, between the Hindus and Mohammedans, in consequence of some unauthorized aggression attempted by the latter sect on the sanctity of certain Hindu temples at Ajooddea, three miles distant from Fyzabad, on the banks of the Gogra." Man Sing placed himself at the head of the Hindu party, and, but for the interposition of the British Resident, a fierce collision would have ensued. The Mussulmans having been dispersed, Man Sing remained victorious, and he is said to have then declared, that, but for the support which the king would be sure to receive from the British, he would have marched to Lucknow, destroyed the Mohammedan dynasty, and established a Hindu government in its place."

It may be well, as he is before us, to trace a little further the history of this man. The introduction of British authority into Oude found him in circumstances of great embarrassment. "The large number of followers which he had maintained had involved him in debt; the special immunities which he had received from the weakness of the Oude court, and the corruption of its minister, were questioned; the old proprietors of the villages comprised in his talookah all sued him to recover their lost rights, and the demand for payment of government revenue was instant. Under these circumstances Man Sing fled the province, and remained absent five months." *

No sooner, however, did the disturbances commence, than he appeared on the scene of action. In the beginning of the memorable month of May 1857, in consequence of information telegraphed from Calcutta, he was arrested by order of the Chief Commissioner, and placed in confinement at his fort of Shahgunge. Sending for the British authorities, he warned them that the troops would rise, and "offered, if released, to give the Europeans shelter in his fort. Seeing the critical state of things, Colonel Goldney released him, and Man Sing at once commenced to put his fort of Shahgunge in order, and raise levies." Matters looking very ominous at Fyzabad, the civilians sent their families to Shahgunge, where they were sheltered for a few days, when Man Sing, "either from zeal or pretended fear of the mutineers, desired them to depart. He, however, provided boats for them on the Gogra, to which they were escorted by night, and a party of Man Sing's levies accompanied them some way on their journey. They all reached the station of Dinapore in safety."†

Man Sing remained at his post, "organizing and increasing his levies, which he maintained by forced contributions from the merchants of Fyzabad and others." Overtures had been made to him from both sides. The Fyzabad mutineers invited him to place himself at their head: the British Government offered him a "perpetual jagheer, secured on land, of 25,000*l.* per annum, if he remained stedfast and rendered active aid."‡ His replies had been evasive. Nor, so long as General Havelock's forces remained on the Oude side of the Ganges, did he declare himself. But when, on August 13th, Havelock, falling back on Cawnpore, recrossed the Ganges, Man Sing, thinking the British cause hopeless, marched in from Fyzabad, and joined the mutineers at Lucknow. The attack of September 5th was especially heavy. Assaults were made on various points of the defences, and a storm of round shot and musket balls was kept up. Our men considered that the matchlock-men of the enemy had increased, and this was attributed to Man Sing's reinforcements.

In the middle of October, when the British prospects began to improve, a message was received at the Presidency from Man Sing, offering the troops an escort of 10,000 men, if they would evacuate the place and retire to Cawnpore.

It is pleasant to find another name in the history we have sketched which contrasts favourably with that of Man Sing: we mean the young Rajah of Bulrampore. When, in the beginning of June, the native troops at Secrora were ripe for mutiny, Mr. Campbell, Commissioner of the Baraitch division, was enabled to place confidence in the friendliness of this Rajah, Dirg Bijehsing, and to arrange that the European officers should seek refuge with him when the crisis came. This was done, and after a few days' stay at Bulrampore, the whole party, under an escort, reached the Gorruckpore district in safety.

But we must go back to Oude and its mismanagement. We have dealt with the *izarah*, or co tract system. Before we leave it, it may not be amiss to mention an extreme measure not unfrequently resorted to by the landholders, when they could in no other way free themselves from the iron grasp of the contractors. The proprietor retired into the jungles, compelling the cultivators to accompany him, and plundering their villages if they refused to do so. The whole estate was left untilled, and yielded nothing to the contractor, who, after a season or two, found it his policy to come to terms.

The *amanee*, or trust system, alone remains to be mentioned. Under this arrangement, instead of a fixed sum, the Amil was trusted to pay into the treasury what he could fairly and justly collect. It required, however, honest men to work it; and as these were scarce in Oude, and, when available, the least likely to be appointed under the Court *régime*, the system was found to be, on the part of the ryot, equally oppressive with the *izarah* system, and more prejudicial to the Government.

In another Number we hope to pursue this subject.

---

* Gubbins' " Mutinies in Oude," p. 208.
† Ibid. pp. 135, 136.
‡ Ibid. p. 169.

INDIA—WHAT IS TO BE OUR POLICY?

QUESTIONS of primary importance in relation to India press for a solution. We shall specify one or two of them. First—are the officials of the Government in that country to continue in the enjoyment of that Christian liberty of action which they have enjoyed since the coercive despatch of 1847 was quietly put aside by the prudence and consideration of the local Government? Are they, so long as they discreetly use their liberty, and carefully abstain from interfering by force or bribery with the consciences of men, to be regarded as possessing the same freedom which belongs to every private Christian, of avowing their attachment to Christianity, and their sympathy with its persuasive progress? So long as they faithfully render to Cæsar the things which are Cæsar's, are they to be uninterfered with while they reverentially render to God the things which are God's, and conscientiously fulfil the obligations which devolve on them as Christian men?

The Royal Proclamation was, in this respect, strongly and imperatively worded—"We do strictly charge and enjoin all those who may be in authority under us, that they abstain from all interference with the religious belief or worship of any of our subjects, on pain of our highest displeasure." This clause, designed to secure liberty of conscience, and leave every man free to pursue that course, in matters of religious inquiry and profession, which best accorded with his own convictions, is as binding on the highest functionary, as on the man whose sphere of responsibility was of the most limited kind. There was to be no coercion in matters of religion. The native was to be free to inquire and decide; the European was to be equally free to profess Christianity, and, as an essential part of that profession, to speak of its truths, and commend them to the acceptance of others. Authority was neither to compel the one to silence, nor preclude the other from inquiry. The European functionary, whether of high or low degree, was neither by force or fraud to dissever the native from his old religion, if he desired to retain it, nor to discourage and obstruct him, if he felt desirous to inquire into the truth of Christianity; and this is all which the friends of Missions ask of Government, never to interfere with the religion of any one, so long as it does not interfere with the equal rights of others. But if the authorities should conceive themselves bound, not only to abstain from every thing that wars against the religion of the natives, but to prevent anybody else from teaching or offering them any other religion, then, under the pretext of not interfering with the religion of the natives, are they guilty of an interference with the rights of conscience of the most direct and positive kind. While professing compliance with the Proclamation, they expressly violate it.

In our Number for October last we referred to the spirit of inquiry on the subject of Christianity which had manifested itself among the Muzabee Sikhs, who had been embodied in the 24th Punjabee Infantry. The following *résumé* of the facts, as reprinted from the "Lahore Chronicle," will refresh the recollection of our readers.

"Amongst the plunder taken in Delhi, the men of that regiment found a number of Christian books, and became interested in reading them. This stock of books having been exhausted, leaving that interest unsatisfied, they applied to one of their officers for more books. He, to gratify his men, availed himself of the first opportunity that offered of obtaining books from the Missionaries, which happened to be those of Umritsur, on the return of the regiment to that place. The Missionaries, very properly, availed themselves of this opportunity of communicating oral instruction also to those to whom they gave books, and the officers of the regiment very properly refrained from all interference with the work of the Missionaries, or with the religion of the men, retrospective or prospective. The consequence was, that a number of books were distributed, some instructions given, several men offered themselves as candidates for baptism, and one was actually baptized. The men continued to read, and talk about what they read, and other Missionaries, as opportunity offered, went and instructed them; the interest increased, and others avowed themselves Christians. At this stage of the business we understand that one of the officers commenced reading the church service on Sundays to the native Christians and inquirers of the regiment, and any others who chose voluntarily to attend. If there has been any further interference with the religion of the men than what appears in the above simple summary, we are not informed of it."

The Viceroy of India in Council has deemed it his duty to express his disapprobation of the course pursued by these officers and to prohibit further interference on their part with the religion of the men.

Let the facts of the case be clearly understood. The initiative was not taken by the officers. The men came of themselves. The Christian books did the mischief. Had the authorities been aware of it in time, perhaps they might have ordered the removal of the books. Awakened to inquiry, the men came to the only persons who could give them any information on the subject—their own officers. What were these gentlemen to do? To be silent, and thus discourage them from further inquiry? They did not dare to do so. This would have been to violate the essential principles of Christianity, which enjoins, "Be ready to give to every one that asketh you a reason of the hope that is in you." To have acted so might have pleased the Government, but it would have displeased God.

But some of the men openly professed Christianity, and were baptized, and to these their fellow-Christians, when a clergyman was not available, the officers read prayers. Other men of the regiment attended. They did so entirely of their own accord. The officers did not invite them, neither did they prevent them; that is, they did not interfere with their freedom of action in this matter. In so doing, the officers complied with the Proclamation, but, nevertheless, they have been reproved by the Viceroy in Council. The following letter from our Missionary, the Rev. R. Clark, dated Shumshabad, Nov. 2, 1859, will show the effects produced by this uncalled-for and unauthorized interference on the part of the Government—

"I have been staying here on my way, for the last two days, with the Christians of the 24th Punjab Native Infantry. I have often told you of them, and of the orders which have been issued by the Supreme Government in Calcutta, cautioning the officers against taking any part whatever in the spread of Christianity in the regiment. It was an unchristian order and an impolitic one; for the officers were doing nothing more than Christian men should do, and were in no ways unduly using any official influence to the prejudice of the native religions. The effects of the order have been, however, most unfavourable to Christianity. Before it came, the men were pressing forward, eagerly and earnestly inquiring into the subject of Christianity; but from the moment they heard that the Governor-General in Council had interfered, and had written through official channels to their officers about it, they naturally understood this to mean that the English Government directly discouraged the spirit of inquiry, and were averse to any further baptisms in the corps: from that time to the present not one soldier has come forward to ask for either instruction or baptism. The Christians stand dismayed at seeing the interest in their spiritual welfare suddenly lost, and the school has dwindled down to less than half its numbers. The officers may not converse with the native Christians about Christianity; they may not hold a service for them, or even worship God with them, although they are their fellow-Christians, much less speak to any who are not yet baptized. Every thing is in a state of doubt and uncertainty, even as regards what a Missionary may do in the corps; whether he may enter the lines at all, and, if so, whether he may hold a service in a native-Christian's house; and, above all, whether he may admit those to his service who are still heathen. I was certainly grieved to find that the orders were of such a nature as to leave every one in doubt whether a Missionary might or might not visit, as a pastor, a large native-Christian flock of thirty persons, including ten Sepoys, because they happened to live in the lines of a regiment; but it was thought better that our services should be held away from the lines, in one of the officers' quarters. I held one full service and two shorter ones with them, and administered the Lord's supper to five adults. I also married two native Christians belonging to the regimental band; but even there the officers could not be present, although they take much interest in the parties, and although none but Christians were present at the wedding. Our Government surely cannot know the consequences which such orders lead to, or they would be more careful in making them. No rule had been ever transgressed, and nothing had been done to call for such an order. The only apparent fact was, that some of the soldiers had been baptized; and no sooner does the Government hear of this, than it steps in with its veto, and checks the whole proceeding, as if the baptism of ten Sepoys was something dangerous or something out of order; and a summons is forthwith sent, not to this regiment alone, but to every Punjab regiment, for every officer to hold himself clear of such untoward events. If it had been another plot against their very existence they could hardly have done more. The little band of thirty Christians, however, still remains, and they have a catechist and schoolmaster. May they be upheld and strengthened, and, even though European Christians are obliged for a time to seem to forsake them, may they find that help, which never fails in times of trial?"

Here, then, is an important question, which seems to be pending in the balance at this moment; and we are persuaded that it only requires a broad and manly expression of opinion, on the part of the Christian public of the United Kingdom, to decide it satisfactorily, and for ever.

The other question is not less momentous. Is the system of Government education in India to remain just the same as it was before the mutiny, and be subjected to no ameliorating process? Has it been found to work so satisfactorily? has it exercised such a tranquillizing influence on the native mind, caused them to be so well affected to the British rule, and, in other respects, carried with it such evident tokens of the divine blessing, as to forbid any interference with it?

A great alteration is required. The rule which interdicts the Bible must be withdrawn, and the Christian Scriptures be free to enter every Government College and Institution; so that, if the students wish it, they may read and be instructed therein, and voluntary Bible-classes be formed for this purpose. It is suggested by some that pupils are at liberty to study it, and obtain instruction from their masters as to its facts and doctrines out of school-hours, if they desire it, and that with this we ought to be contented. We must decline to accept this compromise, even although—which we doubt—this out-of-school instruction was permitted under the roof of the Government building. It is an authoritative permission of its use in school-hours that we require. On this point—its refusal or concession—depends the whole character of our educational system in India. This must give the key-note to the entire process. With an excluded Bible, Christianity is under a ban. It is pronounced to be an alien element which must be searched out and carefully banished from all books and studies. All traces of it, and all references to it, must be erased. And this adverse principle, thus ruling within the walls of our educational buildings, will from thence sway the whole governmental policy. The one-sided neutrality which has hitherto prevailed will continue to mar the hopes of India, and Christian men will be conscience-troubled in the service of a State which expects its officials to to be as cold-blooded and indifferent to Christianity as it is itself. We agree thoroughly with a remark in a recently-published paper —"The whole principle of Government conscience and Christianity is involved in the question of the authoritative admission of the Bible, during school-hours, as part and parcel of the Government system of education."

We repeat, then, that this is a point of primary importance, which must not be permitted to recede from a prominent position before the public mind, but which must be perseveringly kept there until it has received, by the blessing of God, a satisfactory solution. The defect which has vitiated our educational system is the same which has hitherto pervaded the whole of our national policy in India; and if there is to be amendment, and a national policy of a more candid character on the subject of Christianity is to be adopted, as the becoming expression of our gratitude to God for a great national deliverance, it must begin with this specific point, the admission of the Christian Scriptures into our schools; for in this, in fact, the whole question is included.

Let us ask ourselves solemnly, as in the presence of God, Has our national policy, as hitherto carried out in relation to India, been blessed or prospered?

Important legislative ameliorations have been introduced from time to time, in the hope that they would carry with them the mind and sympathy of the people for whose good they are intended. Demoralizing customs, and even crimes of deepest dye, in many remarkable instances have been repressed. Thuggee and Dacoity have been put down with a high hand; infanticide rendered penal; suttee prohibited. Witchcraft, Tragga, Meriah sacrifices, slavery, forced labour, have been summarily dealt with ; the civil rights of religious converts secured ; the re-marriage of widows legalized ;—have these measures been so duly appreciated as to ensure contentment and tranquillity? We cannot say so. The solemn events of 1857 established too plainly the want of this necessary agreement between legislative action and national sympathy. Measures suggested by a real interest in the welfare of the vast population placed under our rule in India, and a sincere desire to promote their happiness, were misunderstood. Instead of exciting the gratitude, they aroused the hostility of the people. How far may this be attributed to our defective system of education? Instruction and enlightenment on the various points, in connexion with which alteration is required, ought always to precede and prepare the way for legislative acts; so that when they are promulgated they may not take people by surprise, but may carry with them such a measure of popular approval as may suffice to countenance and sustain them in their action.

Again, our native *employés* have been raised up, in a great measure, out of our governmental institutions. This was one of the results which they were expected to yield—one confessedly important to the prosperous course of India's government, namely, that the state should be supplied with servants in whom perfect confidence might be reposed, to whom offices of trust might be committed, and who should be possessed, therefore, not only of intellectual fitness, but of moral character. Without such native *employés*, we do not see how the government of India can be successfully carried on. They constitute the medium through which the character and proceedings of the superior authorities are presented to the people.

How shall reliable natives, in whom we have confidence, be obtained? Some reply, By the advance of European knowledge in India. To that thesis we readily subscribe, if interpreted not narrowly, but generously, and in the fulness of its meaning, as not excluding the most important element of European knowledge, Christianity. Abstract this from European knowledge, reduce that knowledge to a mere secularity, and it is left destitute of renovating power. It cannot so raise the human character as to render it trustworthy and reliable, and prepared to participate in the great work of national progress. There exists no room for doubt on this subject. Secular European knowledge has been tried, and its fruits have been yielded in sufficient quantity to enable us to form a just estimate of their value. There is a large class of natives at Calcutta who have been educated on this principle at English schools and colleges, and who, while keeping on good terms with their families and priests, by observing the outward forms of Hindúism, are either Vedantists, i.e. professors of a cold Unitarianism, or have advanced to the rejection of all religious belief whatever. There are, perhaps, 5000 of these persons "speaking and writing English in perfection, whose minds have been trained to reason and reflect, and who have a general knowledge of the history and claims of Christianity, while all belief in the old idolatry and mythology has dropped away." Let us examine into the character of these men, who have had education in European knowledge apart from Christianity. We take the testimony of Mr. H. Pratt. He states this as a prominent characteristic of the Bengal Hindú, a want of earnestness. This appears, indeed, from the ambiguous and compromising position which he occupies on religious questions. He conforms outwardly to a system of idolatry, which, in his heart, he despises and rejects. He holds himself aloof from Christianity, not so much from the absence of intellectual belief, as because he is disinclined to put himself "under the restraint of the Christian life, and incur the sacrifices involved in the avowal of the Christian name." Where, then, is the probity of character to which it is so necessary the native should be raised? Surely it is a part of probity to be honest to our convictions, and not to compromise ourselves with that which, in our hearts, we disbelieve. Surely this disingenuousness is the opposite of probity, and there is a leaven of insincerity introduced which is likely to pervade all the actions of the man.

Let us look a little further into the sketches given us of this class, and thus ascertain whether the system under which they have been trained is the one which is fitted to ensure the regeneration of India.

"They would rather not believe Christianity. They seek eagerly for infidel works; have reprinted cheap editions of 'Tom Paine;' ask for Parker's Sermons, because they hear that he writes against Christianity; and will not read works on the Christian Evidences, or visit Christian Missionaries. In fact, these men speak even more contemptuously and bitterly of the converts than the Hindús of the old school. Prosunno Coomar Tagore (a near relative of Dwarkanath Tagore, who went to England), the principal pleader of Bengal, and a man of great wealth, disinherited his son for embracing Christianity, though calling himself a 'Liberal Freethinker," and supporting one of Rammohun Roy's congregations. If his son had called himself an atheist, and merely ridiculed Hindúism, drunk champagne, and eaten beef-steaks, as he himself does, he would have kept his inheritance! Of course, I am speaking generally."

Again, in refering to the Society of Reformed Hindús, or of Brahmas and Vedantists, the same writer observes—

"As regards the test of life and moral conduct, I see no difference between the members of these societies and those who repudiate all forms of religious belief whatever. Both classes are men of good education, who have carefully and intimately studied our highest literature at school and college, have clearer notions of right and wrong, a better appreciation of what is honourable, greater benevolence and patriotism; but neither have or can have that which a living belief in Christ's mission, and the divine source of his teachings alone can give, viz. those firmly fixed principles of conduct, in obedience to which the true Christian will offer himself as a living sacrifice. For want of them, so little progress has been made in truthfulness; so little in respect to child-marriages, and exposure of the sick, &c.; so little in female education; so little in incorruptibility, honesty, fair dealing, and integrity."

These are not the men we need for India: they will not advantage their countrymen; they will not advantage us. There is in their knowledge no healthful reproductiveness. Yet they are the fruits of education without Christianity, and they are the best it can yield. Education, such as this can never raise a man out of his low selfishness. In fact, it is valued only because it panders to the selfish tendencies.

"'Education' is in the mouth of every Hindú in Calcutta. It means, preferment, high salaries, distinction, and honour; for by it all these are made accessible. Every year Government throws open to the natives fresh posts, of higher and higher emolument and honour, making their selection from the most distinguished students of the colleges; while the increase of European trade, railways, telegraphs, &c., creates a constantly growing demand for the services of men of tolerable education. It is true that even the best students read but little after they have obtained the great object of desire—'an appointment'—and that many never open an English book for the rest of their lives."

Yet it is on education of this kind that Government has hitherto relied. "We most emphatically declare that the education which we desire to see extended in India is that which has for its object the diffusion of the improved arts, science, philosophy, and literature of Europe."* And is that great element to be studiously omitted to which Europe owes its intellectual development, and without which it never would have reached its existing attainments in arts and sciences? Do our statesmen really think that secular education is sufficient to raise the human character to that sterling principle and moral tone which will render it reliable and trustworthy? Will it suffice at home? Can it be sufficient amidst the still greater difficulties of India's moral degradation? And if Christianity be necessary for India, why should any state documents be so worded as though it might be dispensed with? Her Majesty's proclamation is far more truthful and becoming. She does not suppress all mention of Christianity, as though it were something to be ashamed of and kept out of sight. There is an honest avowal of her personal conviction, while at the same time she disclaims any design of imposing it on any of her subjects. No, undoubtedly. Forcible interference, the setting aside the convictions of any man, however erroneous they may be — this would be unchristian, short-sighted policy, one that would obstruct instead of facilitating the action of Christianity. But are we to do violence to our own convictions, and studiously ignore that great element of true religion to which we owe all our greatness and our glory, and which we know in our inmost souls to be that which the nations of India need? This we believe to be the great and serious defect under which our Government education has hitherto laboured, that it has dispensed as completely and decidedly with Christianity as though it was in no wise necessary for the amelioration of India. We gain nothing by this disloyal action. There is quite enough in our private acts to convince the native, that, as a nation, we are Christians, not only by profession, but by conviction, and our studied avoidance of all recognition of it in our public acts renders the native suspicious of our sincerity, and causes him to distrust us.

Instruction in Christianity is what India wants. Nothing less will suffice to raise her. If this be wanting, we may subvert Hinduism amongst the higher classes, set up Vedantism in its place, but India will be no happier, and England's dominion over India, instead of being consolidated, will become less secure. What then should Government do? Let it recognise Christianity; honestly avow its convictions of its truth and excellency, and afford opportunities of Christian instruction in its schools or colleges to such as may be willing to use them. As to his improvement or otherwise of such opportunities, let the native be left entirely to his own judgment and convictions. But that numbers of the native youth will esteem such opportunities a privilege, and hasten to improve them, may, we think, be concluded from certain interesting facts connected with the city of Benares, which we now place before our readers.

The following communication from H. Carre Tucker, Esq., recently Governor-General's Agent and Commissioner at that city, appropriately introduces this part of our subject.

"In the summer of 1856, the late lamented Lieutenant-Governor of the North-West Provinces, John Colvin, sanctioned my establishing a normal college for village teachers in Benares. Upwards of one

---

* Educational Despatch, 1854.

hundred of the most promising indigenous teachers from the different districts of the Benares division were collected in a large two-storied building, together with a number of intelligent candidates. All of them resided in the building and its outhouses, as I was very anxious to prevent the young men becoming corrupted in such a licentious city as Benares. Two of the most earnest and pious Christian teachers I could find (one of whom has since become a Missionary) were located in the same building, with their families, and the whole instruction was carried on in the vernacular. The progress made in six months was so great as to excite the surprise and astonishment of all who visited the institution, including good Bishop Dealtry of Madras. Its most marked distinction, however, was, that although a purely Government school, the whole of the young men regularly studied the Holy Scriptures in Hindi and Hindustani, and to such good purpose, that some thirty-four of them ventured to compete with the Mission schools at a general Bible examination which I caused to be held for the whole Division. A few Mohammedans demurred at first to join the Bible class; but even these came round in three or four weeks, finding it easier to swim with the general stream of the school, than to go against it. So hard did they study the Bible at night, that the mother of one of the teachers declared that it made her quite ashamed of herself, as a Christian woman, to hear them poring over the Scriptures at midnight. Mr. Colvin himself presided at our examination, where great stress was laid upon Biblical knowledge, and the classes examined in his presence, not only by Missionaries, but by Timothy Luther, the energetic native-Christian schoolmaster of the Church Missionary Society at Azimgurh. So entirely did Mr. Colvin approve of all that had been done, that he presented Mr. Tresham, the head master, with a gold watch. I am glad of an opportunity of bearing this testimony to the Christian character and boldness of that fine fellow, John Colvin, as it has been somewhat overlooked in the eulogium written by Sir C. Trevelyan.

"While speaking of Timothy, I may mention that the parents of his most advanced pupils, including the Government treasurer and other leading men in Azimgurh, allowed their boys to come in to Benares, a distance of fifty-six miles, to compete in the Bible examination, under the sole care of their native-Christian master, in whom they had full confidence that he would not do any thing to cause them to break caste."

Mr. Tucker, in this extract, refers to a Bible examination held at Benares. We must now explain to our readers what this was. In the hope of inducing, on the part of the natives, the perusal of the Christian Scriptures, and thus increasing the amount of scriptural knowledge throughout his division, he decided, with Mr. Colvin's sanction and concurrence, to offer prizes for the best scriptural knowledge, to be competed for by all the students, native teachers, and monitors of the Educational Institutions of the Benares Division. Notices to this effect were issued in March 1856, the examination to be held in the beginning of 1857. The principals of the different Institutions—the Benares College, Jay Narayan's College, Central School of the London Missionary Society, &c., made known to the students under their care what was intended to be done, and invited them to compete for the prizes. The questions being in English, Urdu, and Hindi, and thus affording the candidate the opportunity of drawing up his replies in whichever of these languages was the most facile to him, enlarged considerably the area of competition, and enabled all who were under instruction, whether in English or the vernacular, to come forward, if disposed to do so. But the success of the movement depended entirely on the inclination of the natives themselves. No official influence was brought to bear upon them, nor was any displeasure from the principals of the different institutions at all likely to supervene, if so be they felt themselves indisposed to prepare themselves for an examination which necessitated an attentive perusal of the Christain Scriptures. It is true there was the stimulus of prizes; but, according to the scale originally proposed, they were neither numerous nor of high amount. Mr. Tucker's notice offered fourteen prizes, the highest of the amount of fifty rupees, the lowest of ten rupees—inducements not sufficient to overcome any bigoted antipathy to the subject of Christianity, or aversion to the Christian Scriptures, had such existed; and therefore the facts connected with this movement afford a very fair criterion by which to judge how far the youth of India would be disposed to avail themselves of opportunities of Christian instruction, if fairly presented to them, and left to their own option.

The notice was widely circulated, and a lively interest awakened, which, as weeks and months advanced, appeared rather to increase than to diminish. A large proportion of the pupils of the Missionary schools throughout the district addressed themselves energetically to the work of preparation. Native teachers, and others, engaged in schools, caught the spirit of the movement, and applied themselves diligently to the same studies.

An examining Committee had been appointed, consisting of Professor Griffith, Head Master of Benares College, and Inspector of Government Schools in the Benares division, the Revs. M. A. Sherring of the London Mission, J. Gregson of the Baptist Mission, and C. B. Leupolt of the Church Mission, with Mr. Tucker as President. By these gentlemen a final notice was issued in November, announcing that the Prize Fund had risen to 1252 rupees, besides books; that the written examination had been arranged to take place on January 5th, 1857, in the Mint, a large and admirably-suited building belonging to the Rajah of Benares; to be followed by an oral examination, at which Mr. Colvin, the Lieut.-Governor, was expected to be present. This examination, it was hoped, would be attended by the Missionaries assembled about that time at Conference, as well as by a considerable number of gentlemen from the neighbouring stations. In such employments was it intended, at Benares, to commence the eventful year of 1857.

The results were of a character truly satisfactory. They are thus summed up by a Calcutta periodical—

"On Monday morning, January 5th, some time before 10 A.M., the aspirants assembled, in almost alarming numbers, in front of the appointed building, eagerly awaiting the hour of admission. Among them might be seen the almost tottering step of the aged, the grave and manly deportment of those in middle life, and the frolicsome playfulness of youth. Here, too, were assembled the picked boys of almost all the Missionary—certainly of all the best Missionary—schools throughout the district, and boys and young men collected from every point of the compass, and whose residences must have been scattered over a division of country not less than two or three hundred miles in diameter. From Gorruckpore, a distance of 120 miles, there were five candidates. From Chupra, a distance of 110, there was one. The Azimgurh Mission School, distant sixty miles, and entirely under the control of a native teacher, had nine representatives. Ghazepore, forty-five miles distant, nine also; while from Juanpore, thirty-five miles distant, there were eighteen. The majority, however, belonged to Benares. The Normal College alone, only opened about six months previously, sent no less than thirty-six candidates; the London Mission School thirty-two; the Church Mission twenty-eight; and the Baptist Mission School only seven. On first casting our eyes upon this large and motley throng, we were afraid that the accommodation, ample as it was, would be inadequate to meet the large demand upon it; but in this we were happily disappointed, and a few minutes after the opening of the doors all were suitably accommodated; those writing English sitting at tables, and the Urdú and Hindi writers sitting in the native fashion on the floor. As soon as quietness was restored, and care had been taken that all the boys were furnished with pens, ink, and paper, three sealed packets were produced by Mr. Tucker. These packets contained the written questions —printed in three languages, English, Urdu, and Hindi — which the candidates present had now to reply to in writing. These were at once distributed, but, being found insufficient in number, one set of questions had to answer for two candidates. The competitors were allowed six hours, or from 10 A.M. to 4 P.M., to complete their replies, at which hour all replies were given in, each essay, as produced, being marked with a number corresponding to that affixed to the writer's name, in a list of all the candidates previously prepared; and to each writer was given a ticket, bearing the same number as that written upon his essay. During the course of the examination, besides H. C. Tucker, Esq., and the examining Committee, consisting of Professor Griffith and the Revs. Messrs. Leupolt, Kennedy—who took Mr. Sherring's place, he having removed to Mirzapore—and Gregson, a large number of visitors dropped in, many of them being Missionaries drawn from a distance by the approaching Missionary Conference, which was to commence its sittings on the following day, Tuesday, January 6th.

"The business of the Missionary Conference prevented the examining Committee from proceeding at once to an investigation and scrutiny of the essays; nor was it until after a fortnight had elapsed that their task was completed. We must therefore here just say one word in reference to the oral examination which took place in the Normal School, on Monday, the 12th of January, in the presence of the Lieutenant - Governor, H. C. Tucker, Esq., and a large number of the residents of Benares and the neighbourhood, besides many Missionaries who had been attending the Conference. The answers given to a series of searching questions, historical, chronological, geographical, and doctrinal, &c., were, on the whole, remarkably satisfactory; and although, previous to this public examination, several hours had been spent in sifting the candidates, and not a few had been rejected, yet a very large number of superior order remained, and it was found impossible satisfactorily to test their relative capabilities in so brief a space. It was therefore resolved to attach no value to the oral examination, but to test the merits of the candates solely by their written answers.

"On examining the essays that had been given in, it was found that they amounted to no fewer than one hundred and fifty-two. Of these, eighteen were in English; twelve in Urdu, written in the Roman character, and seventy-six in Urdu, written in the Persian character; while forty-six were in Hindi, written in the Nagri character."

Of the intrinsic merit of these writings, and the measure of knowledge on the subject of Christian truth, possessed by the candidates, we cannot enter now. It would lead us away from our direct subject. We shall revert to this point on another opportunity. But as an evidence, therefore, that, if opportunities were presented to them, there would be no unwillingness upon the part of the *alumni* of India to read and make themselves acquainted with the Christian Scriptures, the results of this effort at Benares are in the highest degree satisfactory. We feel fully persuaded that voluntary Scripture classes in the different collegiate institutions would be largely attended. No one can read the accounts which have reached us from Lucknow and elsewhere, without the conviction that the prestige of the old systems is gone; that the native mind, to a great extent, has pronounced them worthless, and is prepared to abandon them. The late great conflict in India was a struggle for supremacy. The expectation was strong that Christianity would succumb, and, driven forth in ignominy from the shores of India, would leave to Mohammedanism the sceptre of dominion, while, relieved of Missionary interference, Hinduism should proceed to wrap, in densest folds of unbroken darkness, the degraded masses of its population. Sudden was the outbreak of insurrection; terrific the effort. Human sympathies were cast by the insurgents to the winds. Acts of hideous cruelty marked their steps. Surprised, taken at a disadvantage, bewildered at the sudden destroy every European in the Baillie guard? And now that the result has proved so different, we cannot be surprised that their minds have undergone a momentous change, and that the confession is wrung from them, "If God had not been for you, and against us, you must have perished."

British supremacy has been restored, and its restoration has been graced by an act of clemency. The native mind is softened, and presents itself under a more favourable aspect than at any previous period. Let there be, then, no more half-hearted policy. Let us not be ashamed of the Gospel of that God who preserved us in a moment of such extreme danger. If opportunities be afforded to the natives, they will use them. Let them have them. We will force no man's conscience; no, undoubtedly: but the waters of life must be permitted to come within reach of every man who wishes to drink of them. Our Government institutions for native education, our colleges and schools, can no longer remain dry places of secular education, where the torch is held up to show the hideousness of idolatry, and then dashed out, to leave the native youth in the gloom and outer darkness of having no religion at all.

On matters connected with religious duty, England has often been led astray. Her statesmen have given a wrong direction to her course. She has been taught that the faithful and unflinching discharge of the responsibilities which devolve upon her as a Christian nation would militate against her interests; and she has been counselled to compromise the one, that she might preserve intact the other. Fatal error! He who would thus steer, endangers the noble vessel of the state. Such a temporizing policy has never yet been adopted by this great nation without unhappy consequences. Ireland was so dealt with. Plain duty was thought to clash with political interest, and, in various ways, it was unhesitatingly sacrificed. Instruction in the vernacular was considered a dangerous perpetuation of national distinctiveness and corresponding jealousies, and the people, left uninstructed, became a disaf-

cording to the interpretation which the native chooses to put upon it; the contempt and scorn of a people, who, in their zeal for false religions, put to shame our lukewarmness in the profession and maintenance of truth? Truly, "*even in a political point of view, we err in ignoring so completely the agency of ministers of our own true faith in extending education among the people.*" So testified Lord Dalhousie: so speak Sir John Lawrence, Edwardes, Montgomery, M'Leod, Colvin; every man of note and power, whose services have given weight to his opinion.

And we may ask, where an open Christian policy has been pursued, has our prestige suffered? have alarming results followed? What ensued at Benares? Let us hear Mr. Tucker's testimony.

"At the time of the Meerut mutiny we had three native regiments, and only thirty European gunners. Surely if any station was to go, Benares should have been the one. Yet, with the exception of the fight with the regiments on the 4th of June, the city, under God's blessing upon Mr. F. Gubbins' vigorous management, remained in perfect stillness, with less than the ordinary amount of crime; the Missionaries pursued their labours without hindrance: and not one single native voice was raised against the various schemes of Christian effort. On the contrary, when I left India, all the principal inhabitants of the division, Hindu and Mohammedan, united to raise upwards of 6000 rupees in testimony of my 'labours for their welfare here and hereafter.'"

In noticing this remarkable circumstance, the "Friend of India," observes—"This reputation has been acquired without the slightest concession to native religious prejudices. Mr. Tucker has never skulked from a profession of his faith. He has energetically supported Christian Missionaries, is known as a personal friend of almost every Missionary in the province, and for months past has devoted his resources to their aid in a manner even liberal men find incomprehensible. No temptation would induce him to attend a native festival, nor would he dream of refusing a valuable geography in the vernacular, because like all other geographies, it was opposed to the Shasters. Mr. Tucker did justice without trampling on the cross, and the people who have honoured his virtue do not respect him the less for avoiding a humiliation."

The men to whom, under God, England is indebted for the conservation of her rule in India, who stood forward unflinchingly in the time of danger, and, with combined courage and wisdom, stemmed the torrent of insurrection, ought to be heard on questions such as these. Their services entitle them to speak, and give weight to their opinion. Let us hear one of them, Col. Edwardes. We quote from a speech delivered at Shrewsbury, on the occasion of a crowded and influential meeting of the Shropshire Church Missionary Society, held about a month back, the Lord Bishop of Lichfield in the chair. It is of importance at the present moment, and we extract largely from it.

Referring to the objections usually urged against the admission of the Bible into Government schools, Colonel Edwardes observed—

"The first peculiar objection of the Government is, that the Bible is not necessary as a basis for the education of man. It is actually said that there may be morality without the Bible. Reference has, indeed, been made to eternal principles antecedent to revelation. I know not where they are to be found, or what nation set them forth. Did the Egyptians, the Assyrians, the Persians, the Buddhists, the Greeks, or the Romans? Has not the world long since agreed to reprobate the immoral religions of those people? What people in the new world have them? Have the savages of the Pacific, the Bushmen and negroes of Africa, the civilized Chinese, the Mohammedans and Hindus of Asia, or the savans of the first French revolution? The Bible gives a different account of the morality of man without revelation. Job, the oldest work in the world, in chapter xiv. verse 4, says, 'Who can bring a clean thing out of an unclean? Not one.'

"I come next to a much stronger objection — the objection which is made that we stand pledged to be neutral in religious matters. The question whether neutrality in religion be a nation's duty is best answered by asking if it be the duty of an individual. No one will be bold enough to say that it is. We do not ourselves, nor do we see our neighbours, saying, 'This question of Christianity and infidelity is really nothing to me. It does not affect me in any way. It seems my duty to remain neutral!' We cannot use such language. There is that within us which, whether we will or no, takes cognizance of religious truth or error, which stands on tiptoe in the breast, and 'looks before and after,' peering into the sky with intense anxiety to find some certainty for eternity. We hear God himself declaring that 'he that is not with me is against me,' and the words find a loud echo in our hearts. We cannot—dare not—be neutral about our own soul. How, then, is the case changed when we join the throng of our fellow-countrymen, and act together as a nation? Has one relieved another of his responsibilities? Have thirty millions of Christians conglomerated into one neutrality? Do two and two make nothing, or do they make four? Because each Englishman is brave, does the British army become cowardly and run away? or does it, in the mass, preserve the self-same virtues, and press on irresistibly to victory with the united valour of 10,000 soldiers? We are not atoms that we can be isolated thus. We have a national existence in every other sphere—in arts and arms, science and commerce, laws and civil government, and foreign polity, and as yet, thank God, we have a national religion, and a Queen whose title is 'Defender of the Faith.' To ask us, then, to be neutral in India, between the religions of Christianity, and the false prophet, and the gods of the Hindu, is to ask us to denationalize ourselves, to do abroad what we have not done at home, and cease to be Englishmen and Christians when we cross the line. But these things we cannot do. We cannot be neutral. We must desire that our native subjects were not Mohammedans and Hindus, but Christians like ourselves, or better; and it is our duty to avail ourselves of every lawful opportunity to promote the spread of Christianity among them. Another argument for neutrality is based upon some supposed pledge that we have given, no one knows when or where. The despatches of Lords Ellenborough and Stanley to the Governor-General speak of 'good faith' requiring us to be neutral. But I have never yet found any one who could produce the bond. It has, indeed, been the traditional policy in India, not merely to be neutral towards native creeds, but to be intolerant of Christianity. But if we have hitherto done wrong, good faith does not require us to go on doing it. It is well to be consistent; but it is better to be true. We once were partners with the priests of Juggernaut, and derived an annual revenue from the temple; but the indignant voice of England forced the Indian Government to break off the idolatrous connexion. Was that a breach of faith? No Government can be carried on upon such a principle. As we find out our past errors we must correct them. We cannot nail them to the mast and sink or swim with them. There is, indeed, a document of very recent date, of the very highest importance, pledging the Queen of England to a particular line of conduct towards her English subjects—I mean Her Majesty's Proclamation on assuming the direct government of Hindustan. In that Proclamation is the ambiguous term 'interference,' and it has been seized upon by the advocates of the traditional policy; and the passage has been quoted in India by the Governor-General himself as affirming that policy of 'neutrality,' and enjoining it upon every public servant. But the Proclamation has been submitted in England to a close and critical analysis by a great Christian lawyer, whose published judgment I now hold in my hand; and he pronounces that it is impossible, by any sound and constitutional principle of interpretation, to attach an unchristian meaning to any passage in the Proclamation of Her Most Gracious Majesty—she having prefaced the expression of her sovereign will by acknowledging her own title to be derived from the Christian's God, and her own reliance on the truth of Christianity. We have, then, the Governor-General of India interpreting the Queen's Proclamation (as it has been interpreted by the Hindus of Madras) in favour of neutrality; while an eminent lawyer, accustomed to weigh words, interprets it in a totally opposite sense. It becomes necessary, therefore, that this question should be set at rest; and I hope that some one may be found to ask Her Majesty's Minister, in the coming session of Parliament, which is the official interpretation of the Proclamation — Lord Canning's or Mr. O'Malley's. The people of England will then know what action to take in the matter.

"Another argument for the 'neutrality' policy is, that the natives of India are taxpayers, and we cannot apply their money to teaching the Bible without a breach of trust. . . . The fallacy of this argument has been well exposed by Sir John Lawrence, who has in effect pointed out that we are not trustees for the people of India, but trustees for that Providence which gave India to us, and that we are not to rule India according to the light and conscience of the natives, but according to our own. . . . . While, therefore, we earnestly desire and strive to rule India well, and for its own benefit, we do not put our measures to the vote of the natives; and the acts and resolutions of our Government reflect the image of our mind, not theirs. On this ground, therefore, we say it is our bounden duty to place the Bible before the pupils of our Government schools; not, indeed, to compel them to read it, but to give all who will read it, and do not object to it, an opportunity of sharing with us in that knowledge which we deem the best and highest that we have—the knowledge which has 'the promise of the life that now is, and of that which is to come'—the only knowledge which can regenerate either an individual or a nation—which has lifted Europe out of paganism, and is able to lift Asia, if we will only apply the lever. . . . .

"The last argument for 'neutrality' that I know of is of a totally opposite character. We are no longer invited to treat the natives as if they were free, but we are asked to turn round and face the real fact, that they are a conquered and a slavish people—a people who have for ages been under despotic forms of government, and habitually bow to the will of their rulers. For the British Government to declare itself a Christian Government, by basing its education on the sanctions of God's word, would, we are told, carry too great an influence with such subjects, and would partake of the nature of bribery or force, and be akin to persecution. This sounds very well in England, but, to any one acquainted with the people of India, is perfectly ludicrous. They are, indeed, a slavish people, accustomed to despotic governments, but the British Indian Government is not exactly the personification of their idea of a despot. They know very well what religious persecution is, and don't require us to teach them. All classes and creeds in India have had their share of it in days gone by, and preserve lively traditions of it now. The mass of the Hindu people has been for many ages groaning under the heaviest religious persecution that the world ever saw—the system of caste—imposed by the Brahmins on four-fifths of their fellow-countrymen. A system like this, which denies the equality of men, and carries degradation and pollution into every house, could never have been submitted to had it not with infernal art appealed to the pride of each successive caste, by giving them a caste below them—an inferior being to look down on. In Upper India there are whole districts of Mohammedans whose ancestors were Hindus, but who were converted by Moslem emperors by that famous alternative, 'the Korán or the sword!' In the Punjab, where I have been for the last twelve years, the whole country is scarred with the religious persecutions of our predecessors. At Umritsur, which is the religious capital of the Sikhs, there is a sacred pool which the Mohammedan invaders invariably defiled by the slaughter of kine, which are objects of Sikh worship; and hard by are Mohammedan temples, which the Sikhs, whenever they were victorious, defiled with a hecatomb of swine. Under the rule of Runjeet Singh no Mohammedan could raise the cry for prayers; and the life of a man was taken by law for the life of a cow. I remember one day an old Mohammedan soldier of the Sikh service coming into my court to give evidence. He had no arms, and I said, 'I fear you have been a thief in days of yore, and the Sikhs cut off your hands for you.' 'Oh no,' he said; 'I am one of a guard of five. We were firing off our muskets one day, and wounded a cow. Goolab Singh, who was commanding in camp, sent for us, and asked who did it. We could not tell; so he chopped off all our arms!' This is religious persecution if you like; and this is what the slavish natives understand by that term. But if the British Government opens a school, and first of all leaves it quite optional with all the children of the country to come to school or stay away as they choose, and then begins the day with an hour's reading of the Bible, with full liberty to the scholars to attend during that hour or not, the people of India may like it, or may not like it, and they may doubtless wish that the Korán or the Vedas were read during that hour instead, but they would not regard it as a religious persecution.

"Having now shown that the policy of 'neutrality is unreasonable' I come, lastly, to show that it is an impossible policy—a policy which we go on violating year after year; and consequently an untruthful policy, which the natives can only view as a deliberate deceit. 'The Government,' says Lord Ellenborough, in his despatch of April 13th, 1858, to the Governor-General, 'will adhere with good faith to its ancient policy of perfect neutrality in matters affecting the religion of the people of India.' But how stands the fact? It is notorious, not only to us in India, but to you all in England, that the British Government in India has made laws for the abolition of some of the most treasured rites and usages of the natives. 1. Suttee, or the burning of widows on their husband's funeral pile. 2. Human sacrifices to idols, and plunging men, women, and children to sharks at certain holy bathing places. 3. Domestic slavery. 4. The abolition of Brahminical jurisprudence, and assertion of equal justice in criminal cases. 5. The removal of all disability of inheritance incurred by Hindus on changing their religion. 6. The legalization of re-marriage by Hindu widows. 7. The slaughter of oxen by the English. All these are quoted by Mr. Kingsmill in a late work; but others could be mentioned. Why do we deprive Mohammedan husbands of the religious luxury of murdering their own wives? And why, if we are really neutral in matters of religion, do we open secular schools and teach sciences which give the lie to Hindu cosmogony and mythology, and make infidels of the pupils? All these are instances in which neutrality in religious matters has been violated by Government in India. Every one of them was right to do, and not to do any one of them would have been an offence against humanity. But does not this show that the policy of neutrality as between us and India is an impossible policy? Why, then, profess it? It is a great evil for a Government to profess to be neutral and not to be so; and to tell the natives that it won't permit interference with their religions, and then proceed to crumble their religions down piecemeal by legislation. The result of such a course has been to fill the minds of the natives with distrust. I do not mean to attribute dishonesty to the Government. I am quite sure it meant to be neutral, and that it never would have abolished any of the native customs, unless driven to do so by the voice of European public opinion. But the result is the same. Government has professed one thing and done another; and in the eyes of the natives it has become an object of suspicion. It would have incurred far less odium had it from the first taken the manly and open course, declared itself a Christian Government, bound by its own Christian principles to tolerate all religions, but not indifferent—not neutral—between good and evil, truth and error.

"I have now done with those who plead the duty of neutrality as a reason for excluding the Bible from the schools; and I turn, lastly, to those who oppose it from motives of expediency. They fear that one or other of these two results must follow—1. Either that opening the Bible will close the schools: or else, 2. That the conversion of the pupils will alarm the people and create an insurrection. I boldly maintain that neither of these results will follow. The effect of putting the holy Bible into native schools is not an untried experiment of which men are free to conjecture and prognosticate according to their own opinions. It has been tried in every Presidency and every province in India, and the result is open to everybody who chooses to inquire. It is a *sine quâ non*

from the experience of all whom I have ever conversed with on this subject—and I even believe that it will be admitted by our opponents—that the Mission schools in which the Bible is taught are more popular than the Government schools, from which the Bible is excluded. Do not misapprehend me. I do not mean to say that the Mission schools are more popular because the Bible is taught there. I admit at once that the Mission schools would be still more popular if the Bible were not taught in them. But I say that, notwithstanding the Bible being taught most prominently in those schools, and in spite of all the Bible instruction, the Mission schools are freely resorted to by the people. And this is all that we want to ascertain; for this is a complete answer to the apprehensions of a timid Government. You will naturally ask why this is so, for it is a curious fact. The reasons are two: Firstly, because the standard of education in a Mission school is generally higher than in a Government school. The Government school is usually conducted by natives; the Mission school by a European gentleman; and not merely a European gentleman, but a Christian gentleman, free from the pride and sense of superiority, which are the prevailing faults of most of us in India: a gentleman who, day after day, undeterred by a burning climate, devotes many hours to the task of teaching some hundreds of native children, with unwearied patience, and humility, and kindness, and displays a real earnest interest in their welfare, watching their dawning intellect with delight, rejoicing over their good, and grieving with a personal grief over their evil; thus rearing them up into useful men, and exhibiting before the eyes of scholars and parents a bright example of a Christian, 'a living epistle known and read of all men.' Is it not wonderful, then, that parents prefer to send their children here? Their object is education, and they simply choose the school which gives the best. The other reason is, that the native does not believe in conversion by reading the Bible. The Hindu religion has long since had its heart overlaid by caste, and it is

any part in it. It is a common trick for Muhammedan Missionaries to disguise themselves as Hindus, get into the society of the Hindus of the caste they have assumed, get them to join in a common meal together, and then, when it is over, inform the horrorstricken Hindus that they have eaten and drunk with a Mohammedan, and are Mohammedans from henceforth. The argument is considered quite conclusive, and Mohammedans they become. A great orator in the House of Commons was thought to have said a very good thing in the debates on the Sepoy mutiny of 1857, when he denied that its origin was the greased cartridge. 'Revolutions,' said he, 'are not made of grease.' But that only showed his entire misconception of the Hindu and Mohammedan mind. I say Hindu and Mohammedan, because the Mohammedans of India have come as nearly as much under the yoke of caste as the Hindus; and when told that the Enfield cartridge was made up of pigs' fat as well as beef fat, they considered that it would take away their religion as much as the Hindu did. A people such as this, sunk in superstition, is a prey to the most childish fears, and every thing new, no matter what it is, is suspected to be a trick to deprive them of their faith by surprising them into a defilement. Every now and then the rumour spreads like wildfire that Government has mixed a quantity of beef and ham-bone dust in wheat flour, and is selling it cheap in the bazaar to turn the consumers into Christians. The electric telegraph is a perfect puzzle to them. They think that when it has got thoroughly spread over the whole country, some day the wire will be pulled and the people converted in a moment. And what does all this teach us? that the people are afraid of the Bible? No. It teaches us that they are afraid of every thing else but the Bible; and that if we really want to calm their fears, we must give them the Bible, and explain our Christianity, and show them that Christianity is not made of grease, though revolutions are. Lastly, I have to reply to the opposite objection—that there will be so many conversions in the schools if the Bible be opened, that the people will be alarmed into insurrection. I have two replies to make to that: one in all sadness—that one need not be under any apprehension that the progress of Christianity will be too rapid. If it were a grease affair it would spread fast enough; but being a heart affair, it is slow indeed. It is a common taunt to the Missionaries by worldly people that they have spent so many years, and so many thousands of pounds, and made so small a number of converts. Both arguments cannot be true. The Bible may be efficacious or inefficacious, but it cannot be both. Look at home, at the schools in which English boys have the Bible daily. Does it make too many Christians? 'The wind bloweth where it listeth;' and the Bible is efficacious where God blesses it. What we have to do is to sow it in faith, and pray that we may reap in joy. But I have another reply to make to these alarmists. For one hundred years they and their party have had their own way in India. They have not merely been 'neutral,' but they have been intolerant to Christianity. They have entered into partnership with Juggernaut. They have sacrificed at shrines. They have pandered to Hinduism and Mohammedanism, endowed their temples, administered their funds, and been a nursing-father and nursing-mother to them. They kept Missionaries out of India as long as they possibly could. They would not let Judson land within their territories, and they gave the honour of tolerating him to the King of Burmah. And what was the end of their coward policy? The most hellish insurrection that the earth has ever seen, and the blood of our Englishmen and women spilt like water over India. Who made the insurrection? from what class did it raise its horrid head?—from some Mission school where the Bible was being read?—from some agricultural district or populous city where the incendiary Missionary was at work converting the poor natives? No, from none of these, but from the ranks of the native army —that army which had ever been made the stronghold of caste, and from whose proud and undefiled ranks was driven the polluting Christian convert. Yes; their sin has found them out. They have sown the wind, and reaped the whirlwind. They sought for an unhallowed peace, and they found a desolation. Let us do what is right, and nought but good will come of it."

We know not what the national course may be on these eventful questions: but whatever it may be, the duty of Missionary Societies and Missionary agents is clear.

India must be raised: her population must be improved. On all hands this is now admitted. Their ignorance and fanaticism have already caused us great calamities. The same causes, if permitted to prevail, will be productive in due time of like evils. They must be enlightened. Christianity alone can do it. This also has been tried, and has produced its results. Native converts in India have been a despised class—despised not merely by the religionists from whom they had separated, but by many of those who profess the

Christianity which they had embraced. They were regarded as the true pariahs of India, as the refuse of Hindú society, who, for the sake of contemptible worldly advantages, had done violence to their connexions, and sold their faith. They were shunned as men who were not trustworthy, and in whom no reliance could be placed. The experience of 1857-58 proved the contrary. They were the only natives who were thoroughly to be depended upon. Their change of religion was found to be the result, not of bribery or inconstancy, but of conviction; for, rather than apostatize, they preferred to suffer. Throughout the dread ordeal, their identification with the European was complete, and the genuine influence of pure Christianity was found to make the native conscientious, attached, and enduring. We repeat it—Christianity is what India needs, and to communicate the Gospel to India is the work of the Missionary—of the Christian evangelist. He can do more for India than the statesman. He can do more to secure for us a peaceful rule over India than disciplined armies. They may repress and overawe, but the Gospel which he preaches changes the character, removes disaffection, and implants kindly feeling in its stead.

"The great difficulty of our task lies in the moral, not in the geographical distance. The great problem is, how to diminish that distance, to create greater sympathy of feelings and aims between the rulers and the ruled. . . . . We neither can serve or rule with success a people who either hate us, or even regard us without attachment. All notions of holding India by fear, by mere physical force, are as mistaken as they are unchristian. We cannot rule by bayonets alone. If once the mass of the people become permanently disaffected towards us, no amount of military expenditure would enable us to hold the present Indian empire. If there had been any thing like active sympathy or complicity with the mutineers on the part of the civil population last year, not an Englishman would have been left in India, outside the three capital cities, by the end of June. But notwithstanding many serious blunders in our administration, the people acquiesced in our rule, because they believed that we really desired to do justice, and to protect the rights of all classes.

"But, on the other hand, there was little active sympathy and support on our behalf, and, consequently, the mutiny produced the instant disruption of civil government, anarchy, and confusion. And this was the consequence of that wide interval between us and the people which prevents them from understanding our character and the nature of our policy. Universal ignorance, the observances of caste, a different language, and race prejudices, have kept the rulers and the ruled wholly apart, in dangerous ignorance of each other. How, then, to bridge over this terrible chasm is the great problem for the British Government to solve. It is clear that this object can only be accomplished by bringing the people to our own stand-point; by bringing them, in fact, to our own highest standard of moral and religious life."

By what powerful medium shall results of such importance be secured? One suffices: Christianity, in its penetrative, renewing, and winning influences. Thank God we need, in this respect, no change of policy. Our mode of action has long since been determined: only let us increase our efforts, and where we have been contented to send one Missionary, let us plant first ten, and then one hundred; not Europeans merely, but what will be, after a time, more easily attainable, and more serviceable in detail, native evangelists.

THE POPULATION OF EASTERN BENGAL.

The forty-sixth Report of the Calcutta Bible Society contains copious passages by Missionaries and other persons engaged in the ful inquiries were instituted as to the religious state of the people, and their earnestness or carelessness in the observance of the forms

The results of these inquiries was far from satisfactory.

"A kind of inanity and listless fatalistic ignorance is very prevalent. The reason seems to be asleep. There is no desire to inquire into the origin, utility, or truth of any established notion or custom prevalent in the villages. The mind appears to be devoid of the powers necessary for such inquiries. The methods in vogue for eating, drinking, dressing, working, and worshipping seem to be the result, not of thought and judgment, but of passive unthinking humanity cast into a mould, invented and established by the ancients. This mental inability or inertia extends, not the action of the mind in petty intrigues and low cunning regarding the tangible, but only to the higher sphere of thoughts, and more rational and ennobling duties of man. In spite of reason, I frequently found it difficult to keep my thoughts from hovering between the rational and irrational creation whilst conversing with the villagers. The number of their ideas, and the circle of their thoughts, seemed to be so limited and confined, that it was difficult to decide whether reason was not wholly displaced by mere instinct. The darkness is certainly grosser than that of the feudal ages and the millennium of Popery in Europe.

"The people have no higher standard of moral actions than the custom of the village. It is true they say that right is right, and wrong is wrong; that truth-telling is good, and falsehood is bad. A Patagonian, a Flathead, or a Naga, does the same, and does it often on a higher principle than a Bengalee villager. The latter, as far as I could find, never thinks that his morality has any thing to do with his volitions and his judgment. It consists, as he thinks, in the conformity of his actions with the *lokáchar*, 'custom,' in his village. The villager seemed surprised at our teaching that morality consisted in the conformity of man's thoughts, feelings, and actions with the will of his Maker; and that it had to do with the training of the nursery, with the habits and regulations of the domestic and social circles. The nobleness of sentiment and feeling connected with the purity, benevolence, simplicity, manliness, and delights of the higher walks of Christian morality, is unknown to him. Even the lower morality which emanates from a half-obliterated natural religion, he comprehends not. The spiritual, rational, and divine ethics of the Gospel he can neither know nor practise, without a long course of training. From birth to death he is doomed to inhale the noxious vapour of his gloomy atmosphere, and closes his existence without morality and hope.

"As regards mental culture and intellectual enlightenment, Hindus and Moslems are in the same state. The latter, perhaps, are a shade lower in social morality, and are more illiterate. Neither class seem to have any clear notion regarding the nature and requirements of a spiritual religion. With both, religion consists of a set round of ceremonies and outward forms. In reference to religion, these people seem to be like the compositors of Newton's Principia; each part must be attended to as prescribed, without the slightest idea of the work as a whole—of the adaptation of one part to another, or of the whole to its ultimate object. It is true, the spirituality, excellency, and glory of Christianity are far from being properly exhibited by the conduct of its professors. The Christianity of Christendom and that of the Bible are very different. But in these two religions, the book and their votaries agree in making religion a form instead of a principle. The religions of the books and of the professors are alike mechanical, formal, and immoral."

Various difficulties to the progress of Christian truth amongst these benighted masses are pointed out.

"The obstacles to the success of the Gospel in India are very great. The most formidable difficulty is the immobility and servility of Asiatic society. The native community in Eastern Bengal is made up of a large number of small circles. At the head of each circle stands the Zemindar as the liege lord, surrounded by a number of religious teachers, of his own faith. The views and opinions of these are paramount in all moral and religious matters. The rayats included within these circles are as much at the will of their liege lord and teacher as Abraham's trained servants were at his will. No feudal lord ever had greater influence over his serfs. . . . . In and around Missionary stations, light is slowly penetrating into the recesses of errors and evil customs. But the myriads In rural districts are still in utter darkness. The people are in ' the snare of the devil, who are taken captive by him at his will.' "

It is our comfort to know that the Gospel has often made its way amidst difficulties as great as those which have been just enumerated. Only let the proportion of effort be in some degree commensurate with the greatness of the work. British Christians need to gird themselves for the momentous undertaking of India's regeneration.

OUDE AS IT WAS BEFORE THE ANNEXATION.

We proceed to introduce our readers a little further into the arcana of Oude mismanagement; and, taking Lucknow as our starting-point, shall commence with a description of that city. When Asuf-ood-Dowlah became Viceroy of Oude, Lucknow was but a village of little importance. The Sheikhs, who had risen in rebellion against his rule, built there a castle, the Muchee Bawn, from whence they infested the surrounding country. The Viceroy in person expelled them from their stronghold, and, being pleased with the locality, selected it as the site of his future capital, removing thither from Fyzabad.

In 1824 it was visited by Bishop Heber, Ghazee-ood-Deen Hyder being at that time king. Lucknow then possessed a considerable population, crowded together in mean houses of clay, traversed by lanes of the filthiest description, and so narrow, that even a single elephant did not pass easily. Swarms of beggars occupied every angle and the steps of every door. Of the remaining population, almost all were armed—a sure index of prevailing turbulence and general insecurity of life and property. "Grave men in palanquins, counting their beads, and looking like mollahs, had all two or three sword-and-buckler lacqueys attending on them. People of consequence, on their elephants, had each a suwarree of shield, spear, and gun; and even the lounging people of the lower ranks in the streets and shop-doors had their shields over their shoulders, and their swords sheathed in one hand." Gradually, on advancing further, the buildings improved, although the streets remained narrow and dirty. Pretty mosques appeared, large houses, built like the native houses in Calcutta, and bazaars well filled with people. At length the principal street was reached, of commanding appearance, "wider than the High Street at Oxford, but having some distant resemblance to it in the colour of its buildings, and their general form and Gothic style."

Several of the localities, which, in connexion with the late disturbances, have been so often mentioned, were visited by the Bishop; the Dilkoosha (Heart's Delight), a small summer palace of the king's, about three miles from the city, situated in an extensive park, "sufficiently wild and jungly to offer a picturesque variety, and in parts sufficiently open for air and exercise, as well as to show off its deer and neelghaus to advantage;" Constantia, subsequently called the Martinière, "a very large and most whimsical house and grounds, in the worst possible taste . . . . built by the late General Martin, a Frenchman, and originally a common soldier," who entered the service of the King of Oude, and died a millionaire. This eccentric man, apprehending that, after his death, the king would seize the house, and appropriate it to his own purposes, directed his body to be buried in a vault made under the foundation of the building. The king being thus constrained to abandon his intention, inasmuch as no Mussulman will sleep in a house where any one lies buried, the building, according to the General's will, was devoted to the purposes of a college, under the name of the Martinière.

Many stately khans and handsome pagodas and mosques were found dispersed amidst narrow streets and alleys, far dirtier than those of Benares, the most striking being the tombs of Saadut Alee and his consort; the Gate of Constantinople ("Roumi Durwazu"); and the Imambara, or cathedral, consisting of two courts rising with a steep ascent one above the other, and containing, besides, a splendid mosque, "a college for instruction in Mussulman law, and a noble gallery, in the midst of which, under a brilliant tabernacle of silver, cut-glass, and precious stones, lie buried the remains of its founder, Asuf-ood Dowlah."

Such was Lucknow in Heber's time. Upwards of thirty years have elapsed, during which brief period four Kings of Oude have passed away from this earthly scene, leaving the last occupant, Wajid Alee, on the throne. Let us endeavour to sketch Lucknow as it appeared in his reign, two or three years before the annexation.

We shall select as a central point the Residency, "a very extensive and beautiful brick building, with lofty rooms, fine verandahs, and splendid porticoes. Besides having a ground floor and two upper stories, it had a tykhana, or cellar of splendid apartments, as lofty and well-arranged as any in the house. These were built to shelter the residents during the summer from the extreme heat of the day. Sky-lights and cellar-windows gave an excellent light to them." Such was the commodiousness of the house, that,

L

during the time of trouble, it afforded accommodation to very numerous families, about eight hundred to a thousand souls, men, ladies, women, and children, all finding place in it."

The ground on which the Residency stood being of much higher elevation than that of the houses surrounding it, a spectator on its flat roof commanded a fine panoramic view of the city. Let us conceive ourselves placed on this eminence, at the date already indicated.

"Two-thirds of the city are as completely buried in foliage as the suburbs of Damascus." To the east stands the king's new palace, the Kaiser Bagh, presenting "a line of white walls and terraces, about half a mile in length, and topped with a mass of gilded towers and domes." Across the Goomtee, whose sinuosities may be traced from west to east, a champaign country extends itself, so embowered in foliage that only a few domes and towers are visible above the sea of sycamores, banyans, tamarind, acacia, neem, and palm-trees. Not far from where the Residency gardens abut on the river, it is crossed by an iron suspension-bridge, which, having been sent out in 1816, remained thirty years without being erected. Below this is seen a bridge of boats, over which passed the road to the Badshah Bagh, or King's Gardens, on the plain beyond. Higher up, the river, which flows with a gentle current between grassy and shaded banks, is spanned, near the Muchee Bawn, by a stone bridge with ancient arches. Viewed from the iron bridge, the left bank rises gradually from the water, "forming a long hill, crowned with palaces and mosques, stretching away into the distance, where a crowd of fainter minarets tells of splendours beyond."

An early morning excursion exhibits crowds of people passing to and fro, the gaudy dresses of many of the natives indicating the presence of a native court, "some borne on palanquins, some mounted on elephants, and a few on fine horses of Arabian blood." Emirs, cadis, writers, and the like, attired in silken raiment and splendidly turbaned, pass continually to and fro, with servants running before them, dividing the crowds for the passage of the elephants. "The country-people are pouring into the city by thousands, laden with their produce; and the bazaars of fruit and vegetables, which seem interminable, are consta tly thronged."

Let us visit the heart of the city. "A splendid gateway spans the street, over which a forest of tall minarets and gilded domes rises in the distance. Passing through the arch, an open space is entered, with a large mosque and hospital on the left side, and a magnificent gate of white marble beyond. This is the Roumi Durwazu, or Constantinople gate, which leads into a scene of unexpected splendour. The visitor finds himself in the midst of "a group of mosques, tombs, and pavilions, all of marble, or covered with white stucco, and surmounted with swelling oriental domes, shining like solid gold—fitting crowns to the slender arches, and the masses of Saracenic filagree and fretwork from which they spring." In the foreground of the picture is seen a huge stone tank, with flights of steps descending into it on all sides, "a boskage of roses in full bloom running around its banks and between the dazzling pavilions, while a few tall palms in the midst of them shoot up into the sunshine." On the left stands the gate of the Imambara, or tomb of Asufood-Dowlah. Entering, the visitor finds himself in "a quadrangle surrounded by the same dazzling white architecture, with gilded domes blazing against the intense blue of the sky. The enclosed space was a garden, in which stood two beautiful mausoleums of marble." Ascending the marble steps at the bottom of the garden, leading to the edifice, the tabernacle of chandeliers, to which Bishop Heber has referred, presented itself. "Through the open marble arches nothing else was at first visible. The whole building was hung with them: immense pyramids of silver, gold, prismatic crystals, and coloured glass; and where they were too heavy to be hung, they rose in radiant piles from the floor. In the midst of them were temples of silver filagree, eight or ten feet high, and studded with cornelians, agates, and emeralds. . . . . . There were ancient banners of the awabs of Oude, heavy with sentences from the Korán, embroidered on gold; gigantic bands of silver covered with talismanic words; sacred shields studded with the name of God; swords of Khorassan steel, lances, and halberds; the turbans of renowned commanders; the trappings of the white horse of Nuzeer-ood Deen, mounted on a wooden effigy; and several pulpits of peculiar sanctity."

With such a lavish expenditure on a tomb, we cannot be surprised that the treasury of Oude became rapidly exhausted, and that venality and extortion were brought into requisition to supply funds for new extravagance.

Saadut Ali established a reserved treasury in A.D. 1801. Up to that period he had been dissipated and unfit for the responsibilities of a throne. At that time his character underwent a change, and having vowed at the shrine of Huzzut Abbas, at Lucknow, to cease from all such indulgences, he applied himself so diligently to the affairs of state, as to leave, on his death in October 1814, fourteen crores of rupees, or fourteen millions sterling in the reserved treasury.

Saadut Allee's son and successor, Ghazee-ood Deen Hyder, spent four crores out of the reserved treasury over and above the whole income of the state; and when he died, on the 20th of October 1827, he left ten crores of rupees in that treasury. His son and successor, Nusseer-ood Deen Hyder, spent nine crores and thirty lacs; and when he died, on the 7th of July 1837, he left only seventy lacs in the reserved treasury. His successor, Mohammed Allee Shah, died on the 16th of May 1842, leaving in the reserved treasury thirty-five lacs of rupees, one hundred and twenty-four thousand gold mohurs, and twenty-four lacs in our government securities—total seventy-eight lacs and eighty-four thousand rupees. His son and successor, Umjid Allee Shah, died on the 13th of February 1847, leaving in the reserved treasury ninety-two lacs of rupees, one hundred and twenty-four thousand gold mohurs, and twenty-four lacs in our government securities—total, one crore and thirty-six lacs.

The present ex-king, when in possession of royalty, was accustomed to spend, out of the reserved treasury, over and above the whole income of the country, twenty lacs of rupees a year. The glass chandeliers in the Imambara were some of the costly luxuries in which he indulged, two of the principal ones costing him 50,000 dollars each; while generally, to the buildings and decorations of new palaces and gardens may be debited the one crore which his majesty found in the reserved treasury, and the twenty-two lacs of annual deficit of the first five years of his reign. The result was as might be expected. The stipendiaries, troops, and establishments, were all deeply in arrears, and more especially the various members of the royal family who were stipendiaries on the crown, one of the first petitions presented to Colonel Sleeman, on his becoming Resident, being from the surviving ladies of Asuf-ood Dowlah, and Shuja-ood Dowlah, to which the seals of 216 of those unfortunate persons were affixed, representing that their stipends had not been paid for three and four years, and that they were literally starving, and driven to the extremity of distress.

But recurring to the city, let us imagine ourselves one of a party accompanying the British Resident on an excursion to its more thronged part. The party is mounted on three of the king's largest elephants. These have gilded howdahs, long crimson housings, with drivers in resplendent dresses, and umbrella-holders sitting behind the Europeans on the elephants' backs. It is the fashionable hour for appearing in public, and the broad street leading to the Roumi Durwazu is filled with a long string of horses and elephants advancing slowly through the dense crowd of pedestrians. The Imambara is reached, and a new mosque, in course of erection by the king's mother, attracts attention. It is large and picturesque, but showing a decline in architecture. We then plunge into the heart of the city, and reach the "dark, narrow, crooked streets of the Lucknow of the last century. The houses are three stories high, projecting so that the eaves almost touch, and exhibiting the greatest variety in their design and ornament. The street is so narrow and crooked, that we run some risk of crushing our howdahs against the second story balconies." The windows are all latticed. Passing the place of execution, "a muddy bank overhanging a sewer, filled with the drainage of the city, and the gate, where the heads of malefactors were wont to be exposed, we return through "the Choke, the main street of the old city, and of tolerable breadth. Here, on the second story balconies, are to be seen unmistakeable evidences of the deep immorality and sensual degradation which characterized Lucknow under its kings." But see, we are descending "the slope towards the river. The sun is setting, and the noises of the great city are subdued for the moment. The deep green gardens lie in shadow; but all around us, far and near, the gilded domes are blazing in the yellow glow. The scene is lovely as the outer court of Paradise; yet what deception, what crime, what unutterable moral degradation fester beneath its surface!" Lucknow, as it used to be, was in truth a Sodom. The description given of old was applicable here: "it was well watered everywhere, even as the garden of the Lord, like the land of Egypt as thou comest into Zoar; but the men were wicked, and sinners before the Lord exceedingly." And what a tempest of iron hail descended on this city, what a storm of fire and brimstone! A season of dread calamity came upon it—" the new wine mourneth; the wine languisheth; all the merry-hearted do sigh. The mirth of tabrets ceaseth; the noise of them that rejoice endeth; the joy of the harp ceaseth. They shall not drink wine with a song: strong drink shall be bitter to them that drink it. The city of confusion is broken down; every house is shut up, that no men may come in. There is a crying for wine in the streets; all joy is darkened; the mirth of the land is gone. In the city is left desolation, and the gate is smitten with destruction." Great indeed have been the calamities of Lucknow. But the earthquake has broken down obstructions, and the Christian Missionary has now free entrance. Let us hope that the Gospel will cleanse the city of those evils which Mohammedanism nurtured and developed.

Once more we shall endeavour to place before our readers a panoramic view of this remarkable city. It will be necessary to transfer them to the roof of the Chuttur Munzil palace.

On the relief of the pent-up garrison in the Residency and adjoining posts, by the force under General Havelock and Sir James Outram, the old position was extended, and a new line of defence taken up, on the north, as far as the Goomtee, and eastward, so as to include the Tehzee Kotee, Furhut Buksh, and Chuttur Munzil palaces. These are lofty and extensive ranges of palaces, built of solid masonry, and rising nearly from the water's edge. The following extract graphically depicts the view which is obtained from the top of the Chuttur Munzil palace.

"Standing on this elevated position, and facing eastward towards the Dilkoosha Park, you look perpendicularly down upon the Goomtee, which skirts the building on your left. Beyond this extends a level plain, covered with green sward, broken and bounded by various royal residences and gardens. The nearest of these is the 'Dilaram,' or 'Heart's Ease' house, which stands near the river bank, and is now unoccupied. Further on, but thrown back at the distance of a mile, is the Badsha Bagh, or king's garden, comprising buildings of some size and elegance, embosomed in a thicket of orange and other fruit-trees. Further on, and near the river, lies the Hazuree Bagh, or breakfast garden. The eye then glances down a long reach of the river, till it rests upon the Chukker Kotee. On the right bank of the Goomtee the country is thickly wooded, as far as we can see, with mango groves and fruit-gardens; the eye resting in the distance on the double-storied mansion of the Dilkoosha, which looks like an old French château. Nearer, and a little to the left, are seen the lofty and fantastic stories of the Martinière. Nearer still, but yet distant, we distinguish the walls and gateway of the Secundur Bagh, marked by its gilt-topped turrets. Still nearer, and to the left, stands that old renovated tomb, high on a mound overlooking the river—that is the Kuddum Kusool; and closely adjoining it, that flat white dome marks the site of the Shah Nujeef, which is the name given to the tomb of one of the former kings of Oude, Ghazee-ood Deen Hyder. It is a strong massive building, standing among a number of low mud huts, and surrounded by trees. As the eye withdraws to the nearer vicinity, it now catches a conspicuous and solid-looking building of two stories, distinguished by four towers at the corners. This, afterwards known as the mess-house of the 32d regiment, was named, under the native rule, Khoorsheyd Munzil, or happy Palace. Its structure is massive. All the windows on the ground-floor are furnished with strong iron gratings, and it is surrounded by a moat, passable only at the two entrances, of which the principal one immediately faces us. A garden of low trees and bushes surrounds it, which is itself enclosed by a mud-wall, separating it from the high road. Crossing the road to the nearer side, what is that extensive range of building abutting upon the river, and distinguished by a pavilion with four richly-gilded domes? This is the Motee Munzil, or Pearl Palace, and that pavilion is the Shah Munzil, or royal hall. It is the prettiest building of the kind at Lucknow, spacious and airy. Here European guests used to be invited to banquets, and to view the fights of animals on the opposite side of the stream. Close on the other side of the Motee Munzil stands a European-looking building in an extensive orange-garden. This is called Martin's house, but was the royal library in the king's time. To the right of the Khoorsheyd Munzil, and separated from it by a narrow lane, stands the Tara Kotee, or observatory, a handsome and classically-designed building, erected by the late astronomer, Colonel Wilcox. And now the eye falls upon the gilded domes, and cupolas, and archways of the Kaiser Bagh palace, which forms a picture of itself. Its numerous buildings and squares cover a very large area, and it is chiefly the creation of the present exking. Those two large mausoleums, however, belong to a former age. The larger is the tomb of Saadut Alee Khan, the most sagacious ruler that Oude has had, and the smaller one of his mother. Their substantial masonry contrasts strongly with the less modern edifices; and they are destined, unless they are destroyed by the hand of war, long to survive them. It is indeed a lovely view which is obtained from the top of the Chuttur Munzil. But the city of Lucknow is beyond doubt very beautiful, and surpasses every city in India that I have seen."*

* Gubbins' Mutinies in Oude.

We have endeavoured to make our readers conversant with Lucknow and its localities, because we may have again occasion to refer to it, in connexion with the great struggle between British power taken at a disadvantage, and Mohammedanism rising up suddenly, like a hooded snake, and committing the unwary passenger to a deadly conflict. But for the present we must leave behind us the city, with its marble palaces and gilded domes, and, in the anarchy which prevailed throughout the country districts, show how utterly its rulers, amidst their luxury and self-indulgence, were regardless of the sufferings of the people.

In our last Number we referred to the evils of the revenue and finance system, and the extortion, accompanied with ruthless barbarity, perpetrated by contractors and Amils. We were necessitated to confine ourselves to a few examples: they were incidental selections from amidst a mass. The contractors unduly burthened the talookdars; the talookdars, driven to extremity, laid waste their own estates, and, driving off the peasants, kept them unproductive until the Government officials came into their terms. The suffering entailed on the labouring classes may be conceived. So soon as harvest was finished they had to take to the jungles for shelter, until the season for sowing recommenced. Then, remaining in the fields, and houseless during the night, they worked during the day in fear of their lives, not knowing the instant they might have to flee into the jungles again. The examples of injustice and oppression set by the king's *employés* was eagerly followed by the talookdars, each one of them, as he had opportunity, preying on those who were weaker than himself. Sleeman mentions a family of Kumpurrea Rajpoots, whose sole possessions, in 1814, consisted of nine villages. By degrees they drove out or murdered all the other proprietors, until they held not less than 150 villages, for which they paid little or no revenue to the Government. The rents they employed in keeping up large bands of armed followers, and building strongholds, from whence they infested the surrounding country. As the family increased, it divided itself into several branches, each branch having a fort or stronghold in the Nye jungle, and acting independently in its depredations on its weaker neighbours, but all uniting when threatened by the Government. Yet proceedings of this kind were not considered as any stain upon the character of the depredator; nor, so long as he complied with the requisition of the Government officials, did he lose credit, influence, or good repute in the estimation of the authorities. "Men who augmented their estates in this way purchased the acquiescence of temporary local officers, either by gratuities, or promises of aid in putting down other powerful and refractory landholders, or they purchased the patronage of court favourites, who got their estates transferred to the 'Huzoor T hseel,' and their transgressions overlooked."* Thus robbery became the trade of every considerable landholder in the country, of all of them occasionally, and of a great many of them perpetually, the murder of men, women, and children generally attending their depredations. If, on the repeated remonstrances of the Residents, some especially-notorious offender was seized and sent as a prisoner to Lucknow, he soon contrived to bribe the courtiers, and orders were forthwith transmitted to the authorities on the spot that his son should be kept in possession of all the ill-gotten lands, and favoured and protected in every possible way.

In such a disorganized condition of society, where individuals were being continually dispossessed of house and home, gangs of robbers were soon formed. Ready materials were found in the Pausee bowmen, who, in the absence of any protection from Government, were paid by the towns and villages to serve as a guard. When the wages thus received did not suffice for their expenses, they thieved in the neighbouring or distant villages, robbed on the high-roads, or formed gangs of professional robbers. Officers or Sepoys, discharged, whether faulty or otherwise, from the king's service, also recruited the companies of freebooters; and so soon as a band became formidable, it found a patron in some talookdar, who wanted its aid in resisting the king's officers, or for some deed of spoliation. These lawless men spared nobody except such as were able to defend themselves. The plunder of villages, murder of travellers, and carrying away of brides and bridegrooms from marriage processions, were things of every-day occurrence. Sometimes towns were attacked, the principal inhabitants seized as hostages, and liberated only on payment of heavy ransoms. If they refused to pay, or pledge themselves to pay, the sum demanded, they were murdered. If they paid part, and pledged themselves to pay the rest within a certain time, they were released; and if they failed to fulfil their engagements, they and their families were murdered in a second attack. Sir W. Sleeman, in his journal, records numerous instances of such atro-

---

* Sleeman, vol. i. p. 243.

cities. One specimen may be given. Thakur Purshad, one of these daring freebooters, in 1836 attacked the village of Molookpore, two miles east of Dewa, plundered it, took possession of the land, seized and carried off the proprietor, and put him to death in his fort. Three years after, he attacked the house of Janoo, a shopkeeper, plundered it, and tortured him until he paid a ransom of two hundred and fifty rupees. Three months after, he seized and carried to his fort another shopkeeper, and confined and tortured him till he paid a ransom of three hundred rupees. In 1849 he seized and took off another man from Dewa, and extorted forty rupees from him. Next year he attacked a marriage procession in Dewa, plundered it, carried off the bridegroom, and confined and tortured him till he paid eleven hundred and fifteen rupees. This man, and some others of like character, "had created a jungle of nine miles long by four wide for their own evil purposes, preserving it with so much vigilance that no man dared to cut a stick, graze a bullock, or browse a camel on it, without their special sanction: indeed, so much were they dreaded, that no man or woman, beyond their own family or followers, dared to enter the jungle."

Such a state of social disorder would soon have laid waste and utterly desolated any part of India less naturally favoured. In the valley of the Nerbudda, an estate left of its cultivators, from the richness of the soil and humidity of the air is soon covered with rank grass, where deer and other animals find a covert, soon to be followed by beasts of prey—tigers, leopards, wolves, wild dogs, &c.; malaria follows, and it becomes alike dangerous and unwholesome. Thus extensive tracts of the richest soil, and most picturesque scenery along the banks of the Nerbudda have been rendered desolate for ages by the misrule of only a few years.* The same is true of the Tarae forest, which separates Oude from Nepaul. "But in the rest of Oude, from the Ganges to the belt of the forest, no such effects follow misrule, however great and prolonged." The grass does not grow too rankly, the deer are but few in number, and the beasts of prey are not attracted thither. The cultivators migrated from the locality where life and property had become insecure, but the cowherds and shepherds remained, feeding their flocks and herds over the rich and abundant pasture lands which grow rich from the respite they receive from grain production. After a time, things quieted down, the storm having drifted in some other direction, the cultivators returned, and, in two or three years, the lands became carpeted with a beautiful variety of spring and autumn crops.

Still, amidst all its fertility, the country exhibited the traces of misrule. Sir William Sleeman speaks of the beauty of various portions of it, the surface undulating and well cultivated, adorned with groves and fine solitary trees; but he adds, "Everywhere it is devoid of all architectural beauty in works of ornament or utility: not even a comfortable habitation is anywhere to be seen. The great landholders live at a distance from the road, and in forts or strongholds. These are generally surrounded by fences of living bamboos, which are carefully kept up as the best possible fence against attacks. The forts are all of mud, and, when the walls are exposed to view, they look ugly. The houses of the peasants in the villages are, for the most part, covered with mud, from which the water is carried off by tubes of wood or baked clay, about two feet long. There are parapets around the roof a foot or two high, so that it cannot be seen, and a village appears to be a mass of dead walls which have been robbed of their thatched or tiled roofs. Most of the tubes used for carrying off the water from the roofs are simply branches of the palm-tree without their leaves." In another place he adds, "No respectable dwelling-house is anywhere to be seen, and the most substantial landholders live in wretched mud-hovels with invisible covers. I asked the people why, and was told that they were always too insecure to lay out any thing in improving their dwelling-houses; and, besides, did not like to have such local ties, when they were so liable to be driven away by the Government officers, or by the landholders in arms against them, and their reckless followers. The local officers of Government, of the highest grade, occupy houses of the same wretched description, for none of them can be sure of occupying them for a year, or of ever returning to them again when once removed from their present offices, and they know that neither their successors, nor any one else, will ever purchase or pay rent for them. No mosques, mausoleums, temples, serais, colleges, courts of justice, or prisons, are to be seen in any of the towns or villages. There are a few Hindu shrines at the half-dozen places which popular legends have rendered places of pilgrimage, and a few small tanks and bridges made in olden times by public officers when they were more secure in their tenure of office than they are now. All the fine buildings raised by former rulers and

---

* Sleeman, vol. ii. p. 42.

their officers, at the old capital of Fyzabad, are going fast to ruin. The old city of Ajoodhea is a ruin, with the exception of a few buildings along the bank of the river, raised by wealthy Hindus in honour of Ram, who once lived and reigned there, and is believed by all Hindus to have been an incarnation of Vishnu."*

It may be observed here that no native gentlemen from Lucknow, save such as held office in districts, and were surrounded by troops, ventured, during the native rule, to reside in the country. They could not have done so with safety. They would have been either suspected and destroyed by the great landholders about them, or suspected and ruined by the court. There existed in Oude a class of native gentlemen which, had the Government been such as to secure tranquillity throughout the kingdom, would have been specially fitted to "build houses in distant districts, take lands, and reside in them with their families, wholly or occasionally," until Oude had been "covered with handsome gentlemen's seats, at once ornamental and useful." It consisted of those who enjoyed hereditary incomes under the guarantee of the British Government. The former monarchs of Oude, fearful of revolutions which might exclude their families from the succession, and anxious to make for them a more secure provision than 'the circumstances of their own kingdom rendered possible, were in the habit of lending large sums to the East-India Company, which, in fact, were thus vested in European securities, the interest on these sums being duly remitted to the appointed heirs. Thus, for instance, Ghazee-ood Deen Hyder lent to Lord Hastings, in October 1814, for the purposes of the Nepaul war, the sum of one crore, eight lacs, and 50,000 rupees. All the interest of this money, amounting to six lacs and fifty-one thousand, was distributed, in the manner described, amongst the members of his family, the principal being paid back as the incumbents died off.

This class of gentry might have been very useful in promoting a kindly feeling between the higher and lower classes, and between the capital and rural districts, had the circumstances of the country been such as to permit the prospect of their settling down in tolerable peace and tranquillity. But the disturbed state of things concentrated them at Lucknow, which thus became filled with an overgrown aristocracy, absorbed entirely in court pleasures and intrigues, and having no sympathy whatever with the surrounding population. In fact, this city aristocracy, instead of becoming an useful medium through which the king might communicate with the people, surrounded him with an exclusive circle which obstructed that reciprocal action which is so needful between a ruler and his subjects. Without any ennobling pursuits, they became absorbed in the dissipation of Lucknow, and wasted their means and energies on trifling or vicious pursuits. Hence the capital was in a perpetual turmoil of processions, illuminations, and festivities. On these the sovereign expended himself, without the slightest wish to "perpetuate his name by any useful or ornamental work beyond the suburbs. All the members of his family and of the city aristocracy followed his example, and spent their means in the same way. Indifferent to the feelings and opinions of the landed aristocracy and people of the country, with whom they had no sympathy, they spent all they could spare in gratifying the vitiated tastes of the overgrown metropolis."

Thus in the capital there reigned a showy sensuality, and, throughout the country districts, sanguinary broils and general insecurity. Amidst all, the peasantry—an industrious, brave, and robust people—were the great sufferers. Sir William Sleeman gives a pitiful detail of the numerous applicants who crowded to him for help and restitution. Every day, as he travelled throughout the country, scores of petitions were wont to be presented him, "with quivering lip and tearful eye, by persons who had been plundered of all they possessed, or who had their dearest relatives murdered or tortured to death, and their habitations burned to the ground, by gangs of ruffians, under landlords of high birth and pretentions, whom they had never wronged or offended;" some merely because they happened to have property, which the ruffians wished to take; others because they presumed to live on lands, which they coveted, or had deserted, and wished to have left waste. In these attacks neither age, nor sex, nor condition, were spared. The greater part of the leaders of these gangs of ruffians were Rajpoot landholders, boasting of descent from the sun or moon, or from the demi-gods who figure in the Hindu religious fictions of the Puranas. The peasantry of Oude, harassed as they were on all sides, might not inaptly be compared to the *exocetus volitans*, or flying fish, which, pursued by dorados and other fishes of prey, endeavours to escape by rising out of the water and skimming through the air, but which, so soon as it emerges from

---

* Sleeman, vol. ii. pp. 26, 27.

the water, is met by new enemies, gulls and and albatrosses, who pounce upon it from above. Their best position was when they became settled on the estate of some powerful talookdar, who having, by means however unscrupulous, acquired large properties, was enabled to set alike at defiance the Government and his unruly neighbours, and applied himself with diligence to the improvement of his spoils. Such was the family of Bukhtawar Sing, Dursun Sing, and Maun Sing, referred to in our last Number. Their estates, studded with trees, hamlets, and villages, were well cultivated and peopled. The landholders and peasants, protected from thieves and robbers, the attacks of refractory barons, and, above all, the ravages of the king's troops, pursued their occupations without being molested. As we have now guaranteed the talookdars in the possession of their estates,[*] this is so far satisfactory. We have not committed ourselves to the troubled sea of disputed titles, nor attempted to restore the old proprietors. This would have been to unsettle every thing, and involve the whole country in confusion. The policy adopted has been a wise one. The lands have been dealt with as escheated to the Crown, because of the insurrection and by virtue of conquest; they have then been restored to those whom we found in occupancy, unless the case, for special reasons, was an excepted one. We trust that the talookdars of Oude will now apply themselves honestly and industriously to the improvement of their estates : but at the same time we should have little hope for the future if they were not under the curb and rein of a strong-handed Government.

But even supposing that, under British rule, external tranquillity be secured, there are other evils, and other sorrows, which can only be reached by higher and more penetrative influences; evils which lie hid in the domestic life and relationship of the heathen, and which legislation cannot correct. Their sources lie in individual character, and divine truth, in its renewing influence, can alone change this fountain-head, and make it a source of sweet instead of bitter waters. Amongst the Rajpoot talookdars of Oude the crime of female infanticide has been fearfully prevalent. We have traced it amongst the Rajpoots on the other side of the Ganges, and wherever the same soil has spread itself, we cannot be surprised if the same noxious weed be produced. The king of Oude, in 1833, prohibited suttee and infanticide, yet, in defiance of the law, the latter continued to be practised. Nor has our own legislation, in this respect, been altogether as repressive as some have hoped. Between the Oude Rajpoots and their brethren on the southern side of the Ganges there is an understanding and complicity. They intermarry, and the female infants, born of daughters given in marriage to Oude families, have been destroyed in Oude without fear or concealment, while the daughters received in marriage from Oude families were sent over the border into Oude, when near their confinement, on the pretence of visiting their relatives. If they gave birth to boys, they brought them back with them into the British districts; but if they gave birth to girls, they were destroyed, and no questions were asked on their return home. Now that Oude has been annexed and that both sides of the Ganges have been placed under the same vigorous administration, this, with many other border irregularities, will be put an end to ; but as to the crime itself, law may diminish it, but can never eradicate it. So occult is the domestic life of the Hindu, that if the father be disposed to take the life of his babe, the facilities for the perpetration of secret murder are innumerable. The domestic life of the Hindu is a dense and gloomy forest, where many an evil deed is committed, and the wail of human anguish, so far as human help is concerned, is uttered in vain, for there are none to hear who feel—none except God, who will not fail to help in

---

[*] The following is the sunnud which bestows their estates in perpetuity :—

"Know all men, that whereas by the proclamation of March 1858, by his Excellency the Right Honourable the Viceroy and Governor-General of India, all proprietary rights in the soil of Oude, with a few special exceptions, were confiscated, and passed to the British Government, which became free to dispose of them as it pleased, I, Charles John Wingfield, Chief Commissioner of Oude, under the authority of his Excellency the Governor-General of India in Council, do hereby confer on you the full proprietary right, title, and possession of the estate or estates of   , consisting of the villages as per list attached to the kuboolyut you have executed, of which the present Government revenue is   . Therefore, this sunnud is given you, in order that it may be known to all whom it may concern that the above estate has been conferred upon you and your heirs for ever, subject to the payment of such annual revenue as may from time to time be imposed, and to the conditions of surrendering all arms, destroying all forts, preventing and reporting crime, rendering any service you may be called upon to perform, and of showing constant good faith, loyalty, zeal, and attachment to the British Government, according to the provisions of the engagement which you have executed ; the breach of any one of which at any time shall be held to annul the right and title now conferred on you and your heirs. It is also a condition of this grant that you will, so far as is in your power, promote the agricultural prosperity of your estate, and that all holding under you shall be secured in the possession of all the subordinate rights they formerly enjoyed. As long as the above obligations are observed by you and your heirs in good faith, so long will the British Government maintain you and your heirs as proprietors of the abovementioned estate or estates, in confirmation of which I herewith attach my seal and signature."

his own time and way. When shall the daylight penetrate those dark recesses, and put such deeds to shame?

The motives to the crime are the same as among the Rajpoots in other parts of India—family pride of the most insufferable character, and the expenses connected with marriage ceremonies.

In the Byswara district there is a class of Rajpoots, the Byses, from whence the district has its name, sometimes called Talookchundee Byses, from Talookchund, the founder of the family in Oude. From his two sons descended two families, Nybassas and Synbunzies—families ever at war with each other, except when resistance to the authorities rendered union necessary. They have a singular notion among them, that no snake has ever destroyed one of the family. They never condescend to hold the plough. The females of the family, if they cannot afford to wear silk or satin, never wear cotton cloth of any colour, but plain white, the one piece of white cotton cloth forming the waistband, petticoat, and mantle or robe (the dhootee and loongree), without any hemming or needlework whatever. On the ankles they wear nothing but silver, and, above the ankles, nothing but gold; and if not gold, nothing, not even silver, except on the feet and ankles. These people "take the daughters of other Rajpoots, who are a shade lower in caste, in marriage for their sons, but do not give their daughters in marriage to them in return. This is the case with the Ditchit Rajpoots, who live just beyond their boundaries. They give their daughters in marriage to the Bys Rajpoots, but cannot get any of their's in return. Both families practice infanticide, especially the Byses. The crime brings its punishment even in time." Old Bukhtawar Sing informed Sir William Sleeman, that "scarcely any of the heads of these landed aristocracy were the legitimate sons of their predecessors: they were all adopted, or born of women of inferior grade. They unite themselves to women of inferior castes for want of daughters in families of their own rank, and there is hardly a family among these proud Rajpoots unstained by such connexions."

Hence arose another crime. Great numbers of girls were purchased or stolen from the British territories, brought into Oude, and sold to Rajpoot families as wives for their sons. The assurance was invariably given by the kidnapper that they were of the same or higher caste, the parents being constrained to part with them from poverty, but the reverse was usually the truth. The great expenses consequent on marrying their sons to a high-caste female is another reason why the purchase of wives brought from a distance was resorted to. A singular instance of this occurred in the case of the Rewa Rajah: a family of Rajpoots, the Bhudarees, a shade lower in caste, gave one hundred thousand rupees with one daughter to his only son, as the only condition on which he would take her; and another high Rajpoot of Oude, Rajah Hunmunt Sing, of Dharoopore, by caste a Beseyn Rajpoot, with difficulty accomplished a union between his daughter and the same son, on the payment of one hundred thousand rupees. But it costs the Rewa Rajah still more to dispose of any daughter he may have on hands to some member of a higher-caste family, not less than ten or twelve lacs of rupees having been given by him to induce the Rajah of Oudepore, Joudpore, or Jypore, to take away, as a bride, a daughter of Rewa. This, as well as the prevalence of infanticide, induced the stealing of young girls from other districts.

It is remarkable that the Rajpoot family, in which a deed of infanticide has been perpetrated—the usual mode of which is burying alive as soon after birth as possible—considers itself to be, in consequence, an object of divine displeasure. On the twelfth day, therefore, the family priest is sent for, and, by suitable gratuities, absolution is obtained. The mulct varies in cost according to the means of the family. A rich man has to give food to many Brahmins to get rid of the stain; but, for a poor man, a little food, presented in due form to the village priest, suffices. Caste customs constitute, indeed, a burdensome ritual. To give their daughters to wealthy people of a lower clan is to lose caste for ever by so doing; while to give them to those who are above them entails such an expense as to reduce, in many instances, the father to beggary. Those who have property must give all they have with their daughters, while they can take nothing in return, as it is a great stain to take such from any one. They solve the difficulty by infanticide, the crime increasing in intensity according to the restrictions on marriage with which the family is burdened.

Sometimes natural affection is stronger than the tyranny of caste. A Rajpoot landholder of the Sombunzie tribe had a daughter born to him "when he was out in the fields, and the females of the family put her in an earthen pot, and buried her in the floor of an apartment where the mother lay, lighting a fire over the grave. Meanwhile a messenger reached him with the news of his wife's confinement, which was sooner than he had expected. He had given no directions that the child should be put to death; but concluding such would be done unless he interposed, and feeling a wish to save the child, he hurried home, removed the fire and earth from the pot, and took her out. She was still living, but two of her fingers, which had not been sufficiently covered, were a good deal burnt. That child was reared. The mothers are said to weep and scream a good deal when their first female infants are torn from them, but become quiet and reconciled to the usage, and say, "Do as you like." "The infant is destroyed in the room where it is born, and then buried. The floor is then plastered over with cow-dung, and on the thirteenth day the village or family priest must cook and eat his food in that room. He is provided with wood, ghee, barley, rice, and tillee (sesamum). He boils the rice, barley, and sesamum in a brass vessel, throws ghee over them when they are dressed, and eats the whole. This is considered as a *hom*, or burnt-offering, and, by eating it in that place, the priest is supposed to take the whole *hutteea*, or sin, upon himself, and to cleanse the family from it." "After the expiation the parents again occupy the room, and there receive the visits of their family and friends, and gossip as usual."

It is said that the crime prevails among the Rajpoots only, and that other classes, Hindus as well as Mohammedans, are averse to it. "But the Rajpoots are the dominant class in Oude; and they can disregard the feelings and opinions of the people around them with impunity." The answer of a Brahmin to Sir William Sleeman, when he asked him, "Do you ever eat or drink with Rajpoot parents who destroy their female infants?" was, if he spoke truth, vigorous and decided—"Never! We are Brahmins; yet we can take water in a brass vessel from the hands of a Rajpoot, and we do so when the family is unstained by this crime; but nothing would ever tempt us to drink water from the hands of one who permitted his daughters to be murdered." They also declared their abhorrence of the village priest, who gave absolution to the parents, with whom nothing would induce any one of them to eat or to associate. They considered him to have taken all the sin upon his own head, and to have become, in consequence, an outcast from the tribe, and accursed. "Tigers and wolves," exclaimed the Brahmin speaker, "cherish their offspring, and are better than these Rajpoots, who, out of family or clan pride, destroy their's. As soon as their wives give birth to sons, they fire off guns, give largely in charity, make offerings to shrines, and rejoice in all manner of ways; but when they give birth to poor girls, they bury them alive without pity, and a dead silence prevails in their houses."

Such, then, was Oude before the annexation; the detached points, which we have put together from various authorities, sufficing to show the anarchy and suffering which prevailed. The time at length arrived when the British authorities determined on decisive action. Lord Hardinge, in his personal interview with the king in 1847, had urged upon him the necessity of a speedy reformation of manifold abuses, and a probationary period of two years was assigned, in which the much-called-for improvements might be made. They passed away; but the King amidst his favourites, and the minister amidst his peculations, were alike insensible to the necessities of the country. Meanwhile the talookdars were increasing in strength. Each refractory baron, who by fraud or violence had amassed an estate, provided himself forthwith with one or two mud-forts, and, as indispensable to his security, turned the country around him into a jungle. Each fort was surrounded by a ditch and a dense fence of living bamboos, through which cannon-shot could not penetrate, and men could not enter except by narrow and intricate pathways. These fences were too green to be set on fire, and so completely under the range of matchlocks from the fort, that they could not be cut down by a besieging force. Eighteen miles north-east from Lucknow one of these jungles had sprung up, occupying sixty-four square miles on the bank of the little river Reyt, in which several of these hereditary robbers had their forts. Thirty-four miles to the north-west stood a similar fastness, occupying thirty-six square miles; another on the east, forty miles' distant, a tract of sixty-four square miles. In this manner they were spread over the face of the country, the entire aggregate covering a space of not less than 886 square miles, beyond the Terae forest, and within the fine climate of Oude. In these jungles the landholders found shooting, fishing, and security for themselves and families, grazing-ground for their horses and cattle, and fuel and grass for their followers; "and to such an extent had this element of armed independence established itself, that in the year 1849 there were in Oude 246 forts or strongholds, mounted with 476 pieces of canon, all held by landholders of the first class, chiefly Rajpoots."

At the end of the year 1851, Oude, its existing

state and future prospects, were to have been brought under the special consideration of the home authorities; but the war with Burmah unexpectedly broke out, and, occupied with the prosecution of this, it was impossible for the Government of India to address itself to so large a question as the remodelling of the administration of Oude. At length, in June 1855, a minute of the Governor-General indicated that the time was come, and that the authorities were prepared to take action on this long-deferred difficulty, Sir James Outram at that time officiating as Resident at the court of Lucknow. He had unhesitatingly expressed his conviction that it was no longer possible to uphold the sovereign power of an effete and incapable dynasty at the cost of five millions of people, for whom the British Government was under obligation to secure a beneficent administration.

In his minute, Lord Dalhousie expressed his indisposition to the extreme measure of requiring from the King the abdication of his royal power, and his consent to the incorporation of Oude with the British territories. "In their adherence to the British power, no wavering friendship has ever been laid to their charge. They have long acknowledged our power; have submitted, without a murmur, to our supremacy; and have aided us, as best they could, in the hour of our utmost need. Wherefore, although we are bound to dissolve our connexion with a Government whose oppression is sustained only by the countenance we lend it; and although we are entitled to seek, by all means in our power, to amend the lot of a people whom we have so long indirectly injured; justice and gratitude nevertheless require that, in so doing, we should lower the dignity and authority of the sovereigns of Oude no further than is absolutely necessary for the accomplishment of our righteous ends.

"The reform of the administration of the province may be wrought, and the prosperity of the people may be secured, without resorting to so extreme a measure as the annexation of the territory, and the abolition of the throne.

"I, for my part, therefore, do not advise that the province of Oude should be declared to be British territory."*

Experience had shown the impracticability of attempting to govern Oude through native officers under British superintendence, and Lord Dalhousie, rejecting a renewal of the vain attempt to govern by a divided authority, proposed that the sovereign, retaining the rank and title of King, should be required to vest "the exclusive administration of the civil and military government of Oude and its dependencies in the hands of the Company, with such ample powers as shall enable the Company to act with vigour and promptitude in every branch and department of the state."

In recommending this course his lordship followed the opinions and suggestions of Sir William Sleeman—.

"If our Government interpose, it must not be by negotiation and treaty, but authoritatively on the ground of existing treaties and obligations to the people of Oude. The treaty of 1837 gives our Government ample authority to take the whole administration on ourselves, in order to secure what we have often pledged ourselves to secure to the people; but if we do this we must, in order to stand well with the rest of India, honestly and distinctly disclaim all interested motives, and appropriate the whole of the revenues for the benefit of the people and royal family of Oude. If we do this, all India will think us right, for the sufferings of the people of Oude, under the present system, have been long notorious throughout India; and so have our repeated pledges to relieve the people from these sufferings, unless the system should be altered. Fifty years of sad experience have shown to us and to all India that this system is incapable of improvement under the present dynasty; and that the only alternative is for the paramount power to take the administration upon itself. . . .

"We should derive substantial benefit from the measure, without in any degree violating our declaration of disinterestedness. . . .

"Oude would be covered with a network of fine macadamized roads, over which the produce of Oude and our own districts would pass freely, to the benefit of the people of both; and we should soon have the river Ghagra, from near Patna on the Ganges, to Fyzabad in Oude, navigable for steamers; with a railroad from Fyzabad through Lucknow to Cawnpore, to the great benefit of the North-West Provinces and those of Bengal.

"Were we to take advantage of the occasion to annex or confiscate Oude, or any part of it, our good name in India would inevitably suffer. . . . We are now looked up to throughout India as the only impartial arbitrators that the people generally have ever had. . . . We must show ourselves to be highminded, and above taking advantage of its prostrate weakness, by appropriating its revenues exclusively to the benefit of the people and royal family of Oude. We should soon

---

* Blue Book on Oude, p. 184.

make it the finest garden in India, with the people happy, prosperous, and attached to our rule and character."

From this proposed solution of the affairs of Oude two members of the Council differed in judgment from the Governor-General, preferring that the King should be compelled to abdicate.

The Court of Directors abstaining in its reply from affirming in preference either of these propositions, it was eventually resolved that the king of Oude should be invited to enter into a new treaty with the Company. This treaty consisted of seven articles. The first embodied its main intention, namely that

"It is hereby stipulated and agreed, that the sole and exclusive administration of the civil and military government of the territories of Oude shall be henceforth vested, for ever, in the Honourable East-India Company, together with the full and exclusive right to the revenues thereof; the said Company hereby engaging to make ample provision for the maintenance of the royal dignity, as hereinafter mentioned, and for the due improvement of the said territories."

Of the remaining six articles there were five which secured to the King and his legitimate successors the royal title and other privileges and immunities. These were calculated to induce him, from personal considerations, quietly to sign the treaty. In this case a proclamation was to be issued, announcing that, with the King's consent, the sole and exclusive administration of the Government of Oude, together with the full and exclusive right to the revenues thereof, were henceforth vested for ever in the Honourable East-India Company. But should the King, after a period of three days permitted him for deliberation, refuse to sign the treaty, then the necessity for it, as a preliminary condition to the assumption of authority by the East-India Company, was to be dispensed with, and, without the King's consent, the following proclamation was to be issued announcing the transfer of administration.

"Proclamation is hereby made that the government of the territories of Oude is henceforth vested, exclusively and for ever, in the Honourable East-India Company.

"All Amils, Nazims, Chuckledars, and other servants of the Durbar; all officers, civil and military; the soldiers of the state; and all the inhabitants of Oude, are required to render, henceforth, implicit and exclusive obedience to the officers of the British Government.

"If any officer of the Durbar—Jageerdar, Zemindar, or other person—shall refuse to render such obedience; if he shall withhold the payment of revenue, or shall otherwise dispute or defy the authority of the British Government, he shall be declared a rebel, his person shall be seized, and his jageers or lands shall be confiscated to the state.

"To those who shall, immediately and quietly, submit themselves to the authority of the British Government—whether Amils or public officers, Jageerdars, Zemindars, or other inhabitants of Oude—full assurance is hereby given of protection, consideration, and favour.

"The revenue of the districts shall be determined on a fair and settled basis.

"The gradual improvement of the Oude territories shall be steadily pursued.

"Justice shall be measured out with an equal hand.

"Protection shall be given to life and property; and every man shall enjoy, henceforth, his just rights, without fear of molestation."

It will be observed that the course adopted by the British authorities was at variance with that recommended by Sir William Sleeman in this important particular, that the revenues of the country were not appropriated *exclusively* to the benefit of the people and Royal family of Oude. The whole proceeding must be regarded as an act of annexation, the name and shadow of royalty being permitted to remain.

The following documents, now matters of historical record, and deposited amongst the archives of our country, detail the circumstances of those memorable interviews with the King and his minister, in which the Resident announced the final and irrevocable determination of the British Government.

The first of these papers refers to the interview of the Resident with the prime minister of Oude, Alee Nukkee Khan Bahadoor, Jan. 30, 1856.

"On the arrival of the Resident at the suburbs of Lucknow, he was met by the Prime Minister, who was present to pay his respects, according to established usage. During a brief conversation, the Resident requested the Minister to accompany him to the Residency, in order to converse on matters of public importance. . . . .

"The Resident then proceeded to acquaint the Minister that the time had at length arrived when the British Government felt necessitated to adopt a policy towards the Government of Oude, which could no longer be averted. This policy had been dictated by the Honourable the Court of Directors, and had received the sanction of Her Majesty's Ministers. The king could not be ignorant that, soon after the Resident's arrival at Lucknow, he was called upon to report on the state of the administration, and the general condition of Oude. After patient and searching inquiry, it was the Resident's painful duty to confirm, in all particulars, the deplorable and distressing details which his predecessor, Colonel Sleeman, had been obliged to submit to Government, of the anarchy and misrule existing in Oude. The Governor-General had likewise deemed it imperative to forward that report, with his lordship's sentiments, for the consideration and instructions of the Home Government, and, within the last few weeks, the orders had reached India, and would now be carried into effect.

"The Resident then, in general terms, informed the Minister of the contemplated changes, and of the explicit instructions with which he had been honoured by his lordship; and mentioned that, in order to prevent the chance of a disturbance on the part of evil-disposed persons, a strong brigade of troops was directed to cross the Ganges, and march on the capital.

"The Minister appeared much surprised and distressed at this intelligence, and declared that the presence of any British troops was altogether unnecessary; that his Majesty was in the hands of the Resident, who had simply to express his wishes to ensure their fulfilment.

"The Resident assured the Minister that his Majesty might implicitly rely on the favour and consideration of the British Government, which would guarantee that nothing should be done which could in any degree detract from the King's rank, position, or personal comforts, or in any way diminish his Majesty's dignity or honour....

"The minister then attempted to contrast the reign of the present King with those of his predecessors, and to point out the manifest reforms which were to be seen on all sides; but the Resident replied that it was now useless to discuss that, or any other question, and that he was compelled by the tenor of his instructions to offer his Majesty either of the alternatives to which the Resident had already alluded.

"The Minister again declared that the march of the troops was entirely unnecessary, and begged that their presence might be dispensed with.

"The Resident declared that the advance of the troops was indispensable, and suggested that some confidential servant of the King should be deputed to meet the force, in order to arrange with the commanding officer for compensation for whatever damage to the fields the encampment of the troops might have occasioned. ...

"As it was late in the afternoon, the Resident requested the Minister to be good enough to call at the Residency on the following morning, in order that he might peruse, in detail, the various documents which would be laid before the King, and thus have an opportunity of fully and fairly imparting to the king the object of the interview which the Resident would be obliged to seek with his Majesty in a few days. This would enable the Minister to give the fullest information on all points to the King, and prevent the possibility of his Majesty being kept in ignorance of the wishes and policy of the British Government, or of stating that the King had not received timely and adequate intimation of the determination of the Government, and of the changes which the Resident was charged to carry into execution."*

The second paper contains the notes of a conference with the Queen-mother.

"On the 1st of February 1856, at the request of the Jenab Aulea Begum, mother of his Majesty, the Resident, Major-General Outram, paid her a visit, at the Zurd Kothee Palace, at 4 P.M., when a conversation passed between the Resident and the Queen, of which the following is a summary.

"After the usual compliments, the Queen, who appeared deeply moved, entreated the Resident to inform her what his Majesty had done, and why he had incurred the wrath of the British Government, and implored the Resident to intercede for the King, and to avert the destruction of the King's authority, by the adoption of any measures which might afford his Majesty the opportunity of showing how anxious he was to administer the government of his country in a manner satisfactory to the British power, and advantageous to his Majesty's subjects. The Resident, in reply, deeply regretted that he was wholly incapable of opening the question, or of acting in any way save by the tenor of his instructions: he had, that very day, in reply to a communication of his Majesty, stated, in terms the most unequivocal and explicit, that the resolution taken by the Government was irrevocable and final; that it was based on the orders of the Court of Directors, supported by the unanimous decision and approval of Her Majesty's Ministers, one of whom was the future Governor-General of India: moreover, that the present Governor-General of India had been directed to carry out the policy alluded to, prior to his departure from India; consequently his Lordship was unable

---

* Blue Book, pp. 279, 280.

to alter in any one tittle the orders received from the Home Government.

"The Queen implored the Resident to reflect on the utter ruin to the King; that he would be degraded in the eyes of the world, and be deprived of every thing which he had been accustomed to and brought up to; but the Resident assured the Queen that the British Government had been pleased to declare that his Majesty should be dealt with in the most liberal and honourable manner; that nothing should in any way detract from his Majesty's rank, honours, dignities, or high position; that he should have placed at his Majesty's disposal, solely for the King's personal expenses, 1,00,000 rupees per mensem, which sum would be guaranteed to his Majesty's heirs for ever and ever; moreover, that 3,00,000 rupees per annum would be assigned for his Majesty's guards, of whom he might retain as many as he pleased; that his Majesty's relatives of the blood-royal would be amply provided for, and those of his Majesty's principal and confidential servants would have no reason to regret the contemplated changes; that the Resident felt perfectly assured that, in a very short time, his Majesty, relieved of the care, anxieties, and responsibilities of the Government, would gratefully thank the British Government for relieving him of so responsible and harassing an anxiety; and would, surrounded by all that could afford comfort and happiness, and fully provided with all that could maintain himself and family in affluence, rank, and distinction, gladly acknowledge that the British Government had been his benefactor. .... The Resident was well aware that his Majesty was personally incapable of afflicting any of his subjects; but, as the King had devolved his duties and responsibilities on worthless and undeserving favourites and ministers, it was obvious that the British Government had no alternative but to look to his Majesty, and to hold him responsible for the enormous evils which had impoverished the country, and necessitated the policy which was now imperatively commanded, and about to be carried into effect.

"The Queen begged that a further period might be allowed, during which the King might be enabled to show to the world, by the adoption of vigorous reforms, how anxious and eager he was to obey and follow out the instructions and advice which the British Government might point out. The Resident again declared that it was useless to argue the matter: he had no authority whatever to act in any way but according to his commands; and he therefore must decline to enter on that subject. The Queen reiterated her entreaties that the impending measures might be delayed, and protested against their adoption; but the Resident assured the Queen that it was impossible the measure could be deferred; and that, by procrastination, or refusal to accept the treaty, the King would needlessly jeopardize the liberal maintenance now offered to him: in that case, it followed that the King could have no security for title or stipend, and would have to be content with whatever might be granted for his support by Government. The Resident was empowered to lessen the grant which had been determined on by the Government, should his Majesty not have the good sense to sign the treaty, and to cause his subjects to afford that aid and co-operation to the new administration which it was confidently hoped his Majesty would never hesitate to afford: on the other hand, the Government was prepared to treat his Majesty with all possible courtesy, liberality, and munificence, should his Majesty sign the treaty, and realize the expectations of the British Government.

"If the Queen-mother really felt interested in the welfare and prosperity of his Majesty, her son, she would not fail to urge, with all that good sense and intelligence for which she was so remarkable, the evil consequences which most assuredly would blight his Majesty's prospects, by the adoption of any measures which would be displeasing to the Government, but which could not avert the change of the policy about to be carried out. After some further conversation, and protestations on the part of the Queen-mother, the interview terminated, and the Resident took his leave, with all the usual honours and ceremonies."

The third paper contains the notes of an interview between the King and the Resident at the Zurd Kothee palace, on the morning of Feb. 4, 1856.

"General Outram, accompanied by Captains Hayes and Weston, proceeded, at 8 A.M., to visit his Majesty, by appointment. The approaches to, and the precincts of, the palace were unusually deserted; the detachments of artillery on duty at the palace, together with the detachments of his Majesty's foot-guards, were unarmed, and saluted without arms; the artillery was dismounted, and not a weapon was to be seen amongst the courtiers and officials present to receive the Resident on his entering the palace. The Resident was received at the usual spot, by his Majesty in person, with the customary honours.

"During the conference, in addition to the

Prime Minister, his Majesty's brother, Sekunder Hashmat, the Residency Vakeel Mushee-ood-Dowlah, his Deputy Sahib-ood-Dowlah, and the Minister of Finance, Rajah Balkishen, were present.

"The Resident, after assuring his Majesty, that, from kindly consideration to his feelings, he had been induced to forward, through the Minister, a copy of the most noble the Governor-General's letter, two days ago, to afford the King ample time to peruse and reflect on the contents of his lordship's letter, now felt it his duty, in pursuance of his instructions, to deliver to his Majesty in person, the Governor-General's letter, in the original. His Majesty, after attentively perusing the letter, observed that he had already been made acquainted with its purport and contents, not only by the Minister, but by the copy of the letter which the Resident had been good enough to transmit, and for which the King expressed his obligation. After a brief pause, his Majesty turned towards the Resident, and said, 'Why have I deserved this? What have I committed?'

"The Resident replied, that the reasons which had led to the new policy were explicitly, clearly, and abundantly detailed in his lordship's letter to his Majesty, and that he was unable to discuss the subject, or to deviate in any way from the tenor of the instructions with which he had been honoured; but the Resident had little doubt that, on mature reflection, the King would readily acquiesce in the proposals made by the British Government. His Majesty should consider how amply and liberally the Government had provided for his Majesty's maintenance. The King's titles, honours, rank, and dignity would be scrupulously preserved and transmitted to his Majesty's descendants, in the male line, in perpetuity. His Majesty's authority would be absolute in his palace and household, always excepting the power of life and death, over the King's servants and subjects thereunto appertaining. His Majesty's relatives and confidential servants would likewise be adequately provided for; and the Resident had every reason to hope that his Majesty's good sense would induce him to meet the wishes of Government. The Resident was bound, by the solemn discharge of his duties, to announce to his Majesty that the treaty of 1801 no longer existed. The systematic oppression and misrule which had existed in Oude ever since its ratification—the violation of all the solemn obligations which the rulers of Oude had faithfully bound themselves to perform, as one of the high contracting parties to that treaty—had necessarily caused its infraction, and rendered it imperative on the British Government to adopt a policy which should secure the lives and property of his Majesty's suffering subjects. That policy had been commanded by the Honourable the Court of Directors; it had been sanctioned and approved of by Her Majesty's Ministers unanimously; and the Most Noble the Governor-General of India had been directed to carry into effect the measures alluded to prior to his lordship's departure from India. Under these circumstances, the Resident was persuaded that his Majesty would readily acknowledge that the British Government had no authority whatever but to give effect to the commands of the Home Government, and, with this view, had directed that a treaty should be prepared for submission to his Majesty, which, embracing every suitable, adequate, and ample provision for his Majesty's maintenance, and omitting nothing which could in any degree redound to the King's honour, titles, and dignity, transferred the administration of the Government of Oude into the hands of the East-India Company. . . .

"His Majesty received the treaty with the deepest emotion, and handed it to Sahib-ood-Dowlah, with directions that it should be read out aloud; but that confidential servant of the King, overcome by his feelings, was unable to read but a few lines; on which the King took the treaty from his hands, and carefully perused each article.

"His Majesty then gave vent to his feelings in a passionate burst of grief, and exclaimed—

"'Treaties are necessary between equals only: who am I now, that the British Government should enter into treaties with? For a hundred years this dynasty has flourished in Oude. It has ever received the favour, the support, and protection of the British Government. It had ever attempted faithfully and fully to perform its duties to the British Government. The kingdom is a creation of the British, who are able to make and to unmake, to promote and to degrade. It has merely to issue its commands to ensure their fulfilment: not the slightest attempt will be made to oppose the views and wishes of the British Government: myself and subjects are its servants.' . . . .

"His Majesty then again spoke of the inutility of a treaty: he was in no position to sign one. It was useless: his honour and country were gone. He would not trouble Government for any maintenance, but would proceed to England, and throw himself at the foot of the throne to entreat a reconsideration of the orders, and to intercede for mercy. The Resident begged his Majesty to reflect that, unless the King signed the treaty, he would have no security whatever for his future maintenance, or for that of his family; that the very liberal provision devised by the British Government would inevitably be reconsidered, and reduced; that his Majesty would have no guarantee for his future provision, and would have no claim whatever on the generosity of the Government. The Resident's instructions were concise, clear, and definitive; the resolution of the Government irrevocable and final; and the Resident entreated the King to consider what evil consequences might alight upon his Majesty and family by the adoption of any ill-judged line of conduct. The Prime Minister warmly seconded and supported the Resident's advice, and protested that he had done every thing in his power to induce his Majesty to accede to the wishes of the British Government. Hereupon his Majesty's brother exclaimed that there was no occasion for a treaty. His Majesty was no longer independent, and in a position to be one of the contracting powers. His office was gone, and the British Government was all-powerful. His Majesty, who was moved to tears, recapitulated the favours which his ancestors had received at the hands of the British Government, and pathetically dwelt upon his helpless position. Uncovering himself, he placed his turban in the hands of the Resident, declaring that, now his titles, rank, and position were all gone, it was not for him to sign a treaty, or to enter into any negotiation. He was in the hands of the British Government, which had seated his Majesty's grandfather on the throne, and could, at its pleasure, consign him to obscurity.

"He touched on the forlorn fate which awaited his heirs and family, and declared his unalterable resolution to seek in Europe for that redress which it was vain to find in India.

."The Resident felt himself unable to act in any other way than by the tenor of his instructions, and assured his Majesty that, at the expiration of three days, unless his Majesty acceded to the wishes of the British Government, the Resident would have no alternative but to assume the government of the country.

"After some further conversation, and the expression of the unalterable reluctance of the King to sign the treaty then and there, the Resident intimated that no further delay than the three days could be permitted, and then, with the usual ceremonies and honours, took his leave of the King."

The only proclamations, which his Majesty could be induced to issue are the following—

"To all Amils, Talookdars, Malgoozars, Zemindars, Military Officers, Thannadars, Kanoongoes, Chowdries, and to all his Majesty's subjects—

"Be it known, that, according to the orders of the British Government, the servants of that Government have been appointed for the administration of the kingdom of Oude, and will assume the Government; therefore, take heed to obey all orders which may be issued, and to pay the revenue to them, and to become faithful subjects to them : on no account resort to resistance or rebellion. The army ought, on no pretence, to revolt or mutiny, because the servants of the British Government have the power to punish.

"No date of the month, but simply, Jemad-ul-awal, 1272."

"To all the officers of the army—

"Be it known, that you ought to remain at your post and on your duties in readiness as usual, and on no account are you to commit any violence or lawless act, and on no pretence allow of any unsoldier-like conduct.

"The balance of your pay, after the deductions made for advances received, will be paid to you by the East-India Company (Sirkar Kampani).

"Let no man leave his post ; and pay particular attention to these orders."*

All efforts to induce the King to sign the treaty proved ineffectual, and, carrying out his resolution of proceeding immediately to Calcutta, accompanied by the Queen-mother, his brother, and other relatives, for the purpose of laying his case before the Governor-General in Council, and, in the event of this proving unsuccessful, of sailing for England to prosecute his claim before the home authorities, in less than a fortnight's time, Wajid Allee Khan took his departure from Lucknow.

* Blue Book on Oude, pp. 279, 280; 284—286; 287—289.

DISMISSAL OF MISSIONARIES TO THEIR SPHERES OF LABOUR.

At a general Committee of the Church Missionary Society, held at the Society's House on Monday March 12, 1860, Admiral Sir H. Hope, K.C.B., Vice-President, in the chair, the Committee took leave of three Missionaries, two of them returning to the Mission fields where they had already laboured, and one of them going forth for the first time. The Missionaries were the Rev. J. Bilderbeck, returning to Madras, where he has laboured with zeal and perseverance for many years; the ordained African, J. C. Taylor, to the banks of the Niger, where, in his fatherland among the Iboes, he has been instrumental in laying, at Onitsha, the foundations of a new Mission; and the Rev. R. H. Weakley, designated to Constantinople to strengthen the hands of Dr. Pfander. On that occasion the following instructions were delivered by the Honorary Clerical Secretary.

DEARLY BELOVED IN THE LORD—

You are going to widely different spheres of labour: your circumstances will be as various as it is possible to conceive. Your modes of operation must be distinct. Yet you go forth on one work—guided by one spirit—having each one and the same aim in view—to win perishing souls, whether in Asia, Africa, or Europe, to the Lord Jesus Christ.

To you, Brother Bilderbeck, the Committee have no specific instructions to address. You will, upon your return to Madras, re-enter upon your former work; and the Committee have only to pray that you may be enabled to carry it forward in the same wise, persevering, prayerful, and faithful spirit as before. The Committee have earnestly desired to make up the full complement of the Madras Mission, by appointing four Missionaries to that station. But through the failure of the health of several labourers, they have been hitherto defeated in their design. They fully acknowledge the importance of possessing a strong and complete Mission at the Presidency; and they will do all in their power to secure that object. You will carry back with you many new and encouraging associations. Your visits as a Deputation to different parts of the country have secured for you and your work many praying friends and much sympathy; and the Committee trust that the fruit may abound to the glory of God, upon your re-entrance into your work.

The Committee are thankful, Brother Taylor, that God has permitted them to see you face to face, and to confer with you on many important points connected with the Niger Mission. Your visit to England will, they trust, prove a great benefit in this respect to the Mission. They pray God that it may also prove a great spiritual benefit to your own soul: that when you return to your countrymen, your sympathy with them may be as entire as before: and that they may perceive in you nothing but deeper humility, as the fruit of enlarged intercourse with the church of Christ; and a more lively and patient compassion for the spiritual thraldom of Africa, upon the comparison which you will draw between this Christian country and your own dark land. Let all European habits, European tastes, European ideas, be left behind you. Let no other change be visible in your tone of mind or behaviour than that of a growth in grace and in the knowledge and love of God.

The good providence of God has provided you with the inestimable advantage of such an able, wise, and Christian philological guide as Mr. Schön. By his help your translation of St. Matthew's Gospel has been carried through the press, and you take out 500 copies as a noble gift to your tribe. You also carry out the Book of Common Prayer in Ibo, together with tracts and other translations, which will be the foundation of a native literature. The Mission will be furnished with a printing press, and the Committee trust that a taste for reading will rapidly spring up, as it has done in Abbeokuta.

You will be joined in Sierra Leone by the European catechists whom the Committee have set apart for the Niger Mission; and probably others besides Mr. Coomber, the native schoolmaster, will also join you: so that the Committee trust that you will return to Onitsha a goodly company of Evangelists, to build up a spiritual temple upon the foundations already laid on the banks of the Niger.

But here the Committee are checked in their full satisfaction by some apprehension lest your numbers, and the union of Europeans and natives, should possibly give occasion to misunderstandings and jealousies. Such is our wretched human nature, that even the Lord's servants too often suffer wrath, and evil-speaking, and backbiting, and contention to arise amongst them, and to mar the work of God. These are the poisonous serpents which lurk in the dwelling. These are the white ants that destroy the spiritual building. These are the works of Satan, by which he strives to counteract the light of the glorious Gospel, lest it should shine into the hearts of men. To you, and to all the other members of the Niger Mission, the Committee affectionately, but most earnestly, say, "Let brotherly love continue." As you stamp out the burning spark which falls upon your dry thatches, so put out as vigorously the sparks that are "set on fire by hell." They are soonest quenched by kneeling together at the throne of grace, and each one imploring the Lord's forgiveness of his debt of ten thousand talents. Open your hearts to a Saviour's love, and the expulsive power of the new affection will clear them of the works of the flesh.

And not only must you live in love: you must *keep up united action* in the spirit of love and mutual forbearance. You will act in Committee on all matters in which the business of the Mission is concerned, and in these respects all of you must be subject one to another. Let all your Committee meetings be sanctified by the word of God and prayer. Avoid all attempt to carry a point by voting. Seek the middle course, in which all may concur. If a spirit of contention and disputation arises in such meetings, turn them into prayer-meetings. United action in a holy, loving spirit of mutual confidence and self-sacrifice is the glory of a Mission, and gives it a strength which will overcome all obstacles. Here, therefore, Satan will ever direct his assaults—to sow discord among brethren, and so divide and conquer.

Onitsha will be your station; and it is to be regarded as the basis of the Ibo Mission. Strive to make it strong before you take up out-stations. Let all unite to raise up a body of converts in Onitsha, and to form them into a native church, able to read for themselves the word of God, to supply native teachers, and to consult with you upon future extension. Such an established body of Christians at Onitsha will be of inestimable value for future extension. Be not too hasty, therefore, to comply with the invitations which distant towns may send you for a white man or native teacher to dwell with them. If they are urgent, propose to them to send a few young men to reside for a time at Onitsha, to learn to read, and to be instructed in the new religion; who may afterwards return to their native town, and carry back a few elementary truths, which may suffice to keep up an interest in Christianity till the Onitsha Mission is strong enough to occupy out-stations with effect. This course was pursued in New Zealand, and it was one means of spreading the knowledge of Christian truth far beyond the range of Missionary tours.

Strive above all things to awaken amongst the new converts a spirit of self-reliance and activity in spreading the Christian knowledge amongst their countrymen. In matters of personal holiness, and love, and zeal for Christ, the Evangelist is to place himself before his people. As it is written, "Be thou an example of the believers in word, in conversation, in charity, in spirit, in faith, in purity." But in other matters—such as the management of affairs, the serving of tables, the exercise of discipline, the building of places of worship and schools, the extension of the Mission—avoid putting yourself before the people as a leader: rather stand behind them as a prompter and counsellor. Prompting to self-action is more important than inducing men to follow a leader. It is possible that by this course of action a teacher may think that he will be lowered in general estimation; that bold spirits may take the lead. But things will soon rectify themselves. The forward spirits must soon fall back upon the mature wisdom and powerful aid of the teacher. His influence will be greater than ever. He will be the real spring of action. Whereas, if the teacher attempt to take the lead in all things, the whole Mission will hang upon his responsibility. The forward and bold spirits will foment jealousies against him, and thus the spirit of self-extension and self-government is checked and stinted, and the Mission becomes stationary as soon as the teacher's hands are full of employment.

The Niger Mission will be furnished, by means independent of the Society, with the opportunity of introducing industrial employments amongst the natives, especially the cleaning and pressing of cotton. But let this department be kept in subordination to the spiritual work of the Mission. Let it be so conducted as to make it of the widest benefit to the people. The object of such industrial establishments is only to teach the people to work for themselves, and to secure employment for converts who may be thrown out of their usual occupations by embracing Christianity. The success at which they aim is to be superseded by the general introduction of industrial habits: then their connexion with the Mission may be cast off.

One further instruction the Committee desire to impress upon you. Act as you have hitherto done in showing great respect to native authority. The system of native government may appear in many things very defective; but it holds society together, and gives you protection. Show that Christianity enjoins submission and obedience and respect to rulers, as a cardinal duty.

And now the Committee commend the Niger Mission to God and to the word of his grace. It is a great experiment. It is essentially a Native Mission. The Committee believe that they have been led step by step in its formation. They have confidence in its stability, because they have confidence that it will be carried on in a spirit of prayer and faith. Take as your motto the noble saying of an old Red-Indian chief—" Our Mission is strong—Prayer is the stability of a Mission."

You, Brother Weakley, were introduced to the Society with a view to the Mission among the Turks. A zealous friend of that nation had first directed your attention to that field of labour, and awakened your sympathy in it, as one too long neglected by the Christian church, and holding out peculiar promise at the present time. You have already had a brief specimen of the kind of work to which you are called, by your visit to the Turkish sailors at Plymouth, and by witnessing the labours of Messrs. Bennett and Williams. In order that you may be the more fully equipped for your Mission, the Committee have directed you to reside for a few months in France or Geneva, to study the French language, as all the educated Turks prefer that language for their first inquiries.

While you have been thus preparing at home for the work for the two past years, a preparation of the most encouraging kind has been going on abroad, especially in Constantinople. This preparation may be noticed in three particulars.

1. There is evidence of an increasing spirit of inquiry abroad among the Turks. The reports of the American Missionaries furnish many instances. A body, comprising probably several hundred, have withdrawn their faith from the Koran, and are making inquiry respecting the truth of the Gospel. This is just one of those providential helps to an advancing Gospel which is often found in Missionary histories. Several Turks have also visited Dr. Pfander who were acquainted with his works in Persian, and had evidently studied them. These instances are indeed few, and for the most part isolated, but they are streaks of the dawn.

2. There is evidence that the effect of the Hatti Hamayoun is real, though at present very partial. There is testimony from many quarters that the prison-bars are unloosed, though few go abroad. Remarks are now made in the *Cafés*, and in common intercourse, which startle the ears of the old Missionaries, and show that "thought" is set at liberty.

3. The commencement of a Mission has been most wisely and auspiciously effected by Dr. Pfander. A room has been engaged in the midst of the population, where two native agents reside. There they sell their books and invite visitors. The Missionary occasionally attends. Already Dr. Pfander's admirable works addressed to Mohammedans are in a course of translation from Persian into Turkish. One of these is finished, the second has received its first revision. The utmost caution is required in order to obtain permission for their being printed in Constantinople, which would be a great step gained; but if this is refused, they can be lithographed elsewhere, and may soon become available for the use of the Missionaries.

These substantial encouragements strengthen the faith of the Committee in now sending you forth on your Mission; and they trust that your own faith, and prayers, and expectations will be enlarged thereby; and that you will go forward with the calm self-possession and firm perseverance of one who knows assuredly that the Lord has called him to the work.

On two specific points the Committee give you their directions.

You will find on the field of Constantinople and its neighbourhood a noble band of American Missionaries, whose labours there, as well as throughout all Western Asia, have been greatly owned and blessed of God. While this Society only paid occasional visits to Constantinople, and maintained a feeble Mission in Smyrna, and published Missionary researches, the American Society threw into that field a large force of men, erected printing presses, organized churches, and may fairly claim the credit of having opened the country to Christian Missions. To them, therefore, let the first place of honour be given. Avoid scrupulously any appearance of interference with their work. Let no root of rivalry and envy spring up amongst the subordinate agents of the Mission. Check any approach to questions or comparisons of ecclesiastical systems. Let it be your highest honour to follow them, as they have followed Christ. All questions of church organization are utterly out of place in the present state of our Mission in Turkey. Let nothing at present appear but points of agreement. The Committee hope that you will be assisted by the son of the native minister whom the American Missionaries employ. You will desire him to behave with reverential affection towards his honoured father. Set an example in your own conduct towards your American brethren of the same deferential affection towards those whom Christ has called into the field before ourselves.

The second special instruction which the Committee address to you is to submit yourself, in all Mission questions, to the judgment of Dr. Pfander. The Committee are fully aware of the critical nature of Missionary operations in Turkey. They thank God that our Mission has been formed by a man of ripe and solid judgment and of large experience. You, as a junior and inexperienced Missionary, will find it your highest privilege to labour with him as a son with a father. Dr. Pfander is to be regarded as the head and the Secretary of the Mission. In laying upon you this injunction, the Committee rejoice to know that it entirely coincides with your own wish and predetermination.

The Missionaries having respectively and in a deeply feeling and earnest manner acknowledged the instructions which they had received, they were addressed affectionately and impressively by the Rev. W. Cadman, the Epistle to the Philippians being taken as the basis of his observations, and the more salient features of it, as presented seriatim in the different chapters, being brought home with great felicity of application to the circumstances of Missionary labourers, their responsibilities, and supports, their trials and encouragements. They were then in prayer commended to the favour and protection of Almighty God by the Rev. D. Wilson.

CUSTOMS OF THE HINDUS AND MUSSULMANS OF INDIA.

A SERIES of papers bearing upon this subject have been placed in our hands. They have been drawn up by an officer many years resident in India. Frequently, in reading publications having reference to India—the papers of statesmen, books of travels, the journals of Missionaries—the reader meets with terms having reference to native rites, civil and religious, with which the writer is perfectly familiar, but which, to persons who have never visited Hindustan, convey no definite ideas. The fact is, our acquaintance, generally speaking, with the actual condition of the Hindu population is but superficial. We are scarcely aware of the complex nature of that idolatrous ritual with which they are tied and bound, of the manner in which it has interwoven itself with the details of domestic life, and the heavy exactions of time and attention which it requires from those who are ensnared in its meshes. Nor are we aware how well fitted these ceremonies are to quicken into action the depraved tendencies of the human heart, and facilitate their indulgence. The native mind is shut up in a gloomy prison. Were we convinced, how piteously enslaved it is, we should labour more strenuously for its emancipation. We shall be happy if the perusal if these papers induces more commiseration for the people of India, and prompts to more effort for their emancipation.

" I will endeavour to give a brief account of the customs observed by the Hindu population, both in their religious ceremonies and at the births, deaths, or marriages of their relatives. I will describe from the actual scenes which I saw myself, or from what I heard corroborated by the testimony of numbers of natives. The opportunity of being present at any of the remarkable sights or processions I never neglected. I have not trusted to the accounts given me, nor have I read any English author on the subject. The greatest number of the travellers who have, as it were, glanced at those details in their hasty progress through the country, and written their comments upon the sport or the society which they have found there, have not treated upon the manners, customs, religions, or language of the inhabitants of this large portion of the globe, who number about 120 millions. The late dreadful disturbances which for a season arrested the inquiries of those who were anxious to become more acquainted with the details of the modes of life which characterize the inhabitants of India, now that they have passed away, will probably make individuals more anxious to ascertain with precision the moral and social condition of a people who could be guilty of such great atrocities; and as they have been in times past, such, in great measure, shall we find them now; for so unchanging and so invariably superstitious is their general tenor of conduct, that the description of the habits and ceremonies which, in their worship, their families, and their daily intercourse used to obtain years and centuries ago, is still prevalent amongst them. When we reflect upon this, and also upon the

BURNING THE DEAD IN NORTH INDIA.

difficulty which exists of finding means or men to carry the tidings of Gospel truth amongst such immense multitudes, it would appear desirable to extend as much as possible the information likely to throw light upon the actual condition of these people. With regard to the habits of the Mussulmans, there are books which are written, and which give information with reference to the zenana, or modes of life which exist amongst the female population of the Mussulmans of India, and their secluded state, and the habit of immuring them in their dwelling-places, where they can neither communicate with any one, nor obtain any information from any who are not servants or slaves, or from their lord and master, who treats them as slaves. These exhibit the lamentable fact that they can neither read or write, or have any education whatever, and that their general ignorance is deplorable. There are also books written, treating of the Mussulman male population, but giving accounts which are mere translations from native descriptions, and which are too much interlarded with native jargon to be interesting. There are some of the descriptions of the modes of ejecting evil spirits practised by the ingenious and enlightened doctors of Islam, which I think would defy the patience of the keenest inquirer into native customs.

"Most of the customs practised by the Hindus will be found detailed in the 'Asiatic Researches,' but I am not aware that they have been explained and laid before the public systematically. I shall begin with the customs which are observed as religious rites, and put into practice by the higher classes, viz. the two castes called Brahmins and Chatrees invariably, and by such as value their character, and respect the degree of estimation in which they are held by their brethren of the other castes. Without mentioning here the great festivals which engage the attention of all classes universally, whether as festivals of joy or as commemorative of some gloomy event, we may first advert to the regular observances practised at fixed periods of the month.

"It is considered imperatively necessary on the last day of every month, or the first of the ensuing month, for all the male population to go to the Ganges, Jumna, or any river which is deemed holy, and bathe; and generally the higher classes—the Brahmins and Chatrees—stain the body, and breast, and forehead with sandal wood after having left the water. This is sometimes red, sometimes yellow, and there are also other colours. It appears that the order of things is frequently reversed in this country; for whereas a civilized person would suppose that painting the face and body was a rite indicative of debased intellect and prostrate superstition, and one likely to be practised by the most ignorant and degraded wretches, here he would be brought to the knowledge of the fact that those who perform it are the most respected amongst the general community. After this they go to the toolsee plant (that plant which naturalists call *ozymum sanctum*) and cover it with Ganges water. They sometimes throw flowers into the Ganges, and sometimes those who can afford it throw milk. The toolsee is used by every Brahmin, who gives the vessel containing the Ganges water to any person whom he wishes to take an oath. When the plant is in the water, and the person swearing holds the vessel in his hand, it is considered a most solemn manner of taking an oath; and the natives who go through these observances constantly affirm, that, after death, the reward of adhering to them will be great, and their state of life happy.

"On the fourth of every month a very great number of the inhabitants fast inviolably during the whole of the day, and at night, when the moon comes out, they break their fast. This is called the *chath*.

"The 11th of this month is called the *ekadshee*, and on this occasion the most religious will fast during the whole of the day and night; but some fast during the day, and at night eat sweetmeats. Many send invitations on this day to the Brahmins, and feast them sumptuously, but they themselves refrain all the time from touching a morsel. During the feast one of the Brahmins, takes a *pothee*, or book containing extracts from Shasters which treat of the customs of the *ekadshee*, and reads to all the party assembled, both when they are at meat and also during the rest of the day. The next day is called the *dooadshee*, and this day is the occasion for all the worshippers of Brahma to give the Brahmins what is called a *seedha*, which means a present of any kind of grain or provisions undressed. The quantity requisite to form this present must be a sufficiency for one man's consumption during the day, and also they put upon it half an anna, and then it is given to the Brahmin, or priest of their religion. It is considered also right, that, at the change of the moon, viz. when the light fortnight, as it is called, commences, which goes by the name of *amawus*, or 'the dark fortnight,' which is called *punnoor*, begins, that on that day every true Hindu should bathe in the river. This usually occurs about the middle of the month.

"On every Saturday, called by them *su*-

neechur, of which there are four in the month, there are a sort of Brahmins called *canogees,* or the class nominated *doobys,* who go about from house to house, and it is considered necessary to propitiate them by giving them presents of grain, cord, and oil, together with the usual accompaniment in such cases, viz. some pice. Those who give in this way believe that the star of that particular day is most unpropitious and unfavourable, deem it expedient to propitiate their evil destiny, and suppose that calamity to them, or to their family, may be averted by this act of giving presents to the wandering Brahmin. On Wednesdays, those who are the richest, make a great day of rejoicing. This festival day, which they call *boodh,* is considered a wrong day to begin any business upon, but proper for making merry. They carry their belief so far as to say that any thing commenced upon Wednesday will never be perfectly accomplished..

" They consider Friday as the most fortunate day for commencing any business, and think that their fate is likely to be favourable to them if they begin any work on that propitious day. But the day of the month which they look upon as the most propitious for the commencement of any business, is the 10th. These customs of the Hindus with regard to dates and days of the week obtain more or less amongst all parties according to the different degrees of superstition which prevail. In no part of the world are such superstitions stronger or more widely diffused, nor have they been shaken by our long intercourse with them.

" The year commences with the month called Bysakh, answering to our April. I have ascertained that the first custom which takes place during the year is called by the Hindus the *Beas Pooja.* The exact date for its observance is usually about the middle of July; but as it depends upon the change of the moon, its observance is decided by the directions of the Hindu astronomers, who fix upon the fifth day from the commencement of the light fortnight of the month: the time of its celebration is different in different years.

"Very early on the morning of this day the Hindus go to bathe in the river. The Ganges is always held the most sacred of all streams, and therefore the best adapted for the purpose; but when the distance from their abode is too far from it, the worshippers must take some river, tank, or stream, which is nearer them; and such as are pious give alms to poor Brahmins, and make a basket filled with mangoes and fruit called jamun, and sweetmeats, and present it to their family priest, or their gooroo, as he is called in the country. They make their obeisance to him by touching his forehead with tolee, the name of a species of red earth, which is common to the country, and sandal-wood. And after the gooroo has washed his feet, they fill a brass vessel with water, and make him put his feet in it. They then drink some of this water thus consecrated, and the rest they sprinkle on their faces. Of such a slavish nature is the debased and prostrate superstition of this land. The votaries of idolatry drink the *churna-mittur,* or the water which a Brahmin has put his foot into. The Brahmin then puts the *tiluk,* or mark, composed of a sort of paint, mixed with clay, on the centre of the forehead of each worshipper; and they are then bound by religion to give him, in return, presents according to their means.

" There are, throughout Hindustan, a species of pious men called *Bhuguts,* who bind themselves to abstain from fish, meat of any kind, all intoxicating drugs, and every sort of spirituous liquor. They are known by wearing a necklace of wooden beads, which, from its coming in front of the windpipe, is called *khunthee,* and the Brahmins, on this day of the Beas Pooja, invest the persons who are to assume this order with the necklace, and give the necessary injunctions.

" The origin of this ceremony is believed to be, that many thousand years ago, on the anniversary of this day, there was a great sinner, who had committed numberless atrocities and murders, but in a repentant mood he went to bathe in the Ganges; that he became very sick, and could not stir; that one of the holiest of the order of Brahmins came to him after he had left the water, and told him to say the name of God twice; that he did so, and became perfectly well.

"The next ceremony which is observed by the Hindus takes place about the 17th of our month of July, corresponding to the 8th day of their month Jawun. It is the anniversary of the birth of Krishna, the Indian Apollo, whose praise is the theme of so much of the Hindu poetry. He is very highly esteemed and especially worshipped by the women, and his birthday is kept all throughout Hindustan. On this occasion the men decorate thir *muths,* or idol houses, with jewels, carpets, and whatever ornaments they can procure, and they dress up their *thakoors,* or idols of brass, in fine clothes, and' put jewels upon them. And some men go thither at the rising of the sun, and sit near the temple, singing their *bujins,* as they call the songs, and neither eat nor drink from the rising of the sun till the middle of the next night. There is no provision made for the relief of the hungry worshipper; but if extreme or annoying thirst should come on, then he may drink the water of the Ganges, or, as they call it, the Gunga, but nothing else. In the middle of the ensuing night they get a large cucumber or pumpkin, and open it, so that they may enclose a small idol inside it. When they have put this small idol into it. and having left it there for about half an hour, they take it out again, and commence a great uproar with blowing shells, beating drums, sounding cymbals, and, by other means, evince their worship by making a clamour. After the idol has been taken out of the pumpkin they may break their fast.

"The reason which they assign, both for the fast and for the different ceremonies is, that the mother of Krishna, Jussodu, at the time of his birth, suffered extremely, and they fast in remembrance of this. And they think, also, that the deities, at the time of the birth of this divinity, made a great clamour of applause when it occurred; whence the hubbub which is kept up during the whole of the day. On the morning of this day, and on its evening, one may see in every direction groups of Hindu girls in dresses of all sorts of colours—yellow, red, crimson, blue, and white—singing, at the very highest pitch of their voices, songs in praise of Krishna. Those even of the highest rank, in point of birth, go out very early in the morning to bathe, and come back singing the praise of Krishna; and, as it is the general custom of women of rank to conceal themselves, these women do not allow any one to see their faces, and wrap themselves, head and all, carefully under a scarf.

"In this month also takes place the custom which is called the *goorea teohar*. The first thing which they are called upon by their creed to do is to eat rice-milk. After this they dress themselves in their best clothes, and assemble on a plain near their respective villages, and the wrestlers, called by the Hindus *Pahulwans*—similar to the athletæ of the Greeks—begin to exhibit the feats which are acquired in their art. This is done, not for any money, or reward, but merely as a trial of strength. All those who wish to become wrestlers learn the active exercises—the *dur palna*, which is a sort of exercise in which a person continues moving his body up and down in a horizontal position, with his face to the ground, and the *mooydur hilana*, which is a way of moving the heavy club so as to acquire strength in the loins. The tailors in the villages make dolls of cotton, and the boys of the villages beat them to pieces with sticks. These dolls are called *goorcas*, and the day, the *goorea teohar*, or the day of the dolls.

"The reason which the old men of the country assign for this is, that the devil, with an army of little creatures, invaded the country of the king of gods this day, and that the army of the gods defeated them; and they who chiefly practice this rite being the lowest of the people, conceive that they should, in commemoration of this event, make one idol resembling a man, and beat it to pieces, as, by doing so, they commemorate the defeat of the host of devils.

"On the next morning the Hindus purchase eight annas' worth of rice and milk, and, going to the river Ganges, make their proper worship of it, which, being finished, they throw the rice and milk into the water. I have seen many of the oldest amongst them with the dolls in their hands, which they either destroyed themselves, or gave them to the boys to tear to pieces. Had I not seen such things I would hardly have believed that their credulity could have been carried to such an excess.

"Towards the end of this month—the Lacoun of the Hindus, being our July—there is another holiday which is called the *raki teohar*. The Hindus commence the observance of it in the morning by eating rice-milk. However, previously to doing so, they are bound by their religion to bathe in the Ganges—an operation which, happily, being both salubrious and cleanly, is generally enjoined in their forms of devotion. When they have finished eating the rice-milk, they call upon their gooroo, or family priest, and the priest puts on their arm, tied above the elbow, the *raki*, or string. This is a sort of amulet or charm, which they consider as powerful to avert calamity, and they carry their superstition so far as to bind a ring of the same kind round the foreleg of their horses. When it is bound round a horse they give it the name of a *gunda*, or 'circle,' and it is considered efficacious in preventing any of the diseases to which a horse may be subject. When the Brahmin binds the string round the man's arm he reads some extract from the Vedas. The *raki* is composed of silk, or of a thread called *hoolee*. After it is bound on, the Hindu gives the priest some money, and the regulation of the day is, that every Brahmin he may meet binds a new string to the *raki*, and, in return, receives a new gratuity. The Hindus do not usually wear them longer than a few days.

"They believe the origin of this custom to be, that, a long time ago, in the *Treeta joog*, or, second division of the Hindu chronology, there was a king called Bul, who was in the habit of giving away every morning, to the poor of the Hindu persuasion, a hundred pound weight of gold. One morning a *jogee*, or beggar, came to see him, and the king gave him an entertainment of rice-milk, which, in those primitive days, was considered a great delicacy. The beggar was pleased with his repast, and said to the king, 'I am a man whose prayers are listened to, and I can cause you to get whatever you wish for.' Then the king said that there was an epidemic which raged in his dominions every year, at a peculiar season. The beggar then tore some hair from his temples, and, making it into a band, tied it round the arm of the king, and said, 'You must keep this round your arm for a month, and all the people in your kingdom who wear these kind of bracelets, having had them tied on by Brahmins—the Brahmin, at the time of tying them, reading the *Shasters*—will be free from the plague. They must be made of silk and red thread.'

"The next Hindu custom, taking them in the order that they happen during the year, takes place in the month of August, or the Hindu month Badun, on the sixth day after the change from light to darkness in the moon. On this day, called the *Shunka choth*, all the Shunka Hindus practise a rigid fast. They then take out of their houses an image of Ganesa, or the god of gain, which every householder in Hindustan preserves with the greatest care, and they place it in the cleanest part of the house. They get necklaces of flowers, and flowers in parcels, and these, with some ready money, they place as an offering before the image. When the appearance of the moon gives them intimation that the time for breaking the fast has arrived, all the family go and prepare a mess of a small grain called *zill* and sugar. They then proceed to look at the moon, and do so in a solemn way, as one of worship; and after having gazed on it sufficiently, they return to the house to eat the mess.

"This holiday is kept in commemoration of Mahadev—another name for the destroying spirit or devil—and of Ganesa. The story is, that Mahadev left his wife, Purwuttee, on the anniversary of this day, and promised to return in a very short time. The faithful spouse, seeing that she had no protector, placed an image of Ganesa at her door, telling him to admit no person inside the house. He observed the injunction most strictly; so much so, that when Mahadev himself came back, and attempted to enter his own house, the god Ganesa forbade him. Mahadev at this, like Apollo, in his wrath, attacked the guardian deity, and cut off his head. Having done so, he went in, and his wife, on seeing him, asked him how he had obtained entrance. He then told her of his act. Purwuttee was extremely sorry, and swore that she would eat nothing till Ganesa was made whole. She observed a fast from the morning until the moon appeared at night: then Mahadev got an elephant's head and put it on Ganesa: thus all the images of that god throughout the country have an elephant's head.

"The *tej* is the ceremony which is observed by the Hindu women on the third lunar day from the beginning of the light fortnight of the month of August. In the evening they make an image of Mahadev, which they call a *moorut*. They then send for a very learned pundit and he brings a book containing an account of Mahadev in Sanskrit. The women put in a basket some *soorma*, which is the antimony used by the women in India for staining their eyelids of a black colour, a comb, and a looking-glass: these are all symbolical of marriage, and are presented to the pundit.

"They believe, that on the anniversary of this day Mahadev was married to Purwuttee, and the day is therefore much thought of by the Hindu women. The death of a husband is known to be the greatest calamity to a wife. Although, in the districts under the British rule, she is not permitted to be burnt upon the funeral pile of her husband, still her life from that time commences to be one of dependence and, indeed, of infamy. She is taken into the house of her husband's brother, or into that of his nearest male relative, and she is treated as a slave, both by him and by his wives. She is not allowed to wear her ornaments. Thus the commonest mode of salutation to a Hindu woman is, 'May the ornaments of your husband's pride, the nuth and the bracelet, be always in safety!' and, 'May the turban of your husband be never unbound!' This last refers to the husband's never taking off or unbinding his turban in his waking hours. But speaking figuratively of his death, it is said, 'His turban is unbound.' At his death, the turban and the rest of his clothes are left at his couch. In the tombs of the great kings and chiefs who have ruled in Hindustan, one invariably sees the sword and the turban of each laid at the head, and the mute and simple pathos of this mode of appealing to his memory is more touching than the most studied devices and elaborate epitaphs.

(*To be continued.*)

ENGLISH POLICY ON THE COAST OF CHINA.

New complications have arisen on the Chinese coast, and our relations with that singular people are again disturbed. In the opinion of many it is strange that it should be so. We had just achieved a great triumph. The forts at the entrance of the Peiho, which the Chinese had so laboriously strengthened, having succeeded in erecting earthworks, sand-bag batteries, &c., for a distance of nearly a mile in length, were carried with a dash by the united British and French squadron, and at "the temple of Oceanic influences" in the plain near Tientsin, Lord Elgin had constrained the Chinese Commissioners to the signature of a treaty, the provisions of which were in the highest degree distasteful to every Chinese functionary, from the Emperor down to the lowest mandarin in the suite of Kweiliang and Hwashana. The treaty secured to the English special advantages, and the congratulations of the home country were loudly expressed at the important stipulations secured at so slight a cost. But that treaty in its integrity the Chinese had no intention of keeping. It had been wrung from them by force; and, taken at a disadvantage, they had signed it to get rid of a present difficulty. As to conscientious scruples they had none; nor in refusing to give it practical force did they consider that they acted with greater injustice than the English, who, at the point of the sword, had compelled them to it. Their only object was to gain time, and so soon as the Western ships had withdrawn themselves, they began to reconstruct, on more scientific principles, the forts at Takoo, and, out of the ruins of a recent reverse, to learn those lessons which, on a future occasion, might enable them to a more successful resistance. And so it must continue to be so long as we pursue our present unhappy system of flogging the Chinese into good behaviour. We shall find John Chinaman like an intractable schoolboy. He will wince under the rod; irritated for the moment, attempt to defend himself, and, means by which he may evade the obligations which we compel him to contract, and, as a people whom he dislikes and whose incidental visits are as disagreeable to him as those of the piratical Danes to the former inhabitants of the British isles, keep us at the greatest possible distance. Meanwhile these corrections, which we, in our high character of a great and civilized nation, think it our duty to administer to the erring Chinese, are to us rather of a costly character. We have been, and still continue to be, subjected to a vast military outlay. The great rebellion of India, and its cost of forty millions; the home preparations against a coming struggle, which all are anxious to avoid, and which, nevertheless, all fear may supervene; these have necessitated increased taxation and a great expenditure. And now to these is to be added the expense of a new expedition to China, one which, for the moment, will be irresistible, and to which the Chinese will not fail to yield with all the impressibility of water, but, like water, so soon as the stroke is removed, only to become precisely what they were before. In truth, China is like the ocean, not only in the vastness of its population, but in the facility with which it yields to the momentum of an effort sufficiently strong to overcome its negative resistance, and the rapidity with which it relapses into its usual state of sluggishness, and that in total forgetfulness of recent and painful experiences. So long as we persevere in our present system we go to write characters upon the water.

In fact, we have got into a wrong position on the coast of China. We may succeed in opening China to free intercourse with other nations, but we are closing the national mind against ourselves. We may force her into closer amity with Russia than she desires, and to which she would never resign herself but with the view of avoiding a greater evil; but to the Chinese, as a people, we are rendering ourselves increasingly distasteful, and the

barked with us in our decisive course of action. Why should he do so? We are breaking open the gates for him. We shall have the obloquy, and, as he expects, that will leave him a monoply of the benefit.

The truth is, and let it be told—let the nation know it—there is no object to be gained by disguising it—of all the foreigners on the coast of China, the English are disliked the most; and yet, had we pursued a different course, one more congenial with our professed principles as the great Protestant nation of our earth, we might have gained the goodwill of the Chinese, and obtained an influence over them which would have distanced all competition.

Does any one smile incredulously? Assuredly the persuasive influence of a just and honourable intercourse has never been tried by us, and we cannot, therefore, predicate of it that it would have been a failure. Our whole course upon the coast of China has been one of injustice and of unsound policy, in which, for the sake of a present gain, we have sacrificed our future prospects, prejudicing against us a vast multitude of people, and, so far as their sympathies and goodwill are concerned, closing against ourselves a boundless field of operation, which will eventually prove to be one of the finest openings for philanthropic efforts and commercial intercourse which the world has ever known. Of nations, as well as of individuals, is it true, that whatsoever each soweth, that shall he also reap. On the coast of Africa, England has sown good seed, but on the coast of China she has sown evil seed, and her harvest on either continent must be accordingly. Already, at the mouth of the Peiho, the first reverse has been sustained, and the first rebuke administered.

How have we distinguished ourselves upon the coast of China? We are the great opium-producers, the great poison-vendors of the East. It is not merely a matter of private speculation—a few private individuals, who, lost to all sense of honour, have sacrificed their own character, and the character of their country, for the sake of gain: it is in our national capacity we have acted. We have raised a large revenue on the opium, and that, not by placing a heavy export duty on the sale of a drug, whose liability to be abused renders the increase of it beyond the limited quantity needful for medical purposes prejudicial to the interests of humanity, but by becoming ourselves, in our governmental capacity, opium-farmers. The ryots who grow it are the *employés* of our Government; to this, as the great factor, they bring the harvest which they gather in; and other agents, skilled in the manufacture of it, prepare and flavour it so as to adapt it to the purpose of vicious indulgence. The Hon. James Wilson, in his financial speech before the legislative council of India (February 18th, 1860), candidly admits, "It is the only instance I remember at the moment of one country having succeeded in raising a large revenue from the subjects of another." The truth is here fairly put forward. Our opium revenue, at present amounting to five millions a year, is raised from the subjects of the Chinese crown; and what is it we vend to them? China exports to England articles which are promotive of the health, comfort, and convenience of European life. Her teas promote amongst us temperate habits, and a large portion of our population preferring this, distaste stimulating fluids; but we vend that to the Chinese which exercises a most dissipating influence on the physical and mental system, and destroys the *morale* of the man. We have nursed the morbid appetite, and developed it into large dimensions; we have advantaged ourselves of their weakness to vend our poison.

This heathen people, devoid of Christian truth, and destitute of any conservative principle or power which would enable them to offer effectual resistance to so dangerous a temptation, we nevertheless classify as free agents, unnecessitated, unless they choose to do so, to become the purchasers of our opium; and thus adroitly evading our just responsibility, we perpetrate the wrong, pocket the money, and then wipe our mouth and say we have done no wickedness.

How grave the responsibility, how heavy the guilt connected with the opium transactions of a long series of years! The Portuguese commenced its sale on the coast, and we followed greedily in their steps. The high authorities of China denounced it, but the local officers found the bribes of the foreign merchant more influential than the denunciations from Pekin, and the extent of the contraband trade at Canton was indicated by the floating dépôt of receiving ships at Lintin, an island between Macao and the Bogue. We have found the Cantonese of late years especially turbulent. They have been rendered so under the demoralizing influence of a contraband traffic in which our people were the tempters. Not content with the sale established at Canton, the opium-traders diligently sought out new places along the coast where they might find purchasers. In 1832 the ship "Lord Amherst" was sent out, at the desire of the factory of the then East-India Company in China, to facilitate commercial enterprise, opium constituting a leading feature of the cargo. The Rev. C. Gutzlaff was on board, and in his "Three Voyages along the Coast of China" a narrative of the voyage may be found. It is singular that the cargo and its sale are frequently referred to in the narrative, but the fact that opium was on board is carefully suppressed. Scriptures were distributed, and opium sold, as there was opportunity. In October 1832 the "Sylph," a fast-sailing vessel, well manned and armed, with opium on board, proceeded northward on a like expedition. The same Missionary was on board, and occupied himself, as he had opportunity, in distributing Christian books, while the supercargo vended the opium. They were all near being lost. Off the great wall the ship ran upon a sand-bank, and as she fell over on her beam-ends, a fierce north wind, blowing from the ice-fields of Kamtschatka, disabled all the Lascars. A sudden change in the wind saved the vessel, and, returning leisurely down the coast, at Shanghae, Chapu, Pehkwan, Namoh, and other places, a ready sale was found. To Namoh and Chinchoo small vessels continued to be despatched, until affairs became ripe for the receiving ship, and the same system of bribery, and connivance, and deceit, which had so long prevailed at Canton, was extended along the coast.

Finding themselves unable to carry out the restrictive policy, some of the Chinese ministers, in 1837, recommended to the emperor its abandonment, and the legalization of the traffic. Nai-tsi in particular, the president of the Sacrificial Court, advocated this course; but others as earnestly opposed this proposition, amongst them Chu Tsun, a cabinet minister. The removal of the restrictions he compared to breaking down the dikes which prevented the overflowing of water, because they had grown old. In particular he adverted to the great encouragement which would in consequence be given to the native growth of the poppy, and the loss of fertile lands to nutritive purposes. This policy he compared to the error of a physician, " who, when treating a mere external disease, drives it to the heart and centre of the body." The anti-legislation policy prevailed, and the efforts of the Pekin Government for the suppression of opium smuggling became, in 1838, more stringent than at any previous period. The trade, encouraged by the memorial of Nai-tsi, and the prospect of speedy legalization, had become more active, and the Canton river was in a state of ferment. Then arose the Elliot-Lin controversy, the subsequent collisions, and the war of 1841. That war is justly denominated the opium war. It was avowedly commenced, not only "to obtain indemnification for the losses the merchants had sustained under threats of violence," but to get security that persons and property trading with China should in future be protected from insult and injury. No reference is made to the contraband trade in opium, and our continued violation of international relations. There is no admission that if the Chinese had acted intemperately, they had been subjected to extreme provocation. In the demand for the future security of persons and property trading with China, there is no exception of opium and the opium smuggler. The drug and its salesmen had caused all the complication, yet both must be protected. For the past there must be reparation, for the future security, and for the attainment of such objects the war commenced.

That war was carried on with great suffering to portions of the coast which were wholly innocent of any offence against the English. The port of Canton having been blockaded, the British fleet moved northward, and, anchoring in the harbour of Tinghae, demanded the surrender of the town and island, "stating the grounds of the attack. The Chinese officers in command of the place and its defences, though confessing their inability to cope with such a force, declared they should do their best, and, during the night, placed the town and shipping in the best position for defence. They complained of the hardship of being made answerable for wrongs done at Canton, upon which the blow should properly fall, and not upon those who had never injured the English."* In the engagement which followed many of the principal Chinese officers were killed. The chumpin, or admiral, had his leg carried away by a round shot, and died a few days after. On board his junk were found five wounded men who had been unable to make their escape with their comrades. One of them, a young mandarin, who had accompanied the admiral on a visit to the "Wellesley" the day before, was writhing in agony; and seeing the operations the doctors had performed, he pointed to his shattered limbs, and, clasping his hands, implored them by signs to do something for his relief; but it was too desperate a case, and past all human remedy, so that in a few hours he breathed his last. Twice Tinghae was attacked and taken, the second time with a loss to the Chinese of 1000 men. At Chinhae a body of Chinese, in utter ignorance of military operations, allowed their flanks to be turned and fled into the sea, where hundreds were

---

* Williams' "Middle Kingdom," vol. ii. p. 52

shot down and hundreds drowned, the water being covered with dead bodies. The defences at Chapu were taken, 1500 Chinese being slain, with a loss to the invaders of thirteen killed and fifty-two wounded. "This was the first time that the Mantchus had ever come into conflict with the English, and either fearing that indiscriminate slaughter would ensue on defeat, or unable to brook their disgrace, they destroyed themselves in great numbers, first immolating their wives and children, and then cutting their own throats." The fleet now proceeded up the Yang-tze-kiang, und, on the defeat of the Chinese troops, and the capture of the city of Che-keang, the same pitiable scenes followed. "The destruction of life was frightful. Some of the Mantchus shut the doors of their houses, while, through the crevices, persons could be seen deliberately cutting the throats of their women, and destroying their children by throwing them into wells. In one house a man was shot while sawing his wife's throat as he held her over a well, into which he had already thrown his children: her wound was sewed up, and the lives of the children saved. In another house no less than fourteen dead bodies, principally women, were discovered; while such was their terror and hatred of the invaders, that every Mantchu preferred resistance, death, suicide, flight, to surrender. Out of a Mantchu population of four thousand it was estimated that not more than five hundred survived, the greater part having perished by their own hands."*

At length the war was brought to an end, Keying and Ilipu being the Chinese commissioners. During the conferences which ensued, the subject of the trade in opium was introduced. Well aware of the complications in which it had involved them, and the double injury which it was inflicting on their native land, by destroying the morals and draining the resources of the people, the Chinese Commissioners eagerly appealed to the British Plenipotentiary, praying him that the growth of opium in the British territories might be prohibited. His reply was explicit. Of any restriction being placed upon its growth in India there was no prospect. It was in China that remedial measures ought to be applied. The Chinese people needed to become virtuous, and then, as the demand ceased, the growth of the poppy would be abandoned. But surely this was a harsh and unsympathizing reply. If we had not actually engendered the morbid appetite for opium, we had availed ourselves of a pre-existing weakness, and, in order to raise a revenue, had nurtured it into gigantic dimensions. Surely it was too late to admonish the Chinese statesmen to teach their people to become virtuous, when we had helped to make them vicious, and were resolved to persist in affording them every facility for the indulgence of their vice. What element of improvement could they bring into requisition which would be so rapid and potent in its action as to overtake the injury which the opium had been aggravating throughout so many years, and produce a reaction of a healthful character? Had the British statesman been addressing himself to a nation possessed, like England, of the leaven of Christian truth, there might have been some force in the counsel which he gave: he might have urged, "You have amongst you the great conservative element, that which can strengthen man to the resistance of the most powerful temptations. Bring that into more active requisition." But he was speaking to the representatives of a heathen nation, lying powerless before us: a vast unwieldy body, without tone or vigour, unable to resist either the seductive influences with which we approached them in the time of peace, or the military force with which we overpowered them in the time of war. All that they could do was to cast themselves on our sympathy and compassion, but they found no response. The British Commissioner recommended the legalization of the traffic. The Chinese court had refused to do so; her statesmen had hitherto been unwilling to give imperial sanction to a great national vice, against the overpowering influence of which, fed and fanned as it was by Christian England, they had earnestly yet vainly struggled. Nor did England only refuse her sympathy as to the future, but required indemnity for the past; and the opium which Lin had destroyed was compensated for by a payment of six millions of dollars. "How much nobler would that Government have stood in the eyes of mankind in that war, if its head and ministers had instructed their Plenipotentiary, that when their other demands were all paid and conceded, no indemnity should have been asked for smuggled opium entirely destroyed by those who had, it may be illegally, but with honest intention, seized it?"*

The new arrangements professed to give the Chinese authorities free action to prevent all smuggling transactions. Article 12 of the supplementary treaty of October 8, 1843, imposed on each British Consul the duty of apprising the Chinese authorities of any

---

* Williams' "Middle Kingdom," vol. ii. p. 562.

* Williams' "Middle Kingdom," vol. ii. p. 571.

smuggling transactions which had come to his knowledge, while they were free to take immediate action, and might proceed to seize and confiscate all smuggled goods of whatever value or nature. But this authorization was merely nominal. The Chinese authorities were mocked by a permission to deal with an impracticbility. They were free to do that which it was well known they could not do. The opium receiving ships were all powerfully armed, and set at defiance the native authorities. The British Government permitted the smugglers to adopt this course, and in doing so evaded its most solemn engagements.

This treaty of 1843 did not heal the breach between the nations, or lay the foundation of a good understanding for the time to come. It not only left all the pre-existing causes of irritation unremoved, and ready to break out again on the first opportunity, but it introduced the seeds of new complications. The 6th article of the supplementary treaty provided for the residence of British subjects and their families at the cities and towns of Canton, Fuh-chau, Amoy, Ningpo, and Shanghae, without molestation or restraint. This right, at the ports of Amoy, Ningpo, and Shanghae, was conceded without difficulty; at Fuh-chau and Canton it was resisted. After a time the unwillingness of the people of Fuh-chau was so far overcome, that a Missionary of the Church Missionary Society, the late Rev. W. Welton, who had won good opinions by his readiness to use his medical knowledge in the alleviation of Chinese misery, especially that portion of it which originated in the use of opium, obtained permission for himself and his colleagues to live within the city; but the people of Canton remained immoveably obstructive on this point. Assuredly they knew far more of Europeans than the people of Fuh-chau, and the experience of former years was not such as to conciliate their goodwill. As a people, they had become fearfully demoralized by the contraband traffic. It had taught them lawlessness and disregard of authority: they had become an opium-tainted people, and ready for the perpetration of any crime. They distrusted and disliked the foreigner, and, except so far as commercial transactions were concerned, wished to keep him at the greatest possible distance. China had hitherto wrapped herself in a rigid exclusiveness, and her Government, absurdly assuming a position of superiority to which it had no claim, offended other nations by its superciliousness. All felt how desirable it was that China, in her state-craft, should become more affable and courteous. The only question was, how this might best be accomplished. One is reminded of the old fable of the traveller and his cloak, and which should prove most successful, the gentle or the violent course of action in effecting its removal. We have not had patience to wait the result of persuasive action. Our arm is strong, and it seemed the shortest way to force the door open. We have not yet succeeded, and the question is, whether our national procedure on the coast is not engendering an anti-English feeling, which will prove a more serious difficulty to beneficial intercourse with the Chinese people than the exclusiveness of their Government.

Canton, according to treaty, was to have been opened after April 6th, 1849, but, as the period approached, the unwillingness of the Chinese officials became more apparent. They asserted that this concession, so far from being advantageous to British merchants, would be, in reality, injurious, and that the Chinese Commissioners who had permitted its introduction into the treaty would have disembarrassed themselves of it if they could, but were obliged to yield to the force of circumstances. Governor Bonham, in a letter to Lord Palmerston, dated July 20, 1848, frankly stated the difficulties which presented themselves— the Cantonese were turbulent, and opposed to the entrance of the Europeans: the Chinese authorities were unable to coerce them. If, therefore, the treaty-right was to be insisted upon, a military demonstration on the part of the English would be necessary. In other words, if we wished to enter in, the door must be forced open. It was admitted by Govenor Bonham, that the right to enter the city was a matter of comparative unimportance. In a letter addressed by him to Lord Palmerston, under date of December 29, 1848, we find the following frank acknowledgment of this—

"It is my belief that no material advantage to our commerce would be gained by British subjects being admitted indiscriminately into Canton; at all events, none commensurate with the danger to be risked of involving the British Government in hostile discussion with that of China, for I am satisfied that, with the present temper and feeling of the populace in regard to this change, not one month would pass without some gross act of insult or violence being committed against any British subjects who might avail themselves of the privilege; such, in all probability, ending in bloodshed, and rendering it necessary for us to take steps which would certainly tend very much to embarrass our position.

"I have endeavoured, as far as possible, to make myself acquainted with the views of some of the principal of the mercantile community on this important point, and I have come to the conclusion, that although they are quite alive to the inconvenience, politically speaking, that may possibly arise from our foregoing claims to a right which has been the subject of much negotiation, it is, notwithstanding, their impression that their particular interests, and those of commerce generally, would suffer less by allowing the question to remain in abeyance, than by enforcing what we demand by an appeal to arms."*

Yet, while its unimportance was admitted, it was thought by many on the coast that it ought to be insisted upon, otherwise fresh complications would arise; and a morbid sensitiveness of this kind so exaggerated the difficulty, that, rather than forego our claim, Governor Bonham suggested the desirableness of proceeding to Pekin to submit the matter to the consideration of the emperor; or, if this were found impracticable, from want of water in the river, to blockade the mouth of the Peiho, or the fort of Tientsin, or the great canal at Chekeang on the Yang-tze-kiang. Lord Palmerston's answer to these propositions deserves to be placed on record—

"I am clearly of opinion that it would not be advisable to proceed to hostile measures against Canton, or to take the unusual step of a mission to Pekin, in regard to a privilege which, like the admission of British subjects into the city of Canton, we have, indeed, a right to demand, but which we could scarcely enjoy with security or advantage, if we were to succeed in enforcing it by arms. It may be true that the Chinese might be encouraged by their success in evading compliance with their engagements in this matter, to attempt to violate other engagements; but this consideration does not seem to me to be sufficient to determine Her Majesty's Government to put the issue of peace and war upon this particular point."†

That a collision would ensue if the treaty-right of entrance was enforced became increasingly evident. The populace of Canton were getting into a high state of ebullition. A medical Missionary, who had expressed an opinion that the disputed point might be gained by firmness on our part, having resided some months in the suburbs, at a considerable distance from Europeans, daily mixing and conversing with the inhabitants, was led to disown all his former views. The aversion of the people was far stronger than he had imagined, while, in the numerous forts in the vicinity, stores and ammunition were being accumulated. The point, however, continued to be pressed on the attention of the Chinese Commissioner Seu, and, with a view to its adjustment, a conference took place, February 21, 1849, between him and Governor Bonham, on board Her Majesty's ship "Hastings."

On that occasion Seu frankly acknowledged the difficulty of his position. He declared that he had no hope of being able to ensure the peaceable entrance of the English, and that, rather than engage in the matter, he would prefer being removed to another place, or even retiring altogether from the service. He also insisted on the necessity of a reference to the emperor. Pending that reference the aspect of the Cantonese became more decidedly hostile. Large bodies of militia, or braves, continued to be enlisted, the expenses connected with which were met by a voluntary taxation. Numerous placards of an inflammatory character were spread abroad; the woollen trades published a table of resolutions to forego, or prevent trade with, or brokerage on behalf of, the barbarians; while all guilds were ordered to break off connexion with any hong merchant who should act otherwise. Meanwhile, the emperor's reply to Seu's memorial arrived. It avowed the impossibility of granting admission into the city contrary to the wishes of the inhabitants. "The decrees of heaven are in unison with the aspirations of the natural mind. Since the people of Kwang-tung [Canton] are now unanimous in their determination, and do not wish foreigners to enter the city of Canton, how can, then, an imperial order be stuck up everywhere, and a forced proclamation be issued? The central empire cannot oppose the people in order to yield to men at a distance. Foreign nations ought also to examine into the feelings of the people, with a due regard to mercantile interests." At the same time documents were forwarded from the Privy Council at Pekin, deprecating any rash movement on the part of the Cantonese, and dealing with the whole subject as a matter of trifling moment, which ought not to be magnified into a cause of war, and misfortune to the frontiers of the empire. "Would the annoyance by barbarians solely be confined to Canton? Would it not likewise extend to Fokien and Che-keang? How could we oppose them then? Those barbarians are, moreover, exceedingly cunning, crafty, and expert in war. .... Some years ago the said barbarians invaded Kwang-tung, Fokien, Che-keang, and Keang-se: the slaughter was terrific, and

---

* Parliamentary Papers relating to Naval Proceedings at Canton, 1857, p. 160.

† Ibid., p. 158.

their tremendous power was sufficiently displayed. Owing to the sacred penetration of our emperor, which embraces heaven and earth, we entered into a good understanding with those barbarians, that was to last ten thousand years. Our people were thus protected, and, by this means, lasting quietness was insured by a single effort."*

Mr. Bonham now addressed to the Home Government a lengthened *resumé* of the complications and correspondence on this subject. He expressed his conviction that the time was come when the claim must be either abandoned or enforced. To the adoption of the latter course he was disposed; not because he thought that any important advantage to commerce would accrue from our admission into Canton, or that there would be any increase of insolent bearing on the part of the Cantonese, in consequence of our foregoing the claim, but from an apprehensiveness that in matters of future discussion our position would be prejudiced. He thus advocates the policy of coercion—

"Believing, as I do, that the hostility of the people is encouraged by their officials, it is only by coercing the latter that we can make them so exert their influence upon the middle, as to produce through these a change in the demeanour of the lower classes. The last must, in my opinion, sooner or later, be taught a lesson which has perhaps been too long delayed; and I am only deterred from recommending that it should be given immediately by the serious doubts which I entertain whether the good we hope to obtain as an end, by enforcing the fulfilment of the treaty, justifies the possible destruction of the city as a means. Your lordship will understand that I am not suggesting a military expedition, but the employment of a part of the naval force in these seas, which can be easily assembled here, and at small cost. The presence of this force at Canton might extort what we require; but, failing this, it would be necessary to proceed to extremities. Since the emperor's ultimatum has been received, I foresee no good in making, without a formal mission, such a reference to Pekin as I had inconvenience to the local trade, greatly ameliorate our commercial condition."*

To either of these extreme courses the Home Government felt disinclined. Lord Palmerston, in a despatch dated June 25th, 1849, considers that a formal renunciation of the treaty-right would be undesirable, while he deprecates a recourse to force of arms and the coercion of the Chinese authorities into a fulfilling of their engagements.

"A renunciation of the treaty-right would be inexpedient, because, though the exercise of the right may not for the present be attainable without efforts which would be disproportionate to the object, or without risks in the enjoyment of it which would counterbalance its value, yet at a future time the state of things may be different, and the privilege may be willingly granted and safely enjoyed.

"An enforcement of the treaty-right by military and naval operations would require an expensive effort, might lead to loss of valuable lives on our part, and much loss of life and destruction of property to be inflicted on the Chinese, while the chief advantage which it seems, by your account, we should derive from a successful result would be, that by giving such an example of our determination and power to enforce a faithful observance of the treaty, we should deter the Chinese from attempting future and other violations of that treaty. But Her Majesty's Government are not disposed for this object to make the effort, or to produce the consequences above mentioned; and they prefer waiting to deal with future violations of the treaty, according to the circumstances of the case, if such violations should occur."†

In a reply to the chairman of the London East-India and China Association, in which the Committee of that body had called upon the British Government to adopt energetic measures for the purpose of securing to British subjects all the benefits stipulated for by treaty, Lord Palmerston thus sustains the policy he had prescribed—

"I am to state to you, in reply, that Her Majesty's Government have no intention to

derived by British trade from free access into the interior of Canton is probably not very great, while the effort to obtain the immediate fulfilment of the Chinese engagement, in this respect, would be costly, and might lead to a great loss of life and destruction of property, and to a considerable interruption to British trade in that quarter of China, and might, moreover, seriously affect the trade at the other ports, Her Majesty's Government are of opinion that the general commercial interests of the country are best consulted by not pushing matters to extremities on the present occasion."*

Meanwhile Seu had very adroitly availed himself of an ambiguous expression in a communication from Mr. Bonham of April 9th, the intention of which was to convey to the Chinese commissioner the Governor's conviction of the inutility of further negotiation, until he had obtained fresh instructions from home as to the course to be adopted. The communication ran as follows—"The question at issue rests where it was, and must remain in abeyance. The discussion of it cannot be further prosecuted between your Excellency and myself." Seu immediately replies—

"I received, on the 19th day, 3d month (April 11), a communication from the honourable Envoy, to the effect that the question about the entrance into the city should not again be agitated in future. These words are still as in our ears: not only have the Chinese who have eyes all seen them, but also all the nations that carry on commercial intercourse who have ears have heard them. . . .

"You, the honourable Envoy, judging the times, and considering the circumstances, put immediately a stop to the question of entering the city; the trade and commercial intercourse have thus been peacefully carried on as customary, and this may be called the very essence of the deepest wisdom. It would be inexplicable if any one looked upon it as weakness (on your part). If one is acquainted with the aspect of affairs at the time he would not do so."†

Seu soon communicated to the people of Canton, as well as to the court at Pekin, the successful issue, as he conceived it to be, of his negotiations. The gentry and literati of Canton resolved to erect a tablet in honour of Seu, and Yeh the Lieutenant-Governor, bearing upon it an inscription derogatory to the British Government; while from Pekin honours came thick and fast. Seu was rewarded with a double-eyed peacock's feather, and the fourth rank of nobility; the Governor of Kwang-tung with a single-eyed peacock's feather, and the fifth rank of nobility. An imperial edict was also promulgated, commending the people of Canton for their firmness in resisting the demands of the English—

"Nearly ten years have elapsed since the barbarian affairs rose (into importance), during which the country along the coast has been involved in troubles; the public revenue exhausted; the army wearied with toil; and although of late years a state of quiet has been in some degree attained, still in the measures taken to manage the barbarians, the equipoise between inflexibility and complaisance has not been maintained, and evils flowing from them have gradually made their appearance. We, having been seriously apprehensive that the inhabitants of the seaboard would be trampled down (if we acted otherwise), have for that reason tranquilly endured all, abiding our time. For it is unquestionably a principle of reason that slight oppression must be followed by great redress.

"The English barbarians having again preferred their request that they might enter the city of Canton, some days back the Governor-General, Seu-kwang-tsin, and his colleague (the Governor Yeh), sent in several reports to us detailing the measures adopted, which were in perfect accordance with good policy. To-day they have again reported by the post that the merchants and people of that place being fully alive to a high feeling of patriotism, have subscribed money to make preparations for preventing the insults (of the barbarians); that the gentry and literati had really exerted themselves in giving assistance; and that the proposals to enter the city were at rest, the barbarians in question carrying on trade as before, and both natives and foreigners being in a state of quiet and tranquillity, while not one man had been lost, not a single shot fired."*

Six triumphal granite arches had been raised in the city and suburbs of Canton, in order to record the wisdom and patriotism of the imperial Commissioner, the inscriptions conveying the Emperor's admiration in the most flattering and emphatic terms. About thirty miles from Canton there is a magnificent temple, called the Polo temple, covering a large space of ground; it is regarded one of the wonders of the province of Kwang-tung, and is dedicated to a god who is supposed to exercise a great influence over distant nations. In times of national danger this god is the object of special invocation, and when the

---

* Papers on Naval Proceedings, &c., p. 194.
† Ibid. pp. 205.

* Ibid. pp. 200.

peril has passed away, libations and offerings are made up on a magnificent scale, to testify the gratitude of the rulers and people for his auspicious interference. Here Yeh had erected a temple, with an inscription to "the god of the southern seas," some extracts from which, as illustrative of Chinese ideas and practices in the important concernment of religion, we introduce—

"The Leke classic (or Book of Rites) tells us, in regard to the sacrificial system, the organization of which devolves upon the sacred prince (emperor) that oblations should be offered to those (powers or spirits) who can guard against the evils (originated by men), or are able to avert the direr calamities (inflicted by heaven.) . . . .

"But how great is the difference between the early and these latter times! The usages of past antiquity were simple and pure; the numbers of natives and sojourners were then but limited, and the blessings which they derived from the watchful aid of the deity may be said to have been confined to those of an ordinary nature, such as rich harvests and profound tranquillity, which each succeeding year brought them. Now, however, the manners of the present age are becoming daily more removed from those which preceded them. Numerous cities have arisen along the coast; the territory has increased in extent; productions have multiplied; and the ports are frequented by the merchants and their ships. But these great benefits are attended with evils of corresponding magnitude. Intrigues from without are coupled with conspiracies within; (some men) are injured by sinister design, whilst others are ensnared in (their neighbours') wiles, and commotion oft ranges the maritime frontier. How imposing, then, is the majesty, and how great the honour due to the deity who continues (at such a time) to preserve harmony among the masses of the people, who prevents the growth of evils (inherent in mankind, and averts the infliction of calamities (from on high), and who shares the responsibility which weighs on those to whom the local guardianship is entrusted.

him, in conjunction with Seu, and their successful character, and then tenders his obligations to the god of the Polo temple.

"On these occasions the strength of the deity availed us, when it was indeed needed. At the same time plenteous harvests were reaped, and an abundance always recorded : not only, therefore, have the blessings bestowed on us been bounteous, but likewise of such a nature as shall endure for endless ages. Great, indeed, have been the exertions of the deity on behalf of the people of this province.

"Arms have now been laid aside, and the progress of the storm arrested; the public are in the enjoyment of peace, and their affairs are flourishing and prosperous, and the spirit of satisfaction and delight reigns among the people. It is at such a time that they should turn towards their gods, and render to each one of them the proper sacrifices. In the Sheking particular mention is only made of 'the river' as one of the objects of general public worship throughout the empire; but the preface (to that work) explains that (the rule for this worship) comprises within its application the sea, towards which all rivers flow.

"In person, therefore, I offered up a pure acceptable sacrifice (to the deity of this temple), and rendered to him thanks for the efficacious protection he had granted us. By the wish of the gentry I presided over the repairs of the temple buildings. These were commenced in the Keyew year of Taoukwang (1849), and their completion was announced in the Kangseuh year (1850). And I now compose this inscription to be engraven on stone, in order that the great virtue of the god may become widely known, and inspire proper respect."*

Thus Yeh, in his inscription, curiously blended his own praises with the praises of the god, and vaunted himself over the barbarains. It was translated by Mr. Interpreter Parkes, and duly forwarded to the ministry at home. But these lucubrations, if they showed any thing, made us cognizant of this fact, that the admission of the foreigner into Canton was a much more serious matter with the Chinese than we had imagined, and that

court, in which the emperor expressed his desire, "that the merchants of foreign nations, coming as they do from far across many seas, and in all instances dwelling in quietness, and delighting in their vocations, are to receive the same support as those of China, with a view to the establishment of perpetual amity, and to the enjoyment, by both in common, of universal tranquillity;" and thus, through the temperate action of the Home Government, which refused to go to war with the Chinese for the purpose of enforcing a treaty-right, which carried with it no real advantage, difficulties were smoothed over, and commercial intercourse resumed.

In January 1852, Sir Samuel Bonham returning home on leave of absence, Dr. Bowring, the Consul at Canton, was appointed Superintendant of Trade, receiving, at the same time, very explicit instructions as to the course of policy to be pursued—

"It is the anxious desire of Her Majesty's Government to avoid all irritating discussions with that of China. It will, of course, be your duty carefully to watch over, and to insist upon, the performance, by the Chinese authorities, of the engagements which exist between the two countries. But you will not push argument on doubtful points in a manner to fetter the free action of your Government, and you will not resort to measures of force without previous reference home, except in the extreme case of such measures being required to repel aggression, or to protect the lives and properties of British subjects."*

Dr. Bowring, however, in a despatch dated April 10, 1852, resumed the old question of admission into Canton. It was a pity to resuscitate it: it had been decently buried. What though the Chinese had erected over it a somewhat vain-glorious inscription: it was not worth while, because of this, to disinter it. The new Consul, however, insisted on the importance of admission into Canton. He considered that it might be effected without any serious difficulty. The moment also, in his opinion, was very opportune for such an effort. "The city of Canton had been, for two years, in a state of universal tranquillity. The popular passions, so long and so systematically excited against foreigners, under the encouragement of the mandarins, have been allowed to subside. No longer administered to by violent placards, public meetings, ostentatious displays of rude military organi-

zation for the so-called 'defence of the city,' the fear, and, to some extent, the hatred and distrust of strangers, have been moderated by a more friendly and habitual intercourse." Some would have thought that these were weighty reasons why the *vexata quæstio* should not be re-agitated. The new Superintendant was of a different opinion. The mandarins were in difficulty: they were menaced by the insurrectionists in the neighbouring provinces, and, dreading a collision with foreign nations, would, it was thought, be disposed to yield to a comparatively slight pressure. We must confess that the proposal to take advantage of the new emergency in which the Chinese authorities found themselves does not comport with the generosity and highmindedness which ought to mark the proceedings of a great nation like England. So confident was Dr. Bowring of obtaining ready entrance into Canton, that the despatch of Earl Granville, which put a wholesome restraint on his proceedings, appeared to him to constitute the only difficulty to a happy solution of the question. Before, however, his despatch of April 19th had reached England, the home ministry had been changed, and Lord Malmesbury, from the Foreign Office, prohibited still more peremptorily all incautious interference with Chinese affairs—

"I have received your despatch of the 19th of April, and I have to state to you in reply, that it is the intention of Her Majesty's Government that you should strictly adhere to the instructions given to you by Earl Granville, by which you were enjoined to avoid all irritating discussions with the Chinese authorities; and in conformity with the rule thus prescribed to you, you will abstain from mooting the question of the right of British subjects to enter into the city of Canton.

"You will likewise abstain from pressing to be received as Her Majesty's Plenipotentiary at any other description of place, or in any other manner, than your predecessors.

"I have further to remind you that you were enjoined by Earl Granville's instructions to take up your residence at Hong Kong for the period of Sir Samuel Bonham's absence; consequently you will not be authorized to visit the various ports of China, as you seem to intimate your intention to do, and you will therefore abstain from so doing."*

A subsequent despatch, a month later in date, reiterated, in an unmistakably decided tone, the injunctions which had been laid on the new official—

---

* Correspondence relative to entrance into Canton, p. 3.

* Correspondence, &c., p. 10.

"With reference to the possible occurrence of circumstances which render personal intercourse with the Chinese authorities indispensable, I have to repeat to you the injunction contained in my despatch of the 21st of June, not to press to be received by them at any other description of place, or in any other manner, than your predecessors.

"I have further to enjoin you not to raise any question as to the admission of British subjects into the city of Canton, and not to attempt yourself to enter it. In my opinion no solid advantage could be gained which would compensate for the risk of provoking an insult to Her Majesty's Plenipotentiary, and bringing on, as a necessary consequence, a collision between England and China."*

And thus for two years longer Canton remained at peace.

In February 1854 the Earl of Clarendon was at the Foreign Office, and Sir J. Bowring was appointed Her Majesty's Plenipotentiary and Chief-Superintendant of British trade in China. His lordship's first despatch to China recalled all the old questions, the rights to which we were entitled by treaty, more especially "free and unrestricted intercourse with the Chinese authorities, and free admission into some of the cities of China, especially Canton."† These, he was of opinion, it was desirable to secure, although, in dealing with such questions, much caution was required. Thus empowered, Sir J. Bowring was not long in forwarding a missive to Yeh, in which he was reminded of the accumulated injuries under which the English were suffering, the most important grievances being "non-admission into Canton city" and " personal intercourse between the officials of the two countries." He sought a personal interview with the commissioner, for the discussing questions of so great gravity; an interview which, after some delay, Yeh was willing to concede, specifying Howqua's packhouse on the Canton river as a suitable rendezvous. This afforded the British plenipotentiary the long desired opportunity of bringing matters to a point. He at once declined any but an official reception, at the public office of the Viceroy, within the gates of the city. Yeh, in his reply, very properly deprecates the revival of so irritating a subject, and reminds the British official of the tranquillity which had prevailed since this question had ceased to be agitated. Finding Yeh immoveable, Sir J. Bowring proceeded to Shanghae, and there addressed a letter to the Viceroy Eleang, in which he complains of Yeh, and the danger to which his incautiousness exposed the friendly relations between the two countries. Eleang's answer is worthy of note.

"I have no means of knowing what kind of treatment your Excellency or your predecessors received at the hands of the Commissioner at Canton. It is to my mind a matter of more consequence that we, of the central and outer nations, have made fair dealing and good faith our rule of conduct, and thus for a length of time preserved entire our amicable relations. Familiarity or otherwise in social intercourse, and all such trifles, are, in my opinion, to be decided by the laws of conventionality. As your Excellency cherishes such a dislike to discourteous treatment, you must doubtless be a courteous man yourself; an inference which gives me sincere pleasure, for we shall both be able to maintain treaty stipulations, and continue in the practice of mutual goodwill, to your Excellency's everlasting honour."*

Canton now became endangered by the proximity of the rebel forces, and Yeh addressed himself to the British Governor, in the hope of obtaining from him some seasonable help. He referred to the joint action which had been adopted in the pursuit and destruction of the Ko-lahn pirates, and expressed his hope, that as the thieves in the river had become strong and troublesome, the English ships of war might be available for their destruction likewise. In this expectation, however, he was disappointed. A notice, signed by the consuls of the Western Powers, was immediately put forth, in which they declared, that as they and their countrymen were resident at Canton only for the purposes of trading, they were resolved to take no part in the movements now agitating China, and that, as they purposed to maintain a strict neutrality in all respects, they claimed that all foreign residences, and the avenues leading to them, should be respected as neutral ground.

It would have been well, however, if no attempt had been made to take advantage of the perplexity in which the Chinese authorities found themselves, for the purpose of constraining them to the surrender of points which they had hitherto been unwilling to concede. As they had felt it their duty to decline affording any assistance in the present critical circumstances of China, the greater delicacy was needed on the part of the B...

authorities; and we cannot but think that the determination "to take this opportunity of compelling the Chinese to give effect to certain measures which had been provided for in Sir John Davis's convention with Keying, in April 1847, but which had been either neglected or imperfectly carried out—such as the removal of boats and other nuisances in front of the foreign residences; clearing the navigation from barriers and other obstructions to free communication" was neither generous nor wise. It must have served to confirm the Chinese officials in the view they had already taken of the restless and grasping tendencies of the English. These changes would have involved the removal of a considerable Chinese population, and to this Yeh positively objected—

"The boundary of the foreign residences has always been well defined. The natives who live within it are mostly engaged in foreign trade, and there are also some who have shops for the sale of miscellaneous articles, which are much resorted to by foreigners. These are all harmless people, and there need be no apprehension of their creating any disturbance. It would be inexpedient to compel them to remove without their consent, and such a measure would excite suspicion and alarm."*

Sir John Bowring had also flattered himself with the idea "that the extreme perplexities of the Chinese authorities, with the country all around them in confusion and conflagration, and the city menaced daily by the rebel forces," would have induced the mandarins to grant him "an official and amicable interview, in order to discuss matters which interest them so deeply." But on this point they continued to manifest the old determination. The superintendant plied them with verbal messages and formal communications; but he was not successful. Compelled to return to Hong Kong without having succeeded in carrying out this favourite point, he addressed to Yeh the following peremptory note—

"I came hither with the confident hope that by my presence the friendly relations between the Governments of China and Great Britain might have been consolidated and extended, and I expressed to your Excellency, through your deputed officers, my willingness officially to meet you, and personally to discuss those arrangements which the disordered state of China, and the position of Canton and its neighbourhood, seemed to demand from your Excellency on the one hand, and from me as the plenipotentiary of a friendly power on the other.

"My Government will learn with sorrow and surprise that your Excellency has not appreciated the motives which brought me hither, nor the amicable spirit which has been the guide of all my proceedings.

"I cannot, however, quit Canton without reminding your Excellency, that if I have not insisted on a proper reception within the walls of Canton, according to the engagement entered into by his Excellency Keying, in the month of April 1847, it is solely because I was unwilling to take advantage of the embarrassments which surround your Excellency, and to add to the many complications and difficulties with which you have to struggle.

"But in order to remove any misunderstanding on the part of your Excellency, it is my duty to inform you that I possess sufficient means peremptorily to enforce the obligations entered into by your predecessor to admit me into the city, and that nothing but extreme forbearance has prevented my employing the powers at my disposal; and I ventured to believe that the experience you have had of the power of that Sovereign whose representative I am, would have led to the adoption of a policy far different from that in which your Excellency has seen fit to persevere, notwithstanding the lessons of the past, the perils of the present, and the uncertainties of the future.

"It would not, however, be becoming in me to leave this neighbourhood without again formally advising your Excellency that the state of our intercourse is most unsatisfactory and intolerable; that many great grievances remain wholly unredressed; and that Her Britannic Majesty's Government, who have already been informed of the results of my visit to Tien-tsin, will be further advised as to what has taken place at Canton, in order that such measures may be adopted as in its judgment become the dignity of a great nation, and as may be deemed necessary for the assertion of rights secured by solemn engagements, and for accommodating our relations to the exigencies of present circumstances."*

This communication must be acknowledged to be sufficiently threatening. The British nation, through the unwise action of its officials, was placed before the Chinese in a most truculent aspect, as prepared to have recourse to war, in order to carry a point, which was virtually of no consequence, and which Lord Palmerston and Lord Malmesbury had wisely

---

* Correspondence, &c., p. 33.

* Correspondence, &c., pp. 34, 35.

put aside, as provoking needless irritation, and unduly disturbing our relations with the Chinese Government.

On the defeat of the insurgents by the imperialists in the vicinity of Canton, Sir J. Bowring, with a perseverance which had better have been reserved for a more suitable object, again importuned Yeh to concede to him an official reception at his yamun within the city. Yeh's good fortune was now in the ascendant, and, emboldened by his successful operations against the insurgents, he responded to the British official with a curt and decided negative.

"As regards the question of personal intercourse between the officials of our two nations, to which it refers, when I undertook to meet your Excellency last year at the Jin-sin packhouse, you declined the interview. The rebels have been causing trouble and disquiet ever since, and I have been so occupied with the movements of the military necessary to their suppression, that I have not had a moment's leisure. Even now, although tranquillity is perfect restored to the city, still the movements of the troops for the extermination of vagabonds throughout the other departments and districts of the province all so require my personal attention as to keep me busier than before.

"As regards the arrival of the British Consul at Canton, there is no precedent for an interview with him. There never was a deputation to receive your Excellency for instance, during the many years that you were Consul here. The Commissioner of Finance, again, is charged in no way whatever with the administration of foreign affairs, and as, in addition to this, the Commissioner Tsuy is dead, and his vacancy has not yet been filled up, there is no use in the consideration of the question. I accordingly reply to you, availing myself of the opportunity to wish that prosperity may daily increase to your Excellency."

In all these proceedings Sir J. Bowring appears to have carried with him the full approval of the Foreign Office.

Our readers will readily perceive, from the preceding digest, that the train was laid, and that a trivial circumstance would be sufficient to ignite it. The "Arrow" was the ignitable spark. It bore the same relation to events on the Chinese coast, as the greased cartridge to the disaffected elements which had accumulated in India. Yeh, by the seizure of the lorcha, only precipitated a crisis; and if there had been no other point in dispute it might have been arranged. It was not, at best, a very clear case. The vessel had been for a time in the hands of pirates, and then had become the subject of litigation between the parties whose property she had been before her seizure by pirates, and the subsequent purchasers. The register under which she was authorized to use the British flag had run out, and she was, at the time of seizure, in an irregular position. The Chinese authorities accused one of the crew of piracy, nor does the accusation appear to be disproved. Yeh, on being remonstrated with, liberated nine of the crew, reserving three for further examination.

Not much time, however, was permitted for negotiation. The British authorities were prompt to act. An opportunity long looked for had occurred, and they were determined to break ground, with a view to the settlement of all those great grievances which, as Sir J. Bowring informed Yeh in his letter of December 27, 1854, remained unredressed. The "Arrow" was seized on the morning of October 8, 1856, and, on the 15th, Her Majesty's ship "Barracouta" made a reprisal by seizing a large junk flying Government ensigns, and mounting ten or twelve guns. On October 22d Yeh gave up ten of the crew, and, finding this unsatisfactory, forwarded the entire twelve; but this was one only of three things which had been required of him, and, therefore, Mr. Consul Parkes refused to receive them. Now the other two required reparations were of mere nominal value, namely, that Yeh should apologize for what had taken place, and give assurance that the British flag should in future be respected. They might have been dispensed with. The remittance of the twelve men was the most practical apology, and as for Yeh's assurance, it was worth as much waste paper. But, nevertheless, because of these two valueless points we went to war with China, and how much this insisting on a letter of apology has cost us, let subsequent events testify.

On October 23d the British admiral took possession of the four Barrier Forts, as well as the Macao passage Forts, and the next day the true gravamen was avowed, and the real object of the war unmasked. Sir J. Bowring, writing to Mr. Consul Parkes, October 24, 1856, says, "I have conveyed to Sir Michael Seymour an opinion, that if his Excellency and yourself agree on the fitness of the opportunity, it would be well if the *vexata quæstio* of our entrance into the city should now be settled, at least as far as to secure us an official reception there. This would be a crowning result to the successful operations of Her Majesty's naval forces."

On the 24th Yeh addresses to the Consul a

letter of remonstrance on the subject of the "Arrow:" he pleaded that she had been originally a Chinese vessel, and was supposed to be such at the time when she was boarded; that he had remitted the twelve men of which the crew consisted. He then proceeds, and with justice, to remonstrate against our precipitate proceedings, which, without any formal declaration of war, had already involved some loss of Chinese life.

"Who could have incited you, the said Consul, to attack, on the morning of the 23d instant, the Barrier Forts, burning the forts, and wounding and killing six of the soldiers? And again, on the 24th instant, to attack and burn the Macao Passage Forts, when three of our soldiers received contusions? It was because I, the minister, am at peace with your honourable nation, that the soldiers, in no instance, offered resistance. But if you, the said Consul, should thus, of your own will, again resort to violence, and occasion commotion among the people of this city, who will not submit to such proceedings, then I, the minister, shall find it difficult to employ persuasion on your account. I therefore inform you of this beforehand.

"Furthermore, your honourable nation has hitherto reverenced the spirits of heaven and the Sabbath-day, and justice and propriety are held by you in esteem. But does the destruction of forts correspond with your professions? You, the said Consul, should well consider this"*

And, on the 25th of October, he adds—

"On the morning of the 22d October I addressed you a declaration, and with it sent you the twelve men, thus, therefore, returning to you the whole number that had previously been seized. You, the said Consul, received (the letter and men), and thus had knowledge (of the fact). Was not this proceeding in accordance with (the demands made in) your letters of the 8th and 12th October? Why then did you, as before, refuse to receive them, and proceed without reason to burn and destroy the forts of this city?

"But I, the Minister, also know full well what you the said Consul have in view. For a certainty it is nothing less than a desire on your part to imitate the course taken by the Envoy Davis in the spring of 1847. Little, indeed, you know, that in China the people form the basis of the nation, and that the people of Kwang-tung are very different from (other communities)."*

Yeh's mind was soon made up. He saw the real question at issue. It was the old question of admission into Canton. That disputed and irritating point, which a wise and conciliating policy had for a season put aside, was now placed in the foreground of the controversy. It was a point carrying with it no real advantage to us. It was a point of unquestionable difficulty to the Chinese officials, for to yield it would be to embroil themselves with the population of Canton. If, then, to gain what was of so little value to us, we were prepared to go to war, we cannot be surprised that Yeh, with whom it was a vital point, was prepared to go to war rather than concede it. He issued, therefore, in true barbarian style, the following proclamation—

"Yeh, the Governor-General, proclaims the following—

"The English barbarians have attacked the provincial city, and wounded and injured our soldiers and people. Their crimes are indeed of the most heinous nature.

"Wherefore I herewith distinctly command you to join together to exterminate them, and I publicly proclaim to all the military and people, householders and others, that you should unite with all the means at your command, to assist the soldiers and militia in exterminating these troublous English villains, killing them whenever you meet them, whether on shore or in their ships. For each of their lives that you may thus take, you shall receive, as before, thirty dollars. All ought to respect and obey, and neither oppose nor disregard this special proclamation."†

It was accompanied by a Chinese notification to the following effect—

"A public announcement of all the gentry and scholars of the city of Canton.

"When, some time since, native banditti had raised disturbances, our soldiers swept away every one of them to destruction, and merchants and people, both native and foreign, were then enabled to live in peace, and pursue business with satisfaction. Could there be a better state of things than this? Lately, however, we have heard that the English authorities have suddenly forced their way into the river with ships of war and steamers, setting fire to and destroying batteries, and wounding and killing soldiers, with the utmost degree of unreasoning perversity. Fortunately, however, the soldiers

---

* Papers relating to Naval Proceedings, &c., p. 35. It does not appear that any violent action on the part of the English occurred on the Sabbath.

* Papers relating to Naval Proceedings, &c.,

of our batteries did not return their fire, to prevent (its being said that) we have turned our backs upon the treaty and disregarded the claims of friendship.

"It appears that heretofore many of the lorchas which run upon the Canton river have been breaking the laws, both by smuggling and trading in salt: there are records of their repeated offences, and they are universally detested by the mandarins and people. On the present occasion, lorcha No. 27 had the audacity to afford concealment to Leming-tae and other robbers on their passage to Canton; but the English authorities in the first place, if they respected the treaty, ought, according to it, to hand over persons discovered to be robbers to the Chinese mandarins to deal with, and as the master who was in charge of the said lorcha secreted (robbers), and concealed the circumstance from the Consul, if there was an irregularity the fault is his and not our officer's.

"The lorcha in question, moreover, was in the employ of Soo-a-ching, a Chinese, its sailing letter having been obtained under false pretences through the master aforesaid: it was in no respect an English lorcha, having nothing at all in common with those genuine ships of war or trading vessels that come from foreign countries. And further still, those military officers of ours, whose duty it is to search for robbers, though adroit in seizing them, do not understand treaties, which is a thing, indeed, of every-day occurrence.

"When our mandarins heard the circumstances, with an uncalled-for indulgence they set free all the twelve criminals in a way, it may be said, the most friendly and the most courteous; but—who would have thought it?—the English authorities have openly violated the treaty in attacking our batteries with cannon, setting fire to and destroying them, and wounding and killing our soldiers. Is there also, we would ask, any principle of right in operations such as these?

"In our humble opinion, the batteries all along the river banks were erected originally for the protection of the people, and now that they have been suddenly burned down, it is to the people in truth that the injury has been done.

"Everybody's blood is boiling with indignation, but we can only ask the officials and merchants of other countries, and the principal English merchants themselves, to look into and consider the unreasonable perversity of the English authorities, and the manner in which they have disregarded treaty obligations. Do not say that we Chinese have not observed the principles of right."*

It will be our duty, in our next Number, to trace the progress of the war so far as it has advanced, and to show how, with its progress, our demands have increased. We commenced by requiring free admission into Canton; we next insisted on a concession still more repulsive to the dynastic sensibilities of China, and equally barren of advantage to ourselves—the residence of a British ambassador at the Court of Pekin.

* Papers relating to Naval Proceedings, &c., pp. 45, 46.

RUPERT'S LAND—ITS PROSPECTS.

SIXTEEN years past the Red-River Colony was a secluded spot, a home in the wilderness, where a mixed population of Europeans, Indians, and half-breeds had met together, and a colony had been formed along the banks of the Red River and its tributary, the Assineboine, which straggled down to no great distance from the shores of the great lake Winnipeg, into which the united stream discharges and distant north, the door of entrance to their territories having been placed by the Company at the icy portals of Hudson's Bay.

The necessary result was, that, as they increased, the settlers began to seek out some other channel of communication with the world outside, and faint threads of intercourse began to form between the United

together, perhaps 200 carts and men, with horses and oxen, for the accomplishment of this lengthened journey of 1700 miles to and fro. This route is being increasingly used. St. Paul's, Minnesota, presents a very different aspect from what it did twenty years ago, when the first shanty was set up for the purpose of selling bad whiskey to the Indians. It is a place of business-like aspect, with its daily lines of steamboats crowded with passengers and goods. Substantial stone buildings adorn its principal streets, while on many others in rapid progress the sound of the workman's hammer is heard. The best mode of conveyance across the intervening flats is the Red-River cart, which, unlike other vehicles, has not a particle of iron in its composition. "It is made with two high broad wheels, admirably adapted for crossing soft, swampy places. Loaded with six hundred or even nine hundred pounds of stuff, these carts are drawn from St. Paul's to Red River by single oxen, at the rate of twenty-five to twenty-eight miles a day.

But it is not only in the American direction that the strong impulse for intercommunication has been felt, but on the Canadian side likewise. Canada, with its increasing population, begins to feel its way in the direction of the Red River. The lands in the western peninsula of Canada, between lakes Ontario, Erie, and Huron, had been gradually taken up, and many of the settlers began to look wistfully towards the prairies of the Western States, as preferable to the labour of clearing the forest. When, therefore, the Select Committee on the Hudson's-Bay Company was sitting, in 1857, the government of Canada deputed two of its officers, the Chief Justice of the Court of Common Pleas in Upper Canada and another gentleman, to watch over their rights and interests in this question. The natural outlet of the Red River appearing to be rather in the direction of the United States, it became the more necessary to encourage the Canadas to open communication with that territory, and render it available for the purposes of British colonization, otherwise there was reason to fear, lest in some way or another it might cease to be British territory; and the Committee recommended the cession to Canada of the districts on the Red River and the Saskatchewan, provided the province was prepared to open communications with them, and provide for their administration. At the time when that resolution was adopted, the gold deposits of British Columbia had just been touched upon, and the value of the intermediate districts between Canada and the Rocky Mountains has proportionally increased. The line of country on the British side of the frontier presents the most feasible route for a railway across the continent. On the American side, the country is intersected by the tributaries of the Missouri; but the water-shed to the westward of the Assineboine lies a little to the north of the frontier, and, northward of that, the prairies extend, with scarcely an interruption from the Red River to the Rocky Mountains. The competition, therefore, between Canada and the Americans, with reference to this important field for emigration, is becoming more intense. The Americans have had the start, and are availing themselves of the advantages which the Red River affords as a practicable route to the gold fields of British Columbia. In the summer of 1859, the good people of the Red River, who had hitherto lived in such seclusion from the rest of the world, were startled by the unexpected appearance amongst them of about two-score Americans. They were on their way to the auriferous regions beyond the Rocky Mountains, and rested at the Red River for a brief season, to obtain a renewal of strength, preparatory to the further prosecution of their lengthened journey.

But Canada, also, is rapidly pushing forward her roads and communications. "A road has been completed from Thunder Bay, Lake Superior, to Dog Lake through a section of country which was believed to be the most difficult on the whole route; and from the head of Dog River, a line has been opened across the summit of the water-shed to the Savane River, which, with the Lac des Mille Lacs, into which it discharges itself, presents an unbroken navigable reach of seventy-five miles. This important link of communication has been effected by the efforts of a few spirited individuals, who have undertaken the work and risked the outlay pending the organization of the North-west Transit Company. Lac des Mille Lacs is within sixty miles of Rainy Lake, from whence an unbroken navigation of 200 miles extends, by Rainy River and Lake of the Woods, to within sixty miles of the prairie region."

The local paper * from whence the foregoing extract has been taken is the first publication which has been attempted at the Red River, and marks the new era which has dawned on that colony. It is with reference to these altered circumstances that it has been commenced.

"Exploring parties, organized under the direction, respectively, of the Canadian and

---

* The "Nor-Wester," published at the Red-River Settlement.

British Governments, have established the immediate availability for the purposes of colonization, of the vast country watered by the Red River, the Assiniboine, and the Saskatchewan; and private parties of American citizens, following Captain Palliser, are engaged in determining the practicability of rendering this the great overland route to the gold deposits of British Columbia. The Red-River Settlement is the home of a considerable population, hardy, industrious, and thrifty; occupying a fine farming country, with all the advantages of prairie and timber combined. It has churches many, and educational advantages which will endure comparison with those of more pretentious communities. And, for hundreds of miles beyond, stretches one of the most magnificent agricultural regions in the world, watered abundantly with lakes and navigable rivers, with a sufficiency of timber, with vast prairies of unsurpassed fertility, with mineral resources, in some parts, of no common value, and with a climate as salubrious as it is delightful. Such a country cannot now remain unpeopled. It offers temptations to the emigrant nowhere excelled. It invites alike the mechanic and the farmer. Its rivers and rolling prairies and accessible mountain-passes, secure to it the advantages which must belong to a highway to the Pacific. It has mail communication with Canada *viâ* Fort William; and regular communication with the Mississippi *viâ* steamboat and stage to St. Paul. What can impede its development? What can prevent the settlement around Fort Garry from becoming the political and commercial centre of a great and prosperous people?"

The seclusion of the Red-River Colony is at an end. For better, for worse, it must come forward and be known. Busy emigrants and gold-finders from Canada and the United States will make it a halting-place, in the first instance, and a *point d'appui* as they locate themselves in the regions beyond towards the Rocky Mountains. The settlers and Indians of these remote regions will come within the reach of those dangerous influences which are inseparable from free and unrestricted intercourse with white men of every variety of character.

"Temptations," observes our Missionary, the Rev. W. W. Kirkby, in one of his late communications, "are fearful things for a weak-minded, half-civilized people, and often astonish and confound us by the discoveries they make. And temptations we shall have. Indeed, we have had them for some time past; but they are very much on the increase. We are every year brought nearer to the civilized world, and at present are receiving more of its vices than its advantages. We have Canadian soldiers and Commissioners here, whose influence is not at all what we could desire. Then there are Canadian and American traders continually visiting the Settlement, who fill the minds of our young people with notions of pride, extortion, and ungodliness, which they never before had. And in addition to this, some 700 or 800 carts go every summer to St. Paul's (at least they have now reached that number: four or five years ago they were only fifty) for goods. These are chiefly attended by young men, whose principles are not formed, and the effect upon their character is but too manifest. Last year some of the American traders, and, I fear, our own people too, brought in a great deal of whisky, which they sold here, and to the poor Indians in the interior, at an immense profit. This induced a great many of the free-traders and others to fetch some this year, that they may do likewise. From the pulpit and the platform did I beseech all connected with this parish to abstain from such wicked and unlawful traffic. Yea, to every one going from here did I go, and, almost on bended knees, implore them to spare us the sin, the shame, and the wretchedness that will certainly follow the promiscuous and unlimited sale of ardent spirits; and, thank God, I for the most part prevailed. I am not aware of one man from this parish (St. Andrew's) bringing any for sale here. One man, who was to have brought forty gallons, assured me he would not bring a drop; but the carts are just returning, and I hear that the people from the Settlement, and the American traders together, are bringing in not less than 8000 gallons. The result must be ruinous. It is a critical period for the Mission. Earnestly am I endeavouring to warn the people of it, and to strengthen them in those things wherein they have been taught. Pray for us, my dear friends, that our people may stand firm in their allegiance to the Gospel of Christ, that they may be preserved from being carried away by the temptation of the wicked one. The enemy is indeed coming in like a flood : may the Spirit of the Lord lift up a standard against him, that he may not prevail over us!"

The above extract tells us of the dangers which must be met, and of the only influence by which they can be effectually resisted. Let us, then, ask what measure of influence has scriptural Christianity attained over the mingled population of the land, or what amount of conservative influence is it likely to exercise at a crisis such as this? A long period of quietude has been permitted, during which it might take root and spread. Has it been diligently improved? and is it exercising sufficient power on the hearts of Indians and Europeans, to justify us in entertaining the hope that the transition period will be passed in comparative safety?

The population of the Red River will be the first to be visited by the tide of emigration, with its mingled good and evil, and, next, the Saskatchewan districts. Beyond that limit, we do not think it will advance. The remoteness of the northern districts, and the severity of the winters, will probably, for a lengthened period, deter settlers from occupying the cultivable spots, which are by no means infrequent. But the Red-River districts will be the first to be tested, and they ought to be the best prepared to meet the trial. They have been longer under Christian cultivation, which has not yet extended itself beyond the Missinipi or English River. What, then, is the condition of the settler population of the Red River? We shall take one parish, that of St. Andrew's, as a specimen, the more so, as it is a station of the Church Missionary Society, and the resident Minister, one of our Missionaries, The Rev. W. W. Kirkby had charge of the parish during Archdeacon Hunter's visit to the Mackenzie-River district, where he now occupies the Archdeacon's place, being the only Protestant Missionary in the vast regions which lie beyond the English River and York Factory. His statements as to the spiritual condition of this Mission station are very encouraging—

"I am thankful to say, that during the past year, on all the services, but more especially on the Sunday services, the attendance has been extremely good—almost all that we could wish. I do not think that we have one wilful, habitual neglecter of the means of grace in the whole parish. Almost every stranger that has passed a Sunday with us has been impressed by its devout observance; and frequently has the question been asked, 'Are your Sundays always so well observed, and your services so well attended?' And on being answered in the affirmative, the inquirers have felt astonishment and delight.

"I am thankful to report that the communicants are on the increase: several have been admitted during the year, and four more are waiting for admission the next time the Lord's supper is administered. This I feel to be a source of comfort and joy. They now number over 200, and might have been much more had we not weeded them most unsparingly.

"The parish being ten or twelve miles in extent, it is impossible to keep up a regular and systematic course of visitation; but I have done the best I could under the circumstances. The sick have always been promptly and regularly attended, and the others as time and opportunity served. In my last course through the parish, I made special inquiries respecting family prayer, and the private reading of God's blessed word, and was delighted to find both more extensively practised than I had ventured to hope. Diffidence, or fear of incompetence, had refrained many from erecting their family altar; but upon my giving them a little book of family-prayers, they promised at once to do so. Some I found were in the habit of reading a chapter and saying the Lord's Prayer; others using some of the prayers of our church. Many, very many of our dear people are, I believe, endeavouring to glorify God in their bodies, and in their souls, which are his. 'The life which they live in the flesh is a life of faith upon the Son of God, who loved them, and gave Himself for them.' When in the house of God, or when one visits them in their homes, and questions them about their souls, the truth comes out. The quivering lip, the heaving sigh, the falling tear, and the downcast look, bear abundant evidence to the work within. And happier death-beds I never sat beside, than some which I have witnessed here. But when I have said this, I must add that there is a great deal in the parish which I could wish to see otherwise. And I fear worse is yet to come. A testing season is at hand, which recent events in New Zealand and Kishnagurh cause me to dread."

Now we do not mean to give any exaggerated views of the Red-River Settlement, or endeavour to persuade our readers that they are all real Christians, and that there are no bad characters among them. We do not think this. But we believe that there is much genuine Christianity among them, and we doubt not, if the trying times of which some are apprehensive should arrive, that it will come forth into decided action, and manifest its conservative power.

If we look to the native population, we find that, through the blessing of God on the faithful and persevering efforts of our Missionaries, scriptural Christianity has obtained a decided influence over the Indian nation called the Crees. Numbers of them have been led to renounce heathenism and profess the Christian faith; so much so, indeed, that not less than from 8000 to 10,000 Indians and halfbreeds are computed to have been brought under the instruction of our Missionaries: no slight result, when it is remembered that the entire population of the Hudson's-Bay territories, east of the Rocky Mountains, does not amount to more than 140,000. If we had such a proportion of Christian converts in India, they would amount to fourteen millions of souls.

From amongst these people Christian congregations have been raised up: some of them are now settled congregations, and present features of much interest. The most prominent are the Indian congregations at Red River, the Christian Indians at Christ Church, Cumberland House, 500 miles distant from Red River, in a north-westerly direction, and the congregation at Moose Fort, at the bottom of James' Bay, 1200 miles east by north from Red River.

We have space only for a few brief notices of the state of these congregations; but let our readers judge from a few sentences. At the expiration of the first week of the new year the Rev. A. Cowley is enabled to bear the following testimony, "Although this generally is a season of great festivity, I have not seen a drunken Indian, and have heard of but three cases of drunkenness among the people, heathen and Christian Indians, of the station." The value of this testimony will be more strongly felt, when it is remembered that drunkenness was the besetting sin of these tribes. Again, on Easter Sunday 1857, he remarks, "Morning congregation large: a goodly number were present at the sacrament. The usual solemnity and decorum prevailed, and we trust the season was profitable to all. Several partook for the first time."

One other congregation we shall so far refer to as to introduce one extract from the communications of the Rev. J. Horden, of Moose—

"*April* 30, 1859—During the greater part of the month I have been constantly engaged on the Indian books, except while fulfilling my pastoral duties. On Easter Sunday a large number met around the table of the Lord, after preparing themselves, by prayer and supplication, by assembling in the church for that purpose. But that which I think has, more than any thing else, caused me to feel deeply grateful to my God, is the having been enabled Watkins. They were very well executed, and required, for the most part, only the change from the pronunciation of one dialect into that of the other. We had made arrangements to translate together the whole of the New Testament, but his removal to the Cumberland district prevented our carrying our intentions into execution. These books, and the Prayer-book I have sent home, will provide the Indians with much of the life-giving food. I dedicate all to God. In a desire to extend his kingdom they were undertaken, that the inhabitants of this quarter of the world may be able to read, in their own tongue, of the wonderful works of God; that they may see what has induced the white man to pity their condition, what reason they have to fear and love God, the abundance of the mercies obtained through Christ—happiness below, happiness and eternal life above. I hope my spiritual children will be deeply grateful for all that is done for them, and that they may grow in grace and in the knowledge of our Lord and Saviour Jesus Christ. Many of them are now increasing in knowledge. They had first put into their hands the First Catechism of Dr. Watts, then the Bible and Gospel history, the Gospel of St. Matthew followed, and now the whole of the Gospels are printed for their use. Glory be to thee, O Lord!"

Let it be remembered, that from these more settled points the influence of scriptural Christianity is extending itself in various directions. The work which has been accomplished among the Crees has excited among other tribes a desire to be possessed of similar advantages. Taking the Red River as the basis of operations, the Missionary stations are spread abroad, like an expanded fan, from west to north and east. Some of them are very distant. One of our most advanced stations to the north, the English River station, was visited by the Bishop of Rupert's Land in the summer of 1859. This is a frontier station, the Chipewyans being found on the northern bank of the river and the Crees on the south. There the bishop was met by a deputation from the first-mentioned people—nearly fifty adults, with their wives and chil-

.... They spoke with great animation and earnestness, and listened with attention to what was laid before them. In their language there is a near approach to the click of the Hottentots, which recurs at intervals, coupled with a great abundance of the liquid L. To my own ear it is not inharmonious: some of their names are thus pretty enough, as, for instance, *Chillousa, Basilinné.*"

The bishop promised his utmost efforts on their behalf, and appeals to the Parent Committee to send out help. He says—"I only wish that all the Parent Committee had been in my place, and had heard the Chipewyans face to face. The result then would have been, I am convinced, that they would unanimously, without one dissentient voice, have acceded to the petition, and granted the prayer. Though absent, I trust they will act in the same spirit, and send a Chipewyan Missionary."

It is gratifying to be enabled to add, that before the bishop's appeal reached us, a Missionary was already on his way to strengthen the English-River Mission.

Thus the seed of the divine word is being scattered throughout the wilderness, and we doubt not that portions which we thought were lost are springing up, and will be found when least expected. The following fact may be adduced as an instance of this.

The Earl of Southesk has been travelling extensively throughout these regions. Proceeding by Fort Ellice and Qu'Appelle Fort, he and his party crossed the south branch of the Saskatchewan, advancing westward into the plains some thirty miles. From hence they passed, *via* Carlton and Fort Pitt, on the north bank of the Saskatchewan, to Edmonton, about 299 miles from the base of the Rocky Mountains, where they left their carts, using, in their stead, pack-saddles on their horses. Diverging from the Saskatchewan at this point, they pursued a north-westerly course until within about a day's march of Jasper House, where they struck the Medicine Tent River, the principal tributary of the Athabasca, and went up the river, some fifty miles, to its source in the mountains. "The scenery in this portion of the mountains was of the grandest description. The valley ran north and south, masses of rock, of an enormous height, towering above it on either side; and as it was situated at least 3000 feet above the level of the sea, with a view almost unobstructed, a charming prospect of the country was obtained. From the absence of any axemarks, or other indications of the presence of travellers, it is supposed that this valley has not been explored before."

But another and more encouraging discovery was made by him. At a Missionary meeting held in January last, in St. John's schoolhouse, his lordship, who was requested to address the audience, stated, 'that while on his trip, in the neighbourhood of the Rocky Mountains, he fell in with about twelve families of Assiniboine, or Stone Indians (a very wild and savage tribe), who professed Christianity, and, so far as he could judge, were acting up to their profession. These families were far from any Missionary station, and had not even seen a Missionary for many years. Still they showed considerable acquaintance with Scripture, and were regular in their morning and evening devotions. A little bell was always rung as their signal for assembling to worship, and the singing of hymns formed part of their religious exercises. At their earnest request his lordship wrote out for them several passages of Scripture. Their knowledge of religion is supposed to have been imparted to them by the Rev. Mr. Rundall, a Wesleyan Missionary, who went to Fort Edmonton in 1839, and left the country in 1847, on account of ill-health. They have, however, a regular teacher in one of themselves, who has been set apart by them for that purpose."

CUSTOMS OF THE HINDUS AND MUSSULMANS OF INDIA.

(Continued from p. 96.)

"On the 14th of Badun, which answers to our 23d day of August, there is a ceremony held in commemoration of Vishnu, or 'the preserving spirit.' The Hindu males begin the day by preparing all sorts of sweetmeats, and they then twist a sort of band, made either of silk, or cotton mixed with silk and silver threads. In this are always tied fourteen knots. This is called an *ununth,* and it must be fastened to the upper part of the arm. At one o'clock in the day they send for the Brahmin, their family priest, without whose presence no rite or ceremony can be performed, and they throw the *ununth* into a brass cup filled with milk and Ganges water, and make oblations of red clay and flowers, and burn incense. After this the Brahmins read from the Shasters an extract treating of the customs of the *ununth*. They believe that this custom has descended from time immemorial.

"The next custom which takes place in the Hindu year is a very remarkable one, and occurs usually about the beginning of our October, on the 25th day of the Hindu month, called Koobar; but as it must ensue during the light fortnight, it is of course variable. It is called the *Dusserah Leela*, which means, 'the ten days' sport,' although it usually continues eleven days. It is attended with the most profuse expense of money, laid out in making images of pasteboard dresses, and all manner of pyrotechnic display. In some cases the English officers have been known very largely, to contribute, *proh pudor!* to the grandeur and the effectiveness of this 'barbaric solemnity.'

A short history of the tradition will be necessary, to show the meaning of the different actors in the scene, which is often an enigma to numbers of spectators who flock to view it, unless they actually belong to the country, or have had it explained to them by an intelligent native.

"The Hindus, then, believe, that 81,000,000 of years ago, in the country of Lunka—which is the Sanskrit name for Ceylon, which they assert to be 10,000 miles from the shores of Bengal—there was a great king, of supernatural powers, whose name was Rawun. He had authority over all the spirits which disturb the peace of humanity. He had the power of walking on the sea as upon dry land, and was in the habit of making frequent journeys to India. Having seized on all the living creatures he could catch, he used to take them over to his own country, and to feast upon their flesh. Thus the world was much oppressed by his cruelty, and, from his being endowed with supernatural powers, no one could sufficiently make head against him. The divinity Vishnu, seeing the condition of the sons of men, and that they were suffering much, was grieved, and told Rawun that he would be destroyed by a human hand. He (Vishnu) assumed the incarnation of a human being, and became born as one of the sons of Jessurut, who was then reigning in Ujoodhea—or, as we call it, Oude—and had the whole world under his control. The name that was given him at his birth was Ramchund, and his brother Lachmun was born from the same birth, though two days after him. When Ramchund was twelve years old, he was married to Leta. Some time after this, Ramchund had a quarrel with his mother, and, in consequence, he left the abodes of men, and lived in the desert along with his wife and brother. They lived a rambling life: they subsisted upon hunting and fishing, and Leta dressed for them the food which they procured in their hunting and sporting excursions. On one occasion they left Leta under a tree, and went into a neighbouring jungle to hunt. It happened that Rawun had been making his excursions that day, and arrived at the place where the lady alone, seated under a tree, was waiting for the return of her brother and husband. Having the power of assuming whatever form he chose, he took that of a beggar of a religious kind, and approached to where she was seated. When he saw her close he became enamoured of her beauty, and, seizing her in his arms, mounted a stag which was at hand, and went along, with the speed of lightning, to his own country.

'Thus Pluto, seizing Proserpine, conveyed
To hell's tremendous gloom the affrighted maid.'

"On his progress he met two birds, who were the favourite allies of Vishnu, the one a vulture and the other a crow. He defeated them, and killed them both, and left their bodies on the ground, and went on to Luuka, or Ceylon. When Ramchund and Lachmun had come back, they were heartbroken to find that Leta was gone. They made every possible search for her, and travelled into the country far and near. When, in the course of their travels, they found the bodies of the vulture and crow, they knew them to be propitious to them. They burned the bodies, and, from the ashes, they were shown, by a divine spirit, where Leta was borne to. When Ramchund had ascertained this, he collected immense armies of bears and of monkeys, and went to the shores of Bengal. He chose one amongst the monkeys of prodigious stature, called in the Sanskrit Hunooman, or the Chief of Monkeys, and made him cross over to Lunka. On Hunooman's arrival there, he commenced destroying the houses in the island with fire. When he had proceeded to some extent in his work of destruction, Ramchund and Lachmun crossed over the sea to Lunka. Rawun sent his brother Krimkurrun to fight with Ramchund and Lachmun. In this combat they fought with stones, and rooted up trees to use as weapons. There was much slaughter amongst Rawun's subjects, and at last Krimkurrun was killed by an arrow from Lachmun's bow. Then Rawun sent his son Indurjeet against them, and he was killed by an arrow fired by Ramchund. At last Rawun came to fight in his own person, and there commenced a great combat, and Lachmun was killed. There was a physician in the army of Ramchund who declared that if some grass of the kind called *jeewun bhootee* were procured, and Lachmun were made to smell it, he would revive. Hunooman, the monkey, went into the forest for the grass, and having procured some, restored Lachmun to life. Towards the close of the fight Ramchund killed Rawun with arrows, and his army, with the exception of a small number, were routed. After this, another brother of Rawun's, named Baber, came and acknowledged his submission to Ramchund. Then Ramchund ordered that no further depredations should be committed; and having got back his wife, he returned to Oude, and, after the death of Jessurut, became king of the country.

"This story, incredible and absurd as it is, is most strictly believed, and all the characters who are mentioned in the course of it are represented either by living actors dressed conformably, or by immense figures of pasteboard. The representation is in a rude kind of theatrical style, exhibited

'Midst horrid shapes, and shrieks, and sights unholy,'

All the monkeys, the chief of them included, Hunooman, the bears, and the living actors in the story, are represented by Hindus. In the same semi-barbaric theatrical manner is acted the combat, the fire, and the destruction of the houses. The very large concourse of people, the thousands of instruments playing, the noise of acclamations, and the grotesque character of the scenes, are things which one does not soon forget. The whole transaction takes up eleven days, which have their Sanskrit names. The first day is called the *Bun ou bas*, abode in the forest. It represents the departure of Ramchund, Lachmun, and Leta to the desert, and parties from all quarters trying to dissuade them from it. The second day shows the abduction of Leta; the third, the killing of the vulture and crow; the fourth, the burning of vulture and crow; the fifth, the cutting off of Rawun's sister's nose. This punishment, the commonest in the country among native governments for a woman's infidelity, was supposed to be inflicted upon Rawun's sister for her brother's fault. The sixth is called *Lunka Julu*, the burning of the houses and property in Lunka by Hunooman. The seventh *Krim Kurrun ke biraee*, the fight between Krim Kurrun and Ram's army. On the eighth the people celebrate the fight between Ramchund's army and Indurjeet, and great quantities of the grass called *serhee* is burned. On the ninth day is represented also the combat, and the actors in the scene throw about earthen vessels called *kicopees*. On the tenth day there is a fight with Rawun, and it ends in the evening by his being killed. On this day the people commence the celebration by throwing stones over the large pasteboard body of Rawun; and towards night they set fire to him, to Indurjeet, and to Krim Kurrun; so the three hideous-shaped masses of pasteboard are turned into gigantic lighthouses, and so bright are the flames, that for a quarter of an hour the scene in the vicinity is as light as day; great quantities of fire-works are also let off during the combustion. On the eleventh day they celebrate the return of Ramchund to his family, the meeting of his kinsmen, and his re-establishment upon the throne.

"The next observance which occurs during the Hindu year takes place about the 13th of their Kohar, or 23d of our November. The first day kept holy is called *Dhuntaris*, from a Sanskrit word meaning the flowing in of wealth. On this day all the Hindus, whether of high or of low rank, make their houses altogether clean, apply the lime called chunam, to the walls, and have them put in the best possible order. They brush and clean their furniture, and spread out their best carpets, and, if they can afford it, they buy new dishes and goblets. The second day, being the next day to this, is called the little dewalee (*chotee dewalee*). On this day they make ready all sorts of sweetmeats, and partially illuminate their houses. The third day, which is the *dewalee* or great day of all, they make what they call a *puteree*, or clay image of Luchmee. She is the wife of Vishnu, and is the Hindu goddess of abundance. Round the image are twenty-five departments for lamps, and when it is night they light these lamps and illuminate the whole of the house, so that not a corner of it may remain in darkness; and having taken one of the new basins, and put thereon a gold mohur, or a rupee, according to their means, they assemble all their family, and send for a Brahmin. They will borrow money rather than not go through this ceremony, to omit which they consider as highly unfortunate. When they have put flowers, and sweetmeats, and wet rice upon the place on which the money is laid, they repeat the words of adoration to Ganesa—

'That Ganesa sublime
May bless with joy his own propitious clime.'

The basin or plate, and its contents, are all given as a present to the Brahmin. This pri-

ment is called a *duchma*. On the departure of the Brahmin they may eat, but they dare not touch a morsel till the offering is completed. They pass away the night in gambling, principally at *gunjeefa*, a game played with round cards, on which are pictured the Hindu deities; *brat chosar*, a game played on a piece of cloth having twenty-two divisions, three dice, and sixteen counters; at *solihi*, in which sixteen cowries are brought into play; or at *pacheesee*, a very common game in India, played with cowries and counters on a cloth piece of checked work. They must not, on any account, lie down during the whole of this night, and, until day-dawn, they must keep the lights burning in their houses. These observances they consider proper and necessary to propitiate the goddess 'Suoheree' or 'Abundance' for one years' prosperity. The *dewalee* is the most generally observed of all the festivals.

"On the 30th day of their month Ragh, or on our 8th of February, the festival of the *Sanka Nath* takes place. On that day all the Hindus go to the river and bathe. Then they collect a quantity of grain and rice mixed together, which is called in the country *kicheree*, a sort of crisped cake made of grain, salt, and clarified butter, called *pooper*, and the seed called zill, and these, together with some ready money, they give the Brahmins; and they believe that if, on this day, they obtain a rupee, it is as good as a hundred on any other day. They believe the origin of the custom to be, that, according to the Hindu chronology in the *sutjoog*, or first division of time, which is their idea of the golden age, there was once a certain traveller passing through the country, and, after enduring three long fasts, which, from poverty, he was unable to break, he found a vessel containing *kicheree*; he sat down and was about to eat it, when Mahadev, whose name is also Shunka, appeared. The god was in the guise of a beggar, and he asked from him the food, saying, he was very hungry. The traveller, notwithstanding his own wants, gave the beggar the food. The beggar solicited him not to do so, but

"On the 5th day of Phagoon among the Hindus, corresponding to our 14th day of February, is the ceremony of the *Busunth*. This is even observed partly by the Mussulmans. In the morning the Hindus bathe in the river, and afterwards, during the day, have large assemblages, and collect a number of dancers and singers, and make merry. All denominations of people on this day wear yellow clothes, if they can afford it. This is the colour of festivity. The custom, they assert, had its origin in the golden age, the time of the *Sutjoog*, Ramchunder was going to war, and appointed an assembly; when Hunooman, the chief of the monkeys, came into the assembly, and brought with him a large number of followers, and Ramchunder was well pleased, and gave them all splendid dresses. The meaning of the word 'Busunth' is 'spring,' and it is used also to express a time of pleasure.

"The next festival day is called the *Holee* and, like most of the other ones, it is determined by the moon, but it usually takes place about the beginning of March, which is the Hindu *Jyte*, and is the last month of their year. It is certainly remarkable as one of the most extraordinary customs ever practised among any people: it more resembles the description of the Roman saturnalia than any thing else which I recollect having heard of. On this day, throughout India, servants, masters, soldiers, porters, labourers, all associate and mingle promiscuously in the jokes and familiarities, when the master sinks all his authority. The world is made slightly acquainted with this observance from the notoriety of the interview, described so often, which happened some years ago between Runjeet Singh and Lord William Bentinck. The interview took place while the natives of Lahore were celebrating this holiday, and the astonishment of the noble parties at finding the people composing his court amusing themselves with flinging gold-dust at one another, and at the noise and licence which prevailed all throughout the palace, may well be conceived. They consider it an honour to throw dust on all whom they see, consequently they did not

scurrilous epithets to each other. These, which the language is most prolific in, are some of them, even when literally translated, unintelligible to any one who has not been long in the country. Thus it is known to be a most abusive thing to call a man your brother-in-law. But all the ribaldry, which takes place this day, is taken in jest. Then all ranks of people begin pelting each other with dust, which is of three kinds of pulverizing clay, viz. the umber, which is brown; the grolal. which is red; and the tesse, which is yellow, A short time after this, no matter where you go, every person you see has his clothes covered with some of these colours, and you find parties in every direction singing, dancing, and flinging about the various coloured dust. In one place you may see groups laughing immoderately and chewing pawn, or smoking; in another, a group quite senseless from the intoxicating influence of *bhung* or *subzeé*. The lowest order of the Hindus are all of them, on this day, generally drunk from spirits. The song, which is sung by all parties, is most licentious, and is generally shouted by them at the topmost pitch of their voices. It is called the *holee*. This custom, which is so generally practised by all parties from Lahore to Calcutta, and which obtains among all classes, is most lamely accounted for; but what the natives have told me I have put down and had it reiterated by many of all classes. They keep it in commemoration of the first appearance of fire upon earth. They believe this to have been the gift of the Almighty. They think that when they were first created they had no occasion for fire, but subsisted upon roots, fruits, and such unsophisticated diet as did not require fire to prepare it for eating; that a number of these aborigines, having assembled upon a large plain about the same time of the year as the *holee* occurs, some amongst them saw a flame of fire issuing from the ground in the form of the root of a tree; that they who saw it differed much in opinion as to what it was, and begun to dispute, to abuse one another, and to pelt each other with clay; that fortunately there came among them some Brahmins, who, having held a consultation, decided that the favour of Vishnu had thus given them fire; that the Brahmins addressed the multitude, and told them to approach the flame, which they accordingly did, and, when they were by its side, they threw into it wood, barley, wheat, and other kinds of grain; and, seeing the effect produced, they begun worshipping it and making merry, dancing and singing.

"The next observance which they generally attend to takes place about the middle of March, and again, during the next year, some time before the sowing of the autumnal crop. There are two harvests in Hindustan, one vernal, which is called the *rubbee*, and the other autumnal, which is called the *khurrieef*. The highest orders of the Hindus begin to observe this festival by sowing barley, or other sort of grain, in a small space of ground allotted for the purpose, and near the place they put a small lamp of oil, which is kept burning night and day, and they place near it flowers and roles, and some sweetmeats, and every morning early the guru, or family priest, reads out some extracts from the Vedas, to carry a blessing to it; and the eighth day from this is called the *tistummy*, and all the little boys and girls in the neighbourhood, who are about three years old, are assembled, and given a mark to their foreheads called a *tilk*, and the people prepare quantities of pastry, which they give to the children, and a little ready money, and they go to some place where there is a goddess's shrine, and make what is called their *durshun* by going up to the idol and depositing flowers before it. And on the tenth day from the first planting the corn, the seed has grown up, and the corn is some inches out of the ground, and it is rooted up and thrown into the Ganges; but the Brahmins do not throw away their roots, but receive a large sum of money from their followers for putting it into their turbans. On this day all merchants and traders commence their accounts. They believe that, many thousand years ago, there was a person, who was very poor, who bought some ground and sowed barley, but it did not spring up; that at last he kept calling on one of the goddess's names as he sowed in the ground, and that then the seed sprung up; that on the eighth day the goddess herself appeared, dressed in red, and holding in her hand lamps decorated with flowers. She remained there till the tenth day, when she disappeared.

"These customs of the Hindus apply to those of Hindustan Proper."

ENGLISH POLICY ON THE COAST OF CHINA.

In our last Number we indicated the *vexata quæstio* in which has originated our present serious and expensive war with the Chinese government—the right of entrance into Canton. The treaty of Nanking, the ratifications of which were exchanged at Hong Kong, June 26th, 1843, did undoubtedly provide for the residence of British subjects at the cities of Canton, Amoy, Fuhchau, Ningpo, and Shanghae, and that "without molestation or restraint." But this was subsequently modified. Such was the opposition of the Cantonese, not only to the entrance of foreigners into their city, but even to the enlargement of the space allotted without the city for the European hongs or factories; and such the inability of the local authorities to overcome their refractoriness, that Sir John Davis advanced to Canton with several vessels of war, capturing the Bogue forts, and compelling the Chinese to yield a sufficiency of room. On that occasion a convention was agreed upon at the Bocca Tigris, April 4th, 1846, which dealt specifically with the points in dispute. Our right of entrance was recognised, but its execution deferred. The following paragraph of the convention is explicit on this point—

"His Majesty the Emperor of China having, on his own part, distinctly stated that when, in the course of time, mutual tranquillity shall have been insured, it will be safe and right to admit foreigners into the city of Canton, and the local authorities being for the present unable to coerce the people of that city, the Plenipotentiaries on either side mutually agree that the execution of the above measure shall be postponed to a more favourable period; but the claim of right is by no means yielded or abandoned on the part of Her Britannic Majesty."*

The conviction of the Plenipotentiaries who signed and sealed that document is here clearly expressed, that the time had not arrived when the admission of foreigners into the city could be attempted with safety. The people of Canton would not suffer it except under coercion, and to this the local authorities felt themselves unequal. To insist upon it under such circumstances was not regarded as a becoming course by the British plenipotentiary. It would have neither been safe or right; and therefore, with his consent, it was postponed until the arrival of a *more favourable period*, when, through commercial intercourse and other conciliatory influences, irritation might subside, and "mutual tranquillity be insured." Of the wisdom of this decision no doubt can now be entertained, and it is to be regretted that the just principles laid down therein have not been persevered in. But it shadows out the line of policy which, so soon as circumstances permit, ought to be resumed on the coast of China. They who, in that quarter, are charged with diplomatic interests, need to be thoroughly acquainted with the idiosyncracy of China. Its formalism is excessive. Points of etiquette, of no real value in themselves, but handed down from time immemorial, such as the mode of communication between their high officials and those of other nations, the ceremonial to be pursued on the introduction of foreign embassies to a personal interview with the sovereign, constitute with them just those vital points on which they have resolved there shall be no surrender. There is an assumption of superiority in the Chinese, and a haughty reserve towards foreigners; but it is a portion of the national character, and is exhibited as well in their intercourse with each other as with us. If Canton was a prohibited city to the foreigner, the inner city of Pekin is a prohibited city likewise to all save the privileged classes who are admitted within its precincts. Pekin consists of two portions, the northern or Tartar city, called Nui Ching, and the southern or outer city, where the Chinese live. The northern city consists of three enclosures, one within the other, and each surrounded by its own wall. The inner area is called Kin Ching, or Prohibited City. When it is necessary to bring Chinese workmen into this interdicted city, they are conducted in blindfold; and when the work is done, they are again blindfolded and taken out. And here, within this reserved area, the *sanctum* of the Chinese system, in which the Emperor is not merely chief, but divinity, to whom universal homage is to be rendered, there is one point of more intensified reservation, the Kien Tsing Kung, or Tranquil Palace of Heaven, into which no one can enter without a special licence. This principle of reserve and exclusion is the pervading principle of the national organization. It centres in the Emperor, and extends from

---
* Papers relative to Naval Proceedings at Canton, p. 223.

him through the varied grades of officials in continually expanding circles, until at length it exhibits itself in the demeanour of the Chinese towards other nations. All this no doubt is very inconvenient and offensive. But what is to be done? We have resorted of our own accord to the coast of China for commercial purposes; and we have done so because such is our interest. It is just one of those peculiarities of national character which, under the influence of kindly intercourse, would have modified itself, given way by degrees, and finally have disappeared; and until this consummation had been attained, it would have been our wisdom to have avoided, as much as possible, collision on those points. But we have not had patience to wait; nor is this surprising, for nothing can be more contradictory to an Englishman's straightforward mode of action, than the official cunctation of Chinese diplomacy. We have got impatient, and have proceeded to put it aside by force. These ceremonial delays and obstructions to direct and prompt intercourse have been estimated by us at their true value, as useless, nay, mischievous, and to be got rid of as quickly as possible. But the Chinese are not of the same mind with us: they think just the opposite. And we have come into collision with them on these points. We have proceeded to deal with them as with the obstructions at the mouth of the Peiho. A little of our strength, it was thought, would suffice for the purpose, and so we set to work. The Cantonese would not give us right of entrance into Canton. We resolved to wait no longer. We summoned the high officials to give way to our demands. We asked of them more than, if they were ever so much disposed, they dared to concede. The high Chinese official knew well what would be the result to himself personally, if he ventured to admit the English—a popular insurrection, a displeased court, an angry menace from the vermilion pencil, and his own death by suicide. If they must needs fight, better to fight the English with their own people to back them, than, by concession, get rid of the pressure from without, and thus subject themselves to a worse pressure from within. Again we resolved, not only to have entrance into Canton, but to have free entrance into Pekin, and to hold direct communication with the Emperor himself. We resolved to come as no other ambassador ever had. English embassies had visited Pekin, but matters had been so managed as to save appearances, and to leave intact the prestige of the court. The flags pendant from the yachts and land-carriages of Lord Macartney's embassy had inscribed upon them, in large Chinese characters, "ambassadors bearing tribute from the country of England;" and when, on his interview with the Emperor at his summer residence in Tartary, his lordship, at the instance of the President of Rites, ascending the steps which led to the throne, bent on his knee, and lifted above his head, between both his hands, the square box of gold, adorned with jewels, which contained the letter of the British King to the Emperor of China, he was regarded at that moment as presenting the tribute. But now, in these modern days, we will go on no such terms. We must needs visit Pekin, and visit it as recognised equals: these ridiculous ceremonies must not interfere. But ridiculous as they may seem to us, they are vitalities to the Chinese, and, rather than yield, they are prepared to fight for them. We had to force our way into Canton at the cost of much blood. We shall, if persistent on these points, have to do the same at Pekin. Are we, as a Christian nation, justified in the sight of God in beating down by force the peculiarities of the Chinese system? Are the results which we would compass such as to justify the shedding of human blood? That is a question which, as a nation, when we give account of our stewardship we shall find it difficult to answer. All our perplexities at Canton have been ascribed to the want of free entrance into the city, and immediate access to the Chinese Commissioner. All our difficulties with the nation generally we now ascribe to the want of free access to Pekin, and direct communication with the Emperor himself. Are they not rather attributable to other causes, with which we are ourselves far more intimately concerned? Is no self-correction necessary? Has our conduct along the coast always been innocuous and praiseworthy? Have we given no cause to the Chinese officials to complain? Has the advent of the Englishman on the coast inaugurated that benignant period which has introduced ameliorating influences into China? Or have we not rendered the Chinese worse than they were previously? "The Chinese at first feared and respected those who came to their shores, and whom they saw to be their superiors in the art of war, and in the spirit of enterprise; and if means and conduct befitting the superior knowledge and civilization of their visitors had been taken to enlighten them, such efforts, it cannot be supposed, would have been useless or unappreciated." But we first wrong them, contravene their fiscal regulations, grow opium for contraband purposes, and smuggle a large revenue out of China. They grow savage and retaliate, and then we flog them.

It is necessary we should have a just perception of our actual position in China, and that with a view to the adoption of such a policy on its coast as may be more considerate towards the Chinese, and more becoming as regards ourselves. It is with such views that we attempt an analysis of recent events there. It is not at all with the intention of imputing blame to any of those individuals who have occupied responsible positions in China. All, we are persuaded, has been done with the best intentions. But political and commercial interests on that coast are like the oceanic tides in the same region: there are currents and countercurrents; and the politician from Europe finds himself like the shipmaster when he has to deal with the *Kuro-Siwo*, or "Black Stream," which at the best is but little known. Hence the judgment becomes warped, and able and humane men get wrong without intending it.

So also with respect to our naval and military operations on the coast: they have always been conducted with the greatest forbearance and humanity, and by none more so than by Admiral Sir M. Seymour. But our commanders on the coast are the executive of our diplomatists; and when they are informed that, diplomacy having failed, the solution of the difficulty devolves on them, however they might wish it otherwise, they must bring into requisition the force at their disposal. Still it must be remembered, that there is no European nation which has derived so large a revenue from China, and by such indefensible means, and that there is no nation which has shed so much Chinese blood as England. This is an unhappy notoriety which cannot be regarded without the deepest pain by every well-wisher of his country.

To resume our review of events as they occurred—Sir John Davis's convention with Keying neither yielded nor abandoned the treaty-right of entrance into Canton: it only deferred its execution until a more favourable period. In the meanwhile, British subjects were to enjoy full liberty and protection in the neighbourhood, *on the outside* of the city of Canton, within certain limits fixed by treaty; freedom to make excursions on the two sides of the river, where there were not numerous villages, being also granted. We have stated accurately the articles of the convention, and it certainly guaranteed for the suspension of the treaty-right, until the time came, when, in consequence of an alteration in the feelings of the Cantonese towards us, it might be carried out without provoking popular tumults, and endangering in consequence the peaceable relations of the two countries. In fact, until the hostile feelings of the city population had become altered towards us, the fulfilment of the provision of the original treaty remained impracticable. If the British insisted on their treaty-right, and entered the city, the local authorities declared that they could not protect them. The execution, therefore, became impossible, except under the protection of British troops in such force as to overawe the city population, and amounting to a military occupancy of the city: and such, in fact, has been the course of events. Yet the convention of 1846 pledged us not to compel an entrance; and it ought to have been remembered and adhered to. Nor does the force of it appear to be invalidated by the fact, that, at a subsequent period, Keying, in answer to a proposition that the British officials should visit him at his own residence in the city, got rid of a present difficulty by undertaking that, at the end of two years from April 1847, British officers and people should have free access into Canton. It was done in the hope that, during the intervening period, the Canton population would have become better affected towards foreigners, and such perchance would have been the case, had we conducted ourselves in all respects as became a Christian and civilized people.

As, however, the appointed period of April 1849 drew near, it became obvious, that whatever might be the feelings of the local authorities, they had no power to compel the people, who retained all their hostility to the measure, "to behave themselves in a quiet and peaceable manner;" and that, therefore, "without some military demonstration, it would be useless to attempt an entrance into the city."* It was then that Lord Palmerston sought information as to the practical disadvantage in regard to commerce under which British residents laboured in consequence of exclusion from free entrance into the city, and the practical advantages which they would gain by admission, receiving from Mr. Bonham the decisive reply which we introduced in our last Number, "that no material advantage to our commerce would be gained by British subjects being admitted indiscriminately into Canton."

This decided the Home Government as to the course which ought to be adopted. It

---

* Mr. Bonham to Lord Palmerston, July 20 1848.

consisted in an adherence to the principles of Sir John Davis's convention, deferring thus to a more favourable opportunity a question which was not yet ripe for solution. This was the temperate line of policy enjoined on Sir John Bowring, when he was invested with full powers as Her Majesty's Plentipotentiary on the Chinese coast, and that both by the Earl of Granville and the Earl of Malmesbury, the representatives of different administrations. The British official, however, felt strongly on this point. In a letter to the Earl of Clarendon, April 19th, 1852, he expressed his conviction that the importance of admission into Canton, and of access to the high authorities, had not been sufficiently appreciated. He also considered that it might be obtained without serious difficulty. Hence the re-agitation of this question in April 1854, and the continuous and irritating discussions maintained with the Chinese officials on the subject, engendering suspicion and bad feelings, which at length exploded in the affair of the "Arrow." Hence the quick and peremptory action of the British authorities on the coast, the seizure of the Government junk, and the commencement of military operations. A very little pressure, it was thought, would suffice to obtain the point so long contended for, of free entrance into Canton. With each fort, as it yielded, it was thought Yeh would yield. But these demonstrations, instead of overawing him, only served to bring out his obstinate and savage temper, until, on opening our eyes, we found that we had drifted into a war with China, which no one wished for or intended, but which unhappily has continued ever since, and which, so far, has cost us much, and profited us nothing.

Resuming our sketch of events as they transpired, on October 25th, 1856, the British admiral took possession of the Dutch Folly, a fort with fifty guns on a small island opposite the city. Letters and missiles continued to be expended, the one on Yeh, the other on the defences; but the Chinese Commissioner maintained the same imperturbability. The defences yielded, but he did not. The *iron* arguments were therefore brought to bear somewhat more closely upon him. Fire was opened on Yeh's yamun, a large space of ground within the old city which contained his residence. It was done in such a way as to show that it was done reluctantly, and merely with the object of inducing him to yield, a shot being fired at intervals of from five to ten minutes from the 10-inch pivot gun of the "Encounter." The irritated barbarian responded to these importunate knocks at his yamun's gate by issuing a proclamation, having appended to it his own seal, in which he offered a reward of thirty dollars for the head of every Englishman. The document runs as follows—

"YEH, the Governor-general, proclaims the following—

"The English barbarians have attacked the provincial city, and wounded and injured our soldiers and people. Their crimes are indeed of the most heinous nature:

"Wherefore I herewith distinctly command you to join together to exterminate them, and I publicly proclaim to all the military and people, householders and others, that you should unite with all the means at your command, to assist the soldiers and militia in exterminating these troublous English villains, killing them whenever you meet them, whether on shore or in their ships. For each of their lives that you may thus take you shall receive, as before, thirty dollars. All ought to respect and obey, and neither oppose nor disregard this special proclamation."*

This sanguinary document rendered the prospect of an adjustment more distant than ever. One attempt, however, in that direction the admiral resolved to make before he advanced further. Modifying the demands, which had hitherto been preferred, he acquainted Yeh that he would be satisfied with this simple concession, that at Canton the foreign representatives should have the same access to the authorities as at the other ports. Had this moderation been used at the beginning, matters might have been arranged; but now that blood had been shed, and savage tempers aroused, were the Cantonese more likely to concede a point, to which already, as included in more extended demands, they had given the most decided opposition? Had the shots so freely bowled from the British ships into Yeh's yamun conciliated the people, or rendered them better disposed to give a friendly welcome to the British officials? If Yeh had found it impracticable to persuade the Cantonese before a shot was fired, how was he likely to prevail with them now? Yeh, in his reply to Sir John Bowring, refers to the increased difficulty in which he found himself.

"The proposition made before was objected to by the entire population of Canton; the people affected by the present proposition are the same Canton people; the city is the same Canton city; it is not another and separate Canton city. How can it be said that there

* Papers, &c., p. 40.

is no connexion whatever between the two propositions? "But more than this, the Canton people are very fierce and violent, differing in temper from the inhabitants of other provinces. Admission into the city was refused you in 1849 by the people of Canton, and the people of Canton of the present day are the people of Canton of the year 1840; and there is this additional difficulty in mooting the question of admitting British subjects into the city now, namely, that the strong feeling against your Excellency's countrymen having been aggravated by the terrible suffering to which the people have been subjected, without a cause, they are even more averse to the concession than they were before.*

Offensive operations were in consequence resumed. Two guns were placed in position on the Dutch Folly, and, the fullest warning having been given to the inhabitants in the vicinity to remove their persons and property, an occupation in which they were engaged during the whole of the previous night, opened fire in the direction of the city wall, which was quickly followed by the conflagration of the houses in the line of attack. A practicable breach having been opened, preparations were made for storming, and about 3 P.M. the English colours were planted on the wall by Captain Bate. A field-piece placed in the breach cleared the approaches to the yamun of the Imperial Commissioner, which was duly entered by the admiral at the head of the marines. Yeh, however, was not there to receive him, and the position, being found untenable, was abandoned at night-fall.

The city population began now to be thoroughly roused. A notification was issued by all the gentry and scholars—"The English authorities have openly violated the treaty in attacking our batteries with cannon, setting fire to and destroying them, and wounding and killing our soldiers. Is there, we would ask, any principle of right in operations such as these?.... Everbody's blood is boiling with indignation; but we can only ask the officials and merchants of other countries, and the principal English merchants themselves, to look into the unreasonable perversity of the English authorities, and the manner in which they have disregarded treaty obligations."

A counter notification was issued by Mr. Consul Parkes "for the removal of misconceptions by declaration of the truth, to the end that confidence may be restored to the public mind." To its two concluding paragraphs we direct attention—

"To conclude—this quarrel is not with the people: our proceedings have not originated in any thing done by the people. They have been caused by the obstinacy and discourtesy of the chief authority, and for any calamity that may result from them the chief authority is singly responsible. There is but one means of escape from it, and this is in the hand of the chief authority, who, if he lose no time in meeting our high authorities, will be enabled, by arranging matters on a satisfactory footing with them, to put an end to the existing peril, and to prevent the recurrence of like misfortune in the time to come.

"Think how completely at our mercy are the lives and property of the entire population of the city; and with what facility, in one moment of time, we could effect their utter destruction—a terrible contingency! You are told this in no spirit of boasting: the power of our nation is too well known to require that we should indulge in self-glorification; but simply because we have no wish to see a long continuance of these hostilities, so cruel to the feelings of the people and so injurious to their interests."*

Surely, if we had no quarrel with the people, and the collision had not been caused by any thing which originated with them, it ought to have been felt that we had no power over their lives and property; and that, although force was at our command, we were powerless to use it against a people who we acknowledged had committed no injury against us. With one breath we tell them they are innocent, and, with another, terrify them with threats as though they were guilty persons. The inconsistency of the document exhibits the falseness of the position into which we had been betrayed.

The Chinese now closed up to the conflict, firing with desultory matchlocks and wall-pieces from the south-western angle of the city wall upon the inmates of the factories. They were answered by shot and shell thrown by the ships, at moderate intervals, into the yamuns of the Tartar-General and Governor of the province, situated at the back of the city, and surrounded with large trees and open courtyards, which separated them from the more populous and densely-built dwellings of the people. Heavy guns, placed upon the Dutch fort, were also directed against the Kwang-yin-shan hill, to the great amazement of the Chinese, who had imagined that position secure against all attacks.

On the morning of November 5th, a docu-

---

* Papers, &c., p. 89.

* Papers, &c., p. 69.

ment was sent in triplicate to the British Consulate, from the house of the Chinese merchant Howqua, one copy being intended for Her Britannic Majesty's Plenipotentiary, one for the naval Commander-in-chief, and one for the British Consul. It purported to be an address from the inhabitants of the whole city. The following is a translation of this document, in which, not without reason, an entire population prayed that their case might be considered, and that they might be spared from the destruction which threatened them—

"Every question has its rights, every position its contigencies of advantage and disadvantage. We cannot refrain from stating those incidental to the present one for the benefit of your Excellency's nation.

"We, the Cantonese, who have been born and brought up in this place, some of us in the public service, some of us in trade, whatever our vocation, have each one and all our property, our very food and raiment, in this city, and to all of us, hundreds of thousands in number, the city is our base and our foundation.

"Your nation has traded at Canton for more than a century, during which it may be said that between you and ourselves, the Cantonese, there have been relations of friendship, and not of hostility.

"The late affair of the lorcha was a trifle; it was no case for deep-seated animosity, as a great offence that could not be forgotten: yet you have suddenly taken up arms, and for several days you have been firing shell, until you have burned dwellings and destroyed people in untold numbers.

"It cannot be either told, how many old people, infants, and females, have left their homes in affliction. If your countrymen have not seen this, they have surely heard, have they not, that such is the case?

"What offence has been committed by the people of Canton that such a calamity should befal them?

"Again, it has come to our knowledge that you are insisting on official receptions within the city. This is, doubtless, with a view to amicable relations; but when your only proceeding is to open a fire upon us which destroys the people, supposing that you were to obtain admission into the city, still the sons, brothers, and kindred of the people whom you have burned out and killed will be ready to lay down their lives to be avenged on your countrymen, nor will the authorities be able to prevent them.

"The authorities are able to accord you admission into the city, but they are not able to assure to such of your countrymen as do enter a perfect immunity from harm.

"If, then, your countrymen were admitted, could you always have a large force here for their protection? A protecting force cannot remain here any great length of time; and if death and wounds were to be the condition of your entering it, what boon would your admission into the city be, even were you to obtain it?

"There is another point. Although shells have been flying against the city for several days, burning buildings and destroying life, no fire has been returned by the troops. This is really friendly and conceding: it is enough to content you. And as you resorted to hostilities for a small matter, so now, for the sake of the people's lives, you may suspend them; and, considering what has been achieved at the present stage of proceedings, there allow them to terminate. Why add another difficulty to the existing one, and so cause an interruption of the friendly understanding between our countries?

"To conclude: it is not well to trust power too far; neither is it right to let a feud so confirm itself that it cannot be ended.

"There is one point of which you lose sight. You do not remember that our authorities are subject to promotion, translation, and similar changes of office, which may remove them from Kwang-tung: in the twinkling of an eye its whole establishment may be changed. But the native trader has been here, generation after generation, from father to son, from grandsire to grandson, for hundreds and thousands of years, without interruption of the line. You do not reflect upon the distant future, that to inflict injury on the Canton people is to make enemies of thousands and millions of men; that the longer the feud endures, the deeper rooted it will be; that the more protracted the struggle the more impetuous will be the zeal for it. Is it in your power to go the extreme length of injury that can be inflicted?

"To resolve on this is truculently to contemplate the extermination of every living being in Canton—is to contemplate the total abandonment of its trade. What in that case would be your gain? And if resolved to go this length, how are you to dispose of the French, the Americans, and other foreign nations?

"This is the unanimous declaration, made with sincerity and earnestness, of the Cantonese. We submit it in the hope that your Excellency will deign to consider it, and we respectfully present our wishes for your Excellency's peace and prosperity.

"Representation made by the whole population of Canton."

This was followed by a respectable deputation of the gentry of the city, who waited on the Consul with a view to the adjustment of difficulties. But to the accomplishment of this, one thing was requisite—concession upon the part of Yeh. The British, with their ships and guns, had done their best to overcome his obstinacy, but in vain. The gentry were now told, that if they desired peace, they must constrain him; and that, if they could not do so, the war must go on: in other words, that they must continue to suffer for the delinquencies of Yeh, whose obstinacy they declared themselves to be as incapable of overcoming as the English found themselves to be. They "urged that the Imperial Commissioner's obstinacy was altogether uncontrollable, and that they could not influence him; and they deprecated injury to the population of the whole city for the fault of one man."

Once more the indomitable Yeh was summoned to surrender, and twenty-four hours were given him for deliberation, before active operations were recommenced. In his answer he concedes nothing, but defends himself. He stated that when fire had been opened on the city forts he had refrained from any hostile rejoinder, in consideration of the peaceful relations which for many years had subsisted between the nations. But when fire had been opened on the city, by which, as he asserted, numberless houses had been consumed, with considerable loss of life, the people had come crowding to his court in thousands, demanding why they should be subjected suddenly to such suffering at the hands of the English; and at their demand he had issued a proclamation, offering a reward for the head of every Englishman. That we justly considered a most barbarous proceeding, and not only the British authorities, but the French representative, the Comte de Courcy, remonstrated with Yeh because of it. But when, without warning, shots were plumped amidst the crowded houses and dense population of a Chinese city—when individuals, who probably never had any intercourse with us during their whole lives, saw their homes wrecked, and their friends killed or wounded—did we not, in their eyes, appear just as barbarous and cruel? It is not surprising that heathen people, who had no guiding principle, should proceed at once to avenge themselves by every means in their power, however unscrupulous and sanguinary. If we disturb and irritate a nest of wasps, it is not to be wondered at if the insects use their sting. It is their nature, and we must expect it. We are at liberty to destroy the insects, but it is rather a serious thing to deal with multitudes of men and women after the same fashion, more particularly as we profess ourselves to be the followers of One, who came not to destroy men's lives, but to save them.

On November 12th, the admiral proceeded to possess himself of the Bogue forts, which command the entrance into the Canton river. Previous to attack, a flag of truce was sent to the principal fort, summoning the commanding-officer to surrender, on the condition of their being restored, without injury, when difficulties should be adjusted. This, however, he declined to do, stating that he had orders to fight, and that he should open fire on any ships that approached within a certain distance of his batteries. The engagement accordingly commenced, but, on account of the strength of the forts, they had to be attacked in detail, and those on the north and south Wang-tung, mounting 200 pieces of cannon, fell on the 12th; those of Aneanghoy, mounting 187 pieces, on the 13th.

The capture of the Bogue forts was followed by the destruction of the Shamun forts at the south-west angle of the city. These were dismantled and blown up, the working parties being fired upon by the Chinese troops in the adjoining houses.

Yeh was duly informed of these new calamities, and the admiral again called upon him to comply with the requisition which he had made; but the Chinese Commissioner, in his answer to Mr. Consul Parkes, declares that the measures pursued by the British commander had rendered all concession upon his part impossible.

"As to your proposal in the same letter, that we 'should meet as becomes, &c.,' an interview might of course have been practicable in the first instance, but do the proceedings of Admiral Seymour, who has commenced hostilities without cause, show any acquaintance with what 'becomes?' He has come to Canton, and, at a moment's notice, he has destroyed habitations without number, with considerable loss of life; the sufferers are crowding to my court, complaining of their distress, and entreating me to do them justice; and such, at this moment, is 'the opposition of the gentry and the turbulent violence of the people,' that not only would your Excellency have some difficulty in entering the city, but, for the time being, I, myself, should have equal trouble in getting out of it. It is the admiral's wanton proceeding that has provoked all this irritation. Let your Excellency once again well consider it."*

---

* Papers, &c., p. 107.

On November 18th the British guns from the Dutch Folly re-opened fire on the Tartar buildings in the Tartar city, but ceased at noon, to allow time for a reply to a note sent in by Sir John Bowring, proposing an interview with the High Commissioner in the city; a request which, if granted, was to ensure the cessation of hostilities. The British Plenipotentiary declared, that if Yeh was unable to control the people, he could protect himself. Yeh, in his answer, after referring to the feeling of animosity with which the population was pervaded, replies to the British official—

"You say in your letter that you are quite able to provide for your own safety: it is, I think, but too probable that, so far from having your safety in your own hands, you are incurring mortal danger. Would your Excellency but follow the course of the late Plenipotentiary, Mr. Bonham, you would, in so doing, be following the policy of safety. Your Excellency, during your service (here) as Consul, must have seen with your own eyes the real condition of things. To conclude, I request your Excellency, once more, to ponder well on this—that in the management of all matters, we must act as reason teaches is right before heaven and due to man, before we can arrive at any satisfactory result."*

It now appeared but too plainly how great the misapprehension had been under which this series of aggressive operations had been commenced, when it was thought that a little pressure would suffice to overcome the reluctance of the Chinese Commissioner, and obtain for us entrance into the city. This Sir John Bowring now clearly perceived. In a letter to the admiral, dated November 8th, 1856, he observes—"Whatever may have been the importance of the question which necessitated the first appeal to hostilities, it has assumed a character seriously involving all our present and future relations with China." Undoubtedly it had done so, and that this would be the issue had been foreseen by many.

The war now commenced in right earnest. Yeh had been taken by surprise, and was at first wholly unprepared for a conflict with the English. But he lost no time in collecting all the forces within reach of Canton, and summoning to his aid all the village braves, who are recruited mainly from among the idle and dangerous classes of the population. The results soon appeared. On the night of Dec. 14th the Chinese set fire simultaneously, in several places, to the houses surrounding the Factory buildings, and all the foreign establishments, with the exception of the English Factory, were burnt to the ground. The whole of Old and New China Streets, with the contiguous portions of the suburbs, were consumed. The admiral, feeling the importance of holding the position at Canton, the church and barracks being preserved, proceeded to entrench a portion of the Factory garden, and garrisoned it with 300 men. They were not suffered to remain unmolested. The Factory being threatened, the British proceeded to burn the suburbs to the right and left, in carrying out which operation a party of the 59th was repulsed with loss from the city wall. A retrograde movement now became necessary. The admiral, finding it impossible, with the handful of troops at his disposal, to bear up against the increasing pressure of his assailants, withdrew from all the advanced positions in the immediate vicinity of the city, falling back upon the Macao fort, which remained for a considerable time our advanced position in the Canton river.

Tidings of these events soon reached England. So serious were they considered to be that they caused a defeat of the ministry. More than this, they had to be accepted as a disagreeable necessity. Chinese barbarity had broken out fiercely, and every method which an unscrupulous hostility could devise, even so far as the attempt to poison the English community at Hong Kong, was brought into requisition by Yeh and his Cantonese, who now appeared intent on one object, the entire expulsion of the English from their waters. The western powers also had come to their determination. Their relations with the Celestial Empire had long been unsatisfactory. The suitable moment appeared to have arrived when China might be constrained to abandon her peculiarities, and to throw open, not only the vast interior, but even the sacred city of Pekin, to the entrance of the inquisitive foreigner. France and England were to unite in a military demonstration so imposing as to overbear all resistance, while from four countries, England, France, Russia, and America, Ministers Plenipotentiary were to be accredited to the Court of Pekin, who, following up diplomatically the successes of our fleets and soldiers, were to content themselves with nothing less than access *ad libitum* to the imperial presence, on such terms as might befit the representatives of equal powers, and therefore without the kotow. They were to have free entrance into Pekin; how far does not appear to have been fully understood. To be

---

* Papers, &c., p. 108.

there, and yet be detained in the Chinese city, would be to subject our representative to a degradation greater than if they had continued to negotiate outside. Even if they were admitted into the Tartar city, while the vermilion city remained interdicted, they would still be stamped with inferiority in the presence of the high officials of the Chinese empire If the representatives of the western powers were to approach his Celestial Majesty on terms of equality, they needed to have access, not only into Pekin, but into the Kien Tsing Kung itself. But the British Ambassador was to require, not merely access to His Imperial Majesty, but the permanent residence of a British official at Pekin. This was not a new demand. On the occasion of Lord Macartney's embassy, the same request was preferred. Kien-lung, on that occasion (in his 58th year, 1793), communicated with George III. in a very patronizing document—

"The Emperor makes this communication for the information of the King of England—

"'You, oh king, who are distant by the breadth of several oceans, while your yearning heart inclines toward our transforming influence, have sent a special envoy respectfully to present a memorial and gifts. Having crossed the seas, he has reached our Court and made the prostrate salutation: he has also presented the productions of your country, thus exhibiting your loyal devotion. I have looked over the document, and find the expressions are truthful and sincere, exhibiting the honesty of your Majesty's respectful obedience, which is deserving of the highest commendation.'"*

He then refers to the proposal of a resident Ambassador at the Court of Pekin—

"As to the request in your Majesty's memorial, to be allowed to locate one of your people at the Celestial Court, to watch over the commercial interests of your nation, this is opposed to the constitution of the Celestial Court, and cannot, by any means, be permitted. Hitherto Europeans of every nation, who have desired to receive employment at the Celestial Court, have been permitted originally to come to the metropolis, but, having once come, they respectfully complied with the etiquette of the Celestial Court in their clothing; they remained quietly within their churches; and were never permitted to return to their native lands. These are the unalterable regulations of the Celestial Court, as I presume your Majesty is well aware. Now your Majesty wishes to be allowed to place one of your people to remain in the metropolitan city; but since he cannot come to the capital in the character of a European in the Imperial service, and remain in the capital, never to return to his native land, and, moreover, as he cannot be permitted to come and go, or to carry on constant communications, there would certainly be no advantage gained. Further, the territory under the dominion of the Celestial Court being most ample and extensive, when envoys arrive at the capital from any of the outer dependencies, the provision for them at the intepreters' hotel, and their various movements, are all controlled by fixed rules, so that they are never allowed to follow their own option. Now, should one of your people be left in the capital, his language would be unintelligible, his dress would be strange, and there is no place where he could be located. If he should come to the capital, and enter the Imperial service as a European, he would be compelled to change his garments in accordance with the regulations; but the Celestial Court is unwilling to force people into such difficulties. Should the Celestial Court wish to send a man to reside in your country, would your nation permit such a thing? Besides, as there are a great many countries in Europe, and not your country alone, suppose, like your Majesty, every country should request to be permitted to place a man in the capital: how could permission be granted to every one? So that this affair is beset with difficulties. How can we, at the request of your Majesty, a single man, alter the laws of the Celestial dynasty, which have been in force for more than a hundred years?'"†

We were about to ask much; we were scarcely aware how much. We decided to demand a change in the ceremonial of the Chinese Court—with sacrilegious touch to approach that which is most sacred in the estimation of the Chinese. We were about to interfere with the queen bee of the Chinese hive. Perhaps we had in our minds the example of the bee-charmer of some fifty years ago, who had such power in the management of that peculiar insect, that he could possess himself of the queen bee without exciting her resentment, and, by placing the queen wherever he wished the bees to settle, manage the whole hive. Perhaps we had a latent thought that our Ambassador, if resident at Pekin, could possess himself of such influence over the Emperor, as, through him, to manage the vast hive of China. But we have not yet exhibited the skill of the bee-charmer, and the

---

* "North-China Herald," February 6, 18:6. † Ibid.

queen bee is not yet in our hand. Meanwhile, not finding his Celestial Majesty quite so amenable as the royal insect, we have set to work to break down the hive, and in so doing have got severely stung for our pains.

In short, we have been asking for a revolution in the Government of China. So the Chinese regard it. Can we be surprised if they resist, until, finding we are too strong for them, they profess to yield in order to gain time, and then exhibit a more determinate resistance? Probably they will again be defeated, and again agree to prescribed stipulations. How shall we ensure their fulfilment? Have we resolved on the permanent occupancy of Pekin? Certainly, for the resident Ambassador, that would be a very desirable arrangement, and would place him personally on a much more secure footing. But we shall find such an embassy rather expensive, and in other ways inconvenient in its character.

Meanwhile, in sending forth our Minister Plenipotentiary to insist on such concessions, we have been as sanguine of success as Sir J. Bowring in the matter of entrance into Canton. Nationally we adopted his principles of action. A little pressure brought to bear upon a well-selected spot, one nearer the organs of vitality than Canton, and all would be well. The Chinese emperor would come forth from his seclusion, resign without a sigh all his arrogant pretensions to superiority, and concede to us readily all the privileges we should ask, and this, not to obtain from us corresponding advantages—for neither he nor his subjects wished to visit our shores—but to dissuade us from smiting him with the naked sword which we held *in terrorem* over him. We should have known otherwise. We should have known that the Chinese never will yield these points except on compulsion; a fact which suggests two very serious considerations—is it right to use it? and then, can we so use it as permanently and effectually to secure the objects which we have in view?

RUPERT'S LAND—ITS PROSPECTS.

It is the distinctive feature of genuine Missionary work that it cannot stand still: it must needs go forward. It is like the flow of the tide, which, though met by numberless obstructions, still continues in some direction to open a passage for itself, with an impulse at first feeble, but which, slowly gaining strength, isolates the projecting rocks, and then, burying them in its depths, establishes its uninterrupted dominion far as the eye can see. The great evangelistic effort has commenced, and it must needs go forward. A Divine Power urges it on; and therefore wherever, amidst the wide range of heathenism, we find a standing-point won for Christ, we discover there a vitality more or less powerful which will not be satisfied unless it put forth new efforts and make new conquests. Thus, in the Rupert's-Land Mission the more settled points become centres of more extended action. In the direction of the Plain Indians, where the Indian tribes are most numerous, advances are being made, and opportunities sought for the extension of the Gospel. An effort of this kind made from the Nepowewin station by our native Missionary, the Rev. H. Budd, presents an interesting specimen of these tentative efforts to our readers—

"*Feb.* 20, 1859—As we got ready last night, we were up in time this morning for an early start, with two young men and three trains of dogs. The thaw will soon commence, and we must make all possible haste to make this trip before the thaw. I want to see the chief of the buffalo-hunters, 'Mistowasis' by name, or 'Big-child.' I have heard something of this chief before, and I had a wish to see him. He has always been considered kind to our men when out there with him; and he always has a band of Indians about him, which I wish to see too. To-day it was snowing, and made travelling very difficult, for the snow had already covered the road. We had to go with the snow-shoes on our feet all the day, and at night we felt very weary. When we had camped and made our fire, we took our suppers, fed all our dogs, had our prayers, and made ready to lay down.

"*Feb.* 23—We came up to the camp of Indians soon in the afternoon of the following day: the man, however, was not at home himself, but the women and children were. After resting ourselves in the tent for some time, and getting something for our dogs, we proceeded on our way, and went on till night overtook us, when we had to put up for the night. We started early in the morning, and reached the edge of the plain by noon, the plain (properly so called) commencing from here. We took our dinner, and made ready to cross the wide

CHURCH, &c., OF THE BISHOP OF RUPERT'S LAND, RED RIVER.

plain, which is like one vast field of snow. Late on the evening we came to the first woods on the south branch of the Saskatchewan. Here we found a little wood, and were glad of it, encamping for the night. Resuming our journey, we proceeded on to the Moose-woods: the snow being less in the wide, plain our dogs came on much better. We met three of the Company's trains in the evening: they had come off from the Moose-woods, and are on their way to Fort-à-la-Corne. In the evening, rather late, we at length arrived at Mistowasis' house. We found quite a comfortable house to lodge in, and every thing that I could expect to find in a civilized place, was to be found in this house. There is quite a village of houses. The free-traders occupying a row of houses, and the Company also having houses there, the place looked quite inhabited. We soon had a comfortable supper. I found that the chief man was not at home. He was away hunting the buffalo, but was expected to be home soon. I resolved to go after him, for he was the principal person I came here to see. I called the people together in the house, and I read a portion of God's word, and endeavoured to explain it to them. There were a mixture of Canadian half-breeds, and Indians, who came to join us in our evening prayers.

"We got up early, and were soon ready to go off after Mistowasis. The Company's men started off with us, and kept us company for part of the way. Our route lay towards the Eagle Hills; but the Company's men were going in another direction looking for provisions to trade. I sent off two of our sleighs in company with them, to try for some provisions too. However, when the sun got hot, a regular thaw came on, and we were all stuck, and none of us could move. We all remained together, and waited till the night came on, when we could have nice travelling. As the sun was setting, it got colder, and we all started off, and travelled all the night. Just at break of day we reached the chief's encampment, and I saw him for the first time. He is not a pure Indian, but a half-breed, an elderly and intelligent man. He soon made his wife get up, and commence with the cooking operations, and pieces of the best buffalo meat and tongues were soon boiling in the kettle. When we had breakfasted we were all soon under way, the chief coming with us towards his house. He had seven carts all loaded with fresh meat. Pushing on before him, we reached his house late in the evening, and rested all the next day, waiting for his arrival. He arrived in the evening with all his carts and horses. When all was quiet, we again assembled all the people, and invited them to come in and join us in the evening prayers. All the neighbours being free-traders, though Roman Catholics, came in, and joined us. I had the honour of addressing them, in the name of God, in their own tongue. They were exceedingly attentive, and, after prayer was over, some of the Canadian half-breeds remarked, 'This is the first lecture in Cree I have heard in all my life.'

"*Feb.* 28: *Lord's-day*—A very nice morning in this wilderness. I found plenty to attend the two services with us this day, when, by the help of God, I freely spoke to them of the freeness and fulness of the salvation of God in Christ, and of the necessity of at once closing in with the offer of mercy, while yet it is the accepted time, and the day of salvation. I had a long conversation with Mistowasis in the evening. I find him quite favourable, and willing that his children should be taught to read, &c. I went into the other tents in the evening. The next day we remained in Mistowasis' house, to get our sleighs ready loaded for a start the following morning. I went to see more of the people, and got into some of the houses. In the evening we called in the people again for the evening prayer. I addressed them in the Cree, and bade them farewell. I was talking to Mistowasis with regard to my coming out to them and staying for a few months in the summer, that I might have a better opportunity of speaking to them of the things which regard the next life, and likewise to do something towards teaching his children to read, &c. The chief said, " I would like it very well if you can come and live with us for a short time, and I shall ever feel thankful if you take the trouble and teach my children to read." I told him that I would see, and whenever I was able to come to them I would. I told him that when I came I should expect to have every liberty, and be under no restraint whatever, but have room in the tent to hold prayers in every morning and evening. He said, ' I shall be very glad to take you into the tent: I will take care of you, and feed you with the best meat I have.' Would that I could manage to leave my Mission for a little time every summer, for there is plenty of work for a Missionary to be even always with them."

The greatness of the efforts made by the Missionaries for the extension of the Gospel may be estimated from the extent of the journeys made for this purpose. We have before us the notes of a Missionary journey of 500 miles on snow-shoes, accomplished by our Missionary, the Rev. T. H. Fleming. It extended from Moose Fort to the East-Main district on the east shores of St. James' Bay, whither wandering parties of Esquimaux came down from the Labrador coast. Some sketches of this journey we shall introduce, that our readers may understand something of Missionary travelling in Rupert's Land. The first night was passed upon a bed of brush, and beneath the open sky. There was plenty of dry wood to burn; and a good fire, with a barricade of snow to windward, were the defences against the cold. In the morning "it blew a hurricane, and drifted so thick that it was impossible to see which way to go; so I was obliged to make the barricade my home for that day, and a wretched home it was. I was half blind from smoke, and but for my blanket, which I stretched on two or three poles stuck slantingly in the snow, and extending roof-like over my head, I should have been wholly covered with snow, so great was the drift. This was impossible to bear, and I told my Indians so; but they said they could mend matters no other way than by going farther into the woods, and striving to make a sort of tent with the few coverings we had for our respective sleds. It took hours to perform, as the deep snow had to be cleared away from the site of the tent, the poles cut, firewood chopped, and brush obtained for carpeting and bed. Then the sled coverings were too small, and the holes had to be stopped with brush and snow, and a bank of snow raised all round to keep out draughts at the bottom: a blanket made the door. Just at sunset we got into a capital tent, where we slept well, resolving, before we lay down, if spared, to be on the move early next morning, and strive to make up for lost time. But we were doomed to disappointment; for, when the morning came, the storm had not lulled, nor the atmosphere cleared. We were confined to our house in the woods for that day also. Thus two whole days were lost; and dreary days they were.

"On Tuesday morning we got under way again, but the coldness of the weather, which usually forbids talking, or, at least, suffers little more than the exchange of common civilities between winter voyagers, and the almost utter barrenness of the whole route, must excuse my omitting to mention particular spots and camping-places. Suffice it to say, that, at seven o'clock P.M. on our eleventh day from Rupert's House, we arrived at Fort George, I must not, however, omit to mention, that as far as camping-places and firewood, this coast has far the advantage of the opposite, at least that part which lies between Moose and Albany, which I have good reason to know. We had no difficulty in getting good places to put up at, and this settles the question of wood, for no place is good without that. The monotony of my daily walk was now and then agreeably broken in upon by the excitement of shooting white partridges, or a chase after a band of reindeer which emerged from the woods; but these on the coast, and the isolated whiskyjack, the lonely tomtit, and the cheery chattering squirrel in the woods, were the only signs of animation along the dreary waste which lay before and around us. All animated nature seemed dead. I did not see a living soul besides my Indian companions, while passing over the 210 miles which lie between Fort George and Rupert's House."

Leaving Fort George, our travellers advanced on their way. Provisions were not to be procured, and scanty food was added to other hardships. On one of the nights an Indian tent afforded poor shelter—

"The tent that night would have been a strange sight for those who are unaccustomed to scenes in Indian life, and the various circumstances under which the Missionary in this desolate region of the world is enabled to make known the saving truths of the Gospel to its wandering inhabitants. The tent was made of deerskin, now black with soot and smoke, and only adorned here and there by a white fox, or an otter skin, which was suspended from its low slanting sides to dry. A round hole in the centre, where the tent-poles converge at the top, answered the double purpose of window and chimney, although, on the present occasion, the smoke seemed to be disposed to go anywhere but through it. Twenty-two individuals, of various ages, sexes, and conditions in life, sat crosslegged all around on a carpet of brush, listening most intently to the hissing and bubbling of at least half a dozen kettles which were suspended over the cheerful fire, which burned in the middle. Again the scene changes: supper is ended, the kettles are removed, and the tent arranged. Then we lifted the voice of prayer and praise, confessed our sins, and sought for pardon through the blood of Jesus. Then I refreshed the memories of those poor, forlorn, and forsaken ones in the blessed truths of the Gospel."

The Great Whale River post was next reached, from whence, after a few days' rest, our Missionary proceeded on his journey in a sledge, drawn by nine Esquimaux dogs, and thus Little-Whale River was at length attained, where he expected to meet the Esquimaux. The census forwarded by him from this place contains the names of seventy-one families, num-

being 430 persons, and of these Mr. Fleming saw 351, in little parties, for they were continually coming and going on their sleds, and earnestly did he occupy himself during the time of his continuance with them in communicating divine instruction. "I strove to explain to them how God extends pardon and forgiveness to the most guilty sinners who turn and repent of their sins, believing on Jesus. Oh! it is most painful to find them so attentive, manifestly desiring to hear more of the word of life, and yet be able to communicate with them in broken accents only. I cannot, however, but acknowledge the hand of God to be with me, for they have caught up my meaning in a wonderfully quick manner."

The great object of the Missionary was to teach them to read the syllabic characters, which in so short a time are learned, and then to place in their hands rolls containing the Lord's-prayer and Ten Commandments, and brief portions of Scripture, such as John iii. 16, 17, verses which most of them had learned by heart. After nearly four months' residence among them, during which we may trust much precious seed was sown in the hearts of these poor wanderers, our Missionary left, with many a *chimo* ("Good bye") from the Esquimaux.

Beyond the English River, and far away to the north, through the zeal of Archdeacon Hunter, the standard of the Gospel has been planted at Fort Simpson, the dépôt for the Mackenzie River, and the head-quarters of the Hudson's-Bay operations in the north. Until this forward movement had been made the priests of the church of Rome were spreading themselves over the country, and, instead of the bread of life, distributing among the poor Indians their miserable counterfeits. There are two priests at Isle à la Crosse; two at Athabasca; two at Fort Resolution, Great Slave Lake; one has recently gone down to Fort Good Hope, situated in latitude 60° 16' N., and consequently not far from the Arctic Circle; besides which, a bishop is to be consecrated for the north, and a staff of Sisters of Charity is to be sent to Isle à la Crosse. Perhaps all this was needful to stimulate us to effort. In 1857 the entire Indian population of the Athabasca district amounted only to 2000 souls. We might perhaps have thought these numbers too few and scattered, and, especially in consideration of the teeming multitudes of tropical lands, have been tempted to leave these few sheep in the wilderness without a shepherd. If the church of Rome thinks them worthy of her notice, shall we contemn them? Let one extract be given from Archdeacon Hunter's journal—

"I feel it a great privilege so far to have carried the tidings of the blessed Gospel down this mighty river, and thus to become a witness for Jesus 'to the uttermost part of the earth.' May He graciously crown this feeble attempt with abundant success: for the first time, since the command was given to his disciples, has the Gospel been proclaimed here, and we cannot but believe and hope that He has many souls here which shall become jewels in his royal crown, who shall be built into the living temple of the living God, and be numbered among those who have washed their robes, and made them white in the blood of the Lamb. I cannot, I will not think that my visit thus far has been in vain, but will indulge the pleasing thought that I am only opening the way for others to enter in and reap an abundant harvest of immortal souls. Surely the time to favour these poor benighted Indians is come; surely these smiling faces I see around me will no longer be left in darkness, no man caring for their souls. They look all energy and intelligence, and listen gladly to the message of redeeming love. Surely we will never allow the idolatry and superstition of Rome to be chained around their souls, and the mark of the beast to be imprinted on their foreheads! Having advanced to this point, no thought of retreat must be entertained. We must not show our back to the enemy, but go straight forward and possess the land. I feel, however, that all events are in the keeping of our faithful and covenant God; that in his gracious providence He has brought me here to proclaim his truth; and I cannot but believe that He has purposes of love and mercy towards these poor benighted Indians, and that He will, in his own good time, raise up and send his faithful servants to preach among them the unsearchable riches of Christ. Labour is our's, results are his; and I therefore leave all in his hands."

This brief review of the existing circumstances of Missionary work in North-West America, will prepare our readers to peruse with the more interest the following extracts from a charge of the Bishop of Rupert's Land addressed to his clergy on Jan. 6, 1860.

"My Reverend Brethren—It was not without some reluctance that I gave up the idea of meeting you as usual on St. John's day. But from the almost additional solemnity connected with Christmas and New-Year's Day, as falling each of them on a Sunday, it was found inconvenient and unadvisable to withdraw those from more distant spheres during any portion of that week. I deemed it best that you should enjoy both those hallowed seasons in the bosom of your flocks, and that you should come up with all the freshness of an opening year for mutual counsel and communion. Nor could I have much doubt in the choice of the Epiphany instead, as a bright and blessed season for all associated in any way in Missionary labour and in the ingathering of the Gentile church.

"I have read somewhere of the celebration which takes place at Rome at about this time—an exhibition of the various languages among which her emissaries are labouring over the face of the earth. In something of a similar spirit we might reckon up to-day the different tongues to which the ministrations of our church are extended in this far reaching land. The Crees and the Salteaux, the two largest tribes, with their cognate dialects, have been long embraced: to these have been added during the past year a large body of the Chipewyans, and a very few of the Sioux;* while in the eastern district, the Norwegians† have regularly, and the Esquimaux occasionally, heard the message of the Gospel. These, with the original settlers, and, as yet, a very small number of emigrants, form our care, and along with them will be associated, we trust, gradually, a remnant from other numerous tribes,‡ as we penetrate yet farther to the mountain ridge of the west and the icy barrier of the north. Planted in the midst of these, accommodating itself to their varied tongues, 'the little one' may, in accordance with the divine promise which we have just heard, 'become a thousand, and the small one a strong nation.'

"With such a field of labour before us, it is an unspeakable pleasure to find our ranks still unbroken by death. Indeed, the healthiness of the land for the European may now be established upon grounds which place the matter beyond dispute. When I look around, and see one of you who has completed his thirty-fourth year in this country—when I take the average of the seven who have been the longest on this continent, and find it seventeen years—when I remember that it is the eleventh year of my own episcopate, and think of the short period in that office of many most signally marked out by God as possessing every qualification for their high work—I feel that no common gratitude ought to be ours for the amount of health and strength which God grants us here in his service.

"Now, if God, while mysteriously cutting short the thread of life elsewhere, prolongs so graciously the span of our existence, He has surely work for us to perform; and we are naturally called upon to review our position, and to ask how we stand at the point of time which we have now reached.

"Politically, no change has as yet passed over the land. Several social improvements have taken place, marking a new era, and betokening progress. The river communication has been opened up; the road over the prairies has been traversed; and the appliances of modern science have rendered more easy the production of some of the necessaries of life.* But the greater change has not yet come. There is a general expectation that the present year may usher it in, and that, during its course, the southern portion of the land, or at least our own settlement, may become a direct colony of the Crown. The boon was granted with great promptitude by the late Colonial Secretary to British Columbia, and I can scarcely doubt that the nobleman who has succeeded him in office, and whose attention has for so many years been directed to the subject, will be prepared ere long with a comprehensive measure bearing on the condition of this territory. For this, as a body, we have ourselves petitioned the two Houses of Parliament, from the persuasion that the highest interests of the country may in this way be best promoted. Whenever the change shall take place, a new class of duties and responsibilities will arise. It will be your part, brethren, to guide and direct the minds of the people in the new channel, so that there may be a healthy and hearty co-operation from all—so that they may exercise the privileges which may be committed to them, to the good of their fellow-men and the glory of God.

"Ecclesiastically, we ought to feel in a measure strengthened. Two new dioceses,

---

* It seems not unlikely that more of this tribe may penetrate into this country. As the territory of Dacotah becomes settled, the Sioux (or Dacotahs) will in all probability be driven northwards.

† It is not a little creditable to Mr. Horden that, in addition to preaching in the Indian tongue, he has also acquired the Norwegian, so as to be able to preach in it to the Norwegians in the Hudson's-Bay Company's service at Moose Factory.

‡ Among these would be the Blackfeet, towards the Plains; the Siccanees and Loucheux, towards the extreme north.

---

* Besides these might be specified the publication of this Charge on the spot, for the first time.

the eighth and ninth in British North America, have been formed since we last met; so that we have an additional one on either side of us—that of Huron on the east, and that of British Columbia on the west. The uncertainty regarding the extent of our own jurisdiction has been removed; our boundary is now marked and definite, and the Rocky Mountains would limit our view in looking towards the Pacific. We have, too, a third new diocese immediately adjoining us to the south—that of Minnesota, in the sister church of the United States. All this has a tendency to support us. And yet, in comparison of all the other dioceses, we are still of a very unwieldy shape, and, though small in population and number of clergy, our distances are almost as great as before. In each of the other eight dioceses, the clergy can, on all such occasions as this, meet almost all of them together: here we can scarcely ever expect to succeed in gathering more than a half. In this diocese alone can it be said that one is absent from us two thousand five hundred miles distant to the north-west; that another is unable to be with us, being twelve hundred miles to the east. Ungava Bay, the Rocky Mountains, and the Arctic Sea, our present limits, are limits rather for the eye and the imagination to rest upon, than possible to be overtaken by any amount of personal labour. And at the heart and centre we remain very isolated; we are still the oasis in the wilderness. After repeated efforts, the difficulty is found to be great to bridge over the intervening distance on each side—to throw out branches which may connect us with our neighbours in Canada and Columbia, and make us to be, in something more than name, the highway of the west.

"With this measure of apparent outward strength there are some causes and hindrances which, I think you will agree with me, tend to cripple and retard our work.

"There is the very migratory character of our most settled population. This may, in the good providence of God, carry onward the tide of population, and scatter it over the wilderness. It may thus ultimately answer a good purpose; but its tendency at the time is felt by us very painfully. It weakens parishes and very materially checks education, rendering it more expensive and difficult to be extended to all. It keeps the mass in a state of greater poverty, and prevents their growth and rise. It lessens the amount of public spirit and local attachment, and perpetuates many of the habits of Indian life. It parts and separates, where, if united, all would be combination and strength.

"There is, too, the want of a deeper religious life, even amongst the more advanced Christians. Here there is stagnation instead of movement. The word is heard with joy and received with readiness; but it is the development of the rich fruit which the minister looks for, and looks too often in vain. Measuring themselves rather by that from which God hath saved them—the condition of the heathen who know not God—than by the standard of by-gone generations and of other countries, they are satisfied with smaller attainments—they rest contented with a lower level, and do not press forward to the measure of the stature of a perfect man. Their condition is a matter of rejoicing to the minister of God, at first, as they are eager to hear. It is in their after course that he suffers disappointment. The building stops before he is prepared: the growth terminates suddenly, after advancing for a time with rapidity, and there is not the higher experience of the divine life.

"There is, moreover, an additional check in the Indian work. It is a transition period: change is anticipated. An excitement has seized the Indian mind, and he is little inclined to give a calm and patient attention to the claims of the Gospel. A wider competition is afloat; and baits are held out by the unscrupulous which the poor Indian is too weak to resist. A greater difficulty has thus been found in selecting and planting new stations, while at the old-established Missions the stedfastness of the convert has been very sorely tried, if not, in some cases, too successfully shaken. Direct conversions have, in consequence, been less numerous during the last two years, and I much fear that the next two or three may continue to tell the same tale. At all events, the Indian is less hopeful and more difficult to act upon than he was found to be five years ago.

"With these and other causes impeding the progress of our work, and materially affecting its character, the testimony of all of us would, if I mistake not, be somewhat similar to-day: our common acknowledgment would be, that the interval since we last met has not been marked with such distinct success as previous periods—that some of our more sanguine expectations have only been faintly realized. Now, if such be your feelings, brethren, is there no deeper agency to which we may trace this? is the condition peculiar to ourselves, or may we throw it under a wider classification, and identify it with what we notice elsewhere on a wider scale? The answer to my own mind is sufficiently clear: the explanation which alone appears to me to account for it is a greater measure of power put forth by Satan in the days in which we live, not only here, but over the whole earth. Can we then substantiate this in the world, so as to prove it more than an idle dream?"

In proof of this conviction on his part, that the god of this world is putting forth special energy at the present time (Rev. xii. 12), the bishop refers to the respective conditions of the civilized world, the professing church, and heathendom. We pass on to the last of these divisions, as the one in which we are more especially concerned.

"If, then, we turn to heathenism, has Satan stirred and aroused it in like manner? No. Here, and here alone, his object is to rivet the soul in its chains—to lull with the opiate of a false security—to prevent inquiry and to seal up in darkness. Fearing lest the light should shine into their prison-house, he would stay the hand of Christian charity and silence the voice of the preacher. No interference with the systems of idolatry and superstition —neutrality would be the watchword which he would seek to instil into the minds of all. How clear his unwillingness to allow any one to escape from his bondage and thraldom; how plain the cry of the spirits which 'work in the children of disobedience,' anxious to retain them a little longer in their grasp, 'Art thou come hither to torment us before our time?'"

The charge then refers to those encouraging considerations which show, that when the "enemy comes in like a flood," the Spirit of the Lord never fails to "lift up a standard against him."

"Is there, then, this growing power in the world, the church, and heathendom? If there be, then, judging by the analogy of God's providence and the promises of his word, we might expect to find that there would be a corresponding outpouring of the Spirit. Can we, then, brethren, discern side by side any thing of this?

"And surely here we may place first among the phenomena which force themselves upon our notice, the symptoms of revival in so many different spots in the United States, in Ireland, Scotland, and elsewhere. Whatever there may be of physical or nervous excitement connected with it (as there will often be when the masses are concerned in a religious awakening), I cannot doubt that there is beneath a work of God. This, on our own continent, is attested by two bishops of the highest character, and is made by one of them, the subject of his annual charge; while in the north of Ireland it is fully recognised by the bishop in whose diocese the occurrences have chiefly taken place, who has himself taken part in many of these devotional meetings.* Visitors to the spot, and even judges on the bench, all concur in the same testimony. And surer almost than all these is the proof from the changed life, the wonderful disappearance from districts of sin and vice, the wide-spread prevalence of prayer. The very scorner can scarcely deny that the hand of God is here. But the believer, turning aside to behold the sight, recognises in it something of an effusion of that same Spirit which was poured out on the day of Pentecost; he looks hopefully for times of refreshment from these premonitory tokens. He sees from the droppings the proof of the willingness of God to give the plenteous shower: he hears almost the very voice of God saying to him, 'Prove me now herewith, if I will not open the windows of heaven, and pour you out a blessing, that there shall not be room enough to receive it.'

"Connected with this spirit of awakened seriousness, there is the ever-widening spirit of zeal for the souls of others, whether at home or abroad. How manifest this in the special services at Exeter Hall and elsewhere, designed to bring all within the sound of the Gospel: how manifest in the opening of cathedrals, where thousands listen together to the glad sound, and fill the lofty dome with choral praise; how manifest where, under the open canopy of heaven, the ambassador of God declares the same message, whenever he can assemble hearers—on the steps of the seat of commerce, or in the neighbourhood of the densely-peopled alley. Nor has this in the least tended to weaken the activity of Christian charity for dying souls abroad. We had all, perhaps, thought with anxiety regarding the future, when we heard of the efforts made to succour the Indian sufferers—the large sums raised for their temporal relief. We thought it must necessarily curtail and lessen the receipts of the various Christian Societies, on which we were so largely dependent, and we were prepared to find it so. But we hear of no diminution. Many seem to have acted on the conviction, that whatever their previous contributions to the cause may have been, they must now be doubled. The insecurity of the past has been felt: it has taught the necessity of building on a surer foundation, and proved, with a force clearer than that of lengthened argument, that the open avowal of the Christian faith must ever

* Bishops M'Ilvaine and Eastburn.—See Charge of the latter, "The Signal Work of the Holy Spirit in the United States."

be the surest defence of a professedly Christian nation.

"And already the power of the Spirit is manifesting itself in those very portions of the earth where Satan had erected his trophies, and from which he thought he had gathered in his triumphs. We noticed on a previous occasion that war had given us noble and cheering specimens of the beauty of holiness—convincing proofs of the efficacy of divine grace. It has been so again, brethren, and on a wider scale. Some of the names most conspicuous recently in military prowess are to be handed down as very memorable examples of a living faith. Religion has been seen to be the brightest ornament on the brow of the victorious general; it has been seen giving energy and decision to the civilian, investing him with a power and influence greater than that of the sword;* and elevating with the bright hope of heaven the patient and enduring female, as she bends under the stroke, willing either to suffer or to die. Already we receive from the land tidings which speak encouragingly of the future, and tell of a greater willingness to entertain the message. It is as if the darkest hour had come, and God were now ready to bless. Seeds of light have been sown on the very spots bedewed with blood, and the names of places associated with fierce and foul deeds seem likely to be hereafter connected with the records of grace. And in that other land, since rendered desolate, the land of poetry and song, is a similar dawn of hope. The older superstitions of Italy, under which she has so long groaned, seem fast decaying. Many, unwilling to dwell longer in darkness, seem calling for the light. There is a growing demand for God's blessed word, and, while seeking to cast off their shackles and assert their nationality and independence, they appear in some quarters to manifest an anxiety for that liberty wherewith Christ makes his people free. The slumbering truth may revive, the hidden witnesses who have long prophesied in sackcloth may awake as from the dead, and the pure Gospel of Christ may carry healing and cure to the wounds of that stricken people.

"Thus have we taken a rapid glance at the growing power of Satan, as seen at present in the world, and the yet mightier power of the Spirit which God shows Himself so willing to exert on the side of his people, in answer to their prayers. May we not, brethren, learn something ourselves from this double view? May we not, on the one hand, do well to remember that our very calling is to make inroads on the kingdom of Satan, that 'mysterious, ever-working power, which is entrenched in heathenism as in a stronghold?' Let us never forget his personality, his power, his wiles, as now more than ever necessary to be borne in mind. Let us remember, that at the basis of all Missionary effort lies the declaration, 'the whole world lieth in wickedness,' or rather in the wicked one. From it—that is, from his grasp—we are to win souls for Christ, bringing them to the foot of his cross and the knowledge of his salvation now, that we might present them to him hereafter, to receive from his hands their crown. And, on the other hand, let us seek more of the power of the Spirit. We cannot, it is true, look for it in the mightier gatherings of the saints, where numbers add a quickening energy to prayer; but let us look for it where the promise is still sure of fulfilment, where two or three are met together. You have felt the profit as well as the pleasure of those monthly clerical meetings for prayer and the study of God's word, and conference on ministerial duties and trials, at most of which I have been able to be present and take part with you. Their object is to remind of ordination vows, to plead for a Pentecostal blessing, to give point and unity and purpose to separate and scattered effort. You felt, too, the advantage of the social meetings with your parishioners during the past winter—the cottage or family lecture from house to house. Now, at all such seasons, whether meeting ministerially, as brethren whose toil is for souls, or periodically, as the shepherd with a portion of his flock, let us with yet deeper fervency pray that the agency of the Spirit, felt elsewhere, may be more and more felt among ourselves; that while refreshing other spots, it may also 'drop upon the pastures of the wilderness.'

"And now I might almost pass to the recapitulation of our own work, were it not that there are two subjects which have of late been much before the public mind, which seem to call for a passing notice, and some expression of opinion. The one concerns all the churches of the Reformation, which speak our tongue; the other is connected with our own branch of the church of Christ, and limited to it. The first is a question regarding the Bible, which is the guide and manual of the redeemed people of God, to whatever

---

* The names of Lawrence, Montgomery, and Edwardes will readily occur as instances of great personal influence; as well as the singular fact, that when all means of getting supplies failed, the Rev. C. B. Leupolt was sent out to Benares, as the one most trusted by the natives, and succeeded.

earthly communion they may belong; the second is concerning the form of prayer in which we worship our heavenly Father, as we trust, in spirit and in truth."

The bishop then proceeds to touch upon certain points of commanding interest at the present day; the authorized version of the Bible, the Prayer-book, the subdivision of services, &c., as to avoid needless repetitions, and then returns to the circumstances of his own diocese. As the charge has been separately published, it is not necessary we should introduce it *in extenso*, and we limit ourselves to those portions which refer expressly to the Mission work.

"I must now, however, hasten to the consideration of events more closely connected with ourselves and with the progress of the Gospel in this land. Of these, the most prominent would be our own temporary absence, the commencement of the Mission on the Mackenzie River, and the anxiety of the Chipewyans for the permanent ministrations of our church.

"For our own absence some reasons were given before leaving you—reasons which justified the step to ourselves, and made it in some degree necessary. In addressing you to-day, I would say unhesitatingly that the expectations I then formed were very fully realized. The spiritual refreshment, from intercourse with Christian friends, I found, and found abundantly. It is the compensation which God has graciously provided for a sojourn in a distant wilderness; it is a part of the 'manifold more in this present time,' which the Saviour holds out in promise, and will ever give, to those who forsake home and kindred. If the visit be at sufficiently long intervals, and the land of adoption be kept as the one object uppermost, it is then, I think, alike beneficial to yourself, to the land from which you are for a time an absentee, and, as I was repeatedly assured, to the land which you visit. It renews half-severed links, it revives connexions, it kindles fresh interest and sympathy; in a word, it readjusts that electric chain of communication along which mutual spiritual blessings flow.

"In looking back upon the period, how many the tokens of God's peculiar and providential care! Surely it was his hand, in answer to the prayers of many here and elsewhere, which, on our homeward voyage, interposed to deliver from a disaster which might have been attended with much trial and suffering. It could only be his hand which brought me back to the very Sabbath of appointment, strengthened both in body and mind. And, to take but two intermediate cases, it must have been the good hand of God which, without concert or pre-arrangement, brought from China and Rupert's Land those who had been sent forth to their work together, and placed us so often on the same platform, the visible representatives of the churches of the East and the West. It was the same hand which carried me to England in sufficient time to be present at the consecration of a beloved friend and companion of early youth to his high and weighty office, the charge of what he has truly designated as 'the greatest diocese in the world,' the metropolitan see of London. These, brethren, are the way-marks to be set up—the never-to-be-forgotten causes of gratitude which sweeten the pilgrimage of life.

"It was not, as you well know, a period of rest and activity: it was one of more unceasing employment and greater mental strain than when among yourselves. The preaching and speaking in public were, indeed, without intermission. But the occasions of preaching gave to the labour an agreeable variety. It was no little pleasure to preach, soon after arrival, the ordination sermon before my own University; to lay, by invitation, the foundation-stone of the new chapel of my own college. It was pleasant to preach, as it happened, on successive Sundays in St. Patrick's and St. Paul's cathedrals; and, not least of all, it was pleasant to ordain a labourer for this land in the very church which I had left on coming out hither.* Nor was the public speaking less diversified. Whether it were the village gathering in the parochial schoolroom, in the spreading tent, or on the green turf, or the crowded assembly of those of quicker intelligence and more sharpened powers in the hall of town or city; whether it were the University meetings, now so fully attended, where one longed to be able to discern a Martyn or a Fox, a Ragland, or a Tucker, among the youthful throng; or whether it were those largest meetings of a more mixed and general audience which mark the months of April and May; there was always that eagerness to hear, that anxiety to receive tidings from afar, which at once carries forward the speaker, and makes the effort comparatively easy.

"But there was much of detail beneath. In the way of necessary business, I would assign the highest place to conference with those great Societies which bear up and sustain our work. They are the fountain-heads from which the rills flow over our land. They are the wonderful agencies of this century; for though some of them existed a century

---

* The Rev. T. H. Fleming, Church Missionary, at All Saints', Derby.

before, their sphere of operation has more than doubled during it. On their practical wisdom, on their prayerful zeal, on their being guided in each deliberation by the Holy Spirit, would depend, in no ordinary degree, the welfare of the colonial and Missionary church. One to whom the Missionary church at least, and, consequently, our own diocese, owes a large debt of gratitude, has lately given up his position of very extended influence; one whose instructions are treasured up and remembered at many a lonely station, the respected Principal of Islington College. I am sure that I am but giving expression to the feelings of those here present who were trained by him, in saying that our best wishes would go with him on his retirement; that our prayers would accompany him, that, while blessed in his parish, he may ever retain the happy consciousness that the seeds of truth scattered by him are bearing good fruit in many a distant clime. God, we doubt not, has filled up his place, and, to his devoted successor, who had, even beforehand, furnished an unusual number for the Mission field, one looks with unabated confidence for a supply of duly-qualified Missionaries, men of God, full of faith, and wisdom, and prayer.

"To thank for the sums collected is far beyond my power. With the fulness of a grateful heart, I always find words but feeble to express such feelings. Very various were the donors. Some gave, and gave, we fear, almost beyond their ability; very many, the fruits of much self-denial and self-sacrifice; some, 'whose hearts the Lord stirred up' from simply hearing the tidings, although previously unknown to ourselves; others from personal regard and affection; some, anxious that their names should be concealed, content to lay up treasure in heaven. Not a few are already gone to their rest, and, as we trust, to their rich reward—to that Saviour who remembereth the cup of cold water given to a saint in his name. How doubly sacred their legacy and parting gift! The amount collected might have been more had I made this my only object, but this I could not think of doing. As we are still a Missionary church—as every ministerial income, except the endowment of the bishopric, comes from home—I placed my services, in a great measure, at the command of those Societies which feed and support us. To all of them, I trust, some services were rendered in pleading their cause; nor did I willingly decline to undertake labour in any direction for them, but, most of all, as the Church Missionary Society furnish so large a proportion of my clergy, I felt that all I could do for them was but little in re-

would say that my admiration of the wisdom of their Committee, my affection for their office-bearers, has much deepened from those months of unreserved confidential intercourse.

"On my way out I had an opportunity of seeing, and that for the first time, our church in Canada and in the United States. In the former I was welcomed, on arriving, by him who made the first episcopal visit to Rupert's Land, and was in a manner its first bishop. It was delightful to notice the warmth with which he made minute inquiry after many here, and the deep anxiety which he manifested for the progress of the church in this land. The recollection of his wanderings in the western wilderness is, he seems to feel, a bright and sunny spot in the memory of the past. He was the only Canadian bishop at home as I passed through. From the Bishop of Toronto I have since heard, having received a letter of commendation on behalf of one who has come amongst us. For it I feel grateful, as the intercourse now opened will, doubtless, rapidly increase. I hope that all my brethren, as well as the clergy generally, will send such introductions with those of our own church who may come in, whether to visit or to settle.

"In the sister church of the United States I saw also but one bishop, it being the season when most were absent from the larger towns on their visitations through the country, but he was (if I may say so) the one whom I most wished to see, the bishop who, for four-and-twenty years, has been the Missionary bishop of the north-west, and who, after organizing six new dioceses, has now retired, as he well deserves to do, from the wider field, and will henceforward limit his labours to the diocese of Wisconsin. He has thus been a standard-bearer, carrying forward the banners of the cross for nearly a quarter of a century, and yet he has still an undiminished freshness and activity. At his request I preached the opening sermon at the annual convention of the diocese of Minnesota, and remained with them throughout its session. We cannot wonder that the late triennial convention should have tendered to him their warmest thanks, and should have felt unwilling that the office and title should disappear. They have elected in his room another bishop of the north-west—an unattached bishop, if we may use the term— or, rather, a purely Missionary bishop. He would, in strictness, make a fourth new diocesan, if not a fourth new diocese, adjoining us, and our best prayer for him would be, that on him might fall the mantle of Bishop Kemper.

others, and spoken much of them, it would be very ungracious and ungrateful were I not to thank you from the very depth of my heart for the very cordial welcome which you gave me on my return. Often had I spoken, when away from you, of my possessing, if ever bishop did, an affectionate body of clergy; and on my arrival I found that I had not over-estimated the personal attachment to myself of either laity or clergy.

"Ready as I was myself for travel, if necessary, the following summer, the task seemed naturally to devolve in turn on others. In the winter the proposal came from one among you: a plan for a very long and distant enterprise, to plant the Cross in a new territory, and penetrate towards the Arctic Sea. He came, not sketching a plan for others, but willing to start himself, wanting but an answer to his offer, 'Here am I, send me.' We have surely reason to thank him to-day for the commencement of a good work there, and however difficult its continuance may be, ours will be in great measure the blame should the station be abandoned, and the citadel, thus gained, be given up. With the results of the Mission, so far, we have much cause to be satisfied. It has been hailed by all the officers of the Hon. Company, and it will tell, I hope, happily hereafter on some of the poor scattered tribes. The Archdeacon has returned among us in the fulness of God's blessing, and will, by his presence, tend to keep alive the interest in the work. He has seen what we only bear of; he feels as one yearning for souls without a shepherd. To him, therefore, peculiarly, do we commit the work, and trust that he may yet live to see the pleasure of the Lord prospering in that bleak and barren portion of the earth. One has gone to relieve him, to occupy the advanced post, and we await with eagerness the tidings from him which may reach us in a few weeks. May they be, that, undeterred by difficulty, he is willing to continue and abide there, scattering the seed of life.

"During the last summer I have myself gone in the same direction, but only about a third of the distance. Anxious as I was to stand on the height of land, and meet the gentlemen of the district, according to their wish, at Portage la Loche, I felt that the time was not yet—that my presence at a future day would do more good. And the event proved to my own mind that I had judged rightly, from the very favourable journey which God gave me. It was the lightest and easiest trip I have yet made in the country— seven weeks, and not wind-bound one whole confess to have started with a greater measure of despondency than usual. These stations have been passing through much trial for some winters. To them may indeed be applied those pregnant and forcible words of the Apostle, 'pressed out of measure, above strength.' I found all, however, more encouraging than I had expected, and I then fondly trusted that I had passed through the worst. But I would scarcely say this now. The non-arrival of the supplies from England, through the loss of the ship, will, I fear, renew and aggravate their difficulties, and throw them back again. The brightest and most cheering sight was that of the canoes and tents of the Chipewyans, on the bank of the English River. Their naturalness of manner, and frank and open cordiality with Mr. Hunt, left on my mind the most pleasing remembrance. They seemed the first-fruits of a tribe. With pain I declined to admit to baptism many who importunately sought it. I took their little ones as a pledge, and promised that, God willing, they should soon have some one to preach among them in their own tongue.

"For the two spheres—the Mackenzie River and the Chipewyans—I have written for help, pleading for two able and active men; the one to relieve Mr. and Mrs. Hunt (for in speaking of Missionary labour they must always be named together), and then to direct his efforts to the Chipewyans; the other to assist in carrying on the work on the Mackenzie River. The burden of secular care is still felt at the stations which I visited, so as to weigh down almost beyond the power of endurance. I found in the United States, that in their Missions among the Indians (and I believe it is the case also in their Foreign Missions), they have an officer called an Economos—a layman entrusted with the pecuniary and wordly concerns, the household and the farm. This, doubtless, tends to lighten care. But if the office were created among us, the difficulty would be great to find the man, or rather the men, as they must be multiplied for the several stations. The conviction, too, I found gaining ground in the north, and, I think, probably among us all, that more must be attempted by itinerating; that in districts where distances are counted by thousands of miles, we cannot cover the surface with large and expensive stations; that we must rather take a centre, and, from it, carry the truth in diverging lines. Such is the nature of the work at Moose and in the Eastern District, and such must be the aggression on the Mackenzie River and in the

you want, brethren, some actual statistics, and to see the sum in intelligible figures. We have, then, held nine confirmations since our return, and confirmed in all 831, giving what is a very fair average in each church of thirty-six, or very nearly thirty-seven. We have still to confirm at La Prairie, if God permit, in March, and at Moose in July. We have held four ordinations (including that already referred to in England), at which three were ordained deacons and two priests. Two additional labourers came out the year of my return — one for each district — one of whom is at present at York; the other has already traversed the greater part of the Moose quarter. A third, whom I cannot forbear to mention, offered her gratuitous services for the work, and, with all the heart and devotedness of a Missionary, came out at the same time. She is now labouring assiduously at Fairford, as a fellow-labourer in the Gospel. A candidate for ordination is, we hear, on his way; and another has already reached the land, under circumstances which call for much sympathy and prayer—one of our own party, as one of my own children, for years previously under my care.* He had gained the love and affection of all at the Missionary college, when the hand of God laid him aside, and he returns weakened in body, but, I trust, much ripened in spiritual things. Happy should I be if, through the Divine blessing, his native air should restore him during the winter, so that I may yet lay hands on the son as I have done on the father, and that the name introduced among us may pass down to yet another generation, and become rooted among us.

"We are thus in all twenty-one to-day—one, and one only, in deacons' orders. We have lost one since our last visitation, who has recently been appointed to a living in the diocese of Norwich. I have an additional grant from the Colonial Church Society, and only regret that they have not yet succeeded in finding one to relieve me in some measure of the heavier parochial duty. The work of translation is still going on. The only labourer absent from the country is actively employed in carrying through the press the Syllabic Bible, at the joint expense of the Bible and Church Missionary Societies. He is at the same time superintending two editions of the Prayer-book in the same character, the one the translation of Archdeacon Hunter, for York and the Saskatchewan; the other that of Mr. Horden, for Moose and the East Main. For both of these we have to thank the Christian-Knowledge Society. The work not having been fully completed, the Parent Committee of the Church Missionary Society determined to keep Mr. Mason a year longer in England, and, as the event has proved, most providentially. The large supply of copies for York has, we fear, been lost; but he is on the spot to continue the work, and to throw off additional copies to repair in some degree the loss. On his return, Mr. Gardiner will, we hope, pass on to a new station, and occupy Fort Churchill."

We conclude with one extract more

"We labour in a land of difficulty and paradox. Our double trial is, its vastness and its smallness. Its vastness—so that we often strain the eye until lost in the contemplation of the untrodden soil to which no messenger of peace has yet penetrated, and for which we are in a measure accountable, The bold and daring mariner braves the peril of the Polar Sea in search of those who have perished; and there, from time to time, he meets with some living men. How emphatically may such say, 'No man careth for my soul!' Its smallness, too—so that we often ponder over the thinness of its population and our inability to produce mighty results, or work on a large scale, until we are almost tempted to relax our energy, and cry, 'By what shall Jacob rise, for he is small?' We cannot traverse the land in its length and breadth; and if we could do so, over hundreds of miles, we should not meet a fellow-creature. We cannot plant the wilderness with settlers and thriving villages, for this is not our vocation, and would require far mightier resources. Our best support would be found in the ever-present recollection, that each single soul saved is a gem in the Redeemer's crown, and that each such soul, effectually rescued from Satan's grasp, is a magnet to draw other souls, to increase the ever-widening circle on earth, and add to the number of the redeemed in heaven."

---

* Mr. H. Budd, son of the Rev. H. Budd.

CUSTOMS OF THE HINDUS AND MUSSULMANS OF INDIA.

(Continued from p. 120.)

"I PROCEED to relate some Indian customs regarding births, marriages, and deaths.

"*Births.*—The customs prevalent among the Hindus on the occasion of a child's birth are not very remarkable, but are characteristic of their bigotry and superstition. When the mother has ascertained that such is to happen, she devotes a great portion of her time to looking at herself in the glass, in the certain belief, as told her by the 'wise women' amongst them, that this will occasion the infant's resembling her. This, in common with women of most countries, she most anxiously wishes for. She almost always is possessed of a thumb-ring, in which is set a small looking-glass: in this glass she is perpetually gazing. It is called in the native language an *ursee*.

"At the time of the birth the parents distribute a great quantity of sweetmeats amongst their friends; and they pour down the infant's throat a medicine composed of spice, called *umultas*, a grain called *ujwaeen*, and sugar. These are mixed together in water: it is called the *jinum guttee*, or birth-draught. They then bathe the child in warm water. The fifth night is the time fixed for the pundits and astronomers to assemble at the house. When they have all met and saluted each other, they go out into a court together to look at the stars, and, agreeably to their decision, after a long contemplation of them, the child is given a name. The pundits make then what they call the *jinum puthur*, which is a paper on which is written the names of the child's parents, its grandfathers', grandmothers', and the date, hour, minute, and instant, in which its birth took place. This costs the lower orders a rupee and a quarter; but the higher in rank and the richer pay according to their means. The first name of the child, which is given to it by the pundits, is usually after one of their gods, such as Ram, Luchmun, Sheo, Gunesh, for a male. The women are also named after some of Krishna's mistresses, or some Hindu divinity who is a female. But with regard to the other name which the boy receives from his father, it is usually the name of some idol, tree, river, or remarkable person or animal; but the girl seldom receives more than one. There is a *jinum puthur* also written for a girl, which, as well as that which is written for a boy, is treasured up by her parents with the greatest care. After the boy is born, they take the most especial care that it may not be seen by a cat, as they consider such to be the most unfortunate thing that can betide it; but if a girl, they do not care for cats.

"*Marriages.*—But the mode of life, and the absurd and abject superstitions of the country, is nowhere more shown than in their forms and the bridal processions attending the union in marriage of their boys and girls. The bridegroom and the bride, at the time of these ceremonies taking place, are not more than nine and seven years old respectively: they are sometimes even younger. When a marriage between two families is in contemplation, the parents of both parties take their *jinum puthurs* to the astronomers, and ask whether their stars of destiny are conformable. If the astronomers decree that they are so, then the affair is settled; otherwise they give it up. In the event of their not being propitious, even the astronomers who are pundits receive a present of two or three rupees; but if, as is almost always the case, they consider it advisable, then the parents also give them a present, and go home, taking with them the *jinum puthurs*. Then first the father of the bride sends the bridegroom's father a present of rupees and a large quantity of sweetmeats, called a *tuka*. Then both families remain in the habit of giving and receiving presents, until the time for the commencement of the *beah*. This ceremony begins by the boy's going to the house of the girl, and he there finds prepared for him a small chair, placed upon a throne. Around this are seated his *marriage brothers*, as they are called, and his family priest. On his arrival they welcome him, and place him on the throne. They then, when he is seated, ask him to repeat some appropriate verse, poetry, or ode, for the occasion. He does so, and then all the relatives of the bride perform the *arta*, which consists in circling a plate round his head, in which is a lamp, and give him presents, in amount from one to one hundred rupees. Then the boy-bridegroom asks his father-in-law and mother-in-law for presents, and they give him in money, according to their means, from two to one hundred rupees; and, if they can afford it, presents of elephants, horses, and jewels. After this they make him open his scarf, and they throw therein sweetmeats and cocoa-nuts; and the Brahmin, or family priest, puts a *teeka* on his forehead, and takes his leave. Then the Brahmin receives some presents; also the relatives of the bridegroom receive some, and they, in return, give blessings to the bride's relatives, their donor, and are bound to ask for more than they at first receive. They then (the relatives of the bridegroom), making a great clamour with cymbals and other musical instruments, take him away to his own house. Then, when he has arrived there, he calls the rest of his relatives who have not accompanied him, and the Brahmins who are his acquaintances. The latter, when they have sat down together in a room, begin singing the Shasters with a loud voice. Next one of them draws a good many figures on the ground with coarse flour, and on each makes the boy place pawn-leaves, fruit, betel-nuts, and pice; and in this way they generally make out about twenty figures. The relatives, when the figures are finished, make a reverential salutation to them, which is called a *dundhout*, and place over each some wet rice. This form is considered as an offering to the star of his destiny. The young bridegroom then gives them some rupees, and the Brahmins take the pice from the figures. The Brahmins then begin to congratulate him on the occasion, and they, together with the barbers, who are generally used as Mercuries between the different families, make solicitations for more money. They receive a further donation of some pice. The next night, when it is quite dark, the boy gets on horseback, and puts on a sword, a red turban, and a yellow cloak, and, taking his relatives with him, goes to the door of his father-in-law's house. He finds that inside are assembled a great number of the bride's relatives making merry with mirth, music, and dancing. Then the father of the bride and all his relatives collect a sum of from fifty to two thousand rupees, according to their means, and the jewels sufficient for one girl—which in this country amount to a large sum—her slaves, her elephants, and her horses, and present them to the bridegroom. They also give presents, sweetmeats, and clothes to his relatives; and these they send to his house. He is then conducted by Brahmins into the girl's house, and they make him sit on a chair, and begin several prayers and forms *of mummery*. After this the Brahmins select a place near the house, generally an adjacent court, and plant therein four trunks of a plantain tree (the tree which is considered by the Hindus to be emblematic of fecundity, from its producing so many bunches of fruit), and place over them a red-coloured cloth, so that this has the appearance of a canopy, or small tent. They then put underneath this a cocoa-nut and some small almonds and dates coated with silver. Then ensues the time for inviting a very large concourse of people, dressed in their holiday attire, friends of both parties. The men sit in the outer rooms, and the women, hidden from their gaze, are inside, either in the interior or in some upper rooms, from which they can view what is going on. The women sing and play on their numerous instruments, and call out loudly their jokes, songs, and ribaldry to the male exclusives. After this the Brahmins assemble in the small canopy, which is called a *mundha*. They then go into the apartment where the girl is, and bring her out entirely concealed with clothes. They afterwards go and bring the boy, dressed in his ordinary clothes. They make the young couple sit inside the *mundha*, and say prayers. After this the Brahmins make a great many figures on the ground with coarse flour, kolee, pawn, betel-nut, and rice; and they cause the girl to urge the boy to place wet rice on those figures. Then they kindle a fire, and sing the Shasters, making a great clamour. They pass the night in singing, and when it is near dawn of day, the Brahmins give the girl leave to make her agreement of marriage. She then solemnly promises before them that she will remain obedient to her husband all her life; that she will never allow another man to see her face. This is kept true to the letter. She adds some other expressions indicative of her state of submission. The boy then makes his agreement to the following effect—That he will make all his property subservient to his bride's welfare; that he will protect her; that he will always endeavour to please her, and conduct himself in no way contrary to her interest. After this the Brahmins tie their clothes together, and drag them four times round the *mundha*. During the whole time of dragging them round, they roar out the Shasters at the highest pitch of their voices. After the fourth turn, the marriage ceremony is completed. Her relatives then take leave of her with much weeping. The Brahmins send for a palanquin, and having concealed her well in it, they make the boy get on a horse, and, sounding all manner of instruments, he, together with her male relatives, departs to his house. He there lives with his mother's friends, and when she is about thirteen, and he fifteen, they commence keeping house together. But in this country a girl of thirteen is as much considered eligible for marriage as one of eighteen is in England, and this precocity seems to obtain all over the East. They look on girls of twenty-two as if they were old women. Boys seldom learn or get taller after seventeen, and at thirty seem past the meridian of life.

The first marriage which a man makes is called the *beah*. Should he die and leave a widow, the poor woman, in former times, was urged to burn herself at her husband's funeral; but now that horror is done away with, she is obliged to live with her husband's brother. This occasions a great deal of immorality, and the expenses attendant upon a marriage is another source of the same. It is almost incredible the sums which are laid out in the wedding ceremonies: parties think nothing of expending three or four years' income on them. If a woman, after her husband's death, marry another man, it is considered a great degradation: in fact, she loses caste by doing so, and sinks to the lowest grade. The husband whom she marries is called a *deraychu*. None of the disgrace consequent upon a woman's doing so can fall upon a man when he is placed in similar circumstances; but, on the contrary, if his wife dies, he may marry a virgin. They also attach not the least blame to him if he takes a maid and makes her the resident of his *rungwas*, or seraglio. This is called *butt ke kurna*, or *ghur men daltena*, but he is bound to support the person whom he thus makes his inmate. There is a proverb in the country to the effect that a man of high caste who has daughters has a fortune, because of the very large sums he gets from the bridegroom at the marriage of each. There are many instances, on the other hand, of Brahmins who, by marrying girls, the daughters of people beneath them in caste, have made their own fortune.

"There are many stories told of the extravagancies which are committed by people of high caste when one of their number takes a bride from the daughters of one whom they consider beneath them. I recollect one which came under my immediate notice. The case was of a man of the rajpoot, or military caste, who had gone to the house of some low-caste man to seek a bride. This had been without the consent of his elder brother. In conformity with the customs which I have mentioned above, the bridegroom was seated in his father-in-law's house when his elder brother heard of the news. Having listened to the recital of it, he ate a quantity of bhang, or intoxicating hemp, and, taking his sword, he ran furiously to the house where his brother was seated. When he arrived there, in frantic passion, he drew his sword and cut indiscriminately at all whom he saw. Before he could be disarmed by the police he had severely wounded thirteen people, seven of whom died afterwards. He was brought bound to the English magistrate, who asked him where he had procured a sword which could wound so many in such a short time. His answer was, 'Lord of my life, unbind the arms of your slave, and, by the waters of Gangoutrie, I will show you what the same sword can do.' He did not evince the slightest remorse, either then or at his execution, which took place some time afterwards. I was witness also to the following circumstance, which shows the jealousy with which they regard their wives: it was on a court of inquest of which I was interpreter. The inquest was upon the body of a woman who had been murdered in the most inhuman manner. Her hand, the smallest I ever remember to have seen, was lying beside the body. It had been severed when she raised it to avert the cut of the sword which had been first aimed at her. On her neck had been inflicted three deep gashes, any one of them sufficient to bring on death. The face was beautiful, and the figure symmetrical. After examining several witnesses, apart from each other, it was ascertained that the murder had been committed in open day by her husband. I asked the magistrate for leave to speak to him, which was granted, and then asked him how he had been so inhuman in his conduct. His answer, which was delivered with coolness and self-possession, was to this effect, 'Sir, what would you have a man of my caste do when his wife is known to be unfaithful?' He was of the Bunneah caste.

[*To be continued.*]

A MICA MINE IN BEHAR (See page 150.)

GONDWANA, AND ITS ABORIGINAL TRIBES

BETWEEN the Vindhya range on the north, the eastern chain of ghauts, and a line connecting these drawn from the mouth of the Godavery to the centre of the valley of the Nerbudda, lies a vast territory, very dissimilar to the great plain country of the Ganges—a region composed of lofty and rugged mountains, impenetrable forests, swampy woodlands, and arid wastes, interspersed with extensive tracts of open and unproductive plain. It abounds, too, in varieties of climate as well as of physical aspect.

There are mountains covered with forests, grass-clothed uplands, spring-watered valleys, and low alluvial lands, fertilized by tropical rains. In some places there are winter frosts, and in others, heat that is at all seasons oppressive. This vast plateau, which overhangs Bengal and Orissa, and to the south forms the northern extremity of the Deccan, is usually designated Gondwana. So imperfectly is it known, that, in the best maps, large blanks occur, of districts which have never been explored, and where civilization has not yet penetrated. Within its limits are comprised the British districts of Saugor and Nerbudda, and also the states, British and native, which are known as the South-Western Frontier agency, the Cuttack Mehals, and the greatest portion of the northern part of Nagpore. Its great elevation may be concluded from the fact, that the rivers which have their sources in these uplands flow down, some with a northward course to meet the Ganges; others, as the Mahanuddy, eastward to the Bay of Bengal; and others westward, as the Nerbudda, and Taptee, with their tributaries, to the Indian Ocean. In these regions the Vindhya system appears to centralize, and to send out three ranges to the west, the most northern of which only is called by Hindus the Vindhya; the next being the Satpara mountains, which divide the Nerbudda from the Taptee; and the most southerly being the Mahadeo hills.

The south-west frontier agency of Bengal comprises a considerable portion of this rugged north to south, and 85 in breadth, rises 500 or 600 feet above the adjoining district of Chota Nagpore, itself a table-land, the general level of which is between 1200, and 2000 feet above that of the sea. The Damooda river flowing south-east into the Hoogly, and the Sooburno Rekha and Bamunee flowing more southerly into the Bay of Bengal, have their sources within a short distance of the station of Chota Nagpore. "The table-land extends in a north-eastern direction from Ruttunpore (1539 feet above the sea) of great Nagpore through Juspore, the north-west extreme of Singhbhoom, Tamar and Pachete, to the trunk road east of Parusnath. The southern termination is generally rather abrupt from Ruttunpore to the neighbourhood of Singhbhoom, where lofty ridges stretch south from it." About 100 miles due west from Chota Nagpore, lies Juineera Pàt, the most elevated spot of an extended table-land, being 3200 feet above the level of the sea. From the brow of the hill a beautiful view of the Koosmee valley is obtained, beyond which are the hills of Koorea and Sirgoojah, the country in that direction being very beautiful from the intermixture of extensive and fertile valleys, and well-wooded hills. And such is the general aspect of these districts: picturesque groups of hills, deep groves, clear and rocky streams, all things that are graceful in landscape, in varying succession, meet and charm the eye at every turn. The products of the country are manifold: of metals, gold, copper, and iron; of precious stones, the diamond; and here are ample coal mines, from which, in time to come, unlimited supplies will be drawn.

These mountain-fastnesses have been the home and shelter of wild tribes, remnants of the aboriginal population, whose forefathers fled hither when the successive waves of Aryan invasion swept over the plain country. Here they sought and obtained a refuge and a hiding-place, and here their descendants are to be found at the present day. They are split into manifold tribes, and are known by vari-

tion to be entirely concentrated on the Hindus and Mohammedans of the plains, while these are passed by? Is such a course in harmony with the prescribed action of the Gospel? Surely "these outcasts from the general family well merit the attention of the Christian Missionary. The very genius of the Gospel bids him condescend to men of low estate, while the number of these tribes, their political condition; their freedom from shackles which bind the orthodox Hindu, their evident capacity for improvement, the bearing which their conversion must have upon the evangelization of the whole people of the land, point them out as deserving of serious attention." There are probably not less than eight or nine millions of this people, which occupy the most secluded portions of the Indian peninsula. Their religion is "a simple system of superstition, resting as much on the natural and suggestive fears and desires of the human mind, as on traditions which are handed down from sire to son, alike without the embellishments of song, or the precision of the established chronicle or exciting romance. Their imagination fills their gloomy forests with malevolent spirits, human, superhuman, and infrahuman, and particularly the ghosts of their own ancestors, and of the divers beasts of prey, which were their quondam companions. Their worship is principally a deprecation of evil, conducted by bloody sacrifices and peace-offerings to the beings, seen and unseen, from whom they apprehend injury. When they rise above this devotion, it is principally to take cognizance of the multifarious powers which they suppose direct and control the various objects of nature, and occurrences of Providences, and occupations of savage life, with which they are most familiar."

We shall refer briefly, as we pass along, to some of the wild tribes inhabiting the various sections of this vast area of territory, that their condition and need of the Gospel may be better understood.

And first

THE GONDS.

"The Gonds inhabit the hill districts on the borders of Orissa and Ganjam. Their country naturally divides itself into two parts; lying as it does partly above and partly below the Ghaut range. In the lower districts the hilly wastes, clothed with deep woods and interspersed with extensive valleys and undulating downs gradually come down to the level plains of Orissa near the sea. From these the higher districts are separated by the steep and precipitous ghauts; and form an extensive plateau above them, somewhat similar to that of Mysore, stretching far away into the territories of Central India. These hill regions, termed Máliás, are distinguished by different names. Bordering on the Orissa territory and the river Mahanuddy, lie the *Boad* Máliás; next toward the south the *Goomsur* Máliás, including *Hodzoghoro,* the the *Bara* and *Atháro* Mutahs, and *Chokapad;* south of these are the *Surádá* and *Corada* Máliás; and west of these, the extensive Máliás of *Chinna Kimedy*. These are the chief divisions of the Gond country. Of these only the Surádá Máliás entirely, and Goomsur partially, lie below the ghauts: the rest are entirely above them.

"The country thus divided presents a varied aspect to the traveller's eye. Below the ghauts, the villages are somewhat scattered; the valleys appear poor, bleak, and barren; water is less abundant than in the higher lands; the country displays no varieties of scenery; and the hilly slopes under the great range are thickly covered with the dammer tree and the bamboo. The districts on the plateau above are far more picturesque. The tableland is much broken by valleys, sometimes deep and rugged, and is crossed by ridges of hills of varied height, some being 4000 feet above the sea. Many parts are bare of wood; in others are groups of forest trees; in others a jungle rich in flowers; the valleys and glens furnish sites for the villages and fields for culture; while in the higher and deeper recesses of the hills thick forests grow, inhabited by the tiger and the bear. In the Máliás of Chinna Kimedy a thick forest of timber trees covers the whole surface, and extends westward without a break for more than a hundred and forty miles. Portions of this forest have been cut down by the people, and the cleared land in the valleys cultivated. The soil is everywhere fertile; and if the land were all cleared, and the numerous waterfalls and springs properly turned to account, it would yield the most abundant harvests. Numerous vegetable products are raised, which furnish materials for traffic in the plains.

"The people are in general divided into two great classes; those living on the lower ranges of the ghauts, and those in the districts above them. The former are called *Bennia* Gonds; the latter, the *Máliá,* or highland Gonds. The Bennia Gonds were apparently permitted by their Hindu conquerors to retain their lands on a rent tenure, or on that of feudal service to their zemindars. Living nearer the plains, and in subjection to Hindu governors, they have of course been brought into constant intercourse with the Hindus who people them: they attend the markets and bazaars, and witness much of a life and habits different from their own. The consequence has been a partial adoption of Hindu manners. The most changed among the Bennias are very like the Hindus; and between them and the pure Gonds may be seen all grades in the change from the habits of the latter to those of the former. They wear the Hindu dress, speak the Oriya language, build houses after the Hindu plan, use the Orissa plough, refuse to cultivate turmeric, drink milk, eat ghee, and abstain from the barbarous practice of dancing, of which their less refined countrymen are extravagantly fond. They have even adopted *Káli* as one of their deities; while the Hindus in the same districts have adopted the Gond god, and call him *Gondini*. In the worship of the deity both people unite together; while the Gond priest and the Brahmin serve together at his altar.

"The *Máliá* Gonds, on the other hand, living on the plateau and in the valleys above the ghauts, exhibit all the characteristics of Gond society in their purest form. They have, it is true, always been in intercourse with the zemindars of the lower country; sometimes making a raid or foray into their territories to levy black mail, but acting usually as independent allies and friends, never as subjects. Separated from the Hindus of the plains by the broad belt of hill zemindaries, filled with men like themselves, and shut out by their inaccessible hills and jungles from all attempts at conquest, they have remained the same people in manners and pursuits for many hundreds, it may be thousands, of years.

"The dress of the Gonds, both male and female, is very scanty, and resembles that of the poorer Hindus. The men wear their black and shiny hair in a knot fastened by an iron pin above the forehead or on the side of the head: both men and women wear ornaments of iron or bone, or of dyed wood. Agriculture is considered the only honourable employment, and, drawing to itself the people's greatest energy, is exceedingly productive. The land of every community is apportioned into a great number of petty freeholds, and each proprietor cultivates for himself. Several good-humoured. They have an unconquerable love of personal freedom, and are very impatient of restraint. They are faithful to their engagements when made; but have no idea of any rights except their own. Hence their readiness, both singly and in bands, to make a foray on others' territories or districts, and seize 'whatever they like best' (as they term it); which means, the most valuable property of others. They are selfish, ferocious, and dreadful drunkards. Like the Arabs, they are remarkable for their hospitality, and rather suffer loss and danger than violate its sacred rites. Marriages only take place between the members of different tribes. The women, though they do not eat with their husbands, are yet treated with some respect: they attend to domestic duties; hold ammunition for their tribe on the battle-field; and, by their advice, exercise much influence on their councils."*

Their religious notions, and the sad results to which they lead, may now be referred to—

"There is one Supreme Being, self-existing, the source of good, and the creator of the universe, of the inferior gods, and of man, This divinity is called in some districts, Boora Pennu, or the God of Light; in others, Bella Pennu, or the Sun God; and the sun and the place from which it rises beyond the sea are the chief seats of his presence.

"Boora Pennu, in the beginning, created for himself a consort, who became Tari Pennu, or the Earth Goddess, and the source of evil. He afterwards created the earth. As Boora Pennu walked upon it with Tari, he found her wanting in affectionate compliance and attention as a wife, and resolved to create from its substance a new being, man, who should render to him the most assiduous and devoted service, and to form from it also every variety of animal and vegetable life necessary to man's existence.

"The creation was perfectly free from moral and physical evil. Men enjoyed free intercourse with the creator. They lived without labour upon the spontaneous abundance of the earth; they enjoyed every thing in common, and lived in perfect harmony

world of every form of moral and physical evil. She instilled into the heart of man every variety of moral evil, 'sowing the seeds of sin in mankind as into a ploughed field,' and, at the same time, introduced every species of physical evil into the material creation—diseases, deadly poisons, and every element of disorder. Boora Pennu, by the application of antidotes, arrested and held in abeyance the elements of physical evil; but he left man perfectly free to receive or to reject moral evil.

"A few individuals of mankind entirely rejected evil, and remained sinless; the rest all yielded to its power, and fell into a state of universal disobedience to the deity, and fierce strife with one another. Boora immediately deified the sinless few without their suffering death, saying to them—'Become ye gods, living for ever, and seeing my face when ye will, and have power over man, who is no longer my immediate care.' Upon the corrupted mass of mankind, Boora Pennu inflicted high moral penalties; and let loose the myriad forms of physical evil by the withdrawal of the antidotes which had arrested them. He entirely withdrew his face and his immediate guardianship from mankind. He made all who had fallen, subject to death; and he further ordained, that, in future, every one who should commit sin should suffer death as its consequence. Universal discord and war prevailed, so that all social and even family ties were broken up. All nature became thoroughly tainted and disordered. The seasons no longer held their regular course; the earth ceased to bear spontaneously fruit fit for the food of man, and became a wilderness of jungle, rocks, and mud. Diseases and death came upon all creatures; snakes became venomous; many flowers and fruits grew poisonous; and many animals became savage and destructive. Man now went clothed, lost the power of moving through the air and the sea, and sank into a state of abject suffering and degradation. Thus the elements of good and evil were thoroughly commingled in man, and throughout nature. Meanwhile, Boora and Tari contended for superiority in fierce conflict, their terrible strife raging throughout the earth, the sea, and the sky; their chief weapons mountains, meteors, and whirlwinds.

"Up to this point, the Gonds hold the same general belief; but from it they divide into two sects directly opposed upon the great question of the issue of the contest between Boora and his rebel consort, involving the whole subject of the practical relation between the two antagonist powers with reference to man, the source and subject of their strife...

"Boora Pennu, say his sect, resolved that, for his own honour, his work should not be lost, but that man should be enabled to attain to a state of moderate enjoyment upon earth, and to rise after death, through the practice of virtue, to a state of beatitude and partial restoration to communion with his maker. To accomplish these purposes, Boora created a subordinate divine agency, in addition to that of the first sinless men, who, when deified, were made guardians of man; and he appointed all the inferior gods to carry out the first object, one excepted, to whom was assigned the duty of administering justice to the dead. It was the office of all these gods to regulate the powers of nature for the use of man, to instruct him in the arts necessary to life, and to protect him against every form of evil.'"*

In these statements will be found indistinct traces of the belief transmitted by Noah to his descendants; the original innocence and happiness of man; his fall through the temptations of an evil spirit; the penal consequences of his sin, and the need of a divine interference for his recovery. At that point, however, the human mind, uninstructed by the light of revelation, goes astray, and loses itself in a gloomy forest of superstition. Tari required human sacrifices. "See," she exclaimed, "what hills, and waste lands, and jungles are here: worship me with human blood, and the whole shall become a cultivated plain, and you shall have vast increase of numbers and of wealth."

Victims, called "Meriah" by the Oriyas, and Tokki or Keddi, by the Gonds, were persons of any race, or age, or either sex, either kidnapped or otherwise procured. Sometimes they were Gond children, whom the parents had sold under pressure of distress. They were not unfrequently permitted to live until they had attained years of maturity, being regarded by the people as consecrated beings. But when the appointed moment arrived, and the Meriah victim was made fast to the post, none spared him, nor were they satisfied until their fields had been sprinkled with his blood. Then Tari was with confidence invoked—

"O Tari Pennu! You have afflicted us greatly; have brought death to our children and our bullocks, and failure to our corn ;— have afflicted us in every way. But we do not complain of this. It is your desire only to compel us to perform your due rites, and

---

* "Account of the religion of the Khonds in Orissa," by Capt. S. C. Macpherson, pp. 13—16.

them to raise up and enrich us. We were anciently enriched by this rite: all around us are great from it: therefore, by our cattle, our flocks, our pigs, and our grain, we procured a victim and offered a sacrifice. Do you now enrich us. Let our herds be so numerous that they cannot be housed; let children so abound, that the care of them shall overcome their parents, as shall be seen by their burned hands; let our heads ever strike against brass pots innumerable hanging from our roofs; let the rats form their nests of shreds of scarlet cloth and silk; let all the kites in the country be seen in the trees of our village, from beasts being killed there every day. We are ignorant of what it is good to ask for. You know what is good for us. Give it to us!" *

It is with thankfulness and gratification we refer to the energetic efforts put forth by the British authorities for the suppression of this rite, and the great degree of success with which they have been crowned. A mode of procedure was adopted at once decided and conciliatory. The despotic plan of crushing the system by bullets was rejected as impracticable and cruel. Simultaneously with the efforts to put down the Meriah sacrifices, measures were adopted for the suppression of female infanticide.

These were necessary measures; yet enforced by authority, and, carried out against the customs and wishes of the people, they were resisted. An armed intervention became requisite, and blood was shed. In this the Gospel procedure stands pre-eminent. It accomplishes wondrous changes in the customs of races, without the necessity of resorting to carnal weapons. It is by a gentle persuasive influence on the man, enlightening his understanding, and so correcting his views and feelings, that such changes are effected. The man becomes convinced of the enormity of his old practices, and of himself abandons them.

On the restoration of tranquillity the British authorities resumed their efforts for the suppression of the barbarous practices which had so long prevailed amongst this people, and with increasing success. Tribe after tribe yielded obedience. Since the first war in Goomsur upwards of 2000 Meriah victims have been saved, and female infanticide has greatly diminished. In the infanticide district of Suradah, containing 2150 families, there were, in 1848, less than 50 female children. In the beginning of 1853, in the same district, there were 900 girls under four years of age.

Barbarous, however, as were the customs of the Gonds, there are portions of these wild tribes to be found in a still greater depth of social degradation. Such is the forest race called Puttooa, inhabiting the jungles of the tributary mehals to the south of Singhbhoom. Their stature is diminutive, not exceeding five feet two inches in the men, and four feet three inches in the women. The latter are the household drudges, their spare and emaciated condition bespeaking forcibly the hardship of their daily life. Their costume is such that they have obtained from their neighbours the name "Puttooa," or the people of the leaf. Their villages are small, seldom containing more than six or eight families; the houses are mean thatched huts of wattle and dab: the site selected is generally some opening in the forest, some pretty spot on the skirt of a jungle, where the eye wanders over a small cultivated valley—the out-fields of a distant Orissa village—to the huge mass of the Satusjea mountain, its peaks rising to an elevation of 1800 feet.

Their pursuits are chiefly those of the chase. They use the bow and arrow, and hunt with dogs, killing deer, hogs, and not unfrequently snakes, of the flesh of which they are very fond. Their usual food, however, consists of roots, and the seeds of jungle grapes. Their religious homage appears to be confined to the nameless spirits which they believe inhabit the woods and mountains. "When they find a wild grape-vine or wild plum-tree more than usually fruitful, or when they chance upon a spot rich in the roots and grapes upon which they subsist, they make an offering to the *genius loci* of a fowl, a goat, or a little rice and spirits, and address to him a prayer, in which the terror which overshadows the lives of this forest race with touching expression—' Lord, let the bears and tigers flee when they see us: let them not meet us.' The only festival of a religious character, which they appear to have, occurs in the month of Bysakh, when they offer sacrifices, and pour out libations to the manes of their dead ancestors."

On the northern face of the Vindhya hills, where the three districts of Behar, Monghyr, and Ramghur meet, are situated the principal Mica mines of Behar. "The most westerly-situated mine is thirty-seven miles in a south-easterly direction from Gya, and is in the district of Behar; the most easterly mine is about sixty miles distant in Zillah Monghyr; the whole of the intermediate sixty miles being more or less productive of the mineral. The average distance from the Ganges of the whole aggregated group of mines is sixty miles.

---

† Macpherson, p. 47.

"Rajowli, a small village, in Pergunnáh Jarráh, of Zillah Behar, is the great mart for the mineral, and the spot whence it is dispersed to all the great markets on the Ganges: this village is situated on the left bank of the Dhunarjeh Nullah, which stream, together with the Tillyá Nullah, unite four miles south of Rajowli, flow from the southern hills in deeply-wooded valleys, and completely intersect the mines. The beds of these streams, the roads through the passes and valleys, and indeed the whole surface of the country around the mica formation, sparkles with the bright mineral.

"Leaving Rajowli, and proceeding four miles in an easterly direction, a deep-wooded valley is entered, situated amongst and surrounded by quartz hills: through this valley, in the rainy season, a mountain torrent descends with great violence, bringing with it great quantities of mica. After ascending the course of the torrent for about a mile, the valley terminates in an amphitheatre of low jungle-covered hills; the soil forming the superficial covering of the country is composed of a harsh dry gravel, composed of quartz, schorlaceous schist, detached and silvery mica; through which soil are seen protruding huge naked masses of quartz and gneiss, the latter both plain and garnetiferous. In the beds of the torrents, bushels of minute garnets may be gathered, but, from their very insignificant proportions, they are quite useless. A very beautiful schorlaceous schist, consisting of crystals of schorl of a delicate fineness, embedded in mica, as well as larger crystals of raven-black schorl, varying in size from that of a finger to that of a man's arm, embedded in a bright glassy quartz, and affording, by the contrast of the two minerals, a very beautiful object, are found in great abundance: such is the nature of the minerals in the immediate neighbourhood of the mines, which are always opened in low detached hills. The mica appears in amorphous masses, varying from a few inches square, to four feet in length, embedded in an incoherent soil composed of schorl and comminuted silvery mica, the whole mass filling up extensive interstices between large and widely-separated quartz rocks.

"The mode of opening a mine is as follows: a small and convenient hill having been chosen as the spot for commencing operations upon, a party of the wild hill tribes, named Bandáthis, the members of which party have freely propitiated the local tutelary god or goddess, both by sacrifice and by getting very drunk, ascend to the top of the hill, and commence sinking a series of pits, the whole way down the profile of the hill, about three feet in diameter each, and a few feet apart. These pits are not continued vertically downwards, but in a zig-zag shape, but nevertheless not so much out of the vertical proper, as that a basket containing the mineral cannot be hauled up from the bottom of the pit to the top; the zig-zag shape of the shaft being formed by sinking the shaft, first inclining to the left a few feet and then to the right a few feet, the head of each cut or notch forming a landing-place or step, and thus the necessity of ladders is obviated; the projecting of salient angles of the notches forming a perfect flight of steps from the top to the bottom of the pits, which seldom reaches to a greater depth than forty feet, when darkness interfering with the workman's progress, the pit is forsaken, and another commenced upon a few feet further down the hill. A slight frame-work of faggots cut from the neighbouring trees is placed over the mouth of each pit, upon which a man sits, waiting till the signal from below is given to haul up the basket containing the mica and rubbish, which has been dug from the sides of the pit by the aid of a rude pick. On arrival at the surface, the good and bad materials are separated; the earth and rubbish are shot down the precipitous side of the hill; the good mica which arrives at the surface of the pit in ragged masses about one foot six inches in length, six inches broad, and three inches in thickness, after having its ragged edges trimmed off with a reaping-hook-looking instrument, is placed by itself in a heap, and the bad or refuse, that is, the softer kind, is also placed aside in a heap by itself.

"The mica reaches the surface in three different states, viz. the good, hard, and serviceable mineral; the soft, wet, and flimsy mineral; and the chipped and powdered mineral.

"The plates of the superior kind are used in all the large Gangetic cities and towns, by the native draftsmen, whose beautiful productions in body colours must be familiar to most people; by the lamp and toy-makers; by the Mohammedans for ornamenting their tazias; as well as for ornamenting umbrellas, boots, and for making artificial flowers.

"The second and third kinds are pounded and used for ornamenting toys, pottery, the inside of houses, for sprinkling over clothes and turbans at feasts, the sparkle from which by torch-light resembles diamonds: but the great consumption of the inferior mineral takes place during the Hoolee festival, during which period the 'ábeer,' or pounded mica, mixed with the flour of the small grain, 'Kodo' and coloured with some red colouring matter, is freely sprinkled over the maddened and intoxicated votaries of those bacchanalian orgies.

"The mines are worked by Mahajans or native merchants, who reside at Patna and depute agents to the spot to superintend the mining. The excavators or miners are Bandáhis, or inhabitants of the hills, a race allied to the Kôls, Bheels, and Santhals: they are a wild-looking set of demi-savages, slightly clad, the forepart of their head shaved, the rest of their hair standing up in wild curls: they have the high cheek-bones, thick lips, and small eyes of the Vindhyan races; they are also a hard-working and merry race. The miners receive as monthly wages one maund (80 lbs.) of rice, and a piece of cloth, the whole valued at two rupees.

"The mines are worked during the months of January, February, and March only; for during the hot months, or from the latter end of March or June, the great heat dries up all the water for many miles around the mines, and during the rainy season the pits fill with water; and subsequent to the rains the unhealthiness of the dense miasmatic jungles in the neighbourhood prevent the work commencing before January."*

Hitherto these tribes have been greatly neglected, nor have they been permitted, in any considerable degree, to share in the efforts which British Christians have put forth for the evangelization of India. Perhaps we should have forgotten their existence altogether, had we not been unpleasantly reminded of it by various outbreaks and incursions on the more civilized districts, inflicting extensive injury on life and property, and requiring, in order to their suppression, the interference of an armed force. Such has been the Santhal outbreak, that of the Khasias of Jyntiapore, which has been just suppressed, and the recent disturbances in Cutch and Guzerat. And such occurrences precisely what might be expected. As a Christian nation, scriptural, and Protestant in our profession of Christianity we shall never be permitted to settle down quietly on our lees in the presence of heathen tribes, for whose evangelization we are doing nothing. They will continue to be scourges in our sides, and thorns in our eyes, until we become convinced that they are restless because they are without the great corrective which it is the office of Christians, and especially in this case, of British Christians, to supply.

All recent events in India have urged upon us this lesson, if only we be teachable enough to receive it—that if we would rule in peace

* Journal of the Asiatic Society of Bengal, 1851, pp. 295—7.

over the heathen entrusted to our charge, we must give to them the Gospel. Neither by the Government, nor by private individuals should any thing be done which tends to the disparagement of Christians in the eyes of the natives. Like the Queen in her royal proclamation, our authorities should avow their personal conviction of its truth, and recognise it as that true religion which can alone reach the heart, renew the character, and secure the domestic and social happiness of man; while private Christians, in well-considered organizations, heartily and munificently sustained, should give themselves to the direct work of Gospel propagation.

We indulge the hope that Christians at home will feel more strongly than ever the duty, the wisdom, and the charity of Missionary exertions, and that amidst the increase of effort, the hill-tribes of Gondwana will not be forgotten. These elevated plateaux, the strongholds of aboriginal heathenism, are even now being approached from different directions. The Missionary force is beginning to compass it about; and although the operations be yet incipient, yet from the very nature of the work, which possesses in itself an inherent self-sustaining energy, independent of external circumstances, they will increase, until upon the highest hill-tops, and in the midst of the most secluded valley, the standard of Gospel truth shall be raised triumphantly.

On the Orissa side we find Baptist Missionaries in the Ganjam collectorate, which comprises the most southern extremities of Orissa, and large portions of the Gond territory; and also at Sumbulpore, a large populous town, situated in the hill districts of Orissa, and lying in the dâk or post route from Calcutta, via Midnapore, to Bombay.

We soon hope to see the Missionaries of our own Society amongst

THE HILL TRIBES OF THE UPPER GODAVERY.

Colonel Cotton, who has taken a deep interest in the adoption of this new field of labour by the Church Missionary Society, is particularly anxious that the upper country should be occupied. The reasons may best be given in his own words—

"Two Missionaries having been nominated to the Telugu Mission, the first question seems to be between the Delta and the Upper Godavery: the first would be to Hindus, the latter to aborigines.

"If only a small addition can at present be made to the Church Missionaries on the Godavery—so that the question is between the country on that river, west of the hills, and that near the coast—I am of opinion, that for the following reasons the Missionaries should rather be sent to the upper country—

"Because the people there are aborigines. The great success has certainly hitherto been among those races, as the Shanars, the Kavers, and the Kōls in Chota Nagpore. It seems to me that God thus points out the way to the Mission Societies. The freedom of those races form an established and deeply-rooted system of false religion, and still more their freedom from caste does certainly leave them much more open to the truth. Three men, who have visited the Koiys, all bear testimony to the complete difference between these Koiys and Hindus, as to the teachableness and friendliness of the former, and their being sensible that they need instruction.

"The Koiys have no written language, and consequently no literature: whether they have any forms of religion at all among them I am not certain, but I saw none in their villages, though those that are near Hindu pagodas sometimes go there on festival days.

"They thus offer, as far as possible, a *tabula rasa:* the Missionaries can introduce the Roman character, and supply them with a pure literature. They will thus have the greatest advantage in commencing a Mission among them.

"No other Missions are established among them. There are at present no Missionaries in all Gondwana, from the Godavery to Chota Nagpore, and from Nagpore to Cuttack. There will thus be no interference with the Missions of other bodies.

"The works of the Upper Godavery, which, however, are not yet extensively taken in hand, will no doubt draw to them workmen from every part of Gondwana, as well as from the Telugu districts of Hydrabad, and the Mahratta people of Nagpore, and the assigned districts; so that there will be good opportunities of dispersing the truth over a wide expanse of country, and especially over Hydrabad, as yet untouched by the truth. Budrachellum, especially, is a place of pilgrimage, to which people come from every part of the country.

"The distance of the first barrier, from Rajamundry, is 120 miles. This is the spot where the first works will be constructed, and where, consequently, the head-quarters of the engineers' officer will be established. And most probably it would be the most eligible place to establish the Mission on the east bank of the river. This bank is indeed, as well as the opposite, in the Hydrabad country, but orders have been sent to this Government to see what arrangements can be made with the Nizam to exchange it for other territory. It is only a narrow strip, and I was told that in one place, near the first barrier, it is only one mile wide, and, if that is the case, the Mission might be established on British territory, without being too far from the bank of the river. There can be little doubt, however, that arrangements will soon be completed for transferring this bank to our Government.

"There are already five steamers on the Godavery, and two or three more are now being put together at Dowaleshwaram, so that there can be no doubt that this year there will be constant communication between the first barrier and Dowaleshwaram. The first barrier is fifteen miles above Budrachellum.

"On these grounds I would strongly urge the occupation of the Upper Country rather than the Delta, where the people are Hindus, and where there are already some Missionaries.

"In occupying this ground, two languages will at first be required—Telugu, which is the language spoken all along the banks of the river, and which is generally understood even by the Koiys there, and the Koiy language, which appears to be spoken for a considerable distance to the northward. Beyond, in that direction, Goundu seems to be the language spoken almost throughout the upper basin of the Mahanuddy. As the Mission spreads to the northward, of course the latter language must be acquired. I conclude that there must be considerable similarity between it and the Koiy, but I do not know this. From the small vocabularies of the Koiy obtained, it appears that there are more Tamul than Telugu words in it; and Mr. Walter Elliot says that this is the case generally in the languages of the aborigines.

"If one of the present Telugu Missionaries, who has already mastered that language, were to go with one of the new Missionaries, in the first instance, the latter might give himself up to the acquisition of the Koiy, for which he would require the aid of one who could talk Telugu, as that would be the only medium of communication with the Koiys in the first instance. It would, of course, be a work of great labour and patience to acquire the Koiy, as the people are astonishingly ignorant, and no doubt it would be very important to select a man, if possible, who had a natural talent for such work. But no doubt, on looking about, he would find some Koiy man, above his countrymen in intelligence, who, after a little training, would understand how to give the information about the language that was required. In the mean time the other new Missionary might remain at Ellore, to study Telugu.

"The country northward has been very little explored. It is a forest country chiefly, and very thinly inhabited. Mr. Heles, of the Plymouth body, has gone up the Savery, the northern feeder of the Godavery, the confluence of which is thirty miles below Budrachellum; and the Government are now establishing a salt dépôt at the first British village on that river, about twenty-four miles from its mouth. The country, from the first barrier to near Raipore, has scarcely been seen by a European. It is traversed by the Indrawutty, flowing from the north-east, and entering the Godavery not far from Mahadupore, at a point about eighty miles above the first barrier, where the British territory comes down to the bank of the Godavery, and where also the Government have ordered the establishment of a salt dépôt. How far the Indrawutty is navigable has not been ascertained. Another smaller feeder, the Tal, falls into the Godavery about ten miles above the first barrier: its navigability, also, has not been ascertained.

"All this part of the country has been hitherto in the most lawless state, oppressed by the petty rajahs subordinate to Hydrabad and Nagpore, and the Koiys have been terribly oppressed, so that there can be no doubt that the people generally will appreciate the establishment of Europeans among them, and be prepared to treat them as friends, just as the Karens did. When Point Tavoy was taken, and some Karens ventured into the place, they were brought before the General, and were astonished at their friendly treatment, and at presents being made them, so different from what they had been accustomed to, and a great impression was thus made throughout the Karen tribes, which no doubt prepared the way for a willing hearing of the European Missionaries.

"The whole tract, from the Ganges to the Godavery, is, I believe, occupied by aboriginal races, viz. the Santhals, Puharis, Coles, Gonds, Koiys, &c. Considerable num- throughout one of their most satisfactory converts and powerful preachers.

"I feel persuaded myself that this appears one of the most promising fields of Missionary enterprise, though no doubt there are great difficulties, such as the extreme ignorance of the people, the unopened state of the country, the feverishness of some parts of it, the want of grammars and dictionaries of the language, &c. Ignorance, however, is a far less obstacle than false learning, and no religion than false religion. The Godavery forms a grand highway, superior to any thing in other parts of the country, and probably the other rivers will be soon navigated.

"The neighbourhood of the first barrier has been found extremely healthy, both to natives and Europeans, though very hot for about two months. It is a fine pasture country, and very fertile. The population is considerable on the banks of the river; and it appears to have been kept down solely by the want of protection of life and property.

"*P.S.* I am told that there is a grammar of the Gond language, in English, and that the Koiy language is, in fact, the same as the Gond. If so, it will save a great deal of time."

Again, at Nagpore, there is a Mission of the Free Church of Scotland. They have the Mahrathi language on the west; a corrupt dialect of Hindi on the east; in the south, a sprinkling of Telugu; and, in the jungly tracts, various aboriginal dialects, which, with the exception of that spoken by the Kurkus, or Moosis, may all be classed as Gondi, and bear a close affinity to Tamil. And may not Tamil evangelists be permitted to share in the evangelization of Gondwana? Have not the Tamil churches entered on the great work of direct evangelizing efforts among their countrymen? and are they not preparing themselves for future usefulness in the Missionary field?

At Jubbulpore, 156 miles N.E. from Nagpore, we find Missionaries of our own Society. The hill-tribes are in the neighbourhood, and Gonds and other aborigines are occasionally to be met with in Jubbulpore. At Chota Nagpore, occupied amongst the Kōls, and penetrating into the very heart of

station, one belonging to our own Society, from whence energetic efforts are being put forth for the improvement of the hill-tribes in its vicinity. We must pause here, and endeavour to present to our readers a correct view of this field of labour.

BHAGULPORE.

"The district of Bhagulpore, comprising 7801·04 square miles of territory, is situated in the fertile valley of the Ganges; which river divides the district into two unequal portions, the larger portion lying to the south of the river.

"The district lies between the parallels of North latitude 24° 02' and 26° 27'; and meridians of 86° 13' and 88' of East longitude. The length of the district is 168 miles, or, from the southern boundary of Nepal on the north of the district to the northern boundary of the district of Beerbhoom in the south, the average width south of the Ganges is 112 miles, and north of the Ganges it has an average width of 20 miles.

"Under the Mohammedan kings, the district of Bhagulpore formed the most eastern portion of the Soubah of Behar; its southern and eastern boundaries abutting upon the province of Bengal Proper, of which territory the districts of Beerbhoom and Moorshedabad form a part, and where the official accounts, fiscal and judicial, are kept in the Bengali language; whereas, in Bhagulpore, the accounts are kept in the Hindustani or Urdu.

"The climate of Bhagulpore is peculiar to itself: situated between the parching hot winds of Western and Central India, and the damp soil of Bengal, it appears influenced by both. The heat is not so great or so parching as it is a few degrees to the westward, nor so damp as its neighbouring districts, Moorshedabad, Purneah, and Maldah. The heats of summer, or from April to June, are, nevertheless, very great—too great to allow the natives themselves to be freely exposed to the direct rays of the sun: to the European, such exposure would most likely be fatal in a few hours. During the hot weather, the thermometer ranges from 80° to 100° during the day: a steady west wind generally sets in at nine A.M. and continues to blow till sunset; this wind is warm, approaching to hot, but cannot be compared to the true hot wind of North-Western India. The weather from June to September, or what is styled the rainy season, is much more pleasant to the feelings, from the immense quantity of moisture suspended in the air but the sun being unobscured by dust as it is in the hot weather, strikes down its rays in a peculiarly dangerous manner; especially when an assemblage of clouds favours the formation of a focus for the rays to descend in a concentrated manner, such a sun has the power of blistering the skin as if actual cautery had been applied. During the rainy season, an east wind generally prevails. During the cold weather, or from October to March, the weather is peculiarly fine and well suited to the European constitution: a steady light westerly or easterly wind blows, the air is cool, and the thermometer in December descends as low as 33° during the night.

"A spectator, standing at mid-day during the hot weather in any of the Pergunnahs that lie to the eastward of the Rajmahal hills, may distinctly observe the termination of the hot winds, and the commencement of the humid atmosphere of Bengal. The hot wind is seen on a level with the highest peaks of the Rajmahal hills, which rise to 2000 feet, and up whose western flank the hot wind has been driven from the plains of Monghyr and Bhagulpore; and is represented by a huge, yellowish-brown stratum of heated air, highly charged with minute particles of dust, and peculiarly electrical; this bank, or stratum, extending to near the base of the Himalaya mountains, never descends again, but, lifted up and there retained by the damp atmosphere of Bengal, is lost or cooled in the upper regions of the air: the mark of separation between the heated electrical, and dust-charged atmosphere of Western and Central India, and the damp air of Bengal, is so defined and so nearly stationary during the day, that its height, limits, and rate of progression, are all capable of measurement. The climate of Bhagulpore is peculiarly suited to the growth of rice, which forms the staple agricultural produce of the district.

"The aspect of the district is pleasing, from the great abundance of mango plantations and palm-trees that are scattered over the whole surface of the country, and from the numerous detached hills, and connected ranges of hills, that break the monotony of an otherwise level country. The principal hills are the Rajmahal range, a fine mass of basaltic and carboniferous hills, lying meridionally near the eastern boundary of the district, shutting out the fertile but dry kunkurferous plains of Bhagulpore from the pure alluvial soil of Bengal. This range extends from the Ganges river on the north to the Brahminee river on the south, (and which river forms the boundary between Moorshedabad, Beerbhoom, and Bhagulpore), a distance of seventy miles, with an average width of twenty miles. These hills occupy 1366 square miles; their greatest height does not exceed 2000 feet.

"From near the south-western extremity of

the Rajmahal hills, a tract of elevated land sweeps across the whole district, with a bold curve to the west and north-west, until it unites with the Kurrukpore hills, which terminate in the bed of the Ganges at Monghyr, and which range of hills separates Monghyr from Bhagulpore.

"The mass of low level country thus shut in by the Kurrukpore hills on the west, by the Rajmahal hills on the east, the Ganges river to the north, and by the great curve of high land to the south, consists of a mass of rich, cultivated, and highly productive land, amounting to about 3125 square miles: this is the finest portion of the district, the most densely populated, best cultivated, because it has the finest soil, is level, well watered, and is free from rocks or unproductive ground. The upper or high land, which consists of highly-contorted gneiss rock, is about 500 feet above the Ganges, and is rocky, hilly, broken into deep ravines, covered with forest, or is so dry as to be generally unproductive, and is consequently in a state of nature. This high land is nevertheless not without its uses and benefits to the district, and that to no small extent: it serves as the grazing ground for cattle during the hot weather, when every particle of vegetation is scorched up in the plains; it produces an abundance of wood for ploughs, for building purposes, and for firewood; it produces bamboos, grass, barks, gums, tusser silk, slates, building stone, honey, copper, lead, antimony, silver, iron and coal, besides numerous sorts of grain, but these latter in very limited quantities. The mahooa petal (*Bassia tatifolia*) is largely collected and used in the distilleries; catechu is also manufactured from the mimosa catechu, and is exported to Europe."*

Bhagulpore, the principal town of the district, situate on the right bank of the Ganges, is a miserable straggling collection of huts, extending over four miles of ground, cut-up, and divided by fields, gardens, plantations, and numerous roads, "the whole place resembling an inhabited forest rather than a town. Chumpanuggur and Luchmeegunje, two large contiguous towns, lie immediately mound nearly two miles in circumference, is the site of the cantonment of the Bhagulpore Hill Rangers: it is a high, dry spot commanding a fine view of the river Ganges: it appears to have been originally built upon a kunkur bank, though much raised by rains, rubbish, pottery; and a section lately cut in making a road up to the fort showed remains of pottery to the depth of ten or twelve feet: according to Buchanan, the fort appears to have been built by the Kurna Rajahs. At Chumpanuggur, which is at the extreme west of the town, are the remains of Jain temples."†

Near the southern boundary of the pergunnah lies the Mundar hill, named also Mudsoodun, a mass of naked granite, about 800 feet in height; "the summit of which is gained by a flight of steps cut in the solid rock. Remains of tanks, temples, walls, statues, fortifications, inscriptions, and other marks, show this to have once been a place of note: at the present day a modern Hindu temple stands on the summit of the hill, overhanging a fearful precipice, from the summit of which the base is not visible by reason of the bulging-out of the polished granite rock. The temple is dedicated to Mahadeva. It is visited every year during the month of January, during which period there is a fair held at the village of Bowsee, three miles south of the hill, at which village there is a collection of temples. The most remarkable image on the hill is an Egyptian-looking figure of a gigantic size, cut from the solid rock, but is in an unfinished state: it measures eight feet four inches across the forehead, and is fifty-two feet eight inches in height.

"On the summit of the temple is a Trigonometrical Survey station, and from this spot a fine view of the country is obtained. Looking to the north, or towards the Ganges, the eye wanders over the fertile plains of Bhagulpore, one mass of cultivation extending for hundreds of square miles, prettily varied with villages and mango plantations; but to the west and to the south, looking over Pergunnahs Chundweh, Pussye, Chandun Kutooreea, Daora Sukwara, and Hondweb, far into the Beerbhoom district, is seen an uninterrupted re-

great Vindhya range, and in their recesses we shall find portions of aboriginal tribes similar to those which we have already traced on the eastern, southern, and western confines of the great central fastness, Gondwana.

We shall commence with the Kurrukpore hills. This group of hills, lying immediately to the south of the station of Monghyr and named after the town of Kurrukpore, which is situated to their east, is an offshoot from the northern face of the Vindhya range, and measures 30 miles in length, with an average width of 24 miles. The greatest elevation does not exceed 1100 feet, which is the height of the table-mountain, Maruk, thirteen miles to the south of Monghyr. In the interior are extensive valleys, forests, precipices, hot wells, mountain torrents, &c. Ascending through deeply-wooded valleys of great beauty, and dense forests of fine trees, with ferns growing parasitically on them, the traveller reaches the summit of this table-topped hill, from whence he has extended before him a splendid view of Monghyr station; the Rajmahal hills, seventy miles to the east; some one hundred miles of the course of the Ganges, winding through the highly-cultivated districts of Patna, Monghyr, and Bhagulpore, and beyond, if clouds do not intercept, the Himalaya mountains spread out in one vast panoramic view. The inhabitants of these hills consist principally of Santhals. They collect the iron ore, which is common over all these hills, smelt it in the rudest of furnaces, and exchange the metal with the lowlanders for salt, tobacco, or rice.

To the south-west of the Kurrukpore hills lies the pergunnah of Purbutpara, the summit of a series of rocks connecting the Kurrukpore hills with the Vindhya range to the south. The larger portion of its surface is covered with rocks, hills, ravines or low scrubby jungle, which occasionally rises into fine timber-trees. The cleared spots are in the neighbourhood of the villages, producing rice, juneera, Indian corn, poppy, murroon, muhooa petals, and mango-trees in abundance, the soil between the hills and rocks being a fine black kewal, a rich mould, mostly composed of decayed vegetation. The cultivators are Santhals, Bhoonyahs and Ghatwals, besides a race called Korah and Nyah, engaged in smelting iron, which the pergunnah yields in abundance.

The pergunnahs of Waseela, Chandun Kutoorea, and Danra Sukwara, all lying in a south-westerly direction from Purbutpara, and forming a portion of the great upland curve, which encloses to the southward that plain of Bhagulpore, are of the same character, cultivation being seen only in spots around the huts of the Santhals and other half-wild races. "The forest affords them wood, grass and bamboos for their dwellings. A few goats and cows supply them with milk. Their land yields rice, juneera, ahur dal, and mustard, the oil of the latter being used in their food. The berries of the byne, or zizyphus jujuba, and capsicums constitute their stock of condiments, and a little salt and tobacco their luxuries. Their clothes are either made at home, or are imported from the lowlands. They are mostly armed with bows and arrows, with which they kill bears, birds, and hares, the latter at full speed, the birds when on the wing, and the bears when brought to bay."

To the south-west of Danra Sukwara, and extending in that direction until it reaches the Rajmahal hills, lies the pergunnah Hendwoh " (566 square miles), situated upon the high rocky land forming the water-shed of the series of streams flowing respectively to the north and south. About one-third of the whole area is cultivated; the remaining two-thirds are in a state of nature, being occupied by either hills, bare gneiss rocks, ravines, patches of unproductive iron-clay, kunker beds or sakua jungle. The cultivation, with the exception of large and extensive tracts on the north-east and eastern boundary, is generally confined to small patches around the village sites, which are exceedingly numerous though small; the population for so badly cultivated a tract is immense, and consists principally of Ghutwals, Santhals and Bonyahs. The principal villages are Noni Haut, a fine flourishing village with a weekly market, a thannah, a Hindu temple, a very fair bazaar, and some fine mango groves. It is situated on very high ground near the banks of a small stream which falls into the More river, three miles from the village. To this village numerous Santhals resort from their jungle homes to purchase salt, tobacco, beads, or grain, or to effect an exchange for those articles, giving in return, bamboos, wood, iron, gums, and barks, the produce of the jungles. This village, in former unsettled days, was probably the mart for salt for all the surrounding hill people and Santhals, whence its name Noni Haut, or salt market. The village is situated upon the high road leading from Bhagulpore on the Ganges to Soory the capital of Bheerbhoom: the road, being over hard and gravelly soil, is naturally good, though very tortuous, having constantly to avoid deep ravines and dense patches of jungle.

"The hills that lie scattered over the pergunnah no where rise into distinct ranges, except east of Noni Haut, where two small parallel and contiguous ranges are seen, the western one extending four miles north and south, the eastern one five miles north and south: the detatched hills are in general bare and rounded masses of gneiss penetrated by caves, and filled with numbers of the common black bears, who commit great devastation amongst the crops, principally devouring the juneera. The jungles swarm with jungle fowl, black partridges, peafowl, and bush quail."*

"The Rajmahal hills, the extensive and hitherto unexplored tract of hilly country, extending from the banks of the Ganges at Sikrigalli, in latitude 26° 10′ North, and 87° 50′ East longitude, to the boundary of the district of Beerbhoom, a distance of seventy miles, and known as the Rajmahal hills, form the most north-easterly shoulder or portion of the Vindhya mountains; which range, extending from near the mouths of the Nerbudda and Taptee rivers in Kandeish in longitude 73° 30′ and latitude 21°, and after having travelled 850 miles in an east-north-east direction, or quite across India to Sikrigalli, here turns to the south, passes through the districts of Beerbhoom, Burdwan, Midnápore and Cuttack, and eventually merges into the ghauts or mountains running parallel to the Coromandel coast.

"The hills are inhabited by two distinct races, the mountaineers, or a race living on the summits of the hills, and who are, with rare exceptions, never found residing in the valleys; and the Santhals, who reside in the valleys. Both these races have distinct languages, neither of which are understood by the Hindustani man, nor are the two languages understood by the two races.

THE SANTHALS.

"The Santhal, or lowlander, is a short, well-made and active man, quiet, inoffensive and cheerful; he has the thick lips, high cheek-bones, and spread nose of the Bheel, Köl, and other hill tribes of Southern and Central India: he is beardless, or nearly so: he is moreover an intelligent, obliging, creature, and an industrious cultivator of the soil, and as he is unfettered with caste, he enjoys existence in a far greater degree than does his neighbour, the priest-ridden and caste-crushed Hindu.

"The Santhal eats his buffalo-beef, his kids, poultry, pork, or pigeons, enjoys a hearty carouse, enlivened with the spirit 'Pachúi,' and dances with his wives and comrades to express his joy and thankfulness; and when the more substantial good things of life, such as meat and poultry are scarce, he does not refuse to eat snakes, ants, frogs, and field-rats. The cow is also eaten by the Santhal, as well as all other animals, whether slain or those that have died a natural death, or that have been shot or torn by wild animals.

"The women are fat and short, and although not pretty according to the European idea of beauty, have a very pleasing expression of countenance, with none of the affected or mock modesty of the Hindu.

"The working dress of the male Santhal consists of a mere strip of cloth: the women, on the contrary, are well clothed with an ample flowing cloth, one end of which is fastened round the waist, the other is passed over the left shoulder, leaving the right shoulder, part of the breast and arm, entirely free, and is allowed to hang down in front. When the women can afford it, they load their limbs with zinc and bell-metal ornaments: the men wear small zinc ear-rings, a few finger-rings, and occasionally an iron wrist-bangle: both male and female tie their long hair into a knot on the crown of the head.

"The religion of the Santhals consists in prayers, sacrifices, and religious dances, the whole of which are generally performed and attended to by the votaries whilst in a state of intoxication. The only prayer I have heard of amongst these people is a supplication to an invisible and powerful spirit for protection from famine and sickness; from disease amongst their cattle; for defence against wild animals, especially the tiger; and that their children may be defended from all dangers, amongst which are enumerated the attacks of wild animals, snake bites, scorpion stings, and all kinds of accidents. This simple prayer points out in a forcible manner the condition of the Santhal and his wants: he first prays for protection from famine; for as he is an inhabitant of the jungles, and generally cut off from all communication with his fellow-men, a failure of his scanty crops would be ruin and starvation to him. Their plough cattle being the grand instruments by which their crops are insured to them, and as a murrain or a total destruction of these animals would leave the Santhal in a starving state, his prayers are also directed to their preservation.

"That a portion of their supplication should be directed against the attacks of wild animals is not surprising, for the Santhal, being a denizen of the forest, as before observed, he is himself, as are his cattle, in constant danger from the attacks of tigers, bears, leopards, and

---
* Sherwill, pp. 18, 19.

wolves; and his crops are also in danger from the ravages committed by wild elephants, buffaloes, monkeys, and deer; and as the Santhal never manures his land, and as he generally occupies an indifferent soil, a constant change in his abode is necessary, and thus, in his onward move, he constantly comes in contact with these his great enemies. The Santhal, however, with a proper spirit, does not supplicate without endeavouring to help himself, and no opportunity is allowed to escape of destroying these animals, which is effected, with bows and arrows, poisoned and not poisoned.

"Children, being the Santhals' great pride, comfort, and assistance, are not forgotten in their short prayer. Santhals in general have large families, averaging perhaps eight children to each couple: the male children plough, herd the cattle, reap the harvest, build and repair the family houses, make the carts and ploughs; distil the spirit Pachúi from rice, and perform all out-door work; whilst the female children husk the juneera and rice, express oil from the mustard-seed, cook the household food, attend the markets when near one, look after the poultry, pigs, goats, and pigeons; and, when the parents are old and infirm, the children become their support.

"Almost all nations on earth, savage or civilized, appear to have an intuitive feeling or knowledge that blood is required to be shed for the propitiation of sins, nor do we find the Santhal ignorant of the fact; and in order to propitiate the invisible spirit, they freely sacrifice the buffalo, pig, goat, and poultry, the blood of which animals is sprinkled over the offerings made by the worshippers.

"The Santhals are governed by Pergunnites and by Manjis chosen by themselves from amongst their numbers: the Pergunnite has charge of perhaps twelve villages, from which he collects the rent and makes it over to the superintendant; the Manji has immediate charge of his own village and is answerable for all the misdeeds of his brethren; but as they are in general an orderly race of people, their rulers have little more to do than bear their honours and collect the rent."*

In the notes of a tour through the Rajmahal hills, Captain Sherwill introduces various notices of the Santhal people, which are graphic and interesting—

"Direction north, twelve miles to Burwa. The road over very broken and raviny ground, passes through numerous Santhal villages, around which were fine sheets of cultivation, comprising mustard, gram, cotton, and juneera, the latter cut and stacked. The views along this march are particularly pleasing, especially near the Bokraban bungalow, which stands on the banks of a small hill stream, and buried in a dense jungle, in which I observed some very fine sál and semul trees. The numerous pure and gushing hill streams met with on this march, have a most pleasing effect upon the Indian traveller, who is generally doomed to dry water-courses and drier roads.

"The village of Burwa, where I halted, is under a small gneiss hillock, which, together with its small patches of cultivation, are buried in a pretty forest.

"Observing a tuft of straw tied to a tree in the jungle, I inquired of the Manji the meaning or use of it. He informed me, that whenever a Santhal is desirous of protecting a patch of jungle from the axes of the villagers, or a patch of grass from being grazed over, or a newly-sown field from being trespassed upon, he erects a bamboo in his patch of grass or field, to which is affixed a tuft of straw; or, in the case of jungle, some prominent and lofty tree has the same prohibitory mark attached, which mark is well understood and strictly observed by all parties interested. . .

"In the afternoon I entered a thick forest of asan and chironji at the base of the Tatukpara hill: half an hour's sharp climbing by a steep foot-path brought me to the summit of the hill. The hill village of Tatukpara, which the year before had stood on the summit of the hill, had, consequent upon the death of a villager, been removed half-way down into the valley. From the old site there is a capital view to the eastward of a fine cultivated valley, which has been occupied and cleared by Santhals: this valley is backed by a range of hills, studded in every direction with hill villages, the sides and tops of the hills cleared and occupied by large sheets of cultivation, cleared by the indefatigable hillmen, and cleared in spots where it is barely possible to walk, as I had good proof in returning to my tents down by another road. From Tatukpara I counted thirty hill villages, perched either on the summits or on the slopes of the hills, whilst the villages of the bashful and quiet Santhals were seen far down in the secluded valleys. On this hill there is a fine collection of trees, of a very large growth, the principal of which are mango, fan-leaf palm, tamarind, kurm, pipal, al or moringa, asan, and cheronji: of crops there were the remains of tobacco, Indian corn, juneera, bora bean, and kabar dal: the level ground had been ploughed. . . .

---

* Sherwill, pp. 30—32.

"Direction, north.—Passed a bungalow at Chandna, and from thence struck in under the hills, through a series of wild jungly ravines, and amongst gneiss hillocks and over greenstone dykes to Sundari Kulan, a fine large Santhal village situate close under the hills, and surrounded by sheets of mustard cultivation. The village is about one mile in length, being one long street one house deep, with about one hundred family enclosures, each enclosure occupying from four to five log-wood houses. These enclosures are made with the green boughs of the sakua: planted in the ground and tied together, they keep each family distinct from its neighbours: they generally contain a man and his wife, several married children and their families, a pig-sty, buffalo-shed, and a dove-cot: a wooden stand holds the water-pots, the water from which is used for drinking or cooking: there is also a rude wooden press for expressing oil from the mustard-seed. In a corner of the yard there will probably be a plough, or a couple of solid-wheeled carts, whilst numbers of pigs and poultry are seen in every direction. Each of these enclosures contained on an average ten souls, thus giving a population of 1000 to Sundari.

"The street is planted on each side with the pungent sohajna, which tree is a great favourite with the Santhal. The numerous pig-sties, and great abundance of poultry in the village, proclaim the absence of caste amongst this free and unshackled and un-priest-ridden tribe."

In Captain Sherwill's narrative are found occasional notices of the hill-men, a race of people of whom a description is given in our volume for 1852, p. 107, &c. The following paragraph refers to one of their villages—

"In the evening I crossed the Gumani nullah, a deep hill stream, which has cut its bed through contorted gneiss, and ascended the basaltic hill, on which is situate the hill village Jola: the view to the north and east is very beautiful, every hill appearing capped by a village surrounded by fine mango and fan-leaf palm-trees: much jungle has been needles, thread, buttons, beads, bodkins, and lastly, a dram of brandy; this last gift opened his heart and set loose his tongue. Presents were then distributed to the women, who now flocked in numbers to the spot where I stood, the presents consisting of bead-necklaces, needles, and sewing cotton for the women, and bright metal buttons of all kinds of gaudy patterns for the children. The young man, at my request, showed me the interior of his house, and introduced me to his wife, who was busy cooking in the centre of the one room which constitutes the entire house. The hill houses in general are very neat, being composed of either matting, hurdle, or thin sticks, sometimes smeared with mud to keep out the wind, the whole supported by stout timbers, upon which rests a lofty hog-backed roof with very low eaves; the doors are in the gables, and are protected by verandahs; the roofs are pitched at a singularly obtuse angle, giving great width to the house. The rafters of the present house were covered with heads of Indian corn, juneers, and beans: against one of the mat-walls hung a pair of small antlers with four tynes each, serving as brackets for holding bows and arrows, and a few other light articles. A large drum hung in one corner: a fire was burning in the centre of the room, the smoke from which had blackened every rafter, beam, and bamboo in the house: across the hut was slung a grass hammock, in which the hill people sleep during the rainy and hot seasons; the hammock was twelve feet in length, six feet in width when opened, and was netted, each mesh being a foot in length. I examined the fabric, and found it to consist of the fibre of the Bauhinea scandens: a small fishing-net and creel hung in another corner, for the hill-men descend the hills and fish in the small torrents, but they never capture any thing larger than a moderate sized minnow. . .

"Direction north-east to Burhyte.—Passed through several fine Santhal villages, namely, Kusmah, on the banks of the Gumani, which stands at the ford; Kadmah, Gopladih, Hindoadih, and Sonajori.

"Burhyte, the capital town of the hills, is a

carriage roads have been cut, there are numerous footpaths leading over and along the hills.

"From Burhyte, large quantities of rice, bora beans Indian-corn, mustard, and several oil-seeds are conveyed away in carts by Bengalis to Jangipore, on the Bhagiratti; and in return for these grains, the Santhals are paid in money, salt, tobacco, beads, or cloth. The soil around Burhyte is the deep black cotton soil, producing luxuriant crops of rice, Indian-corn, juneera, beans, koorthee, tobacco, gram, and mustard.

"This valley, viewed from any of the surrounding hills, affords an admirable example of what can be done with natives, when their natural industry and perseverance are guarded and encouraged by kindness. When Mr. Pontet took charge of the hills in 1835, this valley was a wilderness, inhabited here and there by hill-men; the remainder was overrun with heavy forest, in which wild elephants and tigers were numerous; but now, in 1851, several hundred substantial Santhal villages, with an abundance of cattle, and surrounded by luxuriant crops, occupy the hitherto neglected spot. The hill-men have, with a few exceptions, retired to the hills, being either unwilling to be near the Santhal, whom the hill-man despises, or courting that privacy they could not enjoy in a cultivated plain, have yielded up the fertile plain to their more industrious and energetic neighbours.

"I attended the Friday market at Burkyte, which was established a few years ago. The amount of grain, the produce of the valley, exposed for sale was very great: numerous carts from Jangipore on the Bhagiratti were in attendance to convey it away towards Moorshedabad, and eventually to Calcutta, from whence much of the mustard that is grown in these hills is exported to England. Besides grain of various kinds, there was a fair display of sugar-cane; salt, lac, dammer or rosin, brass pots and bangles, beads, tobacco, sugar, vegetables, chillies, tamarinds, and spices, potatoes, onions, ginger, cotton, thread and cloth, the latter in great abundance.

"Two miles north of the village, and extending croscopic fineness to several inches in length, and of a corresponding thickness. The Santhals have ploughed in amongst this curious collection of natural gems, any one of which would be an ornament to a geologist's cabinet; many of the globes have been fractured, displaying in the sunshine a brilliant assemblage of sparkling crystals. The agate balls are of all sizes, some only a few ounces in weight, whilst others weigh several hundred pounds. At the village of Khurwa, and underlying this bed of agates, is a bed of wacke enclosing small balls of chalcedony and stilbite: the wacke passes into a very beautiful clinkstone, of a homogeneous texture, of a pale salmon or dove colour, rings under the hammer, is easily broken, and fracture highly conchoidal: it is found in large slabs six and eight feet in length, also in small parallelograms and wedge-like splinters. If this stone could be found in any quantity, it would be a highly valuable discovery, as, from its natural fracture or stratification, the stone would be highly prized for many domestic purposes.

"A quantity of this stone was taken a few years ago to Bhagulpore for the purpose of ornamenting a tank, but at a fearful sacrifice of bullock life, many of which animals belonging to the Santhals perished from being overloaded. The Santhals have a bitter recollection of the transaction, as they say they were never remunerated for the loss of their cattle. . . .

"Buffaloes from their superior strength, are preferred by the Santhals, both for agricultural purposes as well as for draught, to the common grey cattle, which latter animals are readily exchanged with the Hindus from the plains, who import buffaloes for that purpose: all the solid-wheeled carts, if possible, are drawn by buffaloes.

."The Santhal, in the construction of his solid-wheeled cart, and in the mode of loading it, shows an utter contempt or ignorance of all rules of mechanics: the cart consists of two wheels, composed of two or three pieces of wood, each put together so as to form a solid wheel three feet in diameter: these wheels are supported at a distance of four feet apart by a

packed in huge and ingeniously-made straw baskets, or rather straw rope-balls, five feet in diameter; and as the driver almost invariably adds his own weight by standing on the cart, a ruinous and cruel weight is thus thrown upon the necks of the draught animals and upon the body of the cart, which bends and springs under the weight; whilst the wheels which are at the utter extreme of the bamboos, are pressed outwards and backwards, and seem inclined to fly from their position, which they would do with great force if relieved of their retaining wooden pegs. When it is intended to convey grass, rice in the ear, or any other crop on these carts, a few sticks are interwoven with the two skeleton longitudinal bamboos, so as to form a temporary retaining body to the cart. No iron or other metal is ever used in the construction of these carts, wooden pegs and twisted-grass string serving all the purposes to which metal is put by a wheelwright.

"The plough in like manner is a simple but effectual instrument, consisting of a crooked block of wood, fitted with a still more crooked wooden handle, and a light beam, from six to nine feet in length: the share is a small bar of soft iron, a foot in length and one inch in width, one end of which is hammered into a wedge-like shape: this is the cutting part; the other, or blunt end, is shipped into a groove in the foot of the plough, where, with the aid of two small iron claps laid across the groove to prevent it flying upwards, it is retained by the pressure conveyed to it during its passage through the soil. The deepest furrow ploughed with these instruments is about four inches. Two buffaloes draw the plough, and one man guides it: after the day's work the Santhal shoulders his plough and walks home. . . .

"Direction west, about eight miles, through a very heavy forest of sal, sakua, asun, and dhow, over broken and raviny ground and low hills to Gowpara, the largest village in the hills, containing about eighty houses and 400 souls. The village is situated on the summit of a high range of hills, which here form the central or largest group. The village is surrounded by neat hurdle fences enclosing tobacco, mustard, plantains, date and palm-trees, and in the centre of the village, and around the houses, are numerous fine palm-trees, tamarind, peepul, mango, jack, clumps of bamboos and plantains : the houses are neat: numerous cattle-sheds, pigsties, and well-stocked granaries, bespoke plenty and comfort.

"My arrival seemed to have struck a panic into the minds of the whole population, for on entering the village I could not find a single soul to speak to: every one had fled to their houses and fastened their doors.

"Fortunately a fine old man, who was on the roof of his house, laying out tobacco to dry in the sun, and who was ignorant of our arrival, was caught; his trepidation at the appearance of myself, servants, and elephant, was most painful, and not without much persuasion could he be induced to descend from his house for the purpose of showing us the Manji's residence. A house was pointed out as being that of the Manji, but it was, as was every house in the village, closed. I took up my residence in the verandah, where hung bows and poisoned arrows, deer horns, wild-boar skulls, pea-fowl eggs, and the cocoon of the wild silk, or tusser. The Manji soon arrived from the jungle, carrying on his shoulder the produce of his morning's work, a log of wood. He was so alarmed at my appearance, that he was speechless; but after an hour's persuasion, talking and laughing, he gradually thawed, and told me that he had never before seen a white man, nor an elephant, nor had any one individual out of the 400 inhabitants of his village ever seen one or the other. The ice being now broken, and the reason of his timidity known, I endeavoured to prove to him that a mortal with a white face was not the dreadful creature he imagined: I presented him with an empty bottle, a quantity of beads, gilt buttons, bodkins, ornaments for the women's hair, and told him to assemble all the children of the village, to whom I presented in succession three or four strings of beads, and a handful of buttons. I now had the whole village with me, and, turning round, I perceived the Manji's house-doors wide open, and about fifteen females, old and young, standing behind me, into the midst of whom I threw a quantity of the hair ornaments consisting of tufts of tusser silk, dyed scarlet, and tied with black cotton: to the children in the Manji's house I distributed a quantity of copper money, bargained with the Manji with a quantity of empty bottles and money for poisoned arrows, bows, and grass hammocks, bade him good-bye, and strongly recommended him next time he met a European to be more at his ease, and not to be afraid of him, as no one had the most remote idea of doing any harm to any one in the hills; on the contrary, that we were all desirous of seeing so worthy a race happy and contented.

"I was amused at the Manji's repeated question, put to me in a most serious tone, as to whether I had, of my own free will, given him the empty bottle, my first gift to him.

Upon my assuring him that my gift, a most invaluable one to him, had given me as much pleasure in the making as it had him in the receiving, he seemed partly satisfied, but repeated the question at intervals during my stay at the village.

"The men of these central hills tie their hair much more on the back of the head than do the men further north; neither have they the flattened noses, nor such thick lips as their northern brethren; neither do they pay that attention to dressing their hair or ornamenting their ears or necks with beads and trinkets, which is so striking a feature in the northern tribes: the women, in the same manner, have scarcely any ornaments, are poorly dressed, and untidy in their appearance: their great distance from any market or bazaar may in a measure account for the difference of dress.

"At sunset I ascended the Sendgursa hill by a very steep ascent, from the summit of which I had the finest view of *coup d'œil* yet obtained of the hills. The hill is about 2000 feet above the sea, and from its summit I could see the following remarkable landmarks. The Monghyr hills to the north-west, distant eighty miles, with a Great Trigonometrical Survey Station on the hill Maruk, another on Mundar hill in Bhagulpore half way, or forty miles distant; the Ganges at Bhagalpore, distant sixty miles in N.N.W. direction; the long reach of the Ganges extending to Rampore Bauliah, seventy miles in an E.S.E. direction; the whole of the country lying between the foot of the hills and the military station, Berhampore on the Bhagaetti, extending over fifty miles; to the south another station, on the Satbor hill in Belputta, distant forty miles, appeared topping the whole of the Caticoond carboniferous range; to the W.S.W., distant fifty miles, the Teeur hill, another station, and all the small detached hills of Beerbhoom, as well as the hills of Hendweh and Pusseje appeared; amongst the latter are the Nugwan and Puchpuhar hills, both Great Trigonometrical Survey Stations. In a S.W. direction, the great Parusnath mountain is visible, distant one hundred miles. This mountain, in height nearly 5000 feet, has a station on its summit, and forms the culminating point of the rocks of the great primitive plateau, extending from Beerbhoom to the Dunwah Ghaut.

"To the S.S.W. the view extends over the Burdwan coal-fields, and to the S.S.E. over the whole of the eastern portions of Beerbhoom and Burdwan, with the whole of the southern Rajmahal hills and surrounding forests as a foreground, whilst the view of the hills at my feet was most complete; I could see into every valley, count every village, and trace the outlines of the hills and valleys."*

Missionary operations were commenced at Bhagulpore in 1850, and, amongst other classes of the population, attention was directed to the Puharis and Santhals: the hills were visited, and schools commenced. Then came the great Santhal outbreak, and Bhagulpore was for a time in great danger. A host of 8000 Santhals was encamped, for nearly fourteen days, about twenty-five miles distance, waiting for the subsidence of a small hill stream which, unusually swollen by heavy rains, prevented their advance. So strong was the current that the buffaloes, which the Santhals repeatedly drove in to test the strength of the current, were all carried off; yet these animals swim well. Could they have reached the opposite shore the Santhals would have crossed on them. Meanwhile, troops arrived for the protection of the town.

On the suppression of this fierce insurrection, the local authorities felt how necessary it was that this wild people should be brought under some controlling influences: and what so safe and powerful in its action as Christian instruction? Indeed, the very facts connected with the outbreak pointed out this as the alone means of ensuring future tranquillity; the people of those villages of the Santhals, in which schools had been commenced, having been the last to rise in insurrection, and only doing so at length in being forced into it by the main body; and they first gave warning to their teachers to withdraw and secure their own safety in time, as the friendly villagers amongst whom they were living, were no longer able to protect them. An arrangement was made with the Church Missionary Society. The Missionaries were to commence schools, the Government guaranteeing Grants-in-aid, on the condition that the secular education given should reach a required standard, the Missionaries, as the managers of the schools, availing themselves of the freedom conceded by the Education Despatch of 1854 to carry forward, on such principles as they considered right, the duty of religious instruction. Nothing could be more simple or consistent with the principles of the Education Despatch than this arrangement. The paragraph 50 seemed expressly to provide for such cases—" In so far as the noble exertions of Societies of Christians of all denominations to guide the natives of India in the way of religious truth, and to instruct uncivilized races, such as those found

---

* Sherwill, pp. 41—61

in Assam, or the Cossya, Garrow, and Rajmahal hills, and in various districts of Central and South India, who are in the lowest condition of ignorance, and are either wholly without a religion, or are the slaves of a barbarous and degrading superstition, have been accompanied in their educational establishments by the diffusion of improved knowledge, they have largely contributed to the spread of that education which it is our object to promote." Here then was an opportunity of promoting " improved knowledge" among the Santhals. Missionary schools were to be commenced, which might become affiliated institutions in the Government schemes, and be periodically visited by the Government inspectors. Government was to aid the Missionaries by relieving them of the expense connected with secular education; and the Missionaries were to aid the Government by communicating to the Santhals the alone knowledge, which could effectually tranquillize them. But a despatch from home, dated July 22, 1857, crushed the project, and that on grounds the most feeble and unsatisfactory. " The Santhals, though equally debased in ignorance and devoid of rational religion with the races referred to in our despatch of 1854, differ from them in one important particular; they do not occupy separate regions or tracts of country, so as to form isolated communities, locally separated, as well as socially distinct from the Hindu and Mussulman populations. They are, on the contrary, employed freely by Zemindars, and speculators of land of all classes for jungle clearance, and for other agricultural purposes, and are thus often located in close vicinity with well-inhabited towns and villages, and mix with the general population in many of the relations and concerns of life." Now it is true the advanced stragglers of the Santhals have approached the cultivated districts; but the main body is yet behind, and is sufficiently isolated to be regarded and dealt with as a distinct people. Moreover, the Rajmahal hills are expressly mentioned in the despatch of 1854, and the Santhals occupy the valleys of those hills. But even this indirect recognition

Missionaries, Rev. T. E. Hallett, amidst the Rajmahal hills.

MR. HALLETT'S DIARY.

" *Dec*. 13, 1859—After prayers with our friends, I left Bhagulpore with Mr. Erhardt, at half-past nine P.M., to overtake our tents, which had gone on to Bounsee. May the great God be with me, and give his Spirit abundantly. The more I see of the dense darkness overshadowing this land, the more do I feel that, without his Spirit working with us, and his abundant grace preventing us, our labour is but in vain. But, thanks be to God, we have the assurance that ' his Word shall not return unto him void,' and the knowledge that ' the weapons of our warfare are not carnal, but mighty through God to the pulling down of strongholds, casting down imaginations, and every high thing that exalteth itself against the knowledge of God, and bringing into captivity every thought to the obedience of Christ.' Travelled all night, and, towards daybreak, came up with our carts. Pushed on to Bounsee, and was cheered by the affectionate greeting of some of my Santhals, whom we passed on the road. They asked the Palkee bearers what Sahib was passing, and being told that it was the ' Santhal Padree,' ran alongside my palkee laughing and talking for some time.

" *Dec*. 14—Reached Bounsee, and was most kindly received by Mr. M——, the deputy magistrate, who had his tent pitched for us, and did all in his power to make us comfortable. Our tents did not come up till six P. M., being delayed by having to cross two hill streams. The road is also very sandy and heavy, and, I am told, impassable during four months of the year, the whole country being a swamp. In fact, some parts of the road are, even now, quite soft and slushy. Bounsee appears to be a healthy spot, Mr. M.'s children being pictures of health; but I fear that it would not do for a Mission station, being too far from the hills: no Santhal village within sixteen miles.

" *Dec*. 15—Left Bounsee for Godda at six A. M.; Erhardt in his palkee, and I on horseback. The air was deliciously cold in the

other side of the Dakee Nuddee, as the hill stream is called which bisects the village, who taught some twenty-five boys to read and write. They use no books, his instruction being confined to making the boys write in sand—a very proper medium—the names of the gods over and over again. I asked them whether they would contribute to the support of a master, and build him a house in which to hold his school. They said they would talk it over, and give us an answer on our return. The village contains some 250 children, of whom the Zemindar's headman surmised about sixty would attend school. About two miles further on, came to another village. I stopped to try and buy a tattoo, or pony, for Hunnook, the superintending master of the first circle Santhal schools, who accompanies me. Was unsuccessful, but learnt the state of this and the surrounding villages with reference to education. There is one guru engaged by the Zemindar to teach his own son, who also, 'out of pure love,' as they said, teaches three or four other boys to read and write the names of their gods in sand. 11 A.M.—Found the sun getting rather hot, so rode on in advance of the palkee till I came to a village, most picturesquely situated on the banks of the Gerooa river. Pulled up and dismounted, and sat down on a log in front of the village cow-shed, and was soon surrounded by the village quidnuncs. I heard that Mr. B., who farms the whole of the Godda Pergunnah besides, and several large tracts of country in the Damun, and whose administration I hear everywhere spoken well of, was at the old bungalow of Godda, which was destroyed during the disturbances in 1853. The ryots opened upon me with a long tirade about the new settlement which Mr. B. is making, and which they do not understand as yet, but which is a vast improvement on the system of the native Zemindars. Mr. B.'s plan is to fix the rent each ryot is to pay for the land he occupies, and take neither more or less. The usual plan is—a nominal rent is fixed, which is frequently almost doubled by what are called 'cesses,' that is, certain sums are, by custom, taken as fees for marriage, deaths, festivals, and under twenty other different heads, and added on to the rent named in the lease. This, as may be imagined, is a fearful weapon for oppression in the Zemindar's hand. One man wanted to know whether I was going to the hills for coal; when I took the opportunity of addressing them on what was my mission—' to turn men from worshipping idols, to serve the living God.' One rather intelligent Brahmin, in the course of our conversation, asked the reason why we established schools for the Santhals, and not for them. I endeavoured to convince him that the Hindu villages could well afford to keep a guru for the instruction of their children, whereas the Santhals are a very poor people, and could but with difficulty scrape together funds for such a purpose. Furthermore, that our schools were different from the Government schools, that we had a higher aim than mere secular education, viz. the teaching of morality, and a knowledge of the true God; holding, as we did, that a pure code of morals can never be founded on an impure theology: that the Santhals did not object to our scheme of instruction, whereas the Hindu, or Government for him, did. But he either could not or would not see the force of my argument; his last remark being, that 'the Santhals would not have got schools unless they had fought for them.' It is truly lamentable to see the state in which education is left in places where no show can be made. It may be all very well to have schools for precocious boys, most frequently the sons of the court Umlah, in the large stations; but until some such system as that introduced by the late Mr. Thomason, Lieut.-Governor North-western Provinces, of regular village schools throughout the length and breadth of the land, is instituted in Bengal, but little has been done towards attacking the rule of the giant Ignorance who broods over the millions of the Lower Provinces—Behar in particular. Rode on through a country cut up by watercourses, and arrived at Mr. B.'s tent, where we were most kindly greeted, and, after partaking of some slight refreshment, pushed on for Mr. R.'s bungalow. Found Mr. R. out on tour with Mr. J., the Commissioner, but took shelter in his house until our tents came up, which was not until the morning of the 16th.

"*Dec.* 16—Carts came in at six A.M., having been delayed at the Gerooa Nuddee. Sent them on to Kurmatane at two P.M., and started ourselves at three P.M., leaving a note thanking Mr. R. for the use of his bungalow. I here engaged two coolies to carry a few necessaries, so that we shall not have to wait without food if the carts are unavoidably delayed on the road. We reached Kurmatane bungalow after dark— having to get guides from the last five villages to point out the paths, which lay across rice fields and swamps—very tired, and found that the carts had not come up. The Manji, however, made us as comfortable as possible, sending wood, straw, and two charpoys, or native bedsteads, for us.

The bhangy came in about an hour after us, and after taking a cup of tea, and seeing the palkee bearers and other servants comfortably stretched on the straw, in a circle round the fire, thanked God for his mercies, and slept.

"*Dec.* 17—Carts set up by seven A.M.; so after breakfast, went into the village to see the Manji, and thank him for the things sent last night, and pay for the same. Two boys go from this village to the Soondermore school, one mile distant, where we hope to go after seeing our things fairly started. Heard the Santhal drums for the first time this morning, and pray the God and Father of our Lord Jesus Christ that I may, if it be his will, see the day when this people, who have so many noble and virtuous qualities, may sound their drums in Christian festivals and rejoicings, instead of the superstitious mummeries which stand in the place of a religion to them. Reached Soondermore, after passing through a small hamlet close to Karmatane, in which we saw the roofed platform erected over the remains of some former Manji, generally placed before the existing Manji's house. When not in use for festival purposes, or occasional offerings, it appears to be the lounge of all the pigs, dogs, &c., of the village, and to possess no particular sanctity. It is a custom similar to that of the Mohammedans, of elevating the grave of some fakeer supposed to have died in the odour of sanctity, into a shrine, at which offerings are made, supposed to secure the intercession of the saint. Found the Soondermore school-house, situated at the cross roads, under the shade of a fine kossum-tree, and the boys there present, twenty-five in number, reading aloud, according to the confusing custom of Indian schools. Buriar, the Pergunnite of the Pergunnah, with Dullah, the Manji of Soondermore, and Kharen, the Manji of Bulkal, a very old grey-headed man, were present in the school, and explained the cause of the falling-off in the number of scholars. Hunook, the superintending master, was formerly master of this school, and, when removed, was succeeded by Soona Lull, a Bengalee, who, they say, does not come up to their ideal of a teacher; in short, that they will not have him. The Pergunnite told me straightforwardly, that unless I gave him a Santhal or Puharri (Hill) guru, the school must be broken up; so, after careful investigation, I promised to send them Dalloo, a Santhal, whose training is nearly completed, the Pergunnite and Manjis promising to bring the attendance of boys up to the old number of forty-one, and, if possible, higher.

The school-house is also to be repaired as soon as the harvest is over, and labour obtainable. The boys who were present seem to be getting on fairly, and the two best, one the son of the Soondermore Manji, the other his ward, are to be entrusted to me for training as masters, and I hope to take them in with me to Bhagulpore, on our return.

"The road from Soondermore to Teleband, the next stage, is over a swelling jungly country, rising gradually to the foot of the hills which lie to the east. Soil, red earth, with sand stone, quartz, and basalt, cropping out in boulders at every step. Reached Teleband at half-past one P.M. Heat great, being reflected from the rocks. The road passes between the village and a circular grove of about fifty feet diameter, left standing by the Santhals where the surrounding jungle was cleared, for the devil to go to. In these groves sacrifices are offered to the spirits of evil, to avert danger from wild beasts, sickness, and famine. In speaking to some of the more intelligent of the people, I pressed upon them the absurdity of offering homage and worship to evil spirits, who were powerless for harm, unless permitted by the one great God, who they—the Santhals—acknowledge, and hold to be omnipotent, to whom worship is ever due, and who will, of his good pleasure, avert evil from those of his creatures who obey his laws. I told them that the great God (Purmeshwah) was a jealous God, and that offering the worship due to Him to devils, was the surest way of rousing his wrath, and bringing on themselves the calamities they dreaded and wished to avert. They listen and agree, but I would rather they would argue and dispute, as then some impression might remain in their minds to stir them up to 'search and see whether these things are so.' May God in mercy grant this!

"After dinner went into the village, which is built on the usual Santhal plan of one long street, with kossum trees, forming an avenue on each side, and the houses clean and neat, each enclosed in its own plot of ground. Had a conversation with an old lady, who showed us her family—two girls, one a child at the breast, and two boys, one about eighteen. She is a widow, and her eldest son supports her. This is usual with the Santhals, who are admirable in their social relations. What is particularly noticeable in the Santhals is the respect with which their women are treated, and the consequent freedom from false modesty they evince, when contrasted with their neighbours, the Hindus and Mohammedans. The Santhal women conduct themselves as English peasant women might, and exercise a most salutary influence on the community at large. Their women are chaste, and their men are truthful: God willing, some future servant of His may be able to add, 'and Christian.' They wish to have a school here, and mention one of our Santhal boys, Durgha, who was educated in Bhagulpore, and is now with his father, the Manji of Manuck, as the guru they would like to have. I told them to send over for him, as I should stay over Sunday. This they promise to do, and when he arrives the Pergunnite and Manjis are to come and talk the matter over with me.

"*Dec.* 18: *Lord's-day*—Dhomun, my pundit, came in. It appears that he had been once to see Durgha, who wishes to join me and be employed as a master. I trust God may cause this wish on his part, and the willingness of the men of this bustee, to have him for a teacher, to work together for good and the eventual glory of his church. I am hopeful. Mr. Y. the Commissioner and Mr. R. the Assistant Commissioner came in at 9 A.M. After breakfast, had Hindustani service. Hunnook complained of slight fever, so I gave him some quinine, and trust that he may be well by to-morrow, as he is of the greatest assistance to me. 1 P.M.—Mr. B. came in to see the Commissioner, so that we have quite a large camp for the Santhal Pergunnahs. We all go on to Dhumni to-morrow, where another of the Assistant Commissioners is expected. 6 P.M. —Our servants asked if we did not want a chowkedar, or watchman, for the night; and I felt truly happy to be able to reply that it was unnecessary, as there was not a thief or liar within miles, which could not have been said of a Bengalee village.

"*Dec.* 19—Left for Dhumni, nine miles. The road quite alive with elephants, carts, &c., belonging to the Commissioner's camp. The road branches off from Teleband direct into Dhumin, or Rajmahal Hills, and was frequently cut by hill streams, which made it heavy work for the cattle. Passed two coal wains on the left of the road country: beautiful, with Santhal hamlets most picturesquely planted in the valleys. Reached Dhumni about eleven A.M., and went over to the school. Found the house blown down, but the boys still able to read under the roof. The register gives thirty-six boys, but we found only seven present, on account of this being the harvest season, and the children being required to help in stacking the crops. The progress made seems fair, and what most pleases one is the willingness of those boys, who are sufficiently advanced, to go to the training school at Bhagalpore. Eight boys expressed their readiness to return with us, their parents consenting. The mother being the great obstacle, I make a point of asking whether she is willing, as the preliminary step. Satisfied on this head, I have hopes of the boys being ready to accompany us on our return. Eight boys wish to go with us.

"Our tent was pitched by direction of the Manji in the circular grove before alluded to as being outside every Santhal village. In it we found certain small pebbles daubed with red ochre at the foot of several of the trees. These are termed 'gossain.' Also by the side of each of four trees, forming a square of four feet, was a forked stick stuck into the ground, on which the offerings are hung, and which, I have little doubt, we might have used as fire-wood, without offending the religious prejudices of the Santhals, they being innocent of such weaknesses, and, from all I can see or learn, singularly apathetic as regards both God and the devil. Thanks be to God, the evangelization of this people will not be opposed by a priestly race like the Brahmins, who have a vested interest in the continuance of the present darkness and idolatry.

"The great difficulties we have to contend with are, the language, which is undeniably most difficult, and the dense ignorance of the people. But by the help of our God, and his blessing on our efforts for the education of the rising generation, these will be in time overcome. Had a slight touch of fever, and, whilst I took some rest, Erhardt had a long conversation with the boys who wish to come with us, in order to ascertain whether there were any objections raised on the part of their parents. I shall feel more certain of the boys when we get them across the Damun boundary line. They all seem to have a natural turn for music, and repeatedly express the wish to learn singing and hear our music. I could not very well gratify them out here without a musical box or a barrel organ, neither of which, I regret to say, are amongst my goods. Dhomun complained to-day of pain in the eyes. I now felt the want of a medicine-chest. It is absolutely necessary that a Missionary, situated as I am, often sixty miles, and such terribly bad miles, from any medical aid, should be supplied with a proper stock, both for himself and those who come to him for help, often from a distance.

"*Dec.* 20—Left Dhumni for Kooamah road, passing over swelling ground very fairly cleared and under cultivation. Mr. Y. tells me, that since his last visit, some two years ago, the Santhals have cleared extensive tracts of jungle, and brought the land under cultivation. About two miles from Dhumni, passed on the left the collieries which supply the railway officials with thousands of maunds of coal daily for the works. The hills all round are rich in iron ore, pronounced by competent judges to be equal to the finest Swedish, being smelted with charcoal, not with coal as in England. The workings are entirely conducted by the natives, who in each furnace average about a half cwt. of pure iron per day; being the result of two turnouts. This is sold to Bengalee traders, and sent down to Calcutta. 10 A. M.—Reached Koosmah, most beautifully situated on the banks of the Goomanee, about two miles below the falls, where the river debouches on the large central valley of the Rajmahal ranges, twenty-five miles long by five average breadth. After taking a cup of coffee at Mr. B.'s, who has charge of the collieries, I rode over to Choonchi, where the school is. Found the house in good condition, and sixteen boys in attendance, who passed a very creditable examination. The register gives thirty-six boys, but all the schools are empty at this time, on account of the harvest.

"Mr. Droese had, for this reason, as also because the season of Christmas fell at the same time, usually closed the schools for a short vacation from the 10th of December to the 1st of January. This rule was broken through this year, in order to enable me to inspect the schools. I have to-day given leave to Hunnook and the masters of the school already visited for fourteen days. Three boys at this school expressed a wish to accompany us to Bhagulpore for training.

"Their parents came to us in the evening; and it was quite affecting to hear the mother of one, an old woman, wife of the Manji of Choonchi, deliver over charge of her boy to us, to be taken care of in 'sickness and in health,' as she put it.

"Dec. 21—Left Koosmah for Burbait, four miles, where there is the only Government school in the Santhal country. Found seventeen boys present, who read and write Bengalee well, but appear to be entirely ignorant of any thing else. The number of boys on the register is forty: average attendance twenty-five. The master is a self-taught Bengalee, who, we were informed by several gentlemen, and also learnt from the boys themselves, carefully instructs those under his care (Santhals) in all the mysteries of the Hindu religion, as far as he knows himself, and causes them to perform Poojah, or worship, with him to his strange gods.

"Dec. 22—After dinner we strolled into the village, and came upon the preparations for the feast, one cow, three fowls, four sucking pigs, and five kids, lying slaughtered in front of the Manji's house. The blood from the victims was collected in copper vessels and leaf cups, and set apart by itself, and huge fires were blazing by the side of the enclosure, fed by boys who had evidently an interest in the approaching feast. I entered into conversation with the men and women assembled, as to the reason for the sacrifice. They call it 'Bōgh,' or a feast of the dead, and believe that it propitiates the gossain, or evil spirits. Endeavoured to point out to them the plan of salvation in Christ Jesus, who was offered a sacrifice for our sins. They argued very fairly with me, but as I was obliged often to use an interpreter for the Santhalee, I am not sure that they comprehended all the argument. The chief spokesman concluded with the remark that 'I might be right, but that their fathers had always had a Bōgh when any one died, and why should not they ?' To be able to address them fluently in their own mother tongue is what we require, without which but little impression can be made.

"Dec. 28—I had a most interesting conversation with the Manjis, about a custom the Santhals have, of taking the ashes of their dead to the Damoodah river in Chota Nagpore. It is nothing more than sending the remains of those who die in the strange land back to their own country; and most probably originated in the first immigrants from the west requesting their children, like Jacob and Joseph, to take their bones back for burial in their fatherland. The ashes are collected in four small pots, and thrown into the stream of the Damoodah. This custom points to the south-west as the direction from which the Santhals inhabiting the valleys of the Damun-i-Koh, or Rajmahal Hills, originally came, and goes far to connect them with the Kōls and other tribes inhabiting the ranges as far as the Coromandel coast. Five boys having arrived, I took leave of the Manjis, who appeared to feel very kindly towards us, and started, accompanied by Mr. B., to look at the Toosifoolie colliery, which lies a little off the road. The coal they are at present taking is obtained from headings driven into the hill, and is at present inferior to the Raneegunge coal. Three lacs of maunds (a maund being eighty-four lbs.) is turned out yearly from this colliery. 1 P.M.—Reached Dhumni, suffering much from illness Found Mr. W., Assistant-Commissioner, in camp. Our tents were not yet up, so we lay down under some trees till they came. The eight boys who are to go with us came in about an hour, bringing the pleasing intelligence that five other boys wished to join us, making thirteen in all from the Dhumni school. This school is more advanced than any of the others, Rumoo, the master, a Santhal, who has applied for baptism, being a really zealous hard-working man, who will, I trust, be a great aid to us in our efforts for the civilization and evangelization of his countrymen. Most of the Santhal and hill boys who have been trained in the Bhagulpore Training School have shown a decided Christian tendency. Four—Dhomun, Herna, Dallu, and Ramoo—have applied for baptism, and, if they satisfy me as to their fitness, will be baptized this year; and one hundred hill boys have been baptized. Thus I trust, under God, that the boys who now go in will eventually receive the truth as it is in Christ, and, when converted, strengthen their brethren. Mr. W. came over in the evening, and kindly placed his stock of medicine at my disposal. He is trying to establish a school at his station, Pukour, on the edge of the Damun, and will, I trust, succeed. The great point is a good master.

"*Dec.* 29—After waiting some two hours, we were rewarded by finding our thirteen boys ready to accompany us. I rode on in advance, as I wished to reach the end of the stage before the sun got high, but was obliged to stop about eleven A.M., and lie down under a tree for an hour. Erhardt then came up, and we proceeded on to Teleaband, which we reached about half-past one P.M. Dhomun here made his appearance, having been absent without leave since the 23d.

Dec. 31—Reached Ummerpoora about two P.M., and pitched the tent on the border of a fine tank partly covered with the small white water-lily. Overhead waved the heavy boughs of a large mahood tree, the trunk smeared half-way up with mud, and daubed in two places with streaks of red ochre, in honour of Dauwee.

"The last Santhal village was left some six miles back. The distinction between Santhal and Hindu villages is most marked. In the latter the houses are pitched hither and thither, without any pretension to order, and you cannot go five yards without stumbling into a cesspool or puddle of stagnant water. In the Santhal village all is order and pleasing neatness, each house, cleanly whitewashed, standing in its own enclosure, surrounded by a garden and shrubs for the fowls to take shelter under when threatened by kites. At night all is life and activity; the cattle coming in to be penned up for the night, the women busy cooking the evening meal, and children, fowls, and pigs, all adding their quota of life to the scene. After the evening meal is finished, the drum, pipe, sitarah (native guitar), may be heard on all sides; and though distance lends enchantment to the sound, the Santhal drum is by no means a despicable instrument, and the time kept is very good. The scene in our camp is quite cheerful to-night: my boys, twenty-two in number, have divided themselves into messes of five, and after making their bazaar (as 'going shopping' is called in India), have sat down to cook in detachments, one party of five being told off to make the plates, which they do very ingeniously out of leaves, fastening them together with reeds out of the tank. At the corner of an old river stands Dhomun, who has charge of the boys. He has made himself a pipe out of a leaf, and is smoking in quiescent contentment, watching the Santhal Soyers through the smoke curling up over the wall. Most of the boys are of the aristocracy of the Santhal country, and pleasing-looking. All look bright now at the smell of the rice boiling and bubbling in the earthen pots over the blazing wood fires, which are reflected from the tank in front, and throws a flickering light on the rustling foliage over head. Two annas, or about threepence per diem, is what I allow each boy, and with that they keep themselves in splendid condition, in fact, were able to indulge in luxuries.

"To sum up. We have in the Damun, or Rajmahal hills, twelve schools in connexion with the Church Missionary Society, with a register of 422 boys under instruction. The class of boys training for masters in the Bhagulpore Training School, will open this term with thirty-two Santhal boys. Three or four of these boys are so far advanced as to lead me to hope that they will be fit to take charge of new schools by the end of the current year, by which time I trust, under God, to have some Hindu gurus—who I am placing under Mr. Erbardt, for a few months' training—in charge of schools in villages which have expressed a wish to have their children taught. It will from this be seen that the scheme for educating and civilizing the Santhals so nobly undertaken by the Church Missionary Society when the Government shrank from doing its duty, is steadily making headway, and promises, with the blessing of the Almighty, to stand recorded in the history of a nation as the turning-point, where civilization and a knowledge of the true God first confronted and overthrew the ignorance and devil-worship under which their forefathers had groaned for ages. May God in His infinite mercy grant this."

MISSIONARY DEDUCTIONS FROM THE PARABLES.

In the 13th chapter of St. Matthew's Gospel we find a number of deeply-interesting and instructive parables, the utterances of our blessed Lord Himself, of Him who spake as never man spake, so grouped together as to constitute one of the most beautiful of those constellations which grace the firmament of revelation. And as astronomers, in their survey of the heavens, discover that the stars have distinctive colours—some insulated stars being of a red colour, others, as the double stars, one more and the other less brilliant, so that the fainter one is in its hue complimentary to its fellow, the latter having generally a bright red or orange colour, the smaller appearing bluish or greenish—so with these parables, they have each their own distinctive beauty.

They are seven in number, and have as their main subject the progress of Gospel truth, its mode of action, and the difficulties and obstructions it has to contend with. They are eminently Missionary parables, embodying principles of the very first importance in the prosecution of Missionary work, preparing us for the trials which are inseparable from so great an undertaking; instructing us in the character and extent of the results, which we are justified in expecting, and which in due time will be sure to follow; moderating over-sanguine expectations, and thus preventing disappointment. The first of the series dwells, not so much on the seed, as on the difficulties which must of necessity arise from the condition of the soil in which it is to be sown—the human heart—one unfavourable to the willing and effective reception of it, and requiring, therefore, that the seed should be sown, not merely in the strength and eloquence of man, but in the power of the Spirit of God, regenerating the heart, and changing it into an honest and a good heart: and so Paul says, "My speech and my preaching was not with enticing words of man's wisdom, but in demonstration of the ble energy, making itself felt, until it rises into a position of ascendancy, and exercises a commanding influence over the minds and affairs of men. The two remaining parables deal rather with the inward working of the Gospel on the heart: they show us how, when a man is divinely taught, so that he is enabled to perceive the surpassing excellence of the one great object, which, in its promises, is commended to his acceptance, there will be, on his part, no hesitation in renouncing all else in order to secure Him, who is all in all to the human soul.

One of these parables, as presenting various points of interest in connexion with Missionary work, may be more closely examined—the tares and the good seed. The salient points appear to be as follows—The field; the seed; the sower; the enemy; "his devices;" the mingled crop; the danger of attempting any thing like a coercive separation of the mixed elements; the need of patient waiting, until He comes with his fan in his hand, who can best distinguish between the precious and the vile.

1. The field.—The field, we are told, is the world, and the true proprietor is indicated: "the kingdom of heaven is likened unto a man which soweth good seed in his field;" and then, v. 37, "He that soweth the good seed is the Son of man." The field of this world belongs to Christ. It is his by an inalienable right, that of creation; as his own world, which in co-operation with the Father and the Holy Ghost, He called into existence out of nothing, "so that things which are seen were not made of things which do appear;" and subsequently, after a lapse of ages, re-organized into an habitation suitable for man. But not only so; in another sense also, it is his property, in virtue of his office of Mediator, and as the reward of his work and sufferings; according to the stipulations of the covenant entered into before the foundations of it were laid, between the Father and the

act, placed himself beneath the heavy burden of human sin, and undertook to suffer. "Sacrifice and offering thou didst not desire: mine ears hast thou opened; burnt-offering and sin-offering hast thou not required. Then said I, Lo, I come: in the volume of the book it is written of me, I delight to do thy will, O my God; yea, thy law is within my heart." And if thus to suffer, behold "his reward is with Him, and the recompence for his work before Him." This was secured to him in the stipulations of the covenant. So runs the second Psalm — the Father's purpose that He should reign; the opposition manifested where least expected, from the kings, and princes and people, of the earth; the fulfilment, notwithstanding all hindrances, of the divine intention—"Yet have I set my king upon my holy hill of Zion;" and then the promise of the heirship of the world— "Ask of me, and I shall give thee the heathen for thine inheritance, and the uttermost parts of the earth for thy possession."

The same divine arrangement of extreme sufferings, to be followed by high exaltation, pervades the twenty-second psalm. The first twenty-one verses describe with minute prediction the extreme anguish of the great Mediator's vicarious sufferings; and then follows his enthronement and kingship over that world, where He had so unsparingly poured out his life unto the death—"All the ends of the world shall remember and turn unto the Lord, and all the kindreds of the nations shall worship before Thee. For the kingdom is the Lord's, and he is the governor among the people."

Now, it seldom happens in the ordinary procedure of human affairs, that a field or property is permitted to lie waste. It possesses productive energies which ought to be made available to the use and benefit of the proprietor. The process of husbandry is forthwith commenced; the fallow-ground is broken up by the action of the plough; and when such preliminary operations have been thoroughly wrought out, and the soil is become soft and mellow, then commences the sowing time, good seed being carefully selected, because "whatsoever a man soweth, that shall he also reap."

And so precisely with "the field of the world," by which we understand, not the earth we tread upon, but man, the inhabitant of it. The human element in all its variety is the field which is to be sown. It ought to be productive, for it has been endowed with great energies and capabilities of action. Man alone, of all earthly existences, is capable of knowing God, of appreciating his excellencies, and rendering to Him the tribute of grateful affections: and if all men were as heartily disposed to glorify God, as unhappily they are indisposed to do so, what a revenue of service might they not render to Him! It is not as yet so. Let any individual cast his eye over the face of the earth; let him trace out the outlines of countries on a map, and mark what vast portions of territory lie waste. Some abandoned to barrenness, when a careful use of the means of irrigation, so bountifully provided, would change them into a garden; others expending their productive energies on a waste of vegetation, where the beasts of the forest have their hiding-places, and the poisonous malaria is generated. The application of human industry has been wanting. And so, in a moral sense, how extended the wastes which yield no revenue to God. As the earth requires to be brought under the cultivation of man, so the man requires to be brought under the cultivation of God. And the great proprietor of the world has therefore commenced his husbandry. There are the preliminary processes of ploughing and breaking up. Individuals and nations are found in a state of utter indifference to matters of spiritual import. They have no consciousness of any such necessities as the truths of the Gospel are fitted to supply. They are built up in pride and self-complacency, and treat the message and its bearers with contempt and scorn. They will not even hear. This was the burden of Jeremiah's lamentations when proclaiming the Lord's word to the Jews—"Hear ye, and give ear; be not proud, for the Lord hath spoken: give glory to the Lord your God, before He cause darkness, and before your feet stumble upon the dark mountains, and while ye look for light, He turn it into the shadow of death, and make it gross darkness. But if ye will not hear it, my soul shall weep in secret places for your pride." And because they would not hear, national calamities were to supervene—"Mine eye shall weep sore and run down with tears, because the Lord's flock is carried away captive."

Often has the Missionary found himself similarly circumstanced in the presence of a regardless people. That they may willingly hear, nations require to be brought low. They must be dealt with in the way of preparatory discipline. National reverses are permitted to come upon them, times of heavy affliction, that, under such subduing dispensations, they may become teachable and docile, and the favourable time for the sowing of the precious seed be expedited. Hence the siftings and changes of the nations: they are the providential up-breakings of the long-lying fallow ground, which go before the sower to prepare his way. "Lord, when thy hand is lifted up, they will not see, but they shall see and be ashamed for their envy at the people." "Lord, in trouble have they visited thee, they poured out a prayer when thy chastening was upon them." "O inhabitant of Lebanon, that makest thy nest in the cedars, how gracious shalt thou be when pangs come upon thee, the pain as of a woman in travail."

Such a process appears to be at this moment going forward amongst the mountains of Lebanon, from whose hoary tops and flanks the rain-storms of ages seem to have washed every trace and colour into the blue waters of the Mediterranean, which rolls its long line of white-crested waves up to its craggy base, so that

'It is a fearful thing
To stand upon the beetling verge and see
Where storm and lightning from that huge grey wall
Have tumbled down huge blocks, and at the base
Dash'd them in fragments, and to lay thine ear
Over the dizzy depths, and hear the sound
Of winds, that struggle with the winds below,
Come up with ocean-murmurs.'

Lebanon divides into two parallel ranges. "The western range runs nearly in a straight line north-north-east, and is called Jebel Libnan by the Arabs, but simply and *par excellence*, Libanus or Mount Lebanon. The eastern runs still more to the east, curving slightly round to the north-east, and is called, in contradistinction to the other range, the Lebanon over against the other Lebanon, or Anti-Lebanon." Between these two ranges lies the long and broad valley of Cœle Syria, designated by the present inhabitants Buka'a, or the valley, the floor of which is about 2000 feet above the level of the Mediterranean. The inland range divides again near the sources of the Jordan, so as to enclose on the east and west the prolonged basin which contains the Jordan and its lakes.

The main road from Beyrout to the great valley traverses a mountain-pass, having on its south the peak of Jebel Rihan, the last mountain ridge of the Lebanon on the south; and on the north of the pass is the high peak of Jebel Kuyieniseh, 6825 feet in height, east of the Jebel Rihan. At a distance of about thirty-two English miles, lies Mount Hermon, the most southern mountain ridge of the Anti-Lebanon, both ranges converging until there is left just sufficient opening for the Leontes river to pass out from the long valley of Cœle Syria,

"The highest ridge of the western Lebanon is marked on both sides by a line drawn at the distance of two hours journey from the summit, above which all is barren: but the slopes and valleys below this mark afford pasturage, and are capable of cultivation by virtue of the numerous springs which are to be met with in all directions. Cultivation, however, is chiefly found on the seaward slopes, where numerous villages flourish, and where every inch of ground is turned to account by industrious natives, who, in the absence of natural levels, build terraces to level the ground, and to prevent the earth from being swept down by the winter rains, and at the same time to retain the water requisite for the irrigation of the crops."

In these mountain regions we find located the Druzes, the Maronites, and the Ansariz.

The Druzes occupy, besides other places, "a large tract east of the lake of Tiberias, and north of the lake, with a little exception, as far as the Lebanon, and on the coast of the modern Jebeil, twenty miles north of Beyrout." These singular people, the descendants of a schismatic offshoot from the great Mohammedan delusion, which sought shelter from persecution amidst these mountains and fortresses in the tenth century, grew stronger and more daring, rushing down from time to time upon the people of the plain country, until, in 1585, they were subdued by Ibrahim, a Slavonian in the service of Amurath III. Recovering themselves after a season, they again became troublesome, subjecting themselves to new coercions, until they became tributary to Mohammed Ali, and then, in 1840, to the Sultan.

"Their religion has less of mystery in it than formerly, though they still keep their form of worship secret. But several of their sacred books and catechisms have, during their troubles, fallen unto European hands. These show that they believe in the lawfulness of marriage between brothers and sisters, and, to some extent, in the transmigration of souls. They eat pork and drink wine, observe no festivals or fasts, and, in truth—among the masses especially—have very little religion of any kind which exhibits itself, beyond what are called the mysteries, which are confined to the initiated, called 'Akal,' all others being called the ignorant, or 'Djahel.' An English translation of a Druze catechism, made by a Missionary in Syria, was sent to Dr. Wilson of Bombay. There is in it considerable indistinctness, to say the least, if not positive absurdity; yet with the exception of some very objectionable ceremony in their worship, this catechism contains their entire religion.

with scarcely an exception. They are not permitted to declare their faith to any one*." In 1840, from the best information, based on the Pasha's list, they numbered 70,000.

North of the country of the Druzes is that of the Maronites, stretching for forty miles to the Nahr el Kebir, or great river, the Eleutherus: and again, north of this tribe is another mysterious sect, of which little is known, called the Ansarians or Ansariz, whose land, covered with a chain of mountains, extends from the Nahr el Kebir to Antakia, on the far north.

The Maronites are a papal sect, and although not quite orthodox on some articles of faith, are the ardent admirers of the Pope, and have always strenuously resisted the teaching of the Missionaries, persecuting in the most vindictive manner such individuals from amongst them as desired to embrace the pure faith of the Gospel. One of the most remarkable of these sufferers was Asaad-el-Shidiak, a young man of some property and influence on the mountain. He had undertaken to teach Syriac to Mr. King, one of the American Missionaries at Beyrout. They read the Old Testament together in the ancient Syriac, and the result was his conversion to the pure faith of Scripture. The Maronite ecclesiastics took the alarm. Inveigled into the mountains, he was conveyed to the Convent of St. Antonio, and, on his escape from thence, to the Convent of Canobeen. "Built on a steep precipice, it appears as if suspended in the air, being supported by a high wall built against the side of the mountain. There is a very deep rupture or chasm, running many hours walk directly up the mountain: it is clothed with wild verdure from top to bottom, and many streams fall down the sides. Canobeen stands about mid-way down on the side of the chasm, at the mouth of a large cavern: some small rooms front outwards, and enjoy the light of the sun: the rest are all underground." In one of the latter the prisoner was confined. There he endured a lingering martyrdom, now assailed with arguments and invectives, and then, when he remained resolute, cruelly beaten,† until at length death released him from his suffer-

Greeks has been to fill them with pride and a spirit of persecution, so that, had they been powerful enough to do so, the Protestant Missionaries would have long since been driven from the country.

Many instances of this bitter hatred to which the Gospel and its messengers have been exposed in the region of the Lebanon might be mentioned. The little congregations of Protestants have been intruded upon, and their members beaten. In May of last year the Missionaries attempted to locate themselves in Zahleh, a town situated at the foot of Lebanon, near Labeka. The Greek Catholic Bishop was determined it should not be so. He denounced them in the church, and, through his priests and council, sought to prevent them from engaging a house; and when disappointed in this, proceeded to more summary methods of ejection. The house was assaulted; stones thrown in at the windows; and several persons severely injured; the Missionaries were seized by the mob, and with their wives and children, hurried out of the town.

We have before us the Report of the American Board of Commissioners for the year 1859. It speaks of some hopeful symptoms. In the villages around Hashbeyia, a beautiful village at the foot of Hermon, and close to the sources of the Jordan, the number of inquirers was decidedly increasing. Yet the history of this movement suffices to show the heavy pressure of opposition and persecution which have been brought to bear upon the Mission. When it first commenced, in 1845, the Protestants were publicly insulted, and beaten in the streets, their houses attacked and injured, until one by one they yielded to the storm, and made their peace with the Greek ecclesiastics. Almost simultaneously with this act of persecution, one of the old struggles broke out between the Maronites and Druzes, which ended in the defeat of the former, and their expulsion from the Druze quarter of Lebanon. The persecutors at Hasbeyia, were stoned and driven out by the Druzes, and great numbers of them killed, so that the whole combination was completely broken up and dispersed. The

in Beyrout, the composition of which exhibited the peculiarity of Missionary work in this region. It consisted of twenty-seven members: ten of whom were from the Greek Church, four were papal Greeks, four Maronites, five Armenians, three Druzes, and one a Jacobite Christian. But, soon availing itself of a brief respite, the Mission extended, and a new church was formed at Abeih, while incipient efforts were advanced to Tripoli. In 1851, a church was organized at Hashbeyia, but it was planted in the midst of persecution. Before the close of the same year, all was again in confusion. Anarchy prevailed, robbers infested the roads, and property and life were at the mercy of lawless and marauding bands of people; a state of things which continued throughout the greater part of 1852 and 1853, producing a most disastrous effect upon the church at Hashbeyia, so that it was often impossible for the Missionaries and native assistants to visit the people in safety. "At a communion in 1853, the Protestants came fully armed, and stacked their guns, and hung their swords in the court of the chapel, forcibly reminding the Missionaries of scenes often witnessed in the early planting of churches among the savages of the American wilderness."

Amidst circumstances so adverse the growth of the Mission-work has been feeble. It commenced in the year 1823, when two American Missionaries, Messrs. Goodall and Bird, arrived at Beyrout. What, then, at the present moment, presents itself as the tangible result of thirty-four years of labour? The Americans, in their Report for last year, state—"The number of churches continues to be four: which are at Beyrout, Abeih, Sidon, and Hashbeyia. But three additions were made during the year 1858, and there were two excommunications. The number of members at the end of that year was ninety-three. The whole number from the beginning is 131: nineteen were received during the first six months of the year 1859."

Here, then, the sowing of the Gospel seed has been obstructed. The great purpose of the Lord has been presumptuously interfered with, namely, the promulgation of the Gospel to all nations. That great purpose must take effect—"This Gospel of the kingdom shall be preached in all the world for a witness unto all nations; and then shall the end come." If man raises hindrances, whether they originate in the intolerance of rulers, or the fanaticism of priests and people, they must be removed. We must be prepared to find it so. This for some years past has been, and still continues to be, the special character of the time in which we live. The facilities for inter-communication between man and man have been wondrously increased. Railroads have caused the intervals between distant termini to be calculated, not by leagues, but by hours, and mighty steam-ships bridge the seas. "Many shall run to and fro; and knowledge shall be increased." When, therefore, nations place themselves in antagonism to the free circulation of the one great message of reconciliation from God to sinners, and the heralds who are charged to make it known are opposed and hindered, then must follow convulsions of society, more or less violent according to the necessities of the case, until the obstructions which have been raised have been swept away like the embankments which children raise upon the sea-shore to keep back the advancing tide.

If hindrances are to be levelled, it is only necessary that events should be permitted to take their course. The cyclone of human passions soon arises. The electrical spiral, as it descends, rotating and working like a screw, produces a reaction, until a reversed spiral of air working upwards coils, itself within and around the other, and as they struggle like contending giants in the dread embrace, they pursue with mad impetuosity their cyclonal course, darkening the heavens, and inflicting ruin by sea and land. So arise the storm and conflict of human passion. So rose the fearful mutiny in India, advancing in its rotatory action from one station to another, and inflicting stroke on stroke, until it had exhausted itself. It subjected us to many sorrows, and wrung with anguish many an English heart; but it has done its work: it has levelled obstructions, and has destroyed the prestige of the old religions of the land. Christianity has come forth out of the ordeal, uninjured, endued with new vigour, prepared and resolute for action, while Mohammedanism and Hinduism, like wounded giants, are scarcely able to lift themselves up from the earth where they have been prostrated.

The storm has now reached the Lebanon, and the contending gusts of human passions are in fierce commotion. The Maronites, and others of the corrupt churches of those regions, have hitherto prevented the Gospel from free entrance into the land. Had it been otherwise, who can say how tranquillizing its influence might have been! But they have sown the wind, and now reap the whirlwind. The confusion of events is as yet too intense to permit us with precision to indicate the immediate cause of these bloody frays. The Maronites have always given their neighbours, the Druzes, more or less trouble; and their Patriarch, by evil advice, instigated his people to such innovations upon them, that, in 1841 and 1845, the most terrible bloodshed occurred. The old feud seems now to have reached a crisis, and, in conjunction with a motley horde of Moslems, Bedouins, and Metwalis, the Druzes are inflicting fearful calamities on the Christian population.

Hashbeyia has been amongst the first to fall. It contained a population of 5000 souls, chiefly of the Greek orthodox church. For two days the armed men held their own against the Druzes, when they were induced, it is said through the interference of the Turkish commander, to surrender their arms. In this defenceless state the Druzes were permitted to wreak their vengeance on them. They were butchered in the court of the seraglio, their wives and children witnessing from the windows of the upper chambers the awful scene of blood. Some few succeeded in concealing themselves beneath the bodies of the slain, and escaped to Beyrout.

Zahleh next suffered. Thither had fled the surrounding Christian population, and thither flocked an immense horde of Druzes from the Hauran and Anti-Lebanon, as also of Kurds and Arabs from the desert.

The pasha of Beyrout, at the urgent and repeated representations of the five consuls-general, sent off a small force of 300 soldiers and two guns to drive away the Druzes. They might without difficulty have reached the scene of action next day, the distance being only thirty-two miles, of which twenty-five are over an excellent road, but they lingered on the way, and rendered no help. For several days the defenders held their ground, time being thus afforded to a large body of Christians to make good their retreat. On the sixth day the Druzes, having been strongly reinforced, attacked the place with unprecedented fury, burning it, and committing great slaughter.

Deir-el-Kamr, seven hours' journey from Beyrout, was the next point to which the rage of these motley hordes directed itself. This town contained a mixed population of Maronites and Druzes. It lies, not among the beauties, but among the gloomy and repulsive places of Lebanon, its bald houses climbing up the rugged declivities, and almost resting on each other's roofs, while above tower the mountain summits, bold and striking, but barren and precipitous. On a commanding site stands the Maronite convent; while in chapels scattered throughout the mountains, and concealed from observation, the Druzes celebrate their mysterious worship. In the gardens around a number of Maronites and other refugees had encamped, as in security, Tahir Pasha, with 400 Turkish soldiers, being in the town. Here they were attacked by a large body of Druzes, and while defending themselves, as best they could, were assaulted in the rear by Moslems from the city. On endeavouring to retreat within the walls, they found the gates closed against them, and numbers were killed by the Druzes.

There is no discrimination made by the infuriated Moslems between the Papist and Protestant Christians: all alike suffer. In Hashbeyia, the preaching of evangelical truth had borne more fruit than anywhere else in Syria. "The Protestants in the village numbered upwards of 200: they had a native pastor and a church, the latter having been built chiefly by their own contributions. Of that Protestant community, which a few weeks ago was full of spiritual as well as material life, two men now live to tell the tale of butchery, while of the 4000 Greek Christians, but 33 men have survived."

And yet this would not be permitted, unless high interests precluded the possibility of the Protestant congregations being exempted from the general suffering. They have shared the tribulations of the other Christian bodies in the Lebanon, and in this fellowship of sorrow the bitter prejudice hitherto entertained against them may be quenched. When the disturbances have been arrested, and tranquillity is restored, the Lebanon may no longer prove to be a rugged and difficult Mission field. Broken up by the plough, the soil will have a soft and mellow quality, and native evangelists may go forth with acceptance to sow the seed of the kingdom.

Meanwhile, the whole of Syria and Palestine is in alarm. Damascus is threatened.* What shall be the issue? Are we about to witness an outbreak upon an extended scale, a crusade on the part of Moslems of the Arab race, and the tribes who sympathize with them, against all who bear the name of Christian? Is it the same rancorous spirit of fanaticism which showed itself so unmistakably at Jedda, that is now convulsing and alarming the province of Syria; and the same fierce struggle for the mastery which deluged the plains of India with blood—is this about to be re-enacted in those territories of the Turkish empire which once formed a portion of the vast empire of the Caliphs? Whence arise these disquietudes that are ever appearing, now in one, now in some other province of the Turkish empire?

---

* Since taken, and the Christians slaughtered.

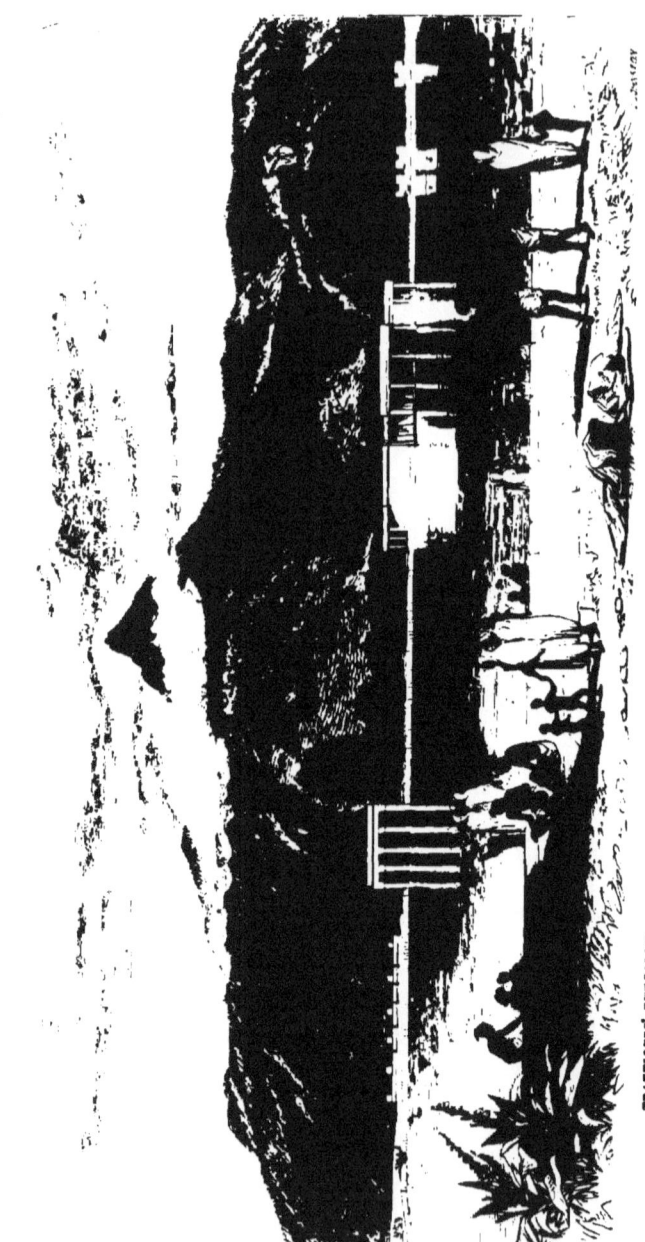

TRAVELLERS' BUNGALOW.   THE GREAT TANK AT STRIVILLIPUTTHUR, NORTH TINNEVELLY.   SHAUMICAL BATHING-PLACE.

Bosnia, the Herzegovina, and Bulgaria, have presented a threatened aspect; and while the Turkish army is being concentrated in that direction for the purpose of preventing disturbances, they break out suddenly in the southern portion of the empire. And now that the Turk appears unable to preserve peace amongst his subjects, and uphold the dignity of the law, an intervention on the part of the European powers becomes necessary. How critical this proceeding? Shall it accomplish just what may be requisite, and no more? How shall it be so directed as that no fresh complications shall arise? Are we on the eve of the dissolution of the Turkish empire, and about to witness the division of the spoil? "Where the carcase is, there will the eagles be gathered together." The vital power seems to be rapidly diminishing throughout the ponderous frame of the Ottoman empire. The old giant has lost his force. He who once wielded his battle-axe with overwhelming power, is now reduced to such weakness, that circulation in the extremities can no longer be sustained. The eagles from the north and south are hovering around. High in the air, as they had hoped, perhaps, out of sight, they have been describing their gyrations, watching with eagle eye the progress of events, and prepared, when the moment came, to swoop upon the prey.

How critical the position of human affairs! How grave the responsibilities of public men! How sensitive the feelings of nations! What jealousies prevail on questions of international right! Who can define the future, or promise the nations a happy era free from the intrigues of ambition, and the sudden convulsions in which such deep-laid mines explode? Amidst all this, when men are looking for the things which are coming on the earth, what a comfort to know that the Lord reigneth, and that nothing shall prevent the fulfilment of his purpose; that the wrath of man, and the devices of the enemy, shall alike be made to praise Him; and that his Gospel shall yet go forth in its majesty and power over the wide earth, producing by its renewing and persuasive influences, those wondrous changes which are promised in the page of Revelation, when "the wolf shall dwell with the lamb, and the leopard lie down with the kid; and the calf and the young lion and the fatling together, and a little child shall lead them:" when "they shall not hurt nor destroy in all my holy mountain, for the earth shall be full of the knowledge of the Lord, as the waters cover the sea."

Press of other important matter compels us to interrupt this article. On resuming it, other nations may be referred to as explanatory of the preliminary process, the breaking up of the fallow ground.

THE REVIVAL IN NORTH TINNEVELLY.

The work of the Missionary is the work of a sower. Two processes are necessary to a perfect harvest. There must be the planting of the seed, and there must be a quickening influence to call forth the blade and the ear, and the full corn. "I have planted, Apollos watered, but God gave the increase." This saying is usually employed to describe, as it justly does, man's impotence without God. But the text is also a text of promise. It contains God's assurance of blessing and success on the planting of the seed, as surely as the statement of men's helplessness without Him. It is "God that giveth the increase," and He has said, "My word shall not return unto Me void."

It was a saying of the middle ages, "To pray is to labour;"* whilst some who felt that this was only a half-truth preferred rather to say, "He who labours prays."† But this, too, was only a half-truth: they who used it let go the old maxim to grasp the new, and the whole truth lies, as it so often does, in the combination of the two opposites. It was truly said by a great forerunner of modern Missions, "Prayer and pains, through faith in Jesus Christ, can do any thing." Prayer without labour is enthusiasm. Labour without prayer is presumption. Duties are ours, events God's. Labour and prayer united make up that spirit of true humility, that dependent, trusting, faithful spirit, which God will not despise, which is sure of success. This view invests Missionary work with peculiar hopefulness. Labour on, and wait in prayer for a blessing, and in due time the blessing must come, for God hath said it. Persevering prayer is never lost.

The recent Revivals in America and Ireland have witnessed to this truth. In America there was a free Bible, and much head-knowledge, the sowing of the "precious

---

* Orare est laborare. † Qui laborat, orat.

seed" through wide-spread Sunday schools. It pleased God to awaken a large spirit of of united prayer. The blessing descended. The seed, which had been deposited by human hands, was quickened into life by the Divine Spirit, and the desert rejoiced and blossomed. Just so, too, in Ireland. The work has gone forward chiefly amongst the Bible-reading Protestants of Ulster. It has very slightly affected the Romanists, who had had but little scriptural teaching. A spirit of united prayer breaks forth: so little was it called out by human effort, that its very origin is hardly to be discovered. The promised answer to prayer is given, even " the Holy Spirit to them that ask." And the truth becomes at once "quick and powerful." There is deep anxiety for the soul, genuine sorrow for sin, absorbing love to the Saviour, the fruits of repentance in a new life.

Blessed be God, His Spirit is as " the wind that bloweth where it listeth." He worketh in India as well as Ireland, and we have now the privilege of laying before the friends of Missions another striking illustration of the Lord's power and love. The scene of it is North Tinnevelly, a district hallowed by the prayers and labours of the beloved and now sainted Ragland. The spirit of united prayer in which the work was sustained by him and his colleagues, English and native, was thus described by an eye-witness in 1855—" The great secret of the happy working of the itinerancy is the prayerfulness that pervades it. Prayer is the atmosphere that surrounds it. In the morning, before setting out to preach, the brethren kneel to ask for thoughts, words, fluency, skill, audiences not blasphemous or indifferent. The first act, on returning, is to commit what has been done to the hands of the Lord, who can make it effectual. Then comes a mid-day Tamil service for the servants; afterwards, the Bible and prayer. Before evening preaching the Lord's presence is again implored, and the day closes with commending the work once again to Him. This is each day's history. Can He fail to bless it who has encouraged and commanded 'us so to work? Will He not bless what is thus done in Him and for Him? He does bless it; refreshes jaded spirits; gives energy, perseverance, hopefulness; and, in his own time—the eye of faith sees it—will authenticate and crown the labours of His prayerful servants, and make this barren wilderness smile and blossom like Mengnanapuram or Nulloor."*

---

* See Annual Report for lviith year pp. 125—128.

North Tinnevelly had been the scene of various evangelistic labours. Some of the earliest German Missionaries appear to have formed congregations there, but the work had not been sustained, and the people had generally lapsed from their profession. The late eminent Missionary, Rhenius, who separated from the Church Missionary Society in 1835 on a question of ecclesiastical organization, also extended his labours into the same locality; and a few native teachers have been maintained there since his death by the contributions of some who sympathized with him in Madras. Of late years, only one such has been labouring there, named Arulappan, in the neighbourhood of a village, called by the English, Wartrap, among the mountains in the northwest corner of the district, his own station being called Christianpettah. His relatives reside in a village called Ukkirankottei, in the Surandei district, the birthplace also of a connexion of his, Moses, one of the Society's schoolmasters. These places and persons will often re-appear in the subsequent pages.

A few sentences may be desirable to explain the subsequent narratives, and to show the extent and wide diffusion of the Revival.

The itinerating (or Sivagasi) district of North Tinnevelly contains about 1230 square miles, embracing about 1200 villages, in most of which the Gospel has been perseveringly and prayerfully preached for five or six years. It is about thirty-five or forty miles from east to west, and rather less, perhaps, from north to south. Two high roads pass through it in a southerly direction towards Palamcotta. On the eastern road lies the small town of Virdupatty, and south of it Satthur. On the western road, about twelve miles from the western ghauts, the larger town of Strivilliputhur, with its numerous and lofty Hindu temples. Sivagasi lies nearly midway between Virdupatty and Strivilliputthur, and another town of 10,000 inhabitants Rajapaliam, a few miles south-west of the latter. Surandei is the nearest Missionary station in South Tinnevelly, about forty miles below Rajapaliam. The present staff of the Mission consists of the Rev. David Fenn, and the Rev. W. Gray,* with three native helpers, Joseph Cornelius, Vedhanayagam Devanayagam, and William Thomas Satthianadhen, who received Holy Orders from the Bishop of

---

* The Rev. R. R. Meadows is now on his voyage back to India, and the Rev. R. C. Macneoald is preparing study on the spot; so that the number of European Missionaries will soon be doubled. The Committee have also designated two more men to

Madras last Christmas. The native congregations in South Tinnevelly also maintain a number of catechists, who successively visit and itinerate throughout the Sivagasi district. When the Rev. W. Knight visited Strivilliputhur in 1855, in company with Joseph Cornelius, the principal inhabitants waited on him to petition for the establishment of a Native-English school there, *i. e.* a school for native boys, Christian or heathen, where English forms a part of the education. Mr. George Haffton was withdrawn from Palamcotta to undertake such a school, which was first held in the portico of a *maddam*, or Brahminical bathing-place, on the edge of the great tank, the people, though strongly attached to caste, allowing the Bible to be read, and Christian prayer to be offered up there.† A schoolroom has since been erected by the exertion of the natives themselves. The sons of the native preacher Arulappan were amongst the pupils.

We now proceed to lay before our readers the wonderful tidings before us. As in America and Ireland, the Revival has not been confined to any one denomination of Christians. Some of the earliest symptoms were manifested at Christianpettah.

The Rev. W. T. Satthianadhen thus describes his visit to it (March 27, 1860)—

"I have seen all the people who were said to be awakened. They are constantly reading the word of God, and meet together for exhortation and prayer. They go to preach to the heathen (the women also included), but I have not heard them preach. They are very anxious to preach the Gospel to all, particularly to their relatives, and are always ready to confess their sins. On Sunday afternoon, while I was preaching on the sufferings of Christ, several of them burst into tears. All this encourages the hope that they are the subjects of the Holy Spirit's operation. But this work is not very general, only a few being affected by it, one man, his wife, and sister-in-law, the rest being the members of Arulappan's family, his son and two or three of his daughters. I forgot to mention that some of his daughters, and

novel, it was most right and wise. They accordingly paused for a few weeks before expressing their opinion as to the movement. But during that time events begun to occur, which left no doubts upon their minds. Our next letter, from the Rev. Ashton Dibb, a Missionary from South Tinnevelly, then gives us an account of a similar movement in the neighbourhood of Surandei (May 15, 1860)—

"Last Sunday (the 18th) we met at Atchampetty and administered the Lord's Supper to thirty-four persons. The day was a particularly happy one to us, as there were indisputable marks of a Revival among the people, brought about by the influence of five men who had come (voluntarily to preach the Gospel to heathen and Christians) from Ukkirankottei, a village in the Surandei district. These had come under Revival influences by means of those individuals of whom, or rather of the reports concerning whom, I wrote rather disparagingly in my last to you. Of the five Ukkirankottei men whom I saw at Atchampetty, the headman had formerly been on a Mission in the Pannikullam district, but had given up that to attend to his own farming and grazing business. This, he now says, was Satan's device to keep him from meddling with his slaves, but now he is determined, as long as he lives, to work freely to set those slaves at liberty, and make Satan's device of no effect. Certainly the effect of their proceeding hitherto has been extraordinary. The heathen listen to them very attentively, though, as yet, I have not heard of any having given up their heathenism in consequence of what they had heard. Their doctrine, too, is sound and pertinent, exhibiting a right practical understanding both of law and Gospel. Hitherto I have scarcely any exception to make to their proceedings, which is remarkable, considering that they are unlearned and ignorant men, who are exercising so much influence on the people. Nothing, I apprehend, can keep such men from extravagance and forwardness but the guidance of the same Spirit who made the same class of men mighty in former years, and yet kept them from all extravagance

if in any place a member should wish to become a Christian as the result of their preaching, they should refer him to the Missionary, in whose district his village is situated. When all these circumstances are considered, and also the fact that the revivalists are churchmen, we have much cause to hope well, as well as to watch well concerning the movement. It certainly does seem to have at least the merit of being the first entirely indigenous effort of the native church at self-extension."

We now turn to another locality, the village of Vageikulam, in the more northerly part of the district, where a most wonderful work has been going on. The main instrument in God's hands has been our native agent, Moses, whose name we have already mentioned, and who was one of the earliest fruits of the Revival. He is a man of remarkable energy, but was of so indifferent character, that he had been degraded from the rank of catechist, and the Missionaries were thinking of dismissing him altogether. But we will not anticipate the remarkable circumstances which have marked the change of of this Saul into a Paul.

The Rev. David Fenn had thus written of him—

"In a village two miles from him live a man and his wife, relatives of Moses. The man was one of the thirteen I baptized ten days before Mr. Ragland's death. I heard then that his wife was not a Christian, and, indeed, was not at all on good terms with him; but as all agreed he was not to blame I baptized him, and he has gone on quietly and satisfactorily since. She has all along been most obstreperous. Some months ago, Moses, who is a man of very great ability and influence, especially among his relatives, and who at that time was destitute of all principle, beat her severely for quarrelling with her husband. This enraged her so, that she never failed to call him all sorts of names, and to heap abuse on all catechists and schoolmasters generally.

This day fortnight she had, in one of her usual fits, been violently abusing the schoolmaster of the village in the morning. In the evening Moses came. His efforts with many other of his relatives, during the last two months, had been greatly successful in bringing many of them to a better mind. In a humble and prayerful spirit he thought he would try what he could do for her. One or two good Christian women had been speaking to her that very morning. When Moses went to her house she was lying down. He asked her civilly for a drink of water. Instead of rushing away from him as usual, she brought it at once, and a little cake also. He then began very quietly to confess that he had done very wrong to beat her so; asked her forgiveness; and went on to urge her to come as a sinner to Christ. Whilst he was speaking, the schoolmaster of the place came in, whom she had that morning been abusing. He also is one of those who have recently been awakened. He suggested that they should pray. At once she went in, put on a respectable cloth over her head and body, as Christians do at service, and they had prayer. She seems completely softened. Next day the schoolmaster and his wife, having come away to where I was, seven miles off, for the Lord's Supper, she, without a hint from any one, went to their house and swept and cleaned it; and on the Monday after, when I had that interesting service in the little church in Moses' own village, she was present, and was brought up to me after the service, and sat before me beside her husband, looking up at me with a quiet modest face, as one who had been for years a Christian. One thing that makes me feel very happy about many of these sudden conversions is, that the subjects of them show so much love to one another afterwards. Love, you know, is the first of the fruits of the Spirit."

Mr. Fenn was subsequently able to give the following glad tidings—

"*Tent, near Virdupatty, May* 17, 1860.

"The Lord has begun to bless North Tinnevelly in very deed. The shower has begun to fall; not so much, however, on the heathen wilderness, as on one or two of the little Christian oases within it. An hour or two after despatching my last, a fortnight ago, I took leave of dear Gray, clambered into my bandy, and found myself next morning in good Vedhanayagam's village, (Vageikulam) twenty-five miles off. There I heard further particulars of Moses, the schoolmaster, of whom I wrote; and every thing I heard went to prove that a real solid work of grace had taken place in his soul. The apparent instrument was dear Vedhanayagam's own solemn and affectionate admonitions, two months before, which had led Moses to reflection, prayer, and the study of the Bible. He at once abandoned drinking and quarrelling, and instituted family prayers in his own house. At the meetings for study held weekly at Vedhanayagam's house, where all the schoolmasters of his section assemble, Moses shows the greatest humility and teachableness. His prayer-meetings in his own house are attended voluntarily by not only the

Christians, but even some heathen women of the place: his own wife and the monitor of the school (a relative of his) have been brought with tears to the foot of the cross. A schoolmaster of a neighbouring village, who, with his wife (Vedhanayagam's own sister-in-law), were unsatisfactory agents, whom Gray was on the point of dismissing, have both been powerfully influenced by Moses' example and prayers, and, after a season of thoughtfulness and study of Scripture, were visited by extraordinary and overpowering convictions of sin, which have led them to be constantly in prayer, and to labour, the wife as well as the husband, for the conversion of all around them. They also have, I fancy, daily prayer-meetings in their house. In the village in the Surandei district, Ukkirankottei, from which Moses originally comes, and where many of his relatives are Christians, among whom is Arulappan (the native preacher of whom I have sometimes written as settled down in a corner of North Tinnevelly, near Strivilliputthur,) there has been, I hear, a remarkable movement, accompanied with outward demonstrations of tears and sobs.

"But now let me tell you what I myself witnessed in my visit to Vedhanayagam's village. Here were assembled for the Lord's Supper, Moses, the other schoolmaster, both their wives, the wife of a catechist nearly related to Moses, who, within the few preceding days, had been brought to see her sins and embrace the Saviour, and other newly-awakened ones. After evening prayers on Sunday, (May 6) Moses came up to me, and looking up in my face, with tears in his eyes, told me, in a few words, how the Lord had had mercy on him; how utterly unworthy he felt himself; how he knew he had grieved Mr. Every, Mr. Ragland, and myself in times past; and how he begged that I would pray for him that he might hold on to the end. On that Sunday we had the usual services at 7 A.M., 12 noon, and 7.30 P.M. Dear Vedhanayagam preached in the morning, and read prayers, and assisted me at the Lord's Supper at noon. About 150 were assembled at the latter, of whom thirty-five were communicants, and three more stayed on, hoping we would admit them for the first time, though they had not previously told us of their wish. I trembled in the prospect of preaching, having felt very unable all the day before, though I tried to prepare; and I thought these new-born souls would be looking up for food, and would go away unfed. However, Vedhanayagam and I prayed that the Lord would help me, and He did. I spoke from, 'Look unto me, and be ye saved.' Throughout the service and sermon there was the greatest attention: some were in tears. It was a solemn thought, as I administered the Lord's Supper, that some, though they had often before outwardly pressed with the teeth the sacrament, yet were now for the first time feeding on Him in their hearts.

"But if the times of service that day were unusually interesting, the times between service were yet more so. No sooner was the early morning service over, than Moses and two or three others began to perambulate the village, going into almost every house, praying with Christians, and preaching to heathen. Dear Vedhanayagam was in the church with me a great part of the day, but from his house near by there was hardly a moment in the day when the voice of prayer or of Scripture-reading was not heard to proceed. The three women mentioned above, and dear Vedhanayagam's own wife, and another good woman, seemed to employ every moment in either speaking to one another or other Christian women; or, while their husbands were out in the village, in praying: and in the afternoon, the women in one party, and the men in another, went about from house to house praying. At about sunset, I heard the voice of one of the schoolmasters rather loud but very solemn and earnest in prayer. I then took a quiet walk in the fields for about three-quarters of an hour. On my return, I heard loud sobs proceeding from Vedhanayagam's house. My Christian servant told me that 'the Lord was doing a wonderful work.' Vedhanayagam himself I found in the church, walking about in some distress. His own wife had shortly before been powerfully affected, so as to give out quite piercing cries as some thoughts of the judgment-day came over her. I then went with Vedhanayagam inside his house, and there, on the ground, found the six or seven Christian women, most of them with their faces buried in their clothes, two sobbing vehemently, one or two repeating quietly suitable texts, and one or two of the men doing the same. I also did so, and soon there was calmness enough for me to read Psalm cxxx., and to offer a short prayer. We two then went into the church for our tea, during which time I could hear, sometimes a woman crying over and over, 'O Lord, I am a sinner!' 'O righteous Father, have mercy on me!' and then, again, the voice of Moses in prayer. It struck me a good deal to overhear, in the midst of it, that beautiful petition in the Litany, 'O Lord, deal not with us after our sins, neither reward us after our iniquities.'

"Soon after, they all came in to evening prayers. We had only a chapter, exposition, and singing and prayers—the usual custom. The second lesson was singularly appropriate (Rom. v.) I omitted the difficult verses in the middle, being very anxious to fix their minds on leading truths. The first verse was most precious, and so was the sixth and eighth, but perhaps most of all the twentieth, 'Where sin abounded, grace did much more abound.' It was sweet to see every face upturned to me, except those of one or two, who still continued to sob at the end. I said a few words to the two schoolmasters, and to one other good old Christian present, after the rest were gone, about 'trying the spirits,' for they must not think every thing from God. I sat up a good while by myself in that house of God, which had indeed been that day a gate of heaven; but drowsiness overpowered me, while the voices of quiet Christian conversation were yet going on outside, and ere I left next morning, dear Vedhanayagam told me, that till past midnight he had been engaged with such precious communings with his wife and sister as he had never before known. 'Oh,' he said, 'I shall never forget this day!'

"Next day (May 7) I was in a small Christian church some eight miles off, whither came two of the good women who had taken a very prominent part in all the prayers and preachings, and, I must add, the tears and sobs of that Sabbath. I was very glad of an opportunity for quietly investigating their feelings; and you will not be surprised to hear that they were attaching, as it seemed to me, far too great an importance to physical emotions and hysteric swayings of the body, and were also in lively expectation of supernatural gifts, prophesying, speaking with tongues, &c. In the evening I went on to Moses' village, Ukkirankottei. I was very glad to send my pony across the country, and have the last three miles for a quiet walk and meditation. The moon had not risen; all was dark and still: I prayed for strength and clearness of mind. John x. came into my mind, and, as I repeated it all over and over, it seemed to me the very word that the Spirit had given me for the occasion. On arriving at the village, I gave them a little tea I had brought with me: they had milk they said all ready, and I expected that about half an hour as usual would pass before the people assembled. I should have had my tea, and then addressed them; but I was hardly within the little church before it was crammed to the doors. I should think forty people must have squeezed into it. It was as good as a hundred cups of tea to see their waiting, serious looks. So at once I told them my thoughts as I had been walking along, and spoke to them of the Good Shepherd, their happiness under his keeping, their everlasting security, and the need to watch against the voice of strangers. Then I told them what I had discovered that day to be the expectations of some, unwarrantable as they appeared to me; then we had prayer: but whether it was singing, Scripture, or prayer, all seemed to join with all their hearts. Some at the beginning began to sob, but by lowering and calming my voice, I was, through God's mercy, able to check what, it appeared, was more from habit than from actual feeling at the time. Oh, it was a wonderful sight! there, where, a few months ago, all had been so lifeless! And what pleased me as much as any thing was to see Moses, on my rising from prayer, stand up, and in a few words explain to the people that he now understood his error; that he had been teaching them the last few weeks to expect outward signs (I was quite ignorant that he also held the notion); that two signs only were necessary, and these God had given them—(1) Fresh light; (2) a new nature.

"Then the little congregation, after I had read a few verses from the end of Mark xiv., and told them my view of them, dispersed. My tea was brought. Four newly-awakened agents of the district, and two good youths from Mr. Sargent's Institution, just come for a month's preaching, sat before me. All the time I had my English Bible, and they their Tamil ones, and I referred them to texts which they read out, mostly on the preciousness of the word of God and the signs of true and spiritual life. One of them was so hoarse he could hardly read, and when I asked the reason, it turned out, as I had expected, that he had been all day, from morning to night, preaching in the streets of the neighbouring towns, and this was a man who, only ten days before, had written Mr. Gray a really rude letter, complaining bitterly of being removed to his present position, which he said was unhealthy. Now he says, 'Do let me stay, Moses, and I will make an assault upon the place: we will attack every house and every soul, and conquer them for Christ.' As I walked away, I got the youth, who is a monitor in Moses' school, to show me the way, on purpose that I might talk with him of the change which he, too, had felt. It was touching to hear him, in answer to my questions, say, in the simplest words, that he had been a great sinner, but he knew that all his sins were forgiven, for Jesus Christ the Son of God had died for him, and now he must no longer live in sin, but pray for the Holy Spirit to conquer his sins. Then I asked him if he, too, felt bodily tremblings. 'Yes,' he said, 'every day whenever I come to prayers I do so.' 'Well,' I said, 'it was no wonder when you first thought of your sins it should be so. But now all this will only hinder you from thinking about Jesus Christ: you must pray against it.' He at once said, 'Yes, I will pray: O Lord, please do not let my body shake when I come to prayers.' I could not refrain from putting my hand on his head, and blessing him in the name of God.

"The moon was now up. I had a happy walk to where my horse was tied, and thence rode on four miles to my resting-place for the night, and thirteen miles more early next morning to dear Gray's tent. My heart was ready to leap out for joy. I thought of the verse, 'The shepherds returned glorifying and praising God for all the things that they had heard and seen, as it was told unto them.' How kind was it of our heavenly Father to permit me to witness all this! It was not my work, but Gray's, to go and administer the Lord's Supper there; and my tent was moving just then to the farthest corner of North Tinnevelly; but just then this dear loving brother was quite knocked up. I took his place, and thus was able to see with my eyes a blessed work of God, which, to my dying day, I shall never forget. Gray is himself gone to those parts this week. I am longing to hear from him, and expect to do so before this letter has to be posted. And I am full of hope, and, with the little company in my tent, consisting of my Christian servant, and two or three from the south, am trying to pray that the shower of blessing may descend on the congregations of the district, especially Kalbodhu and Paneiadipatty, which are both very sadly in need of it.

"Meanwhile we have such tokens of movements among the heathen as we have never yet known; but as they do not seem to proceed from any definite convictions of the truth of Christianity, and certainly from no sense of sin, I set less value on them. Yet they may, in God's hand, be the beginning of great things. I told you of the Shanars of Menachipuram, and of some three or four families in a village quite on our eastern border, in which I spent a day three weeks ago. These last, I now hear, are going on satisfactorily. As far to the west as Rajapalium, two remarkable dreams, one after the other, simple, and such as one may call, from God, have driven a well-connected Shanar tradesman into Satthianadhen's arms: while here, on the north-east corner, seven miles south of Virdupatty, three families have just placed themselves under instruction, apparently urged to it by a zealous native Christian, who has visited them from one of the Madura Missions; while others, relatives of these three, in an adjoining village—one of the worst in our whole district, where, whenever I went or sent catechists, I felt certain we should meet with abuse—seem really inclined to come over. And when I preached there a few evenings ago, notwithstanding one or two cavillers, I had a fair bearing, and was dismissed with great respect. It will indeed be giving us the valley of Achor for a door of hope, if God raises up a church in that place. I feel very hopeful about the three: they are of the lowest castes, but there is a great look of sincerity about them. Last Sunday the Virdupatty catechist tells me that a man of respectable caste, from one of his range of villages, two miles north, who had begun to be very friendly with him, came to see how Christians worship God, and, at the close of the service, went away saying, with apparent earnestness, 'I never thought you did so. Your's must be the true religion. I shall become a Christian.'

"Since I began to write this, a catechist of Kadachapuram has been with me, who was sent by Gray, with one of our district catechists, to look after some families of Pullars, (five miles south of where I now am, and near Satthur,) who said they wished to be Christians. No fewer than 103 persons, from five or six contiguous hamlets, have given in their names: they have, however, a law-suit with their Zemindar, who has just imposed a new, and, as they say, an unjust tax; and however we may protest, still they cling to the notion, that they will be better able to resist him if they are connected with us. But then, again, all these are persons on whom more than usual labour has been all along bestowed. One of their relatives, who is always working with them, is a staunch Christian, so that I do hope for a remnant, at least, from among them. One of the five villages is that in which, some three years ago, I spent, on two or three occasions, a day in their resthouse with Samuel Sandhosham, and got them to learn several texts, and had a hope one or two would then place themselves under instruction; and one of our permanent itinerants, who lives six or seven milus off, has always looked upon them as the most hopeful in his circuit.

"Is it not a mercy, that, just as my exclusive connexion with North Tinnevelly is coming to an end, all this fruit should be vouchsafed? I have often prayed that success might be granted in such a way that we might not be puffed up, in such a way that God might have all the glory, and He seems to be hearing that prayer. Moses' conversion was altogether irrespective of us, even as instruments. And altogether, it is when our itinerating is, as it were, closed, that the Sun of glory and of righteousness is casting his bright beams on every corner of the wide plain. Oh, as I look across it to that magnificent peak, rising some 6000 feet over Strivilliputthur, thirty-five miles away—the crow's nest of North Tinnevelly—I think that it is destined, are long, to look down on a regenerated region, a territory of peace, and joy, and righteousness; and that all over this Sivagasi district the voice of sorrow for sin, of exultation in a Redeemer, of pleading in prayer with God for lost sinners around, and of loving entreaties that they too will come unto Jesus,—when I think that all this is beginning even now to be felt, and seen, and heard,—is it not enough to make one cry out with Simeon, even though I have not reached half his years, 'Lord, now lettest thou thy servant depart in peace, according to thy word, for mine eyes have seen thy salvation!'"

We complete the circle of our narratives with a letter by the Rev. W. Gray, from Strivilliputthur, dated May 14, 1860. Those who have studied the history of recent Revivals elsewhere, will be struck with many remarkable coincidences—

"I am going to endeavour to lay before you an account of the wonderful things that our gracious Lord is pleased to show his servants in this district. If the work goes on (as may He grant it!), I will endeavour to keep you in possession of all its phases, by letters written from time to time. In pursuance of an arrangement I have entered into for administering the Lord's Supper to all the assembled communicants of each section of the district once in every two months, we came here (to Strivilliputthur) on Saturday evening last, my dear wife and myself. On Sunday morning, (May 13) Mr. Satthianadhen read the service and preached. At midday, I performed service and preached to a congregation of nearly a hundred people, and then administered the Lord's Supper to twenty-eight communicants. I bless God that I never before felt my tongue so loosed for Tamil speaking. In the morning I held an English service in Mr. Huffton's schoolroom, and we then retired to the bungalow for the night. We were hardly seated when dear Satthianadhen came over in haste, and requested me to go with him to witness a most extraordinary sight. It was, in truth, an extraordinary sight. The boys of Mr. Huffton's school, sent by Mr. Arulappan of Varttheramppa, (Wartrap,) live in a house close to the schoolroom. We went there, and found all three boys, ten in number, wailing and sobbing loudly, some on their knees, some prostrated. I could hardly believe my senses, and I felt an involuntary tremor running over my whole frame. We went round about them all, and endeavoured to know the cause of their weeping so bitterly. In every case it was the bitterness of sin (so they said) that caused the grief. They were all closely huddled together, all with their Bibles in their hand; some kneeling, and, with eyes uplifted, engaged in prayer; some anxiously turning over the leaves of the Bible for some particular passages. I saw one boy (the very worst boy in his school, Mr. Huffton said) thus turning over for a passage, and on finding it, and reading it, immediately falling down and sobbing bitterly. We were by this time all assembled to see this strange and solemn sight—Mr. Huffton and his family, my dear wife, the Satthianadhens, &c. We all experienced the one feeling, that whatever it was, it was certainly an influence of some supernatural kind that had fallen on these poor boys. It was painful to see two or three of them shaking all over violently, and evidently quite powerless to control it. I asked one of them, who was thus affected, whether he would wish to give vent to his feelings in prayer. He immediately prayed in a very loud voice, and most earnestly: 'More, more, more light,' was the burden of it. How far it may be in a great measure the result of communicated sympathy I do not know. There was no cause assignable for the commencement of it. They had attended the two services in Tamil, and we were just concluding our evening English service, when it began with one boy, and almost immediately all were affected. It all began in their own little room. One of the most striking things about it is the extraordinary readiness they all seemed to have in finding out appropriate passages in the Bible. All, too, set it down to the painful feeling of sin: all had the one thought, too, about the sufferings of Christ Jesus for them. We spent some considerable time with them, and, after commending them to God in prayer, we retired, very deeply solemnized—awe-stricken I might say.

"I went over again early this morning, and found that they had had very little sleep during the night. One of them said that he had heard a loud voice saying to him, 'Arise;' but on inquiring of the others, I found that no one but himself had heard it. They were much more calm than last evening, but all armed with their Bibles, in the reading of which they appeared so abstracted, that they would hardly give heed to our questionings and words. One idea had taken possession of their minds, that they must leave school and go to preach to the heathen. These poor little boys are, as you know, some of them very young, most of them perhaps not over twelve years of age. One of Mr. Arulappan's sons, who was in Mr. Huffton's school, left school a little time ago for this purpose. I began to ask them how they would preach—how they would answer the heathens' objections—how they would prove that Christianity was a true religion—how they would prove that the Bible was God's book, and not a new book made by man—how they would manage if the heathen began to scoff at them and jeer at them?

"I certainly was surprised to hear the ready answers they gave from the Bible, as to the way in which they intend to preach. 'How could little children like you preach to grown up men?' 'Out of the mouths of babes and sucklings hast thou ordained strength,' was immediately the answer. 'How will you prove that the word you read is God's word?' 'Holy men of old spake as they were moved by the Holy Ghost,' was at once answered. I said to a very little and very quiet boy, 'The people will laugh at you, and make fun of you, if you go to preach.' He immediately turned to the passage in St. Peter, where the apostle speaks of 'scoffers' coming in the last times. This really was remarkable for boys, who, I suppose, were before rarely even in the habit of opening their Bibles, except in school lessons. I told them how that Jesus Christ, though He loved little children, and though he loved the honour and praise that their young lips and lives gave Him, yet never appointed them to go to preach the Gospel. In miraculous times, when He wanted a man case), and an outpouring attended with miraculous results, because Mr. Arulappan does not appear inclined to discourage boys from this step, and our good friend, Mr. Huffton, is rather of the same view. When Mr. Arulappan's own son (of whom I spoke before) wished to go to preach and to leave school, he (Mr. Arulappan) appears to have said merely, 'If the Spirit does so influence him, what can I say or do? can I resist the Spirit?' Mr. Huffton appeared to be rather of this view at first, with regard to these boys. But as I said to him, there is nothing miraculous in this case. The most we can say of them is (if we can say so much), that they are 'new-born babes:' how we ourselves have been influenced by the self-same spirit for several years. Our judgments are more matured, our minds more expanded, and therefore our duty is to control and direct these boys, and not leave them to themselves. Our suffering them to go to preach could be only possible on the supposition that the boys were under a plainly and unmistakably miraculous influence. But this we cannot of course admit. I think Mr. Huffton sees the matter in this light now, and I hope all will go on well and wisely. May God direct these poor boys aright, and Mr. Huffton, and us all!

"I have mentioned this case now, which has just come under my notice, and I think, that as a simple fact, as a phenomenon, it is well worthy of notice. But we have other proofs that God is working amongst us here in a very wonderful manner. We feel that we know not exactly what to do. Only let God give us wisdom to guide and direct this matter aright. We much need the prayers of you and all our praying friends. In dear Vedhanayagam's section of the district a most remarkable movement is going forward. I don't know whether dear brother Fenn has written to you about this. As I was not very well, he went for me to administer the Lord's Supper at Vageikulam, according to my new arrangement last Sunday (May 6). He saw there a most remarkable sight: a congregation of 150 people had

human appearance, unmistakably the Spirit of God has fallen upon that man and his wife, and wonderful is the change. Naturally a proud and clever man, he is now most truly humble, and giving his whole heart in the most humble manner to the teaching of all his relatives and friends. You remember, again, the Vellalar schoolmaster, (Moses,) about whom I wrote to you my first official letter after I came here. He had been a great friend of the Zemindar's, with whom, to the neglect of his duties, he used to go to hunt. Month after month I have been watching him, intending to dismiss him entirely. Blessed be God, he too has been thus visited, and his wife also, and is now devoting all his time to the reading of the word and prayer, in teaching all his friends and exhorting them. Another man, a catechist of considerable standing, a really clever man, but very unsatisfactory, has been likewise visited in this strange manner. In these three cases there is nothing of extravagance. The fruits of the Spirit are produced in all peaceableness, and this mighty change exhibits itself in the bursting zeal to preach the Gospel to all. I will just mention these three facts now, leaving a more full statement of the case till my visit to the spot during this week. All through Vageikulam the work, I believe, is progressing in a most wonderful manner. We cannot doubt that the hand of God is with us now. Oh, do pray for us that we may have wisdom to throw ourselves into this matter heartily, and to direct it wisely to the glory of God and the great spread of the Gospel!

"I turn now to the Surivilliputthur side, from which I write this. In a congregation of Satthianadhen's (Pattakulam) lives a pious woman, who has of late become most warm in the service of God. I was lately made most thankful by the receipt of a letter from our dear brother to me about her. Along with the letter he sent me all her ear ornaments (worth about eight to ten rupees), which she voluntarily gave to keep the preaching of the Gospel to the heathen. And not only so, but the old catechist there, whom we always looked on as utterly lifeless, had voluntarily taken out his earrings, and sent them for the same purpose. This old man now appears to be really under the influence of the Holy Spirit. Dear Satthianadhen tells me, that last week, at his usual weekly instruction of his agents, when he began to give them some thoughts about God's dealings with men at the present time, the old man violently shook all over, and asked Satthianadhen whether he might address God in prayer. On being allowed to do so, he prayed before all his brother agents in a most touching and affecting way. From that same village of Puttakulam, a young man has lately come to Satthianadhen to be received under instruction. Satthianadhen sent him back, and he is now undergoing a severe storm of persecution, but is manfully holding his ground for Christ. May God uphold him!

"Again, in the large town of Rajapaliam, a very respectable Shanar has come under instruction, and is holding on his way in joy and peace. I saw him yesterday, and there was something most pleasing about his look. He is a fine-looking man, with a fine, open, intelligent countenance. He has since brought over another man with him. They both came here to see me yesterday. The cause of his coming under instruction, as stated by himself, is not a little interesting. He saw in a dream, some time ago, a Missionary holding an open book in his hand. He thought that he asked the Missionary for the book; but the Missionary said it was not for heathen. He awakened, and felt a great longing for that book. Soon after, the catechist met him, and gave him a tract, which fully opened his eyes to the folly of idolatry. He soon after saw, in another dream, a man advising him to read, and be instructed in the Bible. After this, he came to dear Satthianadhen, and has since been a most promising inquirer, and appears truly a Nathaniel.

"I have thus gone over a good deal of space. I don't know whether I have left on your mind the impression that is on my own, that God is doing a great work amongst us in North Tinnevelly. Whence it all proceeds, it is hard to say. Man seems to have little part in it: the Spirit's work is all predominant. Shall we say, that now, at last, the God that heareth prayer is going to give an answer to the strong cries and prayers that have gone up for the last six years on behalf of North Tinnevelly? Shall we say, that now, at last, it is going to be made apparent that the lives of Ragland, and Every, and Barenbruck,[*] and the labours of

---

[*] The Rev. T. G. Ragland died suddenly of hæmorrhage of the lungs, at Sivagasi on October 22, 1858; the Rev. C. Every died of cholera, at the same place, on August 18, 1857, having been recently appointed to take charge of the small congregations of inquirers in the itinerating district; and the Rev. T. G. Barenbruck, after fourteen years of Missionary labour, chiefly in the Sarandei district, had been attached to the itinerancy only a month, when he sank under a short but severe illness on March 29, 1858. "These all died in faith, not having received the promise." See C. M. Quarterly Paper, No. cclxxiii, for Lady-day 1859.

their living associates, have not been offered up in vain?

"Or shall we say that Joel's vial of prophecy is now about to be emptied out to the last on the dead inhabitants of the nations, and that 'all flesh' is about to feel that 'not by might, nor by power, but by my Spirit, saith the Lord of Hosts,' is its quickening into life to be effected?

"We live in strange and startling times. May God give us all to 'watch and pray, that we may be accounted worthy to stand before the Son of man!'"

We may well "stand still, and see the salvation of God." "There is little doubt," writes one of our friends from Madras, "but that the Spirit of the Lord is in an extraordinary manner at work in portions of our South-India Missions. Church-of-England clergy are backward in accepting such movements as these; but the testimony is now pretty decided and unanimous. It is indeed a new era in Indian Missions—that of lay converts going forth without purse or scrip to preach the Gospel of Christ to their fellow-countrymen, and that with a zeal and life we had hardly thought them capable of. What blessings, indeed, are showered down in answer to faithful prayer! How much have we to thank the Loodiana Missionaries for putting forth that call to prayer!"

We reiterate this appeal. Brethren, pray for us that the word of the Lord may have free course and be glorified. We are only at the beginning of this great movement. What might not be hoped, were all or half the native Christians in India to receive such quickening grace as those of North Tinnevelly? The word of the Lord to us is the same as the word to one of His servants of old—"Up! is not the Lord gone out before thee?" May He give us the hearing ear!

We had thus concluded; but the following mail brought with it further tidings of so wonderful a character that we cannot withhold them from our friends. Mr. Gray's letters are so deeply interesting, that we reproduce them *in extenso*, though they refer partly, as it will be seen, to the subject of and where this remarkable work has been principally going on. I will just give you a brief sketch of what has gone on there up to the date of my leaving it on last Thursday, May 17. I told you before of an arrangement I had made for the administering of the Lord's Supper once in every two months at each of the principal stations of the three sections of the district, for the benefit of all the communicants of each section in its turn. Dear brother Fenn went for me for the administration on Sunday, May 6th, as I was not very well. Our two agents, Gnanamuttu and Moses, who had been converted in so remarkable a manner, (as I told you in a previous letter,) had come there with their wives, (also converted,) on the Saturday evening, and from the time of their arrival had not ceased to exhort and entreat most earnestly all whom they met, to turn to Christ for salvation. They also held constant meetings for prayer on Saturday evening and Sunday morning. Such an assemblage as assembled in the church on that Sunday dear V. Devanayagam had never witnessed before: 150 people had assembled: thirty-five communicants partook of the holy Supper of the Lord. Dear Fenn preached a most stirring sermon, and, while he preached, many sighs, and sobs, and tears were observable, but no direct awakenings took place. But during that evening constant prayer-meetings were held, and several conversions took place, and a strange and solemn influence pervaded the whole place.

"Then from the Monday after that Sunday until the day on which I left Vageikulam, thirty-two persons had been awakened, to all outward appearance, and of these, nineteen were women. I will just mark down the days, and the number of awakenings which took place on each, and afterwards generally mention the physical manifestations which accompanied most of these awakenings.

"On Monday, the 7th of May, ten cases occurred, and principally at prayer-meetings held in the Rev. V. Devanayagam's house. On Tuesday, the 8th, five cases occurred on the same occasions, when the prayer-meetings were principally held by the Rev. V. Devanayagam's wife, and some of the newly con-

cases, and their attendant circumstances, as our dear native brother, who stands in the centre of it all, fully communicated them to me. I may mention, that amongst those 'struck down' were six heathen men and women of the village. The Rev. V. Devanayagam remarks generally—'The heathen, also, observing this wonderful work, are amazed. Since the commencement of the movement, twenty of these, including the awakened, have joined us. What a mighty change has come over these people for the better! Those who were at enmity before with each other have become reconciled of their own accord. They show great eagerness to hear the word of God. For these ten or twelve days I have not heard a single word of bad language, either from the new converts, or from the heathen. It appears as if a terror had fallen upon the heathen. But I rejoice with trembling.'

"The outward symptoms attending these awakenings have, for the most part, been of one and the same kind. Generally, the subject of the affection assumes, as if under some uncontrollable influence, the kneeling position, begins to sob bitterly, and to cry out for help against the overwhelming power of sin, sways the body with more or less violence to and fro, gasps, as if from suffocation, sometimes rolls the eyes wildly. I will just mention one case which the Rev. V. Devanayagam told me of, and in his own words—'A married young man of this village had plunged into the depth of iniquity. When it pleased God to show him, by his Holy Spirit, his real state, he was in such an agony as I never witnessed, and this agony continued for three full days. During all this time he continued crying most bitterly for his sin, and, as I heard him, the words in Zech. xii. 10 came most powerfully to my mind. He did not feel backward to tell out before all; in his confession, the most gross of crimes.' Some words of his prayer were as follows—'O God, what a great sinner I am! Oh, my sin! my sin! If I had died on Saturday I would have been now in hell amongst the devils! O Lord Jesus, my burden of sin is great. Thou alone canst unburden my load. Thou alone art my friend!' After a long and continued struggle, and earnest prayer for mercy, he has found peace. Oh! what a different aspect he wears now! His face is bright and cheerful. He is constantly going about in preaching to his friends and relatives.'

"They all came in to see me when I reached Vageikulam on Monday the 15th. It was a truly delightful sight. In the faces of many of them you could read the traces of a bitter, bitter conflict they had gone through, and you could see the calm, and pensive, and subdued, yet happy and joyful look of peace that had arisen out of it. All of them told of the one thing, viz. that Jesus Christ was all-powerful to save, and that they had found it to be so. All were in constant and earnest attendance in the house of God. There was no appearance of extravagance about them. All was calm, and happy, and sober, and I rejoiced particularly at this. Prayer-meetings were held constantly. My dear native brother had hardly a minute in the day to rest from the constant applications for him to instruct, or pray, or comfort, or exhort. All was earnestness and joy.

"I may just mention here, that on the evening of my first day's visit to Vageikulam, I visited a new congregation of about twenty inquirers, who have come over within the last three months, and who are going on most satisfactorily. We have placed no catechist amongst them, but fortunately one of them can read, and he in the most pleasing manner does all he can to instruct the rest.

"During my second day's stay, all the catechists of the section came in to their weekly instruction. Daniel, our permanent itinerating catechist, who has his centre at Putthons, gave us the pleasing intelligence that the movement has begun in that village also. Thus everywhere the word of God seems to grow mightily. 'Unto thy name, Lord, be all the praise.'

"I left Vageikulam on Thursday morning for the village of Kulakottikurichi, about five miles off. I will just mention one incident that took place there. After breakfast I called the schoolchildren together to examine them. Before beginning the examination, we all knelt down together to pray. As I prayed, the young assistant schoolmaster began to sob very bitterly. From that time he continued for two hours in the most bitter agony I have ever witnessed. Such piercing cries as he uttered for mercy I have never heard. At one time he would rise up to his knees and pray most earnestly. Then a bitter thought of sin would start up before him, and he would fall down into a most despairing agony. As I witnessed this strange sight, and this terrible sorrow for sin, I could not let go from my mind the remembrance of that poor afflicted one whom 'the Spirit tare; and he fell on the ground and wallowed foaming.' Visions appeared to float before his mind of an awful lake of fire, and a wave that was rolling him on irresistibly nto it. All his sins were fully and freely confessed before a number of people who had congregated about the doors and in the church. Poor fellow! he describes himself as in this state ever since he had a conversation with Moses, about four days before. His father, who is the catechist of the place, and I, did all we could to direct him, by means of the promises of God, into the happiness of peace. He did, after about two hours, appear to obtain some measure of it. All the day he was constantly at his Bible. There is no other token of good in this congregation. May his example be blessed to the turning of many of them unto Christ!

"I set out the following morning for Neilapatty. I extract from my journal what I saw and heard there. There does really appear a mighty work going on in that village, of which the converted Moses, is under God, the honoured leader.

"'*Neilapatty, May* 18—Rose up this morning at a very early hour. I was hardly dressed when poor Manuel came in, and began talking about the subject—which is now the great subject with him—the salvation of his soul.

"'I pointed out to him a number of texts, which he seized upon with the utmost avidity. I told him how watchful he must be as to whether he is growing and bringing forth more and more the fruits of the Spirit. I then prayed with him and his father and another, and took leave of them. I reached Milepatty at about eight o'clock. Moses met me, looking as happy and cheerful and bright as be could look. We went together to the little prayer-house, and there I saw, to my delight, the little monitor Royappen (who is amongst the converted), with a face beaming brightly like a little angel's. Around him were no less than twenty-three little boys, all as busy as a set of little bees, and making no end of noise with shouting out their lessons. But in one corner of the prayer-house stood a man with a different look about him. This was a poor man (Sangau) to whom Moses had preached a few days before in a neighbouring village. This poor man had come the evening before to Moses, with tears and groans, and had spent the night with him receiving consolation from the word of God. I spoke to him for a while, and then we all knelt together, and asked God's blessing that his Spirit might be poured out on us all.

"'Moses then sat down by me, and began to tell me all about the wonderful things that were going on about here. To illustrate the change that has taken place in himself, I may mention one thing he told me. This very Moses, of whom I am speaking, had been heretofore the very terror of the neighbourhood. Even the neighbouring Zemindar and his people feared him. Whatever lawsuit Moses took up (and they were a few), he was sure to beat, by his ingenuity and unscrupulousness, every opponent. He had been once a catechist with us, but is now a schoolmaster, degraded, I think, by Mr. Barenbruck. Though he had had no sphere for the exercise of his forensic power with us, he has yet been always looked upon as a person whom it was better to leave alone than to molest, and so the Zemindars and he have been on very good terms with each other, the mutual respect for each other's power of doing mischief being, I suppose, the bond of union. What a mighty change is the change the blessed Spirit of God effects! Moses has often been feeling, since his conversion, a great desire to go and speak to the Zemindar about his soul. It lay heavily on his conscience, for he remembered how that all his dealings with him before were in sin and iniquity. He made up his mind at last, and presented himself a few days ago before the Zemindar in his cutcherry. Twenty Brahmins stood round about him. 'Ah, Moses, where have you been this long time? For three months and more I have not seen you.' 'When I used to come to you before, Sir,' replied Moses, 'it was in order to receive worldly favours from you. I have not come with that object now. I am a changed man, I have come to speak to you about your immortal soul.' And thereupon, amidst the extreme surprise of the whole party, he opened his Bible at the 6th of St. Matthew, and warned them all from it against 'laying up treasures upon earth.' They listened to him with wonder and attention, and soon after allowed him to go in peace, the Zemindar remarking as he went, 'Well, after all, what he says is but the truth.'

"'After spending about two hours in examining the boys, we collected the members of the congregation for worship. My dear native brother, V. Devanayagam, had joined me here in the morning. After singing a hymn, and an extempore prayer, I proceeded to address them from Luke xiii. 23—30. I should have mentioned that the little church was quite filled, and that before our little meeting was broken up, eight or nine heathen people had taken their seats with the rest. I had been hardly speaking five minutes when one woman began to sob very violently. Then followed a violent shaking of the body, and a rolling of the eyes, with apparently much mental agony. Then, within ten minutes or so more, no less than six women and one boy were all shaking and sobbing, though not with the same violence and agony as the first woman. Every one appeared to be deeply solemnized. I found that I could not possibly proceed, and so sat down, and dear V. Devanayagam offered up prayer. To quiet and calm them who appeared so deeply afflicted, we began to read out the promises of God to sinners, and all became soon composed.'"

"Now just look at the altered state of affairs in this place, and then judge. First, the most unsatisfactory (and perhaps, in point of ability, the ablest) man in our district is converted. If the 'fruits of the Spirit' have ever been visible, they are so, I believe, in his case. Then his wife and daughters are converted. Then, that once stupid-looking boy, Royappen, has been converted, and his now bright and beaming face does one's heart good to look at it. Then, eight women of the congregation and two men have been visited by the strange influence, and appear now to be in the enjoyment of peace. Then, eight heathen have joined the little body. The verse of the Bible that was most prominent before my mind all day yesterday was—'And there was great joy in that city.' They seem to have only one thought, only one object to talk about. The Bible is now in their hands, and every one of them is furnished with a pencil to take down from your lips any text they may not have themselves alighted on before. If, in the joy and love and peace of these new-born babes, the impress of the blessed Spirit's work is not to be traced, I know not where we are to look for it. There is nothing extravagant about the whole matter. Perhaps in the woman to whom I have alluded above there may be. We have advised her for the present not to attend any meetings, where she might be liable to be excited. But she is the only case I have seen.

"I have much more to say on this wonderful work, but I have already gone on, I fear, too far. In going round amongst these dear people, I have felt myself somewhat like one in a trance. The feeling constantly on my mind was this, the fear lest by my own deadness and coldness I should throw a chill upon the blessed work. For nothing did I feel I had greater need to pray than that I might not be a hinderer by my very presence of all that was going on. I hope that God has ordered it otherwise. To Him be all the glory!"

On the 25th of the same month, the Rev. W. T. Satthianadhen wrote to Mr. Gray—

"Good news from Pattakulam.—Last night, whilst the people were engaged in prayer, several of them were struck down, thirteen cases in all—five women and eight men. A heathen, too, says the catechist, seems touched. One of these new-born babes, Masillamani is his name, is with me just now. Dear fellow, he looks quite altered. May the Lord graciously uphold them, and may this movement prove very salutary to the whole village!"

A second letter of Mr. Gray's, written from Thirnthangal, carries our information down to the 1st of June—

"Just one line or two to tell you how the work, which the Lord has graciously begun amongst us, is going on. On Wednesday evening last, a letter came to me from the Rev. W. T. Satthianadben, from which I extract the following—

"'About an hour after your cooly had left yesterday, Saravané Nadan came with glad tidings about the Rajapaliam congregation. During morning service at Somiapuram last Sunday (Whit-Sunday) many persons were touched, and they all cried out for mercy. Saravané said that the scene was very touching, and very extraordinary. There were eighteen cases in all, and it is very remarkable that the number was equally divided, that is to say, six belonged to Somiapuram, six to Veyalkattupatty, and six to Sevalpatty. Two of these were backsliders. With two exceptions they were women and children. I suppose you know Isaac, the son of Abraham of Sevalpatty, the most advanced boy in our school there. I hear he is a very remarkable case. He used to be very reserved, would hardly speak, but now he preaches to every one he meets, and prays beautifully. So said Saravané Nadan, and his statement was confirmed by Moses, who came in afterwards with the same happy intelligence. Of these eighteen cases, five are the children of our school at Rajapaliam. I am sure you will bless God for His continued goodness to us and our dear people, and pray that they may look up to the Saviour more fixedly, and that they may grow in grace, love, and holiness every day.'

"It is very singular that in no place have we felt more the need, for a long time past, of additional agency than in Rajapaliam. In that great town, comprising in itself a number of villages, with a teeming population of 10,000 people, we have had no agent but one schoolmaster, the man mentioned in the above extract. He has had for a considerable time past two congregations under his charge, from the three villages mentioned above, and also manages a school, one of the best in North Tinnevelly. Mr. Ragland and Mr. Fenn had often thought of making him a reader, but they had never been able to see sufficient evidence of a spiritual work in his heart, nor had he at all learning beyond that of the most common-place description. I always thought that he was an admirable teacher, whatever his attainments in knowledge might be. Every boy was in life and motion when he began to teach. I think now that there can be little doubt of the propriety of making him a reader. I might urge the same in favour of both Moses and Gnanamutta, whose cases you know. This is the most wonderful thing, as it strikes me, in this movement—God's dealings with our agents. Here has He given us four new-born men, of no common power, for the carrying on of his work amongst this people. It is truly remarkable. His name be praised! It may perhaps be better to wait for a little, and see how they get on before promoting them. But I think you will agree with me that, with their present zeal and ardour, they may better be given over to the work of direct preaching than to that of school teaching.

"The Rev. V. Devanayagam, on the same evening, wrote to me, that since the time I left Vageikulam, of which I told you, 'till yesterday, May 25, no new cases of conversion occurred; but yesterday evening, through God's mercy, four persons have been awakened.'

"I was very much delighted to hear of one of them. She was the wife of a young man whom I found in the district, on one of my late tours, and had designed to employ in some useful way. He had been in the Palamcotta Seminary, in Mr. Clark's time, and had left it under a cloud, which, however, has since been entirely cleared away. I found him speaking English pretty well, and reading it very nicely; and accordingly sent him and his wife to live at Vageikulam, under the Rev. V. Devanayagam's care, to try him, and see if he might not be employed as a schoolmaster. Thank God, his wife has been one of the newly-awakened. She had been, before this, a great obstacle in her husband's way, and had kept him very much back. I hope now she may be a real blessing to him.

"But I had no intention of writing at this length when I began. I just thought of mentioning the fact, as it had been told to]me, about the above cases. Let me remind you of our great meeting next week, (Tuesday, the 5th,) and ask your prayers. Macdonald came to us last Tuesday evening, and stays till the close of next week with us. He and Fenn are together now. They come in here on tomorrow night for Sunday."

The great meeting to which Mr. Gray refers is the periodical gathering of all the Missionaries, native clergy, catechists, and other agents at Palamcotta, when the wonderful narrative of the Lord's dealings in North Tinnevelly will be laid before this assembled body in the South. Can we not imagine the eager interest, the fervent prayers, the joyful thanksgivings, with which the rehearsal will be welcomed, and how, when they return to their work, the tidings will penetrate every village and congregation of our 37,000 Native Christians? "Then said they among the heathen, The Lord hath done great things for them. The Lord hath done great things for us, whereof we are glad."

And has not the Church at home her solemn duties herein also? Devout praise for the past is a plain and obvious obligation; but far more are strong and continual intercessions demanded to sustain our Missionary brethren in this arduous time of need, prayers that the work may not be hindered by our coldness or unbelief, supplications for a larger outpouring of the Holy Spirit than has even now been granted. We believe that the strengthening and spread of the great work depends mysteriously on the faithfulness and the expectation of the Church. There was a place where Jesus could do no mighty work because of their unbelief; and has not He said, "According to your faith, be it unto you?" We plead earnestly with the friends of Missions for their constant and believing prayers. If they give us these, we need not fear the lack of men or means to foster the great work to which an Almighty Hand is so manifestly and most graciously leading us.

CUSTOMS OF THE HINDUS AND MUSSULMANS OF INDIA.

(*Continued from page* 144.)

"CONTINUING our review of the Hindu customs, we come next to *deaths*. The rites and ceremonies which the Hindus consider essentially necessary on the occasion of the sickness and death of one of their caste, are, generally speaking, adhered to, as they believe that if they be neglected it will materially deteriorate the repose and well being of the soul after death; so, when one of their caste falls sick, if they believe the disease to be serious, they assemble round the bed, and pour some Ganges water down the patient's mouth; then they make him take a medicine called *rus*, which gives him a temporary renewal of physical power, and they endeavour to make him repeat as often as possible the name Ram Ram, and all his family continue singing the same. These all take place, only after the aid of the physician is considered hopeless. Afterwards they call a Brahmin, who brings with him a selection from the Shastras, which he reads in such a doleful, at the same time loud tone of voice, that it gives the poor sick sufferer great annoyance. They believe that, during this process, if the soul leaves the body—or, to use their own figurative language, 'the spirit leaves its tenement' —the exit will be unattended with pain, and easy. They always remove the person to the lowest apartment they can find, as they believe, that if he dies in a high room his spirit will certainly wander. They believe that if he were to die upon a *charpoy*, (bedstead), his spirit would become evil, so they always put him on the floor. Then, when they expect his death, they get some rice, and a sort of sweetmeat called *jullaybee*, and some money in coins, and leave them near him. A Brahmin gets some Gunga water, and puts into it his hand, and reads a verse from the Vedas to the following effect—'Oh God, may this man's death be happy.' The sweetmeats, the rice, and the coins are taken afterwards as presents by the Brahmins, to ensure the after happiness of the sufferer. When the breath has completely quitted the body, the family put a lamp in the corpse's hand, and make it move in the act of giving it to the Brahmin. If the death occurs after sunset, they leave the body till the next day; but if it occurs during the day, they begin the ceremonies an hour after death. From this arises the proverb so prevalent in the country, 'How long will ye weep for him that died in the evening?' because the weeping and lamentation, which is very violent, generally lasts about an hour only, and is similar to the *keening* which takes place in Ireland, and the death-song which Sir Walter Scott describes as taking place in the Highlands of Scotland. As such loud and bitter wailing cannot, with small effort, last very long, it is generally over in an hour; and, in the case of a person dying in the evening, the deathsong, which is supposed to last till the corpse leaves the house, could not be protracted during the night; so, as it must soon cease, the saying is applied to persons who indulge in unavailing tears. In case of its being a husband, the wife is bound to take off her *choorees*, or hand and feet ornaments, and her nose-ring, and, if she be well dressed, to take off her clothes also, and put on sorry apparel. Then all the male relatives assemble round the corpse, and begin making lamentation. They call to remembrance all the actions of the man's life, and praise him thereupon, and their weeping and sorrow are very great. The wife is not permitted to join in this, but is obliged to sit down disconsolate in a corner, with her head between her knees, and is neither permitted to speak or to weep. At this time, in some castes, all the male relatives of the deceased cut off their hair, their beard, and their moustache, but, generally speaking, only the eldest son does so; and this son, after having put on very fine white *dooties*, and lung a cloth over his shoulder, goes to some Brahmin, and tells him that he is ready for the taking away of the body. The Brahmin who performs this office is of the sort called Maha Brahmins. Then the Brahmin gets a water-pot that was never used, and some of the perfume called *chooa*, some sandal-wood, fresh flowers and twine, and makes a carpenter prepare a board. He then calls all the relatives, and having spread a white sheet over the board, they lay over it the corpse, which has been previously wrapt up in another sheet. If they can at all afford it, they buy a shawl and spread it over the body, wrapt up as it is. The eldest son fills the new water-pot with well-water, and gives it to a servant; then the relatives fasten bamboos to the board, or *charpoy*, and, taking it on their shoulders, go down to the Ganges: four are considered enough to bear this board, on which the corpse is mounted; but a long procession of relatives follow, making a great uproar, saying, *Ram Sutha*, 'He was true to God;' or, *Bola Ram*, 'He calls on God;' or, *Huri bol*, 'God calls him;' or some other expressions nearly to the same effect. On the way they stop at some place where there is a tree, and there they set down the corpse. There the eldest son takes the water-pot from the servant, and passes it round the head of the deceased, and throws it away and breaks it. Then the relatives take up the body and go to the Ganges. There they bathe it well, and, having purchased two rupees' worth of wood, they heap it up in the shape of a funeral pyre. The Maha Brahmin takes the shawl and board for his perquisites. The party then heap some more wood on the top of the body, and, having placed straw underneath, they burn it. They always leave the skull unburned, but the eldest son comes up with a large bamboo, and breaks it: life is considered then extinct, and the son throws the broken skull into the river. There is one extraordinary variation in these proceedings, which takes place in the event of the deceased having been a very old man or woman. It is, that when the relatives bear him or her to the grave, they go on with laughter, noise, and much glee, until they arrive at the river.

"The lowest order, when they cannot afford to buy wood, throw the bodies of their dead relatives into the river; and in Bengal it is common to see the people of the highest caste take their relatives who are dying down to the side of the river, and there leave them to die, or sometimes they will cover his face with the Ganges mud. After the skull has been thrown into the river all the family put on clean clothes, and having gone some paces from where the funeral pyre was made, they gather straws, and begin to break them. This denotes, in their opinion, that their connexion and ties with the deceased are now no more. Then they return, weeping, to their homes, and give the *charpoys* and bedclothes, and every-day raiment of the dead, to a man of the lowest class, a *hulal-khor*, and the greater part of his clothes they distribute among beggars, and the eldest son sits for thirteen days, with his head uncovered, in a solitary apartment, while all the family remain somewhere near at hand, giving him comfort. They burn a lamp day and night, and keep it burning beside him; and on the second day all the relatives assemble and give the widow clothes and money. On the thirteenth day the eldest son may rise and perform his usual business, and the women of the family all assemble and make lamentation, generally for thirteen days. Their incessant and absorbing grief is extraordinary to Europeans or civilized people. It reminded me frequently of the description which Homer gives of the women who were Andromache's handmaidens, after the parting of Hector—

'Αμφιπόλους τῇσιν δὲ γόον πάσῃσιν ἐνῶρσεν.

There is one caste whose women grieve for one year after the death of a husband. There is another who continue it for six months. In all the castes, six months after the man is dead, the family get a fine well-made bedstead, a carpet, five brass vessels, and five changes of clothes, and give them to their guru, or family priest; and on the day of the year after the man's death they give a feast to a number of Brahmins and all his relatives. On every succeeding anniversary they perform what is called a *sradh*, which consists in offering rice and fruits to the manes of their ancestors, and they end the day by an entertainment to Brahmins and relatives. These *sradhs* also take place frequently at pilgrimages.

"The belief which this extraordinary people entertain with regard to what passes to the soul, after it has quitted this life, is as follows— They believe, that when a very excellent soul dies, he goes to paradise (a place which they designate by the name of Byecunth), a place of the greatest luxury and pleasure, abounding in every sort of luxury, and having every gratification which can please the senses. He will there abide for a length of time, and as soon as that period has elapsed, he shall afterwards become incarnate as a man. That then, if he continue in the same good character as that which he originally had, he will not again be sent to paradise, or become incarnate, but be actually resolved into nonentity, and become part of the divine essence, and the particles of his frame shall evaporate into air. But if the person who dies be not a devotee, or any exemplary character, that he will be allowed some time in paradise, and then will be obliged to go to hell, to expiate his transgressions : or even if the saint who was first sent to paradise come from hence to earth, and at his second incarnation be an offender, that he will have to go to hell for a short time. Hell is described as a place beneath the earth, where there are all sorts of fire and torments, and the worst hell is called *Gore-Nirruk*. They believe that its surface is iron, and the atmosphere fire, and that the pain inflicted upon mortals is most cruel; that a longer or shorter continuance there will take place with men, according to the flagrancy of their offences; but that, after this penance in hell, they will become incorporated or resolved into divine essence; that those who, at their first birth, have been pious, but not invariably so, are to become spirits after their death; but this state is held less in estimation than that of being replaced into *Eshur*, as they call the divine essence; but that those who have been great offenders are to become incarnate as animals of all kinds, or as living creatures of every sort—birds, beast, fish, reptile, or insect : that the character of the man is to determine whose body he is to be reproduced in; as, for instance, if a man be malicious without cause, he will first be reproduced as a snake, and that they must go through 84,000 changes, and then become men again : that the change previous to that of becoming a man is a bull, and for this reason, all through India, this animal is held in great reverence. When they then become men, they have a second probation, and may fit themselves for paradise, or for the other places, according to their deserts.

"The Hindu beggars, or travelling mendicants, are held in great repute, and the people of that persuasion are in the habit of giving them large sums. The first, or most honourable class, are called the *Sunyassees*. They are known by their long hair, which they let grow, and never clip. They live mostly in the jungles, and wear usually a long necklace of wooden beads, which they tell with their fingers, and, in doing so, repeat the name of Ram-Ram. This is called the *Mala Jupna*. They are the people most frequently in the habit of making the various pilgrimages, viz. to Juggurnath, for the purpose of *durshun*, that is, viewing it; to Preag, or Allahabad, for the purpose of bathing there; to Buddinath, where there is supposed to be a god and a river, the sight of which two objects is considered as conferring a right to happiness; to Gyagee, where there are many idols; to Dwarkanath, Benares, and Himalaya.

"The second class are the *Nánuks*, who usually live like hermits, and wear coloured clothes, and bathe daily in the Ganges, and they are reckoned well skilled in devotional beggary, and they instruct young mendicants in the same line.

"The third class are the *Byragees*, whose head and bodies are streaked with red sandal wood. These are not learned, but are usually great recluses. They generally live by the side of rivers, and do not take so much care as to the rites of bathing and other superstitions which the other Hindus usually practise.

"The fourth sort are the *Gosayens*, who are very learned, and they call themselves *dervishes*: they will usually transact any worldly business consistent with a high-caste man.

"The fifth sort are the *Jogees*, who will inflict upon themselves all manner of torture. They are always worshippers of Mahadev, and when they meet any one they may be known by calling out *bum bum, Mahadev.* (This expression is, however, used by all those who go to Allahabad on a pilgrimage, and who are called *Kowruttees*). They generally cover the whole body with white ashes, so that its surface, as well as their face, may be concealed. The *Jogees* often kindle a fire in the hottest weather, and hold their hands over it.

"The sixth are called *Tuppusees*, who are voluntary self-tormentors. These, in the coldest season, go into the river, and stand in it the whole day up to their necks. Sometimes, in the hot season, they will stand out in the sun all day, or else kindle a fire as the *Jogees* do.

"The seventh sort are the *Nanukphuttees*, who let their beard and hair grow. The last they let fall on their back as long as a woman's. They support nature upon what they receive, being the voluntary contribution of the pious. They work not, but stay in their own houses all day, praying to their gods. When one of them meets another he says *Wah-Goorw*. These are all respected, and generally belong to high castes; and they make more by their begging than any people in the country.

"After these, class those who are not of the highest order; but the first seven are very much respected.

"The eighth sort: the *Digumburs*. These wear filthy clothes, and live in the most miserable villages. Thus the proverb goes, 'What use is a washerman in a village of *Digumburs?*'

"The ninth sort are called the *Nagas*, and these never on any occasion wear any clothes or integuments of any kind. They have their heads and beards closely shaven. They are very courageous, and their combats, in which they engage on all occasions, are on the subject of religion.

"The tenth sort are the *Primhans*, who run about the country like mad people. These conduct themselves like idiots or insane, but are the more, for that reason, held in reverence. No one will injure them, but the public are always giving them food.

"The eleventh sort, the *Suthurshaees*, who wear a long black rope twisted round their heads, and a necklace of black rope, called the *Selee*, which is divided into three strings, and they carry two sticks, of about a foot and a half long, in their hands, which they strike perpetually, and get from each shopkeeper, as they pass, some alms. They are always marching about from one city to another.

"The twelfth sort are called *Aghorees*. These are an unclean and disgusting class of wretches, who eat filth and ordure, and stand before shopkeepers' doors to induce them to give them alms. They disgust so much, that people generally pay them to get rid of their nauseous presence.

"These are the names of the classes of mendicants who are generally recognised in the country; but there are others who belong to no particular order, and yet who ply no unprofitable vocation by asking alms from all.

THE GREAT WALL OF CHINA.

MISSIONARY DEDUCTIONS FROM THE PARABLES.

(Continued from p. 175.)

The ground, hard and unyielding, broken up by the action of the plough, becomes fitted for the reception of the seed. So it is with the field of the world, the human element in which the divine word is to be sown. Man in his prosperity is indisposed to hear. Afflictions, sent before to prepare the way, break up the ground, and at length the sowing time commences.

We indicated, in our last Number, one region which is passing through this suffering period.

In another direction we see heavy calamities impending over a nation which has dealt superciliously with the Gospel. In recent articles, China has been referred to. Our object was, to show, that in our intercourse with the Chinese we had committed wrongs; and now, as the result of our unhappy proceedings, find ourselves involved in a war, concerning which no one can predict, even if satisfactorily conducted to the humiliation of the Chinese, and the triumph of our arms, that it will yield to us any permanent benefit; but which has already committed us to an expenditure of not less than £6,000,000. Indeed, such is the nature of this embroglio, that our victory may prove our greatest embarrassment. We may find ourselves in the same position with Sir Michael Seymour after his attack on the Takou forts had put them *hors de combat*. It was impossible to fight any longer, simply because there was no one to fight with, save masses of unarmed people, who proceeded to embarrass our authorities with acts of kindness, and disarm them by obsequiousness. As the victorious gun-boats advanced up the waters, which for the first time were ploughed by a foreign keel, "entire populations turned out and saluted them with profound and reverential obeisances." If any of the officers ventured to land, they were forthwith assaulted with earnest importunities that the English should come and reign over them—"Hail, O king! Welcome great King! be thou our Emperor: come thou and reign over us." Provisions of all kinds were brought and money in return refused. On reaching Tien-tsin the way was blocked up by an Imperial decree—"We commend Kweiliang, chief Secretary of State, and Hwashana, president of the board of civil office, to go by post route to the port of Tien-tsin, for the investigation and despatch of business. Respect this." As Mr. Oliphant naively observes, "With any other nation one would have supposed that the capture of the forts at the mouth of one of its rivers, and its subsequent ascent by a hostile force, would have called forth a warlike demonstration, instead of a civil commission." But we do not know the Chinese. They are wiser than we think. They can bend to circumstances. They had already essayed the one, and found it would not answer; they now availed themselves of the other, and found it more successful. We received, as the recompense of our labours, a treaty which, like a bad bill, has been accepted, but never honoured. When presented for payment, we received our answer at the mouth of the Peiho.

We have now, in conjunction with France, sent out another and more powerful expedition. The forts at Takou will be knocked to pieces; the Tartar forces, after a short resistance, will disperse like a flock of sheep. We shall not stop this time at Tien-tsin: an advance on Pekin will be decided upon. Perhaps it may be defended; more likely we shall be met, as at Tien-tsin, with cries of "Welcome, O Emperor, come and reign over us!".

We shall find ourselves masters of China's capital, and the penetralia of the Kin Ching open to us. But what shall we do then? The Emperor is gone, and all his court with him. We must follow him beyond the great wall. In fact, at Pekin we shall find him as inaccessible as when we were at Canton. But what course shall we pursue? The permanent occupation of Pekin? But how shall we preserve order amidst its two millions of inhabitants? The removal of the Emperor, will be the dissolution, for the time being, of all social order. The native authorities will become invisible, and the native police cease to act. Gangs of desperadoes will begin to plunder, and the European military have to do police duty. Meanwhile, Pekin is not a port like Canton; nor is it self-supporting. Its provisions are supplied from the southern provinces, or from the flocks reared in the northern parts of Chih-li. These supplies will be arrested. The streams will be cut off. How long shall we persist in our occupation of Pekin? The Tartars will let us keep it, rather than give free access to the palace and person of the Emperor. How long shall we be able to do so? Shall we accept at last another treaty, and trust to the good faith of the Chinese to observe it, when our ships and soldiers—such of them as survive—come back to England?

The tone, then, of the recent debate in the Commons House of Parliament is not surprising. On both sides of the house there was but one opinion respecting this war. Mr. Sidney Herbert, on moving the vote of credit, said " that he would not enter upon the policy of the present Chinese war, except to say that he believed we could not enter upon a more ruinous war." The Chancellor of the Exchequer declared, "I cannot venture to hold out any expectations, now that we have reason to believe the war has actually broken out, with regard to the limits or amount of the demand which may be made on the House, or the period when those hostilities happily may be brought to a termination. I trust and pray that it may be at an early period. I trust we shall listen to the lesson taught us by these transactions." And what is that lesson? The Right Hon. Gentleman informs us. " I confess the lesson I draw is this, that it is impossible to check proceedings of this kind, growing out of transactions such as the deplorable events at the mouth of the Peiho, when once they begin. What you should really look to is the mode of conducting your ordinary communications with such distant powers, and the responsibility under which they are conducted. It is an extremely dangerous system of policy that sends forth treaties to be exchanged at the sword's point and at the cannon's mouth." It is indeed to be hoped, that as a nation we shall not fail to learn that lesson, although we are paying dearly for our experience. Again, Sir John Pakington confessed, " We cannot regard our present position with respect to China with too much anxiety. It is not only that beyond all question serious doubts have long been entertained, and are at this moment entertained, with regard to the whole justice and propriety of our policy; it is not only that we are now asked to embark in what, to use the popular phrase of the day, is a gigantic expenditure; but, unhappily, in addition to all this, at a moment when we ought to have our resources of all kinds concentrated at home."

The truth is, that the idiosyncracy of the Chinese, the peculiarities of their governmental system, its exclusiveness and intense ceremonialism, have not been fully understood. And it is in this way that national complications arise. The customs of a people are not sufficiently understood; and we forget that points which appear to us to be intensely ridiculous and unnecessarily obstructive, have been consecrated by a lengthened antiquity, and are regarded by those who have received them from their forefathers as matters of the utmost moment, to be adhered to at any cost and with the most unalterable tenacity. We think it unreasonable in the native that he will not yield a custom which, from our standpoint, appears absurd and barbarous: but the native considers it just as unreasonable in us to expect that he should do so. Hence arise misunderstanding and collisions.

It has been so in a great measure on the coast of China.

We shall so far revert to the proceedings along the coast as to place this point prominently before our readers. On the 10th February 1858, the blockade having been raised and trade resumed, the Plenipotentiaries of the two belligerent powers, England and France, and of the two neutral powers, Russia and the United States, resolved on uniting in an earnest and peaceable appeal to the Court of Pekin for a redress of grievances and a revision of treaties. Shanghae was selected in the first instance as the place for negotiation, and thither a Chinese Plenipotentiary, invested with full powers, was invited to be sent. Lord Elgin's letter to Yu, the senior Secretary of State, enumerated the points on which he was prepared to require concession; and, amongst others, these especially—" A resident Minister at or near the Court, and a more extended intercourse throughbout the country." The Taoutai, or Intendant, of Shanghae being absent, it was resolved that the letters of the Plenipotentiaries should be delivered to Chaou, the Governor of Kiangsu, in person, and that the French and English officers who were charged with this duty should proceed to Soo-chow for this purpose. In 1854, the American Commissioner, Mr. Lane, had made a similar attempt, but was prevented from entering the city, having been met by the Governor outside the city walls. On this occasion the Europeans were more successful, the adoption of an unusual water route enabling them to evade the obstructive courtesies of Chaou, and to push within the city walls, despite of the frantic gesticulations of the officials. Oliphant's description of this scene is highly graphic and amusing—

"We appeared so suddenly before the water-gate called 'Foomun,'" that the officials, had they wished it, would scarcely have had time to shut it. However, they contented themselves with making the most frantic gesticulations and expressive signs to us to turn back; but we put on an air of the most obtuse stolidity, and pushed vehemently on; my boat, which happened to be leading, carrying away in a hurry some of the grille which formed part of the gate. Once in the city, we did not venture on an exploration of the lanes of water, which, like those of Venice, opened up in divers directions, but moored at once in the retired spot under the walls. We were not long, however, left in quiet. Almost immediately a dense crowd collected on both sides of the canal, deeply interested in the proceedings of the barbarians. Whenever any of us moved from one boat to another, a general titter of astonishment and curiosity was heard; but they manifested no semblance of dislike or hostility towards us, and were infinitely more respectable in their behaviour than an English mob would have been under similar circumstances.

"We had not been long moored here, before the 'Foo,' a blue-button mandarin, came with a message from the Governor to Mr. Lay, who was an old acquaintance of his, requesting to see him at the west gate. In about two hours this gentleman returned with the welcome intelligence that the Governor would receive us at his yamun in the centre of the city, and would immediately send down chairs for us to a neighbouring wharf. Accordingly we proceeded, the same afternoon, to the appointed place, the whole party, with the exception of M. de Contades and myself, being in uniform. We were received at the wharf by a guard of soldiers, and were accompanied by them during our progress in chairs through the city. We thus traversed a distance of about two miles. The streets throughout were lined with spectators; the windows, house-tops, and bridges were thronged with an eager and excited populace, who gazed with the most extraordinary earnestness at probably the first barbarians they had ever seen in their lives. So wrapt in contemplation of these unknown specimens of humanity were the audience-hall, and seated M. de Contades and myself on the raised estrade which usually forms the centre of a semicircle of chairs on these occasions, and is considered the seat of honour. The Governor himself took a seat to our right, which, in this land of ceremonies, was considered an additional compliment, inasmuch as the further you are to the left of your host, the more highly honoured is your position.

"We went on to inform his Excellency that we were the bearers of notes to the Prime Minister Yu, from the four Powers, which were of the utmost importance, and which, we trusted, he would lose no time in forwarding, as delay in their transmission might seriously compromise the interests of the empire. The covering despatch to himself he opened and read, a crowd of attendants collecting round him, and making themselves acquainted with its contents over his shoulder. As we desired that the whole proceeding should be invested with as much publicity as possible, this mode of conducting business, though rather unusual in western diplomacy, was quite in accordance with our wishes."*

Thus to Chaou, in his own yamun, the despatches were delivered. We may well conceive, that notwithstanding his dignified courtesy, he must have felt no little uneasiness on this occasion—a feeling which was no doubt imparted to the higher authorities at Pekin. There were these barbarians: they had just stormed Canton, and had made a prisoner of Yeh. And now, in a most unusual way, in utter contempt of all prescribed usages, they had forwarded a letter to Pekin, containing an unheard-of requirement, that within the sacred city—one honoured by the in-dwelling of the Emperor himself—a barbarian official should have his residence. How troublesome these barbarians had become; how exorbitant in their demands; what might they not next require! And if their demands were not complied with, they had ships of war and troops; and the coercive measures pursued at Canton would, in all probability, be put in force elsewhere. What course, then, would

capital and the coast, the right of entrance to Europeans belonging to his suite, and the transit of messengers to and fro, was a blow aimed at the very heart and citadel of Chinese formalism, the surrender of which could not be contemplated without horror. Already the Russian Minister had applied for admission to Pekin by way of Kiahkta, and, on being refused, proceeded, on his own responsibility, to the mouth of the Peiho, where he was informed that no communication with the Court could be made on his behalf from that point. Eventually, however, his letter was forwarded, and answered by a decided refusal to see him at Pekin, with an intimation, that under no circumstances could the "kotow" be dispensed with. Such was the reply to Russia, whose relations with the Court of Pekin have always been such as to attain the object in view without having recourse to coercion. Is it surprising that the advances of the European officials to free and friendly intercourse were more rudely repelled? The imperial answer was addressed, not to the Plenipotentiaries, but to the authorities of the two kiangs. It required that these barbarian innovators on Chinese customs should return to Canton, and there submissively await the imperial communication through the medium of Hwang, the new Governor.

This was not the first time that the idea of an embassy to Pekin had been entertained by us; and the experience of the past, had we recurred to it, might have served to remind us of the difficulties which English Ambassadors to that Court have had to endure, and how devoid these expensive undertakings proved to be of any practical advantage.

Lord Macartney's expedition left England in September 1792. Trade grievances had arisen at Canton, which, it was hoped, might be rectified by an embassy to Pekin. A British Ambassador, it was thought, "would be a new spectacle, and his mission a compliment that would probably be well received. Upon general reasoning it appeared that every motive of policy or commerce, which led to the maintenance of ministers from Great Britain at European Courts, and even in Turkey, applied with equal strength to a similar establishment, if practicable, at Pekin."* Such a connexion, it was thought, would tend to put the British trade to China upon a less precarious and more advantageous footing. "The Court of Pekin was understood to be guided by maxims peculiar to itself, being averse to a promiscuous intercourse with foreign states, and inclined, in some measure, to consider its subjects as placed in the vale of happiness, where it was wise to seclude them from a profane admixture with other men." It was therefore the more desirable that there be resident at Pekin "a succession of British subjects, whose cautious conduct and courteous manners would be calculated to gain the esteem of the upper, and the respect of the lower classes of the Chinese, and thus by dissipating their prejudices and conciliating their goodwill, induce confidence."

On the 5th of August 1793, the Ambassador and his suite, with the presents for the Emperor, entered the Peiho, passing the town of Takoo, where large covered barges and boats of burden adapted to the shallows of the river, had been provided to convey them to the capital. Every courtesy was shown them en route, "provisions of various kinds were purchased in abundance, the Emperor charging himself with all expenses." Care was, however, taken, as the fleet advanced, to announce the strangers as coming from afar to pay a compliment to the celestial Emperor, and the impression thus made, that they were tributaries proceeding to Pekin to render homage, was confirmed on the first interview between the Viceroy and the Ambassador, in a pavilion at Tien-tsin. "The Viceroy conducted the Ambassador, with the principal gentlemen, into the pavilion, at the upper end of which was a darkened recess or sanctuary, where the majesty of the Emperor was supposed to be continually residing," and to that majesty it was signified that a respectful obeisance should be paid, "which, however singular, was performed by a profound inclination of the body."

At the time of the Ambassador's arrival, the Emperor was at Zhehol, in Tartary, whither the Ambassador was expected to proceed. At Tong-choo-foo, twelve miles from the capital, where the river ceases to be navigable, the embassy disembarked, proceeding in sedans, on horses, and in waggons, along a road, the centre of which was paved with flags of granite to the width of about twenty feet, an unpaved road of considerable breadth extending on either side of it. Advancing through the eastern suburb of Pekin, our countrymen at length arrived before the city walls, where, at a resting-place within the gate, refreshments had been prepared. The walls were about forty feet high, having no regular embrasures, but, in the merlons, loopholes for archery. They were flanked on the outside by square towers, about sixty yards distant from each other, and projecting from the curtain between them forty or fifty feet. The street

* "Macartney's Embassy to China," vol. i. p. 20.

into which they were introduced was above one hundred feet wide, flanked by houses in general only one story high, and none of them exceeding two stories. Along this they proceeded until they reached the eastern wall of the imperial palace, called the yellow wall, from the colour of the varnished tiles on its summit and that of the public buildings within. On reaching the yellow wall the embassy turned along it to the right, until they reached its northern side, when, resuming the westward direction, they advanced through the Tartar city, until, passing through the western-gates, they emerged into the western suburb, and reached at last the Emperor's villa of Yuen-min-yuen, assigned as the head-quarters of the embassy.

Scarcely had he been installed in his new abode, than the Tartar legate, a man of unconciliatory deportment and prejudiced against the English, began to press the Ambassador on the vital point, the "kotow." The Emperor considers himself as the representative of the gods, and expects to be honoured with the same prostrations. He who would be introduced into the imperial presence, must be prepared to render the kotow; he must kneel and strike his head on the ground, thrice kneeling and nine times knocking the head. Lord Macartney had already borne with patience the flags pendent from the yachts and land carriages, having inscribed upon them, in large Chinese characters, "Ambassadors bearing tribute from the country of England." Now, a still greater humiliation was required from him, a refusal to comply with which would deprive the embassy, carried out at so great cost, of all advantageous results. He resolved, therefore, to try and compromise the matter, and declared himself willing to comply with the prescribed forms, provided that one of the officers of the Chinese court, his equal in rank, "should perform before His Britannic majesty's picture at large, in his royal robes, and then in the Ambassador's possession at Pekin, the same ceremonies which should be performed by the Ambassador before the throne of His Imperial Majesty." The proposed compromise was a modest one. The Ambassador was

Above twenty miles from the capital the country began to rise into hills, the roads becoming increasingly steep and rough, and the scenery presenting a pleasing and romantic aspect. On the morning of the fourth day's journey, a prominent line, or narrow and unequal mark, was observed along the mountain's sides. Soon it assumed the form of a wall with battlements: it was the great wall of China. There it was, "carried along the ridges of hills, over the tops of the highest mountains, descending into the deepest valleys, crossing upon arches over rivers; doubled and trebled in many parts to take in important passes, and interspersed with towers and massy bastions at almost every hundred yards, and as far as the eye could reach." Perhaps, while we write, Tartar reinforcements are pressing forward through the narrow defiles which the gates and towers were designed to defend. The wall, with its multiplied defences and concentric works, is now useless. A danger which the ancient Emperors of China never contemplated now threatens the Emperor's throne. It is not from the lakes and forests of Manchuria that the peril comes; not from the steppes of Mangolia. It is from the sea-coast the empire is assaulted. The barbarian war-ships are again there, and the advanced guard of a disciplined host is already threatening Tien-tsin. Perhaps even now bands of wild warriors are pressing forward to the mighty gathering, which, at the Emperor's command, is occupying the vast plain before Pekin, prepared to strike one stroke for an antiquated dynasty, which, through an obstinate adherence to effete usages, has at length brought destruction upon itself.

As the embassy advanced beyond the great wall into the northern portions of the Chih-li province, the season became cooler, the road more rugged, the mountains less richly clothed with timber, while the inhabitants of the villages, dispersed among the valleys, were found to be afflicted with the goitre. At length, the mountains receding somewhat from each other, disclosed the valley of Zhehol, with the palace or seat of grateful coolness, and its pleasure grounds, designated, in Chinese phraseology,

empire; and one of them is the Li Pu, or Board of Rites, "which has the regulation of the etiquette to be observed at Court on all occasions, on congratulatory attendances, in the performance of official duties, &c., also the regulation of dresses, caps, &c., as to the figure, size, colour, and nature of their fabrics and ornaments; of carriages and riding accoutrements, their form, &c., with the number of followers and insignia of rank. It has also the direction of the entire ceremonial of personal intercourse between the various ranks of peers, minutely defining the number of bows and degree of attention which each is to pay to the other when meeting in official capacities, according as they are on terms of equality or otherwise. It has also to direct the forms of their written official intercourse, including those to be observed in addresses and from foreign states," &c. Ceremonialism at the Court of Pekin is reduced, therefore, to a science: it has its precedents which may be appealed to, and its regulations fixed as the laws of the Medes and Persians. Its nucleus is in the person of the Emperor, and from thence it extends itself through all gradations of society. Indeed, the homage rendered to the Emperor, on certain special occasions, becomes confessedly religious adoration. On his birth-day "the princes, tributaries, Ambassadors, great officers of state, and principal mandarins, were assembled in a vast hall, and, upon particular notice, were introduced into an inner building, bearing at least the semblance of a temple. It was chiefly furnished with great instruments of music, among which were sets of cylindrical bells, suspended in a line from ornamented frames of wood, and gradually diminishing in size from one extremity to the other, and also triangular pieces of metal arrayed in the same order as the bells. To the sound of these instruments a slow and solemn hymn was sung by eunuchs, who had such command over their voices as to resemble the effect of musical glasses at a distance. During the performance, and at particular signals, nine times repeated, all the officials prostrated themselves nine times, except the Ambassador and his suite, who made a profound obeisance. But he whom it was meant to honour, continued, as if it were in imitation of the Deity, invisible the whole time."

The English Ambassador found himself pressed in every possible way to follow the example of the Chinese officials, and to kotow the Emperor as the representative of the gods. At length it was agreed to accept from him an obeisance, "such as he was in the habit of paying to his own sovereign." A spacious and magnificent tent, supported by gilded pillars, was pitched in the palace garden. The interview was to take place at daylight. The Emperor was to break upon the eyes of his expectant subjects as the rising sun, and gladden them with his august presence and favour. Some of the courtiers had been waiting in the gardens all the night. Soon after daylight he appeared from behind a high and perpendicular mountain, skirted with trees as if from a sacred grove, seated in a triumphal car, borne by sixteen men, accompanied and followed by guards, officers of the household, high flag and umbrella-bearers, and music, and preceded by a number of persons busied in proclaiming aloud his virtues and his power. Ascending the throne provided for him, the tributaries and great officers of the state being ranged in their respective places, the Chinese Emperor was prepared to receive the homage of England's representative. The Ambassador, instructed by the president of the tribunal of rites, held the large and magnificent square box of gold, adorned with jewels, in which was enclosed His Majesty's letter to the Emperor, between both hands lifted up above his head, "and in that manner, ascending the few steps that led to the throne, and bending on one knee, presented the box, with a short address to his Imperial Majesty." Little doubt can be entertained as to the interpretation put on this proceeding by the Chinese and Tartar princes around: it was the "Ambassador of England presenting tribute to the Chinese Emperor." The president of the board of rites had dispensed with the kotow, because it was evident that the English nobleman would not submit to it, but he substituted another form, in which the supremacy of China's Emperor appeared to be just as clearly recognised.

Soon after the Ambassador's return to Pekin, he was summoned to the great hall of audience, that he might receive the Emperor's answer to the letter of the King of England.

"The Ambassador, however indisposed at the time, was unwilling to fail to the appointment, and set out, properly attended, in a short time, to the palace, to which he passed through a considerable part of the Tartar city. The palace is encompassed by a high wall, within which he was conducted through spacious courts, along canals of stagnant water, and over bridges of granite, with balustrades of marble, to the foot of the hall, where he found the Emperor's answer contained in a large roll covered with yellow silk, and placed in a chair of state, hung with curtains of the same colour. It was afterwards carried in form up the middle of three flight of stairs, while the Colao and others who had hitherto stood by it, and the Ambassador and his suite, went up the side steps to the hall, a single structure, surrounded by many others, itself of great size and magnificence, though built of wood upon a foundation of granite, and decorated withinside and without with gilding, and in the happiest disposition of the most pleasing and vivid colours. The answer was placed in the midst of the hall, from whence it was afterwards to be sent to his Excellency's hotel.

"At this time came likewise several chests of presents from the Emperor to His Majesty, containing specimens, no doubt of the best kind, of the different articles of the produce and manufactures of the empire. Other presents came also for the Ambassador and all the persons of his suite; and the attention of His Imperial Majesty in giving some small token of his beneficence to the meanest servant who was present, was extended even to persons then absent, in the instance of all the common men, as well as officers of the ships which had brought the embassy to China."*

Soon after, intimations were given that it was time for the embassy to depart. It was suggested to the Ambassador that "the Chinese had no other idea of an embassy, than that of a visit with presents on some solemn festival, and to last only during the continuance of the latter; that accordingly, of the many embassies sent to them in the past and present century, none of them were suffered to pass that period; that in the present reign, the Ambassador of the Portuguese, the most favoured nation, was dismissed in thirty-nine days; that the Chinese had little notion of entering into treaties with foreign countries; but whatever business might be desirable to transact with them, must, after a favourable foundation for it, laid by the compliment of an embassy, be afterwards prosecuted to effect by slow degrees, for that much might be obtained from them by time and management, but nothing suddenly. That such was the nature and practice of the Chinese Government; that however adverse in the beginning to any new propositions, lest it should be surprised into undue concessions, or any improper regulation, the same matters might be brought again, when the offensive novelty of the idea was over, into a more serious and dispassionate consideration; that this even might be accelerated by the means of letters sent from one sovereign to the other by the annual ships, which might be done without impropriety, now that the communication had been opened between them in a fit manner."†

But meanwhile, what business had been transacted, or what advantages obtained for the English merchant on the coast? What well-considered measures had been decided upon, which might prevent unhappy collisions, and consolidate peaceful relations? Nothing of this kind had been attained. No opportunity of transacting business had presented itself. The whole procedure, with its cost, dangers, and discomforts, issued in one conclusion—which it would have been well to have remembered in future dealings with the Chinese—that intercourse with the Emperor may be maintained more intimately and under more favourable circumstances, than by an Ambassador resident in the middle of the Imperial Court.

The next embassy was that of Lord Amherst's. It arrived off the Peiho in August 1816, and proceeded up the river to Tungchau, and from thence to Pekin, the eastern gate of which was reached at midnight. The strangers in this inhospitable land—for so far it had proved to be such—had been assured that it would be kept open for them. Instead of this it was found closed, and their conductors, turning to the right, began skirting the city wall on the outside. Yet the lateness of the hour did not repress the insatiable curiosity of the Chinese, who had provided themselves with multitudes of little paper lanterns, which were very unceremoniously thrust towards the persons of the English, who at length, in self-defence, were obliged to seize one or two of the offenders, and extinguish their lamps. Entering one of the western gates, they found themselves on the high road to Yuen ming yuen, but so slow was the pace at which they advanced, that day had dawned before they reached their destination. But new fatigues and discomforts awaited them.

"It had evidently been the intention of the mandarins to separate as many of the party as possible from the Ambassador and the Commissioners, in order to effect what now, for the first time, appeared to be the object of hurrying us forward during the whole night. The carriage was conducted beyond Hai-tien, to the immediate vicinity of the imperial residence, and as soon as it stopped, (which was before five o'clock in the morning,) Kwang Tajin made his appearance, and requested the inmates to alight. The Ambassador naturally desired to be conducted to his hotel or lodging; but to the astonishment of all the English assembled, several of whom had by this time collected round the carriage, the mandarins very earnestly urged their immediate proceeding, for a short time, to a conference with Duke Ho. The party then were conducted to an apartment on the other side of the court, before which the carriage had stopped. Here the whole truth broke upon them at once. From the great number of mandarins, in their full dresses of ceremony, including princes of the blood, wearing their circular badges, it became evident that this was the moment of an imperial audience; and that the Ambassador and Commissioners had been inveigled by the most unworthy artifices, and the most indecent haste, to be carried before the Emperor in their present unprepared state. They were presently informed that His Majesty had changed the day of audience from to-morrow to this day, and that Duke Ho was waiting to conduct them at once into his presence.

"The Ambassador pleaded, that without his credentials, and the letter he was charged with from his sovereign, this was impossible; requesting at the same time that it might be stated he was ill from the effects of the journey, and required some rest. Duke Ho presently appeared in person, and urged his lordship to proceed direct to the Emperor, who was waiting to give him audience. It was in vain that every argument was repeated; the Duke's earnestness only seemed to increase with opposition, until he at length forgot himself so far as to gripe his lordship's arm violently, while one of the yellow-girdles stepped up at the same time. The Ambassador immediately shook them off, and behaved with great dignity and composure at this trying moment; telling the officer of the guard, that no swords must be drawn. The highest indignation was naturally expressed, and a fixed determination to proceed to no audience in such a manner. The party at length retired, with the appearance of an understanding that the audience should take place on the morrow, as before agreed upon. The Emperor's physician was soon after despatched to see His Excellency.

"The crowd of mandarins had in the meanwhile displayed a very indifferent specimen of their court breeding, by crowding upon the English party, and examining their persons and dress with the most unceremonious curiosity, and another strange scene took place as the Ambassador was quitting the room; for when the crowd of idlers, spurred on by their inquisitiveness, pressed on in such a manner as to impede the doorway, Duke Ho snatched a whip, with which he belaboured them handsomely on all sides. The courtly appendage (some of them with yellow girdles) dispersed like a flock of sheep. When His Excellency reached our intended dwelling, they crowded, in like manner, into the large room, and peeped through the windows of his private apartments, making holes with their fingers in the coloured-paper windows; but when the Ambassador entreated some of our party to clear the place of these intruders, they fled out at the entrance the moment they perceived in what a summary mode the writ of ejectment was about to be served on them.

"On first returning to us at Hai-tien, His Excellency told us that he had successfully resisted the violent conduct of the Chinese, but it was impossible to say what they might do next. Shortly afterwards, it was intimated to us by Chang that the Emperor was in a towering passion, and that we were to go back directly to Tungchau. This certainly was a barbarous, not to say brutal measure, considering that we had only just arrived from a most fatiguing night journey; but I was not altogether sorry to hear the announcement. Whatever might have been the opinion of one or two persons on the subject of the ceremony, there could be no difference of sentiment on the present occasion. The insult offered had been so gross, and so completely developed the disposition of the Pekin Court, as to make it evident that we were to expect nothing in the way of favours. In the meanwhile, a most elegant repast was served up by way of breakfast, consisting of the greatest delicacies, and some really fine grapes and other fruit, laid out on porcelain of the richest description. This formed a singular contrast with our bait of the preceding night in the stable-yard, and the difference between our treatment, when *in* and *out* of favour, was remarkable. A mandarin from the 'general of the nine gates' (a sort of prætorian prefect) came to hasten our departure, saying that 'a million of men obeyed his orders.'

"When the baggage, of which very little had been unloaded, was ready, we set off on our return at four in the afternoon, nearly in the same manner as we had come, except that the Ambassador's carriage was given up to the sick, and chairs used instead. The daylight in the early part of our journey enabled us to take a good view of the lofty walls of Pekin as we skirted them, and some of the party provided themselves with fragments of the blue bricks which compose it. When darkness came on our miseries commenced, and I may safely say that I never passed so wretched a night, except perhaps the one immediately preceding."*

A period of some forty years appears to have obliterated the remembrance of these untoward circumstances. Experience might have served to convince us, that to send an Ambassador to Pekin is to place him in a position of all others the most humiliating, in which he finds himself entangled, in the complicated meshes of Court formalism, powerless for good, and exposed to the superciliousness of ignorant mandarins. It was again however, introduced into our negotiations, and the residence of our Ambassador at Pekin came again to be regarded as an object of primary importance, and as presenting the only solution to the difficulties in which we found ourselves involved on the coast of China, one therefore, which it was necessary the Chinese Government should concede. Yet was it the very proposition which of all others was the most distasteful to them. In their eyes it was a sacrilegious innovation, which they were resolved, by whatever means, whether of force or fraud, to avoid. Hence the refusal to send a Plenipotentiary to Shanghae, and the evasive reference to Canton.

In the beginning of May 1858, we find the French and British Plenipotentiaries at the mouth of the Peiho, endeavouring, by whatever means, to engage the Chinese Government in treaty-relations of a satisfactory character. A summons was addressed to the Emperor, requiring that a duly authorised minister should be appointed to negotiate; otherwise, as Lord Elgin proceeds to state, "if, before the expiry of six days from the date of the present communication, a minister so accredited shall not have presented himself at Takoo, the undersigned will consider their pacific overtures to have been rejected, and deem himself thenceforward at liberty to adopt such measures for enforcing the just claims of our Government on that of China as he may think expedient." A certain Tan, governor-general of Chih-li was designated by the Emperor to this office, having associated with him two other Chinese officials. His refuse to meet him. Count Poutiatine was of opinion that "we could not expect further powers to be granted to a Chinese Plenipotentiary in the pressing difficulties to which China is now exposed, nor do I think that great inconveniences may ensue from references to Pekin, which will not require more than four or five days for answers, though it would have been of immense consequence if negotiations were conducted at Shanghae or at Canton. In my belief, I consider that the Chinese Government has acceded to our last demands in sending a proper person for negotiations to the appointed place, and for the term fixed by us for his arrival." The American representative was of like opinion; but the British and French Plenipotentiaries considered that they would not be justified in opening communications with Tan unless further credentials were given to him, and a delay of six further days was permitted him for this purpose. Not only, however, was Tan left with the same restricted powers which he had before, but, through the Russian embassy, was communicated to the Ambassadors the Emperor's determination not to admit foreign envoys into Pekin. As he was unwilling to be persuaded, the Western Europeans resolved to coerce him; the forts of Takoo were carried on May 19th, and the joss-house where Tan resided was searched for papers. Tan had fled, but within the door was found the body of Tehkwei, the commandant of the forts, who, knowing that he would be punished for his unsuccessful defence of them by loss of liberty, if not of life, had anticipated his doom by suicide. The Ambassadors, without delay, pushed in gun-boats up the river, and occupied Tien-tain. The Court of Pekin, finding the Europeans more rapid and resolute in their moves than they had expected, forthwith advanced two Commissioners, with full powers to stay their further progress towards the capital. It were tedious to introduce our readers into the entanglements of the negotiations. The Russian treaty was the first signed. "The chief concessions gained were the right of correspondence upon an equal footing between the Russian Minister of

required by the English were of a more stringent character, especially in reference to two points, which had not been introduced even into the French treaty: these were, that a British minister should be entitled to reside permanently in Pekin, or visit it occasionally, at the option of the British Government; and the other, that British subjects should have the right of travelling to all parts of the empire for trading purposes. These were stipulations to which the Commissioners were most averse. With importunate earnestness did they pray that they might be dispensed with, and, finding their own efforts unavailing, prayed the other Plenipotentiaries to intercede on their behalf, declaring that an imperial decree, just received, threatened them, not merely with degradation, but decapitation, if they conceded these points. The British Ambassador, however, felt it to be his duty to persevere, and the treaty was signed, "by a curious coincidence, the day of the signing of the treaty of Tien-tsin, being the anniversary of the day upon which the treaty of Nankin was signed fifteen years previously."

Even, however, after the treaty had been signed, did the Chinese Commissioners plead earnestly that its stringency on this point might be modified. In a letter to Lord Elgin, dated October 22d, 1858, they stated that they yielded it under coercion. "When the Commissioners Kwei and Hwa negotiated a treaty with your Excellency at Tien-tsin, British vessels of war were lying at that port; there was the pressure of an armed force, a state of excitement and alarm; and the treaty had to be signed at once, without a moment's delay. Deliberation was out of the question; the Commissioners had no alternative but to accept the conditions forced upon them. Among these were some of real injury to China, (to waive which) would have been of no disadvantage to your Excellency's Government; but, in the hurry of the moment, the Commissioners had no opportunity of offering your Excellency a frank explanation of these.

"In Article III. of the treaty it is laid down that 'the Ambassador, or other such high officer of Her Majesty the Queen of England, may reside permanently at the capital, or may visit it occasionally, at the option of the British Government.' (The employment of) the word 'or' expressing, as it undoubtedly does, the absence of a decision, is evidence enough of the sense and reasonableness of your Excellency, who would not precipitately decide upon an arbitrary course towards any one.

"Now the majority of the inhabitants of the capital are Banner-men, who, never having been beyond its walls, or in intercourse with other people, are quite ignorant of the feelings of men or the ways of the world outside. The business the officials, high and low, have to transact in the capital, again, is entirely metropolitan.

"They have had no personal experience of the popular feeling on public affairs of provinces, and know nothing whatever about them. Then the habits and dispositions of the people of the capital are different from those of the eastern and southern provinces. If foreigners reside in Pekin, it will certainly come to pass, that in their movements something will create misgiving and surprise on the part of the multitude; any slight misunderstanding will be sure to beget a quarrel; and great indeed would be the injury to our country were some trifling cause of difference to attain serious dimensions. China, too, is at the present moment in a crisis of great difficulty; and should the people, as it is to be apprehended they might, be misled by idle words upon this point, they would commence some trouble in addition (to those already on our hands). It would never do, surely, to bring China to such a pass.

"The condition of residence at Pekin is very irksome to China; and as the French and Americans have not this privilege (bis. Article), and it is only your nation that has, we beg your Excellency to consider what compromise may be effected, and to dispense with its peremptory (enforcement).

"Should such an arrangement be agreed on as is proposed, the Emperor will still specially depute, on the part of China, a Chief Secretary of State, or President of a Board, to reside in the provinces, at whatever point the high officer sent by your Excellency's Government may see fit to choose for his residence. When Nankin is retaken, he may, if it suit him, reside at Nankin."*

In Lord Elgin's first answer, on October 27th, the ambassador declined to accede to the alteration which they had proposed; but they were not deterred from a second application, dated Oct. 28th—

"The established reputation of your Excellency for justice and straightforwardness, for kind intentions and friendly feeling, make us place the fullest confidence in your assurance, that when you exacted the condition referred to, you were actuated by no desire whatever to do injury to China. The permanent residence of foreign ministers at the capital would, notwithstanding, be an injury to China in many more ways than we can find

---

* Oliphant. vol. i. Appendix.

words to express. In sum, in the present critical and troublous state of our country, this incident would generate, we fear, a loss of respect for their Government in the eyes of her people; and that this would indeed be no slight evil it will not be necessary, we assume, to explain to your Excellency with greater detail.

"It is for this reason that we specially address you a second letter on this subject, and we trust that your Excellency will represent for us, to Her Majesty your sovereign, the great inconvenience you feel (the exercise of the right would be) to our country, and beseech her not to decide in favour of the permanent residence at Pekin."*

Nor was this second entreaty without effect, Lord Elgin undertaking to submit to "Her Majesty's Government the representations that have been addressed to him by their Excellencies the Imperial Commissioners upon this important question; and humbly to submit it as his opinion, that if Her Majesty's Ambassador be properly received at Pekin when the ratifications are exchanged next year, and full effect given in all other particulars to the treaty negotiated at Tien-tsin, it would certainly be expedient that Her Majesty's Representative in China should be instructed to choose a place of residence elsewhere than at Pekin, and to make his visits to the capital either periodical, or only as frequent as the exigencies of the public service may require." We find, therefore, in a letter to Lord Malmesbury, dated Nov. 5th, 1858, this point specially dealt with.

"In order that your lordship may correctly apprehend the drift of this correspondence, it is necessary that I should state at the outset that the Chinese authorities contemplate the permanent residence of foreign ministers at the capital with more aversion and apprehension than any of the other innovations introduced by the treaty of Tien-tsin.

"In reply to the representations which I have been able, through private channels, to make to them in favour of this arrangement as the best means of obviating international disputes, and of preventing them, when they chance to arise, from assuming undue proportions, they are wont to urge, in the first place, of course, the traditional policy of the empire, and then the difficulties in which, if he were constantly resident at the capital, the idiosyncracies of an individual foreign functionary, of violent temper and overbearing demeanour, might involve them. As regards this latter point (I refer now to communications which have passed between us through officious channels), they are in the habit of illustrating their meaning by examples. 'If we were quite sure,' say they, 'that you would always send to us men thoroughly wise, discreet, and considerate, it might be different; but if, for instance, so and so were appointed to represent a foreign Government at Pekin (and the right, if exercised by you, would, of course, be claimed by all other Governments), a month would not elapse before something would occur which would place our highest officers in the dilemma of having either to risk a quarrel or submit to some indignity which would lower the Chinese Government in the eyes of its own subjects.' No doubt such apprehensions are to some extent chimerical; but I am bound to admit that I do not consider them to be altogether so. . . . .

"In conclusion, I would beg leave to remind your lordship that it is only in the British treaty that the right to appoint a minister to reside permanently at Pekin is provided for. Any other nation desiring to exercise this privilege must borrow it from that treaty under the most favoured nation clause; and if such a claim on the part of any other power were admitted, of course the objection to the residence of a British minister at the capital would be at once, by that fact, removed.

"And further, although I adhere to every opinion I have formerly expressed with regard to the importance of the establishment of direct diplomatic relations with the Court of Pekin,' I am bound to admit that the position of a British minister at the capital during the winter months, when the thermometer, if Humboldt is to be believed, falls to 40 deg. below zero, the river Tien-tsin is frozen, and the Gulf of Pechelee hardly navigable, would not be altogether a pleasant one. And that it is even possible that, under such circumstances, his actual presence might be to the mandarin mind less awe-inspiring than the knowledge of the fact that he had the power to take up his abode there whenever the conduct of the Chinese Government gave occasion for complaint."*

The suggestions of Lord Elgin were acted upon by the Home Government. The treaty-right respecting a British Ambassador was to be retained, but not acted upon. In the instructions to Mr. Bruce, dated Foreign Office, March 1st, 1859, we find the following paragraph—

"Her Majesty's Government were fully prepared at once to carry out the provision of the treaty of Tien-tsin which admits of the permanent residence of a British Ambassador at Pekin; but the observations on this point which Lord Elgin has so ably laid before them, coupled with the fact that the French

Government, on considering Baron Gros' reports, have arrived at the same conclusion, have determined Her Majesty's Government, for the present at least, to fix at Shanghae the residence of the British Mission, and only to require that it should be received occasionally at Pekin. But you will be careful to make the Chinese authorities at the capital and at Shanghae distinctly understand that Her Majesty's Government do not renounce the right of permanent residence, and, on the contrary, will instantly exercise it, if at any time difficulties are thrown in the way of communications between Her Majesty's minister and the central Government at Pekin, or any disposition shown to evade or defeat the objects of the treaty."

It was evident that we had erred in pressing the point of a resident minister at Pekin as of primary importance, and forcing the Chinese officials to introduce it as a conceded point into the treaty. But when we discovered our error, it would have been better to have renounced it altogether. By retaining the clause, we have increased existing complications. This barren treaty-right, yielding to us no advantage, has been taken advantage of by Russia. "Under the most favoured nation clause," which allows to each treaty-nation free and equal participation in all privileges, &c., granted by the Emperor of China to the Government or subjects of any other nation, she has placed a permanent Ambassador at Pekin. This, for her, is comparatively easy of execution, and of immense advantage. Encroaching as she is on the Tartar provinces of the empire, having her bases of operations comparatively near, out of her heterogeneous population she can easily furnish forth an embassy which can without difficulty accommodate itself to the peculiar habits of the Chinese: from the contiguity of her dominions she can preserve it from revolutions, and work it with immense advantage. But important as this privilege is to her, she was not prepared to force it from the Chinese. We did that, and finding the treaty-right, when we had gained it, of little practical advantage, left it to her to reap the harvest. And now we have this new difficulty; we must, it is thought, place ourselves on an equality with Russia in this respect, and thus, new complications arising, we may find ourselves dealing with the treaty-right of having an Ambassador at Pekin, as we dealt with the treaty-right of entrance into Canton, a right which, at first we decided to waive, but eventually, changing our minds, enforced it at the point of the sword.

Perhaps the Chinese foresaw this new complication. They are sufficiently keen-sighted so to do. A full concession on this point would have pacified them. But our retention of our treaty-right as one which it was at our pleasure to insist upon, or otherwise, served only to irritate them, and prepare the way for the unhappy collision at the mouth of the Peiho in 1859.

As the time approached when the ratifications of the treaty were to be exchanged at Pekin, nothing could be more ominous than appearances on the Chinese coast. Every thing intimated the unwillingness of the Chinese to ratify the treaty, and their determination not to permit the advance of the Ambassador to Pekin, except under humiliating circumstances. The Chinese Commissioners were lingering in the south when they ought to have been far on the way to Pekin. Rumours prevailed that the Chinese were preparing for resistance. A conversation between the interpreter, Mr. Hart, at Canton, and a Chinese who had just returned from Pekin, as embodied in the following Memorandum, is decisive upon this point—

"Yesterday evening, a Cantonese, Sen-seen-sang, who has for several years been in the habit of lending money to expectant officials, whom he accompanies when appointed to any post, called upon me. He had just returned from Pekin, viâ Shanghae, having left the former place on the 22d of March. He informed me, that, at the time of his departure from Pekin, the expected return of the British Ambassador to Tien-tsin, and the possibility of his visiting the capital, were subjects freely canvassed in every quarter; that the Emperor was known to be highly displeased with some of the stipulations contained in the Tien-tsin treaty; that he was entirely averse to the Ambassador's taking up his quarters in the capital, and that he had resolved not to grant him an audience on any pretext; that military preparations were going on at Pekin and Tien-tsin; that the Russians had offered the Emperor 10,000 muskets, but that His Majesty had declined to accept the present, fearing that the muskets in question might be brought to the palace by an equal number of Russians; that the arrangement of all matters connected with the reception of the British at Tien-tsin, and the preventing of any visit to Pekin, had been confided to Sung-wang-yay, a Ta-tsze-wang, son-in-law of the last Emperor; that Sung-wang-yay

a way as to render it impossible for foreign vessels to reach that city; that 30,000 'so-lo' troops—men never called out except in cases of the greatest emergency—were under orders to hold themselves in readiness to join Sung-wang-yay if called for; that Sung-wang-yay's orders were to receive the British at Tien-tsin with all civility, but at all hazards to prevent any nearer approach to Pekin; that Sung-wang-yay was very desirous of gaining military renown, and that the Ambassador would be unable to reach Pekin without having recourse to arms; that, according to the opinion of some, the Ambassador, accompanied by a few people, might possibly reach Pekin without bloodshed, but that a fight would certainly ensue if more than a hundred men were landed; that the country between Tien-tsin and Pekin being flat, and the Chinese troops being so much more numerous than any number of men the British could land, it was the general belief that the British could be surrounded and cut to pieces before the completion of one-half the journey.

"Sen-seen-sang further informed me that a Russian Ambassador had visited Pekin on the 2d March; that the Russians in the capital, more than one hundred in number, roamed about just as they pleased, much to the grief of the Emperor and the anti-foreign party; and that it was feared the British, if they once effected an entrance, would take an ell for every inch the Russians had arrogated to themselves; that at Yung-chow large quantities of grain had been bought up by the Russians, but that the Emperor, having become alarmed, had forbidden the traffic."*

On arriving off the mouth of the Peiho, every thing betokened a dogged obstinacy: the river was barricaded, and an armed rabble repelled all attempts to open communications. At length a letter was received from Hang, Governor-General of Chih-li, the successor to the unfortunate Tan, who had been banished to the borders of Siberia, stating that he had reached Pa-tang-ho, a port or harbour to the northward of Takoo, for the purpose of doing honour to the Envoy, and requesting him to proceed there. It was difficult to decide on the

Bruce at once to put away all misgiving on the subject. There is no need for him to feel any anxiety. They would wish, that on his arrival on the mouth of the Tien-tsin river (the Peiho), he should anchor his vessels of war outside the bar, and then, without much baggage, and with a moderate retinue, proceed to the capital for the exchange of the treaties. His mission being a pacific one (or, as he comes speaking peace), his treatment by the Government of China will not fail to be in every way most courteous; and it is the sincere wish of the Commissioners that relations of friendship may be from this time forth consolidated, and that on each side confidence may be felt in the good faith and justice of the other." †

Now at the last moment, when off the Peiho, he is refused admission by the route which had been pointed out; while Governor Hang's letter indicating Peh-tang-ho was evidently penned in a discourteous spirit, the character signifying "Her Majesty" not being placed on a level with that signifying Emperor. Duty appeared to require that Lord Elgin's example should be followed, the passage of Peiho forced, and the Chinese Government, compelled by the intimidation of a second defeat to receive the British envoy with due honours. The issue is known to our readers. It was no doubt the course which the Chinese expected we would take, and they had made every preparation to give us a warm reception. The door of entrance into China, the one which their own Commissioners had indicated, was found closed. A postern gate was pointed out as still open, but the acceptance of which on our part would have been considered by them as an acknowledgment of our inferiority, and would have prepared the way for further humiliation; and when we proceeded to force open the main entrance, their batteries opened upon our boats and men with a force and precision to which as yet, in Chinese warfare, we were unaccustomed. It was a violation of good faith, a violent and treacherous proceeding, but such as might have been expected from a barbarous nation, upon which we had forced a line of policy which they utterly dis-

come the fertile source of new complications; and that as we had compelled the treaty by an armed force, we should be obliged to send out another expedition to constrain them to the observance of it. Had the articles of the treaty been such as they approved of, and which they had signed willingly because they perceived it was their interest so to do, we might have with safety pursued the course we did, and withdrawn our troops while the ink was yet moist on the paper. But coercive treaties, which are acceded to because the vanquished party must either do so or else submit to further buffetings from the mailed hand of the persistent conqueror, will ever prove to be expensive agreements.

An admirable resumé of these complicated events will be found in the following extracts, from a despatch of Mr. Bruce to Lord Malmesbury, dated Shanghae, July 13th 1859—

"I propose in this despatch to give a succinct account of the course I have adopted, and of the grounds on which it is based. It is necessary to allude briefly to the maxims of China in regard to intercourse with foreign nations, as they afford the key to what has taken place.

"In China international relations have been always studiously ignored by the Government, and in no single instance has a Foreign Minister succeeded in obtaining admission to the capital, except on performance of the 'kotow,' or ceremony of vassalage, or in the character of tribute-bearer. The subjects of foreign nations residing in China are represented as belonging to barbarous tribes, and living by trade (of all occupations the one least in repute among the Chinese), as devoid of civilization, and ignorant of the rules of reason, and by all means to be confined to the outskirts of the country.

"According to the maxims of the Government, they are entitled to no rights beyond those accorded by the favour of the Emperor; and though circumstances and the weakness of the Government have led it to acquiesce in the concession of considerable privileges to foreigners in distant sea-ports, it is remarkable, as proving how tenaciously it holds to

equal power, and the Chinese Government, in its treatment of him, is called upon finally to abandon the assumption of superiority which it asserted uncompromisingly during Lord Amherst's embassy, and, so lately as three years ago, when Count Poutiatine first proposed to visit Pekin. He is to be allowed free and unrestricted communication with the capital, not only as specified in the French and American treaties, when he has business to transact, but whenever he wishes to visit it. His diplomatic intercourse is to be conducted according to the usages of western nations, and he is not to be called on to perform any ceremony of a nature derogatory to his character as representing an equal and independent nation. In future, access to the capital is to be recognised as a right the Minister can insist on, instead of its being begged for as a favour, and either refused or conceded on such terms as the Chinese might choose to impose, for the sake of saving their own dignity at the expense of that of the foreign envoy in the eyes of the Chinese population.

"The clauses which permit British subjects to travel in the interior, and open the Yangtze river to British shipping, are equally subversive of the established maxims of Chinese statesmen. To push us back on the sea-board, and confine us to as few seaports as possible; to keep us outside the walls of important cities, and vilify us to the people, in order to preserve a wall of separation between the races, is the policy which the Chinese Government, from its adherence to usage, and from its indifference, if not dread of all progress which can only be attained through novelty, would gladly follow, if it dared to do so.

"It is not surprising, therefore, when the allied squadrons left the Peiho river last year, and the panic produced by their presence began to subside, that ancient maxims and prejudices should have gradually resumed the ascendant at Pekin, and that the Imperial cabinet should have entertained hopes of recovering part of the ground it had lost. There is proof of its language and feeling with regard to foreigners having undergone no change in a decree published in the 'Pekin Gazette,'

river to efface the impression produced by the proceedings of last year, and, by preventing foreign ships from arriving at Tien-tsin, to render Pekin more inaccessible than ever.

"I felt at once that it became necessary either to throw overboard my instructions entirely, to abandon the visit to Pekin, and the attempt to establish, on a proper footing, once for all, our diplomatic relations with the Court of Pekin, or to declare that I would insist on exchanging the ratifications at the capital within the period stipulated in the treaty, and on a personal reception by the Emperor, for the purpose of delivering to him Her Majesty's autograph letter. I could not doubt that the task of extorting a reception at Pekin, in a form implying a surrender on the part of the Emperor of his pretensions to national superiority, would be more difficult than obtaining a recognition of our equality on paper; and that the Chinese Government, in accordance with its usual policy, would endeavour, by prescribing the route I was to follow, by limiting the number of my attendants, and, by bad arrangements during the journey, to put me in the degrading position hitherto occupied by foreign envoys, and recover, by this means, the prestige it had lost by our successful *coup de main* of last year. To prevent such a result, and to receive free access to the capital in future 'on becoming terms, I decided, after mature reflection, on proceeding by the river, the natural highway to Tien-tsin, under the British flag, as its presence at that place would establish in the eyes of the Chinese that our visits to Pekin are a matter of right, not of favour.

"On arriving at Shanghae, where I proceeded as soon as my French colleague was ready, I found, as I anticipated, the Commissioners armed with pretexts to detain me, and prevent my visit to the Peiho. Their letters, though moderate in tone, alluded to the three principal clauses of the treaty, and proposed to re-open the discussion upon them. Had I accepted this overture, and abandoned the course laid down in my letter of the 16th May, they would have inferred that I was to be 'soothed and controlled,' and would have

result of the interviews had been communicated to it.

"I think that the Commissioners themselves were acting rather in obedience to their instructions from Pekin, than in the expectation that their attempts to detain us here would be successful. For as soon as they received my letter, stating that I would not enter into discussion until the ratifications were exchanged, and declining any interview with them at Shanghae, the twelvemonth allowed by treaty for the exchange having almost expired, they changed entirely their tone. They acknowledged the propriety of abiding by the terms of the treaty, and stated that they had memorialized the Emperor to send down a high officer to Tien-tsin, whom we should find on our arrival, ready to conduct us, in time, to the capital. Though they hinted at a journey by land from the river's mouth, and wished me to anchor the squadron outside the bar, they did not state that orders had been given to prevent us entering the river, and making use of it to reach the town of Tien-tsin. . . .

"I have only to remark, in explanation of the course pursued, that we found ourselves off the mouth of the river, which forms the highway to Pekin, within a few days of the expiration of the period fixed by the treaty for the exchange of the ratifications. On requesting a passage to be opened for us, and explaining the peaceful objects of the mission, we were informed that there was no authority on the spot; that the fort and barriers were not constructed by order of the Government, but by the people, who had built and garrisoned them for their protection against rebels, not to keep us out of the river. In proceeding to remove them, we therefore violated no order of the Imperial Government, and, had we been successful, the Government could and would, no doubt, have disavowed entirely the acts of those who opposed us. At the same time we were convinced that the repugnance of the Chinese Government to execute fully the treaty, and to grant us the reception we were instructed to demand, could only be overcome by a sense of their inability to resist us. The

on such a question had expressed doubts as to the result of an attempt to force the passage of the river. But I can state positively, that if Admiral Hope had expressed doubts on the subject, they would not have been shared by the squadron, nor by those who have had most experience of warfare in China; and if it be decided that the means at our command were insufficient to justify us in pursuing so bold a line of policy, it is but right that I should share that responsibility with him."*

It may be not uninteresting to state how the American Minister, Mr. Ward, was dealt with by the Chinese. The right of access to Pekin had not been introduced into the American treaty; but, like the Russians, availing themselves of the stipulations which we had compelled, the Americans claimed, under the most favoured nation clause, to exchange ratifications at Pekin. The mode of action adopted by their Representative was therefore diverse from ours. Isolating himself from our system of intimidation, yet profiting by the impression made thereby on the Chinese, and their disposition to yield on some points which otherwise they would have haughtily resisted, he hoped to reach Pekin pacifically, and be admitted to a personal interview with the Emperor. He proceeded, therefore, to Peh-tang-ho, according to the directions of Hang-fuh. The results are summed up in the following extract from the North-China Herald of August 22d, 1859—

"On the morning of the 20th, Mr. Ward and suite landed at Peh-tang, where they were received by the escort, and conducted to Pekin with every show of respect. They first travelled forty-five miles across the country in covered carts, striking the Peiho at a village called Pei-tsang, some ten miles above Tien-tsin, and thence proceeded in junks to Tung-chow, distant twelve miles from Pekin, of which it is the port. There they again took carts to the capital.

"The entire trip occupied eight days and a-half, five of which were passed upon the river. They passed not less than six or eight barriers between Pei-tsang and Tung-chow, none of them, however, being in repair, or backed by forts. The boatmen said that they were partly to stop the English, and partly to afford shelter to junks when the ice was breaking up.

The legation remained in Pekin fifteen days, during which time they were confined to their quarters; not, however, as prisoners, for they were at liberty at any moment to walk out, but the Commissioners refused the use of horses and guides, leaving it optional with Mr. Ward to grant permission to walk out or not, as he saw fit. They would doubtless, however, have closed the gates entirely, had not that gentleman taken a firm stand at the very first interview, informing Kweiliang that as soon as his movements should be at all restricted he should close all intercourse, and demand his return escort.

"It seems that the Emperor was very anxious to see Mr. Ward, but that he also insisted upon his performing the 'kotow,' which, being against the principles of His Excellency, was positively refused. The result of this was, that upon the fourteenth day of their stay it was finally concluded to receive the President's letter at Pekin, and to send His Excellency back to Peh-tang to exchange the treaty; and the next day they returned accordingly.

"During their stay in Pekin they saw nothing of the Russians, but received several letters from them. The first of these was six days going from one end of the city to the other, having evidently been detained by the authorities.

"Arrived at Peh-tang on the 16th, the treaties were exchanged, and an English prisoner (named John Powell) given up. This man, who was an ordinary seaman on board the 'Highflyer,' and who, with a sapper by the name of Thomas McQueen, had been captured on the 25th June, fearing for his life, had proclaimed himself to be an American. The Chinese informed Mr. Ward of this, and intimated their readiness to give him up as an American, if he would demand him. This, however, the latter could not do, as he had been taken fighting under the flag of another nation. Anxious, however, to serve the poor fellow, he intimated to them that it would be a great personal favour if they would turn him over, and, as such, it was done. He is now on board of the 'Powhatan.' Of the sapper nothing more is known than that he was wounded in the arm, was doing well, and is still a prisoner.

"The Chinese seemed generally anxious to know what the English would do next year."

We have thus endeavoured to bring together within a brief compass, and to place summarily before our readers, the events which have taken place on the coast of China, that thus they may be enabled to observe and duly estimate the still more momentous ones, which may by this time have supervened, and of which, at any moment, we may become cognizant.

We trust that the tone of the debates in

---

* Correspondence with Mr. Bruce: Blue Book, pp. 21—25.

the British Parliament will tell with moderating influence on the coast of China. If in any thing we have erred let us be manly enough to avow it and correct it. If we have insisted upon any point of little practical value to ourselves, but which touches sorely the morbid sensibilities of the Chinese, let us be generous to forego it. Let the demands made in China be precisely that which the necessities of the case require and no more. To use the words of Sir John Pakington in the recent debate, let us beware of "pressing demands on China one iota beyond what the strictest view of the justice of the case and the interests of the country demand." Let all possible allowance be made for the narrow-mindedness inseparable from the condition of a benighted heathen nation. We have been charged with unduly intruding into political matters, and have been told that the object of this periodical is purely Missionary, and should be confined to that. But if this be the case and if it be true that we are to occupy ourselves exclusively with the details of Missionary information, then is this periodical unnecessary; for this very necessary duty is already and effectually discharged by the Church Missionary Record. But our duty is of a different kind. We have to deal with Missionary results gathered together from different fields, and by a careful comparison of them, deduce Missionary principles, and the best mode of action; how benefits may be secured, and difficulties avoided. But we have also to do with all questions touching the welfare of nationalities, and to observe upon all points which have a tendency to recommend the Christian religion to the heathen or prejudice them against it. If England were not a Christian nation, as the advocates of the great Missionary interest we should have nothing to do with her policy, nay, if she were professedly Romanist, it might be sufficient to refer her errors of judgment to the errors of her creed, and find in one the explanation of the other. But she is nationally Protestant. Scriptural Christianity is her national profession. It is the same creed which our Missionaries preach. The heathen looks to our national actions as the true exponents of our national faith; and as jealous for the honour of God's truth, and for the honour of our country, we cannot but be solicitous that those actions should be such as shall commend and not misrepresent the truth. Tender points must at times be touched if good is to be done, although we should be sorry to do it harshly. But, at whatever cost, there is one tendency which must be denounced, one misapprehension which must be protested against, whenever and wherever it shews itself, that we have a right to coerce people into compliance with our views and wishes; and when with the usual habitude of human nature they cling tenaciously to old customs, and are unwilling at our summons to surrender them, that we have a right to employ superior force and bully them into obedience. We have no authority from God to do so. We shall never by such a mode of action attain satisfactory results. We think this to be the quickest and shortest way to the solution of a difficulty, which will ever prove to be the longest, most tedious, and expensive, we can select; and we shall be certain in some way or other, according to the providence of God's retributive justice, to suffer for it. Better far to forbear, and wait, and endeavour to enlighten and instruct. We shall win confidence, acquire influence, and the doors which we abstained from breaking open, will open gently of their own accord, and so open as not to close again.

But while we would deal faithfully with our own national action on the coast of China, we have no wish to cast a veil over the vices of the Chinese character. They are an arrogant and supercilious people; inflated with an high idea of their own importance; and an unutterable contempt for all that is Western as barbarian. In religious matters they are sceptical and obtuse in feeling, nor are they impressible by considerations which powerfully move other sections of men. The wild demon-worshipper of Gondwana and Pegu has his gloomy thoughts and fears, in his estimation the deep forests, the mountain glen, each hill and river, have their *genii loci*, whose wrath he fears, and whose anger he propitiates, sometimes even by human sacrifices. The Hindu is mad after his gods, and flings himself with enthusiasm into the whirlpool of an idolatrous worship, which enlists his vices on its side, and sanctions all the worst propensities of his heart. But in religious matters the Chinese are stolid, perhaps beyond all other men; a utilitarian in the strongest sense, he regards only the present, and disregards the future as shadowy and unsubstantial.

There is no nation which stands more in need of the ameliorating action of the Gospel. It is the alone antidote for numberless vices and defects of character and conduct which prevail there. But the Tartar authorities interfere. They would forbid the Gospel to these suffering masses. They have attempted to arrest that mighty tide of divine truth, the first ripples of which are being just felt on the coast of China. Scarcely had the treaties of 1858 been signed at Tien-tsin, when Yin-shan-yung* and Sang-ko-lin-sing† memorialized the emperor on the subject of Christianity. The first observes—

"As to the propagation of religion, its object is to unsettle the public mind, and secretly effect a revolution. If such were not the case, they would be satisfied with practising their faith in their own country. They bestow charity upon the poor as a stratagem for winning the hearts of the people. Those rebellious barbarians, in swallowing up the lesser foreign powers, have always made use of these agencies."

The latter says, in his memorial—"The Christian religion is utterly subversive of good morals. They make use of the false doctrines of Jesus to poison the minds of the simple; and employ Chinese gold and silver to corrupt the hearts of the intelligent. And, at this rate, in a few years the whole population will embrace the false religion of Jesus. Will not the people of China then become the tools of the barbarians? and then where will the mischief end?"

That these memorials have not been in vain is evidenced in the new spirit infused into the provincial authorities. Native evangelists, sent by the American Missionaries at Ningpo, have been driven away from Hang-chow, the capital of the province of Chekeang. They petitioned the magistrate, but without effect. Nor were the representations of the Missionaries, forwarded through the Taoutae to the governor of the province, more successful. A similar disposition to persecute has been exhibited at Ningpo.

The new American treaty has thus been already violated in one of its most important stipulations. The article 29 provided—

"The principles of the Christian religion, as professed by the Protestant and Roman-Catholic churches, are recognised as teaching men to do good, and to do to others as they would have others do to them. Hereafter those who quietly profess and teach those doctrines shall not be harassed or persecuted on account of their faith. Any person, whether citizen of the United States or Chinese convert, who, according to these tenets, shall peaceably teach and practise the principles of Christianity, shall in no case be interfered with or molested."

Thus there appears to be on the part of the Chinese authorities an increasing prejudice against the Christian faith. This may have been helped by various circumstances. The unhappy wording of the 29th article of the American treaty, to which we have just referred, may have done so; in which the Protestant and Roman-Catholic churches are presented to the Chinese mind as kindred systems. Very probably the former has suffered in their estimation from this mes-alliance, for the Chinese have had long experience of Romanism, and no doubt have seen enough of the intrigues of that politico-religious system to lead them to distrust it. Accordingly, in the Kiang-si province, a proclamation has been issued against the religion of the Lord of heaven (Romish Christianity); in which, to show that the Chinese are not either ignorant or forgetful in this respect, as some suppose, there is a reference to the history of the past.

"It would appear that the so-called religion of the Lord of heaven . . . . . . derives its origin from the Occident. It was only towards the end of the things that one Matteo Ricci opened the way for his proselytes to Pekin. At first, by means of his impositions and tracts, they deceived and misled the Chinese people, and afterwards they employed lucre to gain over the inhabitants, scholars, and officers of the state . . . . the more ignorant respected that religion and believed in it more and more, and from that cause it has spread its venom throughout the land of China, and has paved the way to ruin. Under our exalted dynasty, rectitude and public morality are one and united. They consist in a respectful observance of the family precept of the sacred founder, namely, to root out all false doctrines in order to exalt correct principles."

The singular recognition of Christianity by the Taepings, and the harshness and severity of aspect with which they have invested it, as though the Saviour had come, not to save men's lives, but to destroy them,—this also has no doubt served to the increase of dynastic prejudices against Christianity. To this also we find a reference in the state documents which have been recently promulgated.

"When the rebels of the Canton province, by birth depraved and by nature foul, dared to overthrow the precepts of the present holy rule, they imposed on the simple people by assuming the religion of the Lord of heaven, and calling Him their Heavenly Father. According to them, Jesus suffered an ignominious death; but was, nevertheless, sent down

---

* A high Chinese functionary, who has recently obtained important promotion.

† The Tartar prince who commands the imperial forces, and who occupies the very first place in the imperial favour.

by the Lord of Heaven amongst men, some thousand and few hundred years ago, to be the father, the parent, of rebels and malefactors. Only reflect! There is nothing greater than Heaven! who can presume to become the lord and master of it? Yet, what manner of individual is this Jesus of theirs, who should thus have died, and yet be worshipped as the 'Lord of Heaven?' What extreme blasphemy! what excessive profaneness! Since Jesus, then, died the death of a criminal, by what sorcery did He descend on earth again; and, what is more, become the parent of rebels and malefactors? As rebels and malefactors have no Lord, no parent, in that case their Jesus cannot have been born of the human species, and that is an end of it; because it is plain that if Jesus had been born of man, his spirit also would have been that of a human being."

But besides all this, the Emperor and his subordinates have been hostile to the free action of the Gospel, from the time when our Missionaries first planted their foot upon the coast of China. Any *locus standi* which they have had, has not been willingly conceded by the authorities, but forcibly wrested from them.

Encouraged by their successful resistance to the allied forces at the Peiho, they have become more bold in avowing their hostility, and have proceeded to acts of persecution. Two individuals, apprehended on the charge of embracing the religion of the Lord of Heaven, have been compelled in open court to tread upon the wooden cross, after the example of the Japanese.

It is not improbable, therefore, that we are about to witness in China mighty changes, and such a breaking-up of hindrances and obstructions, as shall open a way for the Gospel into the interior. The existing dynasty may be on the eve of dissolution. It is already weak and tottering, and now dangers increase. After a period of comparative inaction, the Taepings have again put on their strength. Hangchow has been taken and plundered; Soochow has met with like calamities; the coast cities are being threatened; the imperial armies have been obliged to break off their positions before Nanking. From the seaward the storm-cloud is gathering, and the obstinate Tartar is busy in preparing his forts at Taku, in the hope that he shall be able to reiterate the victory which he gained over a handful of gallant men, contending against every possible disadvantage. It may be that the overthrow of the Tartar dynasty is at hand, and that mysterious fingers are even now writing on the walls of the king's palace, "Thou art weighed in the balance and found wanting." Perchance the obstructive barrier is about to be thrown down, and the Mantchou princes, through their own obstinacy, remitted to the solitudes of Mongolia.

Unmistakably it is, all over the world, a time of momentous changes. The decree seems to have gone forth, "I will overturn, overturn, overturn it; and it shall be no more, until He come, whose right it is; and I will give it Him." With extraordinary rapidity the political obstructions which interfered with the onward progress of the Gospel, and shut up masses of men in hopeless ignorance, are being levelled in the dust. In India the stroke of the earthquake has been felt, and the prison-houses of gloomy superstitions, in which the Hindu and Mohammedan have been for ages immured, have been so shattered, that the prisoners have now the opportunity to escape. In Italy, thrones have been ruined, and dynasties broken down. Nor has the mighty energy which is at work yet exhausted itself. The pride of the Moslem must be broken, and the ignorance of heathen potentates rebuked.

It is the breaking up of the field of labour, preparatory to a more universal sowing of the seed, for " the Gospel shall be preached as a testimony to all people."

The next part of our subject—the seed—will open up points of interest of another kind.

NINGPO—A GLANCE AT THE SOCIAL LIFE OF CHINA.

Ningpo, a free port, and a centre of Missionary effort, is in the Che-keang province. "Any good map of China presents a coast-line approaching to a semicircular curve, near the centre of which, in lat. 29° 50′ N., and long. 121° 22′ E. Ningpo will be found." Off the north-east point of the city wall, called Sankiangkow, or "river junction," three streams unite. " To the ning down through the districts of Yuyaou and Tszeke, variously called the Yaou river, the Shun river, or the river of Tszeke. To the east there is another stream, known as the Yung river." These two uniting, "flow north-east and north, in a deep channel, until they enter the open sea at Chinhai, a distance of eleven miles and a half from the point of the confluence."

the most important city in Chekeang, next to Hang-chow. It is regarded as one of the most literary cities in the empire, and inferior only to Hang-chow and Soo-chow in the refinement and taste of the people. It is an ancient city, "its annals affording very full information upon every point interesting to a Chinese antiquarian, although a foreigner very soon tires of the many insignificant details, mixed up with a few valuable statements." Its population, variously estimated from one-fourth to one-third of a million, is industriously engaged, one-fifth in literary pursuits, and the remainder in trade, merchandize, and labour. Its situation is a choice one. "The plain on which Ningpo lies is a magnificent amphitheatre, stretching away from twelve to eighteen miles on one side to the base of the distant hills, and on the other to the verge of the ocean. As the eye travels along it catches many a pleasing object. Turn landward, it will see canals and watercourses, fields and snug farm houses, smiling cottages, family residences, hamlets and villages, family tombs, monasteries and temples. Turn in the opposite direction, and you perceive a plain country descending towards the ocean: but the river, alive with all kinds of boats, and the banks studded with ice-houses, most of all attract the attention. Turn inwards towards the city, and while still upon the ramparts, look within its walls, and you will be no less gratified. Here there is nothing European—little to remind you of what you have seen in the west. The single-storied and the double-storied houses, the heavy prison-like family mansions, the family vaults and gravel yards, the glittering roofs of the temples, the dilapidated official residences, the deserted literary and examination halls, are entirely Chinese. The attention is also arrested for a moment or two by ditches, canals, and reservoirs of water, with their wooden bridges and stone arches."* Of that kind of civilization which prevails in heathen countries, and which, like the lacker ware of Japan, polishes the surface of society, there is much. Temples and monasteries are numerous; assembly halls, Governmental offices and educational establishments, abound. The assembly halls constitute an interesting feature in native society. Residents and merchants from the provinces subscribe to erect on the spot where they transact their business "a temple," dedicated to the patron deity of their native province. Placed under the charge of a few priests, or a layman called "a master of ceremonies," they become places of resort for travellers, and answer the purpose of European coffee-houses.

The well-paved streets are interrupted here and there by honorary portals of considerable size and solidity. Two lagoons within the city, supplied by sluices passing through the gates, are the feeding-places of many canals and aqueducts, by which the suburbs are irrigated and the various portions of the city supplied with water. The walls in circumference approach five miles, the average height being twenty-five feet, exclusive of a parapet, five feet high; the width of the wall, on the top, being fifteen feet, and at the base twenty-two feet; the material solid, the lower part of stone and granite, the upper of brick. Strolling through the streets of the city, the stranger marks numerous indications of settled habits and of organized social life. On the gateways, numerous placards "pasted up, apprise the gentry and citizens, or 'ladies and gentlemen,' of religious services, theatrical shows, magisterial orders, musical feats, &c. The rage for advertisement in China is quite as prolific as elsewhere; and among other curiosities in this class of production, may be seen fiery squibs on public characters, sober admonitions on sundry subjects, and quack papers in every line of business. As in Europe, so in China, objection is taken to the placarding of bills upon private premises; and you meet with notices to the effect, that 'Bills pasted up will be daubed over,' 'Placards will be torn down,' 'You are not allowed to placard,' and sometimes the polite request, 'Pray do not paste your bills here.'"*

The tea-houses are another feature of Chinese social life. "Very large shops, appropriated to tea-drinking, are to be met with everywhere in Chinese towns, occupying extensive flights. On the floors of these rooms there stand square wooden tables, with benches and chairs to accommodate four or six people; and at the further end there is the kitchen, with oven and stoves duly arranged, and bearing huge kettles, massive tea-pots, monster cauldrons, all filled with hot water. Usually there is a goodly staff of waiters moving about, vigilant in their attentions, carrying small trays, with tea-cups of the warm decoction and plates of cakes and dried fruits, &c. Less than a farthing will obtain a refreshing cup of comfort. At every hour, morning and evening especially, the rooms are crowded. There is no prohibition of tobacco-smoking or gambling, but the reverse. Nor is there any restraint on loud

---

* "Middle Kingdom," vol. i. pp. 90, 99.

* Milne's "Life in China," pp. 82, 83.

and noisy conversation. Labourers and passengers are continually dropping in for such appropriate conveniences as are offered in the shape of basins of warm water, and rough, rather coarse towels, for washing hands and face. Often music is conducted within, and often, like resorts of the same class in Europe, the tea-drinking houses in China form the evening refuges of the working-classes for news and gossip, amusement or recreation.

"Eating-houses are sometimes connected with tea-houses. In these a substantial meal can be had at a moment's notice. Some of them occupy large and commodious buildings. These are sometimes two stories high, with the *restaurants* above, and the kitchens underneath. The bill of fare offers every thing in season, at moderate charges."*

Glancing from within to without the walls, there will be found "a moat of some extent that well nigh encircles the city. The northern and eastern faces of the city, supposed to be well enough guarded by the river, have no moat; but commencing at the north gate, it runs along the foot of the wall, west, south, south and south-east, until it stops at what is called the 'Bridge-gate.' This gives a length of about three miles. It is deep—in some places perhaps forty yards wide, well supplied with water from the neighbouring fields and river, and daily navigated by boats."

In this, as in all other Chinese cities, there is one great deficiency. They have canals and aqueducts to disperse abroad abundant supplies of water, but there is no provision for the removal of the moral filthiness, which, engendered in the natural heart, oozes forth from numberless fountains, and accumulates rapidly wherever masses of human beings are congregated. Every human heart is a fountain-head of evil influences, and such it continues to be until renewed and purified. There needs a powerful element abroad which shall be corrective of the depravity of the human heart, and render it a spring of influence and action which will be beneficial instead of injurious to society: and forasmuch as, under the happiest circumstances which we can hope to attain, evil will still accumulate, the cleansing element of pure religion needs to be dispersed abroad, like the streams and rivers of a well-watered city, affording to individuals and families the ready means of spiritual purification. This is precisely what is wanting in heathen cities and a heathen land. The temples of heathenism abound, while places of Christian worship—for Christianity is as yet in the initiative, and just struggling into its birth—are few and far between.

Milne, in his "Life in China," describes the heathen temples of Ningpo as he found them some seventeen years ago, and such, in all probability, they remain at the present moment, or, if they have been succeeded by others, with the usual conservatism of China, the mould and type of the dissolved building has been retained. This description, therefore, will still be pictorial of what may be found in Ningpo at the present time. Let us recur to it.

He conducts us to the temple of Leu-tsoo. "Within the entrance, and under cover, there were seated four huge figures, the four great Kin-kang, probably standing there to the present day. One carried a lyre, at the notes of which they say the ears of the whole world are awakened. Another, with a black and ferocious face, flourished a drawn sword. A third sported a big umbrella, and is said, by the simple elevation of this instrument, to have power to draw down to earth storms of thunder and rain. The fourth twists a long snake round his arm, to denote skill to tame wildness into submission. They were arranged two on each side of the passage. In the centre gateway an image faced you, exactly as you entered, very stout, and with the breast and upper abdomen exposed, seated on a large cloth bag, laughing and looking right jolly, with two words inscribed overhead, *Chih Siau*, 'the ever-laughing one.' This is a representation of the Buddha that is to come. Behind him there was an erect idol called the Wei-to image, or the Hoofah Wei-to, as he is said to be the protector of the Buddhist faith. He was clad in armour, and seemed ready for the offensive or defensive. Within there was a crowd of other images, chiefly canonized heroes and disciples of this popular superstition."

In another part of the city is "the palace of the god of the eastern range." A wicket at the east end of the principal gateway leads into a dark, dreary cell called *teyoh*, "the earthly dungeon." "In the centre of the ground-floor there were images of hideous aspect, in threatening attitudes, and, behind them, groups of small figures in stucco relief, plastered upon the wall, to exhibit the pains and penalties of hell. These were arranged in three or four rows, rising one above the other, until they reached the ceiling. Each group had its judge, criminal, executioner, and peculiar form of punishment. The judges

---

* Milne, pp. 69, 70.

were attired as officers generally are, and the executioners as police-runners. The grade of penalties was varied according to the heinousness of the culprit's crime, and the horrors of future punishment were depicted before the spectator in every possible form. To be whipped, to be bastinadoed, to be seared with red-hot irons, to be strangled, to be speared, to be beheaded, to be sawn asunder, to be flayed alive, to be squeezed, flattened, and crushed between two thick planks, to be slit up, to be bored through and through, to have the eyes dug or chiselled out, to have the limbs torn off one by one, to be plunged from a cliff or a bridge into a dungeon below, or into a rapid torrent, to be pounded in a heavy mortar, to be boiled in a hot-water cauldron, to be burnt up in a furnace, to be baked at the stake, to have hot liquids poured down the throat, &c., constitute the ideas of future punishment indulged in the books of this school."*

Here are no improving influences. Let us look in the direction of another *quasi* religious building—a Mohammedan mosque. It is dirty and dilapidated; the pillars which support the roof are ornamented with sentences from the Korán; a copy of this book may be found within, but the priest, although born in China, may be unable to speak or read Chinese, and the system, such as it is, is powerless and disqualified for action.

May we be permitted to look beneath the surface, and lay bare the domestic life and habits of the Chinese. They are a clothed people, and there is outward decency, more so than in the great cities of Europe. The female tunic, buttoning round the neck and down the side, and reaching to the knee, is peculiarly becoming and decorous, and, as worn by ladies, is as splendid as rich silks and gay colours can render it. The neck of the robe is protected by a stiff band, and the sleeves are large and long. But, alas! the decency is without. As a people, they are, in their habits, vile and polluted to a degree. On land and water the haunts of vicious pleasure, are to be found. It is not safe for young girls to go abroad alone, lest they be stolen for incarceration in these places.

A proud people, as they are, worldly disappointments weigh heavily upon them. An atheistical people, in the time of trouble they have nothing to fall back upon, and, in the exasperation of the moment, suicide is often their desperate resource.

"The popular modes of self-destruction are, drowning, hanging, and swallowing opium or gold-leaf: with officials, the first and the last are the most respectable methods. During the war with England, when their reverses were frequent, the military officers, in numerous instances, effected self-destruction in one or other of these ways. Various accounts are given of the use and effects of gold-foil for the purpose: one has it, that a quantity of the flimsy leaf, made up into a large bolus, is swallowed: when a cupful of water is drunk it expands the gold-leaf in the stomach, which distends so as to occasion speedy death. Another account explains, that a bundle of the loose foil is thrust down the throat to produce suffocation. One other mode of self-destruction is reported among the people as a fact, though it sounds fabulous to us. There is a bird called Seenhoh, on the crown of whose head there is a beautiful scarlet tuft of down, or velvet skin, in which, the natives believe, the poison of the serpent it is fond of eating determines. The downy crest is often formed into a bead, and that bead is concealed in the necklaces of the high officers for a suicidal purpose in case of imperial displeasure, which, as report goes, is easily effected by touching the venomous bead with the tip of the tongue, when death follows instantly."*

Japan, however, affords the fullest developement of the suicidal mania. We shall hope for an early opportunity of dealing with the Japanese, as we are now doing with the Chinese character.

But let us glance at another sad evidence of social depravity—the infanticide of China. Some have denied it, or, at least, attempted to qualify their admission of its practice, and reduce it to the exceptional existence which it must be admitted to have in civilized Europe. But the crime is undoubtedly a *habit* of domestic life in China. The evidence lies within a narrow compass. The births of male and female children in China, as in other countries, are nearly equal. Very considerable numbers of Chinese emigrate to the Straits, California, Australia, &c. They are all men: they are never accompanied by their female relatives. Yet, notwithstanding this drain on the male population, it continues to be, in China Proper, considerably more numerous than the female. How is this to be accounted for? In the Fungwha district, some miles above Ningpo, there are never to be found, in any family, more than two daughters: in Ningpo, three.

---

* Milne's "Life in China," p. 86 – 88.

* Milne's "Life in China," p. 102.

Let us turn to one more trait of character, which may serve to convince us of the deplorable condition of this heathen nation, and their great need of Gospel light.

Fathers of families in China have absolute power over children, even to the extent of taking away life. In allowing extensive power to the heads of families, Chinese legislators appeared to think that parental affection would be a sufficient guarantee against its abuse. The following startling fact will suffice to prove that this is not always to be depended upon.

Some short time back a Missionary and his wife were residing in the city of Ningpo; their house was near the north gate, abutting on the river. It was the month of August, when the heat was intense, and the Missionary was ill with fever. Early in the morning, his wife, who was in the verandah, was startled by a cry, "Save my life, save my life." She looked in the direction of the sounds, and saw two men carrying between them a burden, which she soon perceived to be a human figure, with a sack thrown over it in such a way as to prevent the person from struggling or breaking away. Behind them walked a man, dressed as a Chinese gentleman, bearing in his hands a large stone. Unmoved by the cries which every now and then were uttered by the fettered person, the coolies bore him to the river's brink, and laid him down in the water on his face, where the mud was deep and soft. The gentleman then approaching, placed the heavy stone upon his feet, and withdrew, the Coolies squatting down upon the bank to watch the result. Half an hour having expired, they drew the body out of the mud, life being quite extinct, and bore it in the direction of a contiguous police-office. There it was met by the man who had superintended the murder, and was virtually the perpetrator of it. Standing forward erect, in the presence of the constable and a number of bystanders, he pointed to the body, and thus spake—"That was my son: he is such no longer: take him away, and let him be buried with the burial of a dog." The son had been a spendthrift, and had incurred heavy debts, for which, according to the laws of China, the father was responsible. A domestic murder solved the difficulty.

China, in all probability, will soon be thrown open to unrestricted intercourse with Europe The iron sledge of European power is being uplifted, and is menacing a ponderous stroke, before the weight of which the crumbling walls and dilapidated gates of her exclusive policy will be levelled with the dust. When the way is open, through the breach will pour in European life, with its evil and its good, its Gospel truth, and spurious imitations of that truth. On the extended plains of China, Popery hopes to achieve new victories, and there find compensation for loss of character and decreasing influence in Europe. It is remarkable that Romish Missions and Protestant Missions have alike fixed on the same locality as their head-quarters—Ningpo. It is the door into the great representative province of Che-keang, in whose well-watered soil are found the choicest products of China, and whose population comprises the literary, commercial, manufacturing, and labouring classes; a province so important, that a position acquired there must tell on the whole empire. Here, then, the Romish Societies *Pour la Propagation de la Foi* are sending their priests and *Sœurs de Charité* in considerable numbers. They are continually coming and going, and are busy in the work of proselytizing the natives. The transition from the mummeries of Boodh to the superstitions of the Papacy is easy. The points of similarity between the systems are numerous and obvious. The vow of celibacy taken by persons of both sexes, and their seclusion in monasteries and convents, "the monastic habit, holy water, counting rosaries to assist in prayer, worship of relics and canonization of saints, are alike features of both sects. Both burn candles and incense, and bells are much used in their temples. Both teach a purgatory, from which the soul can be delivered by prayers, and use a dead language for their liturgy, and their priests pretend to miracles." Above all, the female goddess who occupies so prominent a position in Buddhist mythology, finds its fac-simile in the Mary of the Romanists. At the same time, as a corruption of true religion, Romanism carries with it the *debris* of superior doctrines, which remain, like the insulated spots of cultivated grounds, gardens, and vineyards, amidst the desolation wrought by a deluge of fiery lava. These remains of divine truths crop out here and there, amidst the superstition in which they are imbedded, and superior, even in their broken and mutilated state, to any thing which mere heathenism can pretend to, suffice to place the Romish counterfeit in such a position of superiority over Buddhism as to ensure proselytes. But, pervaded as the system is with the most bitter hostility to scriptural Christianity, it leavens its own antagonism, and places them in direct opposition to the Gospel. The Romish Missionaries are proselytizing to a considerable extent, and are employing all their craft, which is by no means little, to push their native adherents into positions of influence in native society. Let it be widely known, that, since 1844, "foreign priests, of Popish persuasion, have reclaimed landed property, have purchased new lands in their own name, and built chapels, &c., beyond the boundaries defined for foreigners. Besides which, it is universally known that Jesuit priests are in every part of the country, prosecuting their Missionary labours."

The village of Zee-ka-wei, in the vicinity of Shanghae, is referred to with much self-gratulation in the pages of the "Annales de la Propagation de la Foi." There is planted a well-organized training establishment for the dissemination of Popery throughout the Kiang-nan province; a school-house, with its pupils, native and foreign, all in native costume, with foreign ushers and native teachers; a chapel, capable of containing 500 persons; the seminarist college, where native catechists and priests are being trained in Chinese literature and Romish theology, &c. A letter appears in the Lyons periodical for May last year, purporting to be from R. P. Gounet, *Missionaire apostolique de la compagnie de Jesus*. He tells the world that the work of *proselytism*—such is the word he uses, and it best expresses the kind of work in which he is engaged, which shifts immortal souls from one kind of error to another, and leaves them farther from God than they were before—this work increases day by day. "At first some few families desired to come under the crook of the divine Shepherd; now entire hamlets are eager to enter his fold; and deputations from the heathen continue to arrive, desiring to have catechists who shall teach them the way to heaven." The locality of the Mission is described as "un pays gros d'esperance, une terre neuve qui, bien défrichée, donnerait des fruits abondants. The father adds, "Vous que êtes si devot a saint Joseph, vous apprendrez avec bonheur que ce grand patriarche en a donné un bon coup de main," and describes a happy thought which suggested itself to him when penetrating to a remote part of the district where heathenism was rampant, namely, that of dedicating to St. Joseph all the chapels which he might succeed in building; and St. Joseph has been so pleased with this purposed arrangement, that neophytes and catechists are already sprinkled abroad through the territory.

However, if the success of the system depended on the aid which St. Joseph is to render it, we might well decide to treat its utmost efforts with indifference; but we fear its crafty adaptation to the requirements of the natural mind, and the unscrupulous way in which it compromises its convictions to its interest.

This we may be assured of, that Ningpo and Shanghae are busy centres of Romish efforts. Numerous foreign teachers are disguised as natives, besides a large staff of Chinese agents. These are spread abroad throughout the villages, where, in the Kiang-nan vicarage alone, there are said to be "spiritual children" to the number of 70,000 souls. There are schools for boys and girls, chapels, monasteries, and to these they have added "the institution of religious women." The young women who compose it dedicate themselves to Mary, and consider themselves as chosen agents for the dissemination of her name and worship. Eight foreign sisters of mercy, in 1850, were smuggled into Shanghae for the purpose of raising up this female staff, and, taking advantage of the Buddhist nunneries, appear to have found materials ready to their hand.

In short, there is, amongst the agents of Rome, no lack of energy. Shall the Protestant church appear in the presence of the Chinese with less zeal, with an inferior organization, and disjointed efforts? Not so, we trust.

CHRISTIANITY IN ITS INFLUENCE ON THE COLONIZATION OF NEW ZEALAND.

In the progress of human affairs, questions occasionally arise of such special magnitude and importance, that any amount of effort and self-sacrifice is well-bestowed in the endeavour to bring them to a satisfactory conclusion. Indeed it usually happens that the objects which may be had with little cost are of no value, while such as are really valuable, require persevering and arduous exertions. Experience shows, moreover, that in all such undertakings, it is precisely as when one addresses himself to climb a steep mountain. The nearer the summit the more precipitous the incline; the severest pinch precedes success. It is just then that the most determinate efforts are necessary, and any faltering in our resolutions, or slackening of our exertions, may undo all that has been done, and involve us in a deplorable discomfiture.

New Zealand has been the stage where, for a series of years, a great undertaking has been carried forward, one which has been attended with many difficulties, and has required, at the hands of those engaged in it, no small amount of labour and patience; but which from the deep interest and importance which attaches to it, has been justly deemed well worthy of being persevered in. The object to be attained has been the preservation of a native race in the presence of a powerful influx of colonization from the old world. The question again and again has been asked, Can the white man colonize without the destruction of the inferior aboriginal race, which, previously to his arrival, had the exclusive occupation of the land? Can colonization be carried on, only at a cost so fearful as the extinction of the inferior races; and is there no way by which a result so calamitous can be prevented, except by thwarting and discouraging that movement towards colonization, which naturally and necessarily arises in prosperous and powerful races, whose vigorous ratio of increase has rendered their native land a homestead too narrow for them? We confess that the history of colonization, so far as it has progressed, casts a gloomy shade on this question, and bears inscribed upon it so many painful records of aboriginal races blighted and perishing before the advancing footsteps of the white settler, that men have pronounced such an issue to be a sad yet unavoidable necessity. There are, indeed, painful and numerous facts extant on this subject. Yet are we persuaded that there exists no sad law of necessity which dooms the native to extinction that the white man may colonize and yet the native survive; and that colonization has been calamitous in its results, only because the white man has been false to the Christianity he professed, and because avowedly Christian Governments have allowed the migratory process to be carried forward on principles which Christianity not only never sanctioned, but plainly and peremptorily condemned. The white man, going forth as a colonist, has been too frequently the oppressor and destroyer of the aboriginal races, because he has acted, not as a Christian, but as a heathen, and has refused to be controlled or directed by the maxims of that very religion, the profession of which he still continued to regard as the great distinctive mark between the heathen and himself. We believe and are persuaded that races can meet, and, with a greater or less measure of difficulty adapting themselves to each other, eventually fuse, provided only that Christianity be permitted to exercise its just measure of control, feeling assured that it has power to restrain the outbreakings of human passions, and so moderate the impatience of selfishness, that the aboriginal race shall be contented to yield enough of territory to constitute a new and ample homestead for the settler, while, by the law of equity and the reciprocity of kindness, the latter is well contented that the native retain a convenient and suitable heritage for himself. The question is, whether Christianity has the power to effect so satisfactory a solution of this difficulty; and it is one on which we entertain no doubt, provided only that the great panacea, when the crisis comes, be afforded sufficient scope for action. Humane men have felt so strongly on this subject, that they have not hesitated to oppose themselves to colonization, and to interfere with its free action. It is in vain to pursue this course. The tide of migration must go on, and the surplus of population transfer itself from the older and densely crowded regions, to those which, while thinly populated, invite attention from their climate, position, and productive power. Enterprising, energetic, and rapidly increasing races must needs swarm when the mother hive becomes too strait for them. Nor is it necessary that so fruitless an attempt should be adventured upon. There is a safer and more suitable mode of action. Let Christianity have free course, going forth on its mission of peace throughout the world; let it anticipate the outgoings of colonization, and prepare the aboriginal races for the coming of the white man. Let it act with more energy at home, and thoroughly permeate the centres of population. There is the opportunity. The Anglo-Saxon race is the great colonizing element, and Christianity in all its original purity has its place in the very midst of that population. Let it then be energetically worked at home and abroad. Home appliances, Missionary appliances, let them be vigorously employed. All that is needed is more holy consecration of pecuniary means, of personal influence and effort, to the work. Let the United Church of England and Ireland occupy the van. Let every individual holding a position in that church, and with the opportunity of being useful, if only he be disposed to use it, remember that the well-being of the world's population is more or less involved in his fidelity to his engagements, and that a dereliction of duty and service on his part, weakening as it does the momentum of home Christianity, is felt to the uttermost ends of our earth. Many an ungodly sailor, who introduces new vices and new miseries amidst the population of some heathen land, might have been, instead of a scourge, a benefactor of his species, if only the home pastor, who had charge over him in his early youth and boyish days, had more prayerfully instructed him. But this is what we want—only let Christianity precede and go forth with the advance of colonization, and the issues of the future shall not fail to contrast strongly and favourably with those of former times.

Christianity has had a fairer opportunity for the development of its peculiar influences, in this respect, in New Zealand, than in any other sphere of colonization which we can remember. In other instances it has not appeared in the field until after the races have met and mischief has ensued. We speak not now of adulterated and corrupt Christianity, such as the Spaniards and Portuguese introduced with them into the new continent. That exercised no restraining influences on the evil tendencies of human nature. Instead of compassion, there was bigotry; instead of persuasion, the sword. But we speak of that Christianity which is by revelation of God, and which, maintained in purity of doctrine by a constant reference to the written word, in the power of the Spirit exercises a holy influence on men's minds. But even this has, in most other instances, been placed at a disadvantage. Instead of preceding colonization, it has followed in its footsteps, and that slowly and at a distance. It has not reached the scene of action, until the alien races have met in fierce collision, and the surge thrown up at the point of confluence has been stained with blood; and yet even thus, under such disadvantages, it has, in more than one instance, vindicated its power, and has been in time to save some aboriginal tribe, otherwise doomed to destruction. It has found, amidst the ashes of once powerful nations, a seed of vitality, which it has cherished and fostered, until, rekindled into a flame, it has recovered the ground which had been lost, and exhibits anew a reproductive power and healthful increase. Such instances may be found in the now permanized stocks of aboriginal nations in the North-American continent, which once, under the effects of colonization, had so fearfully diminished, that their speedy extinction seemed to be inevitable. Yet, under the invigorating influences of Christianity, the remnants have unexpectedly revived, and the old stock, shooting out new branches, promises, after a season, to emulate the luxuriance of olden times. We would specify, as illustrations of what we have advanced, the Cherokees and Choctaws, as well as the Crees of Rupert's Land.

But, in New Zealand, Christianity had this peculiar advantage, that it preceded colonization. Indeed, so true is this, that unless Christianity had gone before, there would have been no colonization in New Zealand. Christianity prepared the way for the settler. The Christian Missionary ventured where none had gone before, except some outcast Europeans; men who, on its wild shores, sought a refuge from the consequences of their own crimes, and who, in order that they might be suffered to dwell among the natives, cast away the shreds of civilization, and became more heathen than the heathen themselves. The Maori was then a bye-word: amongst the fierce cannibals by which those isles were peopled, no emigrant ever dreamed of adventuring himself. Had the original settlers, who landed in Cook's Straits in 1839 and 1840, been aware that the site at Port Nicholson, which they selected for their new town, Wellington, was the *locale* of fearful earthquakes, they would have directed their steps elsewhere; and wasted and desolated as these islands had been by fierce outbreaks of human passions, no Englishman, however anxious to emigrate, ever thought of selecting New Zealand as his new home. Suitable as the climate was to his requirements, its moral aspect was repulsive, and he preferred to direct his steps to Canada, with its backwoods and severe winters. Yet thither went the Missionary. Where other men feared to go, he entered in, not alone, but with wife and children. English families, unprotected save of God, located themselves in the midst of fierce cannibals. We know of no more remarkable exemplification of true courage. When, in the battle-field, the blood is up, and in the strong excitement of the moment the man forgets both danger and himself, great deeds of prowess have been wrought. But the noble Christian man, who, actuated by the simple desire of bringing a savage race to the faith of Christ, entrusted himself to their hands, and fearlessly lay down to sleep amidst the cannibal warriors by whom he was surrounded, presented as grand an exemplification of true courage as the world has ever witnessed. And then to persevere, not for a few hours or even months, but for years, amidst the revelations of new horrors, as, day by day, they came to light; to live on in the midst of a people who seemed more like incarnate fiends than men, with an increasing perception of the danger of their position, and not knowing the instant when some unintentional infringement of native customs might be the signal for their being stripped, ill-treated, and perchance put to death;—this indeed was courage, and the men who endured all this were the conquerors of New Zealand. They won their way, not by law but by love; not by coercion, but by persuasion. They used not the sword, or the rifle, the thirty-two pounder, or serried military array; their weapons were not carnal: and these were the great men of New Zealand. Some from amongst the Missionary body became landowners, and that to a large extent. It is to be regretted that they so far sullied the greatness of their victory, and laid themselves open to reproach; but their circumstances were peculiar. They had large families, and were isolated from their native country. The natives regarded them as benefactors, and readily conveyed to them a portion of their land. They did so as an expression of their gratitude, and as a remuneration for valuable services rendered. They knew these services to be such as to be beyond the possibility of any adequate requital. But it would have completed the grandeur of the moral conquest of New Zealand if these men had kept their hands from receiving earthly recompences for their labours, or committing themselves to any procedure which looked like taking advantage of the grateful feelings of the natives to enrich themselves. Better far, if, resisting the temptation, they had said, "We seek not yours, but you," and had cast themselves, their children, and their family anxieties on the Lord. And many of them did so. In this matter of land acquirement they kept themselves unspotted from the world; and these men are now the most honoured and influential of the Missionary body in New Zealand.

But thus the work was done. Christianity went before, and New Zealand was prepared for colonization. The preparation consisted in the humanizing of the people. They ceased to be ferocious and repulsive. Colonists thought they might venture in where Missionaries so long had dwelt in safety. They did so, and the tide of emigration set in on the shores of New Zealand.

And now we wish to trace the moderating action of Christianity, how it has intervened between the two races, and restrained on either side the violence of human passions. This it has done in a very remarkable manner, and beyond our most sanguine expectations. Difficulties, indeed, have arisen; collisions have taken place; but when affairs looked most angry, tranquillising influences have come in, like oil on the troubled waters, and the swellings of anger have unexpectedly subsided. A mysterious influence has been abroad, gentle and unobtrusive, yet effective to results, which mere human interference never could have accomplished. The colonist has been grasping, covetous, yet has he been restrained. The native has been distrustful, vindictive, yet, except in some few instances, he has not avenged himself. The colonist occupies lands which once belonged to the Maori, and yet the Maori continues to dwell in the presence of the white man. The colonists increase, the aboriginal native is said to decrease, yet the decrease may be incidental, and be soon arrested. The old stock may recover its vigour, and revive; and the sparse population, for such, whether it be regarded as colonial or aboriginal, it must be acknowledged to be at present, may become a mighty and amalgamated people, filling the whole land. At present the acreage is immensely in excess of the population, the area of the three islands amounting to 65,000,000 of acres; the aggregate of population, according to recent statistics, numbering not more than 115,313.* At present, in New Zealand, human beings, whether colonists or Maoris, are more scant than land, and therefore, on the lowest calculation, supposing men and

---

* Vide "Thomson's Story of New Zealand," vol. ii. Appendix. Tables 16 and 22, pp. 331 and 336.

acres to be of indifferently equal value, human beings are more valuable than acreage. To sacrifice human life to get possession of land is then indefensible policy. In all places human life is too costly to be expended in conflicts about land, but especially is this patent in New Zealand. By tact and patience, land may be had there, not only beyond all that the existing colonial population could ever by possibility require, but even if it were five hundred times multiplied. But if the attempt be made to wrest it from them by force, the Maoris will fight for it; nay, they will die to a man rather than surrender it to injustice and oppression. Men may be contented to pay dearly, if it secures to them the attainment of the coveted object; but in New Zealand the most expensive mode of proceeding is the least likely to be successful. But we must not anticipate our subject.

We shall proceed to mention some few of those eventful junctures in which the moderating influence of Christianity has been apparent, and which encourage hope, as to the future, that the same influence will not be wanting, in seasons of difficulty and danger, to produce like results.

The treaty of Waitangi may be referred to. The chiefs of the confederation of the united tribes of New Zealand ceded to Her Majesty the Queen of Great Britain, "absolutely and without reservation, all the rights and powers of sovereignty which they respectively exercised or possessed over their respective territories as sole sovereigns thereof;" while, on the other hand, the British Sovereign "confirmed and guaranteed to the chiefs and tribes of New Zealand, and to their respective families and individuals thereof, the full, exclusive, and undisputed possession of their lands and estates, forests, fisheries, and other properties, which they collectively or individually possessed, so long as it be their wish and desire to retain them."* If at any time it became the pleasure of the proprietors to alienate their lands, it was stipulated that the exclusive right of pre-emption should rest with Her Majesty, the land to be taken at such prices as might be agreed upon.

One article more completed this national compact: in consideration of these cessions, Her Majesty the Queen of England "extended to the natives her royal protection, and imparted to them all the privileges of British subjects."

The moderating influences of Christianity could alone have effectuated this arrangement. Its action on the mind of the contracting parties induced that spirit of mutual concession which rendered such stipulations practicable. Without this, British statesmen would never have recognised the native land-title; and unless this had been done, the native would never have bowed his head to the sovereignty of England, until his power of resistance had been broken, and the sanguinary scenes which have stained other pages of colonial history had been re-enacted in New Zealand. Even as it was, some of the chiefs distrusted the arrangement, and spoke against it. "In speeches, full of quotations from ancient songs and familiar proverbs, they stated that the treaty would deprive them of their lands; that it was smooth and oily, but treachery was hidden under it; and these orations so moved the audience, that an unfavourable termination of the conference was anticipated." Eventually, however, after twenty-four hours deliberation, the treaty was signed by forty-six chiefs, a number which, before the end of June in the same year (1840), had increased to 512. "It was a wise measure, a Christian mode of commencing the colonization of the country." By thus recognising the legal title of the natives to all the land in the country, England disclaimed that grasping and oppressive principle which, in other fields of colonization, has been the frequent source of so many evils, namely, that Europeans have a right to appropriate to themselves, without the consent of the native proprietor, such lands as he has not brought under actual cultivation. The treaty of Waitangi, however inconvenient to the adventurer, who, in distant lands, acts as if he were under no law, and had a right to spoil the native so far as he is strong enough to do so, constitutes a grand national compact between the Crown of England and the people of New Zealand. It is the Magna Charta of their liberties to which our national honour stands pledged; and, at whatever cost, it must be preserved inviolate. On one or two occasions only does there appear to have been any vacillation in the minds of British statesmen on the subject. To these we shall have occasion to refer further on.

But, with such exceptions, the voice of British statesmen has uniformly recognised the force of the treaty of Waitangi, and their obligation to respect it. That such is the fact may be established by a series of references to various Parliamentary Papers and despatches. Thus, Lord John Russell, in his despatch to Governor Hobson, of January 20, 1841, states:—" Her Majesty, in the royal instructions, under the sign manual, has distinctly established the general principle,

---

* Thomson, vol. ii. pp. 19, 20.

that the territorial rights of the natives, as owners of the soil must be recognised and respected; and that no purchases hereafter to be made shall be valid unless such purchases be effected by the Governor of the colony on Her Majesty's behalf."

Again, Mr. Under Secretary Hope to the New-Zealand Company, under date February 1, 1843—

"Lord Stanley is not prepared, as Her Majesty's Secretary of State, to join with the Company in setting aside the treaty of Waitangi, after obtaining the advantages guaranteed by it, even 'though it might be made with naked savages, or though it might be treated by lawyers as a praiseworthy device for amusing or pacifying savages for the moment.' Lord Stanley entertains a different view of the obligations contracted by the Crown of England; and his final answer must be, that as long as he has the honour of serving the Crown, he will not admit that any person, or any Government, acting in the name of Her Majesty, can contract a legal, moral, or honorary obligation to despoil others of their lawful or equitable rights."

Sir Robert Peel, in the New-Zealand debate of June 1845, protests against any attempt to evade the obligations of the treaty—

(Referring to a suggestion made by the New-Zealand Company), he says—"I believe there are a good many lawyers in the New-Zealand Company, and this may be the language of lawyers; but what was the language of statesmen?" .... (After citing Lord J. Russell's despatch, above referred to, he proceeds to say)—

"That was the language held by statesmen. That treaty was entered into with as much formality as their usages permitted; and are you now prepared, because you find the engagements onerous and inconvenient—inconvenient to yourselves, but injurious to the natives even — are you prepared to disclaim and repudiate the act of statesmen, and to concur with the lawyers that the treaty is a mere praiseworthy device for amusing and pacifying savages? .... I ask, will you commence your relations with the colony by an abandonment of the obligations you have entered into? I will say, if ever there was a case where the stronger party was obliged by its position to respect the demands of the weaker, if ever a powerful country, was bound by its engagements with a weaker, it was the engagement contracted under such circumstances with the native chiefs."

Lord Stanley to Governor Grey, June 13, 1845, writes in the same strain—

"I repudiate with the utmost possible that the treaties which we have entered into with these people are to be considered as a mere blind to amuse and deceive ignorant savages. In the name of the Queen, I utterly deny that any treaty entered into and ratified by Her Majesty's command was, or could have been, made in a spirit thus disingenuous, or for a purpose thus unworthy. You will honourably and scrupulously fulfil the conditions of the treaty of Waitangi."

And this assurance on the part of the British authorities was communicated by Governor Grey to a deputation of the principal chiefs, which waited upon him with reference to the land question, and the state of affairs generally. In a despatch addressed to the Secretary of State, dated December 10, 1845, he says—

"I think it only necessary to add, in reference to the natives, that I have, in the most public manner, in the strongest terms, and upon repeated occasions, assured them that I had been instructed by Her Majesty most honourably and scrupulously to fulfil the terms of the treaty of Waitangi; that their welfare and happiness was an object of the most lively concern to the Queen; and that it would be my most earnest desire to carry out Her Majesty's most gracious wishes in their favour; and I am satisfied that these declarations on my part have produced a very favourable impression upon many of the most influential chiefs."

In his address to the Legislative Council, December 12, 1847, the Governor announces the same principles of action—

"I feel it to be due alike to the interests of both races of Her Majesty's subjects within this colony, to take this, the first opportunity which has been afforded me, of stating, in the most explicit terms, that I have been instructed most honourably and scrupulously to fulfil the conditions of the treaty of Waitangi, by which the full, exclusive, and undisturbed possession of their lands and estates, forests and fisheries, and other properties which the chiefs and tribes of New Zealand, and the respective families and individuals thereof, may collectively or individually possess, was confirmed and granted to them, so long as it may be their wish and desire to retain the same."

We cannot but regard the treaty of Waitangi as a grand preliminary arrangement which raised New Zealand above the ordinary level of colonization proceedings, and as a dignified announcement on the part of the British crown of its determination, while it sanctioned colonization in these islands, to provide at the same time for the preservation and well-

mitted to notice one more despatch, of a noble character, from Lord John Russell, in which Governor Hobson "is directed to protect the aborigines from injustice, cruelty, and wrong; to establish and maintain friendly relations with them; to turn into useful channels their hitherto neglected capacities for labour; to avoid every practice injurious to their health or the diminution of their numbers; and to educate the young, and diffuse among the whole population the blessings of Christianity. 'If the experience of the past,' observes his lordship, 'compels me to look forward with anxiety to the too probable defeat of these purposes by the sinister influences of the many passions, prejudices, and physical difficulties with which we shall have to contend, it is, on the other hand, my duty and your own to avoid yielding in any degree to that despair of success which would assuredly render success improbable. To rescue the natives of New Zealand from the calamities of which the approach of civilized men to barbarous tribes has hitherto been the almost universal herald, is a duty too sacred and important to be neglected, whatever may be the discouragements under which it may be undertaken.'"*

Let us proceed to trace the moderating influence of Christianity at another juncture in the history of New-Zealand colonization. Collisions have taken place between the two races. This is not surprising. The wonder is, that, with so many sources of contention, the disputes have hitherto been so few, and of such short duration. The grand cause of disquietude has been land and its possession.

Let it be remembered, that, with the Maori, territorial rights constitute a vital question. "Eighteen historical nations of New Zealanders occupy the country." Thomson, in his "Story of New Zealand," enumerates the names and localities of these tribes, with most of whom the annals of Missionary enterprise have rendered us familiar; the Rarewa, at the extreme north of the North Island, where may be found our Mission station Kaitaia, with its European Missionaries and native catechists; bordering on these, the Ngapuhi, Hongi's renowned tribe, the first to obtain fire-arms, and the first to experience the subduing influences of Christianity; around Auckland, where they are intermingled with the settlers, the Ngatiwhatua; southward of the neck of land on which Auckland stands, and in occupation of some of the finest districts, the Wuikato and Ngatimaniopoto natives, numbering 9800 souls; on the islands and bays of the Hauraki gulf, and along the banks of the Thames, the blood-connected Ngatipaoa and Ngatimaru natives, 5000 in number. We next approach a widely-scattered people, "the bold and adventurous Ngatiawa, numbering not more than 4000 souls;" yet are they to be found along the east coast of the North Island, on the shores of the Bay of Plenty, on the west coast, along the Waitara river, near Taranaki, and on both sides of Cook's Straits. There is no tribe, which, if unjustly dealt with and unhappily alienated, is so fitted to become a seed-plot of disaffection in New Zealand; and this is the tribe with which we have just had a sharp collision in the Taranaki district.

"At Maketu, on the coast of the Bay of Plenty, and around the borders of the Rotorua, Tarawera, and other lakes of that interesting geological district, live the Ngatiwhakaue natives, a people numbering 3200, and distinguished for good noses and Jewish features." These, from their secluded position, are, of all the tribes, the least advanced in civilization. To those already enumerated may be added the Ngatituwharetoa, around Lake Taupo; the Taranaki tribe west of Mount Egmont; tending towards the embouchure of the Wanganui, the Ngatiruanui; on both banks of the Wanganui, the Ngatihau; the Ngatiraukaua, southward of the Wanganui; the Ngatitoa, in the sheltered coves of Cook's Straits; besides the Whakatowhea, the Ngatiporu, and Ngatikahungunu along the east coast from the Bay of Plenty to Cape Palliser. It may be observed, in glancing over these tribal names, that the prefix "Ngati" signifies "offspring." "Ngati, therefore, corresponds with the Irish O and the Scotch Mac."*

These eighteen nations are subdivided into tribes, to such an extent, that the Ngatikahungunu, numbering not so many as 4000 souls, comprises, in its narrow limits, not less than forty-five tribes;† that is, on an average, about eighty-two persons to each tribe. Each tribe comprising several families, has one at its head, "who, with the tribe, acknowledges the chief of the nation as his lawful lord." The land is the property of the tribe by a communal title. Any individual of the tribe, by clearance or cultivation, may appropriate a portion of the land, and transmit it to his posterity, as, so far as use is concerned, specially their own, but without the power of alienating it from the tribe. The individual

---

* Thomson, vol. ii. p. 42; and Parliamentary Papers.

* Thomson, vol. i. p. 93.
† Thomson gives some of the names (see vol. i. p. 93), adding, that he only gives a moiety of the clans.

right had force only so far as it consisted with the communal title. Any alienation of the tribal property required tribal consent. "The individual claim did not give the individual the right to dispose of it to Europeans."* The New Zealanders "are rich as tribes rather than as individuals, most of their natural and much of their acquired property being owned, or at least enjoyed, by a group of families in common, rather than by any one exclusive member in particular. Thus there is neither great individual wealth nor poverty among them."†

Now, colonization, at its very outset, infringed upon this tender point of native character, and that in consequence of the irregular proceedings of the New-Zealand Company. They proceeded to locate their emigrants on land which the natives declared they had never parted with. "On the 22d of January 1840, the Company's first emigrant ship arrived at Port Nicholson, and before the end of the year 1200 settlers disembarked. The natives were transported with wonder at the sight of so many white women and men, and inquired if the whole tribe, meaning all the people of England, had come to New Zealand. The natives instructed the settlers in building huts, and cheerfully sold them numerous pigs and abundance of potatoes. There was no quarrelling, and both races lived in confidence of each other." The entrance to the valley of the Hutt was selected as the site of the first town, but its exposure to the sea rendered this spot unsuitable, and a more convenient locality was selected on the other side of the harbour, but one against the occupation of which the natives protested, as they declared they had never sold it, and that the settlers were acting unjustly in appropriating it. This led the emigrants to institute inquiries "into the nature of the Company's land purchases." It was then found that land to the amount of many millions of acres—Thomson says twenty millions—upon which 10,000 souls were actually resident, had been purchased from fifty-eight persons, of tribes different from the population in occupation of the land, thus ignoring the territorial rights of so large a number of individuals, "each of whom, according to native custom, had a vested right in some part of it." It is not surprising that, under such circumstances, misunderstandings arose between the two races; but the forbearance of the natives, so recently brought to a profession of Christianity, does surprise us. "They did not commit personal violence or steal, but pulled down houses erected on disputed lands, and informed Colonel Wakefield beforehand that such acts would be perpetrated. Singular to relate, none of the property within the houses was destroyed or taken away."

Similar mal-arrangements, on the part of the New-Zealand Company, prevailed at Wanganui, on the west coast, where it was proposed to form a second settlement. The settlers, on their arrival, "took possession of the land pointed out as their own by the Company's agent; but the natives warned them off, and announced that they were ready to fight for their inherited possessions." At Taranaki there arose similar altercations, of which we shall not now speak, as the affairs of that district well require to be separately dealt with. At length, in 1843, occurred the fearful collision in the Wairau valley, province of Nelson. This tract was claimed by the New-Zealand Company as their property: the natives denied that they had ever sold it. The Europeans sent in men to survey the valley. " Rauparaha and Rangihaeta, the proprietors, considering this the act of taking possession, burned down the surveyor's huts, but, before applying the match, they carefully removed, and preserved for the owner's use, all the surveyor's property within the huts." Here it might have been supposed the Europeans would have paused, and looked around for some peaceable mode of settling the dispute. Instead of this, a magistrate's warrant was issued for the apprehension of the great chief, Rauparaha, a mode of proceeding of the nature of which he was wholly ignorant, and to which he was not the least likely to submit, and a posse of armed Europeans, headed by the police magistrate and Captain Wakefield, proceeded to execute it. They found the chief surrounded by his armed followers, and occupying a strong position. A discussion ensued, during the course of which Rauparaha deprecated fighting, and desired that the dispute might be referred to the land-commissioner. Instead of this, the Europeans attempted to seize him. A conflict ensued; shots were fired, one of which struck a Maori female of rank, who was present—Rangihaeta's wife and Rauparaha's daughter. That untoward event exasperated the savage nature of the chiefs, so that they could no longer control themselves. Some of the Europeans had fallen; many more had fled. A few remained upon the field. Finding resistance hopeless, they surrendered, and were all butchered on the spot. "Those who fell in the battle were interred on the banks of the Tua Marina, and those who were massacred lie on a knoll in

---

* Thomson, vol. i. p. 97.
† Hursthouse, vol. i. p. 177.

full sight of the valley for which they lost their lives in vain."

All these conflicts originated in one source, an attempt on the part of the settlers to possess themselves of lands which the native had never sold, and over which he still claimed proprietary; and there is no doubt that they did induce much distrust in the native mind, and an alteration of feeling towards the new comers. The news of the conflict in the Wairau valley "spread like fire among flax from hamlet to hamlet all over the country, and being magnified in the usual manner, gave confidence to the restless and dissatisfied." The settlers, on their side, were equally irritated and disquieted; at one moment fearing lest they might be attacked at a disadvantage by the natives, and then, as the military began to arrive from New South Wales, urgently demanding that hostilities should be commenced, and vengeance exacted for the blood which had been shed. Such was the aspect of affairs on the arrival of Governor Fitzroy in Jan. 1844. "The settlers complained of the natives with bitterness, and the natives stated that the settlers were ill-disposed towards them." The hatred of races seemed to have commenced. In July 1844 there arose, in the Bay of Islands district, the disturbances connected with Heke, who, having married the late Hongi's daughter, seemed to think he ought to be a chief man among the Maoris, and put himself forward as a leader of the disaffected party. His first act was to cut down the flagstaff at Korareka, and carry away the signal balls. The military force at Auckland was forthwith strengthened, and preparations were made to crush this embryo insurrection, when the mediation of some friendly chiefs, who undertook to pay for the flagstaff, and to be responsible for Heke's future good behaviour, prevented the commencement of hostilities; and so matters might have sunk into quietude, and the smouldering fire have died out, but for ill-omened news from England, which reached the islands late in 1844; namely, that a Committee of the House of Commons had declared the treaty of Waitangi an injudicious proceeding. This "produced evil results. Heke made it the means of convincing the doubtful, and of strengthening the zeal of his lukewarm adherents." "He wrote to the Governor that he now believed they were to be deprived of their lands, like the aboriginal Australians." The flag-staff at Korareka was cut down a second time. Set up again, the pole being sheathed with iron, surrounded with a stockade, and guarded by soldiers, it became the point of conflict. "See," said Heke, "the flag-staff does mean taking a possession, or why else should they persist in re-erecting it. "On March 11, 1845, he bore down with his wild bands on the British troops, driving them from their position. Korareka was abandoned, the whole body of Europeans, inhabitants and soldiers, embarking in the ships which were in harbour, and leaving the New-Zealand warriors masters of the field. Yet in the moment of victory were they not forgetful of the claims of humanity: "children left on shore in the hurry of the flight were sent by the enemy uninjured to their parents." Auckland, it was thought, would be the next point of attack, and the panic amongst the settlers was extreme. Such as were in the country districts, "dreading a war of races, congregated around Auckland. Several colonists left the country, and property might be had at a nominal price." Defensive measures were adopted; block houses built, and earthworks thrown up; men trained to arms, and troops and ammunition summoned from Australia. Ultimately it was resolved to take the aggressive, and attack a fortification at Okaihau, where Heke was. The British force consisted of 400 men; but the effort was unsuccessful, the Pa being found impregnable without artillery. Another Pa, of greater strength, was attacked in June 1845, by a stronger force of 630 British troops, with five guns, besides native allies. After a cannonade of brief duration, a storming party advanced to the assault, but was repulsed with a loss of 100 killed and wounded, besides two officers. Subsequently, during the night, the Maoris evacuated the Pa.

The effect of this resolute stand made by Heke and his followers was precisely such as might have been expected. The excitement in the native mind was intense. Great chiefs, such as Te Heuheu, of Taupo, openly sympathized with the insurgent chief. "He told Mr. M'Lean that he considered Heke in the right, and that the English were an insatiable people, desirous of conquering all nations. The inhabitants of remote villages in the interior often sat up until day-light, in expectation of messages from the seat of war, and none of the conflicts lost any thing in splendour from the distance the news was carried. Heke rose high in the estimation of his race: he was the first warrior who had fought against England's soldiery." What prevented an universal rising on the part of the Maoris? It was precisely the opportune moment. The entire European population of these islands did not amount to 13,000. They were dispersed around the coast in eight settlements—Auckland, Wellington, Nelson, in the Middle Island, Taranaki, Bay of Islands, reduced from a population of 609 in 1843, to 10 in 1845; Akaroa, Hokianga, Wanganui: of these, the most populous, Wellington contained 3701 Europeans; the least so, Hokianga, 120. The Maoris in force occupied the centre of the island, its mountain fastnesses, and commanded the gullies, which, opening out into valleys as they approach the fertile coast districts, gave them the opportunity of rushing down like a flood upon the European settlements. They might have attacked them simultaneously, or cut them off in detail. What stayed them at such a moment? The repulse of the British troops from before Heke's pa at Oheawai occurred in July 1845; the expected reinforcements did not reach Auckland earlier than October of the same year; while the new Governor, Grey, was a month later in his arrival. This period of four months would have sufficed, had the natives so decided, to have accomplished the utter destruction of every settlement in the colony, and the expulsion, for a time at least, of the settlers from the land; so that the new Governor should have been greeted on his arrival by the ruins of burned houses, and the bodies of men who fell in protecting the retreat of the aged and feeble to the boats and ships. What preserved the infant colony at such a crisis, and warded off a stroke so disastrous? Christianity. The same gentle, unobtrusive, yet powerful influence which prepared New Zealand for colonization, after that colonization had commenced, preserved the infant settlements from destruction. The Missionaries unceasingly exerted themselves in tranquillizing the excited feelings of the natives, and dissuading the chiefs who had hitherto remained neutral from openly identifying themselves with the cause of Heke. But all these efforts would have been unsuccessful had the native character undergone no change—had there been no substratum of Christian principle to act upon. The old warloving Maori would have grasped his tomahawk and rifle, and preluding by a war dance the work of slaughter to which he was about to commit himself, have rushed forward with fiendish delight to revel in scenes of blood. But however strongly native feelings sympathized with Heke, he was left to stand or fall alone : and Governor Grey on his arrival, proceeded to crush him at his last stronghold of Ruapekapeka. Its fall broke the power of the insurgent chiefs; their followers dwindled away; and they were glad to write penitent letters to the Governor, desiring peace. And although, in 1846 and 1847, partial disturbances took place in the valley of the Hutt, near Wellington, and in the Wanganui district, they were but detached fires, and were soon put out; and in the beginning of 1848 peace between the races was restored.

It was on this occasion the hakari, or feast, was given to which our engraving refers.

"The hakari was a banquet given by natives to each other, for the purpose of making peace, honouring chiefs, talking over important affairs, or in return for a similar feast. Twelve months before the festival, food was planted, and preparations made for it. Previously to the arrival of the guests, the food was piled, either on the ground or on wooden scaffolds. Such erections were square pyramidal towers, having an elevation of fifty feet, or ranges of six feet high, extending from half a mile to two miles. There were several compartments in these receptacles for food, each being filled up with sweet potatoes, taros, maize, fern root, potted birds, dried fish, karaka berries, and other things; but there were feasts where nothing was served but fern-root.

"When the banquet was given in return for another, the quantity of food was expected to be greater than that at the original feast. Taunts of illiberality were cast upon tribes not following this custom. On the day of the hakari, in the presence of the assembled guests, the chief host called out each tribe by name, and pointed out its share of the food; and the guests carried away what they were unable to eat. At several modern banquets the surplus food has been sold to European traders present on the occasion. Six thousand guests have been counted at such banquets. Like battles, they were remembered for years, particularly when the entertainment was sumptuous. The wood of the banquet building was used by the guests to cook their food.

"Like Indians, who fell trees to gather the fruit, the New Zealanders at these banquets overlooked the future for the present. Such feasts are highly characteristic of the people, and were often given to have their hospitality noised abroad. To gain this end, tribes worked hard, and endured hunger for months without repining. Magnificence is displayed by savage races in high piles of food, and by civilized races in banquets where the grand feature is elegance more than abundance."*

We shall ever regard so rapid and comparatively bloodless a termination of a war, which threatened to be internecine, as one of the most remarkable facts in the history of New-

---

* Thomson, vol. i. pp. 189—191.

Zealand colonization. It cannot be ascribed to the superior character of the British force. On more than one occasion the troops had been successfully resisted; nor was their numerical strength at any time enough to overawe the natives, the strongest body brought into the field, on the attack of Ruapekapeke, not amounting to 1200 men. The restraint put upon the native population at such a crisis reminds us of the manner in which the swellings of the Jordan were stayed that the Israelites might pass over—it was at the time when its waters were at the highest, "for Jordan overfloweth all his banks in the time of harvest." Then it was, at the most unlikely moment, that they stood upon an heap, and were marvellously restrained. And it was at the moment of strongest excitement, when their national susceptibilities had been most keenly wounded; when the idea was general amongst them that the British legislature would not keep good faith in respect to the treaty of Waitangi, and that their lands would be unjustly wrested from them; when the breast of many a powerful chief heaved with indignation, and his followers only awaited the signal to commence war—just then, in the time of overflowing, was the flood restrained, and the colonists permitted to remain in safety. An unseen hand interposed, and prevented a catastrophe. When the natives become weak, and the settlers strong, may the latter remember to exercise a similar forbearance!

Twelve years have passed away since the termination of the Wanganui outbreak. The native and aboriginal races still dwell in the presence of each other; and until recently there has been peace. They had tried one another's strength, and the result taught them, for a time at least, mutual respect. "The New Zealanders came out of the conflict with no ill feelings against the English. They admit that some of their positions were taken, but say these advantages were won more by the mind than by the sword. Never was a war with a savage race conducted with fewer excesses and less barbarity; and on the withdrawal of the troops from the Bay of Islands in the year 1858, the Ngapuhi tribe, as if to remove every vestige of defeat, erected the flag-staff at Kororeka, which had been cut down by Heke in 1845."*

Since then, important changes have taken place on both sides. New Zealand has received a constitution—one intended to be comprehensive in its character, to include both races, and to bestow on each alike the elective franchise and privilege of political status. The seventh section of the Act appears to be very explicit on the subject—"The members of every such council shall be chosen by the votes of the inhabitants of the province who may be qualified as hereinafter mentioned; that is to say, every man of the age of twenty-one years or upwards having a freehold estate in possession situate within the district for which the vote is to be given of the clear value of 50*l*. above all charges and incumbrances, and of or to which he has been seised or entitled, either at law or in equity, for at least six calendar months next before the last registration of electors; or having a leasehold estate in possession situate within such district, of the clear annual value of 10*l*., held upon a lease which, at the time of such registration, shall not have less than three years to run; or having a leasehold estate so situate, and of such value as aforesaid, of which he has been in possession for three years or upwards next before such registration; or being a householder within such district occupying a tenement within the limits of a town (to be proclaimed as such by the Governor for the purposes of this Act) of the clear annual value of 10*l*.; or without the limits of a town, of the clear annual value of 5*l*., and having resided therein six calendar months next before such registration as aforesaid, shall, if duly registered, be entitled to vote at the election of a member or members for the district."

This at first was regarded as investing with the electoral privilege all inhabitants of a province, whether colonial or native, who should be of the age of twenty-one years, and who should be possessed of an estate of the indicated value. In the case of the native it has, however, been recently ruled that his estate does not qualify him to vote, unless it be held under a Crown grant. The result of this decision is thus stated by Dr. Martin, late chief justice of New Zealand, in a memorandum on native affairs drawn up at the request of the Governor, dated May 12, 1860—"It is now held that occupation under a native title does not in any case entitle the occupant to a vote; consequently the general assembly cannot claim dominion over a race which it does not represent;" and also by Mr. Swainson, late Attorney-General of New Zealand, in a similar document—"Though the constitution is called 'representative,' it has been decided that it does not confer the elective franchise: they have consequently no voice in the Colonial Legislature; and at the present moment they are subject, under the so-called representative constitution, to the government of a ministry in whose election they have no voice," &c.

---
* Thomson, vol. ii. p. 151.

The first elections took place in 1853. One hundred natives are said to have been on the electoral roll. The only one which could be designated as a contested one occurred at Auckland, the centre of the native population, where there was a severe contest for the office of superintendent, the New Zealanders being the more interested in the election, inasmuch "as both candidates were personally known to them — Colonel Wynyard, of the 58th regiment, from having held the office of Lieutenant-Governor of New Ulster, and Mr. William Brown, from his extensive commercial dealings with the natives. "On nomination-day considerable bodies of natives congregated in the streets of Auckland to witness the ceremony. When they heard the shouts of the electors before the hustings, and saw the violent gesticulations of the speakers, they withdrew to a distance; but when roars of laughter were mingled with angry words they looked perfectly amazed. Suddenly, as if comprehending the spirit of the strange scene, so unlike any thing they had ever seen before in the manners and customs of the English, they joined in laughing at the practical jokes played off on the occasion. When the hustings were vacated, several resident Maoris clambered into them, and with much merriment addressed the mob in a sort of monkey-like mimicking of the speakers."*

On the last day of 1853, Sir George Grey returned to England, having governed New Zealand during a most critical period of eight years. He wielded his power with unflinching firmness. A friend of the native, and anxious, in every practicable way, to promote his true welfare, he yet permitted no trifling with the Queen's sovereignty, and crushed every attempt at insurrection with vigorous promptitude. His was just the character and bearing to command the respect of the natives, and they valued him accordingly. His retirement from the government of New Zealand caused them the deepest regret, for they felt they were losing a friend on whose justice and impartiality they could rely. "From tribes resident near the English settlement, from tribes at a distance, from chiefs who had fought for and against the English, addresses were sent to Governor Grey, breathing a spirit of confidence and attachment. Heitikis, and other ancestral ornaments, almost never parted with, were freely given to him; songs were composed, and speeches full of eloquence delivered. Hone Te Paki said, "Let the meeting make known its unanimous wish to keep Governor Grey: the ashes of our fathers are in their tombs, and he has witnessed their deaths; Te Riepa is dead; Mare is dead; Hori Takiware is dead; Wetere Te Pake is dead; and other chiefs of Waikato. Governor Grey, come back to us whom you have left in grief, or whom you leave in their grief.' "*

On the 24th of May 1854, the first New-Zealand Parliament was opened, and the first step on the part of its members was to agitate for responsible government, for which the constitution made no provision. The executive council, with whose advice and assistance the Governor was to act in the administration of the colony, were not necessarily members of the legislative council. They were persons holding office under the Crown, and responsible only to the sovereign. Thus between the legislative assembly and the Government, there existed no recognised mode of communication. The first act, therefore, of the assembly was to move a resolution, desiring the establishment, without delay, of ministerial responsibility in the conduct of legislative and executive proceedings by the Governor. To this demand the head of the executive for the time being, Colonel Wynyard, the senior officer in command of the troops, felt himself unable to give a favourable reply, as he was only acting *pro tempore* until the arrival of Sir George Grey's successor; nor was this demand conceded until the close of the third General Assembly in September 1855, when Colonel Gore Browne, the new Governor, stated it to be his intention to carry on the government by responsible advisers, and in no other way, all questions of importance being deferred until the introduction of the new principle, after a dissolution of the assembly, and a re-election. In making, however, this concession to the wishes of the colonists, one point was excepted—the Governor reserved to himself the direction of native affairs, a reservation which was approved of by the Home Government, and assented to by the assembly. The justice of such an arrangement is obvious. It was to the Crown the natives ceded the sovereignty. A responsible ministry holds its position by a majority of votes in the House of Representatives. In that assembly no native has as yet occupied a place: they remain unrepresented. The Legislative Assembly is exclusively colonial. Its elective members are chosen by the suffrages of the colonists. They are therefore the exponents of the colonial mind, and must be regarded as necessarily and exclusively devoted to the interests of those whose representatives

---

* Thomson, vol. ii. p. 209.

* Thomson, vol. ii. p. 210.

they are.. The interests of both races are really identical. Whatever conduces to the prosperity of the one is for the advantage of the other, and *vice versâ*. But this is not always and at once perceptible. They not unfrequently appear to be antagonistic. To give to either race the right of administering the affairs of both would be most undesirable. It would place the dominant race under a new temptation, and, even if they rose superior to it, would leave them exposed to obloquy and misrepresentation. The other section of the population would regard themselves as consigned to a position of inferiority, and placed under a yoke. This would render them discontented and distrustful, and induce alienation and disaffection. It was therefore a wise decision that the direction of native affairs should remain in the hands of the Queen's representative. Still it does not seem to have been regarded as a settled point, on which no encroachments were to be attempted. It would have been well, indeed, for the future peace of New Zealand, if the native tabu could have been applied to it, so as to invest it with a recognised inviolability. But it has been far otherwise. The action of the responsible ministry on the reserved point has been like the incoming tide on whatever resists its progress: it still works onward. If obstructed, it retires, but only in order to recover strength for a new effort. If it cannot obtain all, it takes a part, and, step by step, makes good its progress. The Governor, with reference to this his special duty, the direction of native affairs, is placed in very unfavourable circumstances. In financial matters he is in a position of entire dependence on the ministry ; and can carry out the details connected with his important branch of the executive only so far as he may be supplied with funds by the colonial legislature. His position, therefore, has been anomalous and painful. Concessions are required from him, and unless he yields, he is exposed to obloquy, and reduced to an incapability of action. However much to be regretted, it is not surprising that he has given way. The first concession seems to have been made in the year 1856, when the Native Reserves Act was introduced. As the Bill originally stood, the powers conferred were left to the uncontrolled discretion to the Governor, but the General Assembly claimed to interfere, and a clause was introduced, providing that the Governor should act only with the advice and consent of the council, by which we are to understand the responsible ministry. The Governor for a while refused to accede, and at last only gave, to use his own words, a reluctant assent, on condition of the correspondence being transmitted, with the Bill, to the Imperial Government. The Secretary of State's reply settled the question. The Governor was informed, that, in legal strictness, the clause was opposed to the principle of native management agreed upon between him and his ministry; but that, in the expectation he would be able to work the two principles in harmony, the Governor's assent would not be overruled. Thus the Governor has greatly embarassed his own position, and shackled his liberty of action. Moreover, the colonial element was placed, by this concession, in the very position which it was most undesirable it should occupy, namely, that of interfering in native affairs without native co-operation. To this concession we attribute the tendency which of late has unequivocally manifested itself among the natives to separate themselves from the Europeans, and, as a distinct race, with dissimilar interests, to raise up from amongst themselves the elements of government and social order—a tendency which has more specially manifested itself in the king movement. The natives are fully aware of the alteration which has taken place, and however unmistakeably loyal they are to the British Queen, and prompt to recognise her authority in the person of her representative, they are resolved not to submit themselves to the rule of the Legislative Assembly, so long, at least, as it continues exclusively colonial, and not until it becomes sufficiently comprehensive to include the representatives of both sections of the population.

We feel that we are anticipating our materials, and introducing matter which will have to be again dealt with in a subsequent place; but however desirable it may be to lead forth with perspicuity the various matters which require the reader's attention, in order that he may thoroughly understand the position of affairs in New Zealand, it is difficult to avoid entirely the foreshadowing of what is yet future on the subject. We shall at present dwell no further on this point, than simply to introduce one passage from a memorandum of the Secretary on Native Affairs, dated September 20, 1858—

" In ceding the sovereignty of the country, the New Zealanders confided in the paternal wisdom and care of the British Government. It is conceived, therefore, that the administration of native affairs cannot, consistently with good faith, be entrusted to any but Her Majesty's Representative, while the Maoris continue a distinct and separate people. As they become incorporate and amalgamated with the colonists, they should take their proper position under colonial institutions. Nor is it at all desirable to perpetuate the distinction of race? Every effort should be used, and every facility afforded, to induce the Maori gradually to come over from the ranks of his countrymen to those of the colonists, and to exchange his aboriginal right on the soil for one derived from the Crown. Under existing circumstances, however, it is deemed of the highest importance that their relations with the English nation should remain in the hands of the Government by which they were established. The personal influence of Her Majesty's Representative has always been great in the estimation of the natives, who are willing to acknowledge it; and it is believed to be of paramount importance to the general weal that this influence should be maintained. To transfer would be to destroy it, and would shake that confidence in the justice of the Crown which is now held by the natives, who are too shrewd observers to be imposed upon by the mere semblance of power without its reality. A very large physical force would be insufficient to maintain a power equal to that which is now exercised by Her Majesty's Representative."

We must here break off this subject. Much more remains for consideration. The existing condition of the respective races, their increase or decrease, their advancement—the one in colonial prosperity, the other in Christianity and civilization; the difficulties which have arisen in the adjustment of their mutual relations, more especially as regards the retention or acquisition of land; the lamentable collision at Taranaki, and the circumstances which led to it; the perils and calamities in which our New-Zealand dependency must be involved, if force, instead of reason and persuasion, be resorted to as a means of solving these difficulties; the necessity that more consideration be shown to the feelings of the native, if we expect him to consider the necessities of the settler in the matter of land; all these yet present a wide field for investigation and reflection.

With the charter of self-government "Her Majesty granted a seal to the colony. It exhibits a New Zealander with his war-dress and spear, and a European covered with a municipal robe. Religion and justice are represented by a cross and scales. The seal is very characteristic; but the spear in the New Zealander's hand has the wrong end upwards, perhaps to indicate that strife had ceased." That it may be so, let all the emblems grouped together in the seal be preserved intact. If the scales be removed, and justice no longer preside over the administration of affairs, the spear in the native's hand will again have the point erected, and strife be rekindled. Indeed, the first blow has been already struck. Unless by generous and prompt action, on the part of Her Majesty's Government and Representative, the mischief be arrested, we shall have a war of races, in which the native race shall perish, and the colonial be miserably wasted, and reduced to a remnant. The Maori, with his war-dress and spear, will be effaced from the seal, and the European remain alone, impoverished and enfeebled, too much so to need, for many years to come, a constitution and a seal; a poor dependent for a mere existence on the generosity of the mother-country; and, if urgent circumstances should render necessary the withdrawal of her military force, as the Romans were compelled to withdraw their legions from Britain, unable to defend himself from a foreign aggression, and living only to lament, when too late, the pitiless extermination of his Maori brother. The Lord avert all such ill omens! That they will be averted we have this as a ground of hope, *the cross upon the shield*. Christianity, which has done so much for New Zealand, to complete her work will do still more.

THE WAR IN NEW ZEALAND.

the assistance of the Waikato tribes in the war. Hopes were entertained that at this meeting sentiments would be expressed which might lead to overtures for peace. This policy, on the Governor's part, has been highly displeasing to the war party among the colonists. We quote a paragraph from one of the Taranaki papers, which will show the state of feeling on this subject—

"We have alluded in our introductory remarks to the mystery which now envelopes the Governor's policy. Whether its ultimate design has changed we are not in a position to affirm; but that the *modus operandi* by which it was first intended to be pursued has been changed cannot for one moment be gainsaid. It was at first believed by the whole of the New-Zealand public, that the Governor intended, by quick smart blows, to drive the nail home; but having only given a few timid taps, he has so bent it, that it will require a great deal of care to get it straight again, if, indeed, he does not draw it, leaving an ugly hole to show how much injury an unskilful workman may do—how much worse the native question must be if an unsatisfactory peace is now entered upon. When war first commenced at Taranaki every journal was agreed on three points. They concurred in ascribing the cause to be a just one; in allowing that the Governor had commenced a new and wise policy; and in giving His Excellency the fullest credit for adopting decided and vigorous action. But during the three months that have since elapsed, a change has come over almost the whole of the press. While doubts as to the validity of Teira's title have been suggested, nothing has authentically transpired to prove that the utmost caution had not been taken to sift it thoroughly; and the few journals which have given expression to these doubts nevertheless strictly maintain that the rebellion must be suppressed at whatever cost; and until this is done peace cannot for a single moment be honourably entertained. On the second point the whole press is at sea. The Governor's policy, which at one time was supposed to be perfectly intelligible, is now understood by none. Either it was never correctly known, or it has changed. It was believed that that policy only related to the land at Waitara. 'Let William King cease his unlawful interference, and my work is done,' were the words of the Governor's letter to the natives of this province. Now, however, that policy seems to have been shifted, and to comprise either an intention to make war upon the king movement, if reinforcements arrive from India or England, or' to patch up a compromise after the meeting of chiefs in July. Public opinion on the third point has completely changed, and so far from being loud in commending the Governor's energy, there is scarcely a journal throughout the islands but what complains bitterly of opportunity lost, unaccountable tardiness, and ruinous delay. The second point—the obscurity of the Governor's policy—is the only one we need attempt to prove. The assertions we have made with regard to the others are too patent to need a single word being adduced in their support."

The king meeting commenced on May 24th, and lasted until May 31st.

"On the 25th of May," says the 'New Zealander's' correspondent, "the whole camp was early astir, and the prayer-bell was heard sounding in various directions, summoning the respective congregations to their morning devotions, for the great majority of the king party profess to base their movement on religion. The loyal Missionary natives doubt the reality of these professions, but feel it their duty to join with their misguided fellow-countrymen, as often as they can, in the hope of being able to restrain them in their rash and self-injurious agitation.

"Breakfast was discussed with more than usual despatch. Those who were to take part in the military display were everywhere busy cleaning their guns and preparing for the war-dance and rush by stripping themselves to the waist, and binding a shawl round their loins, or appearing in the full costume of a shirt, their heads being, for the most part, adorned with fillets and bunches of white feathers; in fact, their whole appearance, on this first day of 'Maori-dom' being proclaimed, was characteristic rather of a disposition to return to their ancient ways, than to inaugurate their 'new era' by exhibiting themselves in as civilised a guise as they could devise. Still, when the Rangiawhia regiment and William Thompson's men mustered on the bank sloping down from 'the king's mound' to the plain where the conference was to take place, they had a highly picturesque appearance; and the lower Waikatos and other natives, who formed the Aui, furnished a regiment equally lightly clothed, and, though a rather smaller body, they were even finer made men, and their firearms generally appeared to be of a superior description to those possessed by the more decided king's men.

"The combined force consisted of between 500 and 600 men, and a few women: about two-thirds had guns, the remainder canoe paddles. The war-dances were executed with much spirit; but older natives, who were looking on, criticised them rather severely, as, clumsily gone through, owing to the legs of the dancers having grown stiff 'through long sitting' (i. e. the disuse of the dance for many years), and, unworthy of a people who were talking so much of erecting themselves into a separate and independent nation. The affair was understood to have been got up with a desire to rouse the slumbering spirit of nationality among the undecided or wavering, and to stimulate it where it has already taken some root. Many young men joined in it purely for the sake of fun. There was one improvement noticeable—there was none of the thrusting out of the tongue, and very little of those horrid grimaces which used to give the Maori braves such a hideously unnatural aspect. After a war-dance and a rush from both contingents, the hill party advanced to those of the plain, and the two having executed a war-dance together, they broke up with a wild shout, and, after some 'welcome' addresses and songs, the first part of the day's proceedings was at an end....

"The meeting decided on erecting the king's flag, which was accordingly done, the Bishop of New Zealand, the officers of the Government, and the few other Europeans who were present, striking their tents, and refusing to remain to witness this overt act of disloyalty. Some of the Waikato tribes, who still adhere to the Queen, also did the same. . . . .

"With respect to the speeches delivered at this native conference, the greater portion were of such a curiously composite character—partly scriptural, partly political, partly fiercely patriotic, yet, on the whole, cautious and practical—that, even after the enumeration of every tribe and every speaker, we doubt whether more could be said than this, that some were for the Queen and some were for the king, and some were for friendship and others for enmity with the white man; that all admitted they had benefited by intercourse with the white man, but that some now wished to dispense with the white man's aid in any respect, while the more rational (who will eventually be the more influential) party quietly disposed of all this boasting, by asking *how* they would get on without the white man? that while some were disposed to defend the late murders at Taranaki as simply 'accidents of war,' others denounced them as 'murders;' that opinion was widely different as regards Wi Kingi's position at the outset, but, before the close, became almost unanimous in admission that 'the case' of the Governor, as to the purchase of Te Teira's land at Waitara, was unassailable; that therefore the Waikatos should not interfere in *that* quarrel, that they should, as far as possible, preserve peace with the white man, 'unless attacked by the white man,' of which, it was evident, they were in fully as much dread as many of the out-settlers were of them; and that, while they were bent on hoisting the 'new flag' (to which strong opposition was taken by some of the most influential of the native leaders), they were, at the same time, resolved to watch very closely the 'order of events.' That no more land was to be sold to the Governor without 'the king's' consent, was unanimously agreed upon; yet circumstances transpired, before the conference broke up, to show that the Maori kingites have doubtful friends, even in influential quarters. That 'King Potatau,' or, Te Whero Whero, is, to a great extent, made use of by his council, there can be no doubt; that he wishes to see peace preserved between the two races we also believe; and that he would prefer the title originally proposed of 'Father of his People,' to that of 'King,' or all the fulsome and sometimes blasphemous adulation addressed to him, no one who knows him can doubt. And when we have told this, we have said all that can be said as to the apparent results of the late meeting at Ngaruawahia. What may be the real results remain to be seen."

These extracts will serve to show, that at this important crisis in the history of the Maori race, there is far from unanimity amongst the various tribes. In their political feelings they may be divided into three classes : 1st, the Queen's party; 2dly, the moderate king party ; 3dly, the extreme king party. The first party are loyal natives, who wish for British law, and for every tribe to use its own judgment in reference to the sale of their waste lands. The second party would, for the sake of peace, give up to the Government the disputed land at Taranaki, but at the same time expect in future the Government not to purchase; but the third party object to its being given under such circumstances.

Meanwhile, during the time when the meeting was being held, events were being precipitated at Taranaki. "The beginning of strife is as when one letteth out water; therefore leave off contention before it be meddled with." Little wars are dangerous things; for often, little wars become great ones. "Behold how great a fuel (ὕλην) a little fire kindleth!" and the little blaze, which those on the spot think they can put out whenever they please, spreads as amongst the dry fern, until it becomes a mighty forest-conflagration, which will not be controlled. Hot spirits on both sides were impatient under restraint. "Lately," observes one of the Taranaki journals, "when about 250 Taranakis, Ngatiruanis, and Waikatos crossed the ford at the Waitara, the officers and men were most anxious to get at them, and burned with indignation at being compelled by their orders to allow those rebels to pass unmolested, when every one of them could have been picked off as they were crossing the ford." These, we apprehend, were a party of Waikatos escorting back the Taranaki deputation. Had they been fired upon the whole of the Waikatos, who as yet remained undecided, would have risen.

Nor were fiery spirits wanting amongst the Maoris, men who were anxious to put an end to all uncertainty, and decide the tribes for war; men, too, of the old New-Zealand stamp, ready for any savage act. It is the unhappiness of times of confusion that bad men rise to the surface, and compromise, by their evil deeds, others of very different purposes and temper. Towards the latter end of May, Mr. Richard Brown, an old colonist and merchant of Taranaki, riding out from the camp in search of a stray horse, and venturing too near the bush, was shot down by three natives. William King, it is said, and the Waikato natives, repudiate this act. We trust it may be so. This we are sure of, that such atrocities must serve to open the eyes of every well-disposed native, and lead him to say, if Scripture truth has any hold upon him, "Oh my soul, come not thou into their secret; unto their assembly, mine honour, be not thou united; for in their anger they slew a man." It must be observed, however, that this poor gentleman was more than a simple colonist. He was captain of the native irregular force, and had volunteered some time before, in company with two chiefs and eighty followers, to capture Wi Kingi, and bring him back alive or dead. He was therefore a marked man, and should have been more cautious. But there have been other murders, which show that there are bad natives abroad, whose power of exciting additional irritation is excessive, and who deserve condign punishment.

Reprisals now commenced. Towards the end of May an attack was made upon the coast natives by a column of 500 men, under Colonel Gold. They burned down some Maori huts and a mill, carting a large quantity of wheat, and spreading it over the land.* Such proceedings only increase exasperation. When a blow must be struck, let it be well-directed and decisive; until this can be done it is better to refrain. The natives, now becoming bolder, entered the houses which had been erected on the disputed block, destroying the property, and carrying off the stock of the settlers. Parties of military were sent in pursuit of them, but to no purpose. Meanwhile the town of Taranaki appears to have been almost hemmed in. Travelling in the direction of the bush had become unsafe. The outsettlers had come in, bringing their wooden houses with them. A night attack from the insurgents being apprehended, the town was at night doubly guarded, lamps being put up in various parts, dogs also being in request, "the Government getting all the dogs they can. These they are going to chain up, and feed well, placing them in the gullies around the town;" that in case of any attempt on the part of the natives to steal in, they might give the alarm.

The Maoris had by this time restored an old Pa, at a place called Putekakauere, just outside the boundary of the disputed land. It appears to have been strong in position, as well as strongly stockaded. It consisted of two stockades, one upon the entrenchments of the old Pa; the other new, and apparently without entrenchments. They stood on a ridge formed by two gullies, these gullies meeting a little below the Pa, and opening on to swampy ground in the Waitara valley, forming a sort of long Y, the stalk toward the river, and the stockades in the fork.

The details of the attack on this Pa, ineffectual notwithstanding the bravery of our troops, have been published at full length in the daily papers. The repulse must be regarded as highly disastrous, as we fear it will confirm the disaffected portion of the natives in their unhappy delusion that they can successfully resist the British soldiery. The detachment appointed for the arduous duty assigned to it appears to have been numerically unequal to its work—not more than 350 in number—yet a large body of British troops some 1900, was at the time concentrated in the Taranaki district.

The excitement on both sides is great: on that of the colonists intense. Nor is it confined to New Zealand: it has extended itself to the Australian colonies. To quote the language of the "Sydney Morning Herald," "the die is cast. It is plain we have a foe to deal with who is not to be despised; it is equally so that he must be put down at all cost." To what an extent the war ought to be prosecuted, according to the opinion of some, appears, from the language used by a Melbourne correspondent of the "Times" (September 14th, 1860). Writing in reference

---

* This is said to have been done on Sunday.

to the repulse at Waitara, he says, "In one respect our disaster will produce a good result. The Governor is surrounded by many, whose sympathy, just on some grounds, has tended to encourage the natives in their resistance of our authority. This would have continued had the Maoris been often worsted. But this decided success of the natives will arm all instincts against them. The sympathizers will find the ground cut from under their feet; and the conviction is becoming practically universal, that we *must* subdue the natives, and establish the supremacy of the Crown. This has now become an instinct."

That which we most dreaded has then commenced—a fratricidal contest between the native and colonial races; and the same scenes of blood and of reciprocal vindictiveness which have stained other fields of emigration, seem about to be re-enacted in New Zealand. Nearly two years ago we sounded a note of warning on this subject, and insisted upon "the great need which the ministry and legislature of New Zealand have of wise caution and undoubted impartiality in the delicate and highly responsible position in which they have placed themselves. They have it in their power to enact a noble part, and fulfil all the expectations of their friends; but a rash and incautious procedure may be productive of results the most calamitous." And again we said, "What if, through some blundering policy, a war of races were kindled? Would that help forward the prospects of New Zealand? Let there be peace and quietude, and the tide of emigration will not fail to visit these shores, and the wilderness be peopled, if once the emigrant be assured that in the Maori he shall find a friend, and not an enemy. Let it only still continue to be with truth recorded that no property has been wrested from the native owners, that no laws of humanity or justice have been trampled upon, and we doubt not that, with God's blessing, the bright vision will be realized, and New Zealand become the Britain of Australasia."

But let us endeavour to trace out the latent causes of the late disastrous events. For some time past there has been arising, like a mist out of the earth, a growing distrust and alienation between the races. Satisfactorily to account for this would require a more careful and lengthened analysis of what has been going forward during some years in New Zealand than is possible at the end of our Number, and at an advanced period of the current month. But the smoke of the smouldering fire has been too palpable to escape notice.

On the part of the natives this feeling has manifested itself in the Maori king league, and, connectedly with this, a determination to sell no more land to the Europeans. Different views have been taken of the king movement. Some regard it as an attempt to set up an independent sovereignty; others, and these men of experience, whose opinion ought to have weight in New-Zealand affairs, think less seriously of it.

But whence is it that these new elements have arisen in New Zealand, for, some years back, they had no existence?

There was a time when the loyalty of the tribes to the sovereignty of the British Queen was undoubted; so much so, that old Potatau, *alias* Te Whero Whero, the first Maori king, during the time of Heke's disturbances had been a firm ally of the British, and up to the time of his death was in receipt of a pension, bestowed upon him in recognition of his services. There was a time, also, when there was, upon the part of the native, no unwillingness to sell his land. It was not the unwillingness of the Maori, but the inability of the Government to purchase, that prevented the extinction of the native title over a far larger extent of territory. Now the native has grown distrustful of the intentions of the colonists. There must be some cause for this alteration. Let, then, our readers carefully peruse the following paragraph, from a memorandum on the future policy which ought to be adopted towards the native race, drawn up by the Bishop of New Zealand, at the request of the Governor, and dated May 8th, 1860—

"Difficulties have arisen since the partial introduction into the country of a representative system in which the natives have no voice, and but few advocates. They hear of thousands of immigrants brought into the country by the promise of free grants of land; and every vituperative epithet is heaped upon them in the public journals, and even threats used openly in the provincial councils, because they are accused of not selling their land fast enough to supply the new comers. It is but natural that they should cling to their rights with more tenacity the more they are called in question. Land leagues are the reasonable protest of an unrepresented majority against an aggressive minority.

"In what sense it is an offence on the part of the native people, either individually or collectively, to oppose the further sale of land, it is difficult to see. The question is left by the Treaty of Waitangi entirely to their discretion. They may think that they have already sold enough, or they may be waiting until the land has acquired a higher value; or they may dread the unscrupulous use which English settlers make of their neighbours' land, by trespass of cattle; or they may be taking steps to acquire sheep and cattle for themselves, and require a much larger surface than is needed at present for their crops of corn and potatoes. Or they may dread moral evils, such as the establishment of grog-shops in all parts of the country, for the augmentation of the provincial revenue, but to their own incalculable injury. There may be many good reasons to induce the native owners to suspend for a time all further sales of land; and it is enough to say that they have full discretion in the matter."*

Now, even supposing that the natives had no sufficient reason for the determination to which they had come, to sell no more land, yet even thus the settlers might have been contented to wait a while until this distrust and impracticableness on the part of the Maori had passed away. It is not yet twenty-one years since Captain Hobson landed at the Bay of Islands, and the Queen's sovereignty was proclaimed over New Zealand. During this period, the settlers have succeeded in acquiring from the Maoris no contemptible heritage. Out of sixty-five millions of acres which these islands contain, not less than forty millions are at this moment at the disposal of British emigrants. Over more than a half of the entire area the native title has been extinguished. This splendid acquisition comprises the entire of the Middle Island, consisting of thirty-three millions of acres, and seven millions in the North Island; and all these have been purchased from the natives, at prices varying from a farthing to sixpence per acre. These tracts moreover occupy the choicest and most commanding positions, and include within their limits the chief sea-ports of the islands. We quote again from the Bishop of New Zealand's memorandum—

"The surrender by the native owners of all the best harbours has placed the commerce of the country almost entirely in the hands of the English colonists. Here again the provincial system has an injurious operation. The council of each province looks upon the customs revenue of the province as its own. It is not borne in mind that the revenue which the provincial council administers at Auckland includes, in large but uncertain proportion, the proceeds of the industry of 30,000 natives employed in the cultivation of land, in collecting flax and kauri gum, in felling and hauling spars, and in the navigation of coasting vessels. For a long time Auckland had scarcely any trade but that which resulted from native industry."

Fifty-nine thousand and three hundred settlers constituted the maximum of the colonial population in 1858, of whom 33,585 were males of all ages, with an apportionment of forty millions of acres. Surely an impartial observer would conclude, even if the native had become sturdy, and did not choose for the present to sell any more land, that still they had obtained enough for the present to occupy their attention, and that they could afford to wait quietly until the native had changed his mind. And it has been so with some, but not with all. Men have been impatient, and have used threatening language, in meetings and through the press. We have before us reports of public meetings held at Auckland, June 4th and 18th, 1859, on the subject of the land question. According to the statements of the speakers on these occasions, the condition of the colonists of the northern districts was most lamentable.

"We are at present a large city without a country, obliged to import our beef and mutton, butter and cheese, from other provinces, as well as flour, wheat, oats, &c., which this fine province might very well produce, if we only had the lands opened up. Our farmers are obliged to suspend the increasing of their flocks, owing to the want of lands and the scarcity of food. Many of our herds of cattle are bordering upon starvation, from being pent up upon the already overstocked pastures around Auckland, while there are millions of acres of excellent lands in the interior of this province at present unoccupied, large tracts of which are grass lands, nothing inferior to the plains of Canterbury or Otago, and which the natives are quite willing to lease or sell to the pakeha, but not under the present system."*

Now in 1858 there were in the Auckland† province, 10,218 male colonists of all ages, and on January 1st, 1859, there had been purchased from the natives for their use, 1,211,530 acres. Of these they held in actual possession, at the date mentioned, 579,449 acres, 632,081 remaining at the disposal of the provisional government. Yet at this moment they were clamouring for more land, and complaining of the restrictions put upon the purchase of land by the government right of pre-emption, although there were large blocks of land suitable either for grazing or settle-

---

* Parl. Paper—New Zealand, Aug. 1860, p. 7.

* Parl. Papers, July 1860, p. 134.
† Thomson, vol ii. p. 331. Table xvi.

ment, lying unoccupied in various parts of the province. But these would not suffice them. They had cast a wistful eye over lands still in the possession of the native, which he had not parted with, and had exhibited no desire to part with, and they organised exploratory parties into portions of the country where the native title was unextinguished. We quote from a letter addressed by some of these settlers to the Colonial Secretary, in which they detail what appears to us to be their very unwise proceedings, calculated as they were to awaken the distrust and alarm of the natives.

"A party was organized to proceed up the Thames, as far as Wai-waro-wero, examining the banks on both sides of the river: having done this, to cross over to the east coast, and examine the country between Tauranga and the East Cape; to return across the country to the Thames, and proceed to the Matamata there to divide, one half returning by the Thames, the other half by the best overland route they could find: the objects required being good land, a port with easy communication to Auckland, and an overland route for cattle, without any consideration as to distance provided the other objects were attainable.

"Our attention was directed to the Thames district; 1st, from its geographical position, in immediate connexion with the harbour of Auckland; and 2dly, should it prove a river navigable for steamboats, and the land on its banks adapted for agricultural purposes, there must be room for a large population. We were led to suppose, from information collected from persons who had visited this district, that the banks of the river were low, and the whole country was composed of impassable swamps, totally unadapted for agricultural purposes. Our party report, that, after proceeding two days up this magnificent river, they were agreeably surprised to find a country containing from 150,000 to 200,000 acres of superior land, level and dry, containing grassy plains, sufficient in their present state to carry large quantities of sheep and cattle.

"Here, then, was the object of their search, within a journey of two days by steam and three days overland to Auckland. On inquiry, they found this immense plain of excellent land held by a few natives, who made no use whatever of the greater portion, yet were unwilling to sell an acre. They were told that the natives had parted with the shadow of the land to the king, and that it was useless prosecuting the remaining portion of the proposed journey, for the natives, from the east to the west coast, including all the Thames, had decided not to sell to the Europeans, but they were willing to lease.

"We cannot dismiss this subject without expressing our deep regret that former governments had not extinguished the native title over a large portion of this district, which we do not hesitate to state must become, from its position and quality of land, the granary of the province of Auckland."*

But if more land was needed, why not proceed to occupy the portions in the province, over which the native title had been extinguished, and which were available for occupation? We shall give their own explanation, and the Governor's answer to it—

"That a very large proportion of the land purchased by the government is unfit for cultivation, is proved by the fact that many thousand acres, granted as early as 1845, within a radius of twenty miles from Auckland, remain uncultivated to the present day. . . . .

"It is fully proved that, in a young colony, where there are necessarily so many drawbacks both as to capital and labour, the attempt to cultivate inferior soil can only end in ruin to all who attempt it.

"The settlers are informed by the Government that there is land enough of available quality to supply their wants. They simply answer, that they cannot find it. The testimony to the insufficiency of the supply is overwhelming."†

The Governor's reply is as follows—

"It is grass, and not land which is required. Grass grows naturally only in a very small part of the south of this province: the remainder is covered with fern, and can only be made available by the cultivation of artificial grasses, which requires capital. And though this sort of cultivation has been proved to be amply remunerative, less capital is required to occupy vast tracts of waste land capable of maintaining one sheep to six or seven acres, instead of six or seven sheep to one acre."‡

We think our readers will now be enabled to solve the mystery. The available lands required that the colonist, by cultivation, should substitute artificial grasses for natural fern; whereas the grassy plains in the Thames, districts were capable, just as they were, of feeding large quantities of sheep and cattle. What these colonists really wanted, therefore, was not land, but capital and patient industry. It seemed, however, a more facile way to get possession, by some means or other, of

---

* Parl. Papers, p. 136.
† Ibid., p. 143.

those tracts as yet in possession of the native, on which they might proceed at once to feed their sheep, without any expenditure of capital or labour. But could any proceeding be more likely to render the native distrustful of his white brother, and thus either originate a land-league, or strengthen and confirm one if already started? When one gentleman openly declared, in the meeting held at Auckland, "Land we want, and land we must have," and that in the immediate neighbourhood and within hearing of the Waikatos, it is not surprising if that people considered that their only security against threatened aggression on the part of the settlers, was to be found in combination with defensive purposes.

The Colonial Secretary, in his answer to these gentlemen, speaks to them in a very wise and admonitory manner—"That there is within easy distance of the city of Auckland a large quantity of fine land, and that the natives are unwilling to part with it . . . are facts patent to every one possessed of the slightest acquaintance with the subject.

"The best and only sure solution of this great difficulty is to be looked for in an altered state of feeling amongst the natives, signs of which are not wanting. Nevertheless, the Government would gladly embrace any expedient which gave promise of accelerating a change so much to be desired.

"Impatient demonstrations on the part of the settlers are most injurious. So also with regard to the threats held out of the illegal occupation of native land, the Government is satisfied that such attempts would result at once in individual losses and great public injury."*

To show how small an outlay of cultivation had been bestowed by these settlers on the large tracts placed at their disposal, it may just be mentioned, that in the year 1858 we find in the province of Auckland only 60,183 acres under crop; and only 90,448 as the total number of acres fenced; and that, as we have already shown, there were available for their use, in that province, 1,211,530 acres, of which 579,449 had been actually taken up and become settlers' property.

But we think we have discovered another secret in these tale-telling Blue Book documents; the reason of this great haste, at any cost, seems to be to get possession of fresh lands, on which, without waiting for the tedious process of cultivation, the Auckland colonists might proceed to feed their stock. One of the speakers at the Auckland meeting of June 4, remarks—" When he looked on the revenue of Nelson, as lately published, amounting to 60,000*l.*, he could not help wondering how Auckland was to maintain her position amongst the provinces of New Zealand for the future. It was impossible under the present system."

A speaker at another meeting, a week later, touches on the same point—"I hope now that the community, which is fairly roused upon the land question, will look ahead in the election of their representatives in future, so as to make this question one of the leading principles upon which they shall be returned. When such a measure shall have been brought into operation, which will have the effect of allowing the natives legally to sell portions of their surplus lands, then this province will have some chance of prospering: we shall then have inducements for capitalists, not only to come, but to settle amongst us; not as at present, where some of our own, and, I may say, old settlers amongst us, are compelled to go to the southern provinces to seek investment for their capital, as has been of frequent occurrence of late."*

In a letter to the Colonial Secretary the complainants are still more candid and explanatory on this subject—

" We are further stimulated to prosecute some course to enable us to feed more stock at less expense, that we may be in a position to compete with our neighbours in the Southern Provinces, who possess advantages for feeding sheep, that will, with the assistance of steam communication, tend, in a short time, under existing circumstances, to drive the settlers of the Auckland province out of their own markets—the large quantities of natural grass runs that they are enabled to obtain at a small annual sum for their sheep to graze on, leave us without a chance in competition, unless we can obtain good and cheap land and sufficient quantity. There is no lack of argument that might have been used in support of our position; but we thought it better to simply state the facts that forced upon your oldest settlers the necessity for going back. . . . We were under the impression that the quality of land in this province was inferior. . . . This hypothesis is now cast to the winds. Practical men have seen and declared there are tens of thousands of acres of good land of equal quality within three days' journey of Auckland, and that they will no longer continue satisfied to occupy the motley patches hitherto provided for their

---

* Parl. Papers, p. 141.

* Parl. Papers, p. 134.

use. Sheep are arriving from the south, and arrangements have been made for bullocks to arrive from Sydney in our Auckland markets, fat and ready for the butcher. These have been grazed on lands producing natural grass, and held in large quantities at a nominal rent."°

Putting together all these fragments and items of information, some of them incidentally blurted out, we feel ourselves justified in coming to this conclusion, that there has been amongst the colonists of the province of Auckland a strong agitation for the acquisition of more land, and that at a time when more than half of the land, in which the native title had been extinguished throughout the province, remained at the disposal of the provisional government, and therefore, as yet, unappropriated by the settler; that discontentedly refusing to enter upon this, they coveted lands to the southward, which the natives had not alienated, sending exploring parties into them, and openly declaring that they were the lands which they wanted, and were resolved to have; that such proceedings were calculated to disquiet the native population, and lead them to conclude, in their own minds, that the settler, dissatisfied as he was with the ample supply ceded to him for his present wants, would never rest quiet until he had grasped the whole heritage of the Maori, as, indeed, one speaker in the Auckland meeting of June 4th openly declares, "Nearly every acre in New Zealand would ultimately become available." These admissions and discoveries decided a people, naturally sensitive and suspicious, to unite together in a combination against the further sale of land to the European; and it is this landleague which renders the conflict at Taranaki so critical, and induces the apprehension that the outbreak will extend itself to the entire of those powerful and warlike tribes which have entered into that combination, if, indeed, it has not already done so.

Fully to satisfy our readers that we have not presented to them a view of matters which facts do not justify, we shall quote from an authoritative document, viz. a despatch

look with apprehension to the annihilation of their nationality.

"The consequence of this feeling has been the formation of a league to prevent the alienation of land, commenced by the tribes on the Waikato before my arrival in the colony, and which has since been combined with the so-called king movement.

"Assuming the whole of the Northern Island to contain 26,000,000 of acres, and that the native title has been extinguished over 7,000,000, there remain 19,000,000 of acres owned or occupied by about 57,000 Maoris. A large portion of this consists of mountain and dense forest, but the remainder, which includes some valuable land, is greatly in excess of all their possible wants. The Europeans covet these lands, and are determined to enter in and possess them *recte si possunt, si non, quocunque modo*. This determination becomes daily more apparent. A member of the Auckland Provincial Council stated in the Council that 'the fault lay in the system of acquiring land from the natives. We were called upon to leave them the best land, and sacrifice ourselves to sympathy for the natives

"'The settlers had no room for their stock, and would be obliged to set the government at defiance. Hitherto the settlers here had been a law-obeying community; but when once the Rubicon was passed, it was impossible to say how far they might go. There was something higher than the law, namely, the framers of the law, and the source of all law—the people. They had new arrivals landing here every day, and they might say, what right, for instance, had a parcel of natives at Coromandel, like dogs in a manger, to keep everybody out of that rich district? People would soon begin to act on the old principle of letting land belong to those who can keep it. It was impossible to prevent the Anglo-Saxon overcoming the natives; and the Europeans, if they could not get land with the consent, must get it without the consent of the Government.'

"This speech was highly applauded in one of the journals; while another (the 'Southern Cross') keeps up a continued agitation on the

management of a race in a lower state of civilization than the dominant one, which is, in a certain sense, associated with it. I refer to the constant abuse and misrepresentation heaped upon the meritorious department by which native affairs are conducted : in speaking of it, the *post hoc* is too often replaced by the *propter hoc*, and it is not seldom looked upon as an obstacle to be destroyed by fair means or by foul. Among Europeans this sort of language is so prevalent, that it has no other effect than that of rendering those most subject to it callous and indifferent to public opinion, but it has a very injurious effect upon the natives. Ignorant of what the press really is, they lose confidence in those whom (it is the undisputed interest of all) they should trust and respect, and believe every idle and malicious report circulated among them by disaffected persons. Articles headed 'Extinction of the native race,' coupled with attacks on Sir George Grey and the native department, have a most insidious effect. I am well aware that there is no remedy for such an abuse of the freedom of the press, but I allude to it as proving the necessity for a council formed of men thoroughly known and respected by the natives, who would be personally indifferent to calumny, and above its influence."*

Nor is this feeling confined to any one locality. In all the settlements similar views are entertained, and in various ways are published abroad. In Bills introduced into the House of Assembly, the Native Secretary complains of assumptions of a right affecting unalienated native territory.

"Ministers include in the term, 'waste lands of the colony,' native territory over which the aboriginal title is unextinguished. It is conceived, however, that this term should properly be restricted to those lands which, having been acquired by the Crown for colonizing purposes, vest in the General Assembly, under clause 72 of the New-Zealand Constitution Act."

The Assistant Native Secretary in a memorandum, adverts to these assumptions as views generally entertained by settlers throughout the country.

"Nothing will more surely hinder the peaceable acquisition of native territory, and rouse a spirit of opposition and hostility to the Government, than the possession of the native mind by a belief that the appropriation of their lands is a thing resolved on, the mode of acquisition only being left an open question, to be decided as expediency may dictate.

Under such circumstances, however liberal the terms upon which they might be invited to treat for the surrender of their rights, they would be offered in vain.

"The Crown's right of pre-emption over native lands is generally regarded by the native tribes as a protection against undue encroachment by the Pakeha; and while they believe that the cession of their territory is optional, and is admitted to be so by the government, they feel secure from evils which would otherwise be apprehended from the occupation of their country by a more powerful race. Relying upon the repeated promises made by successive representatives of the British Sovereign, that their rights, as secured to them in the treaty of Waitangi, will always be respected, and that their lands will never be taken possession of otherwise than with their free consent, they contemplate without alarm the rapidly increasing numbers of the colonists. It is essential to the peace of the country that the confidence of the natives in the paternal character of the government should not be disturbed.

"For this reason, I think it important not only that any system adopted by the government for acquiring native lands should secure a proper provision for the owners, but also that it should be so presented as to avoid the appearance of seeking to force it upon their acceptance. They should be allowed to feel that they are free to choose between surrendering their territorial rights to secure advantages they cannot otherwise obtain, and, by maintaining those rights, to forego such advantages.

"I have been led to these remarks from observing the view commonly taken in the colony on this question. Few would admit that the extension of European settlement must be contingent on the consent of the aboriginal owners to cede their territory. Their unimproved lands are regarded as the property of the colony, merely encumbered with a certain native right of occupancy, of which it is the duty of the government to clear them, as from time to time they may be required by the settlers. The government is accordingly held to have failed in its duty in every case where lands eligible for settlement remain in the hands of the natives. The existing system of land-purchase is supposed to be in fault, and the adoption of some new scheme is, from time to time, urged upon the Government, which is thus subjected to a pressure from without, calculated to defeat the very object which is sought to be attained."*

---

* Parl. Papers, pp. 78 and 82.

* Parl. Papers, p. 84.

The Rev. R. Maunsell in a letter published in the "New Zealander" in 1856, sounded, even thus early, a note of warning. Referring to various painful cases, in which an inferior race was oppressed and injured by a superior colonizing race, he proceeds—

"Of the depth to which even Anglo-Saxons can descend when they obtain the supreme control of another race, we have a remarkable example in the laws passed against upwards of 3,000,000 of negroes in the United States, and the coolness with which judges of the highest standing in that country expound and enforce them.

"That the tendencies of our Parliament [the New-Zealand Assembly] are in a somewhat similar direction, has been more than once most painfully evident to my mind. True, indeed, it is, that they voted in their first session 500*l*. with a view to the vaccination of the Maori population. This grant we accepted with the deepest thankfulness, not so much for the value of the gift, as for the strong practical proof that it afforded of the goodwill of our fellow-countrymen to the native population. Still, that the spirit of self-aggrandisement is supreme is beyond all contradiction; and that that spirit will, unless carefully watched by the mother country, bring on a war of races, it does not require a prophet's mind to foretell. The wrongs that are now endured, and the measures that are mooted, are amply sufficient to create anxiety. . . .

"Let a sense of injustice enter the mind of the native; let him imagine that the white man only legislates for himself; that he cares not for the Maori; that his desire is to shut him out from advantages that he himself possesses; and changes of the most dark and gloomy character will take place in the island. This impetuous and high-spirited people will soon be ready for any thing desperate; and the white man will, before long, feel that a crooked policy will always recoil on itself. Even though they do continue to keep the solitary settler; even though they extend food and shelter to the weary traveller; even though they continue to sell their lands for a nominal sum, and aid the Government in the arrest of Pakeha and Maori culprits; still, if the feeling of wrong has taken up its abode in their minds, the first spark may produce a conflagration."*

Let us now then inquire, Can this war, the outbreak of feelings of alienation originating in causes such as these, be permitted to proceed, until it becomes a war of extermination? The Melbourne correspondent in the "Times" has taken upon him to be the exponent of the feelings of the people of Victoria, and he informs us "that it cannot now be settled by one signal victory; that there must be a succession of successes; that the war may be a protracted one, and that it must be ruinous to many of the settlers." Are the settlers contented that it should be so? What more disastrous to the peaceful emigrant than this outbreak. For years he has lived on friendly terms with his Maori neighbour. His new home has lost the bare appearance which it had at first: it has become clothed and furnished, and has acquired the look of comfort, which is the characteristic of an English home, and which reminds him of the old country. Around him are the lands acquired by peaceful purchase, and which his own hand has brought under cultivation. Must he leave all and fly, or remain and trust himself to the forbearance of the natives? Such is his dilemma.

For ourselves, we too have had our clearances and husbandry in New Zealand. We found it a barren, heathen tract, and have brought it under Christian cultivation. We are not prepared to see our fences broken down, our Christian churches and congregations thrown into confusion, and a native race, in which we have taken so deep an interest, and on which we have bestowed so much time and labour, thrown back from their advanced position into unknown calamities and evils.

Is England prepared for a war of extermination? Is it not enough that we have a war in China, of uncertain result, and carried forward at a heavy cost, and must we now fling ourselves into a new and protracted contest with the warlike Maoris?

We look to the Home Government. The decision is with them, and we have that confidence in them that they will never suffer so fratricidal a contest to proceed. In a despatch from Lord Carnarvon to the Governor, dated May 18th, 1859, in which is communicated to him the resolution of the Home Government not to recommend to Her Majesty for confirmation a Bill introduced into the House of Assembly by the responsible ministry, under the title of the Native Territorial Bill, the following sentences occurs—

"I am bound to ask myself, whether in case the decisions of the Governor in Council on titles to land should be resisted by the natives, the British Government are prepared to promise such a military force as may be sufficient to enforce them. If any such expectation could be held out, it would be clearly necessary that the decisions which imposed so much responsibility and expense on

---

* Parl. Papers. p. 58.

the Home Government, should be taken by an officer solely responsible to that Government, and not to the colonists. It is more than questionable whether the moral influence of the European Government would not suffer by the issue of certificates of title, which the natives would be at liberty to disregard with impunity."*

The question, then, is, whether the military force of Great Britain is to be employed in a dispute about land, the title to which has never been subjected to any judicial decision, and which, if at all, must have been decided upon by the "Governor in Council."

On the cause of the present outbreak we have not touched in the present Number. Those of our friends who are urgent for some publication on the subject can furnish themselves with a pamphlet just published.† But for ourselves we pause, as well because we have neither time nor space, as also because we desire to give a closer and fuller consideration to the subject. We have read carefully Governor Browne's despatches to the Home Government on the subject of the Maori race, and cannot doubt the real interest he has taken in their welfare. We regret his commencement of hostilities in the Taranaki district, and feel the matter in dispute ought never have been submitted to the sharp action of the sword. But then the Governor's position was one of extreme difficulty, placed between two races, interested in both, yet unable, amidst the increasing jar, to reconcile their conflicting interests: the difficulty, amidst the complication of interests, to preserve an unbiassed judgment; and the danger of misrepresentation and precipitate action.

The important point now is the prompt action of the Home Government. It is for Her Majesty Queen Victoria to interpose her sceptre between these contending races, and say to them, as Moses said to the striving Hebrews, "Sirs, ye are brethren; why do ye wrong one to another?" Nay, indeed, we entertain the hope that this has been done, although we will not disguise our conviction that the recent repulse of our troops at Waitara has made the prospect of a peaceable Maori prosper too — who desire that "Ephraim should not envy Judah, nor Judah vex Ephraim"—to have recourse to prayer. One Missionary writes—" I feel assured that the good and great work effected by the word of God, will not be allowed to be destroyed by the great enemy. The Lord will preserve a seed to serve Him of the Maori race, and, great as the sifting may be, He will not suffer his wheat to be destroyed." Let that sentence be the groundwork of our supplication. Let the remembrance of what the Lord has done encourage us to entreat Him to do still more. While the cries of war are heard in New Zealand, let other sounds—the sounds of earnest prayer — arise from English hearts and homes, that the great Disposer of events, who so often brings good out of evil, and makes the wrath of man to praise Him, would do so in this instance.

Meanwhile, "Sydney is quite denuded of soldiers," and this in the absence of any effective local force, " the colonists having been singularly remiss in this respect." It is rather *malapropos* that it should be so at the present moment, as a visit from the French is expected; and although between us and our Gallic neighbours, a good understanding exists at present, yet it would be quite as well to show them, in case of any unexpected change in the relations of the two countries, that Sydney is not to be molested with impunity. " Two regiments of French soldiers are now on their way to Sydney, *en route* to New Caledonia, and will doubtless come on shore here." Now the French are keen observers. The fact that we have so badly administered our affairs in New Zealand as to disaffect the native population, and arouse a portion of the race, if not the whole mass, to arms and open hostility; the prospect of *protracted war;* the absorption of our entire military force in Australasia to meet the exigencies of that war; all this, no doubt, will be dotted down in a note-book.

One ray of hope breaks in upon our gloom. The Governor has invited to a parley thirty-six native chiefs from the southern ports. That invitation has been accepted by them, and, having arrived by the steamer "Victoria,"

A NEW-ZEALAND FOREST.—*Vide p* 213.

COLONIAL NEW ZEALAND.

In our previous Number we endeavoured to place before our readers the sparse and yet complex population of New Zealand, between the distinctive portions of which, native and colonial, Christianity has hitherto, in so remarkable a manner, prevailed to maintain peace, thus affording to either section the opportunity of improving and making progress. To this point we now wish to direct attention, that either section of population has had abundant room to strike root and make progress. Assuredly it would be preposterous to imagine it could be otherwise. A scanty population of 115,303 persons in the midst of a splendid heritage of sixty-five millions of acres, of which the glowing language used to describe the promised land of the ancient Israelites might with justice be applied—"a good land, a land of brooks of water, of fountains and depths that spring out of valleys and hills; a land of wheat, and barley, and vines; . . . . a land wherein thou shalt eat bread without scarceness; thou shalt not lack any thing in it"—how could they by possibility feel themselves straitened? Already, although little more than twenty years have elapsed since colonization set in upon these shores, there has been a fair division of the land between the original proprietors and the new comer—the emigrants having had placed at their disposal forty millions of acres, and the Maori retaining the remainder for his own use. Surely any straitness, under such circumstances, must be imaginary, and not real!

Let us consider, first, the natural advantages of these islands generally: we may next review the lot which has fallen to the colonists, and examine whether we can discover in that section of the population such symptoms of growth and of improvement as suffice to show that the position which they have occupied has not been otherwise than favourable. We shall then turn to the native population, and examine whether there are to be found in them such evidences of progress as justify the hope, that if preserved from those harsh and blighting influences which have proved the destruction of many an aboriginal race, they will rise to a parity with the European, and become thus fitted for the process of amalgamation. These points when sufficiently dealt with, will prepare the way for further consideration.

The islands are three in number—the Northern, the Middle, and Rakiura, the small South island, the only one which possesses a native name. The Northern and Middle Islands are parted from each other by Cook's Straits, a noble channel, 160 miles in length by 50 in breadth, and the Middle from the Southern by a clear deep channel, 50 miles in length, by 20 in breadth. The coast line of the whole group measures 3120 miles. On this vast range of coast many and magnificent harbours are to be found, but it is remarkable that they cluster together at the northern and southern extremities of the two great islands, the vast extent of the eastern and western shores being in a great measure denuded of them. In the indented coast of the northern projection of the North Island may be found the harbours of Wangaroa, Bay of Islands, and Waitemata, on which Auckland stands. The entrance into the Wangaroa harbour is formed by towering perpendicular rocks, and is only 150 yards broad. These rocks look as if they were rent asunder by an earthquake. The water close to this is of great depth, without sunken rock or any hidden danger below the surface. Spacious and deep, this haven possesses anchorage for the largest fleet, and shelter from all winds. On the west coast the indented north projection is bounded on the south by the Manukau harbour, an inlet fifteen miles long. Here the eastern and western seas are divided by a very narrow portage. South from this, along the western coast, the harbours are suitable only for small vessels, until Cook's Straits are reached; while along the eastern coast, from Cape Colville to the East Cape, there are only two safe anchorages; and from the East Cape to Wellington harbour, only one, Port Napier in Hawkes Bay. So again, in the Middle Island, harbours of first-rate capacity are numerous at its northern extremity; but along the whole eastern coast, from Cape Campbell to the Bluff harbour, an extent of nearly 500 miles, Akaroa, Port Victoria, and Otago are the only safe anchorages; while on the western shore from Jackson's Bay to Cape Farewell, a distance of 300 miles, the coast is open and exposed.

The outlines of these coasts, however, cannot be considered as fixed and permanized. "That there is at present a general elevatory movement extending from the southern pole over the whole southern hemisphere, is now a well established fact. In this general movement New Zealand undoubtedly partakes, and has, moreover, her own special elovatory forces continually going on. . . . . These elevatory forces, where they have been slow, gradual, but continuous, have raised the precipitous chains of mountains from the deep, carrying up with them, as it were in their arms, those extensive plains destined to become the sources of wealth to a new colony. In the same way also, where there were shallow arms of the sea and deep winding bays, the former, by the elevation of a few feet, have become fertile valleys, and the latter have had their dimensions contracted by the narrowing of the gorges at their extremities. In this way have the extensive plains of the Middle Island been formed, and that, too, at a period, geologically speaking, very recent. In this way also have the circular plains to the immediate south of Otago been formed, the first glance of them giving the idea of a bay just dried up.

"These general remarks apply in every way to the province of Wellington. Here all the proofs of recent elevation are very evident. They are to be recognised in the terraces so well defined on the flanks of the hills from Baring Head round the whole coast northwards to Hawkes Bay; and in the formation of the Waidrop Valley, which is but an arm of the sea emptied by elevation of the country generally, and so made dry land, in the same manner as would the habour of Wellington become a grassy plain were an elevation of but fifty feet to take place."* That such an alteration is more than a possibility will appear from the fact, that, since 1848, Port Nicholson has risen to the extent of five feet, and that the last earthquake has given such an additional elevation, that what had been low-water mark is now that of high-water.

"The centre of the North Island of New Zealand is occupied by broad and lofty mountains, which send off spurs in various directions to the sea coast; the valleys formed by these diverging mountain ranges are at first gullies, which open out as they approach the coast into fertile districts, through the centres of which flow the rivers Waikato, Thames, Waipa, Mokau, Wanganui, Rangitikei, Tara Wera, and other streams. It is the abrupt configuration of these mountain chains which renders the land communication between Auckland, Taranaki, Wellington, and Hawkes Bay so difficult. Ruapahu, the highest mountain in this central range, has an elevation of about 9000 feet, and its summit is covered with perpetual snow. Tongariro, one of Ruapahu's peaks, rising upwards of 6000 feet above the sea, is an active volcano, and discharges from its crater smoke and cinders. Primeval forests cover nearly the whole of these mountain ranges from their bases to their summits."*

"The Middle Island is traversed by a mountain range, which commences at its northern extremity, and terminates in the south-west, after forming a sort of backbone to the island. The summit of this range is covered with perpetual snow, and as it reaches an elevation in some parts of 13,000 feet, that portion of it has been called the Southern Alps.

"On the west coast, this range of mountains sinks abruptly, leaving a narrow slip of fertile land between its base and the sea; and on the eastern coast, where it falls in the same abrupt manner, extensive and fertile plains intervene between the sea and its base. Through this eastern plain, upon which the settlements of Otago and Canterbury stand, flow rivers of considerable width, subject to sudden floods, occasioned by the melting of the mountain snow. At the northern and southern extremities of the island are hills covered with primeval forests; and between them plains of considerable extent, upon the northern of which the settlement of Nelson now stands."†

New Zealand is the land of green wood. Vegetation runs riot. Its peculiarities are, the excess of trees and shrubs, the paucity of herbaceous plants, and the almost total want of animals. "In England there are forty indigenous trees; in New Zealand 120. Two thousand species of plants have already been collected, and Dr. Hooker anticipates that 2000 more will yet be discovered. . . . .

"Travellers find themselves surrounded in New Zealand with a new vegetation; the landscape is not soft or gay, but grand and sombre. It presents to the eye a dark green colour, and, except in the tree-ferns, little that is striking. Unfortunately for the beauty of the floral scenery, the tree-fern shuns observation, avoids the sun, lives in solitary places, and flourishes best in stagnant air. Almost all the New-Zealand trees, are evergreens: forests are never leafless, and the change of seasons makes little difference in their appearance: in the winter they are greener than in summer."‡

"The mode of growth, too, the general appearance of a New-Zealand forest, is different from any thing in the old world. Thousands of tall columnar trees, of fifty different species, one to two hundred feet high,

---

* Notes on the Geology of New Zealand. By C. Forbes, M.D.

* Thomson, vol. i. p. 5.
† Ibid., p. 7.   ‡ Ibid., p. 16.

struggle up through a wilderness of underwood—their leafy heads so loaded with tufts of rushy parasites, that the true foliage is almost lost in the rank vegetation of the alien polypiæ; whilst innumerable creepers, from the rope-like supple-jack up to the gigantic rata (a vegetable boa constrictor), coil round every stem, run up every limb, glide from head to head, and entwine the topmost branches of a dozen trees in fifty Gordian knots. The underwood consists of three creepers, and of an equally dense growth of young saplings, mixed with forest shrubs; such as the delicate lady's hair, the kopakopa, an elegant plumy fern, the nikau, and many others. And such is the closeness of the growth, the luxuriance of the vegetation in a New-Zealand forest, that sun and air scarce can penetrate, glimpses only of the sky are caught through the leafy canopy above, and at high noon-day in the fields it is always green twilight in the woods.

"If this underwood-thicket contained any prickly plants like our briars and brambles, or the African wait-a-bit thorn, the New Zealand forest (or bush as it is called) would be a jungle physically impenetrable; and, even as it is, it presents so many obstacles to free step and movement, that none but a patient and accomplished pedestrian, experienced in supple-jack snares, root-traps, and other parasitical impediments, would struggle through it at a greater rate of progress than a mile an hour (with three falls) at most."*

"The smaller trees and tree-shrubs ('light bush') growing about the edges of the great forests, or clothing the dells and valleys of the open country, are numerous. . . . Among the commonest, we find three varieties of that forest houri, the fern-tree, fifty feet high, with coronals of palmy leaves fluttering in the breeze like forest fans; the nikau, more rare but less beautiful than the fern-tree; the fuchsia, thirty feet high; the fruity poroporo, the sweet-scented manuka, the tree-myrtle and fragrant veronica, the ngaio, the elegant titoki, and the laurel-like karara, with its glossy foliage and clusters of golden fruit—the only tree which the Maori-Æneas brought with him in his migration from the sunny shores of Hawaii.†"

"Indescribable is the charm of New-Zealand forests for the lovers of nature. There generations of noble trees are seen decaying, and fresh generations rising up around the moss-covered trunks of fallen patriarchs. The profound silence which reigns in these regions produces a pleasing gloom on the mind, and the scene displays, better than the most classic architecture, the grandeur of repose. No sound is heard save the falling of trees, or the parrots' shrill screech, as birds which enliven the outskirts of forests are mute in the interior. Around the graves of past generations of trees the air is hushed into stillness, while the tops of the living generation are agitated with gales and breezes. At Christmas the pohutukana (*metrosideros*) is covered with scarlet flowers, and is then the most gaudy of forest trees; and the rimu (*dacrydium cupressinum*) possesses a melancholy beauty and an indescribable grandeur. Few of the pines recal to the settler's eyes the same trees in England, and, singular to relate, unlike their congeners, the majority of them grow intermixed with other trees. The celebrated and beautiful kauri (*dammara australis*) is the only pine bearing a cone, and the male and female cones are found on the same tree."*

With reference to the surface character, " New Zealand may be called a 'wooded-highland' country, displaying some half dozen noble plains, and thousands of brook-watered valleys, dells, and dales.

"But New Zealand differs from a highland country in one remarkable feature—that of natural clothing. The common, and, indeed, the correct idea of a highland country, is that of a naked, bare-looking country of mountain, lake, and stream, where the soil is poor, and the vegetation scant. But in New Zealand, the soil, though light, is often rich; and the fertility of the earth, quadrupled by the genial climate, literally produces a 'wilderness of vegetation.' Sea-spray crags, shore-margins, plains, valleys, hill-sides, mountain-steeps, are alike clothed with perpetual verdure; and the expression 'smothered in vegetation' is not a mere figure of speech when applied to New Zealand, but a term truly descriptive of the country. . . . .

"One of the most striking natural features of New Zealand is the abundance of water—the blood of the earth—and water power. Taupo is the only large lake, and New River, in Foveaux Strait, the Clutha, Thames, Hokianga, Fovea, Wanganui, Waikato, and Manawatu, are perhaps the only rivers navigable twenty miles up for any thing larger than a canoe. But there are several smaller lakes and lakelets; and the country from north to south is profusely studded with rivers, rivulets, brooks, and burns of the softest, purest

---

* Hursthouse, vol. i. p. 134.
† Ibid., pp. 134, 135.

* Thomson, vol. i. pp. 16, 17.

water; running over pebbly beds, and bearing a close resemblance to many of our trout and salmon streams, such as the Dove, Tamar, Tweed, Don, and Dee.

"The natural scenery of New Zealand is both bold and beautiful; though to an English eye, accustomed to trim fields, clipped hedges, and to the smooth-rolled, finished look of every acre in England, it would frequently appear more bold than beautiful. Indeed, many a district would strike the Norfolk farmer, or the Cockney sketcher, whose ideal of beauty was the Holkham turnip-field or the highlands of Hampstead, with far more of amazement than delight. The scenery we admire in England is often the costly coat of art, rather than the primeval dress of nature. As regards polish of cultivation, the garden's glories, the plough's court-robes, New Zealand is much in the state that Britain was when Cæsar landed; and if Cæsar's Britain could now be shown us, many a bright champaign country, which we call beautiful, would vanish, to reveal the gloomy forest and repulsive rugged waste.

"Bearing in mind the extent of the country; that the land is equally verdant and leafy through summer and winter; that the bright breezy light-and-shadow-casting character of the climate is peculiarly favourable both to the display and to the enjoyment of scenery; I think we may say, that in combination of those great natural features which constitute the foundation of fine scenery, New Zealand is not surpassed by any country in the world. She displays noble forests, snow-capped mountains shooting up 10,000 feet from a sea of green and wooded up to the line of snow, tracts of rolling champaign country, dells, valleys, rivers, and rivulets innumerable, and 3000 miles of bay and ocean coast.

"New Zealand, too, with all the elements of fine scenery, this stock of 'raw beauty,' is a fertile, cultivable country; where plough, sickle, and mill would singularly enrich and brighten the landscape. The plough could not improve the natural beauty of a country like the Scotch highlands, because the Scotch highlands are not pecuniarily ploughable; and the plough, if every ploughman were a Mechi, could not create the 'beautiful' in a country like the Lincolnshire fens, or the plains of Belgium. But in a wild, fertile, woody country, more re-

for hamlet, tower, and town, homestead cottage and castle, are multitudinous in New Zealand; and when cultivation has given colour to the landscape, and contrast to the universal background of green; when the hills are more dotted with sheep, and the valleys more golden with corn; when the pheasant whirs from the brake, and the fox bursts from the cover, New Zealand will offer a thousand views which even a Turner might cross the seas to paint.*

The climate of New Zealand is well adapted to the Anglo-Saxon emigrant. "It is a climate assimilating to, but better than, his own; a climate which, endowing him with full powers of body and mind, requires and calls forth the fruitful exercise of such powers. . . . . It is a climate favourable alike to the preservation of robust health and the improvement of weak health; a climate most congenial to all pastoral and agricultural pursuits; one in which every domestic English animal thrives and fattens; and in which every English grain, grass, fruit, and flower, "attains full development and perfection."† It is the opinion of those who have sojourned in different parts of the world, that the Anglo-Saxon race can work and expose themselves in the climate of New Zealand without injury, during more days in the year, and for more hours in the day, than in any other country."‡ "The mean temperature of places in New Zealand is lower than that experienced in corresponding latitudes in Europe, ... but higher than that experienced in corresponding latitudes in America. . . . . No single locality in Europe has a temperature during the whole year like that experienced in New Zealand. The North Island possesses the summer heat, tempered with a sea breeze, of Paris, Brussels, and Amsterdam, with the winter cold of Rome; while the Middle Island has a Jersey summer, and a winter in mildness resembling that at Montpellier.§

"Though there are more fine days in New Zealand than in England, yet when it does rain, it rains harder; and the annual fall of rain is somewhat greater. But there is no tropical 'rainy season' in New Zealand; and there is probably no country where those 'golden showers,' which Loudon describes as so favourable to agriculture, are so common, and where even moderate droughts are so rare. Rain generally falls at or about the full and new moon, particularly about the latter. New Zealand cannot be called a damp country, in any injurious sense. Rains and heavy dews are frequent, and there is considerable moisture. But New Zealand is an upland, hilly country, thoroughly drained by rapid streams. There are no fens. Both surface and subsoil are generally light and porous. Wet rapidly drains and percolates away; and moisture is quickly dried up by the combined influence of sun and breeze."*

"Probably in no country in Europe is the atmosphere so frequently agitated by winds as in New Zealand." "It may not blow furiously so often as it does on the English coasts, but it blows 'stiff' oftener; there are fewer tempests, but more half gales. Early winter is perhaps the calmest season; spring and early summer the most breezy."

"In fine winter mornings, a crust of ice is occasionally seen on pools and road-side splashes. Snow is never seen in the North Island, except on the mountain tops; but slight falls occasionally sprinkle the southern plains of Canterbury and Otago.† Fogs and mists are rare, and thunder-storms are less frequent than in England. There is but little twilight; in summer it is dark about an hour earlier than in England, in winter about an hour later. The nights are always proportionately cooler than the days: when a warm coat would be oppressive in the fields by day, a blazing log would be cozy in the house at night.

"Our experience of the New-Zealand climate is, however, at present, chiefly confined to the coasts. In the interior, the climate is more settled and serene, the winters a little colder, the summer a little warmer, the seasons more advanced; and it seems probable that semi-tropical fruits, orange, citron, olive, and pomegranate, might be cultivated with success in sheltered valleys of the Northern-Island districts."‡

"Such, then, are the elements of the climate of New Zealand, and, under its fertilizing influence, every European plant grows in the colony, while the geranium, arum, fuschia, plums, and melons, ripen in the open air side by side with apples and pears; but the temperature in summer is not sufficiently warm in the southern parts of the colony to bring these delicate fruits to high perfection. At Nelson, in the Middle Island, melons, grapes, and nectarines ripen better than in any other part of New Zealand.

"Camphor, spices, and the luscious fruits of oriental orchards do not ripen in any parts of New Zealand, although the taro and sweet potato, originally brought by the natives from the tropics, still survive, and are cultivated for food by the aborigines living north of Banks's Peninsula. Potatoes and maize ripen side by side on the North Island, a circumstance rarely observed in Europe. The aloe, which seeds in South America in four years, and in England with difficulty after a long series of years, seeds in the neighbourhood of Auckland in eleven years.

"An idea of the seasons in New Zealand may be drawn from English strawberries being ripe in November, December, and January; cherries and gooseberries in January; apples, pears, plums, and peaches in February; and melons, figs, and grapes in March and April. Spring, in short, commences in September, summer in December, autumn in April, and winter in June. The summer mornings, even in the warmest parts of the colony, are sufficiently fresh to exhilarate without chilling, and the seasons glide imperceptibly into each other. The days are an hour shorter at each end of the day in summer, and an hour longer in winter, than in England. The beauty of the day is in the early morning, and at this hour, away from the settlements of men, a solemn stillness pervades the air, which is only broken by the shrill and tinkling voices of birds. Summer nights are often singularly beautiful and mild, and on such occasions the settlers are frequently enticed from their houses to wander about in the open air.

"Happily the climate is as favourable to the health of the settlers as it is to vegetation and beauty. Captain Cook, ninety years ago, remarked the healthy state of his ship's crew

enjoyed better health than soldiers stationed in any other portion of Her Majesty's colonial possessions. During the five years ending March 1853, residence in New Zealand saved the lives of eight soldiers annually out of every thousand who would have died had the troops been quartered in the United Kingdom."*

In the presence of advantages so many and varied as those we have enumerated, the New-Zealand settler may well say, "The lines are fallen unto me in pleasant places, yea I have a goodly heritage." And in this land of so great natural advantages, not less than forty millions of acres, which some twenty years back were the property of the native, have been placed at his disposal.

We have before us a map, appended to the Parliamentary Papers, showing approximately the extent of land acquired from the natives. We proceed to examine it, and place the results before our readers. And, first, the Middle Island. A few specks here and there along the northern and eastern coasts indicate the native reserves: but so small are they, that the native title may be regarded as extinct. The great island is exclusively colonial.

This island is divided into three provinces— Otago the southern, Canterbury in the middle, and Nelson to the north. The great mountain range, which constitutes the backbone of the island, approximating, as we have seen, much more closely the western than the eastern coast, attains its culminating point in the province of Canterbury, a little to the north of the 44th degree of south latitude, where Mount Cook rises to the elevation of 13,200 feet. As the range approaches the boundary of the Nelson Province, it strikes more into the heart of the country, travelling into numerous lower ranges, which stretch northwards from the sea at various points on the south shore of Cook's Straits. Thus one range, Kaikora, strikes the eastern shore at Cape Campbell; another range extends along Cape Campbell and Cloudy Bay; a third, forming the north-western boundary of the Wairau plain, subdivides into ridges which enclose the magnificent harbours of Port Underwood, Queen Charlotte Sound, Port Gore, and Pelorus Sound; and a fourth range extends west of Blind Bay, nearly to Cape Farewell. The greater part, therefore, of the Nelson district, which borders on the sea, is mountainous, in general heavily wooded, and steep to the water's edge. Numerous level spots, however, have been formed by the countless streams between the lesser spurs. At the south-east corner of Blind Bay are the haven and town of Nelson, containing about 4000 inhabitants, the European population of the province having increased from 2500 in 1842, to 9272 in 1858. Surrounded by a belt of hills and broken country, nestling beneath which it lies sheltered from cold south blasts, Nelson enjoys a climate of brilliant serenity. Indications of mineral wealth in the encircling hills are already presenting themselves, as well of gold as copper; while at Massacre Bay the first coal-fields have been discovered. These, with the magnificent harbours on the adjoining coast, present the elements of future maritime greatness.

The shores are "indented with a perfect labyrinth of coves, bays, creeks havens, and harbours, of every size, sort, and capacity. Queen Charlotte's Sound, in the centre of the group, twenty-five miles long, with one entrance three, and the other six miles broad, is a gigantic ocean dock, capable of berthing the whole British navy; and Pelorus Sound, a little to the north, is a similar group of harbours, embracing 250 miles of shore and beach."*

Nor are cultivable tracts wanted, notwithstanding the mountainous character of the province. Massacre Bay presents some thousand acres of land desirable for occupation. There is also the fine valley of the Waimea under high and prolific cultivation, and the Motueka, a pleasant district lying across the bay. But the eastern section of the province is that which possesses the greatest agricultural capabilities. Here are to be found the Wairau and Kaipara-te-ao plains, with extensive upland pastures and low grassy downs.

The western portion of the province is a rugged alpine region, a region unexplored, a vast unpeopled tract, where there are "millions of acres, untrodden by human foot since their first upheavement from the sea." Amidst these mountains, in the heart of a very picturesque country, about forty miles S.S.W. of Nelson in a direct line, are the lakes Arthur and Howick, from whence the Buller river has its course, which enters the sea near Cape Foulwind, presenting on either bank a well-wooded and level tract of many thousand acres between the mountains and the sea.

Here, then, throughout the vast interior, lies a noble field of enterprise, awaiting the researches of an enterprising Government. The capabilities of this great island are as yet but little known. But here, without trespassing

---

* Thomson, vol. i. pp. 44—46.   * Hursthouse, vol. i. p. 223.

on the North Island at all, may be found ample space for the reception of all the emigrants which England may send forth for many years to those far southern lands. It is a field well worthy of exploration, and we should like to see the Home Government encouraging the provincial authorities to such efforts, and affording to them substantial help. Here is an immense territory possessing great natural advantages, where no native proprietor exists to obtrude his title on the path of some anxious colonist, who, having left the chalk cliffs of Albion, desires to find a quiet home in the sequestered valleys or sheltered nooks of these imposing regions. Here, where the homestead has been raised, there is no fear of a native insurrection. They who shall subdue these alpine wildernesses and their hidden treasures and beauties to the service of man, shall become a great people. The Nelson province in particular promises to become one of the most commanding positions in the New-Zealand isles. "The present capital of the province in Blind Bay, however grand its local advantages of site, is not the natural and accessible outlet-harbour for the noble granary and wool-store of the Nelson country. If, at an outlay of 100,000*l*. it were practicable to connect a new port-town on any of the noble harbours of Queen Charlotte's Sound with the Wairau, and the Wairau with the line of interior districts and the frontiers of Canterbury, such outlay would be amply justified by the result; for a good port-town in Queen Charlotte's Sound, commanding such a cornucopia as the eastern portion of the province must be pronounced to be, climate, centrality of position, and other advantages considered, would become the real capital of New Zealand."*

"Canterbury, the noble centre province of the island, 200 miles in length from northeast to south-west, by 100 miles in breadth, has a coast line of some 400 miles, and an area of fifteen millions of acres, all of which, virtually, have been acquired from the natives." On its eastern shore appears the remarkable projection called Banks's Peninsula, with its mountains, forests, and deep inlets of the sea, presenting many beautiful landscapes. Here have been formed the infant settlements of Akaroa, Port Levy, and Pigeon Bay, all possessing excellent ports, Akaroa being one of the finest harbours in New Zealand. On the north side of the peninsula, at its junction with the mainland, lies Port Victoria, formerly Port Cooper, a fine, land-locked, ocean inlet, bearing on its margin, where the land is level, Lyttelton, the port-town, containing some 2000 inhabitants. Behind the town rises a ridge of hills about 1100 feet high. Ascending this by a zigzag path, the emigrant beholds extended before him "a noble plain of four millions of acres, watered by twenty rivers, rolling back in gentle rise forty miles to the foot of the central highlands, and spreading north and south further than the eye can reach."* This is the great Canterbury plain, about one hundred miles long and fifteen to fifty wide. Although nearly flat and devoid of trees, the monotony of the foreground is nevertheless considerably relieved by "the fine mountain range which bounds the horizon to the westward, and also by the smaller hills of Banks's Peninsula to the eastward. The great mountain range is distant about forty miles from Christ Church, and, in certain states of the atmosphere, is so clear, that a stranger to the country would suppose it to be within twenty. From the town, in clear weather, the mountains can be seen over a length of two hundred miles, some of the highest peaks in sight being upwards of 9000 feet above the level of the sea. In winter, when the peaks are dotted with snow from their crest half-way down, these southern alps assume an aspect of grandeur and sublimity which can be equalled in but few parts of the world." †

"Christchurch, the rural capital of the plains, about ten miles from Lyttelton, over the harbour hills, containing some 2000 people, is a considerable village, pleasantly situated on the river Avon. The country around is dotted with corn-fields, pastures, orchards, and dairy farms; and the luxuriance of crop, the sleek, full-fed look of the domestic animals which these cultivations exhibit, prove that the ragged-looking tracts of similar soil which surround them need but the magic touch of plough and spade to be clothed with a like mantle of blooming fertility.'‡

The population (colonial) of this province has increased from 3278 in 1851, to 6967 in 1858. The bringing of the land under cultivation has progressed from 803 acres, as the total under crop in 1851, to 13,935, as the maximum in 1858. In the former year there were of acres fenced in 2526; in the latter, 22,936. The increase of stock during the same period is remarkable; of cattle from

---
* Hursthouse, vol. i. p. 224.

* Hursthouse, vol. i, p. 226.
† Hodgkinson's Canterbury.
‡ Hursthouse, p. 232.

2048 to 20,739; and of sheep from 28,416 to 495,580.

"Otago, the southern province, 150 miles in length by 200 in breadth, has a coast line of some 500 miles, and an area of fifteen millions of acres, all of which, virtually, have been acquired from the natives." Perhaps three-fourths of the Otago province consist of interspersed pastoral and wooded agricultural districts of great fertility; and there is probably no province in New Zealand capable of producing a greater annual export of wool, and meal, and corn.

"Dunedin, the village capital of the province, 230 sea miles from Port Lyttelton, (S. lat. 45° 46', E. long. 170° 44'), containing about 2000 inhabitants, stands at the head of a fine loch, thirteen miles in length, which may be said to form two harbours; "the deep or seaward half running up to Port Chalmers, beyond which large ships do not come; and the shallow inland half extending to Dunedin, and accessible only for small craft and light steamers." The beautiful valleys of the Taieri and Tokomoriro, a few miles to the south of the town, and the banks of the Clutha, a fine semi-navigable river fifty miles southward, suffice for the present to meet the agricultural wants of the infant settlement.

In Foveaux Straits, 140 sea miles from Dunedin, a new settlement, Invercargill, has been formed. The combination of natural advantages is such as to render it one of the finest sites in New Zealand. "It is central between two harbours, the Bluff and the New River, and commands a fine river, navigable for twenty miles. These harbours are practically nearer the Australian harbours, and a week's sail nearer to England than any settlement-harbour in New Zealand. There is no large native population in the country to impede colonization, but there is a scattered population of old squatters, civilized natives, and intelligent half-castes, which may materially strengthen the first efforts of colonization; while, as to land, there is probably no part of New Zealand where so great an extent of agricultural country could be found lying in open communication with a sea-board and shipping harbour." This portion of the Otago province is described by those who have visited it as a splendid district, where extend "thousands of acres of beautiful undulating land, with natural grasses, studded with large masses of bush, containing excellent timber, reminding one of a gentleman's park on a scale '*magnifique:*' small streams of excellent water are interspersed through the country. To the westward, beyond a range of wooded hills, appear the snowy southern alps."

Opposite Invercargill, across the strait, lies Rakiura, or Stewart's Island, well wooded, possessing many fertile little valleys, and many excellent harbours. Various little communities of old whalers, natives, and half-castes, are scattered about its bays and coves. Port Pegasus, on its south-east coast, is a splendid harbour, about sixty miles S.S.W. from which lie "the Snares, a land-mark and point of departure, which the Australian homeward-bounders generally sight in running past the south end of New Zealand."

Eastward from Invercargill some hundred miles, a group of splendid inlets and harbours is found, corresponding to those which we have already described as existing in the north-eastern projection of the island, both being formed by the extremities of the great mountain ranges which, at these points, lose themselves in the ocean. An extract from the Admiralty Blue-Book will briefly describe these "ocean docks of New Zealand."

"The only places of shelter for shipping along the whole extent of the west coast of the Middle Island, a distance of 500 miles, are those singular, and truly remarkable sounds or inlets, which penetrate its south-western shores between parallels of the 44° and 46° south latitude.

"The precipitous and iron-bound coast-line which forms the sea-wall, as it were, in which these extraordinary inlets may be almost likened to so many breaches, runs in a N.N.E. and S.S.W. direction; and the whole, thirteen in number, are included within a space of little more than one hundred miles.

"With the exception of Cook's excellent description of Dusky Bay (explored during his second voyage in 1773), nothing has been recorded of this remarkable region; nor, until an examination by H.M.S. 'Acheron' in 1851, was it known to any but a few adventurous whalers, whom stress of weather alone had compelled to seek shelter on its desolate and silent shores. The character and features of these sounds so much resemble each other, that it seems desirable to offer a description of them generally, before entering into any detailed account of their capabilities individually.

"In approaching from seaward, there is so much sameness in the appearance of the land, that unless a vessel knows her position accurately, it is not easy at a distance to distinguish the entrance of one sound from another; and the smaller inlets, at a distance of four or five miles, have more the appearance of ravines between the high and rugged mountains, than the entrance of harbours.....

"The larger of the sounds are generally

divided into several arms, penetrating the coast, in some instances for a distance of twenty miles, with a breadth rarely exceeding a mile, and studded with numerous islets. The smaller sounds generally run in for a distance of from six to eight miles, with a width of about half a mile, and anchorage is seldom to be found except at their inner extremes.

"The shores, which rise almost perpendicularly from the water's edge, are, in the immediate neighbourhood of the sounds, covered with trees suitable for all purposes; among them the red pine, which, although heavier and inferior to the kauri, is well adapted for masts, and a vessel requiring spars could procure them of any size, up to a sloop of war's lower mast, with little difficulty: for this purpose the southern inlets are preferable."

The growth of the Otago settlements suffices to show that they have struck root in a good ground, where they are likely to thrive and prosper. The European population has increased from 1776, in 1851 to 6944 in 1858; the land under crop during the same period from 1015 to 9320 acres; and the fenced acres from 1974 to 19,066; while the stock has augmented—the cattle from 3161 to 20,071, and the sheep from 34,829 to 223,589.

Having thus presented a very cursory sketch of this magnificent island, with all its great natural advantages and capabilities, let us now sum up its population, at the present moment more especially, when, in the North Island, portions of the two races have thrown themselves into bloody conflict with each other, the cause of contention being a few hundred acres of land in the Taranaki province.

The colonial population of the Middle Island amounted, in 1858, to 25,183 souls; to which 2283, the entire amount of the native population, so far as we know, being added, gives us a total of 27,466, for this magnificent island, the area of which is thirty-eight millions* of acres, according to Thomson. In the map appended to the Parliamentary Papers on New Zealand, the area is reduced to 29,000,000 in round numbers. Why here we have an uninhabited land, healthful, temperate in climate, with large productive capabilities, and features of great natural beauty, all the property of England, and a suitable appanage for her emigrant children. It invites the application of human effort, that its energies may be developed, and that the peculiar charm which cultivation gives may be superadded to its natural loveliness. It is this which would render it all that a Briton could desire, "where the charm of our home beauties, suffused over the wild grandeur of this favoured land, would be heightened by a climate, of which the most lovely of English days can scarcely convey an idea." Why, then, pause to struggle with the Maori for the possession of lands, which, for whatever reason, he is unwilling to alienate? With this splendid central gem at his disposal, the colonist can well afford to content himself with such portions of the Northern Island as have been already purchased. If the opportunity of making further acquisitions in that island be for the present precluded, let the tide of emigration set in more decidedly on the shores of the Middle Island, where no such difficulties exist, and which, peopled by British settlers, must rise to the sovereignty of these seas, and become the Great Britain of the southern hemisphere.

Let us now, however, direct our attention to the North Island, and consider somewhat more closely what may be the position and prospects of the colonist, and whether he be so lamentably straitened, that a death struggle with the native is preferable to a continance in his present state. We shall review the provinces in the order in which they present themselves, commencing with that of Wellington, in which we shall include the newly-constituted province of Hawkes Bay on the eastern coast.

Wellington, the southern province, "200 miles in length from north to south, by 100 in breadth, has a coast-line of 500 miles, and an area of some twelve millions of acres." The Parliamentary map reduces the area to less than 8½ millions of acres. "The native title to the whole of the available land in the Wellington province, excepting about one million of acres, is already extinguished."*
The European population amounted, in 1858, to 13,242, the native to 7983; the total, 21,225.

Wellington, the first settlement founded by the New-Zealand Company, and containing about 6000 inhabitants, is situated on the shores of a fine bay-harbour, at the entrance of Cook's Straits, and midway between the northern and southern extremities of the two islands. Central and commanding as its position must be admitted to be, it has serious disadvantages. It is liable to volcanic action:

---

* In our last Number, p. 234, it was stated to be thirty-three millions of acres, the manuscript figure 8 having been read by the printer 3, and the error not having been detected in the correction of the proofs. Had the greater number been introduced, the argument would have been stronger: of sixty-five millions of acres the colonist has now forty-five, and the native twenty!

* Blue Book, p. 36.

"nine-tenths of all the damage ever done in New Zealand by earthquakes has been done in the town and immediate neighbourhood of Wellington." It has also the disagreeable peculiarity of a boisterous climate. "Standing on the edge of the funnel of Cook's Straits, and surrounded by steep hills, pierced by a hundred deep ravines and draught-holes, it enjoys, for six months, an almost continual gale of wind, bursting out into occasional typhoons." Again, "with the exception of the Hutt, a market-garden valley eight miles distant up the bay, there is no cultivable land near the town. Picturesque wooded steeps rise almost perpendicularly from the water's edge, and the country, for a radius of twenty miles round, consists of densely-timbered mountain ranges, cut up by innumerable ravines."*

There are, however, outlying districts which have been secured by the settlers, and with which communication has been opened.

The province is divided into two nearly equal portions by a range of mountains called the Ruahine in their northern part, and the Tararua and Rimutaki further south. Under the shelter of this range, along the western coast, extend a series of fine districts, and here, for a hundred miles, in an almost continuous chain of cultivation, the settlements of Porirua, Kapiti, Otaki, Rangitiki, Manawatu, and Wanganui, have been planted, several of them being situated on rivers flowing from the mountains, two of which—the Wanganui and Manawatu—are semi-navigable. But more than these have been secured. Eastward of the dividing range extend a series of plains called the Wairarapa. These plains, rising gradually from the sea-beach in Palliser Bay, near Port Nicholson, and Hawkes Bay on the eastern coast, to a considerable elevation at about forty miles inland from either spot, and buttressed up from the eastern coast by a mountain range called the Maungaraki and Rumahanga, extend from Cape Kidnapper Point, the southern projection of Hawkes Bay to Palliser Bay. At Hawkes Bay, to which these plains, expanding in their more northerly portion, stretch down tensive producer of wheat and wool, that in November 1858, by an Act of the General Assembly, it was declared to be the seventh province of New Zealand. Almost over the entire of this new province the native title has been extinguished. Lastly, between the eastern range and the cliffs on the seashore, the country forms a table-land, covered principally with open pastures, and watered by several streams. This also has been transferred from the native to the settler.

Thus, with narrow intervals, all the maritime districts of the province of Wellington, those along the east coast from the north shore of Hawkes Bay to Cape Palliser, the Wellington districts on Cook's Straits, and then along the western shores as far north as Wanganui, belong to the colonists. Even of the exceptional districts which break the chain of continuity, considerable portions appear to be under treaty. The native, thus deprived of the coast districts and other more valuable portions of the province, the harbours and embouchures of rivers, is thrown back on the wild interior between the Ruahine range and the Pipiriki river, and towards the great central group of mountains where the Ruapahu and the Tongariro lift their summits to the skies.

New Plymouth now claims our attention. This province, lying along the western shore, and including that projection of the coast which is crowned by the snow-capped mountain Egmont, has a coast-line of some 150 miles, and an acreage of three millions, or with the reduced area of the Parliamentary map, of 2,044,688 acres, being about 100 miles in length by about 150 in breadth. Its population consists of 2652 colonists and 3015 natives, making together a total of 5667 souls. Of the between two and three millions of acres, about 60,000 have been acquired by the settlers, and of these they appear, in 1858, to have had not more than 12,156 acres under crop, and 12,706 as the total number of acres fenced. The colonial population has increased from 1532 in 1851, to 2652 in 1858. Of these, 1414 are males. They possessed, in 1858, 432 horses, 4052 cattle, and 16,000 sheep.

rises the magnificent landmark of Mount Egmont. This remarkable mountain "may be seen from a vessel's deck, in clear weather, from a distance of more than a hundred miles." It rises in a perfect cone from a base of thirty miles in diameter, to a height of 8270 feet above the sea, and presents nearly the same appearance viewed from every point: its summit, which is an extinct crater, is flattened, and is covered with perpetual snow for nearly a quarter of its elevation. About half the circumference of the base, from Sugar-Loaf Point to the mouth of the Waimate river, is formed by the sea coast; and Cape Egmont presents at once the westernmost point of this circle, and the northern headland of the western entrance of Cook's Straits." Along the coast to the south of this commanding feature, a broad track of undulating country extends in a south-easterly direction as far as the Wanganui district; while to the north, a similar tract extends in a north-easterly direction as far as the river Mokau, being separated by a low range of wooded mountains from the country watered by the western tributaries of the Wanganui river." A saddle-shaped eminence rises to the N.W. of the mountain to a height of 4000 feet, as a kind of offshoot, while a low range of hills diverges to the north-east in the direction of Tongariro.

The village-town of Taranaki, or New Plymouth, lies nearly twenty miles north-eastward from Mount Egmont. It is well marked from seaward by the Sugar-Loaf Islands and by the still more remarkable dome-shaped hill Paretutu, or Main Sugar-Loaf, a cone of trachitic porphyry, which rises to the height of 500 feet, with one side of its base washed by the sea. The islands are five in number. One of them, Moturoa, is a conical rock, extremely steep, about one mile in circumference, and 300 feet high. Here, in the days of heathenism and cannibal wars, the vanquished portion of the natives used to find a refuge from the fierce wrath of the more powerful, the huts they were wont to inhabit being perched in niches on different parts of the rock. New Plymouth has no harbour capped mountain towering up from a sea of lustrous foliage 8000 feet in the golden sky.

"The settlement, snuggly planted on the margin of the beach, embosomed amid gentle hills, and watered by the Huatoki, Mangotuku, and tributary burns, displays its granite church and chapels, its little mills and breweries, snug hostelries, customs, post-office, stores, and primitive shops; but affecting no 'town airs,' stands out before the world a robust, hearty-looking village—famed throughout the land for troops of rosy children, fat meat, and rivers of Devonshire cream."*

"There are no outlying little settlements in this province. The inhabitants are concentrated in the village-capital, and in a belt of farms and clearings, lying around within a radius of ten miles." It is well that it is so for war has broken out, and here, in this peaceful spot, as it might be but for the fierce outbreak of human passions, the colonist and the settler have met in sanguinary conflict. The area of land in possession of the settlers appears to be limited, and we doubt not it is desirable that they should acquire more, but not, surely, at a price so costly as that of war. We do not now propose to examine the Taranaki land dispute: it will require separate consideration. But even supposing that more land was urgently required, would it not have been better patiently to have waited until opportunity presented itself, rather than imperil, by a rash collision with the natives, the very existence of this interesting spot?

We insert here as having reference to this point, extracts from a letter written by Mr. Fox, a member of the House of Representatives, dated April 27th, 1860, taken from the "Wellington Independent."

"SIR,—I have been requested to sign a memorial addressed to His Excellency the Governor by settlers in the Wanganui district, which expresses 'the warm approval of the memorialists of the policy pursued by him in the native disturbances at Taranaki;' and states that they 'regard the grounds on which His Excellency has taken up arms to be just

by the General Assembly to say whether the purchase from Teira was valid or not. I do not believe there is an individual of the European race in this province who *knows* the merits of the case; and I think it would be exceedingly presumptuous in me to prejudge a case on which I shall probably have to adjudicate in the House of Representatives, by expressing my belief that this war is either a just or a necessary war, when in fact, neither I, nor any other colonist in this province, has the means of knowing the truth.

"The responsibility which rests upon the Governor for appealing to the sword for the settlement of this land difficulty, without apparently having attempted any milder method of adjustment, is great. Great also is the responsibility he has incurred by plunging the colony into war with so little preparation, and without any warning to large numbers of settlers, whose position was such as to place them absolutely at the mercy of tribes with whom King was known to have intimate relations, and who might, if they had so chosen, have swept away the population of whole districts before their victims could almost have heard that a war was impending. Nor is the responsibility less, which will shortly rest upon the General Assembly, of investigating these matters, and making provision, if they shall think proper to do so, for the very heavy expense which this war must of necessity entail on the colony. My desire is to preserve my mind entirely unbiassed on these matters, that I may come to their consideration in the House of Representatives free from prejudice, and with a determination to see justice done where the right may be.

"For these reasons, Sir, I have declined committing myself by any expression of opinion such as that contained in the memorial referred to. I trust that the explanation I have given will be satisfactory to my constituents."

We have nearly completed our circle, and have reached the Auckland province, the one which is of most importance in our present consideration, because within its limits is concentrated the largest proportion of the population of 800 miles; and an area of seventeen millions of acres, or, according to the Parliamentary map, of 15,456,000.

"The chief local characteristics of this noble province are these — a warmer climate, almost capable of ripening maize and a few semi-tropical fruits; great area and coast line; the possession of Lakes Taupo, Rotorua, and innumerable hot springs and chalybeate waters; numerous fine harbours and facilities of coast and inland water carriage; the exclusive possession of the kauri forests; the presence of nearly two-thirds of the native population, and the absence of great pastoral plains.

"Auckland (south lat. 36° 50', east long. 174° 50') the flourishing capital of the province, containing about 7000 inhabitants, was founded by Governor Hobson, and a body of pioneer colonists, in 1840. One of the finest commercial sites in the world is that of Auckland. Planted in the centre of her province, she stands, Corinth-like, on a narrow isthmus between her two noble harbours and outlets to the ocean, Waitemata and Manakau. An easy canalization of four miles would unite these waters; when, through gay villas and suburban gardens, a line of battle-ships might glide from sea to sea. Indeed, Auckland is the centre of a net-work of marine highways — a young antipodal Venice, surrounded by natural canals. Close to her, on the east, she has the Wairoa, the Thames, and the deep and placid Tamaki; close, on the west, the great estuary of Kaipara, pushing its arms up to the head waters of the Waitemate; whilst on the south she has the beautiful Waikato, meandering a hundred miles through the valleys of the interior, and floating the rich harvests of Taupo and the Waipa down to her very wharfs.

"A chain of military pensioner villages surround Auckland to the south, at a distance of from six to ten miles; and are connected with each other, and with the agricultural suburbs of the town, by excellent roads, displaying a continuous line of beautiful road-side cultivations.*

"At present, four-fifths of the colonist population of the province are centered in

Whaingaroa, Kawhia, and Tauranga, counting from 50 to 100 pioneer settlers, which will grow into considerable importance as the extraordinary natural resources of the province become developed under the magic touch of capital and labour."*

The colonial population in 1858 numbered 18,177, being an increase, in seven years, of 8747. The native title has been extinguished in 1,959,974 of the 15,456,000 acres of the province. These acquired territories are massed together, almost exclusively, in the northern projection of the island, extending from the north bank of that portion of the Waikato which runs from east to west, as far as Land's End and Cape Reinga, the whole of this area, with the exception of a strip extending across the island from Hokianga to the Bay of Islands, having been either actually proclaimed, or being under negotiation for that purpose. Considering the maritime position of Auckland, of which we have just given a glowing description — an antipodal Venice, surrounded by natural canals—all portions of this territory must be regarded as of easy access.

We have already seen, if their own statistics are to be depended upon, that the Auckland colonists consider themselves to be suffering under a great deficiency of land. "Our farmers," observes one energetic remonstrant at the Auckland meeting on the 'Native Land Question,' held June 18, 1859, " are obliged to suspend the increasing of their flocks, owing to the want of lands and the scarcity of their food."† The Superintendent of Auckland, who, from his position, might be supposed to be sufficiently acquainted with the statistics of his own province, appears to have become so strongly imbued with the same idea, as to forward, in November 1858, an official complaint to the Colonial Secretary's office, that, with the exception of 'certain blocks of land situated at the Bay of Islands, which for the present, for certain reasons, were not to be dealt with, there remained but one block of land, over which the native title had not been extinguished, available for survey and disposal"‡ by the Provincial Government.

Land Purchase Commissioner, dated Jan. 25, 1859—

"It appears to me that there must be some misapprehension as to the Provincial Government having no blocks of land to operate on. In 1857, 119,095 acres were proclaimed in the 'Government Gazette,' and of this extent there are several blocks of good land in the Kaipara district alone, which have not been touched by the Provincial Government, such as the Tatararake, of 12,000 acres; Okahu, 19,000; Waikiekie, 12,000; Tokatoka and Wakahara, 7000. During the year 1858, 277,800 acres were proclaimed : of this extent 86,000 acres, near the North Cape, is more adapted for grazing than for subdivision or settlement. There are, however, in this vicinity, two blocks of 16,000 acres of good volcanic soil, the Otengi and Wharemaru, well adapted for settlement, and situated beyond the limits of lands required under the Bay-of-Islands Settlement Act 1858. There are other blocks in different parts of the province that I have not adverted to, independent of 22,000 acres recently handed over for proclamation from this department. I cannot, therefore, conceive how the statement has been arrived at, that there is only one block over which the native title has been extinguished, available for survey and disposal by the Provincial Government."

In this document the Kaipara district is specially referred to. Into the Kaipara harbour several rivers fall, the whole adjoining district being well irrigated, and presenting such a combination of natural advantages as to induce Dr. Dieffenbach thus favourably to report of it—" Kaipara harbour, into which the Wairoa and other rivers fall, seems to me —on account of the number of timber-trees on the shores of the rivers, the length of their navigable course, the extent of the available alluvial land on their banks, and the immediate neighbourhood of the seat of Government (Auckland)—to be deserving of an early attention as a place where capital and labour may be very profitably employed."* Again, the settlers had especially complained of the want of pasture land on which to feed their

conclusive as it would seem to be, because referring to facts which were undeniable, does not appear, however, to have been satisfactory to the Auckland colonists. On May 24, 1859, they again approach the Colonial Secretary on the subject, and repeat their tale of fast-approaching ruin in consequence of the failure of land-supplies. "Difficulties have arisen, and are increasing to such an extent as to render it imperative on the settlers to inquire, How are our increasing stock to be fed? Where is the land to produce wheat and other necessaries for our present population?" And they then proceed to impress upon the Government the necessity of acquiring native land in the district of the Thames, which the colonist considered would be advantageous for his purposes, but which the Maori preferred retaining in his own hands. Thus driven to bay by increasing importunities, the Colonial Secretary, in a letter dated June 6, 1859, requires from the Superintendent of Auckland an abstract of lands, available for survey and settlement, in possession of the provincial authorities on January 1, 1859; and the very same official, who, in November 1858, had declared, "but one block of land, over which the native title has been extinguished, is now available for survey or disposal by the Provincial Government," remits a return by which it appears, that on January 1, 1859, there were in the possession of the provincial authorities no less than 632,081 acres of land, of which, after the deduction of mountainous tracts or of inferior soil, as well as other portions, the settlement of which, from various causes, was deferred, there remained 344,224 acres available for immediate survey.

These circumstances appear strange, and difficult to be accounted for. The colonists complain, first, of there being no available land. This position being untenable, they are compelled to fall back upon the improving of the large tracts which were awaiting their acceptance. But this, also, being found weak and indefensible, the true reason at length is unwillingly avowed—their distance from the provincial capital. We refer to a speech of

be correct, of its average and quality. [Mr Forsaith then read a paper describing the quantity and quality of the land at present held by Government in the Auckland Provinces.]

"Mr. Forsaith did not wish to deny the character of land in this province, for that which he had mentioned, though unfit at present, might become in future ages of very great value; but it was land not at present required, and which the province was not in a position at present to make available. Nearly every acre in New Zealand would ultimately become available, but all of it was not the land to offer to new comers. He believed that if they went on a large proportion of it ruin stared them in the face; and when he (Mr. Forsaith) saw new comers arriving, and finding all their hopes fallacious, he considered it not only as a private, but a national calamity. One asked, 'Was there no land in the country?' and was told that there was at the North Cape. The new comer comes, and says, 'I do not want to go there.' And it was not to be expected that he should till the circle of civilization and colonization had extended so far. It was a mockery and delusion to expect him to go there, and they ought to take measures for preventing the necessity for his so doing."

We have been in the habit of thinking that the emigrant went forth for the purpose of extending the circle of civilization and colonization; that he was to be the pioneer into the wilderness, and, addressing himself to the cultivation of lands which had been left since the deluge in the wildness of nature, to raise up for himself a new homestead and heritage, until others, encouraged by his example, should go ahead of him, and place him eventually in the centre, instead of being in the extreme frontier of a new civilization. So it has been in Canada; but, in Auckland, the colonist waits until the circle of civilization and colonization has so extended itself as to afford to him a safe position within its limits. But by what mysterious process is this extension to take place, and who is to prepare the way for the emigrant? Are we to understand that the

mission to dislodge the Maori from those productive acres which yield the wheat and, maize and garden produce conveyed by native canoes to the Auckland market, and driving the original proprietor further into the wilderness, to enter upon his labours, and quietly proceed to reap the fruits of them? "There are," observes the Colonial Secretary, in reply to the remonstrant colonists of Auckland, "within easy distance of the city of Auckland a large quantity of fine land that the natives are at present unwilling to part with;" and because they are not willing to part with fine land, so advantageously situated, they are pronounced to be very unreasonable and impracticable persons. But we are inclined to think that the native is in a position to show that the unreasonableness is with the European, and not with him. He might justly reply, "Why urge me to the sale of more land, when, of the territories already acquired by you, hundreds of thousands of acres of good land remain unoccupied? You urge the remoteness of their position as a reason why they are so, and desire that we should alienate lands more conveniently situated with respect to Auckland. But the very circumstance which would make them convenient for you—their vicinity to Auckland—renders them convenient to us, for we also are agriculturists. We raise crops of wheat, maize, potatoes; we rear pigs and poultry; we catch fish; and the proceeds of our industry, with fruit, vegetables, firewood, flax, and kauri gum, we bring to your market at Auckland, and, by their sale, benefit you and ourselves too. If you had no land left, and the case was one of necessity, we might be disposed to listen; but if it be merely a matter of convenience, then we are justified in asking, Is it reasonable to expect of us, that, to convenience you, we should inconvenience ourselves? Auckland has hitherto been the great point of reunion between the two races. You are in almost exclusive possession of the territories on the north; considerable blocks to the southward of its site we have also permitted you to acquire, so as to afford you the opportunity of surrounding your colonial capital with a colonial population. Those other districts which you now wish to have, because of their contiguity to Auckland, are for the same reason convenient and profitable to us to retain, and therefore we will not part with them. It may be very disagreeable to the new immigrant to be compelled to enter upon new localities, and erect his homestead in positions remote from Auckland; but we cannot regard it otherwise than unreasonable to disembarrass him of this necessity by inflicting upon us the very disadvantage which he is so anxious to avoid."

In truth, the more we investigate the subject, the less justification do we find for this intense agitation respecting land, on the part of certain Auckland colonists. It appears, that up to December 31, 1857, 568,288 acres, in the province of Auckland, had been alienated, that is, had actually come into the possession of settlers;[*] and yet, that in 1858, the European population of that province had only 60,183 acres under crop, and 90,448 as the total number fenced in. In grass there were only 50,320 acres. These appear to be but fragmentary portions, indeed, of the magnificent area of upwards of half a million of acres actually in their possession; and it seems unjustifiable that men should agitate for the augmentation, *recte si possunt, si non, quocunque modo*, of fresh lands from the natives, when, of the acres over which the native title had been extinguished, upwards of 600,000 remained at the disposal of the Provincial Government; while of the half million and upwards actually in the possession of the colonists so recently as 1858, little more than 50,000 acres were in grass, and 60,000 under crop. At that date, Auckland, with 18,000 population, had only 31,700 cattle, and 58,792 sheep; Wellington, and Hawkes Bay, with a population of 13,000, had 40,291 cattle, and 336,314 sheep; Nelson, with 9000, had 19,485 cattle and 393,041 sheep; Canterbury, with less than 9000, had 20,729 cattle, and 495,580 sheep; and Otago, with less than 7000, had 20,071 cattle, and 223,589 sheep. We are constrained, therefore, to conclude that the European population of Auckland does not want more land; but more of that patient, persevering, industrial action, which, needful as it is in every man, is more especially so in an emigrant, and without which all the acreage in New Zealand will not avail to make a thriving and prosperous colony. The fact is, that Auckland, with all her advantages of early colonization, and largest amount of European population, is not retaining that advanced position among the settlements of New Zealand, which properly belongs to her as the metropolitan province, in which is placed the colonial capital and seat of Government. The other settlements, especially the southern ones of the Middle Island, are fast overtaking her in the race of progress. Statistics of the territorial revenue, published by order of the General Government, have proved beyond a doubt the humiliating fact, that

---

[*] Blue Book, p. 140.

"both in accession of population and increase of exports" the province of Auckland is being left far behind. The territorial revenue of Auckland, arising from sales of land, licenses, and assessments, which in 1855 had reached a maximum of 60,000*l*., in 1858 had sunk to less than 2500*l*; while that of Wellington had increased from 15,000*l*. to 31,000*l*.; Canterbury from 9200*l*. to 38,900*l*.; and Otago from 1800*l*. to 17,000*l*. and upwards.

Hence we conceive the restlessness at Auckland. The colonists there have attributed the falling-off to the want of land-supply. Hence the public meetings in connexion with the native land question, the rash words which have been said, and the rash things which have been done. Hence the ceaseless complaints and remonstrances addressed to the Government officials, praying for an alteration in the laws regulating the purchase of land from the natives, the abandonment of the crown right pre-emption, and the renunciation of those stipulations in the treaty of Waitangi which recognised the native title, and pronounced the land to be the property of the Maori until it became his pleasure to alienate it. We quote an extract from a paper drawn up by certain Auckland colonists, and which appears to have been put into circulation. After advocating the necessity of some system, which would work with greater facility in the acquisition of more land, they proceed to say—"We venture to suggest that the most feasible and promising method by which this object may be obtained, is *the enfranchising of the lands of the colony, now encumbered with the native right of occupation*, and the royal right of pre-emption."*

When such assumptions are thus openly put forward, and a number of settlers append their names to a public document of this character, which asserts that the lands of New Zealand belong to the colony, and that the native is merely permitted to occupy them on sufferance, we cannot be surprised if the Maoris conclude the time is come when they must unite for self-defence. The view prevalent amongst the colonists on the subject is, that "the unimproved lands are the property of the colony, merely encumbered with a certain native right of occupancy, of which it is the duty of the Government to clear them, as, from time to time, they may be required by the settlers;" and "few would be disposed to admit that the extension of European settlers must be contingent on the consent of the aboriginal owners to cede their territory." "The Government is accordingly held to have failed in its duty in every case where lands eligible for settlement remain in the hands of the natives."*

Nor can we be surprised if the colonists adopt such views, when they have been avowed by the responsible ministers themselves. A certain Bill, designated the "Native Territorial Rights Bill," was introduced by them into the General Assembly, the object of which was to empower the Governor to make free grants to individual natives of lands in reference to which they were willing to cede the native title, that they might receive in lieu of it, and as the future basis of their holding, Crown grants. In this a limitation was proposed to be placed on the exercise of the Governor's power, although in a matter purely native, by making the consent of his responsible advisers necessary to his taking action; and this, on its being objected to, the ministry defended by reasoning, of which the following sentence is an exemplification—"The fallacy is in assuming that to be a right in the natives, which is really a gratuitous concession by the Government. The legislature, very properly, will not trust Governor or ministers, or both together, with any such extravagant discretion as an unlimited power of granting away the *colonial territory* to natives in fee simple."†

To return to Auckland and its prospects, we think our readers will conclude with us, that whatever deterioration has taken place, this cannot be ascribed to want of land, for of that, and good land too, immediately available without trenching on the natives' rights, there appears to be abundance. If we might be permitted to point out one injurious element, we would specify the credit system of Auckland, whereby she offers five years credit to purchasers of land. A lease for four years is granted at a yearly rental of sixpence per acre, and at the expiration of the term, rent having been paid, and the conditions of occupancy fulfilled, the occupant receives his provincial Crown grant in fee simple.

"This is offering a direct bribe to labouring emigrants to do that which they are always only too eager to do, but which, for their own good and that of the whole community, they never should do, namely, instantly to throw aside the well-paid axe and

---

* Memorandum from Mr. T. H. Smith, Assistant Native Secretary. Blue Book, p. 84.

† Remarks of Ministers on Memorandum of Native Assistant Secretary. Blue Book, p. 46.

plough, and to rush to the land office for two or three hundred acres of wild land, without having a penny in hand wherewith to aid cultivation." It is not enough to obtain emigrants for the land, and land for the emigrant, but there is a further necessity to be provided for, that when the emigrant is placed on the land he should have the means to cultivate it. A double evil accrues when an emigrant obtains land without any means to cultivate it—the land of the penniless emigrant is left without cultivation, and the emigrant capitalist left without labour. The emigrant who ought to be a labourer instead of a holder of land, becomes a mere squatter on acres, which, from his inability to cultivate them, remain in the wildness of nature; while the man who has the capital to improve his land, if he had the labour, is embarassed and hindered; and thus rich and poor suffer together, simply because, from injudicious arrangements, they are disjointed from that proper relationship in which they ought to stand to one another. The labourer ought to remain a labourer " until the quick savings of his high wages make him a little capitalist, and thus arm him with the one other weapon necessary to enable him to convert his wild acres into golden crops."

We have dealt particularly with this part of the subject, because we cannot but feel that the restlessness on the subject of new acquisitions of land, amongst the European population of Auckland, has engendered amongst the Maoris that distrustful feeling which has exhibited itself in the land-league and king-question, and the further complications in the Taranaki district. Will the prospects of Auckland be improved by the war between the races which has broken out? "The true paramount end and aim of any land and emigration policy of an infant colony, where there is one human being to 1600 acres of fertile wilderness, should be that of attracting population, that of tempting to her solitary shores the *primum mobile* of civilization—people!"* Has the North Island of New Zealand been rendered more attractive by the war which now rages there?

---

* Hursthouse, vol. ii. p. 128.

VALEDICTION OF MISSIONARIES, AND SPECIAL INSTRUCTIONS ADDRESSED TO THEM.

We present to our readers the instructions addressed to several Missionaries going forth to the various fields of labour appointed them. The Special Meeting of the Committee, on the occasion of which these instructions were delivered, was held at the Church Missionary Children's Home, Highbury, on September 28th, General Alexander occupying the chair. These valedictory meetings are of special interest and importance, inferior in these respects to none which are held in connexion with the Society. From the nature and object of these assemblings, and the elements of which they consist, there is a deeper chord struck, one which lies more close to the human heart, than can be the case in meetings convened simply for the purpose of communi- ere they go; the Committee, with all the solicitude of a parent, prepared to address to them a few last weighty, and yet most affectionate words of godly counsel and admonition; combine in a very peculiar manner to move the heart, and call forth earnest and united prayer. The Missionary work, in its importance and amplitude, is brought out as a great reality. It has its representatives there in the men who have been led by the grace of God to consecrate themselves to it. Certain portions of the field have a significant prominence given them, according to the designation of the Missionaries — sometimes Africa; sometimes India; sometimes poor suffering China; not unfrequently several at the same moment; but although the light

is, that there should be much and earnest prayer at home, if there is to be much and successful effort abroad. We believe that these meetings are regarded by those who frequent them as means of grace of no ordinary unction and power, and that they are valued accordingly. We only wish that more of the friends of the Society could be convened on these occasions; but this would require a larger place of meeting even than the noble hall of the Children's Home, and there is a certain private and domestic character pertaining to such meetings which would be lost if they were transferred to more public places of assemblage.

The meeting of September 28th was one of no inferior interest. The number of Missionaries, viewed in the light of the as yet scanty measure of supply which the church at home is wont to yield to us, was large—fourteen, with the wives of some of them. Some were returning to the scenes of former labours; others going forth for the first time; some already exercised in the ministry at home, one of the brethren having been curate of St. Peter's, Southwark; another curate of St. Saviour's, York; four were for Africa, seven, including William Sandys, a Burmese student, were for India; one for China; one for Ceylon; and one for Smyrna. Thus a large portion of the Society's work was brought immediately under the consideration of the meeting; some of the designated localities awakening at the present moment more than usual solicitude, and requiring a more than usual outpouring of prayer on their behalf—the Yoruba country, distracted with intestine war, while along the western coast the slave-trade is being prosecuted with more than usual intensity—India, subsiding after the severity of the great cyclone of 1867, and yet not so settled down as to dissipate all anxiety for the future; but in its Missionary aspect a field from whence the inundation has just retired, and where we are urgently called upon to go forth and sow—China and Turkey, in the throes of great national changes, the old *régimes*, from their utter decay and rottenness, breaking up, but by what new aspects of government to be succeeded no one can tell—all in a suffering condition, and all urgent for help: like the man of Macedonia crying, "Come over, and help us." Never has any body of Missionaries left England at a more momentous period; and they appeared all to feel that it was so, for never have we heard the entreaty to be remembered and helped by the prayers of friends at home more universal and earnest than on this occasion. And so it should be: if some go forth, the home church should watch and pray the more. In this watchfulness and prayer there should be no relaxation. "I stand continually upon the watch-tower in the day-time, and I am set in my ward whole nights."

The instructions were such as befitted the occasion. They dealt more especially with a point which has been for some time forcing itself on our attention, and requiring to be approached with judgment and discrimination. Our readers will peruse them, we doubt not, with interest. There are several thoughts which they have suggested to our own minds, but which the limited space of our present Number will not permit us to introduce.

The Missionaries addressed were the following—

"The Rev. M. S. Jackson, proceeding to Sierra Leone;

"The Rev. G. F. and Mrs. Bühler and the Rev. J. Buckley Wood, returning to the Yoruba country;

"Dr. A. A. Harrison, M.B., Trinity College, Cambridge, proceeding to Yoruba;

"The Rev. Theodore F. Wolters, proceeding to Smyrna to join his father;

"The Rev. T. K. Weatherhead, S.C.L., St. John's College, Cambridge, and late Curate of St. Peter's, Southwark, proceeding to Bombay;

"The Rev. J. M. Brown, B.A., St. Edmund's Hall, Oxford, and late Curate of St. Saviour's, York, proceeding to North India;

"The Rev. J. Barton, B.A., Christ College, Cambridge, proceeding to Calcutta;

"The Rev. E. L. Puxley, proceeding to the North-west Provinces;

"The Rev. Nigel and Mrs. Honiss, proceeding to Tinnevelly;

"The Rev. J. B. and Mrs. Simmons, also proceeding to Tinnevelly;

"The Rev. R. B. Tonge, B.A., and Mrs. Tonge, London University, proceeding to Kandy, Ceylon;

"The Rev. Arthur E. Moule, proceeding to China;

"William Sandys (Shwai tui), a Burmese Student, returning to India.

"DEARLY BELOVED IN THE LORD,

"We are met together to take leave of a large body of Missionaries going to distant and widely differing fields of labour—to West Africa, India, Ceylon, China, and the Mediterranean.

"The Committee have so frequently addressed their Missionaries upon the main principles and chief motives of Missionary work, that they feel justified in omitting these upon the present occasion, in order to touch upon a topic of great practical importance, which the present aspect of the Missionary field brings into prominent notice, namely, the proper conduct of a Missionary in respect of social and political questions which may seem to be connected with the progress of his spiritual work.

"The one object of the Church Missionary Society is to provide for the preaching of the Gospel of Christ to those who have not yet received it; and to train up the Christian converts in the doctrine and discipline of the Church of England.

"But the blessings of the Gospel, when received, tend to elevate the social position of the converts, and to instruct them in the true principles of justice and humanity; and so to quicken in their minds the sense of the wrongs they may suffer through oppression and misgovernment. A knowledge also of Christian duty, while it secures obedience to the sovereign powers, limits that obedience to things lawful in the sight of God, as defined in his word, and so far often interferes with the institutions of heathen and Mohammedan Governments.

"The relation, also, in which the Missionary stands to his converts, necessarily connects him with their temporal welfare. Going among the people with a message of love upon his lips, and with the spirit of love in his heart, he soon wins their confidence beyond all other persons of his race. He becomes their best friend—their faithful adviser. His message embraces their temporal as well as their spiritual interests, for 'godliness hath the promise of the life that now is, and of that which is to come.' They have, therefore, a claim upon him for advice and assistance against injustice and wrong.

"The Missionary has, moreover, a message to declare, on proper occasions, to those in authority, on their responsibility to God, by whose ordinance they exercise the right of government.

"However earnestly, therefore, the faithful Missionary may strive to confine himself to his one great work—the ministry of the Go-

tical, or social excitement. And the fields of labour to which you are designated are so circumstanced. In India, society yet heaves under the recent terrible catastrophe, and questions have been lately raised, in respect of the civil rights of Christian converts, of the system of ryotry and the cultivation of indigo, of the Christian action of Government, and of its officers, in which the Missionary may be more or less necessarily involved. In the sphere of our Missions in Africa and in China, civil wars rage, and in the former country our Missionaries are severally living under Governments at open war with each other. In Asia Minor, and throughout the Turkish empire, social and political affairs are in a state of terrible effervescence.

"Into such fields of labour you are going forth as the messengers of the Prince of Peace —to preach ' glory to God in the highest, and on earth peace, goodwill towards men.' How blessed the commission! yet how arduous and perilous its right execution!

"The Committee would therefore desire to furnish you, by the divine blessing, with advice for the guidance of your conduct, and with an affectionate assurance of their sympathy, to encourage and cheer you in your future difficulties.

"I. The general rule in such cases has been laid down in the printed ' Regulations explanatory of the relation between the Church Missionary Society and the Missionaries connected with it,' in these words—' Every Missionary is strictly charged to abstain from interfering in the political affairs of the country or place in which he may be situated.'

"The terms of this rule are necessarily broad and somewhat indefinite—political affairs is a wide term. There are worldly politicians who would desire to include in their exclusive province national education, the state support of idolatry, the social institution, as it is called, of slavery, the treatment of the aborigines, the private religious action of Government officers. As soon as a minister of religion touches these questions, an outcry is apt to be raised, as if he were meddling with politics.

by any just interpretation, be included in those 'political affairs,' from interfering with which the Missionary is to abstain. A Missionary is bound to remonstrate if he believes the great principles of justice, humanity, and Christian duty to be violated; and the politician is bound, on his part, to vindicate his adherence to those principles, in the course which he thinks it right to pursue. In all such questions, therefore, it were the wisdom of the governing powers to listen to the suggestions of the Missionary body, and to secure their co-operation: if the authorities, on the other hand, decline or oppose their suggestions, the Missionary is driven to an appeal to public opinion as a last resource, and the Government may be, sooner or later, compelled to yield that which Christian principle demands, and too often after loss of time and opportunity, and after controversial discussion equally disadvantageous to all the parties concerned.

"A few specific cases which have occurred in the history of this Society, will serve to illustrate the foregoing statement.

"(1) The earliest political question in which the Society was involved was that of slavery;—first, the abolition of the slave-trade; afterwards, the abolition of slavery. This Society nobly and prominently denounced the sin and evil of slavery, while it was yet maintained as a social institution, and protected by numerous acts of the legislature. Other Missionary Societies, having labourers before ourselves in slave colonies, bore the brunt of the contest upon the spot. Their Missionaries were denounced as political agitators, till at last the Missionary, Smith, was cast into a jail, and tried as a rebel. This act called forth the indignation of the British Parliament, and the authority of the Imperial Government was interposed to vindicate the rights of justice and humanity in the person of the injured Missionary. Through such conflicts the good cause at length triumphed, and slavery was abolished.

"(2) Another great political question, in which Missionaries were involved, was the liberty of preaching the Gospel to the natives in India. Here, again, the first brunt of actual conflict was borne by the Missionaries of another Society—the illustrious Carey, Ward, and Marshman. Their memoirs, lately published, exhibit an instructive example of the delicacy and difficulty of such questions as we are handling, and how gradually the right and liberty were conceded, for which the Missionary and his friends contended.

"(3) So, also, by the Missionary and his friends, the question of Government connexion with idolatry in India was first raised, and was mainly supported by the evidence of the Missionary. Here, also, the advocates of a Christian policy were frequently denounced as disturbers of Government. Even the eminent Christian bishop, Dr. Corrie, received an official rebuke for pressing this question upon the attention of Government. The cause of Christian duty was, however, supported by the voice of the nation, and at length the very principles which had been at first opposed as the theory of fanatics, were embodied in a formal despatch of His Majesty's Government.

"(4.) So also, in Travancore, the Missionaries have thought themselves compelled, on several occasions, to stand up for the civil rights of the converts, and their efforts have been blessed with success. Even when the Government of Madras censured the Missionaries for appearing in courts of justice as the friends of the oppressed Christian, the Home Government reversed the censure, and vindicated the conduct of the Missionary, as being the natural and proper guardian of the just civil rights of the convert.

"(5) On a late occasion, a Missionary of this Society furnished this Committee with a statement of the effects which he had witnessed of an order of the supreme Government of India, in respect of the private action of Christian officers towards Christian inquirers of the 24th Punjab Native Infantry. The Committee thought it right publicly to remonstrate against this proceeding. The Government, in consequence of this remonstrance, issued a despatch explanatory of that order, which has happily removed the difficulties which a misunderstanding of the order had created; and the Committee rejoice now to add, that the good work in the regiment, arrested for fifteen months by that misunderstanding, has been renewed, and the baptism of several soldiers of the regiment has since taken place.

"(6) At this present time a social question is agitated between the indigo-planter of Bengal and the ryot cultivator. When, a few years ago, the case of the ryot was advocated by the Missionary, the Missionary was denounced as a meddler in matters beyond his province. At length, however, the supreme Government has instituted a Court of Inquiry, and has placed a Missionary, as a fair representative of the ryot, among the Commissioners, and has subpœnaed other Missionaries to give evidence on oath of the cases of alleged oppression which have come under their notice; thus vindicating the right of the Missionary to assist in the adjustment of this question. The result of the inquiry is not yet known, and therefore the Committee abstain from further remark upon this particular case.

"These six instances will sufficiently illustrate our position, that there are many questions of a mixed character, which, though partly political, fall within the province of the Missionary, and, in the adjustment of which, the authorities may advantageously avail themselves of the co-operation of the Missionary body. These questions, it is impossible to deny, are becoming daily more and more prominent and important. For it is a characteristic of the age, that the religious element enters into every great question — even in the Congress of European nations.

"II. The Committee now proceed to offer you a few practical directions in respect of such questions as have been described.

"1. The Committee affectionately, but earnestly, warn each Missionary, especially every young Missionary, not to take up supposed grievances too hastily; but to wait and consult with other Christian men till they have ascertained the reality and importance of any alleged social or civil wrong. Remember that these 'mixed' questions form the exceptions to the general rule of strict abstinence from interfering in political affairs. This rule must be applied to all such matters as do not palpably involve the great principles of justice, humanity, or Christian duty. The Committee say *palpably*, because the ingenuity of some minds will see a connexion which is not generally recognised. All political measures might be thus excepted from the prohibition, and the rule become a nullity. But common sense has established a distinction, and it will be well for the Missionary to err on the side of abstinence from doubtful questions, rather than to interfere in matters which will not be allowed by sober judges to belong to his province.

2. When, however, the Missionary is unavoidably involved, in the line of his duty, in questions having a political aspect, let him guard against a political spirit—that is, against the spirit in which the politicians of this world strive together. He must stand clear of all party strife. The apostolic injunction is— 'The servant of the Lord must not strive, but be gentle unto all men, apt to teach, patient, in meekness instructing them that oppose themselves, if God, peradventure, will give them repentance to the acknowledging of the truth.' In conformity with this rule, the Missionary should never assume a position of hostility to the ruling powers, or have re- paper invectives. Let him rather address the authorities in respectful and confiding terms, as those upon whom God has laid the responsibility of upholding the great principles of Christian duty. If such addresses be unheeded, let a temperate statement of the case be transmitted to the Missionary Directors at home, with such particulars as will bear the closest sifting, and as the Missionary is prepared to avow before the public.

"3. Avoid, even in the most pressing cases, being drawn into the vortex of mere political discussions, for it will prove a painful interruption to your happier duties. Much precious time is necessarily lost in those discussions, which might have been spent in winning to Christ, souls, who should have been your crown of rejoicing in the day of the Lord. Even your conferences with your brethren on such topics will be far less profitable to the soul, than if the time had been wholly devoted to spiritual things. And you will be liable to be drawn into still less profitable connexion with the men of the world, who will court the aid of a spiritual man for the sake of a secular object, though they sneer at his religion. All these, and many other considerations, make the true Missionary shrink from political discussions, make him walk very warily while engaged in them, and make him most thankful to escape from their entanglements.

"4. When compelled by a sense of duty to take an active part in exceptional cases, be the more careful to observe the standing rule of the Society, in its legitimate scope and intention, in all other political relations. These will embrace the ordinary course of Government, in respect of which you must exhibit in your own conduct, as well as inculcate upon all others, the spirit of the apostolic injunction, 'Tribute to whom tribute is due, custom to whom custom, fear to whom fear, honour to whom honour.' You must especially strive to stand aloof from all questions of political leadership—of political partisanship. Whether officers of Government be favourable or unfavourable to Missionary work, whether they patronise or oppose, let the Missionary avoid all appearance of political intrigue. The cordial and courteous recognition of the official position of an opponent will be the best means of disarming his opposition. A candid construction of his measures will conciliate, while a severe criticism will raise needless animosity.

"III. The Missionaries who labour under Christian rulers, in the dependencies of Great Britain, will be enabled, under ordinary circumstances, to carry on their work without concerning themselves with the course of

ficult with those who labour amidst uncivilized nations and Governments. The injunction to abstain from all interference with political affairs is obviously not applicable when the native Government is mixed up with national superstitions and social institutions which violate all justice and humanity; when the magistrate's sword is in the hands of every petty chief, or self-constituted oppressor; when human sacrifices form a part of the political constitution.

"In such a situation, the first Missionaries found themselves in the Susu Mission of Africa and in New Zealand. Yet while the rule stood, some conscientious men hesitated to instruct the natives in political maxims, or to protest against their existing atrocities. For the relief of their consciences, the following note was added to the rule by the Committee, and was printed for many years in the 'Explanatory Regulations.'

"'It is not intended, however, by this regulation, to preclude Missionaries who may be stationed in New Zealand, or in other regions which are uncivilized, and which do not enjoy the protection of a fixed Government, from bringing the natives acquainted with such Christian and civil institutions, as, in process of time, their situations may require, or from using their influence in such countries to preserve or restore peace, in conformity with the spirit of a minister of the Gospel.'

"In the spirit of this explanation, the Society at home and the Missionaries in New Zealand took a leading part in the discussion of the great national question of the colonization of those islands. When the first Governor, Captain Hobson, was sent out to negotiate with the chiefs for the transfer of the sovereignty to the Queen of Great Britain, he obtained the assistance of the Missionaries of this and of the Wesleyan Society to bring about that event. No one took a more prominent part than the senior Missionary of the Church Missionary Society. The services of the Missionaries were publicly acknowledged by the Governor and the Home Government; and, on a special occasion, the Governor thus addressed the Legislative Council on its being opened, December 14, 1841—

"'Whatever difference of opinion, may be entertained as to the value and extent of the labours of the Missionary body, there can be no doubt that they have rendered important services to this country; or that, but for them, a British colony would not at this moment be established in New Zealand.'

"The voice of the Missionary, which was thus mainly instrumental in bringing the New-tangi, is now rightly lifted up on the behalf of the chiefs, against, as they believe, the attempted violation of its letter and spirit.

"On a late review of the printed form of the 'Explanatory Regulations,' this note was omitted, because New Zealand had become a British colony, and the Missions of the Society in Western Africa were then under British Government, and it was thought that the good sense of Christian Missionaries would sufficiently qualify the rule in exceptional cases. But the state of the Yoruba Mission recalls one part of the appended note to our attention. In the present day a civil war has broken out between three of the towns in which Missionaries reside. Ijaye and Ibadan have made war against each other, and Abbeokuta has unhappily joined in the conflict. The several Missionaries in these towns have been thus placed in most difficult positions. The Committee are not prepared to judge of the conduct of each Missionary, or of his conduct in all respects. But the Committee have seen quite enough to induce them to urge upon you, who are going to the Yoruba Mission, with affectionate importunity, the old injunction, of 'using your influence to preserve or restore peace in conformity with the spirit of a minister of the Gospel.'

"IV. The Committee will conclude with a few words of general encouragement and advice, suggested by the circumstances which have called forth these instructions.

"1. Remember that seasons of special political conflict, or social excitement, have always been seasons of special promise and hope to the church of Christ. The King of Zion has an iron sceptre to break down all opposition to an advancing Gospel. Political convulsions are the execution of his judgment. At the very time when He thus wields that iron sceptre, He enjoins upon his church to proclaim the message—'Kiss the Son, lest He be angry.' 'When the judgments of the Lord are in the earth, the inhabitants of the world will learn righteousness.' We have seen this most manifestly in the improved prospects of our Indian Missions since the mutiny. And every observer of God's dealings with the world will supply abundant illustrations. It is refreshing to think how often the work of mercy and grace is silently advancing amidst the crash of human affairs. Let the man of faith repose upon this thought. In the darkest hours the eye and ear of flesh may discern nothing but the flash of lightning, and hear only the roll of thunder; but let the ear of faith catch the sound of the still small voice, and let the man of faith then ply in patience, prayer, and faith, his special mission.

that such critical times as they allude to, are also to the Christian times of special trial and temptation, and he needs then to place a double guard upon his temper and spirit, lest he be carried away by the stream into an exhibition of worldly tempers, lest his good should be evil spoken of through his hasty language or exaggerated statements. There will be perils on all sides. The Missionary may be often in personal danger; such a time is an occasion for showing his faith in a special providence; that he does not fear with the fear of men of the world; that he can stay himself upon his God. There may be dangers to his reputation, especially when the Missionary stands up as the friend of the aborigines, in opposition to the oppression of unprincipled European settlers. Those of us who are old enough to remember the agitation of the slavery question can remember the torrents of calumny and of coarse abuse with which the white man attempted to overwhelm Wilberforce, Macaulay, Stephen, and all other champions of the negro race. We can remember, also, the calm and loving composure with which it was borne, as a part of the costs which had been counted.

"3. The Committee do not attempt to give you more than very brief hints on these topics. They have confidence in the reflections which will arise in your own minds; but above all, they commend you to the grace and guidance of an ever-present Saviour, who has promised to send you the almighty aid of the Holy Comforter, who will manifest Himself to his servants who suffer for his name's sake at the present day, as he did to his Apostle Paul. When, 'the night following' the tumult in the council of Jerusalem, 'the chief captain feared lest Paul should have been pulled in pieces,' 'the Lord stood by him, and said, Be of good cheer, Paul, for as thou hast testified of me in Jerusalem, so must thou bear witness also at Rome.'"

"You, Brother Jackson, are appointed to Sierra Leone, with a special view to the educational department of that Mission. You have expressed your entire willingness to accept this commission. The Lord has work there to be done. He calls. He will meet his servants there, and his presence can make all places the paradise of God and the very gate of heaven. You have the advantage of the experience in tropical climates of the excellent prelate now with us, who goes forth to that field of labour out of love to the African race, and in him you will have a wise and tender father in God.

"You, Brothers Bühler and Wood, are the same spirit of patient faith and persevering labour in which you have hitherto carried on your work.

"You, Dr. Harrison, are going out for the first time as a medical Missionary: you have gained medical knowledge and skill by a course of study, first at Cambridge, and then at a London School of Science, and, for a short time, by practising in South Africa. You have nobly offered to carry these 'talents' to the work of Christ in Yoruba; hoping—and the Committee confidently share in this hope—that you may materially promote the social elevation of the Yorubans, by the confidence which your medical skill will conciliate of all classes of the community.

"The present state of the Yoruba Mission is an anxious one. The Committee have already touched upon it. They only here add, let *peace* be the message of the Christian Missionary—peace, peace peace—peace spiritual, peace social, peace political. Some of the Missionaries have asked how far the converts are bound to obey the summons of their rulers to go to the war. This question can only be decided by local usages, and by the necessity of the case. But let all the Missionaries unite in deprecating as an unmitigated evil — as the work of Satan—all aggressive warfare. Let them point out the distinction between the defence of hearth and home, and aggressive warfare. If there be any possibility of choice, let the Christian converts choose the home defensive branch: here let their patriotic zeal find its expression, as in the volunteer movement at home. And let all the Missionaries, when residing under different and hostile governments, be bound together more closely than ever in oneness of spirit: let them sink all differences, especially those of local policy. If a Missionary be not allowed to maintain this neutral position, it is a question whether he should not retire from that place. But as long as they can maintain their Christian independence and unity, let them remain as oil upon troubled waters; and may He who stilleth the madness of the people be their shield and refuge—their guide and friend —their all in all.

"You, Brothers Barton, Puxley, and Brown, are going to North India.

"You, Mr. Barton, are designated by the Committee as a Joint Secretary of the Corresponding Committee. But for the first year or so it is hoped that you may be relieved from all official duties, and be enabled to visit the various stations in North India, to make yourself as far as possible well acquainted with the Missionaries and their

we trust, and you, we know, equally trust, you may ever sustain. You and Mr. Puxley have most generously determined to bear your own charges, though acting in all respects as Missionaries of the Society—an appropriation of your private fortunes which you consider it a privilege to offer, and which many others would be prepared to make, if the providence of God had put it in their power. May the Lord accept your offering, and fulfil all your vows.

"You, Brother Brown, are welcomed by the Committee as the son of one of their own body, therefore as possessing a double claim upon their affectionate interest and sympathy. Your self-devotion to the ministry at home is a good pledge that the work to which you and we feel assured the Lord has called you, will prosper in your hands; and if so, your excellent father will have the best recompense for the sacrifice he makes in parting with a son and brother in the ministry, cheerfully for Christ's sake.

"One word the Committee will address to a native brother, W. Sandys (Shwai-tui), a Burmese by birth, whose parents were the fruit of the labours of the Baptist Mission in that country, and who has been for a time under instruction in Islington College. You are to go, in the first instance, to North India, as you are acquainted with the Hindustanee language. At Benares you will see a Mission in full work, and there you will be trained with advantage for whatever post of duty the providence of God may open before you. The Committee have always much satisfaction in combining on these valedictory occasions the representatives of native agency with European Missionaries.

"You, Brother Weatherhead, after some experience in the church at home, have devoted yourself to the Missionary church, and the Committee have much pleasure in assigning you to the Bombay Mission, with a view of your occupying the post of Secretary of the Bombay Corresponding Committee, when it shall be vacated by Mr. Robertson. Your first work, as in the case of Mr. Barton, will be to make yourself fully acquainted with the Missions, to acquire the language, and to identify yourself with the Mission.

"You, Brothers Honiss and Simmons, are going to South India. The Madras Corresponding Committee will assign you your particular locations. You go to a Mission which, in many ways, the Lord is largely blessing. May your union with your fellow-labourers be an occasion of increased blessedness to them and to yourselves.

"You, Brother Tonge, are to proceed to Ceylon, with a special view of carrying on the Collegiate School at Kandy, at present under the direction of its zealous Principal, Mr. Jones. Your long experience and success in tuition give the Committee every confidence in your future work; and they rejoice to know that you desire to become as much a Missionary as any of the brethren around you, and that all your instruction will have the one supreme end of training up your pupils for Christ. The Committee need not give you any specific directions, for you will be guided by able and now experienced friends of education, Mr. Christopher Fenn, at Cotta, and Mr. Jones, at Kandy.

"You, Brother Moule, are appointed to the China Mission: your station is not definitely fixed. Each mail brings intelligence which throws new light upon that most interesting but now unhappy country. The Committee rejoice in the prospect of your being associated in the same Mission with your brother, our excellent Missionary at Ningpo, and they would gladly place you at the same station, if the exigencies of the work allowed of such an arrangement. But the Lord will direct, in all things, both you and ourselves.

"You, Brother Wolters, have the blessed prospect of association with a revered and beloved father in the Mission at Smyrna. For many years your excellent and veteran father has sustained single-handed his position in that Turkish city and mart of commerce for all nations. His faith and patience have been severely tried while he looked upon the inert mass of dead superstition in the oriental churches, and of stiff and menacing bigotry in the Mohammedan population. The dispensations of divine judgments have now broken up the dead level. Your father's hopes are at length raised of a future harvest, especially among the Turks. He now asks for a coadjutor; and he will have the joy of receiving, as a fellow-helper in the ministry, his own son. You have the great advantage of an acquaintance with the Greek and Turkish languages. You are acquainted with the work, having already laboured zealously and wisely as a catechist at Smyrna. You have diligently improved your opportunities of acquiring knowledge, both at Malta College and at Islington College; and now the Committee trust that you will carry all these advantages, sanctified by the blood of Christ, and by the unction of the Holy One, to the post to which God has called you, to deliver at ancient Smyrna the message of Him 'who walketh amidst the seven golden candlesticks.'"

THE REVIVAL IN NORTH TINNEVELLY.

More recent tidings of the Revival in North Tinnevelly have only served to confirm our previous estimate of its importance and reality. Apprehensions were at first entertained by a few of the more cautious friends of the Missionary work that it might prove only a transient excitement, leaving behind it no practical results. In past years, the history of our Tinnevelly Mission has certainly had to record remarkable movements among the Shánar and Retty castes, which seemed to indicate a national instability, and suggested care in judging of the precise value of the present stirring amongst the dry bones. We exercised such discrimination, according to our ability, in the instance now under consideration, before placing the narrative in the hands of our readers, and we feel assured that we should have been sinful and faithless had we not recognised the presence and power of God the Holy Ghost in the marvellous events of which North Tinnevelly has recently been the witness. Their satisfactory results are the seal of their truth.

There were many points of difference between the present Revival and the movements of former years, to which we have just alluded. They have, in fact, hardly one feature in common. Let us take as an illustration of these previous cases the movement among the Retty caste in 1844, described in Mr. Pettitt's valuable narrative,* as being the case which obtained most notoriety in England, affected several thousands of the population, and was marked by some of the most questionable features connected with such events. These cultivators were for the most part tenants of the Zemindár of Ettiápuram. Zemindárs in South India are large contractors or farmers under the Government, to whom they are responsible for a fixed amount of revenue—an arrangement customary from time immemorial, and adopted by the British from the previous indigenous Indian dynasties. Though no magisterial or police authority is now recognised on the part of the Zemindár, yet it will be readily seen how great a temptation to fraud or force the system offers to any, if unscrupulous or covetous. Custom permitted the employment of compulsion in order to constrain payment of tribute, often illegally demanded. "The party refusing was dragged off by the Zemindár's people, frightened, and even beaten till he had paid it; or else some article of greater value being forcibly taken from his house, was either kept or sold to pay the amount." The advice and aid of an European merchant long enabled these Retties to resist the extortion of their native "Lord of the Manor;" but their English friend having suddenly died, and not without suspicion of foul play, they bethought themselves where they might best find protection elsewhere; and with this design obviously as their main object, they resolved to place themselves under the instruction, and so of the patronage, of English Missionaries of the two Societies labouring in Tinnevelly. "We felt," adds the narrator, dealing very gently with their case, "that the sincerity of persons under such circumstances must, for a time, be a matter of doubt, but were willing to afford them the opportunity of hearing the truth and forsaking error. Too much was said out of Tinnevelly respecting them, and hopes too sanguine were entertained while this doubt continued, and disappointment, not so much to us as to others, was the result. They were unwilling to give up some immoral practices which prevailed among them. Christian discipline, especially where the headmen were concerned, was unpalatable; and when their affairs did not succeed to their satisfaction, they gradually withdrew and returned to heathenism; and only a few, I believe, either in Mr. Pope's district or in ours, retained any real benefit from the small amount of instruction which it was possible, under the circumstances of the case, to afford them. Still, good was done; some seed was sown; and we cannot but hope that 'the bread cast upon the waters will be found after many days.'" We believe that the Missionaries were right in receiving these people under instruction as catechumens, low and ignorant as were the motives that actuated them; for we know that "the kingdom of heaven is like unto a net, that was cast into the sea and gathered of every kind," and the parable proceeds to teach us how the process of discrimination and separation is to go on afterward; but still we cannot be surprised to learn that there was but little satisfactory result.

Such cases as these, however, only make us all the more hopeful as to the recent Revival. It stands out in bold contrast. It is unprecedented in the history of Indian Missions. The labours of William Johnson at Sierra Leone in 1816 offer the only parallel

---

* "Pettitt's Tinnevelly Mission," pp. 353—357.

in the annals of the Church Missionary Society. These previous movements in Tinnevelly originated with the heathen, the present in the bosom of the Native Church. Sordid and worldly objects stimulated the one, spiritual blessings alone prompted and could satisfy the other. The former inquirers recoiled from practical reformation, practical reformation has marked the latter as strikingly as in Ireland.

We are able to lay before our readers some valuable confirmations of these statements. We have received from the Rev. W. Gray voluminous details of the progress of the work since we last noticed it; but they offer but few new features of general interest. It is to the edification of the converts that his attention has been chiefly directed. We learn, however, that no less than 112 candidates for baptism may be traced to the recent movement. At Vāgeikulam and at Rājapāliam two of the native ministers have each a class of thirty inquirers. A most encouraging spirit of attention is manifested among the heathen, as their towns and villages are visited by the itinerant preachers, and a readiness to purchase Christian books and tracts, in places where the Missionary had before been glad to give them away, is a symptom of interest which will be appreciated by any who remember a Hindu's fondness for money.

We turn, however, to other testimony. Some of our Missionaries of the southern districts have now had the opportunity of examining the Revival for themselves, and we rejoice to welcome the two subjoined letters.

The Rev. A. Dibb writes (Sept. 15th) from Mengnānapuram, the important district of the Rev. J. Thomas, to the charge of which Mr. Dibb has been appointed, during the latter's projected visit to England—

"You will have heard," he writes, "no doubt, of the Revivals in the Tinnevelly Mission lately. I am happy to say that the movement is still progressing. It is chiefly observed amongst careless and nominal Christians within the Church; but it is not confined to them. Heathen without the Church have here and there been benefited and brought in under the influence of the movement. But how forcibly does the fact of a larger outpouring being vouchsafed to nominal Christians teach us to use all diligence and forbearance in preaching the word and keeping up the ordinances, even where for a long season no great blessing seems to accompany them. For years and years have some now revived congregations been in an all but hopeless state. It seemed as if they were—to use what I think is one of the most awful words I know—'Gospel-hardened,' or as St. Jude has it, 'twice dead;' and now at last the promise, after long tarrying, is fulfilled. The word does not return void; and we see an illustration of the meaning of Rom. iii. 1, 2—'What advantage hath the merely nominal Christian, or what profit is there in sermons or sacraments? Much every way; chiefly because that unto him are committed the oracles of God.' He has those means of grace which, though long ineffectual through the power of his own corruption, may one day be made effectual by the greater power of Divine grace."

Still more explicit and discriminative is the following letter from the Rev. A. B. Valpy. While our Missionaries thus deal with the question, we may be sure that it is in safe hands.

It is dated September 7th—

"You will, I fear, have felt not a little surprised and disappointed in that, whilst Mr. Fenn, Mr. Dibb, and Mr. Gray have written so fully and so hopefully of the 'Revivals' in their respective districts, I should hitherto have maintained a strange and unaccountable silence, with regard to what has taken place in my own district of Surandei. And this surprise and disappointment will have been increased from the fact, that more than one allusion has been made to the Surandei district in the letters of my brethren above mentioned.

"The reason which made it appear to me essential that I should delay committing to paper my opinion respecting the movement, arose from the way in which that movement commenced. The small band of native Christians from Mr. Arulappen's congregation, who, after the Revival in their own village of Wartrap, set out with the intention of seeking to promote 'Revivals' amongst their own Christian relatives in other parts of Tinnevelly, made their way almost immediately to the village of Ukkirankottei, in the Surandei district. This visit was attended with marked results. There followed much outward expression of deep mental anguish amongst many of our congregation, and they spent whole days in prayers and tears. But the external gesticulations and emotions of these people became at length so monstrous—the heathen around them imagined them to be all under the powerful influence of evil spirits—and those who had been affected appeared to consider them so essential to a proper conversion or revival, that I was fairly at a loss how I should act in the matter. Indeed, for some time the extravagancies of our Ukkirankottei people were bringing almost a scandal, I thought, on the Christian name. After a time, however, many of these excesses began to abate, and the reality of the work became apparent. Still, not having seen any thing of the kind before, and feeling anxious that the whole movement should have time to manifest itself in the *lives* of the newly awakened, I deemed it, on the whole, my wiser course to reserve my report of the matter to a future day.

"Now that the movement has been going on for five months, accompanied too with increasing manifestations of God's blessing, and the outpouring of his Spirit, I cannot any longer keep back from you an account of what our eyes have seen, and our ears heard.

"As you are by this time aware, Ukkirankottei was the first village where the movement commenced in the Surandei district. In this place there is a congregation of about 220 souls. This congregation has been established for upwards of eighty years. The people were originally Romanists. Up to the month of March of the present year, they were, perhaps, one of the most disorderly and unsatisfactory congregations in Tinnevelly. Drunkenness, and other species of the lowest vice—neglect of the Lord's-day—continual quarrelling, &c.—were the striking features here. Nineteen months ago I heard Mr. Pickford's farewell sermon at Ukkirankottei. His address was full of earnest and affectionate entreaty; and his text was, 'Grieve not the Holy Spirit of God.' Blessed be God! I can testify that a marvellous reform has taken place since that time throughout the whole village.

"In the first place, with the exception of four cases, drunkenness has entirely disappeared from amongst them.

"Secondly—There is a general acknowledgment on the part of the heathen, that those who were formerly a disgrace to their religion, have now become respectable and decent living people.

"Thirdly—One fact more than many has been an evidence to my own mind of the reality of this work, namely, their entire desistance from lawsuits, from which, at one time, tendance at the Lord's Supper—and of a deeper interest generally in the concerns of their souls. It is worthy of remark, that on the very Sunday, May 6th, on which Mr. Fenn speaks of having enjoyed such a delightful day at Vāgeikulam, it was my privilege to be ministering at Ukkirankottei. This was after the 'Revival' had commenced there. I seldom remember to have ever witnessed a more animating spectacle than this congregation then presented. We had on that occasion no less than seventy persons assembled for the Lord's Supper.

"Fifthly—There is now scarcely a house in the village in which private and family prayers are not regularly observed. Frequent prayer meetings are also held amongst the people in their own houses, and I must not forget to add, that many of those meetings have been held for the special purpose of interceding for some hitherto unconverted member of their congregation.

"Sixthly—I am thankful to notice a desire to go forth into the neighbouring villages to preach to the heathen. Sunday afternoon is the time that I suggested, as affording the most suitable opportunity for this.

"Their plan is, for several to meet in the church for prayer after the noon service, and then they divide themselves off into little companies of twos and threes, to go and invite others to seek the Lord Jesus Christ.

"I was very greatly rejoiced whilst in the town of Tinnevelly a short time ago, to hear a person say, 'One of your Ukkirankottei people was having prayers with some others in the Peittei here the other day.'

"God has been pleased already to give a measure of blessing on this aggressive effort. A man of the Asari, or carpenter caste, has commenced attendance at their church on Sunday. This is the more pleasing, in that our Christians are of almost the lowest caste, and no others have hitherto ever joined their congregation, though, as I mentioned before, it has been established for eighty years.

"Before concluding, I cannot refrain from mentioning two cases of individual conversion, as tending to show forth more especi-

few of those who are high in Government employment. He has frequently devoted his energies against the cause of the Gospel. He was engaged in a bitter and violent law-suit against the catechists and people of Ukkirankottei almost to the very time of his conversion, whilst his shameless life (for he has always retained his Christian name) has often brought disgrace on our holy religion. But the Spirit of the living God, which had descended on the congregation of Ukkirankottei, where he was residing, did not spurn even this poor slave of sin and Satan: let it suffice to say, that he and his wife were both awakened almost at the same time, and both were for several days under the deepest agony of mind on account of their past sins.

"The sequel of this man's conversion is intensely interesting, as affording an instance, as mentioned by Mr. Dibb, of 'indigenous' effort on the part of the native church for self-extension, so peculiar to this present movement. A short time since, a meeting was held at Ukkirankottei, at which catechists from Nallūr, Paneikullam, Sivagāsi, and Surandei were invited to attend. The result of this meeting was the appointment of two persons to set forth in company to preach the Gospel through the length and breadth of these above-mentioned districts. They are to be out for a month at a time, and then to return to Ukkirankottei, to give an account of their labours. I believe that three rupees a month is ensured to each of them, and they trust to the liberality of Christians and others, for what more they may require for their daily subsistence.

"This newly-converted man is appointed as one of these itinerating preachers, and he and his colleague are now on their first tour.

"If in any village where they may be preaching their message is received with more than usual interest, they are to remain there for several successive days. In case a desire is manifested on the part of any, of becoming Christians, these are to be handed over immediately to the Missionary of the district, and the evangelists are to go forth elsewhere.

"I wish to make it quite clear that this, from beginning to end, is a purely spontaneous movement on the part of our native Christians.

"The second case, which I wish to notice, is that of a man, also an inhabitant of Ukkirankottei, who has been a confirmed drunkard for many years past. All efforts to reclaim him have hitherto been unavailing. Soon after the 'Revival' in his village, he appears to have been alarmed by some words which fell from the catechist during one of the Sunday services. For some days he was under impression of sin, though he did not make known the state of his mind to others. After returning, however, one day from his work, being no longer able to bear the load that oppressed him, he broke forth into the most fearful and distressing paroxysms of grief, and for a time his reason seemed almost to have forsaken him. He rushed to the church, where the catechist and some others happened to be gathered together for prayer, and threw himself down, literally shouting for mercy at the hand of his offended Maker.

"This man has maintained, up to this time, a singularly consistent walk. Though upwards of fifty years of age, and very ignorant, and though he had never offered up a prayer in his life before, he now prays with great fervour and fluency, in the presence of large numbers of the congregation. He is at this time setting himself with great diligence to learn to read, and I have every hope of his proving a great blessing to many.

"In two other villages, the 'Revival' has commenced, and one of them lies within a mile of Ukkirankottei. The chief person who has been awakened in this congregation was formerly a Mission agent, but resigned his employment some years ago, and has since devoted his attention to agriculture. This man is mentioned in Mr. Dibb's letter as the one who, in company with five others, went to preach in the Paneikullam district, at the very commencement of the 'Revival.' This man's subsequent conduct has also given me the greatest satisfaction.

"The other congregation lies far away to the extreme west of the district, twenty-five miles from Ukkirankottei. The people here are poor, though not related to those of Ukkirankottei. The congregation consists of 100 souls. It was visited by Mr. Arulappen's party, in company with one of our catechists, in the month of June last. On my last visit, a short time since, I noticed a very great improvement amongst them. One pleasing feature here, which I must not omit, is a slight awakening amongst the heathen relatives of these people. I look for considerable increase to our numbers in this congregation.

"It is not without some anxiety that I allude to a work of grace which has been going forward amongst some of the children of the Surandei boarding schools.

"At one time we entertained the hope that this awakening had extended throughout the greater proportion of the children. Now that much of the excitement has subsided, I can, I think, speak with confidence of some six or seven of the girls, and nearly the same number of boys: some of these latter belong to the Sivagāsi district. Six of the girls voluntarily came forward this month as candidates for admission to the Holy Communion of the Lord's Supper.

"With regard to our Mission agents, I have observed, during the last three or four months, an increasing spirit of earnestness in several of them.

"I cannot bring this letter to a close without expressing my firm conviction, that the blessing which has been vouchsafed to us in this district is mainly owing, under God, to the efforts of the party of native Christians, of whom mention was made in the early part of it. To God be all the glory!"

The engraving at the head of this Number presents the general features of the country which has lately witnessed such scenes of deep moral and spiritual significance. It is a view from the Missionary bungalow of Surandei,* looking westward over the plains towards the chain of the Western Ghāts—the Appennines of Hindustān. A group of native Christians occupies the foreground. Groves of the tall palmyra are dotted here and there in the middle distance—the tree which is the main wealth and sustenance of the Shānar people farther south. The landscape is bounded by the range of hills just mentioned, a secluded valley towards the centre, leading up to the beautiful waterfall of Courtallam, the resort of Europeans during two or three of the hottest months of the year. To the distant peak towards the left hand, the natives of Tinnevelly attach no little importance. It is called *Agastya-malei* — "Agastya's Hill." Agastya is the favourite poet and philosopher of South India, and some of his verses are in every mouth. He was no Brahmin nor Brahmin's son, but a simple Pariah, and therefore perhaps all the more popular. A very remarkable stanza of his appears to foretel the future triumph of Christianity, and it is at least so regarded among the Tamilians.

Worship thou the Light of the Universe; who is One:
Who made the world in a moment and placed good men in it;

* From a sketch on the spot by the Rev. W. Knight.

Who afterwards himself dawned upon the earth as a Guru (teacher);
Who without wife or family, as a hermit practised austerities;
Who appointing loving sages to succeed him,
Departed again to heaven: worship Him!

Doubts have indeed been thrown on the authenticity of the lines. Even the historical existence of the Tamil poet has been questioned, and the tenth century after Christ has been fixed as the earliest date of some of the poems attributed to him. It may be so; but these critical matters do not affect the social influence of the maxims that go by his name. The natives often refer to them in connexion with the wonderful religion which has reached them from the West: they think that its time is at hand, and begin to forebode the ultimate triumph of the Cross. Similar vague surmises, as we know, in other heathen and Mohammedan countries, attest the present expectancy of many tribes and peoples and tongues. Suetonius tells us how at the first Advent of our Saviour, which we at this season are commemorating, the whole East was pervaded with the anticipation of a great potentate about to arise amongst them. The origin of the rumour is lost in conjecture, but it contributed, we know, to "prepare the way of the Lord." There appears no reason to doubt that it may have concurred to prompt the Magi to go to worship at Bethlehem—those visitors in whom the early Church recognised not only the first-fruits of the Gentile world, but the types of its different races. And can we contemplate unmoved the present attitude of restless expectation, which so strikingly characterizes the so-called changeless East, and the remarkable events transpiring there, political, social, spiritual? Ought not the Church of Christ to be awake and watchful too? "Yet once, it is a little while, and I will shake the heavens, and the earth, and the sea, and the dry land; and I will shake all nations, and the Desire of all nations shall come: and I will fill this house with glory, saith the Lord of hosts." "It seems certain," writes one of our Missionaries from the field we have now been contemplating, "that a strong spirit of inquiry is abroad amongst the heathen. We need your most earnest prayers that the work may be sustained and extended. 'He that sleepeth in harvest is a son that causeth shame.' It is in truth a harvest time from the Lord."

MISSIONARY DEDUCTIONS FROM THE PARABLES.—THE SEED.

We resume this subject, which the critical state of affairs in New Zealand, and the necessity of giving them full consideration, interrupted.

The particular parable which we proposed to regard in a Missionary point of view, is that of the Sower and the Seed, one of great importance, comprehending as it does the history of the professing church from the first preaching of the Gospel until the time of discrimination—the harvest season—when the angels, the reapers, shall go forth to gather together, first the tares, and bind them in bundles to burn them, but to gather the wheat into the Lord's barn.

We have already considered the field which is to be brought under cultivation, the human element in all its variety; a soil, in its natural state hard and indisposed to the reception of the seed, and often requiring to be dealt with in the way of afflictive and subduing dispensations, in order to overcome this reluctance.

The seed, which is to be sown far and wide amongst the millions of the human race, in all their variety of character, language, and country, next claims our attention; and no more important subject could be presented. "The seed is the word of God."

The things which it most concerns us to know—those which relate to our eternal interests—of these we are naturally altogether ignorant; nay, not only ignorant, but no efforts of our own, no exertion of our intellectual powers, could ever avail to remove that ignorance. Of various branches of physical science a man may be ignorant, and yet, by application and mental acumen, he may break through the mist which is around him, and attain to a clear and masterly conception of deep things which he once knew nothing of. But the realities of the unseen world, and our relation with respect to them, are beyond our reach; and of those grand remedial measures which God has instituted in order to bring fallen man back into communion with Himself, we could know nothing, unless by revelation. That God has done. He has adopted that mode of communication which is most suitable to our nature and necessities —He has spoken to us. "God who at sundry times and in divers manners spake in times past unto the fathers by the prophets, hath in these last days spoken unto us by his Son." This revelation of his mind and purposes respecting us, gradually opened out from age to age, until, in the advent and Gospel of the Lord Jesus Christ, it attained its full measure of light and illumination, is the word; a word first spoken, and then written down for our instruction; for "all Scripture is given by inspiration of God;" and this word is the seed of the kingdom. This seed can alone yield such results as God will recognise and deem worthy to be finally reaped and gathered in as an acceptable harvest. There is a determined effort going forward at the present time to depreciate revelation, and, displacing it from the important position assigned to it as the exclusive seed of the Messiah's kingdom, to substitute for it the emanations of the human intellect. No one, in the discharge of a painful duty—for unless duty constrained to the task few would choose to read them— can peruse the elaborately-woven sophistries which, complex as spiders' webs, pervade the "Essays and Reviews from Oxford," without the full conviction that such is the intention of these writings. One essay associates other instrumentalities with revelation in the great *rôle* of educating the world. A sphere of usefulness is indeed assigned to it, but partial, limited; and important lessons, essential to the well-being of mankind, which revelation could not teach us, are taught by Greece and Rome.* And thus the nation which was under the light of revelation was only a class in the great scholastic establishment of universal education. "Other nations also had a training parallel to, and cotemporaneous with, the Hebrews. The natural religions— shadows projected by the spiritual light within shining on the dark problems without— were all, in reality, systems of law, given also by God, though not given by revelation, but by the working of nature, and, consequently, so distorted and adulterated, that, in lapse of time, the divine element in them had almost perished." But originally they comprised a divine element from whence they had emanated; and thus *natural religions* are placed on a parity with revelation; and Greece and Rome, and the early church," "although not friends to one another," are "the three friends whose companionship is most deeply engraven on the memory of the world." Educated to his manhood by these combined influences, "the spirit or conscience of the man comes to full strength, and assumes the throne intended for him in the soul. As an accredited judge, invested with full powers, he sits upon the tribunal of our inner kingdom, decides upon the past, and legislates upon the future, *without appeal, except to himself.*" Yet,

* Vide "The Education of the World, p. 17."

although thus advanced, is he still a learner, and under "the one condition of all learning—obedience to rules." Law may have two forms; external, governing from the outside, "saying you must, and making no effort to make you feel you ought;" or "an internal law, a voice which speaks within the conscience, and carries the understanding along with it."* When revelation is to be placed in this category, we are candidly informed—"a revelation speaking from without, and not from within us, is an external law."† Thus revelation helps to educate the spirit or conscience until it becomes independent of revelation; and then, mature life being attained, the man proceeds ungratefully to discard the friend by whose aid he had progressed towards maturity. Such precisely is the action of these men. But for the light and illumination which revelation gives, the human intellect never could have attained that grasp and power to deal with the various wonders of knowledge and scientific discovery by which it is characterized at the present day. As a nation, we have been much more under Bible education than is generally conceived. The truths of the Gospel have largely benefitted even where they have not converted. There is an indirect influence abroad, flowing from these truths, of the most healthful character. As the sun, when below the horizon, still by his light reflected from his handmaid the moon so illumines the night-time, that even then there is light, so it is with Christ, "the Sun of righteousness." Even when not yet risen in converting power on the soul, he still imparts a twilight; there is a more correct standard of right and wrong, conscience is more determinately active and admonitory, and there is a larger measure of self-restraint; and thus low and debasing vices, which are alike debilitating to the physical and mental powers, being avoided, the intellect becomes more vigorous, and has opportunity to strengthen and expand; and thus we have, at the present day, the painful spectacle presented to us of men of scholarship and ability, who are far more indebted to revelation for their measure of intellectual power than they are disposed to admit, ungratefully using these energies and powers against that revelation to which they owe so much, and labouring to degrade it from that tribunal of appeal (vide Article VI. of the Church of England) which it has so long and so advantageously occupied, that they may set up in its place the vain conceit of an "inner law." According to the first of these essays, the Bible is to be read, not to override, but to evoke the voice of conscience; and "when conscience and the Bible appear to differ, the pious Christian" is immediately to conclude "that he has not really understood the Bible."* And thus, instead of the Bible correcting and adjusting the action of conscience by presenting to it, as the standard whereby it is to be regulated in accusing or excusing the true will of God, the conscience is to decide the sense in which the Bible is to be received; and thus "conscience is the supreme interpreter."† Thus the safe embankments which have so usefully restrained within suitable limits the spirit of inquiry, are being removed, and an endless field of speculation presents itself, in which the educated mind of the world, having reached its maturity, may extravagate. "Precise statements of faith, or detailed principles of conduct," resolve themselves into an "outer law," and interfere with the great work of self-education. They are to be put aside. In that sense, instead of dogmatism there is to be toleration: the spirit is to be substituted for the letter, and "practical religion for precise definitions of truth." "The mature mind of our race is beginning to modify and soften the hardness and severity of the principles which its early manhood had elevated into immutable statements of truth." But these belonged to a time of immaturity. The advanced manhood of the present day cannot be bound by these, for "physical science, researches into history, and a more thorough knowledge of the history of our world, have enlarged our philosophy;" and "all these must influence our determinations of religious truth."

Language such as this is intelligible enough: it aggresses upon the authority of revelation, and cautiously but determinately moves on one side, that the bold and speculative action of this school may not be interfered with. And this is regarded as the evidence of a matured state: rather does it exhibit that impatience of wholesome restraint which is the precursor of declension: "professing themselves to be wise, they become fools."

Learning itself received into a mind,
By nature weak, or viciously inclined,
Serves but to lead philosophers astray,
Where children would with ease discern the way.

Such is the character of the entire series.

---

* Vide "The Education of the World," p. 34, 35.
† Ibid., p. 36.

* Vide Essays, p. 44.
† Ibid., p. 45.

There is a veil thrown over the intention of the first essay, transparent indeed, yet manifesting some sense of decorum; but the others are more bold, and openly aggress upon the truthfulness, and, inferentially, the inspiration of the sacred records. After the fashion of Bunsen, the "long lives of the first patriarchs are relegated to the domain of legend or of symbolical cycle." "The historical portion," that which is reliable, "begins with Abraham." Having adopted certain theories, Bunsen shifts about historical events as may be most convenient, and on his principle that "there is no chronological element in revelation," varies admitted dates according to his pleasure. He puts back Abraham's going down into Egypt by nearly a thousand years, in order to allow sufficient time to account for the great increase of the Israelites while sojourning there, without being necessitated to admit any interference, in the way of a special blessing, with the "laws of matter," and the ordinary operation of physical causes. This is the principle which pervades Bunsen's researches. The miraculous element at any cost, is to be eliminated from the belief of man. The historical facts recorded in the Scripture have been invested, according to his view of them, with a supernatural character which does not properly belong to them. The avenging angel who slew the first-born was "a Bedouin host, akin nearly to Jethro, and more remotely to Israel;" the angel that smote the Assyrian host which besieged Jerusalem, was a pestilence; the passage of the Red Sea is a description "to be interpreted with the latitude of poetry."[*] Nor are we to be surprised at conclusions so startling, which, if they were to be admitted, would deprive us of the alone standfast point in this world of confusion, and, robbing the statements of the Bible of that reliability which has rendered them an ark, a place of repose to the wearied soul in its searchings and inquiries, submerge them with everything else, into one vast flood of vagueness and uncertainty: for the Bible, after all, is but "an expression of devout reason, and therefore to be read with reason in freedom."[†] Availing himself of this self-conferred freedom, or, as it might with more propriety be termed, licence, Bunsen pursues without hesitation his bold career, a modern Phaeton, who, in urging his fiery steeds towards the sun, seems smitten with blindness as his punishment. And as with miracles, so with prophecies: the idea of their being prognostications, and predictive of future events, is openly spurned. In the most audacious manner, the various passages of the Old Testament, which are expressly referred to in the pages of the New, as having had their fulfilment in the facts of the Redeemer's life and crucifixion—such as Psalm xxii. 17—are taken up and lightly turned over as misreadings or misinterpretations, or, as in the case of Daniel's prophecies, "a history of past occurrences;"[*] until at length, in the judgment of the critic, nothing directly Messianic remains, except, perhaps, one passage in Zechariah, one in Isaiah, "and a chapter possibly in Deuteronomy, foreshadowing the final fall of Jerusalem." Even the 53d chapter of Isaiah, which our Missionaries to the Jews have used with such effect, in contending with the unbelief of that ancient people, is no longer to be understood of Christ. If its reference is to a single person, Jeremiah is to be the selection; but Dr. Williams, by whom the review of Bunsen's Biblical Researches is written, prefers to find the interpretation of the writing in "Collective Israel," and thus deserting the Christian standard, ranges himself on the side of the Jewish sceptic, and adopts and sustains the gloss of Rabbinism.

Dr. Williams's review is promptly followed by the late Professor Powell's Essay on the "Study of the Evidences of Christianity." Dr. Williams having, with the aid of Bunsen's speculations, endeavoured to breach the fortress, this writer rushes to the assault with all the ardour of a forlorn hope. He labours sedulously to disprove the idea of miracles being regarded as an evidence of inspiration. Such supernatural interferences are rejected as unworthy of belief. "Any modification whatsoever in the existing condition of material agents, unless through the invincible operation of a series of externally impressed consequences, following on some necessary chain of orderly connexion,"[†] is pronounced an impossibility. He who is the author of physical law is supposed to be so bound by his own laws that he cannot interfere with them. To admit this is indeed an impossibility. There are moral laws which have their foundation in the character of God, and which He could never wish to alter, and therefore they are eternal and unalterable; but the physical laws by which the universe is regulated, are as the rules which a householder has laid

---

[*] Essays, p. 57.
[†] Ibid., p. 60.

[*] Essays, p. 69.
[†] Ibid. 133.

down for the due regulation of his household, and which it is at his pleasure to suspend and modify, if higher interests render this desirable. Such theories of unalterable laws and eternally impressed consequences may agree with the atheistical principle, but are wholly inconsistent with the recognition of God.

To disencumber themselves of miracles and prophecy, *per fas et nefas*, is the grand object of this school, for with them they get rid of an authoritative revelation. These evidences afford no opportunity for the exercise of the speculative principle. They appeal, the one to the sense of the man; the other, to that ordinary understanding which he applies to the every-day transactions of life. They are both facts: the one a sensible fact, the other an historical fact; the unlearned and the learned can judge of them alike. There was no intellectual subtilty needed to decide whether Jesus had truly risen. The appeal was to the senses. "Behold my hands and my feet, that it is I myself; handle me and see." It requires no nice discrimination to read the historical facts of various kinds in which the fulfilment of prophecy stands out patent and public before the world. These evidences once admitted, substantiate the revelation as from God, and the man, without the opportunity of cavilling, is at once assigned his proper place, that of a learner, receiving with the docility of a child the authoritative communications of God. This is offensive to intellectual pride; men who consider they have attained the manhood of intellectualism do not like to be dealt with as children. They forget that it is written, "If any man among you seemeth to be wise in this world, let him become a fool that he may be wise." They would have submitted to them, not the evidences, but the subject-matter of revelation, and, placing themselves in the seat of judgment, proceed to examine and decide upon the doctrines whether they be such, as, according to their conceptions, might be expected to proceed from God. Hence the pains taken by this school to get rid of external evidences of miracles and prophecy, and throw the proof of inspiration

free to question and speculate as they please Such innovators must be withstood.

We have dealt only with the first three essays of the series, because they strike more directly at the foundations of faith. But they are all woven in the same loom. They are like the decoys of the fowler, carefully constructed and adroitly laid, so as to lead on the unwary reader, step by step, entangling him more and more in their subtleties, until, like the bird, when it has reached the purse-net, he is first bewildered and then snared.

The publication of these treatises is marked by sufficient boldness. Sympathizers they must be aware that they have amongst the literati of the land, otherwise the writers would not have so adventured. But we more than doubt whether the public mind is sufficiently *educated*, in their sense of the expression, or sufficiently emancipated from the trammels of what they are pleased to term dogmatism,' as to receive and digest such ultraisms. At the same time they are not to be despised and passed over *sub silentio* as unworthy of notice. They are ominous of the coming struggle for which we must prepare ourselves. They show the force of the reaction which has been produced by the extreme views which reduced the Scriptures to a dead and inoperative letter, except when interpreted and animated by the living voice of the church. In flying from the dreaded restraints of a sacerdotal domination, these men have rushed into the opposite extreme, and refuse to accept of any thing as a guide in religious truth which does not accord with their own inward convictions.

It is remarkable the efforts which are being made in our day to get rid of revelation. "The sword of the Spirit, which is the word of God," is too sharp, too decisive for the enemy. He dreads the naked weapon. He would have those who are against him either not use it at all, or else, if they will retain it, use it in a sheath. He swaddled it for a time in old traditions, so that when wielded it might not hurt; and now that it has cut through these, and gleams forth in its original brightness, he would persuade men, that so far from

may not, in declining to submit our consciences in religious matters to the tyranny of man, refuse to submit ourselves to the direction of God. Ecclesiasticism has attempted to dominate over the Bible, and we have protested against it; but we have not dethroned one tyrant to put up another pretender and usurper in his place. The Holy Scriptures, accredited as the revelation of God by evidence of the most incontestable character, this we receive; by this we desire to be taught; and from this we desire to teach others.

This medium position between two dangerous extremes is the only safe place for us: and it is encouraging and confirmatory to find that precisely at this point St. Paul placed himself. This he selected as his battle-field, and there he entrenched himself as in a secure position. "The Jews require a sign, and the Greeks seek after wisdom; but we preach Christ crucified, unto the Jews a stumbling-block, and unto the Greeks foolishness; but unto them which are called, both Jews and Greeks, Christ, the power of God and the wisdom of God." He takes his stand on revelation; on that which constitutes its chief glory, Christ crucified; one of uncreated dignity, submitting Himself in that humanity which He had assumed to the penal consequences of our sin, and putting away sin by the sacrifice of Himself; that great remedial fact, in which God's hatred of sin, and God's compassion for the sinner, are so wondrously reconciled; which was predicted in prophecy, foreshadowed in promise, verified in fact, and treasured up for remembrance and continued reference in the inspired writings;—by this, as his standard, he plants himself, and that in contradistinction to two errors, antagonistic to each other, and yet each not the less antagonistic to God's truth; on the one hand *wisdom*, or a reliance on the intellect; on the other hand, *a sign*, or a reliance on what is sensible and external.

We need to take up precisely the same position at the present day; for we perceive the same old fallacies which the apostle condemns, forgetful that they have long since been tried, found worthless, and of no power in the great work of man's regeneration, coming forth from the hiding-places whither they retreated on former discomfitures, soliciting support, and preparing to renew the oft-repeated effort to displace and thrust aside, from the pre-eminence which has been so justly conceded to it, that revelation of God which has wrought amongst mankind results of such surpassing value. On the one hand, we are told, that "at this time, in the maturity of mankind, as with each man in the maturity world is knowledge, the great force is the intellect;"* while, on the other hand, the external is preferred to the spiritual and gracious; and symbolism, as more effective to the religious progress of man, is preferred to the preaching of the cross. Thus, while the fabric is sumptuously embellished, the pulpit utters a feeble sound, and men are ready to die as martyrs, not for the truth, but for ceremonies and vestments.

Thus we perceive the old weapons of attack refurbished, and brought once more into action. The wisdom of the Greek seeks to glorify the intellect, and disparage revelation. The object is to get the Bible out of the way, and to cast such a doubt and haze upon it that men shall cease to regard it as a reality. These cavillers would take away from us the firm substratum on which we stand, and set us in the midst of doubts and uncertainties, to which, when men have unhappily committed themselves, they feel as one sinking in a bog. On the other hand, the men of the past, who would resuscitate, if they could, the faded glories of the Hebrew ritualism, forget that these were but figures for the time then present, and necessarily died out when the great reality, whose advent they were intended to announce, rose in his promised glory on the world. But with them the symbol is every thing, the reality of little value. The ritualism, which was of divine appointment, helped men to the realization of that which was yet distant. The poor imitation of the present day, dims and obscures that great means of regeneration which, as now realized in fact, is intended to be placed distinctly and fully before the minds of men. Unlike the sceptic, they do not deny, they do not subtract; they injure by unauthorized additions. Professing to receive with all deference the doctrines of Scripture, they yet deal uncandidly by them, and endeavour to evade their force. Professedly receiving Christ as the one Mediator, they yet interfere with the majestic oneness of this Mediator, and foist in other reliances between the sinner and Him. He is not placed next to the sinner so unreservedly that the sinner may at once lay hold upon Him. Something is interposed. Christ may be had, but yet through the sacraments. Through these alone they teach that He is apprehensible. Not first Christ, and then the sacraments, but first the sacraments, duly administered, and then the Saviour. When Elisha found the dead son of the Shunamite stretched on his bed, he laid his living body upon the dead body of the child, and "the flesh of the child waxed warm." The living

THE SEED.

Saviour, in the teaching of his truth, must be approximated so closely to the sinner that nothing whatever shall intervene, otherwise the dead soul shall not be reanimated.

If, then, the destructive influence of sin is to be counteracted—if sinners are to be converted, and souls saved—we must recognise the *Gospel of Christ as the great lever which moves the world, and the great force, not the intellect, but the Spirit of God;* for it is "not by might, nor by power, but by my Spirit, saith the Lord of Hosts." The wise men of Athens had their philosophical researches, and carried on their disputations with much show of learning; but they did nothing for the world around them, for they lived in a city which was "wholly given to idolatry." The Pharisees were rigid in the observance of their ritualism, yet it left them narrow and exclusive, without compassion for sinners whom they admitted to be perishing. They gave no help themselves, and discouraged others from so doing. The seed of the world's regeneration must be sought elsewhere. It is to be found in that which now, as of old, is to "the Jews a stumbling-block, and to the Greeks foolishness; but to those who are called, both Jews and Greeks, Christ, the power of God and the wisdom of God;" and therefore, however men, wise in their own conceits, may despise them as vain enthusiasts, they who would do God's work on earth, by opening blind eyes, and turning men from darkness to light, and from the power of Satan unto God, must, with the great apostle of the Gentiles, determine to know nothing "save Jesus Christ, and Him crucified." The revelation of God, in this its chief glory, and the kindred truths, this is "the seed of the kingdom," the seed which the Lord of the husbandry has commanded to be broadcast over the field of the world.

Let us briefly consider some of the peculiar and valuable properties of this seed.

It has been prepared with special care, and with a view to the special requirements of the human heart. A seed is the essence of the fruit, and contains the rudiments of a new vegetable. The word is that in which is embodied all the wondrous acts of Christ for the salvation of men. He Himself, in his offices and acts of love, is summed up and presented in the word. There is thus concentrated in this small compass the essence of the Gospel. The heart of the seed, in which its vitality specially resides, is the death of Christ, possessing as it does a peculiar power to lay hold upon and affect the human heart. In this consists, in a great measure, the suitableness of the seed to the requirements of the sinner. No-told of the dying love of Jesus; to have placed before us his great sufferings; and in their intensity to understand what a crushing weight of penalty attaches to sin, a weight so ponderous and overpowering, that even God manifest in the flesh groaned and travailed beneath its burden. That is wondrous love which led one so high above all sorrow to stoop to such a depth of sorrow. It is this which, applied in the power of the Spirit of God, melts the hard heart, until, as from the smitten rock, the tears of godly sorrow flow forth.

Stupendous in its character is the divine act of Gospel interference on behalf of sinful man. It was this which led David to exclaim, "When I survey the heavens, the work of thy fingers, the moon and the stars, which thou hast ordained, what is man that thou art mindful of him, and the Son of man that thou visitest him." And such considerations have lost nothing of their force; with increasing knowledge, our wonder and admiration may well increase, for we know more of the vastness of the creation and more of the wickedness of man. Each century, as it has rolled past, has opened only more of the riches of creation, and each generation, as it has lived and died, has demonstrated more forcibly the measure of crime of which the human heart is capable; and as, in both these directions, our knowledge increases, our wonder deepens and strengthens, that amidst such a vastness of creation, amidst the gradations of glorious and intelligent beings, principalities and powers, angels and archangels, cherubim and seraphim, which occupy its mansions, there should have been bestowed such a measure of the divine regard and concernment on guilty, fallen man, whose sins, could they be materialized, would exceed in bulk the world in which he lives. If the earth was one amongst a few worlds, our own narrow range of thought might afford to us an explanation. If, for instance, the solar system constituted the whole material creation, we could conceive that one world amongst a few was of importance. But it is far otherwise. The solar system lies indeed in the midst of a vast solitude, and around it extend, on every side, vast regions of unoccupied space. This we know from the comets, the *feelers* of the system, which penetrate into vast distances beyond the orbit of Neptune, and yet return without any alteration of their period, which must have taken place if these bodies of extreme levity had approached any stellar body. The minor limit of the distance within which no stellar body lies is 19,595,175,000,000 miles. All those points of light which, in the night sea-

limit. How densely they appear to cluster over the firmament, especially in the galaxy, or milky-way, where, in a space in length not more than thirty times the moon's diameter, and eight in breadth, 50,000 stars may be counted! And yet each one of these stellar bodies is as remote from his nearest neighbour, as the one which is to us the nearest (a in the constellation Centaur) is remote from our sun. Nor is this all. The stars which are dispersed over our firmament constitute one great mass or stratum of stars, together forming a universe of solar systems; and yet this stupendous agglomeration of stellar bodies is only one amongst many, other stellar clusters like our own being dispersed throughout immensity.

In the contemplation of all this we may well pause, and marvel and exclaim, "What is man, that thou art mindful of him, and the son of man, that thou visitest him?" How is it that the Lord of so many worlds has so occupied Himself with one world, this speck in creation, which, if removed from its place, would have been like a leaf falling from the dense foliage of a forest, or a grain of sand taken from the shores of the vast ocean; a world where his authority has been slighted, and man, the inhabitant of it, has so adventured himself into acts of rebellion? It is that there has been with God "philanthropy," *a love toward man* (Titus iii. 4), a love not manifested towards fallen angels, but which rested upon him; and, in the exercise of that love, He who said, "Let us make man," was pleased to add, "Let us redeem man."

For this mighty work of interference Jehovah girded himself with his majesty, and came forth in his triple personality to the deliverance of sinners. Acting concurrently, and yet distinctly, the three divine persons assumed distinct covenant offices, and resolved themselves into new relations towards each other with reference to this great procedure, the recovery of sinners. The Father willed; the Son devoted himself to the fulfilment of that will—"Lo, I come to do thy will, O God"— and became flesh, that in sorrow of the most extreme kind he might fulfil it. The Spirit to the care and concernment of God, that "now unto the principalities and powers in heavenly places might be known by the church the manifold wisdom of God." For the church, consisting of lively stones, built on the one living stone; the temple of redeemed sinners, which shall stand throughout eternity, as a praise and glory to the Lord; is the accumulation of those results which the Gospel has effectuated, of battles fought and victories achieved over the power of the enemy; of sinners converted and souls saved; of evil crushed and God glorified; and therefore the angels " desire to look into these things," that with increasing knowledge of the wonders of God's character, they may turn to Him with increasing adoration, and delight to join in the song of redeemed man—"Worthy is the Lamb that was slain, to receive power, and riches, and wisdom, and strength, and honour and glory, and blessing."

Such is the Seed, the revelation of God's love to sinners, prepared with such special care and at such a costly price; and its properties are such as from its origin might be expected.

It is incorruptible. There is what is called mummy wheat. The seed from which it has been raised was revived after a protracted death. It had lain for centuries buried in the mummies and catacombs of Egypt. But it was discovered, brought to light, and resown; and it sprang up and bore fruit. And so the seed of the kingdom is incorruptible. It was buried in the traditions and ceremonials of a corrupt church, from which vitality had departed, and which, but for the cerements with which it had been swathed, would have lost even the form of Christianity. Out of this grave the seed was recovered at the Reformation, and resown. Need we say that it was found to have lost nothing of its power, because it was incorruptible seed? It sprang up abundantly, and has never ceased to bring forth fruit.

And so we use it now. The sowers go forth to sow it when opportunity presents itself. It disappears and seems to be lost. But it is not so. It is working unseen beneath the surface. Deep in the recesses of the human

THE SEED.

the ground and die, it abideth alone; but if it die it bringeth forth much fruit."

And thus He was, as a seed, put into the ground; He was slain, buried, and his disciples thought that He was put out of the way, and that his death was the extinction of all their hopes. Yet equally strange would it seem, were we not familiarized with it, to put the natural seed down into the earth, that it might die in order to reproduce itself, that thus by a wonderful process, out of death might come life! And so Christ died, that out of his death there might spring life in abundance, and that He might become the parent seed of many.

And now from his personal acts is yielded that seed of truth which is to be sown amongst men. How great its power of reproduction! With what energy it wrought upon the day of Pentecost, when a single sermon yielded to the church three thousand souls! How the work of evangelization continued to extend itself, the seed,- wherever it fell, whether in Palestine, or the provinces of Asia Minor, or throughout Macedonia and the cities of Greece, at Rome, or in Spain, or the far off shores of the Ultima Thule of the then known world, still bringing forth fruit. Nor has this precious seed of pure Gospel truth, taken from the storehouse of the written word, lost in our day its power. It retains all its vitality. It is as new and efficacious as when first fresh from the life and death of Jesus. The glorious work still proceeds; sinners are being converted, souls saved, great changes effected in the most hopeless and far gone characters, invaluable results gathered in, victories achieved. "There shall be a handful of corn in the earth, upon the top of the mountains; the fruit thereof shall shake like Lebanon." It has been so. There was at the first but a handful of corn. But the divine blessing rested upon it as it was sown, and its product is to be found in fields white unto the harvest. A few grains have been dropped on some distant land, and they fell amidst the multitude and seemed lost. A few converts were yielded, and the world despised the poor return; until at length, as the skies dropped work initiated by foreign Missionaries is now being carried forward by native Christians raised up from the midst of the heathen masses that are to be evangelized, and the great difficulties connected of necessity with the commencement and introduction of a work like this having been in a great measure overcome, it will soon advance with an increasing rate of progress, and as the sowers go forth to sow the seed, their feet shall be beautiful upon the dark mountains of heathenism.

The value of a ministry, whether it be for home or foreign parts, depends upon the purity of the seed which is sown by it; whether it be the pure word of revelation, or some mixture of man's devising. Of old it was commanded, "Thou shalt not sow thy field with mingled seed;" but how presumptuous to sow the Lord's field with mingled seed, and thus violate the laws by which the spiritual husbandry is to be ordered! how criminal to deliver to men, as God's message, what He has never warranted! Surely this is the very act of the enemy, who sowed tares among the wheat, and mixed the seed that he might spoil the crop. This is not to do God's work, but the work of his adversary. We repeat, the value of a Missionary Society depends upon the character of the seed it sows, whether it be the pure truth, reverentially taken from the granaries of revelation, or whether it be "another Gospel"—an adulterated seed, over the preparation of which human prejudice, and human folly, under the name of wisdom, have been permitted to preside. "Charge some" says the apostle, "that they teach no other doctrine" ($\mu\dot{\eta}$ $\dot{\epsilon}\tau\epsilon\rho o\delta\iota\delta a\sigma\kappa a\lambda\epsilon\hat{\iota}\nu$); and the same caution needs to be repeated now; for where this unhappily is done, there can be no blessing: no results can be produced that will be acceptable to God or of real benefit to man. No carefulness of organization can make amends for unfaithfulness, and carelessness in the deliverance of the message. Better far pure water in an earthen vessel, than a vitiated liquid in a golden cup; and if the choice lies between extremes, a defective organization with a pure Gospel is better than one ecclesiastically perfect, yet defective

THE TAI-PINGS.

Six years have elapsed since we placed before our readers such information as we could collect respecting the Tai-ping movement and its politico-religious character. Since that period it has been forcing its way onward amidst the density of China's population, sometimes bursting out into a fierce glare of attack and devastation, and then, as though it had exhausted itself, falling back from its new conquests, but only for a time, to gather new strength, and resume, with increased impetuosity, its onward course. At its birth, it appears to have been of an exclusively religious character, the effort of a partially enlightened Chinese desiring to correct the gross idolatry of his fellow-countrymen, and lead them to become God-worshippers. This man, Hung sew tsuen, soon gathered disciples around him, whose inconoclastic zeal brought them into collision with the mandarins. Obliged to take up arms in self-defence, they resolved themselves into a military organization—at first resistive, and then aggressive. To the mission to which they considered themselves called—the destruction of images—was now added the extermination of the imps, or Manchoos; and in carrying out both these objects they have shown an untiring zeal. In March 1853 they stormed Nanking; when, out of a population of 20,000 Manchoos, which constituted the population of the inner city, not more than one hundred escaped. "We killed them all," was their stern cry of triumph; "we killed them all, to the infant in arms; we left not a root to sprout from."

In November 1854 we find them in possession of Tsing-hae, in the Chih-le province, about twenty miles to the south of Tien-tsin, and about one hundred miles from Pekin. Here they met with the Mongol hordes from beyond the great wall, the same barbarous yet fearless troops with which the allied forces have had to contend, and their onward course was arrested. Reinforcements coming up, they stormed the important city Lin tsing in the face of the Manchoo and Mongol cavalry; and in this and the adjoining parts of the Chih-le province they remained for the space of ten months; but they never succeeded in reaching Pekin, and at the expiration of that time retired southward of the Yellow River.

Disappointed in their hope of terminating the contest by the capture of Pekin, they proceeded to consolidate their power on the Great River, occupying its shores from Chin-keang on the east to Yo-chow on the west. To this heart of the Celestial empire the war has mainly transferred itself, the Imperialist and Tai-ping forces acting and re-acting on each other with varying success; and these rich portions of the empire, amidst such interchanges of defeat and victory, being completely laid waste and desolated.

In the latter end of 1858, a British squadron, with Lord Elgin, passed up the river as far as Hankow, not without exchanging shots, on more than one occasion, with the Tai-pings, and a consequent loss of life was caused, which, by due precautions, might have been avoided. On approaching Nanking, the capital city of Ngan-hwui, the insurgents and Imperialists were found to be in action. The British vessels were not recognised by the Tai-pings: they were the first bearing the British flag which had ascended the stream so far. Under the misapprehension that they were acting in concert with the Imperialist fleets of junks which commanded the river, the Tai-pings fired a shot at the leading vessel, the "Lee," and was replied to by the "Furious," "Cruiser," "Dove," and "Lee," in full chorus. The garrison of the forts was soon in flight, the guns abandoned. A little timely explanation might have prevented this collision. On the return voyage, when these forts were again approached, such an explanation was resorted to. The water had fallen so low that the two large vessels had been left behind, and the two gun-boats were alone on their way to the river's mouth. To engage the forts on going up, when the force was strong, was a pleasant *divertissement*; but to venture on the same experiment with two gun-boats, was, if possible, to be avoided; and that the more so, as the nature of the channel compelled them to steer immediately under the city walls, so that the decks could easily have been swept from them by gingalls. On this occasion, therefore, that was done which should have been done before—a communication was opened with the insurgents, and the gun-boats passed the forts unmolested.

Nothing could exceed the desolate aspect of the districts through which they passed. Suburbs of cities levelled, the peasantry compelled to fly, now from the Tai-pings, now from the Imperialists, their houses burnt for fuel. On reaching the termination of the upward journey, where, on the waters of the Great River, cluster together the three cities of Wo-chang, Han-yang, and Han-kow, additional traces of the misery caused by this cruel war presented themselves. The turreted walls of Han-yang enclosed deserted streets, roofless houses, crumbling walls, and grass-grown courts. Wo-chang, the capital of Hoopeh, had also its large areas of desolation strewed with ruins. Han-kow, although again in a flourishing condition, had, two years and a half before, been so completely levelled with the ground, that not one stone had been left upon another. On the return voyage, Nanking was visited; and here also were painfully visible the traces of the sanguinary conflicts which have been fought within and around its walls. "Many of the streets were entirely deserted and the houses unoccupied. A vast portion of the area within the walls had never been built upon, while yamuns and public buildings still existing attested its former magnificence."

The province of Chekeang, in which our Missions lie, had hitherto been spared; but it was known that the Tai-pings were anxious to reach the sea-board, and open communication with occidental nations; and it was felt that this security could not be of much longer continuance. Accordingly, in the beginning of this year the invasions of this province by the Tai-pings commenced from different points. One large body, breaking forth from Nanking, where the Imperialists had for some time hemmed them in, overpowered the besiegers with an utter discomfiture, and, advancing by Chang-chow, established their head-quarters at I-ting, about forty miles from Soo-chow. Another body appeared in great force on the eastern slopes of the hills separating Chekeang from the Kiangsi province, and, descending along the course of the Tsien-tang river, which, rising in Wu-yuen of Ngan-hwui, falls into Hang-chow Bay, they seized upon Ku-chau and Kiang-shin.

Since then, Hang-chow and Soo-chow, those two far-famed cities of the Chinese—of which the proverb says, "Shang yu tien tang; Hia yu Su Hang;"—the purport of which is, that Hang-chow and Soo-chow are fully equal to paradise—have both fallen.

Situated at the southern extremity of the Great Canal, Hang-chow possesses a commanding situation. In its well-paved streets, ornamented with numerous honorary tablets, Lake, the city and its suburbs "including so many canals and pools connected with the Grand Canal and the lake, that it is hard to say whether the land or the water predominates." Renowned for its manufactures of silk, linen, and cotton fabrics, with works in iron, ivory, lackered ware, it was regarded as one of the most prosperous of Chinese cities. It was visited in the early part of 1858 by the Vicompte de Contades and Mr. Oliphant, Lord Elgin's Secretary, charged with notes from their respective Governments, to the Chinese Secretary of State, and which, the better to secure their transmission, and in the hope of breaking down the superciliousness of the high Chinese officials, they resolved to deliver into the hands of Chaou, the Governor of Kiangsu, who resided at Soo-chow. The details of this mission, and of the interview with Chaou, may be read with interest.* The city is described as "built in the shape of a perfect square, each side four miles in length. On two sides the Grand Canal washes the walls, and on the other two sides two smaller canals complete the square." The numerous canals which intersected the crowded buildings were "spanned, rialto fashion, by high single arches, and with houses rising out of the water, as in Venice." The water-way of the Grand Canal "was as inconveniently crowded with boats, as Fleet Street with carriages, and these of every possible form, from the gorgeous mandarin-junks, with the huge umbrella on the top and a gong at the entrance of the cabin," to "the small covered canoe of the costermonger, which looked like a coffin." The omnibus of our metropolis was represented by large passage boats, which plied between Soo-chow, Hang-chow, and Chang-chow; while the light tanka-boats, 'containing "one or two passengers, and deftly worked by a single oar astern, cut in and out like hansoms."

Such was Soo-chow and its rival Hang-chow; rich and prosperous, they were the most luxurious and sensual of Chinese cities. But the thunderbolt of sudden calamity has fallen upon them. The fiery flood of Tai-ping in-

of three years old; for the waters also of Nimrim shall be desolate. Moreover, I will cause to cease in Moab, saith the Lord, him that offereth in the high places, and him that burneth incense to his gods. . . . . There shall be lamentation generally upon all the housetops of Moab and in the streets thereof; for I have broken Moab like a vessel, wherein is no pleasure, saith the Lord."

Hang-chow was captured as much by stratagem as force. Numbers of the insurgents surreptitiously obtained entrance into the city, under various disguises, as ordinary Chinese, or as pilgrims and mendicants. These secreted themselves in private houses and elsewhere, as opportunity presented itself, until the insurgent forces appeared before the town. Then, rushing out with loud cries, they opened the gates to their friends, and the Tai-pings obtained possession of the outer city. The Tartar garrison retiring into the inner city, held their ground for several days, until, on the arrival of reinforcements, they assumed the aggressive, and the insurgents evacuated Hang-chow. But they left behind them, in and around the city, the most lamentable traces of their raid. The suburbs were wasted with fire. On entering the eastern gate facing the lake, the scene that met the view was no less distressing. Street after street might be traversed for miles with no sign of business but some vendor of eatables on a small scale, or a tea-shop here and there.

Soo-chow also has fallen into the hands of the Tai-pings. The pitiable condition to which it is reduced will be found in subsequent pages of this Number. Meanwhile, *sauve qui peut* became the order of the day. Nothing could be more pitiable than the appearance of families flying from the places which the insurgents threatened, and seeking a refuge elsewhere. Driven forth from their comfortable homes, sitting in open boats exposed to the falling rain, they seemed in the most dejected state. Indeed, numbers of these unhappy people, in utter desperation, have had recourse to a Chinaman's last refuge, suicide; and thus, while the Tai-pings smite the Manchoos and their adherents, and the Imperialists, on any retrograde movement of the Tai-pings, execute merciless vengeance on the people, who, without the power of resistance, have submitted for a time to the rebel authority, the population themselves, distressed beyond measure between the conflicting parties, and maddened by their sudden reverse of circumstances, from ease and prosperity into extreme suffering, add to the horrors of the moment by repeated and almost wholesale suicide. At Hang-chow from fifty to seventy of these a large proportion were suicides. Nor is this last fatal plunge reserved for circumstances of actual danger, but the mere apprehension of it is enough. An alarm was given at Shanghae, in the middle of July, that the rebels were approaching, when a panic occurred. "All the Chinese shops," says the 'North China Herald,' "were closed, and the owners were busy in conveying their valuables to unknown retreats away from their homes. Bands of six and eight women might be seen shuffling along with great rapidity, hand in hand, to places of refuge; Coolies on the bund and in the hongs threw down their burdens, and took to flight, some rushing to the landing-places, and offering large sums to the boatmen who would take them to the American side. The bridge by the Consulate was almost choked up by the rush to cross it. All the boats stood out in the river, and refused the most tempting offers from the shore. In fact, the alarm was tremendous, and took many hours to subside. We hear that many women rushed at once into the water from one of the tea factories, and attempted suicide. One lady and two men hung themselves, while another jumped from a high window, and fractured his thigh. Several suicides are also reported within the city."

Such is the Chinese mind. In the direction of God, all is a dead unknown. There is no hope there; and when earthly hopes are broken up, there is no hope anywhere; and the despairing sinner ends his own life. In what a vortex of miseries is not this great nation involved! The prescriptive routine of centuries is at an end. They had been at ease from their youth, these gentry, and *literati*, and rich merchants, of the Chekeang province. Even when the tempest of civil war was raging beyond their boundaries in Kiangsi, Honpeh, and Ngau-hwui, they remained undisturbed; but at length it has reached them likewise, and, lo! they too are spoiled.

In truth, China had fallen into a condition of profound insensibility to every thing except the enjoyments of pride and sense. Earth was all the heaven which this sensuous people wished for; and, lo! their pleasant dream of an easy and self-indulgent life, disturbed previously by one only apparition, that of death, is rudely broken up, and the Chinese finds himself a sufferer, and without a hope. At such a time, when the population is bleeding at every pore, the preaching of the cross may meet with an acceptance it never did before, and Christ be welcomed as the brazen serpent was by the serpent-bitten Israelites. In fact, the time is getting short, and the Lord's work

has long reaped plenteous harvests in China : it is time that life enter in, and seize the sickle, and reap in the living for the Lord. We are persuaded that, out of the present ruins, there will arise a new and better state of things, and that more rapidly than we expect; and we are free to confess that our hope in this respect lies in that pure work of evangelization which, disconnected from everything approaching to politics, has pursued its unobtrusive course, and, so far as the elementary knowledge of Christian truth is concerned, may have penetrated more widely amongst the population bordering on our Mission stations than we have ventured to hope. Many a Testament and Christian book and tract, have been sent forth on their mission of love amongst this reading and careful people, who so remarkably venerate the printed character; and who can say what unexpected movements may break forth under this new pressure of affliction?

Meanwhile the Tai-pings have been brought nearer to the Missionaries and other Europeans on the coast; and that facility of access to them, which had been so long wished for, has been at length presented. Long and anxiously had Christian men wished to have free intercourse with this extraordinary people, whose new religion presented such a strange mixture of truth and error, that they might detach them from what was delusive, and teach them more perfectly the right way. That opportunity now presented itself, not only because of the presence of the Tai-pings at Soo-chow, but of the accession of Hung-jin, formerly a catechist preacher in connexion with the London Missionary Society at Hong Kong, to the office of King-kan, or minister in chief of the Tai-ping-wang.

To this personage, on his new exaltation, a letter was addressed by the Missionaries, Messrs. Edkins and John, expressing their gratification at receiving tidings of his welfare, and their earnest hope that in his new position he would maintain his Christian integrity. His reply came from Soo-chow, whither he had proceeded on the receipt of their letter, that thus an interview with them periodical for November. And we now present Mr. Burdon's narrative. Our readers will remember that the minds of European, Missionaries and others, are at present much interested and divided on the subject of the Tai-pings. Some regard them in a very favourable light, and seem to think that the delusions under which they labour are not to be put in competition with the grand testimony they have borne to the unity of God in contradistinction to the gross idolatry of China, and their publication of the Christian Scriptures as of supremo authority. Others, on the other hand, look only at their versions and new revelations, their merciless butchery of Manchoos, and their polygamistic practices. For ourselves, we desire to look fully both at the good and evil, and to diminish nothing from either. When we look at them in the favourable point of view, we perceive what advantages are afforded to the Missionary for the prosecution of Missionary efforts amongst them. Much that he would desire to separate them from, they have already abjured ; much of which he would desire to convince them they already admit. There is no need to tell them the idols are nothing, for they know it, and break them in pieces; there is no need to instruct them in the truth of one God. They confess all this, and much more. There is no need to prepare and print a version of the Holy Scriptures for this people: this they have already done. On the other hand, when we mark how they place the reveries of their mystic king and the more ambitious inventions of the Eastern King on a level with the written word, as divine relations; and how, while admitting the ten commandments as the rule of moral duty, they yet multiply wives, and without commiseration slaughter their enemies, we at once perceive what a large measure of evangelizing work remains to be carried forward amongst them, before they can be raised to such a position as would justify us in recognising them as fellow-Christians. This is the practical point in which all are agreed, and to this and the best mode of accomplishing it our attention needs to be directed. At the time of this interview with

remonious reception, and complains that, having been invited to come down to Shanghae, he had expected friendly intercourse, instead of which he had been met with big guns and shot. Yet we do not see that he has any reason to complain.

On Tuesday, August 14th, a Tai-ping proclamation was found posted up in various localities, both of the foreign settlement and native city. In this sufficiently lengthy document, Le, the faithful king, announces the divine mission of the Tai-pings to slay and exterminate the destructive imps, and his determination to capture Shanghae, and yet his willingness to spare the inhabitants, provided they hasted to reform. The concluding paragraph runs as follows—

"I have hitherto taken cities without number, and it would behove you to amend your faults, and so be in the way of having your lives spared. From the first outbreak of righteousness in Kwang-si, until the present time, ten years have passed, during which time no enemy could withstand, and no attack could repress us. Should your little place, only a span in size, brave us, and refuse to listen to us? Shanghae is an intelligent city enough: let the people take the good and the evil, and make their choice (of sides). I issue this proclamation strongly to command and advise you: you know that an egg can't oppose a stone: make up your minds, then, speedily, and submit yourselves; and when the soldiers shall have come, not one fraction of any thing shall be exacted from you. If you will not put confidence in me, but run away, every one of you, with the idea that you can withstand me, why, do exactly as you please. I will establish my will firm as a mountain, and my commands shall be as flowing water. Immediately after I have informed you by this, my soldiers will arrive: they are not going to wait for you; do not say that I gave you no warning. Tremblingly obey, and do not slight this."

The allied authorities lost no time in communicating with Le in order to prevent him from such an attempt. On August 16th, a proclamation was forwarded to the camp of the Tai-pings to the following effect—

"*Shanghae, August* 16, 1860.
"Proclamation sent to Rebel Camp at Shanghae.

"Report having reached us of an armed force having been collected in the neighbourhood of Shanghae, we, the commanders of the military and naval forces of Her Britannic Majesty at Shanghae, hereby give notice that the city of Shanghae and the foreign settlement are militarily occupied by the forces of Her Britannic Majesty and of her ally the Emperor of the French, and they warn all persons, that if armed bodies of men attack or approach the positions held by them, they will be considered as commencing hostilities against the allied forces, and will be dealt with accordingly."

That the Tai-ping chief duly received this proclamation is undoubted, for we have his reply before us, and, exemplifying as it does the feelings with which this people met the first interference of the European powers to stay them upon their path of conquest, we insert it as it stands—

"Translation of Reply.

"Le, Imperial Commissioner of the sovereign reigning in virtue of the true decree of heaven, &c., hereby issues a notification.

"Whereas the appointed period of the Tsing (Manchoo) dynasty having expired, the true sacred Lord was sent into the world to save it. And I, having been honoured with his command to perform the work of heaven, by punishing the crimes (of the rejected dynasty), have, from the time I rose in the cause of right in Kwang-si, never fought a battle without conquering, and never attacked a city without taking it.

"A short time back, on our armies occupying Soo-chow, your countries once and again pressed us to come to Shanghae to discuss personally the various matters connected with foreign trade. Hence it was that, after retaking Sing-keang, I came hither, not to seek a quarrel and to fight with foreign nations, but to offer them a treaty of open commerce.

"And, on now perusing the communication of your countries, I am in the highest degree surprised at the extravagant perversity of its language.

"I would submit to you, that I, under the loyal Prince, have the general command of a large body of officers and of an innumerable army, and could have no difficulty in causing the instantaneous destruction of an insignificantly small city such as Shanghae. When I, therefore, come to the place, and station my troops motionless before it, it is really in a spirit of pure regard and of consideration for our common faith. Had I at once ordered a hostile advance, the members of the same house would have been turning against each other, and we could not have failed to incur the ridicule of the Tsing dynasty.

"With the Tsing dynasty your nation have now a quarrel: you cannot have forgotten the battle at Tien-tsin. But our state, in at present carrying on a war, has no other object than to regain our own country. We are at enmity with the Tsing dynasty, but with foreign nations we have no quarrel.

"Your countries attach much importance to open commerce and trade. Now, the advantages to be obtained from us would be greater than those given by the Tsing dynasty, for after the establishment of peaceful relations with us, unrestricted commerce might be carried on at all places without exception.

"But the wild and fallacious nature of the communication which has reached us is such as renders it quite inexplicable. I must conclude that there is no consideration for the feeling that should make us of one mind, in virtue of our common religion, and that there is, it may be, an intention of seeking a quarrel.

"For these reasons, I hereby issue a notification for the common information of the foreign nations (at Shanghae). If you desire to carry on open commerce, in accordance with an agreement, you can at once come and consult on the terms of an agreement. If, however, it is your wish to make difficulties, and to engage in hostilities, then my troops move as a flood, my commands go forth unchangeable as the hills, and we can only await the time when victory and defeat declare themselves. I trust that you will not bring sorrow on yourselves.

The rebel chief, with a force of from 6000 to 7000 men, attacked the city on the 18th of August, and the foreign settlement on the 20th, but was driven back on both occasions with considerable loss, and compelled to retreat. So far then as to our present relations with the Tai-pings. The troops of the same allied powers, which defended Shanghae from the rebels, are forcing their way to Pekin, despite the resistance of the Tartars and the diplomatic craft of Chinese statesmen; and China's great crisis seems at hand.

Narrative of an Interview with the Kan Wang, or Shield King of the Tai-pings at Soo-chow, by the Rev. J. S. Burdon.

"Shanghae, Sept. 3, 1860.

"The past six months have, as you are aware, witnessed a fresh outburst of the Taiping insurgents. It began last spring in a sudden descent on Hang-chow, which was taken and given up, for the few days of its occupation by them, to almost indiscriminate burning of the houses and massacre of the inhabitants. As soon as they had accomplished their object of drawing off the Imperialist army, which was beginning to press them hard at Nanking, they retired, or were driven from Hang-chow, and appear to have attacked those whom they are pleased to call the 'Imps' or 'demons,' being the soldiers or other adherents of the present reigning Emperor, both in front and in the rear, and to have completely routed them. The consequence of this movement was, that the country between Nanking and Shanghae soon fell into their hands; and for the last two or three months the important cities of Chang-chow, Woosih, Soo-chow, Kwunshan, and many others, on the great highway between Shanghae and the southern capital of the empire, have been in their possession.

"These insurgents have excited great interest throughout the Christian world. Connected as their rebellion has been with the destruction of idols, a profession of belief in one God, and in Jesus as the Saviour, and an acknowledgment of the divine authority of the Old and New Testaments, they could not but at first enlist our sympathies, and call forth our prayers on their behalf. The Christian public of England showed unmistakeably that this was the state of feeling in 1854, when a grand scheme for the printing of a million copies of the New Testament was set on foot, and munificently subscribed to. The million scheme is still being carried into effect; but experience is showing us that it was at least a premature step. The Bibles were to have been printed for the benefit of imperfectly enlightened Christians; and with this design the scheme was most honourable to the benevolence of England. But they for whom principally the books were ordered, have, for the last six years, been content with militarily occupying the positions they had previously obtained, breaking out every now and then to do little else than plunder and lay desolate the places visited. They have thus been the means of bringing untold miseries on the people whom they are professing to deliver from the bondage of idolatry and the Tartar dynasty. The military occupation of great parts of the country has neutralized all efforts at Missionary work among the insurgents; and the Bibles hitherto have had to be distributed amongst those who know nothing of, and care less for, the subjects of which the Bible treats, and thus, the rebels having disappointed us, it has been found difficult judiciously to dispose of such an immense number of Bibles in the limited districts of heathen to which we have been confined.

"But during the last few months the Taipingites have come much nearer to us. They have taken possession of nearly the whole country in this region, to the very borders of Shanghae, and they have cleared the way of all obstacles that used to prevent our visits to them. It then became necessary for Missionaries to meet them face to face, and to inquire from the leading men amongst them how far their system of Christianity tallied with that of the Bible. First one party of Missionaries, and then another, found their way to the rebel head-quarters at Soo-chow, and returned with glowing accounts of the high promise held out by the insurgents for the future of China. Messrs. Edkins and John, of the London Missionary Society, having, on a visit to Soo-chow, had an interview with the general in command of the city, called the *Choong wang*, or, 'Faithful king,' when some of the errors of the Tai-ping Christianity were brought out in conversation with him, wrote out a paper on the leading points of doctrine, and presented it to him. This the Choong wang sent to the *Kan wang*, or 'Shield king,' who resides at Nanking, and is said to stand in the relation of prime minister to the insurgent chief. The Kan wang [Hung-jin], immediately on receipt of it, started for Soo-chow, in the expectation of meeting with Mr. Edkins, who had however, in the mean time, returned to Shanghae. A pressing invitation was at once sent to Mr. Edkins to pay another visit to Soo-chow, in order to consult on the points of doctrine mentioned in the letter which had been forwarded to him. Mr. Edkins was not long in complying with this request, especially as the Kan wang, who is cousin to the head of the rebel movemen, was a member of Dr. Legge's church in Hong Kong for three or four years, during which time he was engaged as a catechist, and gave, I believe, abundant evidence of his sincerity. His letter to Mr. Edkins was accompanied by a manuscript book of his own composition, which consisted of an introduction to next year's almanack, and several other articles, advocating, on the whole, correct views of Christian doctrine and practice, and also recommending strongly the adoption of many improvements discovered and used in the west. Mr. Edkins, on this trip, was accompanied by four other Missionaries, of whom I was one, and my account of our visit I here subjoin—

"'*July* 30—After a hard and hot day's work of preparation, I started in company with Messrs. Edkins, John, Innocent, and Rau, the latter a French Protestant Missionary. Between nine and ten P.M. all had arrived at the boats, and we divided ourselves into two parties, Messrs. Edkins, John, and Innocent, occupying one boat, and Mr. Rau and myself the other. As reports have been rife for some time of the intended advance of the rebels on Shanghae, and the foreign authorities have determined to keep them away, guards of English and French soldiers have been for some weeks posted in different parts both in and outside the city.

"'*July* 31 — Made rather slow progress. Anchored for the night just outside a floating bridge constructed by the rebels near Luh-kia-pang, some forty English miles from Shanghae, which marks the commencement of the rebel territory so far as hitherto acquired.

"'*Aug*. 1—Early in the morning we moved up to the bridge, and asked to be allowed to pass. The poor country-people opened the bridge most readily. It consisted principally of the doors of the cottages seized for the purpose, which were placed on bamboos fastened across the river. The houses thus stripped of their doors and windows presented a most miserable appearance. The place of these, which the poor rustics dared not to take back, was supplied by pieces of matting, to shelter the residents from the sun and rain. It was heartbreaking to see the misery of the people. They spoke very earnestly against being thus treated. They said it did not matter to them who held the empire, but the struggle for it should surely be confined to the contending parties, and not be made the means of bringing such miseries on the people. All they wanted was to till their land and eat their rice in peace, and, for all they cared, any one might be Emperor. They complained bitterly of the excesses committed by the soldiers, both of the Imperialists and the rebels. A rebel proclamation was posted up at this place, requiring all to submit to the "heavenly dynasty," and to render tribute. The fate of these poor people is sealed, should ever the Imperialists be able to muster men or courage enough to make their appearance near them; and thus the people, in their present struggle, are the great sufferers. The rebels come down upon them for plunder, and kill indiscriminately where there is any opposition.

"'In the afternoon we passed Kwun-shan, a perfect scene of desolation. We did not think it advisable to leave our boats. A few rebels were posted about one of the bridges as a guard; and their mirth contrasted painfully with the miserably dejected looks of the few natives that we saw. The whole sight was sickening.

"'At dusk, I-ting was passed; and the desolation surpassed any thing that I had before imagined. Here was a large town, containing, when I last visited it, some twenty or thirty thousand inhabitants, made a heap of ruins, without one sound of life, save that of the authors of the ruin. They were stationed at one end of the town, barricaded off from the ruins, from which, however, they had nothing to fear, but from the ghosts of the injured people that might, in indignation, be hovering amidst them. These representatives of the "great peaceful" dynasty had the wicked desperado looks of a band of robbers who had glutted their appetites upon victims powerless to resist them, and were living on the destruction which they had effected. After passing their noisy camp, the silence that reigned in the once busy market-town, the ruins of the burnt houses, joined with the dusk of evening, produced the most melancholy feelings in our minds. A solitary cat, peering out from among a heap of bricks and broken furniture—a few dogs keeping watch over property that lay in terrible confusion all around them, or prowling about to find some food, either from dead bodies or from the filth that Chinese dogs mostly live upon—were about the only signs of life visible in this once thriving mart of trade. One single human being—an old man tottering on the brink of the grave—was seen wending his way over the rubbish. We accosted him with a kindly word of greeting; but he merely lifted his vacant eyes, shook his aged head, and resumed his melancholy and lonely walk. Our hearts bled as we passed this scene; and I cannot say that I wished success to the rebel movement. We anchored for the night a little beyond I-ting, but we were soon ordered off by some voice from the opposite shore.

"'*Aug.* 2—Very early we were on the move, and by seven o'clock we had arrived at Soo-chow, just outside the gate called Leumun. Here again ruins met our eyes on every side, and the stench from dead bodies was almost insufferable. We anchored near to some foreign boats which had come from Shanghae, and were engaged in trading with the rebels in articles of all kinds, lawful and unlawful. Amongst these, opium, which is prohibited by the Tai-ping chief under the penalty of death, was by no means the least esteemed by the rebel soldiers. Immediately after breakfast, we started to pay a visit to the Kan wang; but on reaching the gate we were most unceremoniously treated, and flatly denied admission. Mr. Edkins showed the gatekeeper the letter written on yellow silk received from the Kan wang, but it produced no effect on the mind or countenance of the relentless Cerberus. He was the very personification of wickedness and insolence, and his conduct made it evident that if combination does exist among the insurgents, inferiors did not think it inconsistent with such combination to manifest disrespect to superiors. Mr. Edkins, however, made one other attempt, and was admitted just inside the outer gate; on which we all followed. Some one with a little more politeness—a native of Soo-chow, who was stationed with the Kwangsi keepers of the gate—spoke with us; and after finding that some of us were acquainted with Lieu, the officer in command of that part of the city, at once offered us a guide to that gentleman's residence. This we gratefully accepted; and we were soon on our way to Lieu ta-jin.

"'My walk through the city did not tend to produce any better impressions in favour of the Christian insurgents of China. The desertion of the streets, except by the rebels who were located in the houses that had been spared from violence—the desolation, almost as great in some quarters as that at I-ting—a dead body of a child here and there seen lying on some door-step—the thorough upturning of every article of furniture in the search for treasure—the opening of the very coffins with, no doubt, the same object—and the desperado looks of those who had caused all this evil—all deeply pained me.

"'Very soon after entering the house of Lieu ta-jin he made his appearance. I was expecting a dignified, well-dressed, gentlemanly-looking person. Instead thereof, a common-looking man, who looked as though he had but just turned out of bed, dressed in nothing more than an oilskin short coat and wide pantaloons of the same material, slipshod, moreover, and his legs entirely innocent of stockings, presented himself among the not very good-looking fellows who surrounded us, and announced himself as the great man for whom we were in search, by shaking hands with all of us. We told him that our object was to have an interview with the Kan wang, who had invited one of our number for that purpose to Soo-chow, but that, not being acquainted with his residence, we begged Mr. Lieu to furnish us with a guide. He informed us that our best course would be to send our cards before us to announce our arrival, and to wait at his house till the Kan wang sent for us. Our cards were accordingly sent; and we were kept waiting a sufficient length of time to convince us of the greatness of him with whom we sought the interview. For more than three hours we were detained as unwilling guests in Mr. Lieu's house; and as no one that we saw, from the master downwards, showed the least inclination to talk or hear about religious subjects, the time passed heavily enough. With Lieu's whole appearance and demeanor I was any thing but pleased. Indeed, the utter absence of any thing like a religious element in one who stood in the relation of Secretary to Choong wang made one naturally wonder where, after all, the religion of the Tai-ping Christians is. Between one and two o'clock P.M., the welcome message came at last that the Kan wang was ready to receive us. Ponies had been sent, and were at the door, to convey us to his small majesty, and without delay we mounted our chargers. My unfortunate legs were about twice as long as they should have been to fit the length of the strings (for they had no straps) to which the stirrups were fastened, and consequently my ride was any thing but a comfortable one. I felt something like Pat in his bottomless sedan—"I would rather have walked if it had not been for the honour of the thing." The ride through a long line of streets added to the gloomy thoughts which I have had ever since touching on rebel territory; and in front of the very house in which the Kan wang has for the time taken up his residence, a stagnant ditch, green with the accumulated filth of years, is full of all kinds of house furniture, some smashed to atoms, others broken beyond remedy, others again nearly entire, but lost for ever to their proper owners; and from the smell that saluted our nostrils I should say that not a few dead bodies are rotting underneath this funeral pile. On arriving at the door we were received with a salute of two crackers; and after staying a second or two in an ante-room, we were, amid a complimentary din of discordant music, ushered in before the gentleman himself.

"'The Kan wang was sitting on a sofa, dressed in a long yellow damask robe, embroidered all over with that invariable mark of Chinese royalty — the dragon. On his head was a high pasteboard hat, completely gilt, in which were set, in different places, a few precious stones. It is the revival of the crown of the Ming, or last Chinese dynasty, which, in A.D. 1644, was displaced by the Manchoo Tartars, who have held possession of China till the present day. From head to foot but one colour—the Imperial yellow—predominated in the dress of the Kan wang, his wide pantaloons and his very boots, which had soles twice the ordinary thickness of even Chinese boots, being of the same material with his robe. Behind him stood a few boys, whose business was to fan him by turns; and on each side of him, ranging themselves in two rows in front, stood his ministers, dressed in long green or yellow silk robes, many of them having their hair completely enveloped in a yellow handkerchief. On our entrance, the Kan wang rose; and the manner in which he was dressed gave, as may be imagined, no little appearance of dignity to his person. He bore it, however, with great natural ease; and without insisting on any ceremonial, such as is required among themselves, he stretched out his hand in the most frank manner possible, and gave us a true English reception. He immediately after beckoned to us to be seated on the chairs which were placed in the usual Chinese style on each side of his sofa, motioning to Mr. Edkins to take the seat of honour.

"'Conversation immediately began; but after the complimentary and some other general remarks had passed, it flagged, in consequence of the number of listeners. This was soon perceived by the Kan wang, and a word from him at once halved the waiting company. Those who still hung behind were, in a like unceremonious manner, again ordered to withdraw; and, with the exception of his personal servants, we were, to our great relief, left to as unrestrained a tête-à-tête with our host as we desired. The conversation lasted for three or four hours; and he most willingly, and apparently with no desire to conceal even the defects and evils of the Tai-ping Christianity, answered our numerous questions. Before going to him we had already determined on the leading questions to be asked, and these we put to him just as they occurred to us. Without attempting to give all these questions and their answers, I shall endeavour briefly to lay before you the leading points of the conversation which seem necessary to be known in order to help in forming our judgment on the system of religion held by the chiefs of this rebel movement.

"'It may be well to remind you, that, in the political organization of the rebels, there is no Emperor, but a "fraternity of kings," consisting of the heavenly king and ten subordinate kings, who are principally, at present, engaged in subduing the districts respectively assigned to them. The Kan wang, and one or two others, seem to be the only civil ministers of the kingdom in this list.

"'1. The visions of the "heavenly king," which may be almost said to be the foundation of the whole movement, were stated by the Kan wang to be fully believed in as realities, both by the chief and his subordinates. The Kan wang himself, notwithstanding all his previous Bible instruction, avows himself as a believer in them, though his conscience will evidently not allow him to entertain such gross ideas respecting them as his brethren and his master. These visions— which happened in 1837, and were again repeated in 1848—refer to the actual descent of the heavenly Father to Hung sew tsuen, appointing him to his work of destroying the idols and the demons, alias the Manchoos.

Hung also states himself to have been called up to heaven to receive the same commission.

"'One alarming evil, consequent on these so-called "visions," is the belief by the "heavenly king," as well as by all those who have had no other means of instruction, in a materialistic character of God. The Kan wang knows, of course, that this is wrong; but he at once confessed, on being interrogated, that the "heavenly king" constantly thinks of God under the figure of an old man, and is entirely unacquainted with his spiritual character. In the manuscript book written by the Kan wang, already alluded to, the phrase, *woo hing woo siang*, "without form or bodily shape," had been used by him in describing the true God. The expression, however, was expunged by the "heavenly king," who will not allow contradiction on this favourite article of his faith.

"'Another grievous evil of these visions of Hung sew tsuen is the encouraging, or the inability to deny, the truth of vision-seeing by his followers. Accordingly, Yang, the eastern king, was also favoured with visions which allowed him to lay claim to such blasphemous titles as, "the Comforter," "the Holy Spirit," "the Redeemer from sickness," &c. This man being believed to entertain secret political designs against the kingdom, was murdered, and his whole family nearly extirpated, by another of the assistant kings, who was in his turn put to death by the rebel chief for the crime. When we asked the Kan wang respecting the whole affair, he said, and truly, that it was "nan kiang," or a difficult subject to speak about. He gave us sufficient, however, to lead us to believe, that though the chief and his adherents generally are compelled to believe in the reality of Yang's visions, yet that his motives and secret designs were perfectly understood at court. Still the error is perpetuated, inasmuch as, for certain political reasons, Yang has, since his death, been canonized, and, in all proclamations on the subject of religion, is spoken of by the "heavenly king" with great respect. His blasphemous titles are still retained; but the Kan

the Saviour the appellation of *Ti*, or "Sovereign Ruler," at present used by the monarchs of China, but which he himself repudiates, on the ground that it is a title applicable only to the Heavenly Father. He designates Christ as the "heavenly elder brother," and the only mark of superiority that he allows Him is the placing of his own name one character below the Saviour, while he puts Christ's name in the same relation to that of the Father. There is, therefore, a regular gradation in the writing of the three names which so often come together, as even to suggest the fear that these three are the only Trinity with which Hung is acquainted—"the heavenly father," the heavenly elder brother, and the heavenly king." Whilst freely stating all this to us, the Kan wang assured us that there was nothing more to be alarmed at than that his master did not understand the real nature of Christ, which point might be remedied in course of time. His visions have caused him to believe himself as heaven's commissioned agent, and he does not know that Christ was any thing more. This, according to the Kan wang, was all that he meant in calling himself Christ's "uterine younger brother."

"'2. The Kan wang's views of the Trinity, as may be gathered from the preceding, are those of orthodox Christians generally. In his book he tries to philosophize on the subject, and to explain the relations of the three persons in one God; but, as was to be expected, he goes beyond his depth. He is, moreover, hampered by the views already detailed of those with whom he has now connected himself. But from all we could gather from our conversation with him, he believes in the full eternity and divinity of Christ, both before and after his incarnation, and likewise of the Holy Spirit. He is clear, too, on the subjects of the atonement, regeneration by the Spirit, and the authority of the Holy Scriptures.

"'3. The offerings spoken of in the writings of the "heavenly dynasty" were stated to be merely thank-offerings, with no propitiatory idea attached to them whatever, and intended merely as a temporary substitute for the rites

"'4. Polygamy is practised by all the chiefs, from the head downwards, not even excepting the Kan wang, with all his knowledge of the requirements of God's law, as revealed in the Gospel. The "heavenly king" is said to be fully aware that the practice is contrary to Scripture, but yet is not only guilty of it himself (he has, I believe, a hundred concubines), but compelled the Kan wang, sorely against his will (if we may believe his account of the matter), to join in the sin. He said that compliance had cost him a great struggle, and much sorrow of heart, but he felt he had to choose between losing his position and yielding to the wish of his superior. He chose the latter, in the hope that he might be able, by his position, to effect the changes in the doctrines and practices of his friends which he feels to be needed.

"'5. The Sabbath cannot be said to be observed during their present state. Services are conducted by the chiefs wherever they may happen to be, but they seem only to be attended by a few of their immediate attendants. With the exception of this domestic service, of which, of course, the mass know nothing, and which consists only of the chaunting of a hymn and the reading, and, in some cases, the subsequent burning, of a written prayer, there is no difference made between the Sabbath and other days. The day on which it is kept at present is our Saturday, and this is accounted for by the fact, that among other changes which this "heavenly dynasty" purposes to make on the practice of the Tsing dynasty, not the least important, next to matters of religion, is the change of the year from a lunar to a solar year. In making the necessary calculations for their almanack they made a mistake, and hence their accidental Sabbatarian character. The Kan wang thought that might easily be rememedied by and by.

"'6. The Lord's Supper has never been observed amongst them, and the Kan wang has not partaken of it since his arrival at Nanking. Nor is baptism much observed by them at present. The form which they have adopted is sprinkling on the head, followed by the washing of the breast, as significant of the cleansing of the heart. The ordinance may be administered by any one, though the chiefs seem to arrogate to themselves the offices both of priest and prince.

"'7. All the Scriptures of the Old and New Testament (Gutzlaff's translation) have been published by them. They are said by the Kan wang to be regarded as of supreme authority, and to be constantly and diligently studied by the heavenly king. One interesting fact concerning this strange being, who combines in himself much that is both childish and blasphemous, true and false, is, that he troubles himself very little about political affairs, leaving the management of the war of extermination which he began, and of the kingdom which he has set up, almost entirely to his subordinates, while he is said to apply himself mainly to the study of the Bible and Mr. Burns' illustrated translation into Chinese of Bunyan's Pilgrim's Progress.

"'8. In answer to our inquiries, we were informed that Missionaries would be permitted to have free intercourse with the people everywhere, and that they would be permitted to teach and preach the doctrines that they believe to be in accordance with the word of God. There would be no firmán issued against us, so as to come between us and the people. Books prepared by Missionaries will also be gratefully accepted, and a special request was made for a small book of prayers.

"''Many other subjects were spoken of, but they were principally on minor matters of detail, which it is not necessary for me to recapitulate here. Altogether, the most friendly feelings were manifested towards us by the Kan wang, and I felt in some measure repaid for the trouble we had had to reach him. As it grew late in the afternoon he invited us to stay to dinner; and just before sitting down at the tables spread for us, we joined together in a religious service. An unobjectionable hymn was sung, in which the Kan wang himself led; and he afterwards asked Mr. Edkins to engage in prayer. After dinner we were conveyed to the gate on ponies provided for us, and we reached our boats a little after dark.

"'Aug. 3—Having yet some unfinished business with the Kan wang, we set out this morning for his residence. We had some difficulty in reaching it, in consequence, first, of the utter desertion of the streets by the people, and, secondly, of the equal ignorance with ourselves of the localities, by those who occupied their places. I have already included in my summary of yesterday's conversation all that passed in to-day's; and so, after presenting him with a few corrections of his book, &c., and joining with him in another act of worship, in which he himself offered an unobjectionable extempore prayer, we took our leave.

"'On arriving at our boats, we set sail immediately, and arrived at Shanghae early on the morning of the 6th of August.'"

RECENT INTELLIGENCE.

WESTERN INDIA.

(*From the Bombay Guardian.*)

The inhabitants of Ahmednuggur lately petitioned the magistrate, Mr. Fraser Tytler, to debar the native Christians from all access to the public wells. The following was the Magistrate's decision in reply to this petition—

"The main statement in this petition is untrue. Vishnoo Punt's wife is not a Mhar, or woman of low caste. Vishnoo Punt is a Brahmin, converted to Christianity. His wife is a Coonbee, also converted. Before conversion he and his wife had full right to draw water from the tank in question. He has not forfeited the above right, or any other, by his conversion to Christianity. On the contrary, the law ensures him every right which he possessed before his conversion to Christianity. This law will be enforced, and those acting contrary thereto punished. In Bombay, and in many other places, 'all classes of the community, Christian converts, Hindoos, and Mohammedans, have free access to all the public tanks and wells.' Petitioners seek to debar Vishnoo Punt and his family from the use of the public tanks solely because he is a Christian. But it is well known that if a Mang or Mhar woman marries a Mussulman, she is allowed to use the tanks in right of her having become a Mohammedan. Cattle, horses, donkeys, &c., have all access to the public tanks; and yet this common and obvious right, petitioners seek to deny to a man whose high respectability they themselves dare not and cannot gainsay.'

This decision had the sanction of Government. The promulgation of it produced no little excitement in Ahmednuggur, and the shops throughout the city were closed from Sunday the 16th of October to Thursday the 20th inclusive. It must not be supposed that this was the voluntary act of all the shopkeepers. Persons of influence went round and charged them, as they would avoid a great curse, they must close their shops. If they refused to comply, they should be stigmatized as the offspring of Christians. Accordingly, all classes, Mussulmans as well as Hindus, shut up their shops. There was further some talk of sending a petition by telegraph to Lord Canning, but we believe there was some difficulty in the way of their doing this. The inhabitants all deserted the public wells to which there was any probability of the resort of Christians. Moreover, they instituted *anooshthans*, or special ceremonies, in the presence of idols, by Brahmins paid for the purpose, to bring about the discomfiture of the native Christians. Some of the more prominent of the native Christians were singled out and commended by name to the special wrath of the gods.

It is quite true that a Mhar woman who marries a Mussulman enjoys immediately free access to the public wells, from which, up to the present time, all native Christians have been rigorously excluded. There is a Mang woman in Nuggur belonging to the Christian community, whose sister is married to a Mussulman: the latter has access to the wells, the former has not. This one fact speaks volumes as to the degree of concession made to

RECENT INTELLIGENCE.

the caste prejudices of the Hindus by the Mohammedans and by the British. There is one religion upon which all are now agreed to put the stamp of a peculiar opprobrium, and that is the Christian religion; and the petitioners of Ahmednuggur have done neither more nor less than humbly petition the Christian Government of this country to declare authoritatively that the Christian religion is the most opprobrious of all religions. And they actually expected to succeed; and were intensely disappointed because Christians were permitted to enjoy the rights enjoyed by other classes of the community generally. What an idea must the people have of the indifference of Government to all religious principles! The authorities deserve great credit for their present decision. It is to be hoped that none will take up the idea that caste among Christians is recognised by the Government, or that a converted Mhar or Mang will be excluded from the public wells, while a converted Brahmin is not.

We have great satisfaction in appending to the above remarks the following resolution of Government on the petition of Anundrao Babajee Deshpandey and other Hindu inhabitants of Ahmednuggur—

"The magistrate may be instructed to inform Anundrao Babajee Deshpandey, that Government will not for a moment entertain so absurd and so insulting an application as that contained in the petition signed by himself and a few other misguided persons at Ahmednuggur. The petitioners should be reminded, that, by their own showing, the fountains in question were established by Mohammedan kings; and that, in the days of those kings, no Hindu would have dared to suggest that they were polluted by being used by Mussulmans. If they could be used without pollution by any Mhar or Mang who embraced the Mohammedan religion, how can they be polluted by the use of Christian converts? The petitioners have forgotten their own Shasters, which declare that the caste of the Ruler, whatever it may be, is equal to the highest; and they have perverted the declaration in the Queen's proclamation, which expressly states that none should be molested by reason of their religious faith, into an argument for molesting and insulting those who profess the same faith which the Queen not merely acknowledges, but of which she proclaims herself the Defender."

This is an admirable letter, and we rejoice to see Government taking up its true position with reference to caste. The demand of the petitioners is severely but justly characterized; and we hope that the rebuke thus administered will be sufficient to deter the natives of this country henceforth from asking Government to affix a stigma to the profession of Christianity.

CHINA.

Extract of a letter from the Rev. W. A. Russell, dated Ningpo, Sept. 10, 1859—

The first and natural result of our defeat at the Peiho, as soon as it became generally known, was the gradual decrease of our *prestige* in the eyes of the Chinese, and the consequent insecurity of our lives and property, which hitherto, under God, seem principally to have been secured by it. This has been exhibited to us in various ways, especially by the late wicked attempts of certain parties, both at Shanghae and here—whether with or with-

RECENT INTELLIGENCE.

out the knowledge and sanction of the native authorities it is difficult to say—to exasperate the people against us by posting up, in the thoroughfares of the city and the surrounding villages, anonymous placards of a most inflammatory character, representing foreigners as kidnappers of the worst kind, who are constantly crimping poor honest people, old and young, male and female, without distinction, either to bring them to the Peiho to put them into the forefront of the battle there, or to carry them off to some foreign country to convert their blood into opium and their brains into medicine, which they design again to bring back to China as merchandise to be sold to the Chinese; and, in conclusion, calling upon the people in self-defence to rise *en masse*, and utterly to exterminate the perpetrators of such nefarious deeds.

With the view of furthering their vile object, a particular case of imposture was got up at Ningpo. A man of the name of Nyi Tseng-hae was suborned to come to my house to report, that, on the 9th of the seventh moon (August 7th), as he, with his three comrades, were returning to Seenpoh, their native place, from the eastern district, where they had been employed in reaping the harvest, about ten o'clock at night, as they lay down to rest on the bank of the river, not far from the British cemetery, suddenly a party of men, amongst whom were three foreigners, pulled alongside in a small boat from one of the large foreign ships, rushed up to the place where they were lying, some with bags in their hands, others with knives and swords, and, by threats of violence, succeeded in bagging his three companions, and carrying them off, while he himself, by brandishing a bamboo pole about him, managed to effect his escape.

When this fellow had told me his story, I asked him why he had not gone to the district magistrate to lay the case before him, telling him that he was the proper authority to whom to look for redress, and that I had nothing whatever to do with the matter. He replied that he had already reported it to him, but had been by him referred to me as the only one who would be likely to succeed in getting back his comrades; and, moreover, he thought he had a kind of claim on me to exert myself on his behalf, as they were all persons who lived in the immediate vicinity of our Missionary station at Seenpoh.

Apprehensive of treachery on the part of the authorities, and yet not knowing how far to credit or discredit the above statement as to the alleged case of kidnapping, I thought it best at once to take down in writing, from the man's own lips, all the particulars of the individuals said to be taken off—their names, ages, residences, appearances, &c., so as immediately to set inquiry on foot about them, and then to bring him over to our Consul for further examination on his part. I also volunteered to go down to Chinghae in Her Majesty's gunboat "Algerine," to search the foreign vessels anchored there, in one of which the kidnapped men were said to be detained in irons. The result of all our inquiries was a strong conviction on our minds that the case was an imposture, which the man himself acknowledged the following day, disclosing, at the same time, the names of his accomplices. This subsequently led the English and American Consuls to demand from the native authorities the issue of proclamations explanatory of the whole affair, which has tended much, under God, to quiet the minds of the people, and to restore that friendly feeling which previously existed between foreigners and natives at this port.

During the continuance of the excitement, which prevailed about a fort-

RECENT INTELLIGENCE.

night, our lives seemed placed in the most imminent jeopardy, and doubtless there would have been, as at Shanghae, a very serious outbreak of popular indignation against us, had it not been providentially prevented by the timely exposure of the above imposition, and the punishment, or the *threatened* punishment (for this is all we can as yet say), of the principal parties connected with it. I think I never before realized a more striking exhibition of the power and malice of Satan than in the change from a high degree of goodwill and friendship towards us, to one of undisguised hatred and disgust which he so suddenly and so unreasonably effected on the minds of this people. From being real friends, they seemed almost instantaneously transformed into bitter enemies, doubtless by the great adversary who has especial power over the heathen in blinding their minds and hardening their hearts, and thus leading them captive at his will. Wherever we went we were openly reviled as kidnappers, and not only foreigners, but the native Christians also were equally exposed to danger and abuse. But through the tender care and overruling providence of our gracious God, not a hair of our heads has been injured; and moreover, what seemed so very adverse at the time, would appear rather to have turned out to the furtherance of the Gospel. The false reports about us, so assiduously disseminated by designing parties, are now as much discredited as before they were believed, and we are regarded pretty generally as basely maligned and slandered. The audiences at our chapels, which for a time were considerably thinned, through the fear of appearing to have any conversation with us, are again as large as before, and apparently even more attentive. So that in this, as in other instances, the Almighty, though, for wise but often mysterious purposes, He suffers Satan, for a time, apparently to triumph, and carry on his vile machinations unchecked and unrestrained, yet has graciously appeared on behalf of his people, vindicated his cause in the sight of the heathen, and baffled all the devices of the wicked one. It has also been a matter of interest to us, as well as a cause of thankfulness to God, that at the very time when the excitement was at its height, and danger seemed to threaten both ourselves and the native Christians from a body of desperadoes fom the Seenpoh district, who had banded themselves together against us on the plea of getting back their countrymen, alleged to be kidnapped by foreigners,—at this very time we had the privilege of baptizing two men from this same district, who had heard and embraced Christianity in Dr. Parker's hospital, and who were undeterred by the threatening aspect of things from coming forward and making a public profession of the truth.

The unexpected check to the extension of our Society's operations in the interior, caused by the late unhappy event at the Peiho, will necessarily frustrate the immediate occupation of Hangchow as a Mission station, and all our plans and arrangements with reference to it.

The little body of native Christians here at Ningpo seems now in as satisfactory a condition as I have ever known it. The addition to its ranks during the past six months is also considerably greater than on any previous similar period of its history; a fact solely to be attributed to an enlarged exercise of power and mercy on the part of God, and not at all to the employment of any unwonted effort on the part of man, which probably during the same period have been even more feeble than usual. To our gracious God alone is the praise and glory due.

RECENT INTELLIGENCE.

FINANCIAL AFFAIRS.

THE Committee have in the press a full explanation of the various points in reference to the financial arrangements of the Society which have lately been made the subject of public remark. It will be issued with as little delay as possible.

EAST AFRICA.

Extract from a Letter of Rev. J. Rebmann, dated Mombas, Sept. 10, 1859—

It was on the 16th of April we took our leave, and again stepped into a dirty Arab bagala, to which you are only reconciled by the thought that it is only for a short time. On the 19th, we safely arrived at Mombas, and were but just in time before the rainy season commenced. The first news that met our ears was of a painful and horrible nature, and unheard of among Mohammedans. When visited by the cholera, which, during the dry season, had spread all along the coast, finding all their usual sacrifices insufficient, they at last, in their despair, had recourse to sacrificing human beings, drowning them in the sea, or burying them alive! Some said that all the principal men of Mombas had made themselves thus guilty; but the Cadi, who afterwards helped me in revising my translation of the Gospel of St. Luke into Kisuaheli, acknowledged it only of one, who, soon after the dark deed had been done, died himself. Resignation to God (Islám) is the very name by which their religion is called; but even where it seems to exist, it is apathy, for true resignation is only learnt in the garden of Gethsemane.

The house we formerly occupied had, during our absence, been turned into a garden of Arab soldiers, and was now left in such a wretched condition, that it looked more like a den of thieves than any thing else, and we were obliged to take up our abode in a neighbour's house. All study was now at an end, and once more I had to put my hand to all kinds of manual employment. After about a month, however, I got our former house so far repaired, that we could once more take possession of it, when, alas! the sad tidings of the downfall of our house at Kisuludini reached us. Remembering how good the house still looked when I visited the place in November last, I could hardly believe the message; though, on the other hand, the rains had been long and heavy enough to render it credible. Still I indulged the hope that at least parts of the walls might still remain, over which a thatched roof could soon be made to serve at least for a temporary residence; and on paying a visit to the place on the 7th of June, we had the pleasure of finding still more left than we had ventured to expect. The greater part of the front Mr. Erhardt,

RECENT INTELLIGENCE.

and, after him, Mr. Deimler, had occupied, was tumbled to the ground; but our own side was still standing, though the roof was also partly broken, and threatening to come down No safe dwelling-place remained; but a whole wing, still standing, which only wanted a framework for a thatched roof, was such a relieving circumstance, that we gave thanks to the Lord in the midst of ruins. Mrs. Rebmann accompanied me in this short visit. The work to be done being of such a nature as did not require my presence on the spot, but could be left to natives of Mombas, we had only to make up our minds for a prolonged stay at a place in which we never wished, and had even thought we never could stay for any length of time. But, thanks be to God, with the exception of a slight attack of fever after the rainy season was over, our health has been very good.

To this long stay at Mombas I was the more easily reconciled, as I was anxious to revise my translation of the Gospel of St. Luke into Kisuaheli with the Cadi, from whom, with the Arabic New Testament in his hand, and being perfectly conversant with the Kisuaheli language, I expected to derive considerable help in the clearing up of all difficult passages. In this, however, I was greatly disappointed: a translation made by him from the Arabic would be a complete jargon. The Arabic translation of the Bible is not understood in East Africa; and I have reason to suspect that this is not merely to be attributed to the difference in the Arabic as spoken in different places, but also to the translation being at fault. Only a few days ago I had the passage Luke xii. 49, which, being translated literally, says just the contrary of what it should say. The same is the case in the translation of the Gospel of St. Luke into Kinika; as also the two debtors in Luke vii. 41, are represented as *demanding* money instead of *owing* it. I see more and more how much care and time is needed to make a correct and intelligble translation into a language, the only source of information about which is the mouth of the natives. In February I had thought it would be ready to be sent to Bombay in April, and now it is September, and I still have not done revising it.

The remaining part of our house at Kisuludini being now ready, we are on the point of removing there. Having asked for a fresh Missionary in my letter of December last, at a time when the whole house was still in existence, I think it proper to say it would be the better if he were a single man, for a married man would have many inconveniences to put up with until another house is built.

Dr. Roscher did not go to the Kilimandjaro, but turned to the south, and all I know about him is contained in the following extract from a letter of Captain Rigby, dated Zanzibar, Oct. 23—" Dr. Roscher, when last heard from, was at Kiloa, very ill with the fever. He says, when any Arabs see him they become frightened, and refuse to take him inland, thinking he will die."

CHRISTIANITY AMONG THE NATIVES OF INDIA.

(*From the Friend of India.*)

The *Hindu Patriot* describes the course of "Indian social progress," or the effects of Christianity among the natives of India:—" The wasting has commenced, and the pithy portion of the tree of superstition has a great deal worn

RECENT INTELLIGENCE.

out. We can assure our European friends that the educated natives stand no longer in need of exhortative advices to make them see through and put aside the tainting customs and practices of their forefathers, to learn that the Purans are false, that Menu was a created man, and that the Brahmins have long trodden over the necks of the Sudras; nor do they wholly fail to act upon these convictions. They—at least a great number—have followed in their actions the dictates of reason and conscience; and where they have not done so, it has been and still is with a view to avoid breaking the heartstrings of those they tenderly love." The writer compares "the sneaking sect meetings among the educated natives of India" to the clandestine conventicles of the early Christians, the English Puritans, and the Scotch Covenanters; and asserts that those who, though Christian in spirit, do not profess Christianity, do more to weaken Hinduism than "the whole corps of professed Missionaries do at present." We fear all this is true only of "Young Bengal," and that in a very modified sense. Sceptical indifference has taken the place of superstition, and weakness leads to the hypocrisy of yielding to its forms. The state of feeling among educated natives is somewhat that which prevailed at Rome when Cicero, himself an augur, wondered how one priest could pass another in the street without laughing. Out of the Presidency cities, orthodox Hinduism has not loosened its hold on the national mind.

SIR CHARLES WOOD ON THE MADRAS MEMORIAL*.

The petition of the Madras Native Association, on the subject of neutrality in matters of religion, transmitted home by Sir C. Trevelyan, July 12th, was replied to by Sir C. Wood, Sept. 30th—" 1. Your letter, dated 12th July, No. 56. 1859, transmitting a memorial from the Madras Native Association and others, Hindu and Mohamedan inhabitants of the Presidency of Madras, has been laid before me in Council. 2. The object sought by the memorialists, besides the general one of an undeviating neutrality on the part of Government and its officers in matters of religion, are—1st, the abolition of educational grants in aid, and, 2ndly, the prohibition of Government officers from taking official part in Missionary proceedings on public anniversaries and meetings. 3. Her Majesty has announced in her gracious Proclamation to the princes and people of India, that 'she assumes no right and entertains no desire to impose her religious convictions on any of her subjects; that it is her Royal will and pleasure that none shall be favoured or disquieted by reason of their religious faith; and that all in authority under her shall abstain from all interference with the religious belief or worship of any of her subjects.' To the principles thus declared by the Proclamation the Government of British India will adhere. 4. As to the first of the two objects specially urged in the concluding paragraph of the memorial, the allegations of the memorialists have failed to convince Her Majesty's Government of the injustice or inexpediency of making grants in aid under the existing rules for the promotion of education in India, such grants being available for schools established or maintained by persons of all religious persuasions indifferently, provided that the secular education given be equal to the prescribed standard. 5. In regard to the second point, Her Majesty's Government consider that the announcement contained in the Royal Proclamation, and the communications

---

* Vide "Church Missionary Intelligencer" for 1859, p. 193.

RECENT INTELLIGENCE.

which have already been made to the Governments in India respecting the interference of Government officers *officially* with the religion of the people, render unnecessary any further instructions on the subject." The memorialists had been advised accordingly.

FESTIVAL OF ST. FRANCIS XAVIER AT GOA.

Strongly contrasted with the Gospel simplicity of Protestant Missions upholding Christ before the eyes of perishing sinners, is the profane mockery of the Romish system.

"On the 3d of December, the day of the great feast, the bells rang joyously at the hour fixed for the ceremony of exposition. The litter on which reposes the body of St. Francis Xavier takes out like a drawer from the rest of the case. It was carried by persons of the highest dignity in the city present, and deposited in its shrine in the centre of the sanctuary. The shrine was now surrounded by candlesticks of massive silver, and by beautiful silver lamps. High mass followed, during which, after the Gospel, the panegyric of the saint was pronounced by the most eminent preacher in the city, who concluded his address by three Hail Marys, the last of which was for his lordship Monseigneur Canoz. During the elevation, guns were fired outside the church, as if it had been a military mass. When the most holy sacrifice was concluded, the faithful were permitted to approach the holy remains, and to kiss the feet of the saint. Every thing was so well arranged, that there was no confusion in this ceremony. The people ascended the platform, one by one, by steps at one corner, knelt and kissed the holy feet of St. Francis Xavier, and, walking half-way round the shrine, descended by a different way, and filed off out of he church. But there were few who did not return at some more quiet time, to have a tranquil look at the saintly remains, and an undisturbed prayer beside them."—*Allen's Indian Mail.*

DEPARTURE OF MISSIONARIES.

West Africa, Yoruba, and Niger.—Messrs. Jefferies, Roper, Lieb, and Flad, embarked at Liverpool, Nov. 24, 1859, for Lagos, and Mr. J. Coomber for Sierra Leone; and, on the 24th of December, Messrs. Ashcroft, Brierly, and Oldham, embarked at Liverpool for Sierra Leone, ultimately to proceed to the Niger. ("Church Missionary Record," Dec. 1859, p. 269.)

North India.—The Rev. S. and Mrs. Attlee embarked at Southampton, Nov. 19, on board the "Ceylon" for Calcutta. The Rev. J. Fuchs took leave of the Committee Jan. 3, and on Jan. 4, embarked on board the "Ceylon" at Southampton, also for Calcutta. The Rev. C. and Mrs. Reuther left Germany in December on their return to North India *vid* Marseilles. The Rev. G. and Mrs. Yeates embarked at Southampton, Dec. 12, on board the "Pera" for Bombay, *en route* for Mooltan.

North-West America.—Mr. T. T. Smith embarked at Liverpool, Nov. 26, on board the "Persia" for New York, to proceed from thence overland to the Red River.

RETURN HOME OF MISSIONARIES.

West Africa.—Mr. J. Alcock left Sierra Leone on the 21st of November, and arrived at Liverpool on December 13.

South India.—The Rev. L. Cradock left Madras November 29, and arrived in London January 12.

RECENT INTELLIGENCE.

FINANCIAL SYSTEM OF THE SOCIETY.

A Pamphlet on the Financial Arrangements of the Society is now ready for distribution, and may be had on application at the Church Missionary House.

WESTERN INDIA.

The following extracts from the annual letter of the Rev. C. C. Mengé (Jan. 7, 1860) are deserving of much attention, in connexion with the subject of Bible education in India, and the disposition of heathen teachers towards it.

"I have also met here with another remarkable individual, who was the first person who taught Santosh the way of life; but, strange to say, though this person possesses a vast amount of Christian knowledge, and has composed a great number of Christian poems, and teaches all his disciples the truth as it is in Jesus, he still remains, outwardly at least, a heathen, fearing to lose his influence if he should be an open professor and baptized convert to Christianity. It is, however, a remarkable fact, that he receives presents and money in kind for his teaching the way of salvation. This shows that the Christian truth commends itself to the consciences of men, and would be professed by vast numbers in this country if it did not involve loss of caste. ....

"You will be interested to hear that several of the most efficient native helpers of our American brethren in the Ahmednugger district were originally disciples of Bhulsa-Boa, the same spiritual guide who instructed also Santosh. He has thus been the honoured instrument for the conversion of several remarkable individuals. May he have grace given him to follow now his disciples!"

SOUTH-INDIA MISSION.

The following extract from a letter from the Rev. P. S. Royston, dated Paneivilei, December 20, 1859, gives an account of the ordinations in Tinnevelly, to which reference was made in the "Recent Intelligence" of December 1859—

"Knowing how anxious you and all our friends in Salisbury Square will be to hear somewhat of the events of the past few days, I send you a hasty line, in hope of catching the second steamer of the month. Our dear

RECENT INTELLIGENCE.

Church Missionary Society brethren are still about me, and I write amid many interruptions; but I will endeavour to give you as faithful and succinct an account as possible of this memorable season. Our Bishop said well, in his English sermon on Sunday evening, that no Bishop since our Lord's own time had been so privileged as he had been himself by that day's service. With the limitation of this statement to the present era of Missions, his lordship's words are true indeed. Besides the advancement of three European Missionaries (Messrs. A. B. Valpy and T. Spratt, of the Church Missionary Society, and J. Seller, of the Gospel-Propagation Society) to priests' orders, we had the goodly spectacle of the ordination at one time of thirteen Tamil candidates of approved character — five to be presbyters and eight to be deacons in the rising Tinnevelly church. Of these, all but one (Mr. Christian David, Gospel-Propagation Society), belong to the Church Missionary Society. With the names of the others you will be familiar:—Priests—the Rev. Messrs. Sinivásagam, Maduranáyagam, Mudhusámi Devaprasádham, Madhurendhiram Saviráryan, and Paul Daniel; Deacons—Messrs. Joseph Cornelius, Vedhanáyagam Devanáyagam, William Satthianádhan, Perianáyagam Madhuranáyagam (of Palamcotta), Abraham Isaac (of Paneivilei), John Nallathambi (of Pannikulam), Arumanáyagam Perianáyagam, and Devanáyagam Virarágu (of Mengnánapuram).*

"You are already aware that this station (Paneivilei) was the one selected for the examination and service. The former began on the Tuesday and ended on the Saturday, the Rev. Messrs. Sargent and Tucker being examiners. On my way hither on Saturday morning with my dear young friends John and James Thomas (sons of the Rev. J. Thomas), from Mengnánapuram, we had occasion, after crossing the swollen river, to wait in an adjoining village for our horsekeepers. It was quite clear that the circumstances of the ordination were well known to the heathen inhabitants, who entered into an animated conversation with my companions upon the subject. Indeed, the fact of two elephants and some ten camels being quartered in Paneivilei, and all Sircar (Government) property, and that so many padres had come in from so many quarters, caused no small sensation; and the amount of particular information about the different orders of ministers was really surprising. Of course we found a busy scene at the Mission Bungalow; and the various tents erected for the accommodation of so many visitors were speedily occupied. In the morning we had a special prayer-meeting with reference to the following day's solemn services; and in the evening the candidates and Missionary party, some thirty-six in number, I think, dined together, and afterwards proceeded to the beautiful church of this station, where Mr. Brotherton gave a Tamil address to the accepted candidates. Next day we had the usual Sunday-morning service at seven, shortly after which the congregation, composed principally of Mission agents and scholars, began to throng the large church, to be ready for the ordination service at eleven. And here I cannot but record a mark of the watchful care of our great Father. You will remember that the church of this station has the (in India) unusual addition of a gallery. Some time before

---

* One of the candidates, Michael, was not accepted by the Bishop on account of his advanced age.

RECENT INTELLIGENCE.

service commenced the central supporting beam of this gallery gave way under the weight of the crowded children who had occupied it; but providentially the rest of the wood-work continued firm, and no accident or hurt occurred to any one. Had it happened after service had commenced, a very different story would have had, probably, to be told. The Bishop having been met by the clergy at the porch, and all the European Missionaries, with our venerable native brother, the Rev. John Devasagáyam, having taken their seats, fourteen in number, within the communion-rails, the service began. After the singing of a hymn, the Rev. E. Sargent, one of the examiners, presented the candidates, sixteen in number. It was a truly impressive sight. In front these interesting brethren; behind them the four other native ministers of our Society (already in full orders); then the catechists and various Mission agents and students, who had come over from Palamcotta; and, beyond them, the crowded congregation of native Christians, many of whom were obliged to stand without, for want of room within.

"Mr. Tucker read the Litany, and our honoured senior Missionary, Mr. Thomas, delivered an impressive sermon, of an hour's length, from the very appropriate text, 'It is required in stewards that a man be found faithful.' (1 Cor. iv. 2.) The order and attentive earnestness of that white-robed congregation of at least some 1100 souls were very marked; and one cannot but believe that many a solemn prayer ascended up on behalf of those whose presence there gave the special interest to the occasion. I need hardly inform you that the service was in the Tamil, the Bishop, however, first repeating his own parts in English. Our venerable Mr. John (the appellation by which the Rev. J. Devasagáyam is known in Tinnevelly) joined with us in laying his hands upon those who were being ordained presbyters, and also took part in the communion service, which was afterwards administered to about 200 persons, chiefly Mission readers and schoolmasters, who remained behind to unite with the newly-ordained ministers in that holy ordinance. It was indeed a day much to be remembered in Mission history. May the many prayers which were offered throughout our English, as well as our Indian dioceses, on that ordination Sunday, bring down—what we may surely expect—an abundant blessing from the great Head and Bishop of the Church! Yea, were not its solemn services brought about by His blessing already bestowed upon the labours of His servants in this Southern India for the last hundred years? The contrast, however, presented by the state of things no more than thirty years ago may well be illustrated by what occurred in the church porch while we awaited the Bishop's arrival. While I was talking to old Mr. John upon the subject, an aged headman of the village came up to him, and, after making a salaam, said, 'Ayyer, do you remember what occurred here just thirty years ago? The Missionary built us a small prayer-house, which was destroyed in the night. And now look at this great church, and think of the service about to be held in it.'

"The remark, indeed, was suggestive of many solemnizing but thankful reflections. 'Not unto us, O Lord, not unto us, but to thy name be the glory, for thy mercy and for thy truth's sake!'

"In the evening the Bishop preached a very solemn sermon to the newly-ordained men and the English speakers of the congregation, from 2 Tim. ii. 15,

RECENT INTELLIGENCE.

Study to show thyself approved unto God, a workman who needeth not to be ashamed, rightly dividing the word of truth.' It will, I believe, be printed and circulated, together with Mr. Thomas's Tamil sermon of the morning. My own Church Missionary Chapel Association at Madras had supplied the means of providing every one who could read with the ordination services in the vernacular, an arrangement, you will remember, which was also made on the occasion of the last ordination in March 1850. And so passed away one of the most important days which has yet dawned upon modern Mission work.

"The Bishop has confirmed some 3500 in Tinnevelly, and about 2000 (I think) in Travancore, this time. Upwards of 4000 of these are connected with the Church Missionary Society."

Extract from a letter of the Rev. J. Hawksworth, dated Cottayam, Dec. 2, 1859—

"The whole of our congregation (Tiruwella), I believe, are growing in numbers, and, better still, in spiritual-mindedness. This has chiefly struck me since my return, and it is very cheering. As yet the Mission appears to tell but very little on the higher-caste heathen, though even among them the light is spreading. But the Gospel in all its saving power is spreading still among the slaves, and others of the lower classes. One old woman at Thallawaddie, a convert from the Chojans, and who was turned out of house and home by her husband and sons at her baptism, has ever since laboured and persevered in prayer, and has been the honoured instrument of bringing about eighty souls into the church of Christ. She now rejoices, seeing that all her children and her children's children, except one, have been baptized."

CANDIDATES FOR ORDINATION.

The earnest prayers of the friends of Christian Missions are desired on behalf of the following accepted Missionary students, who have been recommended as candidates at the ensuing ordination of the Archbishop of Canterbury, on the 4th of March next (the second Sunday in Lent):—

Mr. John Martindale Speechly, B.A. . . ; St. John's College, Cambridge.
Mr. Lewin Street Tugwell . . . . . ⎫ Church Missionary Institution,
Mr. Joseph Bishop Wheeler . . . . ⎭ Islington.

DECEASE OF A MISSIONARY.

We have to record the decease of the Rev. H. C. Krückeberg, of the North-India Mission, which took place on the 6th of February at Munder, in Hanover, after an illness of a few days.

RECENT INTELLIGENCE.

TURKEY.

From Evangelical Christendom, March 1860.

We have, in recent Numbers, alluded to the house built at Bebek by the Missionaries for Mr. Williams (Selim Effendi), and to the scene of Gospel labour which that house had become. Recent letters not only tell us of the vast increase of this particular work, but of some remarkable facts connected therewith, which, for obvious reasons, we can only yet advert to in general terms. Even so, however, they will be found deeply interesting. It seems that the house of the Williams' family is beset, not only by day, but by night, by inquiring crowds. Members of the Sultan's household, his private servants, dervishes, mollahs, imauns, colonels, captains, and also the poorest men, women, and even children, are seen crowding the house. Some stay through the night as well as the day, and Mr. Williams is ready to sink under the continual effort needed to supply Gospel information to these inquiring souls. This is general. But some particulars connected with the work are so strange, that one of our correspondents tell us he is afraid to commit them to paper, lest he should be suspected of drawing upon his imagination for his facts; and, besides, some of these facts it would be imprudent to divulge as yet. From other sources we learn that the numbers of Mussulmans amongst whom a very remarkable movement is taking place are not less than twenty to thirty thousand. It seems that for some years past a spirit of inquiry, leading to curious results, had been at work, irrespectively of all Missionary effort. A certain Mohammedan imaun, or priest, had been led, by the mere study of the Koran, to take exalted views of the character of Jesus, the prophet of the Jews. He counted the number of passages in the Koran where mention was made of his name or person, and also he observed the allusions to his supernatural birth, and to the Paraclete that was to follow him. He prayed to the Almighty for illumination, and, it seems, proceeded so far as to become "heretical" to his own faith. He founded a sect called "the Brotherhood," who, some time since, are stated to have amounted to 10,000, with 20,000 more under instruction. For this the leader was banished to Broosa, where he and some of his followers were at the time of the visit of Dr. Hamlin and Mr. Williams to that place, and of the remarkable conversation there, mentioned in a former Number of this journal. The report of that interview with the Turkish dignitaries in the Broosa church, and the narrative of that conversation, soon spread over Broosa, and this banished "heretic" having heard thereof, wrote to some of his disciples at Constantinople, and desired them to go and visit Mr. Williams, and get what further light they needed from him. In consequence of this, boatsful of delegates visit Bebek, receive instruction, and return to the "Brethren," conveying to them what they have learned. Some letters say that the whole of this movement arose by mere study of the Koran, without any access to the New Testament. Others take for granted that the doctrines of the brethren have been taken from the New Testament

RECENT INTELLIGENCE.

by mere reading, without Christian instruction, and therefore have been mixed up with erroneous and fanatical views. It would be a matter of the deepest interest to ascertain which of these two views is the correct one. It is reported that these "Brethren" claim to be so enlightened and guided by the Holy Spirit, as to need no "book" any longer. And they say, that when the Holy Spirit enters the soul, every book is thenceforth shut, and is needless. Of course all statements about their exact views must be received at present with caution: it would seem, however, to be a favourable preparatory work, rendering them more accessible to the truth of the Gospel, which a few of them have actually received. It would seem, if we compare this work with that going on in Sweden, as well as with the curious concomitants of the Irish revivals, that there are grounds for suspecting something like a general spiritual upheaving, which takes or manifests peculiar features, according to the circumstances of localities, and the amount of the truth of God to which access can be had. All these things invite us to dismiss too preconceived notions as to the doings of Him who "moves in a mysterious way his wonders to perform," and to examine and watch with candour and caution all the various phenomena submitted to our notice. Those who can only see men as trees walking, are often incorrectly judged of by the long-accustomed possessors of the blaze of Gospel sunlight. We shall watch and listen with deep interest for the tidings of this remarkable affair.

NORTH INDIA.

The following interesting extract is from a letter of the Rev. J. Vaughan, dated Burdwan, January 1860—

"In speaking of our experience, I shall only give our general impressions. The details of a preaching tour have a good deal of sameness in them. But in going from village to village, conversing with the people and listening to their arguments, certain convictions are formed in the mind of a Missionary. These convictions are rather the result of an aggregate and extended view of the work, than derived from a few special instances: certain feelings and impressions are deepened within him the more he sees and hears, but he might not find it easy, perhaps, to give in detail the data upon which these opinions are founded. One feeling, then, which is shared in common with myself and my brother Geidt is, that God is, in a very marked way, preparing the people of Bengal for some great change: we believe that it will be a blessed and a glorious change. It is impossible for a person to move about amongst this people, and to watch the workings and operation of their mind, without getting this impression. Most assuredly Hinduism is daily losing its hold upon the affections of the people: a deep and wide-spread scepticism prevails on the subject; and perhaps it is no more than the truth to say that a large proportion of the people have no faith in it at all. The trammels of caste, also, are most certainly being broken through, especially with reference to the Brahminical order. The Brahmin is daily becoming less and less an object of superstitious awe and veneration: he is gradually sinking to the common level. And together with all this, it is abundantly clear, first, that the knowledge of Christianity is being widely diffused. You cannot visit a single village in this large district where some of the principles of the Gospel are not known. And further, it is our deliberate conviction that

RECENT INTELLIGENCE.

there is a growing feeling in the minds of multitudes that Christianity must be the true religion. Many a time, in returning from preaching, does the remark spontaneously fall from each of us, 'Depend upon it, God will ere long do a mighty work in this country.' To my own mind, the state of this people is illustrated by the process going before an earthquake: except a few ominous cracks here and there—except now and then the escape of a vapour through the openings—the surface of the earth is little changed; but below, the elements of destruction are hourly increasing in strength and intensity; hourly, too, is the resisting crust becoming thinner and thinner: at length the crisis has arrived, and in one short moment the catastrophe has passed, and left the face of things completely changed. Such will be the history of Hinduism. Whoever lives long enough (and it may not be very long either) will see this system swept away by one fell sweep; and then, if only the church be faithful to its obligations in spreading the truth, that saying may be realized, 'A nation may be born in a day.'"

The Rev. A. Strawbridge, of Umritsur, reviewing the events of the last year, says—

"The past year has been a remarkable one in many respects. We have been permitted to admit into the outward church a larger number of converts than in any preceding year. The leaven is evidently beginning to work. The good seed is bringing forth fruit. Not only are the minds of men being awakened, but their hearts, I hope, are being converted to the Lord.

"Secondly, among those baptized there have been a larger proportion of respectable and well-informed and independent men, from among whom we cannot but hope that, in due time, some will be found fit to go forth to be instruments in the Lord's hands of turning many from darkness to light.

"Thirdly, owing to the almost daily instances of men coming forward asking for instruction—men who apparently have never been in connexion with any other Mission—I have been much pressed in spirit, and have felt the need of being constantly among the people, seeking out Christ's sheep that are scattered abroad. Everywhere doors of usefulness are being opened to us. Everywhere the minds of men appear to be occupied about religion. By means of former itineration, and especially by the distribution of books, a blow has been struck, and everywhere individuals are to be found who are anxious to be instructed in the word of God more perfectly. This, I know, will be to you encouraging, but I cannot convey to you any idea of the feelings it produces upon our minds.

"What is to be the practical result of all this? I mean, so far as you at home are concerned. Will it not be the sending forth of more men? I will not enlarge upon this. What may be said of the Punjab may, no doubt, be affirmed of thousands of other places."

The Rev. R. Clark, in a letter dated Peshawur, January 4, 1860, says—

"It has been my lot to travel in the Punjab, perhaps, more than any other Missionary of our Society, and there are few important cities which, at one time or another, I have not visited. The strong impression which has been left on my mind, after all I have seen, or all I have heard from natives and Europeans, is, that our Committees cannot attach too great importance to their Umritsur Mission. It is one which ought to affect the whole Punjab, and the whole of

RECENT INTELLIGENCE.

North India. The Sikhs are more prepared for Christianity than any other people in India, and they are fitted, more than any other race, to exert influence. Already the principal Rajah on this side the Sutlej is almost a Christian. At Kupurthala, his residence near Jullunder, he has long since established schools, in which his orders are, that the word of God be taught. He has now established a Mission in his own city, and, after inviting the Missionary, he entirely supports him. He has married a Christian wife, and he has but one; and it is thought that he may, ere long, become a candidate for Christian baptism. The consequences of such a step on the part of so influential a personage, ruling, as he does, independently, or rather feudally, over a large territory, cannot be calculated."

SOUTH INDIA.

The Rev. P. P. Schaffter, says, January 10, 1860—

"The outward progress of Christianity in these lands is certainly considerable. There is a strong feeling among high and low that Christianity is destined to continue and prevail in this land. I have made very minute inquiries on this point. During the past year, in my small district alone, more than 450 people have applied to be received under Christian instruction, 300 of whom only have been admitted. The rest attend prayer and divine worship, but, for various reasons, we have not thought it right to insert their names in the list yet."

DISMISSAL OF MISSIONARIES.

At a general meeting of the Committee at the Church Missionary House on Monday, March 12th, the following Missionaries were taken leave of, previous to their departure for their fields of labour—

Niger—Rev. J. C. Taylor, returning to the Mission.

Mediterranean—Rev. R. H. and Mrs. Weakley, proceeding to Constantinople.

South India—Rev. J. and Mrs. Bilderbeck returning to Madras.

The instructions were delivered by the Rev. H. Venn, and the Missionaries having been addressed by the Rev. W. Cadman, were then commended in prayer to God's protection by the Rev. Daniel Wilson.

RETURN HOME OF A MISSIONARY.

North India—The Rev. H. C. Milward arrived in England, from Calcutta, at the end of February.

DECEASE OF A MISSIONARY.

West Africa—The Rev. C. F. Ehemann died at Fourah Bay on the 27th of January, after nearly seventeen years of Missionary labour in Sierra Leone.

On Sunday, the 21st of December last, at Agra, the Rev. Messrs. Shackel and Champion were admitted to priests' orders, and Mr. Wright to deacons' orders, by the Bishop of Calcutta.

RECENT INTELLIGENCE.

PRAYER MEETING IN JANUARY.

THE invitation to prayer in the second week of the year would appear to have been very generally responded to in the most remote portions of the Mission field. We have many allusions to the subject from different quarters. From the Red River, Archdeacon Hunter writes as follows (Jan. 24, 1860)—

"We have lately held united prayer-meetings throughout the settlement. A complete week was devoted to this blessed work. In my own church from 800 to 1000 were present, and addresses were delivered by Mr. Black, the Presbyterian Minister here; also by myself, Mr. Cowley, Mr. Chapman, and Mr. H. Cockran, on the work of the Holy Spirit. All seemed to feel that it was good to be there, and I think we see the first drops of a coming shower. May the Lord revive his work in the midst of our people, and gather in many souls to the fold of Jesus!

"Last Sunday week I had 180 communicants, and last Lord's-day my church was crowded with attentive and devout worshippers. My prayer-meetings were never so well attended, so that my hands are full, being alone, with this large district to superintend."

The Rev. J. S. Burdon, of Shanghae, says (Jan. 21, 1860)—

"The Loodiana invitation to united prayer during the second week in January of this year was cordially adopted by all Christians in Shanghae, and such a solemn, happy, prayerful week it is rarely the Christian's privilege to enjoy on earth. Secret and public prayer was offered simultaneously by Christians of all denominations, and the daily meetings were felt by all to be seasons of blessing to our souls. Ourselves, our families, this land, the church universal, the world, all formed the subject of our thoughts, meditations, and prayers; and scarcely ever before did such earnest, united, believing prayer arise from this dark land to heaven. Native and foreign Christians all met at a throne of grace. At all the open ports, this week, I believe, was similarly observed; and now shall we not look for encouragement in our work? God has been amongst us, and I feel confident that He will soon be, if he is not already, manifesting his power in the salvation of souls around us."

YORUBA.

The following account of the advance of a Dahomy army is extracted from a letter written by Mr. Smith, of Ishaga, to Rev. C. A. Gollmer, February 28. The letter possesses additional interest in that it is reprinted from the "Iwe Irohin,"* the first periodical of the Yoruba country.

"My messengers have this moment returned from Imeko. Olumeko (the chief of Imeko) entertained them well, and related to them the full particulars of the proceedings of the Dahomy army as follows:—They encamped first near Iketu. From their encampment the king sent to Alekutu (chief of

---

* See page 109.

RECENT INTELLIGENCE.

Iketu) to say that he was going to attack Abbeokuta, and not any of his towns. In return, Alaketu sent, as a present to the Dahomy camp, four men and a cow.

"Leaving Iketu, he came to Idanyi, and told the Idanyi people the same as he had told Alaketu. The Idanyi people gave them a present of a sheep and other things.

"The Dahomy army proceeded on from Idanyi, and for some days they were not seen nor heard of. Suddenly they returned in the night, and encamped between Idanyi and Imeko, intending to destroy Imeko, but his guides failed him. He then attacked Idanyi, slew many, took off the heads of the slain, and carried them off, after having laid the dead bodies together in heaps. The Alaketu sent a body of men to assist Idanyi, of whom many were slain, the Dahomians also suffering a great loss.

"It is supposed that there are four hundred deserters from the Dahomy army, of the Egba and Yoruba tribes, hidden in the bush about Idanyi and Imeko: some have been found by the Imeko people and brought in to Imeko.

"The Dahomian army, in returning, sent a message to Iketu, saying that they may be expected back to destroy Iketu."

The Rev. H. Townsend makes use of this little periodical to influence, in the right direction, both the natives the foreign residents in Lagos, Abbeokuta, and the Yoruba country. Addressing the latter he says—

"It is to be feared that the mercantile community will suffer much loss from the actual warfare now going on in some parts of the country and threatened war in other parts, as a great stoppage to trade will be likely to result from it, except in war material. The commercial community are deeply affected by it, and it would be much to their interest to stop these wars and war alarms, and to establish peace between the various tribes and townships of this country.

"The annual alarm of a Dahomy invasion is a standing infliction upon the people of Abbeokuta which, for the time, puts a stop to commerce and other lawful industry. The reports that cause the alarm cannot be treated with contempt. The following reasons will make this apparent. The farming population are scattered over a large tract of country of sixty miles in length and probably thirty miles in breadth; the trading community are extended over the country from Lagos on the south, to Illorin on the north-east of this. It will be apparent, therefore, that a population thus scattered in lawful occupations cannot be gathered together at a short notice in any number sufficient for the defence of the town.

"The Dahomy force is formidable, as it is guided by one head, and in part previously trained to the use of arms. They are remarkable for the cautious and subtle manner in which they approach the place they intend to attack, if possible to take the people before they are aware of their approach.

"The desire of the Dahomians to attack Abbeokuta is a well-known fact, for yearly presents are made to the Yoruba chiefs to buy their assistance or neutrality. The Dahomy alarm was increased this year by the Ibadan people sending a strong party across the Ogun River and another to the Abbeokuta and Ijaye Road, thus cutting them off from their friends at Ijaye. With threatened invasion from the Dahomians, and the suspicious conduct on the

RECENT INTELLIGENCE.

part of the chiefs at Oyo and Ibadan, it cannot be expected that lawful commerce and industry will go on uninterruptedly.

"It is clear that unless the foreign residents, and merchants especially, are content to remain passive spectators of whatever wars mere jealousy or covetousness among the native chiefs may bring about, they must do something by which their influence may be felt and their voice heard for good in the country.

"One mode of putting some stop to these evils is, in brief, that of Europeans presenting themselves as an united body to the chiefs by the frequent interchange of messages, and by the judicious use of presents; with the view of obtaining a name and influence to be used towards suppressing the wars of the country, and towards the removal of certain restrictions on commerce, which hinder the proper development of trade and the true wealth of the country. The prosperity of the foreign residents in their commercial pursuits will depend upon the advance of right principles and honest pursuits among the natives; and their improvement in these respects will much depend upon efforts put forth by the foreign residents on the coast to produce it."

NORTH INDIA.

The state and prospects of the Mission, newly established at Lucknow, will be seen from the following extracts from a letter of the Rev. J. P. Mengé dated October 14th last—

"*Preaching the Gospel.*—This I have always considered the chief duty of a Missionary, and accordingly, from the time that I arrived in India, in 1840. I have always endeavoured to act accordingly. Whatever other duties I had to attend to (and they were many, for a number of years, in Gorruckpore), I never neglected preaching publicly, to Hindus and Mohammedans, the Gospel of life. Now, I can truly say, that neither in Gorruckpore where I spent many years—neither in Jaunpore, nor Benares, which station I often visited — have I been able to collect, day after day, so many in a very short time to listen to the Gospel, as I have done in Lucknow. I have met with but few instances of opposition and real hatred; and on questioning such closely, I generally found that it was on account of some grievance, of which they imagined that they had reason to complain against the Government, they were enraged. Some Mohammedans, of course, expressed themselves strongly, but not bitterly, against the incarnation of Jesus Christ as the Son of God and the Saviour of the world, and generally allowed me to explain this truth in accordance with the Gospel without becoming angry.

"*Visiting natives in their houses.*—A number of the more respectable natives cannot be reached by the public ministration of the Gospel in the streets and thoroughfares of the city, as they do not stop to listen, if they should happen to pass by where the Missionary is engaged in preaching. They therefore must be visited in their own houses, if we wish them to become acquainted with the truths of the Bible; and accordingly I have made it a point to visit as many as I conveniently could during the past year. I have called, among others, on the brother of the ex-king of Oude, several princes and nawabs, Rajah Mann Singh, the Maharajah of Bulrampore, the Rajah of Kupurthala, when on a visit here, the Rajah of Amethi, several pundits, several respectable native doctors, the Mufti of the Shiahs, the Mufti of the Sunnies,

RECENT INTELLIGENCE.

and a few other molwees. I was generally received with great politeness, sometimes even with cordiality, by a few with fear, and by one or two with dislike. Some listened with pleasure, some with great indifference, and some with astonishment. Some argued with bitterness, some with great caution, some with great carelessness, and a few with candour. What the result of these visits may be it is not for me to say, though I believe God, in his infinite mercy, has opened a door of usefulness in a most wonderful manner, and that He alone knows when the sowing and when the reaping-time is to be. Still it is a good sign that several of those whom I visited have returned my visit.

"*Receiving visits in my house.*—The Maharajah of Bulrampore, the Rajah of Kupurthala, the Rajah of Amethi, several nawabs, and a few talookdars, some molwees, a few Brahmins, and several native doctors, have visited me. Some appeared to be much gratified by their visit; others only thought of becoming acquainted with me for purposes of their own. About twenty Hindus and Mohammedans have expressed a wish to embrace Christianity; but as I discovered that their motives were interested, I of course told them that it was nothing but deceit on their part to ask for baptism, and that it would be very wrong in me to comply with their request. I, however, have baptized a respectable Mohammedan, formerly a native doctor in the late Honourable East-India Company's service, and now a Zemindar in the district of Hurdui, about eighty miles from Lucknow. He visited me very frequently, and told me that for many years past he had been persuaded that Mohammedanism was not true, but that he had not been able to overcome the difficulty of believing that Jesus Christ is the Son of God. We read the sacred Scriptures together, and I explained to him the nature of the plan of salvation, and we often prayed together; and on the 3d of July I baptized him. He has promised to do all in his power to make known the Gospel to his relatives and dependants."

RETURN HOME OF MISSIONARIES.

West Africa.—Miss Sass and Mrs. Hamilton left Sierra Leone on Feb. 20th, and arrived in London on March 17th.

North India.—The Rev. Dr. Trumpp arrived in London from Peshawur on March 27th.

South India.—The Rev. R. H. and Mrs. Vickers left Madras on Feb. 14th, and arrived in London on March 19th.

China.—The Rev. M. and Mrs. Fearnley arrived in London from Fuhchau on March 13th.

DEPARTURE OF MISSIONARIES.

Niger.—The Rev. J. C. Taylor embarked at Liverpool in the "Cleopatra" steamer on March 24th, for Sierra Leone and the Niger (p. 108).

Turkey—The Rev. R. H. and Mrs. Weakley have left London on their way to Constantinople (p. 108).

South India.—The Rev. J. and Mrs. Bilderbeck left Southampton in the steamer of the 4th April, for Madras (p. 108).

ORDINATION OF MISSIONARIES.

On Sunday, March 4th, the Archbishop of Canterbury admitted to deacons orders the Rev. J. M. Spechly, B.A., the Rev. L. S. Tugwell, and the Rev. J. B. Wheeler (p. 68)

RECENT INTELLIGENCE.

SIXTY-FIRST ANNIVERSARY OF THE SOCIETY.

THE Annual Sermon was preached before the Society on Monday evening, the 30th of April, at the parish church of St. Bride, Fleet Street, by the Rev. Henry Venn Elliott, M.A., Incumbent of St. Mary's, Brighton, from Philippians i. 12. Collection, 208*l*. 11*s*. 6*d.*

The Annual Meeting was held next day, Tuesday, May 1st, at Exeter Hall. The Chair was taken at ten o'clock by the Right Hon. the President. Prayer having been offered, and a portion of Scripture read, the Meeting was addressed by the Chairman. An abstract of the Report was then read by the Rev. John Venn, and Resolutions were adopted as follows—

Movers and Seconders.

The Lord Bishop of Winchester, V.P., and Abel Smith, Esq., M.P.—Lieutenant-Colonel Herbert Edwardes, C.B., and the Rev. C. F. Cobb, Missionary from Benares—The Very Rev. the Dean of Carlisle, V.P., and the Rev. Emilius Bayley, Rector of St. George's, Bloomsbury.

Resolutions.

—That the Report, of which an abstract has now been read, be received, and printed under the direction of the Committee; that the thanks of this Meeting be given to the Rev. H. V. Elliott for his sermon before the Society last evening; to his Grace the Vice-Patron; to the Right Hon. the President and the Vice-Presidents; and to al those friends who, during the past year, have exerted themselves in its behalf; and that the following gentlemen be appointed the Committee for the ensuing year, with power to fill up vacancies—

Major-Gen. R. Alexander.	John Gurney Hoare, Esq.	Colonel Smith.
John Ballance, Esq.	Lt.-Col. Hughes.	Henry Smith, Esq.
John Bridges, Esq.	John Labouchere, Esq.	John Sperling, Esq.
Lt.-Col. Caldwell.	Arthur Lang, Esq.	Hudleston Stokes, Esq.
Major-Gen. Clarke.	Colonel Lavie.	J. M. Strachan, Esq.
William Dugmore, Esq.	William Lavie, Esq.	James Stuart, Esq.
James Farish, Esq.	P. F. O'Malley, Esq. Q.C.	J. Fryer Thomas, Esq.
Sydney Gedge, Esq.	Robert Prance, Esq.	H. Carre Tucker, Esq.

—That this Meeting desires humbly to acknowledge the duty of this nation to use increased efforts for imparting to India the blessings of Christianity. They rejoice in the labours of all Protestant Societies engaged in the benevolent design of propagating the Gospel of Jesus Christ, and they trust that the Indian Government will fulfil the obligations solemnly recognised by the Imperial Parliament, of promoting "the interest and happiness of the native inhabitants of the British dominions in India," by the adoption of "such measures as may tend to the introduction among them of religious and moral improvement."

—That this Meeting desires to express its humble thanks to Almighty God for the success which He has granted to the Society's endeavours in many lands to establish a Native ministry and Training Institutions for Scriptural vernacular education; and they desire to acknowledge their sole dependence upon the grace of the Holy Spirit to make these a sure foundation of a Native-Christian church, and the superstructure an holy temple in the Lord.

RECENT INTELLIGENCE.

—That while this Meeting deeply sympathizes with the Sierra-Leone Mission in its late bereavements, and while they bow with submission to the Divine will, they humbly rejoice in its spiritual successes as a proof of the Divine favour, and as the result of God's blessing on the preaching of a full and free Gospel, and on the spirit of self-sacrifice in the preachers which have ever characterized, and they trust ever will characterize, this and every other Mission of the Society.

The last Resolution was intended to have been moved by the Lord Bishop of Sierra Leone, V.P., and seconded by the Rev. Canon Miller, but, from want of time, was put to the Meeting with the third Resolution, and carried.

FINANCES.

The financial statement presented to the Meeting was as follows—

General Fund—Total Ordinary Income, including Fund for Disabled Missionaries, &c.	£132,052	5 0
Special Fund for India, for year ending March 31, 1860	13,576	16 4
Total received at Home	£145,629	1 4
Total Ordinary Expenditure on General Fund	£128,134	3 6
India Fund	9448	1 9
	£137,582	5 3

Special Fund for India—Balance from last year	£45,447	3 6		
Receipts of the year as above,	13,576	16 4		
			59,023	19 10
Expenditure	9448	1 0		
On account of last year	3500	0 0		
(See *Report for* 1858-59, p.12.)			12,948	1 9
Balance			£46,075	18 1

The Local Funds raised in the Missions, and expended there upon the operations of the Society, but independently of the General Fund, are not included in the foregoing statement. The amount exceeds 18,000*l.*; making a grand total from all sources of 163,629*l.* 1*s.* 4*d.*

The *ordinary* income of the Society this year, mainly owing to large legacies, is the highest which has ever been received, exceeding last year's by 0094*l.*, and exceeding even that of 1858 by 1286*l.*, though it included a special donation of 10,000*l.*

CONCLUSION OF REPORT.

Your Committee trust that this review of the past year's operations will confirm the conviction which has been expressed on many previous occasions, that a great and blessed advance of the kingdom of Christ is at hand, in all lands.

. . . .

Under these solemn impressions your Committee invite your attention to the fact, that this Society was never so well prepared as now to meet coming events. Never before could they announce that the problem of a Native Ministry in India was solved. Never before could they announce that the New-Zealand Native Church had its indigenous Ministry. Never before could they announce that a Mission had been opened, of great promise, solely by

RECENT INTELLIGENCE.

native agency, as in the case of the Niger, where European agency will only supplement a native pioneering Ministry. Never before could your Committee speak with the same confidence of the efficiency of their Normal Training Schools, by which the Society is prepared to meet even a sudden expansion of the Native Church by the only element of stability—a sound Scriptural vernacular education; whilst they rejoice to add, that there are other Societies—such as the Christian Vernacular Education Society for India, and the Malta College for the Levant—prepared to strengthen and relieve this and all other Protestant Missionary Societies in the work of Christian education.

In these opening prospects of greatly increased responsibility, and of enlarged opportunities, your Committee have anxiously considered what could be done for the perfection of their machinery, and for the more effectual disposition of their means and agency, at home and abroad. But, in respect of fundamental principles, your Committee see no occasion for any deliberation. The Protestant and evangelical spirit which the founders of this Society infused, by the help of God, into its very constitution and framework, have stood the test of sixty years, and have received a blessing from the Lord, and have won the confidence of the Church of Christ, of which the present Report bears abundant evidence. Among these principles, your Committee will specially refer to the Missionary maxims—that the Lord will guide his own work by the leadings of a special providence: that the only solid foundation of a Mission is in the individual conversion of souls to Christ: that the Gospel of the grace of God is to be preached, in its fulness and in its distinctness, by the pioneer Missionary, and by the faithful Pastor of 10,000 converts, in the bazaar, under the shade of a tree, in the capacious Mission Church, in the Vernacular School, and in the Training College: that a preached Gospel is "the power of God" for the formation and the perfection of a Mission: that all other arrangements must give way to the fullest development of a preached Gospel: that the preacher of the Gospel is the true leader of a Mission till a spiritual Church is raised, and the external organization of constituted authorities becomes expedient: that then the Mission has accomplished its work, and this Society will be ready to withdraw its agency;—though, as in New Zealand, it may be difficult on both sides to break the relationships which spiritual principles have cemented and consecrated.

These principles, your Committee now transmit to their successors, uncompromised and unimpaired, to be the guiding star, in a shifting age, of every successive Committee of the Church Missionary Society.

The Bishop of Sierra Leone pronounced the Benediction. Collection 150*l.* 6*s.* 11*d.*

A meeting was held at Exeter Hall on the evening of the same day, the Most Noble the Marquis of Cholmondeley, V.P., in the Chair. Addresses were made by the Rev. J. Ridgeway, M.A., on "The past year;" by the Rev. E. Garbett, M.A., on "Jesuit Missions and their Lessons;" and by the Rev. C. B. Leupolt on the "Hand of God in the Indian Mutiny." Collection, 66*l.* 6*s.* 9*d.*

PROTESTANTISM IN TURKEY.

LORD STRATFORD DE REDCLIFFE, in presenting a petition to the House of Lords from the members of the Evangelical Alliance, made the following remarks—

RECENT INTELLIGENCE.

"He had accepted the duty of presenting this petition to that House, although it was one rather of general representation than of any specific complaint, in the hope that their lordships' attention might be turned to an important subject. Their lordships might not be aware of the extent to which Protestantism had of late progressed in the Turkish empire. There were two classes of Protestants, one composed of the subjects of foreign powers east of the Porte, under the special protection of their respective governments; the other, to which he especially alluded, was formed of the Sultan's own subjects, and had sprung up within the last half century or less, and had now attained a degree of importance and extension which was well worthy of notice. The origin of that class of Protestants might be traced, in the first instance, to the circulation of the Bible by the Bible Society; and in proportion as the inhabitants had felt the want of a purer Christianity, many individuals, respectable both from the simplicity and integrity of their lives, had been induced to leave their respective churches, and to rally round the standard of Protestantism, as upheld not only by those who belonged to the Church of England, but to other denominations. . . . Among the causes which had tended to its progress was the liberality of the reigning sovereign, who, notwithstanding his position, and the infirmities of his education, had, if not with an energetic, yet with a most benevolent mind, responded to the representations of Her Majesty's Government, and had, to some extent, removed the difficulties from the way of Protestants. Notwithstanding these encouragements, however, there were many difficulties still to be encountered, and he was himself a witness to many of them. Some arose from the sloth of his ministers, and some from other causes; and though his own generous heart, and a great view of the interests of his empire, had, to some extent, overcome them, still those who seceded to Protestantism were exposed to great persecution and danger, and it was most desirable that every effort should be made in this country, not only by private individuals, but by the Legislature, to support them. He believed that in giving that support they would not only be gratifying Her Majesty's subjects, but would render an additional service to the Sultan and his empire; for it was remarkable, that those who embraced Protestantism were distinguished by those virtues which generally accompanied a love of truth. Under these circumstances he trusted their lordships would be disposed to view with sympathy the great work which was going on in that country. . . . . The prayer of the petitioners was, that their lordships would sustain His Majesty's Government in their efforts to forward the progress of religious liberty in Turkey, and to protect the native Protestants in the exercise of their rights throughout the whole of the Ottoman empire.

"Lord WODEHOUSE, in reply, said he could assure his noble friend that Her Majesty's Government, without interfering internally with any of the arrangements of the Government of Turkey, were disposed to give every proper advice to the Sultan's Government which might ensure Protestants being placed in an equal position with all other sects. It was only prudent, however, in doing so, that the British Government should be careful not to pursue such a course as would prevent the achievement of those views which they might wish to carry out."

RECENT INTELLIGENCE.

A Petition from the Committee has been presented to the House of Lords by the Right Honourable the President, in support of the Duke of Marlborough's motion on the Bible in India. Up to Monday, June 25, the number of petitions presented on this subject from all parts of the United Kingdom had amounted to 1152.

NORTH INDIA.

In the Recent Intelligence for April we gave an extract from a letter of the Rev. J. Vaughan, in which he expressed the view he had formed of the state of feeling round Burdwan. That letter has been supplemented by another, dated March 22, 1860, somewhat modifying the sentiments he had before expressed, and at the same time bringing forward several points of much interest. It is as follows—

"I wrote my annual letter to the Committee whilst I was out preaching ; and in that letter I gave some account of our experience on that tour. I also ventured to express certain opinions as to the state of the people, with reference to the Gospel (*vide* Recent Intelligence in the April Number). When I wrote that letter we had not got further than some twenty or twenty-five miles from Burdwan. After that we went much higher up, nearly to Raneegunge. My subsequent experience did not materially affect the general character of the opinions I had expressed, but it did in some degree *modify* those opinions. I am glad, therefore, of this opportunity of adding a kind of postscript to that former letter; and this, taken with that, will give what I believe to be a fair and unbiassed representation of the state of things. All which my former communication said about the hopeful signs among the people, *i. e.* readiness to hear the Gospel, kindness to the preachers, an evident loosing of the bonds of idolatry, and a tendency to think that Hinduism will perish and Christianity prevail, besides, to a great extent, an undefined feeling of the truth of our holy religion,—all this was amply verified by our experience up to the period when I wrote. After moving, however, some ten or fifteen miles higher up, gradually the features which pleased us began to diminish, and less pleasing features began to develope themselves,—more indifference, more opposition, and more devotion to idolatry. We found, in short, that the higher we went—in other words, the further we receded from the Mission centre—Burdwan—the less interesting and hopeful did our work become. Up to, say, thirty miles from that station there were undoubted tokens of good, and great good: a leavening process had been manifestly going on amongst the people within that circuit, and very many individual cases came before us, of whom it might with truth be said, 'These persons are not far from the kingdom of heaven.' This fact has struck me forcibly in favour of settled Missionary centres.

"I think that itineration is indeed a glorious work, and every Missionary

RECENT INTELLIGENCE.

ought, if possible, to devote some portion of every year to it, for it, at least, does good to his own soul; but I also feel a strong conviction that Mission-establishments—of course when worked by devoted, earnest men—are very important: every such station is a standing witness for Christ to the villages around: it also presents a place to which any inquirer can betake himself for instruction and guidance; and, all things considered, I am quite sure that a well-worked Mission-establishment does tell very greatly upon the masses. Burdwan is an instance, but many more might be given. One point is of consequence with reference to such a station; it should be a large town, and a town of general resort for commercial and other purposes. Thus the light will inevitably disseminate itself into the region around. The Missionary may not be able himself to go very often from home, but a general knowledge of the truth gradually spreads, and spreads through the means of the people themselves. How many persons we met, many miles from Burdwan, who exclaimed, 'Oh, we know these things quite well; we have often heard the Sahib preach in the bazaars at Burdwan.' Thus they come to such a central place to market or on business, they hear the Gospel, they listen to disputes on religion, and they carry home to their villages a report, of what they have heard; and it really is wonderful (we saw several instances) how much of Christian knowledge thus gets into a village where no Missionary has ever set his foot.

"Beyond the point specified, we found, as stated, the features of hope were in a decreasing ratio. One of the last places I visited was the least hopeful of all. I began to preach by the side of a Siva temple. Presently crowds of Brahmins came together, and the impress of Satan seemed to rest on their countenances. They first tried to argue, but not succeeding in this, they began to abuse and blaspheme. Some of the elder Barbmins stamped with rage, and almost foamed at the mouth. Still I went on, and was enabled to keep calm. Then they got up deafening shouts of 'Hori bol! hori bol!' They hoped I would retire, but I did not; then they tried to drive the people away, but the people were loth to give up the fun; next they dragged an idiot before me, and pushed him forth to make hideous grimaces; next a Brahmin snatched a tract, and tore it to pieces. Such was the scene in this village, very different to the picture sent in my former letter. It truly seemed like casting pearls before swine to stand so long, but yet, I thought, it is no wonder they are so swinish, and do not value the pearls, for perhaps they have never seen them before. It turned out, however, that, several years ago, some Missionary had visited that same spot. This I learned in the following way— During the whole of that scene of confusion I observed one man, a goldsmith, standing at my side, perfectly silent: he never took his eyes off me, and appeared to be drinking in every word. When I finished, he came up to me and whispered, 'Sahib, will you please give me a book? Some years ago a Sahib came and preached, as you have done to-day: he gave me a little book: that I read, and after reading it I could no longer worship the idols. Sahib, I am not Hindu; I never go to the temple, but I worship and pray to the one true God in my own house as well as I can; but I dare not tell the people, for they would all persecute me. This was cheering; and, I thought, who knows but the Lord has reserved to Himself many such hidden ones in the villages of Bengal who refuse to bow the knee to Baal?"

RECENT INTELLIGENCE.

THE SWINGING FESTIVAL.

The following account of the manner in which this barbarous custom is gradually dying out, is taken from *Allen's Indian Mail*, being the substance of a Minute by the Lieutenant-Governor of Bengal. Surely this state of things would make the interference of Government for its suppression easy and acceptable, rather than, as it is said, "inexpedient and unnecessary."

"In several important districts the practice has already fallen into desuetude. In Behar it only occurs at long intervals, when a number of Bengalees have assembled near large towns at the time of the Pooja. In the Tirhoot and Shahabad districts it is quite unknown; and, throughout that division, its entire suppression may easily be effected by judicious conduct on the part of the police. In the Bhagulpore division it occasionally takes place, the swingers being men of a low caste, or rather of no caste at all, and exhibiting themselves as a means of gain, and not from any religious motives. In Assam, Arracan, Darjeeling, and Cachar, no such cruel exhibitions are either tolerated or attempted. Though existing in the Rajshahye division, it does not prevail to any great extent, and the Commissioner expresses a doubt as to the effect upon the spectators being more demoralizing than 'many other constantly-recurring sights which accompany Hindu festivals, such, for instance, as the Hoolee.' In the Nuddea division the custom is still very generally observed; but, according to Mr. Reid, it is nothing more than a huge sham; 'the swingers, for the most part, being suspended, not by the skin, but by cloths passing under their arms and loins. Even where the skin is pierced, and canes passed through it, the swingers are suspended by hooks passed through the latter.' The swinging, besides, is entirely a voluntary act, the motive being usually the prospect of earning one or two rupees, and perhaps a small quantity of sweetmeats. There are instances, however, of its being performed in fulfilment of a vow. Throughout the Burdwan division the exhibition is decidedly popular, though the Commissioner, like Mr. Reid, declares it to be a 'mere make-believe.' The performer, he says, being first drugged to a state of insensibility, the skin of the back and shoulders is pulled up from the flesh of the body, and the hook passed through the cuticle. 'A strong cloth is then passed round the chest and body, and over the loop of the hook. The man is thus suspended and swings,' the whole of his weight supported by the cloth or band, which passes under his chest. Mr. Young does not consider the swinging as so demoralizing as the filthy pictures and images which are exhibited at all Hindu festivals, and recommends that 'its suppression should be left to the spread of education, and to the feelings and wishes of the better classes of the natives themselves.' Much the same opinion appears to be entertained by the Commissioners of the Dacca and Chittagong divisions, but not by Mr. Cockburn, the Commissioner of the Cuttack division.

"'The practice,' he says, 'is undoubtedly a cruel one, and the result of the grossest ignorance or cupidity. The parties who consent to have hooks fastened into their backs, and are raised up to a considerable height above the ground, and swing round until exhausted with pain and fatigue, are usually, he understands, of two classes, viz. those who have made a vow to swing if they get some good or blessing previously denied, and those who take a part in the spectacle for the sake of the pice and cowries distributed by the spectators.

RECENT INTELLIGENCE.

Nor is it less certain that the practice is a demoralizing one, and how, in truth, could it be otherwise, when large crowds of people, of both sexes, young and old, assemble for the express purpose of witnessing their unhappy, wretched fellow-beings suffer, applauding their conduct, and encouraging them to further endurance? There are other practices,' Mr. Cockburn observes, ' of a similar barbarous kind, which should not be lost sight of in considering measures for putting an end to the swinging. Two years ago, for example, he is informed that at one place in this division, in addition to the swinging, no less than 418 fire-trenches were prepared, and, at a given signal, fires were lighted, and as many men deliberately walked over the lighted charcoal. Besides which, there were several men with hooks in their tongues, one of whom appeared to suffer intense pain, while the scene altogether was most revolting, and seemed more like hell than earth.' "

DISMISSAL OF MISSIONARIES.

On Friday, June 8, a dismissal of Missionaries took place at the Children's Home, Highbury, as below—

North India—The Rev. R. B. Batty, M.A., for the Punjab; and the Rev J. B. Wheeler for Jubbulpore.

South India—The Rev. R. R. Meadows, M.A., and Mrs. Meadows, returning to North Tinnevelly; the Rev. Walter Edmonds and Mrs. Edmonds, and the Rev. W. Ellington and Mrs. Ellington, proceeding to Telugu; the Rev. M. Speechly; and Miss Meredith.

New Zealand—The Rev. J. Wycliffe Gedge, B.A., and Mrs. Gedge proceeding to Otaki.

North-West America—The Rev. L. S. Tugwell and Mrs. Tugwell, proceeding to Fort Simpson, on the Pacific.

The instructions were delivered by the Rev. H. Venn; and having been replied to, the Missionaries were addressed by the Rev. T. D. Bernard, and the Rev. W. B. Mackenzie; and then commended to God's protection by the Rev. G. Lea, of Birmingham.*

RETURN HOME OF MISSIONARIES.

West Africa—The Rev. F. and Mrs. Bultmann arrived in London on June 12th from Sierra Leone.

North India—Lieut.-Colonel Martin arrived in London from Peshawur at the end of April. The Rev. J. and Mrs. Leighton left Calcutta on Feb. 1st, and arrived at Gravesend on June 4th.

South India—The Rev. J. and Mrs. Buncher left Madras on March 15th, and arrived in London on April 20th. The Rev. J. and Mrs. Whitchurch arrived in London, from the Cape of Good Hope, on May 26th.

DEPARTURE OF MISSIONARIES.

New Zealand—The Rev. B. K. Taylor embarked at Gravesend on board the "Persia," on May 2, for New Zealand. The Rev. R. R. and Mrs. Meadows, with Miss Meredith, embarked on board the "Nile," on June 12, for Madras. Mr. and Mrs. S. Coles sailed at Southampton in the steamer of May 20, for Ceylon.

---

* For further particulars see the Monthly Selections from Proceedings of Committee, No. VI.

RECENT INTELLIGENCE.

THE BIBLE IN INDIAN SCHOOLS.

WE place on record the Petition presented to the House of Lords, on Monday, July 2, by the Right Honourable the President.

"To THE LORDS SPIRITUAL AND TEMPORAL IN PARLIAMENT ASSEMBLED—

"The Petition of the Committee of the Church Missionary Society for Africa and the East—

"HUMBLY SHEWETH,

"1. That your Petitioners are members of the Committee of the Church Missionary Society, which Society has been engaged for more than fifty years in promoting the moral and religious improvement of Her Majesty's native subjects in India, for which object they have sent out a large body of European Teachers, of whom 116 are now employed in the work: that they have erected numerous Schools and Churches; and that the whole cost of these operations has amounted to one million one hundred and thirty-four thousand pounds.

"2. That your Petitioners gratefully acknowledge the civil protection received by their Missionaries and other Teachers during all this period, as well whilst the Government of India was held in trust for Her Majesty by the Honourable East-India Company, as since the Government has been under the direct administration of the Crown.

"3. That the special object of the Church Missionary Society is the conversion of the Natives to the Christian faith, and the education of their Christian children; and that therefore the education of the masses of heathen and Mohammedan youth is only a secondary object, and can never be carried out to any considerable extent by the agency of this Society: and your Petitioners believe that the same may be said of all other Missionary Societies.

"4. That the moral elevation of the mass of the population of India is a work regarded as obligatory upon Government by the Act 53rd George III. cap. 155. sect. 43., which declares that it is 'the duty of this country to promote the interest and happiness of the native inhabitants of the British dominions in India; and such measures ought to be adopted as may tend to the introduction among them of useful knowledge, and of religious and moral improvement.'

"5. That the Indian Government has acknowledged the duty and obligation of undertaking this work by means of education in the 'Education' Despatch, July 18th, 1854, which declares—'Among many subjects of importance, none can have a stronger claim to our attention than that of education. It is one of our most sacred duties to be the means, as far as in us lies, of conferring upon the natives of India those vast moral and material blessings which flow from the general diffusion of useful knowledge, and which India may, under Providence, derive from her connexion with England.'

"6. That your Petitioners regard it as necessarily involved in the parliamentary obligation thus resting upon Her Majesty's Government, that the Bible should be introduced into the system of education in all Government Schools and Colleges, as the only standard of moral truth for all mankind, and the source of those Christian principles upon which Her Majesty's Government is conducted.

RECENT INTELLIGENCE.

"7. That your Petitioners must further state their conviction of the extreme danger, to the welfare of India, and to the stability of Her Majesty's Government in that empire, of educating the masses of India upon a system which excludes the Word of God; inasmuch as such an education undermines their native religions, and dissolves the social links by which native society has been hitherto held together: while it is powerless to supply any other means by which India can be socially regenerated, or cemented to the Crown of Great Britain.

"Your Petitioners therefore pray, that provision may be made that instruction in the Holy Scriptures may, under suitable arrangements, be permitted to form part of the system of education afforded in the Government Colleges and Schools of India.

"And your Petitioners will ever pray, &c."

At the meeting of the General Committee, July 9, the Secretaries reported that the Right Honourable the President had presented the above Petition to the House of Lords on July 2, in support of the Resolution of the Duke of Marlborough, Vice-President, for the removal of the authoritative exclusion of the Bible from the course of instruction afforded in the Government Schools and Colleges in India:

That the Earl of Shaftesbury, Vice-President, while suggesting the postponement of the Resolution, had expressed his entire concurrence in the principle and in the substance of the Resolution of the Duke, and that it was his belief that it could be carried into effect in India with perfect safety, and with great advantage:

That on the same day, the Duke of Marlborough had moved the adoption of his Resolution, in a most able and forcible speech:

That the Duke's Resolution was met by an immediate moving of the previous question, which was so promptly put and carried as to prevent several other Peers from supporting the Resolution:

That on Friday, the 6th, the Bishop of Oxford and the Earl of Galloway, Vice-Presidents, had expressed their concurrence in the Duke's Resolution.

The Secretaries further stated that the number of Petitions presented to the House of Lords from England, Scotland, Wales, and Ireland, for the removal of the interdict on the Bible, had been more than 1950.*

RESOLVED—

"1. That this Committee are thankful to record the fact that no less than 1950 Petitions have been presented to the House of Lords from all parts of the United Kingdom, in favour of the removal of the restriction upon the Bible in Government Schools in India; that these Petitions were sent up on a very short notice of the Duke's intended Motion, without organized efforts to procure them, and under many other disadvantages.

"2. That the thanks of this Society are due to His Grace the Duke of Marlborough for his able, Christian, and determined advocacy of the cause of Bible instruction; and that His Grace be respectfully requested to print his speech, and to allow this Society to aid in its general circulation.

"3. That the thanks of this Society are also due to the Right Honourable the President, and the Vice-Presidents, who on this occasion have aided the cause in their places in Parliament.

---

* The entire number, up to the date of our going to press (July 24), was 2041.

RECENT INTELLIGENCE.

"4. That this Committee regard the recent expression of public opinion and the proceedings in the House of Lords as having greatly helped forward the cause of Bible Education in India; and being fully persuaded that the removal of the authoritative restriction which now exists will be a safe as well as a Christian policy, they cherish the hope that Her Majesty's Ministers may see it right to provide for such removal before the next Session of Parliament; for should this hope be disappointed, the object, they are persuaded, will be demanded by a far more general and powerful expression of opinion than on the present occasion."

FINANCES OF THE SOCIETY.

The receipts of the Society from Associations for the three first months of the financial year—viz., for April, May, and June—show a falling off of the sum of £1603, as compared with the receipts for the three corresponding months of 1859.

The Committee beg to call the attention of the friends of the Society, and of Country Associations, to this statement; and to express a hope, that though the inclement spring may have affected the usual channels of supply, some efforts may be made to make up the deficiency.

WEST AFRICA—RIOT IN THE TIMNEH COUNTRY.

(*From the African, June 26th.*)

Capture and Plunder of Magbeli, and Sacking of the Mission Premises.

On Thursday, the 14th of June, a party of Kossohs, employed as mercenaries by the Ro Yonni people in their war with the Masimmerahs, suddenly came upon the town of Magbeli, about half-past five in the morning. Most of the male population were absent, and only the old and infirm were in the town. The Pa Suba was at Ro Masettleh, a town on the Port-Lokkoh road. The attacking party numbered about 300 or 400 men, and for the most part were armed only with cutlasses. They divided themselves into small companies, and assigned different parts of the town to each division. We regret to say that the barbarous people showed no regard to the persons or property of the Missionary party. After having forcibly entered the dwelling-house, they seized the Rev. J. S. Wiltshire and his wife, and stripped them of nearly all the clothing they had on. One man aimed a blow with his cutlass at Mr. Wiltshire, which happily fell short. Another pointed his gun at his breast, and demanded his coat, which was of course given up. Mrs. Wiltshire was then seized, tied, and dragged to the water-side, and then forced into a canoe, with the intention to carry her across the river. But the canoe being too crowded with prisoners, and not having been caulked, was swamped, and sank immediately on attempting to shove off from the beach: all, however, came safely ashore. Most happily and providentially, just at this juncture there was heard a sound of musket-shots in the distance. This proceeded from a few Sierra-Leone traders and others, from Ro Gbenting, who were coming to the rescue. The Kossohs at once left their prisoners and retreated, but not without some loss on their side. Mrs. Wiltshire was left tied in the bush, and, after some moments of anxious suspense, was rescued from her perilous condition by a Sierra-Leone trader. In the mean time, other parts of the town had been given up to plunder. Mr. Thensted, an English trader, was robbed of all his goods, and had his shirt stripped from his back, but happily escaped from his captors,

RECENT INTELLIGENCE.

and from further personal indignities. One of the Mission boatmen who was ill at the time of the attack, was cut across the belly and killed. A school boy, about eight years old, refusing to leave the Mission yard and go with the Kossohs, was killed on the spot, his head being severed from his body. Another of the school children (a little girl) was drowned, along with many others, in a canoe, which, from being too much crowded with prisoners, filled and went down with all on board. The precise number is not known. The most painful feature in this whole affair has been the attack upon the Mission party. Hitherto, both sides in this civil war had agreed, it is said, to leave the Mission unharmed. But in the hour of excitement, with hopes of great booty, and possibly maddened by drink, it is not possible to restrain the ungovernable passions that rage in the breast of a savage; and of all the tribes in our neighbourhood, the Kossohs enjoy an unenviable notoriety for ferocity, and the most unmitigated barbarism. On this occasion each one seems to have acted for himself. The sole object was plunder. Had there been any thing like a plan, and the least concert as to their operations, we believe most of the people in Magbeli would have been made slaves of, and carried into the interior. As it is, many of our traders have been caught and taken away. For the present, but we hope only for the present, an end has been put to the operations of the Church Missionary Society among these treacherous heathen. We are not at all discouraged. Difficulties and dangers will but be spurs and incitements to that Society to urge forward its work of faith and labour of love. It may be that greater security in future will result from the recent act of violence.

WESTERN INDIA.
(From the Bombay Guardian.)

Our readers will not have forgotten the decision of the Government with regard to the right of native Christians to take water from the public tanks.(p. 1.) The Hindu inhabitants of Ahmednuggur, or a portion of them, petitioned Government to deny this right; but Government affirmed this right; and expressed astonishment at the misconception that had led the petitioners to suppose for a moment that Government would lend itself to such an unworthy and unjust attempt. Though nothing could be more explicit than the answer of Government, yet the inhabitants of Ahmednuggur have continued to send in petitions on the subject. They lately sent a petition praying that some of the tanks might be set apart for the Christians, and the remainder left for the exclusive use of the rest of the community. In other words, they wished to have Christians treated as outcasts; not merely so treated by Hindus, but by a Christian Government. Mr. Fraser Tytler, reporting on the petition, points out that it is easy for the petitioners, in Ahmednuggur, where there are many tanks to give up a few; but in other places this cannot be done; and that if Christians are denied *in part* their legal rights in Ahmednuggur, they will be denied them *in toto* in the villages.

The following is the decision of Government—

"RESOLUTION—The Right Honourable the Governor in Council fully concurs in the views stated in the Report by the Magistrate of Ahmednuggur, and directs that the Petitioners be informed that the Government will never admit that a tank is polluted by being used by Christian converts. His Lordship in Council sees no reason for any modification of his previous orders, and the intimation now issued must be regarded as final."

RECENT INTELLIGENCE.

THE GOVERNMENT OF INDIA AND CHRISTIANITY.

THE Governor-General of India, Lord Canning, has thought it expedient to publish, in the form of a despatch to the Secretary of State for India, signed by himself and two Members of Council, a reply to the pamphlet of this Society, No. VIII., on "The Effects of Government Orders on the Progress of Christianity in India." This despatch will require more extended notice elsewhere. Meanwhile we reprint a very temperate article from the *Calcutta Christian Intelligencer*, from which the views of our friends in India may be gathered. We regard Lord Canning's statement as a full vindication of the pamphlet to which it attempts to reply. It now appears that *an order* was issued, the precise terms of which were carefully concealed; but the inevitable *effects* of which were precisely those represented by our correspondents in India. Our correspondents have, moreover, correctly described the tenor of it *as communicated by the officer on whom devolved its official promulgation to those concerned* —

"We rejoice most truly that Lord Canning has come forward to explain his policy towards the 24th Regiment Punjab Infantry and its Christian converts and officers, by the publication, in the Indian papers, of his letter of June 18, 1860, to Sir Charles Wood.

"We had previously seen a good part of the correspondence referred to in it, between the Bishop and the military and other authorities on the subject of the alleged dealings of Government with that regiment; and, before we knew any thing of an intention to publish the explanation above referred to, had fully intended to state, in this present Number of the "Intelligencer," that Lord Canning and the Government had been, to all appearance, mistakenly and unjustly charged in the little C. M. S. pamphlet, reprinted in our last Number, as well as in some of the newspapers, with issuing an order forbidding Christian officers to have any religious intercourse with their Christian men, at least when the latter are natives.

"We felt sincere pleasure in having the opportunity to do this. And we can respectfully assure Lord Canning that we should be most truly glad and thankful to be enabled and allowed to place his views and proceedings in such matters before the more religious part of the community in the most correct form; and, further, to lend them any humble support in our power, when they may seem to us to be in accordance with scriptural principle, and the claims of religion on a Christian ruler. We doubt not that his lordship is too wise a statesman (whatever his own religious opinions may be) to be insensible to the advantage of having the religious part of the European public with him in the carrying out of his policy.

"For ourselves, we are but little to blame if we have mistaken the Governor-General's views and measures as touching on the diffusion of Christianity in this country. Disposed, both by political bias and Christian principle, to respect and to aid in upholding the constituted authorities, we made more than one attempt to put ourselves in the way of obtaining such information as might

RECENT INTELLIGENCE.

enable us to act on that disposition; but meeting with no encouragement, the only course was to draw back again, and be content to judge of motives and principles by public acts and other things gathered from the ordinary sources of intelligence. And we must confess, that, from a number of acts and facts—or supposed facts,—great and small, thus gathered, we were led to form a judgment far from favourable of Lord Canning's disposition to favour or encourage the spread of Christianity amongst the people of India; and hence have, perhaps, taken up and repeated some facts, without as much caution as if our previously-formed judgment had not rendered them to our mind *primâ facie* probable.

"The particular matter referred to, as we have said, in Lord Canning's letter under consideration, is the order issued by his lordship on being informed, in May 1859, of the spirit of inquiry, and of inclination to embrace Christianity, which had appeared in the 24th Punjab Regiment, and the account given of that order and its effects in the Church Missionary Society's pamphlet of March 1860.

"The order was (May 23, 1859), "It will be advisable to warn the officers commanding troops at Peshawur against using their authority in any way for the furtherance of conversion."

"Now this order, taken in the barest meaning of its naked terms, can hardly be objected to. No one—at least no Evangelical Protestant Missionary—wants any officer, civil or military, to use his authority in an official or professional way, to make men profess themselves Christians: we leave such practices to Romanists. But we cannot but think that the order, taken with its circumstances, might be fairly considered to extend much further in its application than its precise terms might seem to render necessary, *e.g.*

"1. It must have been known, that just before that order was issued, on May 20th, Lord Canning had seized upon a loose newspaper report of one of the officers of the corps in question, together with two or three civil officers and others, being simply present at the baptism of a few native converts in Umritsur, actually to call upon the Lieutenant-Governor of the Punjab to report upon the circumstance; and what was to be the result of this strange proceeding had not yet appeared. (*See* Occasional Papers, No. VIII., p. 8.)

"2. The mention of officers at all in the order was significant. There was no reference to them in the representation made by Major Hovenden to the Commander-in-Chief, nor in that of the C. in C. to the Governor General. Those representations simply stated that "a strong tendency to embrace Christianity had manifested itself amongst some of the men" of the 24th Regiment, who were "in the habit of going to the clergyman of the place to hear what he had to say;" that the other men of the corps were indifferent to the movement, and consequently that Major Hovenden, the officer in command, had "thought it better not to interfere in the matter." This was all. But upon it, Lord Canning (without expressing a word of satisfaction or even interest in the tendency to embrace Christianity) does not commend Major Hovenden's prudent and cautious conduct in the affair, which might have been a delicate but significant mode of conveying his sentiments, but volunteers what, we must say, appears to us a gratuitous warning to all officers in that quarter, "not to use their authority *in any way* for the furtherance of conversion." Lord Canning may probably regard this as carrying out a "perfect religious neutrality:" to us it appears to be dealing "a heavy blow and great discouragement" to the apparently spontaneous spread of Christianity

RECENT INTELLIGENCE.

just commencing in the regiment, and to any officer taking any interest in the matter. And taken in connexion with—

"3. The impression (correct or incorrect) which had gone abroad, of Lord Canning's hostility to the spreading of our faith amongst the natives, and with his Lordship's action just before taken respecting the baptisms at Umritsur, it must have been felt to be so by both officers and men. In fact, we know it was so felt, from letters of officers, written at the time, now before us, and from the statements of Missionaries that there was a sudden check given to the inquiries of the men: they felt that the Supreme Government was opposed to their becoming Christians. How could officers tell what Lord Canning would consider "the use of their authority *in any way?*" The course then being taken by his lordship seemed to indicate that simple presence at a native baptism would be so regarded, and still more so (it would naturally be inferred) would attendance at any religious meeting with the baptized.

"One of the first results was, that Major Hovenden (himself, we believe, by no means hostile to the religious movement in his corps), in communicating the Governor-General's order to the regiment, which he did verbally, added an order that the European officers were "not to attend any religious meetings with the men." This order, Lord Canning seems to think, may have been misunderstood by the officers, who probably considered it part of the Governor-General's order. We know of at least one who, in his distress of mind, and conscientious doubts, offered to resign his commission; and who, on that being declined, sought counsel of some friends of eminent station in the Church, as to the course he should pursue. And hence it is not much to be wondered at or blamed, that the Missionaries also considered it so, it being not all improbable *à priori*.* We must frankly state, that we can see little or nothing in the remarks of the Rev. Robert Clark that is not fairly justifiable on the almost unavoidable supposition that the account the Missionaries had received from officers, of the tenor of the Government order, was correct, and as stating "the effects of the order," though of course one cannot justify the transatlantic mode of emphasizing his statement adopted by the American Missionary, Mr. Loëwenthal.†

"Lord Canning tells us in his letter, para. 17, that the Bishop is to point out to Mr. Clark " the great harm which is done by believing and circulating such tales without inquiry." Very good; but we hope the Bishop will also point out, to more elevated persons, the great harm which is done by hasty interference with the personal religious freedom, freedom of conscience and action of public officers on the part of the Government, and also by incautious and ambiguous Government orders, which have the effect of disturbing the minds of conscientious men, and of discouraging sincere inquirers after the saving religion of Christ among the natives, in the public service and out of it.

"Opinions will perhaps differ as to which is the greater harm, that of bringing

---

* Not a word of disapprobation, as far as we have heard, is uttered of the officer who added to the Governor-General's order in such a way as to leave it to be regarded as part of it, or a fair inference from it, that "officers were not to attend any religious meetings with the men." Are we to suppose that his act is approved of, or that the inference is a legitimate one?

† The effects of the authoritative order have appeared again within the last few weeks. A Missionary, visiting the native Christians in this 24th Punjab Regiment, was forbidden by the officer in command of the party to hold divine service with them within the lines of the regiment, and they had in consequence to resort to some other place.

RECENT INTELLIGENCE.

some discredit on the Governor-General and the Government of India by statements of Government proceedings, partially but unintentionally incorrect, or that of putting a stop to some hundreds of men seeking after the way of salvation, to say nothing of the "heavy blow and great discouragement" dealt out to those natives in a similar state of mind over the whole of India, and the disheartening effect it must have on Missionaries and their helpers and friends in their benevolent labours, already trying and discouraging enough. With the Bible before us, we can feel no doubt as to which will appear the heavier harm when weighed in the balance of eternity.

"One word more. Lord Canning intimates, at the close of his letter, the probability that Government may issue some order laying down the course that officers must pursue in cases like that here referred to. Now we would earnestly and respectfully implore his lordship, and the Bishop, "in whose sound sense and moderate views" he justly feels great reliance, to beware of interfering in these matters, more than the most imperative state necessity demands. We implore them not to be applying remedies before there is an evil to call for them.* They cannot frame orders that will not open thrice as many questions as they will close. Government orders on matters of conscience are worse than out of place.

"We respectfully press upon the consideration of the Governor-General the advice of a wise man of ancient times—

"Refrain from these men, and let them alone; for if this counsel or this work be of men, it will come to nought: but if it be of God, you cannot overthrow it, lest haply you be found even to fight against God."—Acts v. 38, 39."

We have no additional intelligence of a decisive character from those of our Missions where insurrection and war are prevailing; but the unsettled aspect of affairs in Africa, New Zealand, China, and Syria, is still such as to demand the special sympathies and prayers of our supporters in behalf of our Missionaries, their converts, and the surrounding heathen.

The prayers of the friends of Missions are earnestly desired on behalf of the following Missionary Candidates for Ordination.

BY THE ARCHBISHOP OF CANTERBURY, ON SUNDAY, SEPTEMBER 23rd.
For Priests' Orders.

The Rev. John Bishop Wheeler . . . . } Students at the Institution.
The Rev. Arthur Evans Moule . . . . }

For Deacons' Orders.

Mr. John Barton, B.A. . . . . Christ's College, Cambridge.
Mr. Edward B. Puxley, formerly of Brasenose College, Oxford; afterwards H.M. 4th Light Dragoons.

Mr. R. B. Tonge, B.A. . . | Mr. Jonathan Simmons . . } Students
Mr. J. Jackson . . . . | Mr. Theodore Walters . . } at the
Mr. Nigel Honiss . . . | Mr. Jonathan Buckley Wood, } Institution.

BY THE BISHOP OF PETERBOROUGH.
For Priests' Orders.

The Rev. J. M. Speechly, B.A. . . . . St. John's College, Cambridge.

---

* Let it not be overlooked, that whatever "harm" has been done as yet has not originated from the native converts or inquirers, nor from the officers who have encouraged them, nor yet from the Missionaries, but from Government interferences, and Government orders. How much better had they been just let alone.

RECENT INTELLIGENCE.

INDIA—PROGRESS OF PROSELYTISM.

THE Christianisation of the Kols in the Chota Nagpore district is proceeding at a very rapid rate. Two thousand have already been baptized, or, rather, this was the number some six months ago. The number of those who have broken caste, and have applied for baptism, is also very large. Ninety were baptized in January last. A Missionary writes, that, in the neighbourhood of Ranchee, the Gospel is spreading like a fire in the jungle. As many as 800 villages have received the Gospel. So many Kols were pouring into the station from the jungle that three Missionaries were occupied all day in giving them instruction. The Lieutenant-governor of Bengal visited the district in January, and was greatly astonished at what he saw. His Secretary remarked to the Missionaries, "There was never seen such a sight in India as this." This referred to a gathering of about 2000 native Christians, at which he was present. From the province of Pachete, Kabreepunthees have presented themselves to the number of forty-six, out of eleven villages, asking instruction. They say that large bodies of this sect are ready to embrace Christianity. There are six Missionaries in the Chota-Nagpore field, Germans sent forth originally by Gossner. We see it stated, that in Lucknow and the surrounding villages eighty-nine natives have been baptized since the rebellion.—*Bombay Guardian.*

NORTH-WEST AMERICA.

Mr. Duncan has been on a visit to Victoria, Vancouver's Island. The "Victoria Gazette" of July 13, 1860, furnishes us with an account of a Missionary Meeting there, which will be read with much interest. There are not, it would seem, wanting in that, as in other colonies, men who look forward to the extinction of the native race, not only as the inevitable but as the most desirable result of British colonization, and who would seek to accomplish that result by fomenting intestine strife and bloodshed. We trust the kindlier feelings which prevailed at the meeting will still prevail, and that Britain's sons will impart to the children of the soil the best and brightest of their treasures—the everlasting Gospel.

"We publish (says the newspaper) the following proceedings of the meeting held on Tuesday evening last (July 10), for the purpose of ameliorating the condition of the Indians who are living in the vicinity of this town (Victoria).

"Before the meeting commenced, a large number of persons, collected upon the spacious stairs in front of the Collegiate School, were amused by a most novel and touching entertainment. A considerable number of Indians assembled by invitation, and, led by Mr. Duncan, sang very sweetly, 'There is a happy land, &c.,' and other hymns. The effect was most telling. To hear these poor heathen children time their voices to those melodies was quite enough to awake the sympathies and arouse the energies of the most indifferent amongst us. The singing being over, the audience quickly filled the room.

"Captain Prevost took the chair, and called upon the Rev. E. Cridge to open the meeting with prayer.

"Prayer having been offered up, the Chairman, in a few appropriate open-

RECENT INTELLIGENCE.

ing remarks, explained the object of the meeting, and introduced Mr. Duncan, Church Missionary, who accordingly came forward, and proposed the first Resolution—

"That in the opinion of this meeting the Indians are capable of civilization, and possess many qualities which, under proper training, would render them not only useful members of society, but also subjects of Christian virtue.

"Mr. Pemberton seconded the Resolution, which was carried unanimously.

"The Rev. J. Gammage, after some appropriate remarks, proposed the second Resolution—

"—That the presence of the Indians here entails a heavy responsibility upon the Christian public to set them an example worthy of their imitation, to repress their evil and call forth their good qualities, and to impart unto them that Gospel of which we are the favoured possessors.

"The Rev. A. C. Garrett next rose, and said—The resolution which he was called upon to second was one which carried its own recommendation in the weight of the sentiments which it contained. There was a voice in the bosom of each one present which spoke responsive to those sentiments. But unfortunately it often happened, that though this monitor within spoke, and spoke truthfully, yet his voice was unattended to. Hence it was that the editor of a public journal, in open defiance of this monitor, in his paper urges the public here to encourage enmity and strife, bloodshed and slaughter, among the Indian tribes, in order that we may be safe! Never let us on British soil, beneath the shelter of British laws, tolerate a policy so unworthy of Christianity—so unworthy of civilization—so unworthy of Britain and of England! Away with such a miserable sacrifice of rectitude, humanity, and honour, to a fancied but mistaken expediency! Even if we be not Christians, let us at least be men; and on the ground not only of Christianity, but of common manliness, let us hurl from us, with the most indignant contempt, principles so unworthy of Britons and of men. A simple illustration would show the responsibility which the presence of the Indians here, as a fact, entails upon us. Here the Rev. Speaker graphically described two travellers through a barren desert. When both are on the point of perishing with thirst and exposure to the piercing rays of a tropical sun, one, by the providence of God, discovers an oasis. Shall he recline beneath the grateful shade of the spreading palm, and quaff from the sparkling fountain refreshing draughts, and at the same time turn a deaf ear to the wail of anguish, which, waxing fainter and fainter, is wafted on the desert air, from his perishing fellow traveller? Nay! Shall he not only be indifferent to his sorrows, but, following the advice of the journalist alluded to, shall he consummate his ruin by adding to his miseries? Oh, if such a monster could anywhere be found, let all imaginable horrors be accumulated upon his guilty head!

"The Resolution was then put, and carried unanimously.

"The Rev. E. Cridge proposed the next Resolution. The Resolution says: 'Let a school be built.' Mr. Duncan has kindly promised to remain here for a period of time which he has not specified, to organize something for the benefit of the Indians resorting to Victoria. With him upon the ground, the Indians perishing for lack of knowledge, and the responsibility which the meeting had accepted, shall the school be built? If that could not be done, we must have a very poor opinion, either of our responsibility or our resources. He therefore entrusted the Resolution to the meeting with confidence—

"That as an effort to meet this responsibility, a room be built of sufficient

RECENT INTELLIGENCE.

size to serve as a temporary schoolroom and church, and that a Committee be appointed to make collections for that object; and that clergymen and gentlemen be requested to act as members of this Committee, with power to add to their number.

"Dr. Piers, of H.M.S. 'Satellite,' rose with pleasure to second the Resolution, which was put and carried unanimously.

"The Chairman then rose, and in the course of his very appropriate remarks, told a most touching anecdote, illustrative of the strong and patient affection of the Indian wives. Some years back, a party of Indians in a canoe were attacked by a body of northern Indians. All were killed, with the exception of one woman and her husband. The husband, though not dead, had been shot through the brain. The wife paddled alongside the gallant Captain's ship, the wounded man was taken on board, and attended to by the surgeon. But no Englishwoman could have exhibited greater devotion, and more patient affection, than were manifested by this Indian wife.

"A vote of thanks was warmly passed to the Chairman, proposed by the Rev. E. Cridge.

"The Doxology was sung, and the proceedings terminated."

The following extracts are taken from a later Number of the same journal—

"A feast was given on the quarter-deck of the 'Satellite' (July 19) to the chiefs of the Tsimshean and Nishkah tribes, twenty-eight in number, by Captain Provost. The principal dishes were rice and molasses, strong tea, and biscuit. The object was to make a return to the chiefs for an entertainment given by them to Mr. Duncan on the Naas River. They were shown over the ship, and were astonished by the weight of the sixty-eight-pounders, size of the guns, and quantity of powder in a cartridge. They were particularly struck with a portrait of the Queen, when told she was the great chief of the English nation. They expressed themselves as highly honoured at being invited on board a man-of-war, of which hitherto they have had so much dread, and gave Captain Provost some handsome beaver, ermine, and otter skins. We commend the gallant captain for his judicious endeavours to establish a good understanding with the Indians, and regret he is so soon to leave this station."

Notes on the Indians.

"The Indians are very much misunderstood by many. One misconception about them is, that they are a people living in a state of chaos, having no law or system to guide them. This mistake arose from our witnessing the disorder and riot prevailing amongst them while staying here. But we are to remember that nine-tenths of the Indians about us are not at home, and are therefore seen to great disadvantage; and those prominent vices to which they have become such victims, and with which they so disgust us, are not Indian vices, but white-men's vices.

"For national government, the Indians are divided into tribes. Thus the Tsimshean nation is divided into ten tribes, viz. the Keeshpokshlot, the Keenakangeak, the Keetsahclaha, the Keetwilgeeaut, the Heetandoh, the Heelootsah, the Keenahtohik, the Keetseek, the Kitlan, and the Keetwillukshebah. The latter tribe is now nearly extinct.

"Each of these names has a characteristic meaning: for instance, Keesh-

RECENT INTELLIGENCE.

pokahlot means 'the people among the elder-berries.' The name Tsimshean—with the people called by that name—means simply 'Indian.'

"Each tribe has from three to five chiefs, one of which is acknowledged head. Among the head chiefs of the various tribes one again takes preeminence.

"At feasts and in council, the chiefs are seated according to their rank.

"As an outward mark to distinguish the rank of a chief, a pole is erected in front of his house. The greater the chief the higher the pole. Some chiefs are great enough to require a pole over 100 feet high. The Indians are very jealous in regard to this distinction.

"The head chief of a tribe of Nishkah, or Naas-River Indians, foolishly attempted, about a year ago, to put up a stick which was higher than his rank would allow. The chief, whose head he would thus have stepped over, though an old and helpless man, found plenty to defend his right. A fight ensued, and the over-grasping chief was shot through the arm, which led him to shorten his stick.

"The Indians are subdivided, for the regulation of their social intercourse, under several crests, which are common to all the tribes. The crests are the whale, the porpoise, the eagle, the coon, the wolf, and the frog.

"In connexion with these crests, several very important points of Indian character and law are seen. The relationship existing between persons of the same crest is nearer than that between members of the same tribe, which is seen in this, that members of the same tribe may marry, but those of the same crest are not allowed to do so under any circumstances; that is, a whale may not marry a whale, but a whale may marry a frog, &c."

RETURN HOME OF MISSIONARIES.

North India.—The Rev. H. Stern left Calcutta on June 4th, and arrived in Germany on July 25th.

South India.—The Rev. H. Baker, jun., and Mrs. Baker, left Madras on June 22d, and arrived at Southampton on August 10th.

Ceylon.—Mr. J. Sorrell has arrived in England from Ceylon.

DEPARTURE OF MISSIONARIES.

Rev. W. J. and Mrs. Edmonds, and the Rev. W. and Mrs. Ellington, embarked at Gravesend in the "Renown" on July 11th, for Madras—The Rev. J. W. and Mrs. Gedge embarked at Gravesend in July, on board the "Thames City," for Wellington, New Zealand—The Rev. L. S. and Mrs. Tugwell left Southampton on June 16th, for America, *en route* for Fort Simpson (p. 204).

ORDINATIONS IN THE MISSIONS.

The following Missionaries and native pastors have been ordained to Deacons' and Priests' orders by the Bishops of Waiapu and Rupert's Land—

New Zealand, Feb. 17—Rev. Raniera Kawhia, to Deacons' orders.

March 4—Rev. Rota Waitoa, to Priests' orders.

May 6—Rev. Charles Baker, to Priests' orders.

June 3—Rev. Carl S. Volkner, to Deacons' orders.

North-West America, May 17—Rev. T. T. Smith, to Deacons' orders, at Red River.

July 11—Rev. T. H. Fleming, to Priests' orders, and the Rev. T. Vincent, to Deacons' orders, at Moose.

RECENT INTELLIGENCE.

WEST AFRICA.

INTELLIGENCE had been received at Sierra Leone, that Prince Alfred, in the "Euryalus," might be expected there on Monday, September 23. This had caused no little excitement among the African population. They have subscribed 100*l.* to procure an African gold chain to present to the Prince; and he is to be greeted by 1000 children from the different schools with the National Anthem. "I trust," adds Mr. Jones, "that the youthful mind of the Prince may be convinced of the successful results upon our colony of the benevolent efforts of Christian England."

CHINA.

The last mail has brought intelligence of an attack upon Shanghae by the insurgents, in which they were beaten back, chiefly by the assistance of a volunteer force of Europeans, among whom the French were conspicuous. Great alarm prevailed, and trade, and, we fear we must add, Missionary operations, were at a stand still. Since our last Number, further information has been received of the religious views of the Tae-ping-wangs. It is communicated in the following highly interesting letter from one of the Missionaries of the London Missionary Society. We regret that want of space compels us to omit a long citation from the books of the insurgents, illustrative of their opinion on the important subject of sin—

TO THE EDITOR OF THE "NORTH-CHINA HERALD."

"SIR,—In No. 520 of your paper, a few remarks were made on the revolutionary movement of the Tae-pings. It was stated that Hung Jen had arrived at Nankin, and was promoted to the rank of king; that his knowledge of Christianity, foreigners, and foreign affairs, must be far more extensive and correct than that of his relative the chief; that his position would enable him to do much towards correcting error and promoting the cause of truth; and that we should possibly find that some of the books which have been recently published evince a deeper insight into, and a more comprehensive view of, the true nature of the Christian religion. From certain documents which have since reached us, we find that this conjecture was well founded. A book, containing about fifty pages, and three or four proclamations, all composed and issued by the Kan Wong, prove not only that he himself is well instructed in Christian truth, but also that he is exerting his power and influence in making it known to others. Many truths which have been verbally taught from the commencement, though imperfectly understood, are explained and enforced by him in a remarkably lucid manner. The doctrinal errors into which we supposed the chief had fallen are met with bold and unequivocal positive statements of true doctrine. This fact is very encouraging to all who take an interest in the movement itself, and in the future moral and spiritual progress of this great people. We shall now give a few extracts on various points of interest, which will go far to show that the advent of Hung Jen in the insurgent camp augurs well to the insurgents' cause.

"We have one very interesting chapter on sin. The importance of a

RECENT INTELLIGENCE.

knowledge of sin, repentance, and reformation, on the part of man—God's willingness to forgive sin—the necessity of atonement—the vicarious sufferings of Christ—and freedom from sin being essential to true happiness, are all treated of in a way that would do honour to any Christian teacher, whether native or foreign. . . . .

"Then we have a very clear statement of the doctrine of innate depravity, which comes in direct opposition to the orthodox teachings of the Chinese. One of the first lessons a child has to learn in China, is that which teaches the inborn goodness of his nature. These men, however, tell him plainly, that he is born in sin; and must be 'born again,' ere he can enjoy true peace in this world, or eternal happiness in the world which is to come. Time will show which of these two doctrines—that which tends to inflate man with a false conceit of his own innate purity and importance, or that which discloses to him his real weakness and vileness—is best calculated to rouse this nation out of its moral and spiritual slumbers, and inspire it with new life.

"It was stated in the communication already referred to, that the insurgents do not seem to regard the Saviour as divine. In proof of this, a passage was quoted in which the title God is denied to Him. 'In heaven above and earth beneath, as well as among men, none can be considered greater than Jesus; and yet Jesus was not called God.' In the book now before us, the divinity of Christ is taught emphatically and explicitly. Take the following as a proof 'He thought it no robbery to be equal with God (Shangte). Should any one ask why it was necessary for Christ, being God, and therefore omnipotent, to be born and become man for the purpose of saving men, then let him know that if the Saviour had not become man, He would be merely a pure spirit. In that case, how could He spread his religion, establish an example, be nailed to the cross and shed his blood? Hence it was necessary that *he should* take a human body, that he might instruct men, and become their substitute. If there be sin, there must be punishment. Though it was the sinless Son of God that became a substitute, according to justice, punishment could not be avoided. This is sufficient to show that the law of heaven is just and impartial.'

"In this book much is said about the Holy Spirit. His divine nature is clearly taught; and his work in renewing and purifying the heart is largely dilated upon. Hung Jen seems to have a profound conviction of the deep and radical corruption of the human heart on the one hand, and the absolute necessity of divine power in its regeneration on the other. Faith he speaks of as the means by which the Holy Spirit is to be obtained. It is by faith, and not by birth, that a man becomes the regenerated child of God. But though his views of the divinity of Christ and the Holy Spirit are clear, we doubt whether his notion of the distinction of persons in the Godhead are quite clear from error. Those who have been extensively engaged in teaching the heathen, know how difficult it is to keep them from falling into the extreme of Tritheism on the one hand, or that of Sabellianism on the other. The doctrine is itself a profound mystery to our contracted reason, and must be received by faith. He endeavours, like many before him, to bring it down within the compass of reason, and explain it by arguments and analogy; and this it is (if indeed he be led astray) that has led him astray. On this point however, we would not be positive. It may be that the mistake lies in his way of explaining the doctrine, rather than in his own mind."

RECENT INTELLIGENCE.

"The observation of the Sabbath is inculcated as the day of the Lord. He speaks of it as a day of rest, when, with reverential hearts and pure bodies, the heavenly Father is to be worshipped. Thanks are to be given for all temporal mercies, as well as for the redeeming and saving virtue of the Elder Brother and Saviour.

"Húng Jen has a most exalted conception of the talents and piety of the Celestial King. He seems, moreover, to be a believer in his visions. We have no doubt but that Húng-siú-tsüen himself is a believer in the visions of 1837 and 1848, as revelations from God; and the impression left upon our minds, during our intercourse with the insurgents, was, that all the chiefs are perfectly convinced on this point. That the man had some sort of visions or dreams, corresponding to the account given of them, is highly probable; that he, being an oriental (and the majority of occidentals are not much more sane on these points), should believe in them as revelations from heaven, is very natural; and that his success, so far, should deepen his own convictions, as well as of those around him, in their reality, is what we might have expected. I believe that no mention is made in the book of any other revelation than those already referred to. In this, the chief and his followers are labouring under a delusion. It would be preposterous, however, to condemn them as impostors of the blackest dye on this account. On the third day of the third moon, a festival is to be celebrated in commemoration of the descent of the heavenly Father; and another on the ninth day of the ninth moon, in commemoration of the descent of the heavenly Elder Brother. These, as well as other festivals appointed by them, show that something remains to be done in the way of enlightenment.

"In one chapter Húng Jen enters into a minute examination of the terms used by the Roman Catholics and Protestant Missionaries for the true God and the Holy Spirit. He concludes with the verdict, that 'Shang-te' should be used for the Supreme Being, and 'Shung-shun' for the Holy Spirit. His views on this point deserve to be considered by the Missionaries, having come from a native, who has nothing at present to hope or fear from them.

"In one chapter he treats of questions which pertain to social and political improvements. He advocates the introduction of railroads, steamers, life and fire insurances, newspapers, and other western inventions. Plans are described, and the advantages stated. Who knows but that, ere many decades shall have passed over our heads, this noble country—vast in its extent, and exhaustless in its resources—will be penetrated and intersected by railroads, and startled into life by the rattling of the fire-carriage, and the flashing of the electric stream?

"Foreign nations are to be treated on terms of equality; and foreigners are never to be called by any opprobrious names. Missionaries will be at liberty to go everywhere to preach the Gospel. We have learnt that Húng Jen is extremely anxious that a number of Missionaries should proceed forthwith to Nanking to teach the people, as most of them, he says, are very ignorant.

"We mention this, not for the purpose of inducing any one to rush to the heavenly capital (which would be a very questionable policy just at present), but as an answer to the following remark, which we have repeatedly heard—'Why don't they send for you, Missionaries to teach them? Let them do this, and I will believe in them. "G.J."

RECENT INTELLIGENCE.

NEW ZEALAND.

Since the remarks in the body of this month's "Record" were printed, we have received further letters from New Zealand. Annexed are extracts of an highly encouraging character, from a letter of the Rev. R. Burrows, dated Auckland, July 30, 1860, which will be read with much interest—

"A meeting of the native chiefs, from different parts of the country, has been convened, and they are now assembled at this place. I have attended most days, simply to hear the speeches of the chiefs. As the meeting consists almost entirely of men who have always been friendly to the Government, their speeches have been of course of a friendly character: some of them, however, have not hesitated to speak out on the question of the war at Taranaki, and have very significantly asked why the Governor did not call them together before he commenced hostilities. Not one of them has advocated a continuance of the war, but many have pleaded with great earnestness for a cessation of hostilities between the Government and William King. Several of the chiefs who would be likely to have influence with William King, have offered their services as mediators.

"Another question which has also been discussed is the Maori king movement. A few days before the meeting of these chiefs, Potatau, the so-called 'Maori king' died; they therefore expressed their hope that the name of 'Maori king' might die with him. As far as we know, no steps have as yet been taken to set up another in Potatau's place, but the combination into which various tribes have entered, not to sell more of their land, is still in force.

"There has been one feature in this conference, which, whilst it will tend to cheer and encourage us in our work, will also be gratifying to the Parent Committee. I refer to the testimony which has almost unanimously been borne by the numerous speakers to the positive, as well as the negative good which has resulted from the introduction of the Gospel of peace among them. The 'Gospel came first,' say they: 'we embraced it, and found it good, without any mixture of evil, for it was from God. After, came the law (meaning the Queen's sovereignty): that was also good, but it brought with it some evil, for it came from man.' Thus, while, on the one hand, your Missionaries are being accused by editors of newspapers, and by individuals through those papers, of disloyalty to the Queen, and as being enemies to the colonists on the other hand, we have the testimony of those among whom we have laboured that our labour has not been in vain in the Lord.

"You will be anxious to know what is the general state of the natives. So far as we can ascertain, the great body of them are not only anxious to live on amicable terms with the colonists, and to live also under the protection of British law, but are fully determined not to mix themselves up with the quarrel of the Government with the Taranaki natives. Still we cannot but see that there is much sympathy among many of them with William King. In a religious point of view there has been no falling off in our congregations, and I trust not a few feel wherein their strength lieth, that 'it is better to trust in the Lord than to put confidence in princes.'"

RETURN HOME OF A MISSIONARY.

North-West America.—The Rev. T. H. Fleming left Moose on September 9, and arrived in London on October 19.

RECENT INTELLIGENCE.
CHINA.

VERY conflicting views are entertained respecting the true state of religion among the insurgents. The subject is dealt with at length in the "Record" for the present month; and in its pages a communication received from our Missionary, Mr. Burdon, who accompanied the Missionaries of the London Missionary Society to Soo-chow, will be found at full length. But for the information of those readers of the "Intelligencer" who do not see the "Record," we insert here some extracts, of opposite tendencies, and each propounding the grounds on which the writers have been led to the estimate they have formed of the movement, and its leaders. The first series of extracts are taken from a letter of the Rev. G. John, of the London Missionary Society, dated Shanghae, August 10.

"MY DEAR BROTHER,—By the last mail you were informed that two letters had just been received from Soo-chow; one from Hung-jin,* the Kan-wang, to Mr. Edkins, and another from Chung-wang, to Mr. Edkins and myself, inviting us both to Soo-chow, to meet the former king. We felt that only one course of action was left open to us as Christian Missionaries. We were exceedingly anxious to have an interview with this man, for the purpose of ascertaining the truth on various points of interest—of encouraging him in his praiseworthy endeavours to correct the errors connected with the movement—of learning what might be done towards spreading the truth among his people—and of suggesting plans and improvements for his consideration. . . . .

"We reached Soo-chow early on the 2nd inst., and had an interview with the Kan-wang on the same day. He appeared in a rich robe and gold embroidered crown, surrounded by a number of officers, all of whom wore robes and caps of red and yellow silk. On entering, he stood up and received us with a hearty shake of the hand. He said that our visit made him very happy, and that his heart was quite set free. He then made kind inquiries about his old friends in Shanghae, both native and foreign. He was much pleased to hear of the progress of the Gospel at Amoy; of the recent accession of converts to the church in the neighbourhood of Canton and Hong-Kong; and of the late arrival in the West. 'The kingdom of Christ,' said he, 'must spread and overcome every opposition: whatever may become of the celestial dynasty, there can be no doubt concerning this matter.' He then put off his crown and robe, and dismissed his officers; after which we had a free and confidential conversation on various points. We gladly accepted an invitation to dine with him. Before partaking of the viands prepared for us, he proposed that we should sing a hymn and pray together. Having selected one of Dr. Medhurst's hymns, he himself started the tune, and sang with remarkable correctness, warmth, and energy. After a short prayer, offered up by Mr. Edkins, we sat at table. The conversation turned almost exclusively upon religious subjects; in fact, he did not seem to wish to talk about any thing else. He seemed to feel very grateful to Dr. Legge, Messrs. Chalmers, Hamberg, Edkins, and others, for their past kindness to him. He told us that his object in leaving Hong-Kong for Nanking was solely to preach the Gospel to the subjects of the celestial dynasty; and that on his arrival he begged permission of his cousin to be allowed to do so. The chief, however, would not hear of it; but insisted upon his immediate promotion to the rank of king. Though thoroughly devoted to the new dynasty, and determined to live or die with it, he told us repeatedly that he was much happier when employed as a native assistant at Hong-Kong than now, notwithstanding the dignity conferred upon him and the authority with which he is invested. We were escorted on horses to our boat at a late hour.

"We visited him again on the following day. . . . .

"After the merchant had left, we had a very interesting conversation with him on various matters, but especially the character of Tae-ping Wang, the chief. Before separating, he proposed that we should commend each other to the care of Almighty God, and invoke his blessing in prayer. After singing a hymn, he engaged in prayer. His prayer was exceedingly appropriate, fervent, and scriptural. He prayed that all the idols might perish, that the temples should be converted into chapels, and that pure Christianity should speedily become

RECENT INTELLIGENCE.

the religion of China. This was a most interesting spectacle—a spectacle never to be forgotten. We parted again with a hearty shake of the hand. We were escorted to the boat as on the previous day. A present of a goat and some fowls followed us from the Kan-wang. Having now done what we proposed to do, we turned our faces homewards. We reached home on the 5th instant, in safety, deeply sensible of the kindness of our heavenly Father towards us and our families during our absence.

"We were all much pleased with the Kan-wang. His knowledge of Christian truth is remarkably extensive and correct. He is very anxious to do what he can to introduce pure Christianity among his people, and to correct existing errors. He says, however, that he can do but very little actively in this work, and that hence he is very anxious to get as many Missionaries as possible to Nanking, to teach the people. 'I cannot do much,' said he; 'but if you will come, I will get you chapels, exhort the people to attend, and will attend myself regularly.' He has prepared a prayer for the use of the soldiers, which is remarkably good. He wished us to prepare a series of simple prayers for general distribution. We took with us a number of copies of the whole Bible, and a good selection of tracts—all publicly delivered to his care. These will, I have no doubt, do their work among not a few. He expressed his opinion that the chief is a pious man, notwithstanding all his errors. He devoutly worships God, and is a constant reader of the Scriptures. The Bible and the 'Pilgrim's Progress' seem to be his favourite books. The Kan-wang thinks that much may be done, in course of time, towards putting him right on various points. It is very gratifying to find that he does hold the Scriptures of the Old and New Testaments as the inspired Word of God, and the standard of faith. We were very sorry to learn that piety has materially declined since their arrival at Nanking, and that even Hung-jin himself has given in on one or two points, such as polygamy. We ought to remember this man at the throne of grace, and earnestly pray God that he may be kept from apostacy. He is exposed to five thousand temptations, of which we have but the faintest conception. Though those men will teach a Christianity of some fashion, whatever may become of him, we all feel that the progress of pure and undefiled religion does depend, to a great extent, upon Hung-jin."

Our next extracts are less hopeful. They are from a letter from the Rev. J. L. Holmes, of the American Mission, who had made his way to Nanking, about the same time that Mr. John and his brother Missionaries were at Soo-chow. He was admitted to the audience-hall of the Tien Wong, and there presented to his two brothers, and others of his family, but the Tien Wong did not appear. The impression left upon his own mind as the result of his visit he thus describes—

"I went to Nanking predisposed to receive a favourable impression; indeed, the favourable impressions of a previous visit to Soo-chow led me to undertake the journey. I came away with my views very materially changed. I hoped that their doctrines, though crude and erroneous, might notwithstanding embrace some of the elements of Christianity. I found to my sorrow nothing of Christianity, but its name falsely applied—applied to a system of revolting idolatry. Whatever there may be in their books, and whatever they may have believed in times past, I could not escape the conclusion that such is the system which they now promulgate, and by which the character of the people is being moulded. Their idea of God is distorted until it is inferior, if possible, to that entertained by other Chinese idolaters. The idea which they entertain of a Saviour is likewise low and sensual, and his honours are shared by another. The Eastern King is the Saviour from disease as He is the Saviour from sin. The Holy Spirit they make a nonentity. The whole transformation may be concisely stated in the language of Scripture, 'They have changed the truth of God into a lie, and they worship the creature more than the creator.'" Mr. Holmes then specifies some of the blasphemous notions which had most shocked him. He proceeds: "Furthermore they do hold that Tien Wong is the Son of God, as really and in the same manner as Jesus is. Some of their most intelligent men with whom I conversed defended their worshipping him precisely on this ground, 'He is the Son of God, and in worshipping him we worship God,' they said. That this worship is of the same character as that addressed to Jesus and the heavenly Father there can be no doubt. No one defended it upon the ground that it was not. On the other hand, they defended it upon the ground of his claim to divine worship. The assumptions which he makes in his proclamation,

RECENT INTELLIGENCE.

it appears to me, moreover, would unmistakeably indicate the kind of worship he would demand. The son of the chief is likewise a member of the divine family. He is the adopted son of Jesus, and is appointed to be the head of all the nations. So it is stated in the edict, and so it was explained to us by those familiar with their theories. Polygamy is another dark feature of their system. The Tien Wong has married about thirty wives, and has in his harem about 100 women. The other kings are limited to thirty. The other high officers are also allowed a plurality of wives.

"I had hoped, too, that though crude and erroneous in their notions, they would yet be ready to stand an appeal to the Bible, and to be instructed by those competent to expound its truths. Here, too, I was disappointed. They have a new revelation which is to be their criterion of truth, and are quite competent to instruct us. In fact, they bear in their hands a divine decree to which we are to submit, according to their account. To be sure they invite Missionaries to come : they invited me to remain, or to return and remain with them. But it is easy to see how long they would be willing to tolerate a man who would preach doctrines radically opposed to those which they themselves promulgate, and upon which they found their claim to the obedience of China and the rest of the world. Their willingness—if indeed they are willing—to receive Missionaries among them is doubtless founded upon a misapprehension of their character. They suppose that the Missionary will prove an instrument which they can bend to suit their own purposes. Exceptions might be made in favour of individuals : it is of those who hold the reins of power that I speak."

In reference to the opium patients referred to by Mrs. Gough in her letter of May 22, she writes, August 10, 1860—

"When I last wrote, in the month of May, we were about to send two native Christians into the district from whence the greatest number of opium-smokers had come, and, amongst them, the one whom I mentioned as an applicant for baptism. He was received into the church, and remained as a guest in our house for some days before he returned home. My husband furnished our native brethren with a list of the persons whom he had received from the neighbourhood they visited, and they succeeded in finding out a large proportion of them. There were instances in which they had returned to their old habit, but there were comparatively few, about one in five, and the report they brought was, on the whole, an encouraging one. The most interesting part of the whole, however, was the readiness of the people to listen to the Gospel, as it was declared to them by the catechist and his companion, and they expressed the most earnest desire that some one should go and settle among them. They sent word to my husband that if he or any other would only go, they would provide a house and give their services."

THE SLAVE TRADE.

We regret to state that there has been a great impulse given to this nefarious traffic of late, and that, too, in different quarters and under different forms. We are told in some of our communications from Africa, that slaves are frequently shipped in what appear to be ordinary trading vessels, in parties so small as to escape detection. But the hydra does not always skulk in corners. The "West African" asserts that there is reason to believe, that during the last four months of 1859, not less than 12,000 Africans were carried across the Atlantic into slavery, from ports between St. Paul and Lagos, and from the south coast. On the 12th of August, 1860, a large screw steamer left Whydah (the great sea-port town of the kingdom of Dahomey) with 1200 slaves on board, and got clear off. Whilst embarking them, twenty-five were drowned in their chains in the surf by the upsetting of the canoes. One American ship is supposed to have left Whydah, September 28, with 600 slaves on board, and another sailed a few days previous with a cargo of slaves. The present king of Dahomey has made fourteen slave-hunting expeditions since his accession. The terrible sacrifice which he announced some months since, has, we are sorry to say, been consummated. The message sent by the British Government was not forwarded, the death of the Consul at Lagos having intervened, so that there was no officer on the spot by whom it could be transmitted.

The following is an extract from a private letter from the Bahamas, dated August 4th, 1860—

RECENT INTELLIGENCE.

"I have something worth telling you this morning. We are in a state of great excitement from the arrival of 350 rescued slaves. It appears that the slave captain mistook the 'Karnack' (mail packet) for a man-of-war, and rushed out of the way through the nearest channel, where his vessel ran aground, and the native boats found her, and they are coming in laden with the poor naked Guinea men and women: 350 have landed, and I see another boatfull is coming over the bar. The passengers on board say that the captain and crew jumped overboard, and others that the captain cut his throat: this may be, but no doubt the villainous crew are trying to pass themselves off as passengers from Africa. What a change for these poor creatures, when they realize where they are! They say they are covered with sores from flogging. Many of their countrymen, the Congoes here, have gone to meet them, and the gathering must be marvellous. They have made some of them comprehend their blessed position. Every one is sending them clothes, food, &c.—rather different to being slaves in Cuba. The children on board, it is said, were sold by their parents for debts to the slaver. How such things make us pray from the bottom of our hearts, 'O Lord, come quickly.'

"The slave captain offered 200*l*. to any Bahamian boatman who would take him to Cay West, but not one would listen to him."

A slave ship has also been lately captured and taken into the Mauritius, with 800 of the natives of East Africa on board. Of this number, 100 were children, who have been placed in the Orphan Asylum, under the charge of Mr. Ansorgé.

DISMISSAL OF MISSIONARIES.

THE instructions of the Committee were delivered by the Rev. H. Venn, on Friday, September 28th, to the following Missionaries, at the Missionary Children's Home, Islington—

West Africa.—The Rev. M. S. Jackson.

Yoruba.—The Rev. G. F. and Mrs. Bühler, the Rev. J Buckley Wood, and Dr. A. A. Harrison, M.B.

Mediterranean.—Rev. Theodore F. Wolters.

Western India.—The Rev. T. K. Weatherhead, B.A.

North India.—The Rev. J. M. Brown, B.A., the Rev. J. Barton, B.A., the Rev. E. L. Puxley, and Mr. William Sandys [Shwai-tui), a Burmese Student.

South India.—The Rev. Nigel and Mrs. Honiss, and the Rev. J. B. and Mrs. Simmons.

Ceylon.—The Rev. R. B. Tonge, B.A., and Mrs. Tonge.

China.—The Rev. Arthur E. Moule.

The Missionaries were addressed by the Rev. H. V. Elliott, and commended to Almighty God in prayer by the Rev. W. B. Mackenzie.

DEPARTURE OF MISSIONARIES.

Yoruba.—The Rev. G. F. and Mrs. Bühler, and Mr. Faulkner embarked at Liverpool, Oct. 24th, in the "Armenian," for Lagos.

Western India.—The Rev. T. K. Weatherhead left Southampton in the steamer "Ellore," for Bombay, on October 12th.

North India.—The Rev. J. B. and Mrs. Wheeler, and Mr. W. Sandys, embarked at Gravesend in October, on board the "Lady Melville," for Calcutta—The Rev. B. and Mrs. Batty left Southampton in the steamer of October 4th, the Rev. J. Barton in the steamer of October 20th, and the Rev. E. L. Puxley in the steamer of November 20th, for Calcutta.

South India.—The Rev. N. and Mrs. Honiss, and the Rev. J. B. and Mrs. Simmons, left Gravesend, Oct. 4th, in the "Trafalgar," and the Rev. J. M. Speechley left Southampton in the steamer of November 20th, for Madras.

Ceylon.—The Rev. R. B. and Mrs. Tonge left Southampton in the steamer of November 4th, for Ceylon.

RETURN HOME OF MISSIONARIES.

Sindh.—The Rev. A. Matchett arrived in London from Bombay on November 9th.

North India.—The Rev. T. H. and Mrs. Fitzpatrick left Mooltan, September 21st, and arrived in London on November 9th.—The Rev. A. L. Stern and the Rev. H. Stern have arrived in London, after a sojourn for some time in Germany.